WAX TABLETS OF THE MIND

WAX TABLETS OF THE MIND

Cognitive studies of memory and literacy in classical antiquity

Jocelyn Penny Small

Routledge
Taylor & Francis Group

LONDON AND NEW YORK

First published 1997
by Routledge
2 Park Square, Milton Park, Abingdon, Oxfordshire OX14 4RN

Simultaneously published in the USA and Canada
by Routledge
711 Third Avenue, New York, NY 10017

*Routledge is an imprint of the Taylor and Francis Group,
an informa business*

First issued in paperback 2015

Transferred to Digital Printing 2005

© 1997 Jocelyn Penny Small

Typeset in Garamond by
J&L Composition Ltd, Filey, North Yorkshire

British Library Cataloging in Publication Data
A catalogue record for this book is available from the British
Library

Library of Congress Cataloging in Publication Data
Small, Jocelyn Penny
Wax tablets of the mind: cognitive studies of memory and
literacy in classical antiquity/Jocelyn Penny Small.
Includes bibliographical references and indexes.
1. Cognition and culture – Greece – History.   2. Cognition
and culture – Rome – History.   3. Memory.   4. Literacy –
Greece – History.   5. Literacy – Rome – History.   I. Title.
BF311.S53   1997
153.1'2'0938b – dc21   96–37725

ISBN 978-0-415-14983-9 (hbk)
ISBN 978-1-138-98698-5 (pbk)

Cover illustration: Gustave Moreau, *Arion*. Musée du Petit Palais,
Paris. Courtesy of Association Paris-Musées.
Cover design: Leigh Hurlock

For Lance and Pam

forsan et haec olim meminisse iuvabit.
Perhaps one day it will be pleasing to remember these things.
Vergil, *Aeneid,* 1.203

Write it on the memory wax tablets of your mind.
ἥν ἐγγράφου σὺ μνήμοσιν δέλτοις φρενῶν
Aeschylus, *Prometheus Bound*, 789

CONTENTS

CONTENTS

PREFACE

Once upon a time, all too many years ago, I started to write a conventional art historical book on time and space in pictorial narrative from classical antiquity. Somewhere along the way I had the 'brilliant' idea that you could not have a sense of time without memory. That Aristotle also thought of the same idea is merely, in Robert Merton's astute words, anticipatory plagiarism.[1] The important thing is that I have been 'side-tracked' ever since, though I have every intention of returning, more or less, to the original topic. In the meantime I have decided to keep all discussion of pictorial aspects in this book to a bare minimum for two reasons. First, they deserve a book-length study of their own. Second, I hope that a narrower focus will make my argument easier to follow.

It is, as always, a great pleasure to acknowledge those who have aided and abetted me. First and foremost, I am very grateful to Rutgers University. The University supported me with both research funds and a faculty leave and a half. Without that time off this book would have taken even longer to finish. I am also very appreciative of the encouragement I have received during the whole project from Ryoko Toyama, the Director of Alexander Library. I thank the graduate students in the Department of Art History for being willing guinea pigs and for inviting me to give a presentation in their annual symposium.

I am grateful to the following people for inviting me to lecture, while the project was *in medias res*: Roger Bagnall at Columbia University; William A. P. Childs at Princeton University; A. A. Donohue at Bryn Mawr College; Gloria Ferrari at the University of Chicago; and Susan I. Rotroff for the Princeton chapter of the Archaeological Institute of America. The audiences were lively and their questions helped me refine my arguments. I feel it only fitting to acknowledge the role of *Psycoloquy*, one of the first refereed electronic journals. Not only did they allow me to lurk, but they also accepted two commentaries of mine despite the fact that I was not 'one of them'. These commentaries generated responses from a number of people, with whom I would never have otherwise come into contact. I especially want to thank for their forbearance and willingness to help me

Marilyn Jager Adams, James Hartley, and Bruce MacLennan. Barbara Tversky deserves a special acknowledgment for her time and patience in explaining rudimentary cognitive principles to a neophyte and steering me to so many helpful references. Almost all of our contact has been via e-mail. We live in a truly wondrous age.

I am particularly indebted to those outside my areas of expertise for discussing their fields with me: William A. P. Childs, Roger Bagnall, Robert Bianchi, Walter Burkert, Phyllis Culham, Gloria Ferrari, Eric Garberson, Deborah Goldstein, Archer Harvey, Robert Kraft, Elizabeth McLachlan, Susan I. Rotroff, Laura Slatkin, Peter White, and Froma Zeitlin. A number of people nobly went over parts and, in some cases all, of my manuscript, sometimes more than once. These stalwart souls are: Frank Abate, Dee Clayman, A. A. Donohue, Gloria Ferrari, Deborah Goldstein, Joel B. Goldstein, James Hartley, Ian Hunter, Bruce MacLennan, Brunilde S. Ridgway, Cynthia Shelmerdine, James Tatum, and Barbara Tversky. An anonymous thanks goes to the anonymous friend who read an early draft and requested 'more trivia'. A special thanks goes to James Tatum. He forgave me for reading a manuscript of his too late for its time of publication by making me co-organizer with him of the panel, 'New Approaches to Memory', at the 1993 annual meetings of the American Philological Association. We then jointly published our contributions in *Helios*. He also suggested Routledge as a publisher and put us into contact with each other. Finally, as is customary after one's acknowledgments, I would like to make clear that any mistakes which remain are not my fault, but that of my colleagues. Lord knows I tried. Since it would otherwise be churlish and ungrateful, I have forgiven them. I very much hope that you do likewise.[2]

INTRODUCTION

Major technological changes in the way words are processed provoke equally major changes in the way human memory is viewed and studied. Plato laments that writing will replace memory. Frances Yates, at the other extreme, wonders 'Why, when the invention of printing seemed to have made the great Gothic artificial memories of the Middle Ages no longer necessary, was there this recrudescence of the interest in the art of memory . . . in the Renaissance?'[1] Today we face the same issue with the same intensity: will the computer destroy our traditional memories, both in ourselves and in print? The past fifteen years have witnessed a wide and profound reconsideration of how human memory works by biologists, cognitive scientists, computer scientists working in artificial intelligence, psychologists, linguists, anthropologists, and historians. Here I explore some of the trends and conclusions that I feel have broad implications for the way we study classical antiquity.

In particular I focus on the continuum between literacy and orality as it is mediated by memory. While a continuum captures the idea that neither literacy nor orality is monolithic, it needs to be qualified, for everybody is 'oral', but only some are 'literate'. We still conduct our lives orally not just for our daily living – buying food and clothing, negotiating housing, traveling back and forth to work – but even for our daily literacy. How many times do you read something, because someone told you orally to do so? Even if you look at *TV Guide* to plan your evening's viewing, that viewing is not just visual but also very oral, whether you are watching situation comedies, the news, or sporting events. All of television depends on words. On the other hand, when I went downstairs just a while ago in my apartment building, I rode in an elevator that required me to read numbers and letters to choose L for lobby. A small door above the buttons was labeled 'PHONE'. My mission was to get my mail, which is eminently textual, even if with a healthy dose of pictures in the advertisements. Because our daily lives so thoroughly mix the oral and the literate, we take both very much for granted. Rarely do we consider how one or the other works, much less how they interact with each other.

Literacy and orality are an exchange that uses the currency of memory. Memory is what enables us not to live in a time warp of repeated actions. You do not need to be introduced to your friends every day or to your parents once a week. You remember who they are. This kind of 'oral' memory depends only on what you can 'carry around' in your head. Literacy extends that 'oral' memory to an external store outside of you. You can record things you need to remember in a variety of ways on a variety of media. You can tape the voice. You can videotape the voice and the person. You can scribble a note on a napkin. You can write a reminder in the computer. You can commemorate a worthy event in stone or bronze. What I have said so far is well known and obvious.

Also well known today to both classicists and cognitive psychologists is the phenomenon of oral composition, because Milman Parry revolutionized not only classics but other fields, when he demonstrated the oral basis of the Homeric poems. Today classicists, who have argued over his theory for more than half a century, tend to forget how unsettling an idea it was that Homer was not a writer. Only very close examination of the text and a modern analogue revealed that what looked like, sounded like, and read like a text was not produced in the same way as a text. But how is a text written? Can you tell whether I have written this introduction in longhand, at the typewriter, or at the word processor? And in the case of all three did I do it seated at a desk, at the dining-room table, or lying sprawled on the couch? Does it matter? When I quoted Frances Yates, did I do it off the top of my head because I knew it by heart? Did I look it up in the book or in my notes? Does it matter? In short, does technology affect the product? This is one of the broader issues I investigate.

One aspect of the nexus of literacy, orality, and memory that has received scant interest among classicists is retrieval. We just assume that what was written in antiquity could be found, even though we know in our heart of hearts that we can't find what we ourselves have written much less what others have written. Anyone can store something. Finding it at a later date is a totally different problem. Everyone knows that the one item they will need in the future is the one item they can't remember where they cleverly put it. We are particularly bad at finding words as compared to objects. The techniques for finding words developed alongside the techniques for recording them, but retrieval has always lagged behind, because not until you have accumulated more words than you can retrieve do you realize that you have an unmanageable situation. Today we are aware of the problems without necessarily realizing it consciously. We learn at a young age about libraries and their catalogues, whether on cards or online. We know that books and magazines have tables of contents. We expect dictionaries to be in alphabetical order down to the very last letter of the word, even if it is 'floccinaucinihilipilification', the longest word in the first edition of the *Oxford English Dictionary*. Today science produces the longest words, such as

'*pneumonoultramicroscopicsilicovolcanoconiosis*'. In other words, retrieval is intimately connected to research tools, all of which have taken centuries to
develop and refine.

Defining literacy is a moving target, because what entails literacy changes
with time and context. Scholars tend to consider literacy in antiquity solely
as a greater or lesser ability to read and write rather than as a multi-faceted
skill. Aimée Dorr gives one of the better accounts:

> An exact, widely accepted definition of literacy is hard to find, as is well
> illustrated by the chapters in this book. Traditionally, however, every
> definition centers on the ability to read and write text, to encode and
> decode the symbol system of text, and to interpret meaning in textual
> representations.[2]

Notice how even she leaves out the issue of retrieval. Here I do not
consider the numbers of the literati. Others have done that better than I
can.[3] Instead I focus on the nature of the literacy of the very highly literate
in classical antiquity for two reasons. First, only the fully literate face a
massive problem of retrieval. Second, they provide a relatively large amount
of evidence, especially from the Roman period, on how they worked. As
writers, they were more likely to comment in both formal and informal
ways about their writing habits. For this body of material I take a traditional,
indeed, ancient approach. I use anecdotes, whenever possible, to illustrate
my points, because they offer proof of those points and are in themselves
quite wonderful. I find it appealing to know that Augustus wrote bad
tragedies in his bath, that Titus had speedwriting contests with his scribes,
that Cicero fussed over the decoration of his villas.

Next I combine this philological approach with a much more recent
discipline, cognitive psychology, with its interest in how and why people
think the way they do. Specifically, I consider the ancient techniques for
improving memory in light of modern research on how memory works. I
examine in detail precisely how and why the systems of the *topoi* and *loci*
work. The ways the memory systems are used raise questions about the
other tools used by the highly literate in the process of writing, for I believe
that memory is a tool. In particular, I am concerned with how tools affect
output. While it is obvious that reading a roll written in *scriptio continua* is
different from reading a printed book, I discuss what those differences are
and the kinds of effects those differences might make in both reading and
writing in classical antiquity.

Because this is a book about technology and work habits, I think some
comments about my own may be useful, because they set the stage. I am
very much aware of the major changes our literate tools are undergoing,
and I find the process fascinating. This interest has led to this book. At the
same time, I could not have written the book that I have if I had not been
forced to learn Greek and Latin. That was my feeling at the time, since I am

by inclination a classical archaeologist, not a philologist. Despite the existence of most of the sources I quote in 'standard' and not so standard translations, this work would have been vastly different without a knowledge of the original languages. Too often the 'best' translations try to impart a modern flavor with the result that 'Cicero holds the book in his hand' rather than 'the roll in his hands'. The worst, however, is the translation of the lengthy but extremely crucial passage from the Auctor ad Herennium on the system of *loci* where the translator used the word 'background' rather than 'place' for *locus*.[4] My adaptations are nearly always in the direction of the more literal, because it is in the mundane, literal use that the classical writer reveals his work habits. If no translation is cited in a note, then I have translated the whole passage myself. 'Adapted from' means that I have changed a word or two. While I do not give the original Greek or Latin, I do put the words I think crucial between brackets.

Does it make a difference that the advent of the computer has meant that I have all of Greek literature and most of the inscriptions and papyri, as well as Latin up to AD 200, on CD-ROMs at home? Does it matter that I was an early surfer of the 'net'? On the whole, I am ending this project with a very healthy respect and, indeed, gratitude for my old-fashioned training. Modern technology does not supplant the old, it complements it.

At the same time my attempts at working within two distinct scholarly disciplines, classics (I don't count archaeology and philology as *that* separate) and cognitive psychology, have led to a recognition that each field has not just its own jargon, but its own work methods. These habits range from relatively minor ones like the fact that the psychological literature always includes the publisher in a bibliographical citation, and the classical fields not only do not, but also sometimes omit the place of publication. The philologist absolutely revels in abbreviations for journals, the more arcane the more delight. The psychologist always uses full titles. Since I find full titles useful and had not quite taken in the magnitude of the task of citing the publisher until well along the way, I have adopted a mixed system here. Psychologists are generally content to cite the whole work, even if they are making a specific quotation. My favorite example was the broad citation to Aristotle's works, numbering nearly 2000 pages in the Bollingen edition, for 'The mind is like a catapult'. Fortunately I was able to use the Greek CD-ROM (the *Thesaurus Linguae Graecae*) to find out that what Aristotle really said was something quite different:

> But of what he is doing a man might be ignorant, as for instance people say 'it slipped out of their mouths as they were speaking', or 'they did not know it was a secret', as Aeschylus said of the mysteries, or a man might say he 'let it go off when he merely wanted to show its working', as the man did with the catapult.[5]

And yes, this is one of the references that got away. I didn't jot down who misquoted Aristotle, but I certainly remembered it. Classicists wince at such behavior, often publicly in reviews. I follow the classicists in citing chapter and verse. I follow the classical archaeologists and the medievalists in giving all the particulars to identify an object: city, collection, inventory number, provenience – the use of 'provenience' distinguishes me from art historians who study later periods; they use 'provenance'.

More significant are the dissimilarities in the way the two disciplines organize their published work. Classicists have total freedom, with one minor exception. Abstracts are slowly creeping in. Psychologists have a set format in which they say everything four times: once in the abstract, once in the introductory discussion to the experiment, once in the discussion of the individual experiment, and once again in the summary of the results. The most important difference between the two fields lies in their concepts of what constitutes proof. Cognitive psychologists divide roughly into two camps: the experimenters and the ecologists. The first group tests their hypotheses in the laboratory. The second group believes that the really interesting questions about how we think cannot be tested only in the laboratory, but must be examined in natural, and hence ecological, settings. This second group deals with evidence in ways very similar to classicists, with one major exception. As far as the psychologists are concerned, there is a right answer. There is a truth. And that truth is attainable . . . eventually. Classicists live a Zeno paradox. No matter how hard they try they will never achieve the truth, much less even know if they have. Like Zeno's arrow that logically never arrived, classicists get closer and closer to the truth, but never quite get there. Some practitioners view all as interpretation. I give a personal example. An art historian published an article in which she applied the system of the *loci* to a set of paintings from one house in Pompeii.[6] Unfortunately, she misunderstood the system and believed that you could 'read' the paintings in any order, when the system depends on sequence. When I wrote to the editor of the journal in which the article was published, the editor treated my information as my interpretation. Since all interpretations are equally valid, the editor saw no need for a correction of what I and the cognitive psychologists consider fact.[7]

Straddling two disparate fields has affected not just my thinking, but also a good deal of the way the book is cast. I consider the jargon used in each field as equally abstruse and obfuscatory. As a result, I have tried to keep both jargons to a minimum. I have tried to define alien terms, many of which may not seem to need definition at all to someone accustomed to the terminology.[8] I have included more information about dates and places for antiquity than may be standard for classicists. I have taken the same approach with the bibliographical references: better to give a few extra so that people outside the field can more easily find more information. At the same time, and this is more frequently true for the classicists, I am sure that I have inadvertently omitted some reference. I can only plead for mercy and ask the reader to consider whether or not that reference would have made a difference to my argument. I worked on the final draft during the Summer of 1996, which is the 'closing' date for my citation of recent publications. In some cases, due to lags in library acquisitions and cataloguing I was unable to consult certain books and articles from 1995 and sometimes earlier, even though I had references to them and they looked, on the surface, to be of interest.[9] Despite the length of the bibliography I have been selective, though I do admit to retaining certain references that I found helpful, even if I didn't end up citing them in my text. I also admit that I have omitted some 'standard' and obvious references if I didn't find them useful.

Next, despite the horror this might engender in the breasts of classicists, it doesn't always matter which edition of an author you cite. Last but not least, like every classicist I feel compelled to mention the spelling of Greek. I am idiosyncratic and use the spelling with which I am most comfortable. Hence I write 'Corinth' with a 'c', but 'Herakles' with a 'k'. Knowing now what I know about orthographies I lay the blame totally with the English language. Germans and Italians do not have our problem. They have 'shallow' orthographies; we have 'deep' ones. That's all there is to it.

As you read through the book, please keep two things in mind. First, I am concerned with patterns of process. There are and always will be exceptions. I recognize those exceptions, but I think that trying to paint an overall picture is valuable. Second, in the words of Quintilian, 'If I were to attempt to say all that might be said on each subject, the book would never be finished.'[10]

Part I

LOGISTICS OF THE CLASSICAL LITERATE

1

MEMORY FOR WORDS

We live in a world of visible words. Even if we can't read them, even if we don't seek them out, we are, nevertheless, constantly bombarded by them. Buy Coke. Smoke Camels. Exit. Push. Pull. Like the silent butler and children in the Victorian era, text generally goes unnoticed. It wasn't always this way. In the classical period, when text was still in its formative stages, its usefulness was hotly debated. Its forms were protean. Its potential was not realized. The technologies that writing was to spawn and continues to spawn were still unborn. The tools of the trade were barely there, much less refined. A pen was either a metal stylus or a reed pen and not a fountain pen not a ballpoint not a roller-tip not a felt tip not a crayon not a pastel not a pencil not a mechanical pencil. 'Paper' came in two basic varieties, papyrus and parchment, and these two types were sufficient through the Middle Ages.

In this chapter I consider the technological problems the creation of the written word presented to the classical Greeks and Romans: what their texts looked like and how that look affected their use. As Donald Norman says, 'An artifact [tool] is not a simple aid. That is, you can't just go out and find some cognitive artifact, and there you are, better at something.'[1] I treat the writing of texts as a separate topic that emphasizes the process of composition, although the two processes – composing and replicating that composition in a physical text – dramatically affect each other.

THE PROBLEM OF INTERNAL VS. EXTERNAL STORAGE

Homer never mentions Mnemosyne (Memory), the mother of the Muses. He begins the *Iliad* with an invocation to an unidentified deity ('Sing, goddess'), while in the *Odyssey* he calls upon a slightly more specific inspiration with 'Tell me, Muse, about the man of many ways. . . . Beginning at any point, goddess, daughter of Zeus,/tell us.'[2] The source of these epics does not come from within the poet, for his telling of the tale has nothing to do with memory. So Lucian in the second century AD has Hesiod

3

disown all responsibility for his poetry: 'I [Hesiod] could say that nothing that I composed belonged to me personally, but to the Muses, and you should have asked them for an account of what was put in and what left out.'[3] Gregory Nagy says that it is 'not so much that the Muses "remind" the poet of what to tell but, rather, that they have the power to put his mind or consciousness in touch with places and times other than his own in order to witness the deeds of heroes (the doings of the gods).'[4] Albert Lord describes the process more generally: 'We remember a story without memorizing its words – the idea of doing so is ridiculous. If it be appropriate we may memorize a "punch line", but that is as far as memorization goes.'[5] The best way to understand the distinction Lord is making between memory for words and memory for story is to recall one of our own fairy-tales, such as 'Little Red Riding Hood' or 'Goldilocks and the Three Bears'. At no time did we consciously memorize the story, because repeated listenings and readings are sufficient for most Americans to render the tales in all their gory. Even if we tell a story in different words and with different embellishments at different times, if asked we would indeed say that it is the same story. As Lord puts it, 'They [the oral singers] create the text anew each time they tell the story.'[6]

With literacy comes a greater need for memory for words. It is not that memory is superlative in preliterate societies and wretched in literate ones, as many today and some then assume,[7] because we differ little in cognitive capacity from Mycenaean man and, if anything, being somewhat later on the evolutionary scale, we should have better equipped brains. Children of 'Stone Age' New Guineans fly planes and run computers.[8] As Ulric Neisser puts it, 'By itself, the absence of something has no causal effects. Illiteracy cannot improve memory any more than my lack of wings improves my speed afoot.'[9] Donald Norman addresses the issue more directly: 'Writing something down doesn't really change our memory; rather, it changes the task from one of remembering to one of writing then, later, reading back the information. In general, artifacts don't change our cognitive abilities; they change the tasks we do.'[10] In other words, the real distinction between the Mycenaeans and us lies not in basic brain power, but in the fact that what we choose to remember differs greatly. Michael Cole and Sylvia Scribner conclude that:

> the anthropological reports are correct – their informants do in fact remember things that the anthropologists find it difficult or impossible to recall. But this performance is not reflective of greater powers of memory in *general*; rather it reflects the fact that the things a Philippine native or !Kung bushman finds easy to recall are different from the things that the anthropologist finds easy to recall. In short, how well someone remembers a particular subject matter depends on the subject at hand.[11]

4

Hence it is not just that literacy produced a need for memory for words on a scale that had never existed before. It is that one of literacy's most notable effects is that it feeds upon itself. The more literate you are the more words you need to remember.

Exact wording is rarely crucial in oral societies, but often of great importance in literate ones, though this aspect took centuries to develop. In the absence of a permanent record of a text in writing or on tape or some such medium, how would anyone be able to prove whether or not two performances, separated in time, were the same? One might remember the amount of time a particular rendition took if one had an accurate measure for time, but even then some of the words could have been the same and others not. There simply would be no way to tell. Most oral societies are not only uninterested in the detail of the words *per se*, but even unaware of the unit of the word. Albert Lord reports the following conversation between an 'interrogator' (N for Nikola) and a Guslar singer (Đ for Đemo Zogić):

N: So then, last night you sang a song for us. How many times did you hear it before you were able to sing it all the way through exactly as you do now?

[Đ: Once . . .]

N: Was it the same song, word for word, and line for line?

Đ: The same song, word for word, and line for line. I didn't add a single line, and I didn't make a single mistake . . . .

N: Tell me this, if two good singers listen to a third singer who is even better, and they both boast that they can learn a song if they hear it only once, do you think that there would be any difference between the two versions? . . .

Đ: There would. . . . It couldn't be otherwise. I told you before that two singers won't sing the same song alike. . . . They add, or they make mistakes, and they forget. They don't sing every word, or they add other words.[12]

Lord explains the contradiction in the singer's statements: 'to him "word for word and line for line" are simply an emphatic way of saying "like". As I have said, singers do not know what words and lines are.'[13] Havelock goes even further: 'Greek originally had no word for a word singly identified, but only various terms referring to spoken sound.' He doubts whether 'the isolation of the individual "word" as the basic building block of language is achieved before Plato.'[14]

Psychologists support this conclusion in their studies of the concept of words in two different groups of people: illiterate adults and children. In a study of the former, Robert Scholes and Brenda Willis concluded that 'Such characteristics of the description of linguistic knowledge, previously associated with preschool children, agrammatic aphasics, and the hearing impaired, are now seen to be retained throughout life in the absence of the acquisition of literacy.'[15] Marilyn Adams gives a good summary of the evidence for children, and hence for illiterate adults:

> In fact, many young children do not understand the word *word*. . . . Surprising as it may seem, the evidence concurs that children are not naturally prepared either to conceive of spoken language as a string of individual words or to treat words as individual units of meaning. What they listen for is the full meaning of an utterance, and that comes only after the meanings of the individual words have been combined – automatically and without their attention. . . . In speaking, we do not emit words one by one. We do not pause between them. Instead we produce whole clauses or sentences in one single continuous breath. In print there are spaces between the words. Each is discretely represented. As children become aware of the one-by-oneness of words in print, they begin to notice and isolate the words in speech.[16]

Her explanation also corroborates the formulaic nature of oral poetry. Epithets produced in single continuous breaths would naturally function as whole and indivisible units. Another study of children demonstrates that knowledge of words is not monolithic, but 'continues to evolve and mature – indeed, significant changes occur when children are well into the period of concrete operations.'[17] Something similar happened in classical antiquity: the idea of the word and how it works developed over time.

Linguists further explain why oral cultures and illiterates do not know words:

> Spaces between groups of letters became important as the conventions of writing evolved. In alphabetic systems, spaces are now universal and as a result literate people learn to recognize 'words' as visual rather than auditory units. In a real sense, the first orthographers of a language make the decisions about how words are to be perceived in that language.[18]

Today one can literally see how the spoken word differs from writing by looking at spectrograms of connected speech. The ups and downs of the waves so seamlessly join each other that the breaks between words are often impossible to distinguish.[19] Computers have the same problem in trying to understand speech. Nicholas Negroponte proposes an approach that a Guslar singer could understand: 'the slurring and blurring of words . . . can be partially simplified by looking at language as multiword utterances, not just as single words. In fact, handling runtogetherspeech in this fashion may well be part of the personalization and training of your computer.'[20] He gives the following example: 'A computer should know the difference between your saying "Kissinger" and "kissing her," not because

6

it can find the small acoustic difference, but because it can understand the meaning.'[21]

According to David Olson, 'writing systems were created not to represent language, but to communicate information' with the result that 'writing systems create the categories in terms of which we become conscious of speech.'[22] In other words, writing provides the model that leads to a particular conception of how language works syntactically rather than vice versa. He gives an intriguing instance:

> Chinese readers of traditional character scripts could not detect phonemic segments whereas those who could read Pinyin, an alphabetic script representing the same language, could do so. To learn to read any script is to find or detect aspects of one's own implicit linguistic structure that can map onto or be represented by that script.[23]

Actually the situation may be more complicated than Olson thinks. The Chinese system of writing militates against the concept of a 'word'. John DeFrancis comments that:

> To them [the Chinese], a character (zi in Chinese) is thought of as a 'word,' but linguists properly distinguish zi 'character' from ci 'word,' a new term that did not come into usage until this century and is still not widely known by the general public.[24]

Thus for oral cultures it is not the words but the story or the gist that counts. Lord's results have been confirmed in a study of the singers of a popular North Carolina ballad, 'The Wreck of the Old 97':

> There is no evidence of rote recall of this ballad. Each singer makes changes in the wording of the ballad between the two performances. However, these changes are limited by the constraints in the ballad and in the ballad tradition. End-rhyme sound, number of beats per line, and number of lines per verse remain relatively constant. . . . Yet there are commonalities among singers that are defined by these constraints.
>   Words and music . . . are intertwined . . . [and] constrain each other. . . . The memory for the ballad is not the exact song, nor is it a collection of words; rather it is a collection of rules and constraints. This notion is the same one that Bartlett (1932) labeled 'schema.' Here, however, we have not only a schema for gist but also a schema for poetics, rhythm, imagery, and music. Together these schemata, and possibly others, constrain recall to the extent that it almost appears rote or verbatim.[25]

The idea of verbatim, word for word, repetition occurs without written texts only in a few, rather limited situations. Ruth Finnegan has been exploring the use of rehearsal and memorization in oral societies of the Pacific, but, as Lord rightly points out, the texts, about a hundred lines, are

7

far shorter than the tales of the Guslar singers or the Greek epics.[26] 'Magical' phrases such as 'abracadabra' and certain prayers depend for their effectiveness on exact wording, but, again, the length is short. Further proof comes from Roman prayers, whose exactitude could be maintained only by a written text and not memory. Pliny the Elder records that:

> We see also that our chief magistrates have adopted fixed formulas for their prayers; that to prevent a word's being omitted or out of place a reader dictates beforehand the prayer from a script. . . . Remarkable instances of . . . interference are on record: . . . when a mistake has been made in the prayer itself; then suddenly the head of the liver, or the heart, has disappeared from the entrails, or these have been doubled, while the victim was standing.[27]

A Roman relief from the first century AD with a sacrifice to Mars shows the scene Pliny describes.[28] On the far right behind the altar stands an attendant (*camillus*) holding a diptych open in both hands like a living teleprompter for the sacrificer to read the prayers. In fact, in the face of such overwhelming negative evidence the real question is why literate people attribute lengthy verbatim recall to illiterate people.[29]

Next, so many more words survive to be remembered in a literate world than in an oral society, because the words accumulate over the centuries: not just the business records for today, but those from all the yesterdays; not just the stories you were told, but those of your great-grandparents and their great-grandparents; not just the laws you follow, but the laws your ancestors obeyed; not just the famous speeches you heard, but the famous speeches of your founding fathers and their successors. Obviously some people are better than others at remembering certain kinds of information and they may become the 'remembrancers' in an oral society.[30] They, however, are not necessarily memorizing words *per se*, but rather the gist or content of whatever needed to be known.

The human brain places definite limits on the amount of information we can store. As a result, according to Merlin Donald, the most recent and significant cognitive step in human evolution is the use of writing as an external storage medium.[31] Once such an external store is created, the nature of the problem is no longer one of each official 'remembrancer' having to transfer 'physically' all his memory to a successor. Instead, an external store requires only that the user should know how to 'decode' it, and significantly the time when the decoding occurs is not important. It can be just after a 'document' was created or two thousand years later. The Egyptians recognized this quality of writing:

> they [scribes] did make heirs for themselves in the form of books and teachings which they composed. They appointed [the papyrus roll as a lector-] priest for themselves, the writing-tablet as a devoted executor.

8

Teachings were their pyramids, the reed-pen their child, the stone surface their wife . . . the memory of the one who composed them [books] is for eternal ages.[32]

In contrast, rather than recognizing the possibilities of long-lasting written records, Plato, or at least his Socrates, deplored the fact that the document cannot respond to your questions, much less change itself as a result of those questions. Plato rightly has Egyptians speak for the opposition, when Socrates in the *Phaedrus* tells a story about Egypt:

But when it came to writing Theuth [Thoth] said, 'Here, O king, is a branch of learning that will make the people of Egypt wiser and improve their memories; my discovery provides a drug for memory and wisdom.' But the king answered and said, 'O man full of arts, to one it is given to create the things of art, and to another to judge what measure of harm and of profit they have for those that shall employ them. And so it is that you, by reason of your tender regard for the writing that is your offspring, have declared the very opposite of its true effect. If men learn this, it will implant forgetfulness in their souls; they will cease to exercise memory because they rely on that which is written, calling things to remembrance no longer from within themselves, but by means of external marks. What you have discovered is a drug [φάρμακον] not for memory [μνήνης], but for reminder [ὑπομνήσεως]. And it is no true wisdom that you offer your disciples, but only its semblance . . . . You know, Phaedrus, that's the strange thing about writing, which makes it truly analogous to painting. The Painter's products stand before us as though they were alive, but if you question them, they maintain a most majestic silence. It is the same with written words; they seem to talk to you as though they were intelligent, but if you ask them anything about what they say, from a desire to be instructed, they go on telling you just the same thing forever.'[33]

Three factors are significant about this passage. First, Plato recognizes the connection between memory and writing, one of the recurring topics in this book. As the computer is decried today, so writing continued to be considered a mixed blessing throughout antiquity. According to Caesar: 'it does usually happen that the assistance of writing tends to relax the diligence of the student and the action of the memory.'[34] Seneca the Younger says: 'Wisdom publishes not words but truths – and I'm not sure that the memory isn't more reliable when it has no external aids to fall back on.'[35] Vitruvius even takes the same stance as Plato, when he says: 'Whichever of these forms of death befell him [Zoilus, a captious critic of Homer], it was a fitting punishment and his just due; for one who accuses men that cannot answer and show, face to face, what was the meaning of

9

their writings, obviously deserves no other treatment.'[36] Ovid, on the other hand, while in exile, recognizes the power of writing to preserve: 'no thing has a strength greater than that of time. But writing endures the years. Through writing you know Agamemnon and everyone who bore arms with him and against him.'[37] Seneca the Elder wrote directly on the topic, when he considered the question as to whether Cicero should forfeit his life or his writings. Seneca presents the case by having two different figures argue: 'Antony has realised that so long as the products of Cicero's eloquence survive, Cicero cannot die'; and 'if you do not burn them, the Roman people promises you eternity.'[38]

Second, it is curious that it did not occur to Plato that natural memory is like the silent page of writing. It, too, does not allow the original author to respond to questions if he is not present. Third, Plato did an extraordinary amount of writing, and took great pains in its production. According to Quintilian, 'the reason why those four [Greek] words in which Plato in the noblest of his works [the *Republic*] states that he had gone down to the Piraeus were found written in a number of different orders upon his wax tablets, was simply that he desired to make the rhythm as perfect as possible.'[39] And what did Plato say that took him so much effort? Simply that 'I went down yesterday to the Piraeus. . . .'[40] In other words, Plato's ambivalent attitude towards writing rests, at least in part, in being alive and having to deal with it in one of its great transitional and formative stages.[41]

Acceptance of the new medium was slow, because the ways to use, much less exploit it were even slower in developing. The real problem was not the silence of the written word, but the difficulty of finding what you wanted among all those unspeaking words. The retrieval aids developed in classical antiquity were appallingly few. You can always ask people where something is and they can often tell you immediately, even if only in the negative.[42] That capability still separates us from computers which search their entire store, even if what we know to be the sole answer may have been found early in the search.

2

ANCIENT BOOKS

THE LOOK AND FEEL OF BOOKS

Everyone today knows what a book looks like. While the size and number of pages vary and the subjects differ, most follow a standard format. They are bound, whether by sewing or with the not-so-perfect glue, in hard or soft covers. The spine has the title, the author, and the publisher's name or logo. The dust-jacket or back cover carries 'information' to entice the buyer, such as favorable quotes from famous people or a photograph of the famous person who wrote the book. Inside the book a title page proclaims the author and title, the publisher, place, and date of publication. Some of this information may appear on the back of the title page along with the copyright, but it is all there, up front. Dedications are brief. Tables of contents are at the front or the back, never in the middle; indices and bibliography are at the back. The text comes in between these search aids. The pages are numbered, with the text broken down into chapters that are themselves subdivided into paragraphs, each beginning on a new line and sometimes with the first word indented; then sentences, carefully marked by periods; and finally words, separated from each other by spaces and/or punctuation. Various embellishments are possible: footnotes at the bottom of the page or notes at the back of the chapter or end of the book; illustrations breaking up the page or collected together as a unit. As you read a book, you have an immediate visual idea of how much you have read and how much you have left to go by the amount of pages remaining to the left or right of where you are.[1] By a careful balancing act on a large table, ten books can easily be opened simultaneously for comparative purposes. It has taken over 2500 years to develop this object we take so much for granted.

Now consider the ancient book.[2] Classical terms for 'book' varied, because the format varied. Only context, and sometimes not even that, indicates whether a whole 'work' or merely a 'part' is meant. In Latin, a book, *liber*, may refer to either the whole work or one of the rolls, *volumen* singular and *volumina* plural (hence our word 'volume'), within that work. It took a certain knack to read a roll so that it stayed open to the place you wanted.[3] The most remarkable thing about this format was that a better model was available when writing was introduced to Greece, for writing tablets were known to Homer (*Iliad*, 6.168ff.). They were:

> commonly formed of two or more flat pieces of wood, held together either by a clasp or by cords passed through pierced holes; the central area of the tablet was usually hollowed slightly to receive a coating of wax, while a small raised surface was often left in the centre to prevent the writing on the wax being damaged when the tablet was closed. Writing in ink or chalk was sometimes placed directly on the wood.[4]

It would not seem to take a very great leap of the imagination to use sheets of papyri instead of bulky tablets.[5] Even more striking, however, was that, by the end of the fifth/beginning of the fourth century BC at the latest, still another model existed for the codex, as the early book-form with page leaves like ours is called: the Etruscan linen books (*libri lintei*) which consisted of a single length of linen, folded into a series of 'pages' in accordion style.[6] Yet the first major attempt to produce a codex was not made until the first century AD and even that, according to Roberts and Skeat, was virtually 'still-born'.[7] The codex in its early stages was used mainly for technical writing and by the early Christians.[8] It took 200 years from its first appearance before the codex was used as often as the roll. From Homer in the eighth century BC to only parity and not total displacement of the roll took more than a millennium. I discuss why the codex took so long to become popular in Chapter 10. Moreover, wax tablets remained in active use until sometime in the fifteenth century AD.[9]

The plight of the classical literate worsens because of the format of the text on the roll. Consider the ancient reader who wanted to read the two most famous works from antiquity, the *Iliad* and the *Odyssey*. Each epic comprised twenty-four rolls or 'books', as classicists call them today following the classical terminology; we would call them chapters. Originally these two epics were not divided into books. When first written down, each was one, enormous, continuous mass. To get an idea of their length, it may help to know that Richmond Lattimore's translation of the *Iliad* takes 437 pages and his translation of the *Odyssey*, set in a smaller type, 332 pages. Imagine each of these works without any breaks. I mean that literally. There were not only no breaks for books; there were no breaks for paragraphs, sentences, or even words. In short, there was no punctuation whatsoever. Everything blended together.

Not until the Hellenistic period in the third century BC was Homer divided into books and did poetry begin to be written by the metric line rather than in the same continuous format as prose.[10] The poetic lines, however, remained without interior breaks. All letters were the same height and often the same width. As everyone who has had to read early computer print-outs knows, the combination of upper and lower case letters greatly facilitates comprehension. At the same time it was not always clear where one poem ended and another began – issues which scholars still fight over.[11] Nor were the divisions into books established at one time and set thereafter, but for some authors, like Thucydides, the divisions ranged from the modern eight, to nine, and even thirteen 'books'.[12] The same problem of dividing longer works into 'books' also happened with Latin works. Suetonius, for example, records that 'the "Punic War" of Naevius, which was originally written in a single volume without a break, . . . was divided by Lampadio into seven books.'[13] An intriguing set of psychological tests has examined whether 'people agree in their chunking judgments. That is, are there locations in the stories where most people put slashes to indicate a part boundary, and other locations where very few people put slashes?'[14] Their results reflect the way Greek and Latin books were divided. There is a lot of agreement on the 'obvious' divisions, but dissension on the others.

Occasionally the accents of Greek words were indicated. Aristotle is aware of how an accent can change the pronunciation of a word. He says:

> ὄρος [mountain, boundary] and ὀρός [whey], said with the accent, mean something different. In writing, indeed, a word is the same whenever it is written with the same letters and in the same manner – and even there people nowadays put marks at the side [παράσημα] to show the pronunciation – but the spoken words are not the same.[15]

Reynolds and Wilson find it 'rather strange that they [accents] did not immediately come to be regarded as indispensable' and sum up the situation: 'it is hard to see what principle determines their use in ancient books, and they were not regularly added until the beginning of the tenth century.'[16] Nagy remarks that Aristarchus (c. 217–145 BC) in his edition of Homer considered the accents not to be part of the text proper, but of his commentary.[17] In fact, it is not clear whether Aristotle means that these marks were directly 'on' the letters, as they are today, or in the 'margins' to the side of the word.

As for punctuation – those wonderful marks like commas and colons – according to the *Oxford Classical Dictionary*:

> Punctuation is uncertain and arbitrary: it takes the form either of a single point, generally about level with the top of the letter . . . or of leaving a short space at the end of a clause. A short [generally horizontal] stroke (παράγραφος [*paragraphos*]) was placed, from the fourth century BC on, below the beginning of a line in which a break occurs (often also indicated by spacing); the same symbol is used in drama to indicate a change of speaker. In the Roman period it is usual for the names of the characters to be written in the margin.[18]

Even when punctuation exists it often varies for the same passage from manuscript to manuscript.[19] Literary texts in antiquity remained pretty much an undifferentiated block. Latin sometimes, and especially in inscriptions, separated words with 'dots' or 'points' (interpuncts) or even ivy leaves ('*hederae*'), but in the second century AD, in one of those great misbegotten regressions, adopted the 'continuous writing' or *scriptio continua* of the Greeks.[20] Word separation did not reappear until the eleventh century.[21] Progress is never smooth.[22]

What they chose to mark also differs from today. Diogenes Laertius writes about the texts of Plato in the second century AD:

> And since certain critical marks [σημεῖα] are affixed to his works let us now say a word about these. The cross X is taken to indicate peculiar expressions and figures of speech, and generally any idiom of Platonic usage; the *diple* (>) calls attention to doctrines and opinions characteristic of Plato; the dotted cross denotes select passages and beauties of style; the dotted *diple* editors' corrections of the text; the dotted *obelus* passages suspected without reason; the dotted antisigma repetitions and proposals for transpositions; the *ceraunium* the philosophical school; the asterisk an agreement of doctrine; the *obelus* a spurious passage. So much for the critical marks. . . . As Antigonus of Carystus says in his *Life of Zeno*, when the writings were first edited [ἐκδοθέντα] with critical marks, their possessors charged a certain fee to anyone who wished to consult them.[23]

All these marks or symbols refer to content. They are not aids to guide the reader in the way that punctuation marks are used today. A period tells us that a 'thought' has been completed and, if we are reading aloud, to take a longer pause than for a comma. I do rather like the idea, however, that mere consultation, not purchase, of such texts was remunerative.

ORGANIZATIONAL AIDS WITHIN THE BOOK

Is it any wonder, then, that studies of cross-references within classical authors of the early Empire have found them to be rather broad like 'see above' and 'see below'?[24] The most specific reference authors make is to the book, because that is the most specific division there is. Occasionally the work is of such a nature that a somewhat more precise citation is possible. Juvenal refers to the Second Philippic as that which 'you unroll next to the first'.[25] He would not, however, refer to a line within that Philippic by number, as we might. Columns were occasionally numbered in rolls. Codices, which are late, had numbers centered or on the outside edges of their pages. Editions of poetry sometimes came with total line counts or marks for every 100 lines.[26] The end of a 'book' of Homer might be marked with an end-title and a *coronis*.[27] Occasionally helpful comments, like the titles of poems, could be added in the spaces between columns.[28] Except for the words, consistency in display between different manuscripts of the same work was not a concern.

The *'paragraphos'*, already described, was neither used all the time, nor numbered or counted as a means of referencing. It was used as a fast way of calculating how much a scribe had written and hence should be paid.[29] William Johnson also suggests that in some cases it might have aided a reader in keeping his place, as he read through a text, especially if the text were read aloud.[30] The paragraph, as a regular unit of layout on a page, does not appear until print in the sixteenth century, according to the OED^2. When divisions like the paragraph were marked in antiquity and the medieval period, the first line was extended to the left of the body of the text rather than being indented.[31] The format resembles what we now call a 'hanging indent'. According to Saenger and Heinlen, our format 'was born in incomplete books in which initials and rubricating [highlighting the letters in red] were wanting. . . .The convention of the indented paragraph represents the acceptance of the unfinished book as normative.'[32]

The chapter numbers and divisions within them that we find in modern editions of classical texts were all added by printers long after antiquity.[33] Print led to the 'blackening' of the highly colored pages of medieval manuscripts, which in turn forced the development of a system of referencing dependent not on color, but on layout with fixed positions for page numbers, punctuation, and fonts.[34] In other words, print returned to the two-color scheme of ancient manuscripts, but not quite as it had been in antiquity, because later readers were accustomed to a punctuated and organized text, even if the punctuation varied from codex to codex. Moreover, in order to retain a similar level of information, while maintaining the practical ease of printing in just one color, typographical fonts became important. Today we **bold**, *italicize*, and underline. Sometimes we change the size of the fonts, as well as switch the **font** itself – generally for clarity. When too many of these devices are mixed together, the result is a confused jumble rather than a crystal-clear message.[35]

The computer is fostering a return to embellished text that would please many a monk and, at the same time, it enhances the fixed, silent display of text with touches of orality and visualization. For example, *Creative Writer*, a word processor for children, allows them to 'add audio to their documents, assigning barks, whistles, horns, and other sound effects to specific words. They can even record their own sounds. . . . When it comes to text, kids can make words sparkle, shimmer, and fade.'[36] CD-ROMs have it all:

> Yes, you could get books with similar information, but they'd just have regular old pictures. Electronic CD-ROM books have moving images and audio accompaniment, adding a whole new dimension to books. Videos, of course, have sound and motion, but they aren't browsable;

you have to move through them in one direction. Computer software is interactive, and this makes it more interesting and much more fun.[37]

Richard Lanham has some ideas about what one could do with a CD-ROM version of *Paradise Lost*:

> Wouldn't you begin to play games with it? A weapon in your hands after 2,500 years of pompous pedantry about the Great Books, and you not to use it? Hey, man, how about some music with this stuff? Let's voice this rascal and see what happens. Add some graphics and graffiti! Print it out in San Francisco (the kooky face I used above) for **LUCIFER**, and Gothic for *GOD*. Electronic media will change past literary texts as well as future ones.[38]

The first major group to exploit the possibilities are companies with products to sell. For example, Hewlett-Packard says that 'one study indicates color accelerates learning, retention, and recall by 55 to 78 per cent.'[39] Just in case, however, you miss the peculiarities endemic to hot metal type, a software program, *FF Beowolf Serif*, now randomly adds jaggies and breaks to reproduce the effect of a poorly printed book.[40]

It was not until after antiquity, especially from the Renaissance on, that readers felt a need for precise citation that never seemed to arise in their ancient counterparts. When one classical writer cites another, he uses the same kind of vague reference he uses when making references within his own works.[41] For example, Pliny the Elder (*Natural History* 13.69) refers to the passage in the *Iliad* on wax tablets that I just cited as 'we find in Homer' and even leaves out the name of the work. Aulus Gellius (*Attic Nights* 9.4.13), working in the next century, refers to Pliny by the book within the work: '[Pliny the Younger] wrote in the seventh book of his *Natural History* . . . .' My edition of Gellius has a helpful footnote that gives the specific location of the passage by its modern division as 'vii.23'.[42] There were two ancient exceptions: passages that began a work or less frequently a book within a work. Such lines were later labeled the '*incipit*' (it begins).[43] A concept of the page simply did not exist. Pages could not be cited not just because works were written on rolls, but because each roll was individually produced by hand and could vary tremendously in the amount written in any given width and column.[44] The codex was no better, since it too was subject to the same idiosyncracies of individual, handwritten production. Although different sized fonts may be used for print today, none the less, each edition remains consistent within itself. No matter whose copy and which reprinting is used, Book One of the *Iliad* in Lattimore's translation always begins on page 59. Such fixed formats do not appear until print.

The table of contents appeared in antiquity, but was a rare event. Pliny the Elder ends his 'Preface' to his encyclopedia, the *Natural History*, with an explanation of his reader's guide:

As it was my duty in the public interest to have consideration for the claims upon your [Titus's] time, I have appended to this letter a table of contents of the several books, and have taken very careful precautions to prevent your having to read them. You by these means will secure for others that they will not need to read right through them either, but only look for the particular point that each of them wants, and will know where to find it. This plan has been adopted previously in Roman literature, by Valerius Soranus in his books [*libris*] entitled *Lady Initiates*.[45]

Pliny has dedicated the work to the Emperor Titus, who would have had many demands on his time. More importantly, what has been translated in the standard English edition as 'a table of contents' is actually not our formal term, but rather a description of what Pliny has done. Literally Pliny says 'I have attached to this letter [the Preface, as we call it] what is contained in the individual books.'[46] Similarly, each section of the actual listing starts with a verb, '*continentur*' ('are contained'), and not a noun ('contents'). The concept of a table of contents *per se* did not exist, because there was no means of referring to the precise locations where things were discussed. None the less, that Pliny could have thought of even including something that resembles the great-great-grandparent of our table of contents indicates that at least one standard had been established by the first century AD: parts of works were divided into rolls and what went in each roll was determined by either the author or the compiler of the work and remained constant from copy to copy, even if the column where a section began varied from roll to roll.

Since we find tables of contents so useful, an examination of Pliny's will explain why it was not adopted ever after in antiquity. It takes an entire ancient roll or book, and in one English translation seventy-one pages of small type. Remember that the roll with the contents is not only long, but has no divisions – none for paragraphs, sentences, or words. Assuming for the moment that you are the Emperor Titus with this great new gift, think about the process of reading the seventy-one pages of the contents to find the one item you want, going to the roll (book) that contains that item, and then reading through that until you are lucky enough to come to your item. This is no speedy process. The contents for each of the thirty-six books are treated similarly: first, the number of the book (Libro XXXII), followed by (*continentur*), and then a list of the items covered, a numerical summary, and a list of the authorities consulted.

A small sample set of excerpts in English from one of the books, partially devoted to what we call 'art history', will immediately make clear why the idea never truly caught on in antiquity:

BOOKXXXIVCONTENTSCOPPERMETALSKINDSOFCOPPER
CORINTHIANDELIANAEGINETANONBRONZEDININGCOUCHESON

17

CANDELABRAONTEMPLEDECORATIONSOFBRONZEFIRSTBRONZE
IMAGEOFAGODMADEATROMEONTHEORIGINOFSTATUESAND
THEREVERENCEPAIDTOTHEM . . . INKSTONEIIIDRUGSFROM
COPPERASXIVDRUGSFROMCOPPERASWATEROR
SHOEMAKERSBLACKINGXVIDRUGSFROMPOMPHOLYXSLAGVI
DRUGSFROMTHESESLAGASHESXVKINDSSKINDETERGENT
DIPHRYXTHESERVILIANFAMILYSMAGICSIXPENCE . . . TOTALCMXV
FACTSINVESTIGATIONSANDOBSERVATIONSAUTHORITIESLUCIUS
PISOANTIASVARROCORNELIUSNEPOSRUFUSMESSALATHEPOET
MARSUSBOCCHUSJULIUSBASSUSGREEKTREATISEONMEDICINE . . .
FOREIGNAUTHORITIESDEMOCRITUSMETRODORUSOFSCEPSIS
MENAECHMUSSARTOFGRAVING . . .

I have made only two changes to the Loeb Classical Library translation: all chapter references added by later editors have been omitted and the numbers changed from Arabic to Roman numerals. I have also followed modern convention in using three dots for ellipses. Otherwise the text is as someone might have read it in antiquity, except that, of course, type, even all capitals, is much easier to read than handwriting.[47] Moreover, then as now, certain letters like *m, n, u,* and *i* often look alike, and small but helpful details like the defining dot on top of an '*i*' did not appear until the fifteenth century.[48] Now try the same passage in a modern layout:

> Book XXXIV. Contents: Copper metals. Kinds of copper – Corinthian, Delian, Aeginetan. On bronze dining couches; on candelabra; on temple decorations of bronze; first bronze image of a god made at Rome; on the origin of statues and the reverence paid to them. . . . Ink-stone, 3 drugs from; copperas, 14 drugs from; copperas water or shoe-maker's blacking, 16 drugs from; pompholyx, slag, 6 drugs from these; slag-ashes, 15 kinds; skin-detergent; diphryx; the Servilian family's magic sixpence. . . . Total, 915 facts, investigations and observations.
>
> Authorities: Lucius Piso, Antias, Verrius, Marcus Varro, Cornelius Nepos, Rufus Messala, the poet Marsus, Bocchus, Julius Bassus's Greek treatise on medicine. . . . Foreign authorities: Democritus, Metrodorus of Scepsis, Menaechmus's *Art of Graving.* . . .

While this arrangement is not easy reading, it is amazing how much those punctuation marks, spaces between words, and mixed cases for letters help.

Pliny's *Natural History* presented problems beyond that of no punctuation to the Roman reader. As a scientific work and the forerunner of our own encyclopedias, the *Natural History* included all sorts of arcane information, not arranged in any order, readily discernible by our standards of organization. If you merely glanced at the beginning summary in the table of contents above for 'copper metals', you would not know that it also discusses the origins of statuary and soap. At the same time, if terms like '*copperas*' and '*pompholyx*' seem strange to us, they may have been no less strange to the Romans.

A century later Aulus Gellius produced a much more manageable 'table of contents' for his *Attic Nights* that takes up only twelve pages of print in the Loeb Classical Library, but his work is three volumes in that edition compared to the ten for Pliny. Like Pliny, he too is concerned about making his reader's life easier. He ends his Preface with an introduction to the table of contents: 'Summaries of the material to be found in each book of my Commentaries I have here placed all together, in order that it may at once be clear what is to be sought and found in every book.'[49] His contents is not just a list in prose as is Pliny's, but reads more like modern abstracts of articles or papers. For example, 'Chapter 1' of Book 1 is: 'Plutarch's account of the method of comparison and the calculations which the philosopher Pythagoras used in determining the great height of Hercules, while the hero was living among men.'[50]

COGNITIVE ASPECTS OF READING TEXT

Reading words that are all run together dramatically affects the way a reader processes those words.[51] Psychologists have tested readers with texts similar to the first version of the Pliny passage you have just read – though somewhat easier than in antiquity – in which 'x's instead of spaces are used between words. The results are just what you probably noticed when reading the first Pliny version. You read much more slowly.[52] A reader who has to divide letters mentally into words, into phrases, into sentences, and into paragraphs works much harder. As the concept of pages was present from the beginning of classical writing in the wax tablet, so was the idea of breaks between words, because words in the Semitic languages, the source of the Greek and Latin alphabets, were written without vowels and therefore had to have spaces to distinguish words.[53] The addition of vowels by the Greeks, however, made words sufficiently distinctive to allow them to be run together. While much has been written about the effects of the vowels, less has been said about one of the major causes for their addition. Unlike the Semitic languages, Greek has a large number of words that begin with a vowel sound. Without symbols for vowels, written Greek would not be easily intelligible.[54]

The way our brains are hard-wired explains why these two kinds of alphabetic writing, vowel and consonantal, developed. The consonants with their clicks and hisses not only separate the vowels from each other but make them intelligible to us.[55] Hence it is possible to write in an alphabetic system without the vowels, but it is impossible to do so without the consonants. Cn u rd ths? F u cn, thn u cn str mor txt n ls spc. The question of which system you use depends on how much information is necessary to understand a particular text. In other words, text, as we are accustomed to seeing it, contains a lot of redundancy, which enables us to understand it far more quickly. The trade-offs are between the time to decode and the amount of effort to produce the text in the first place and then the space needed to store it. F u hv t tm, thn u cn rd stff lk ths. If you don't, you prefer whole words with complete punctuation. Today, highly complex algorithms strip redundant elements from computerized text to produce reductions of one-third to a half in storage space, while retaining the ability to reconstitute the text exactly as it was originally, because the computer does not need the same aids as we do. Much of the work being done today depends on 'information theory', especially as developed by Claude Shannon beginning in the 1940s and, not coincidentally, after working on cryptography during the Second World War.[56] He calculated that written English is about 50 per cent redundant. To get an idea of just how little information is really needed to figure out the words, especially in a context, he played a game much like Hangman or Wheel of Fortune. He took a sentence and had friends guess letter by letter what it said.

The issue, however, is not whether you can read such a format, but whether you want to or should have to. In fact, Joseph Shimron and Tamar Sivan examined whether readers equally skilled in both English and Hebrew read English or Hebrew faster. Pointed Hebrew was always read faster than unpointed, but the really interesting result was:

> Even native Hebrew readers read English texts faster. This is true, although not to the same extent, in comparison to both voweled and unvoweled Hebrew texts. This finding is particularly interesting because . . . English texts contain about 40% more words than do their Hebrew translations.[57]

In other words, more information, as in English, does lead to faster comprehension.

Antiquity not only did not have the variety of models to choose from that we have today, but it also did not recognize the separation of the visual and aural aspects of text that enable us to treat print and speech differently.[58] Hence one of the Greek words for 'read' was 'ἀκούω', which more commonly means 'hear' or 'listen' – a point I return to.[59] Furthermore, punctuation functions in two, not always related, ways: prosody or breathing, an aspect of speech; and grammar, an aspect of both speech and text. Paul Bruthiaux suggests that, as writing made the existence of words evident, so writing also made clear the inner structure or syntax of language.[60] In antiquity prosody was emphasized, while the syntactical uses of punctuation do not appear until the Middle Ages.[61] Seneca believes that separating words, as Latin sometimes did, denotes a stylistic difference between the Romans and the Greeks not just in writing, but also in speaking:

20

The pace of Quintus Haterius, a celebrated speaker of his day, is something I should have a sensible man keep well clear of: with him there was never a hesitation or a pause, only one start and only one stop.

But I also think that certain styles are suitable in a greater or lesser degree to different nationalities. In a Greek one will tolerate this lack of discipline, while we have acquired the habit of punctuating what we say, in writing as well as speech.[62]

The run-on style reminds me of some Italian and French lecturers with a machine-gun style of delivery. It always sounds very melodious, but is often incomprehensible to the non-native speaker. The idea that writing in its physical layout should reflect the rhythm of speech foreshadows modern poets with their special printing effects. What is curious is that Seneca found the run-on style a strain to understand, saw the connection between writing and speech, and never thought of reforming the way Latin was written.

Ken Morrison makes the intriguing suggestion that to the Greeks and Romans their texts were never more than a 'variant of oral utterance . . . due to the lack of procedures for transforming *writing* into *text*.' Only in the medieval period with the codex and its page format does 'true' text appear.[63] While the separation of words is helpful, the use of commas and periods greatly aids comprehension by distinguishing phrases and sentences from each other. For example, Quintilian does not mention the unit of the sentence: 'Then with these very syllables let [the student] begin to understand words and with these to construct a speech [*sermonem*].'[64] Although the interpunct marked the unit of the word for Latin in certain periods, the reader still had to read aloud in order to construe the words into phrases and then into sentences. So Quintilian recommends:

In . . . connexion [with reading] there is much that can only be taught by practice, as for instance when the boy should take breath, at what point he should introduce a pause into a line, where the sense ends or begins, when the voice should be raised or lowered, what modulation should be given to each phrase . . . I will give but one golden rule: to do all these things, he must understand what he reads.[65]

Even today, 'inner speech increases when people are reading passages they find difficult.'[66] Erasmus (1466?–1536), writing in a period when punctuation was still a novelty, puts it extremely well:

Just as the principle of symmetry, when properly applied, makes great improvement in the appearance of script, so you would hardly credit how much good punctuation contributes to the understanding of a passage; so much so that a certain scholar said rather wittily that punctuation was a kind of commentary of the text. It is useful therefore that a boy should quickly familiarise himself with this feature also, and that the habit should become second nature so that, even when his mind is on something else, he should, as he writes, attend to the punctuation marks as much as to the letters themselves.[67]

That punctuation can be 'a kind of commentary' may be seen from the line 'GODISNOWHERE' which 'will be read with totally different meanings by an atheist and by a theist ("God is nowhere" and "God is now here").'[68]

I believe that the development of full punctuation, as we have it today, is directly related to the switch between reading texts out loud, as was the general practice in antiquity, and reading them silently, as became increasingly common through the Middle Ages.[69] Scholars now agree that reading silently to oneself did occur in antiquity. They argue over when it began and just how common it was and in what situations. Bernard Knox places it at least as early as the fourth century BC.[70] For example, Plutarch tells the following story about Alexander the Great:

> Once, when he had broken the seal of a confidential letter from his mother and was reading [ἀναγιγνώσκοντος] it silently [σιωπῇ] to himself, Hephaestion quietly put his head beside Alexander's and read the letter with him; Alexander could not bear to stop him, but took off his ring and placed the seal on Hephaestion's lips.[71]

Despite this story, according to Schenkeveld 'the earliest explicit reference to silent reading' is by Claudius Ptolemaeus, the second-century AD mathematician, a contemporary of Plutarch.[72]

Knox believes that more was read silently in antiquity than is often granted. He finds it remarkable: 'That Didymus wrote his more than 3,000 volumes and read the countless books on which he based them, pronouncing every syllable out loud?'[73] While most of what Knox has to say is judicious, his incredulity here is based too much on his own modern reading experiences. Speed in reading was not considered an ideal to achieve in antiquity the way it is today. The sheer quantity of written matter in antiquity, while not insignificant for the time, is nothing compared to the amount with which we are bombarded daily. The issue of silent vs. oral reading remains a hotly debated topic among psychologists and educators. Rosalind Horowitz finds that the 'Study of authentic uses of oral *and* silent reading are few and far between and . . . will ultimately be helpful in teaching and in broadening our understanding of theories of reading and writing.'[74] Although the evidence remains ambiguous for antiquity with both sides interpreting the same passages as proof for their cases, it seems clear that most people then would read texts out loud, albeit probably *sotto voce*, but some, and probably everybody in delicate situations, would always read to themselves.[75] Svenbro offers an interesting analogy:

Their [people in antiquity] relation to the written word might perhaps be compared to our relation to musical notation: not that it is impossible to read music in silence, but the most common way of doing it is playing it on an instrument or singing it out aloud [sic] in order to know what it sounds like.[76]

Saenger maintains that the adoption of word separation began first in the British Isles, because the native readers learned Latin as a second language and needed the extra help of the spaces to parse Latin texts into words.[77] Each element in our current repertory of punctuation marks has a separate introduction and each has generally taken a minimum of a hundred years to be fully adopted. Nor does a particular mark once adopted necessarily continue in the same favor, as the decrease in popularity of the semi-colon today shows.[78] Conversely, there are definite limits to the amount of punctuation and the number of arrangements of words that can increase our understanding of a written text.

For example,
experiments have been done
with the 'visual chunking' of text
to see
if such arrangements would increase comprehension
with varying results.
Beginning and poor readers
are helped.
Adults show
either positive results
or
no difference.[79]

According to Gamble, because early Christian texts were often meant for reading aloud, by the fourth century AD scribes began to arrange the text in visual chunks that matched 'semantic units', although, even in this case, each unit still consisted of lines with no breaks for the words within them.[80]

I think that arranging words in unbroken blocks impeded the development of our rich set of textual search aids, not just because of the absence of uniform pagination, but, even more importantly, because most of our aids depend on the individual word. If you want to find something in a dictionary, thesaurus, encyclopedia, almanac, or almost any reference, including the Web, you look it up by the unit of the word. Antiquity knew the concept of the word as a unit of speech, but did not consider the concept of the written word as a visual unit to be important. Consider Dionysius of Halicarnassus's description of how children learn to read:

When we are taught to read, first we learn by heart the names of the letters, then their shapes and their values, then, in the same way, the

23

syllables and their effects, and finally words and their properties, by which I mean the ways they are lengthened, shortened, and scanned; and similar functions. And when we have acquired knowledge of these things, we begin to write and read, syllable by syllable and slowly at first. It is only when a considerable lapse of time has implanted firmly in our minds the forms of the words that we execute them with the utmost ease, and we read through any book that is given to us unfalteringly and with incredible confidence and speed.[81]

In one respect little seems to have changed in the way reading is taught. Today we also learn the alphabet first and, as in antiquity, often set to song.[82] Yet one crucial difference separates the two methods. Today, children are taught to read either by the 'whole word' method or 'phonics' or some combination of both. The former is based on the idea that reading is a visual process that depends on the recognition of orthographic units, words; the latter resembles the ancient approach to syllables in that it is based on how the letters reflect the sounds of speech. The modern controversy as to which method is best began around the turn of the century and continues today. In a major study of both methods Marilyn Adams concluded that both methods are appropriate, especially in combination. While this recommendation might seem sensible and innocuous, it has generated an enormous, and sometimes quite vituperative, reaction.[83] Edmund Henderson refers to the controversy as a 'holy war' and 'doubt[s] that there is such a thing ever as pure whole-word recognition or pure alphabetic recognition except in the case of some linguistic catastrophe.'[84]

Never in antiquity was the whole word method used. The unit of the word, which is mentioned in the passage from Dionysius, is not considered from the point of view of its meaning, but rather of its pronunciation. In another essay, *On the Style of Demosthenes* (52), Dionysius discusses the same topic in much the same way, but significantly does not mention the unit of the word. Because all the letters were run together, the major problem every reader faced was figuring out what was a word. The only way to do that is syllable by syllable. To get an idea of how the process would work, read the following sentence first as you would normally and then out loud: 'It is difficult to wreck a nice beach.' When you read the sentence out loud, you should have heard: 'It is difficult to recognize speech.'[85] The sentence also points up another issue. Alphabetic transcription is by no means an exact replication of sound, but – and this is the important point – it is good enough.[86] The ancient focus on the syllable as a major unit also affected the ancient view of the nature of words. Instead of analyzing words by their roots and affixes, Varro, for instance, generally based his etymologies on the syllable. Hence he (5.63) connects '*vis*' ('force') with '*vita*' ('life'), even though they are not etymologically related.[87]

One additional cognitive explanation exists for the two major ways of reading. Instead of thinking of them as 'whole word' and 'phonic', think of them as 'visual' and 'aural' respectively. English has a script that sometimes has little correspondence with the way a word is pronounced, but that has much to do with the morphological history of the word. Greek and Latin, on the other hand, have scripts that reflect in a much more obvious and direct way how they are pronounced. These two types of written 'coding' are called 'deep' and 'shallow' orthography. Studies of modern languages, including a comparison of Greek and English readers, show that in a shallow orthography like Greek, with a great correspondence between sound and form, readers tend to read aurally.[88] In a deep orthography like English, with an often arbitrary pronunciation for the letters, processing tends to be more visual. I have qualified the dichotomy, because in neither case is only one strategy used. Some Greek readers will read certain kinds of words visually. Some English readers will read phonically. Most will mix their approaches to suit the text and themselves. Robert Crowder and Richard Wagner note that 'when change [in orthography] occurs, it always has occurred in the direction that carries writing away from the representation of meanings and toward the representation of sounds.'[89] Hence it is entirely appropriate for written English to acquire new spellings like 'thru'.

Since both Greek and Latin have shallow orthographies, their readers had no compelling reason to change the display of their text from the block-like form that dominated for approximately a millennium. Moreover, Joseph Shimron and Tamar Sivan believe that 'It is likely that reading English aloud will not be faster than reading Hebrew for bilinguals whose L1 [first language] is Hebrew.' In other words, because orthography should have less effect when read aloud than when read silently, the ancient display of text in *scriptio continua* was less of a problem than it would be today, when people read silently to themselves.[90]

3

'PUBLICATION'

Without publishers *per se*, with no advertising, and with limited means of replication and distribution, how did the classical writer publish his work? In this chapter, I discuss the intermediate stage between the time the author feels the work is done and when it gets into the hands of an independent reader via a friend, a library, or a bookseller – the subject of the next chapter. I discuss the actual process of writing in Part 3, 'Writing habits of the literate'.

FINAL DRAFTS AND AUTOGRAPH COPIES

The author produces the final draft from which copies can be made. While the author is responsible for the final draft, he does not necessarily write it himself. Marcello Gigante puts it well:

> We gladly renounce the romantic illusion . . . that among the Herculaneum papyri an autograph copy or evidence of Philodemus' own hand could be found. Philodemus was not a copyist or corrector of his own books. Speculating whether an autograph exists cannot be put on the same level of inquiry as questioning the existence of variations overseen by the author.[1]

In the same way, many writers today have another person type or word process the exemplar from which copies will be made. Martial makes it clear that he doesn't write the final version:

> Now learn what are the merits of a concise book [*libelli*]. This first: less of my paper [*charta*] is wasted; next my copyist [*librarius*] gets through it in a single hour, and he will not be wholly busied with my trifles.[2]

As I will discuss in Chapters 11 and 12, producing a written text was often a process for two people, with the author dictating to a scribe. The author could also mark up the final draft with his corrections, from which a scribe would produce the fair copy. In that case the process is the same as writing a draft: either two people, one to dictate and one to write; or one, a scribe, to write only. Next, as today, someone has to proof the fair copy to make sure it has incorporated all the corrections, but has acquired no new mistakes.

Without printing presses, xeroxing machines, and electronic duplication of digitized texts, only one means of mass reproduction was available in antiquity: each and every copy was produced individually by hand, like Torahs today. Copies could be made either one at a time or in multiples, if one person dictated the text simultaneously to a number of copyists.[3] We do not know what that number might be. Do you dictate to five, ten, twenty, or more scribes at one time? Do you make five daughter copies from the one master and give it out to five two-man teams to copy? Do you reproduce only on demand, the way University Microfilms makes doctoral dissertations available today? The only area where we have concrete information is for administrative and legal recorders. Up to four stenographers would take dictation, and then the copies would be compared for accuracy in much the same way as, in the early days of the computer, two cards were keypunched for each item and then compared.[4] The papyri from the Villa of the Papyri in Herculaneum shed some additional light. A single work that required multiple rolls could have multiple scribes. Philodemus's *On Poems* was copied by four different hands.[5] Otherwise we have only hints about the ancient methods and then generally because something went wrong.

Cornelius Nepos gives a brief description of Atticus's staff:

He had slaves that were excellent in point of efficiency, although in personal appearance hardly mediocre; for there were among them servants who were highly educated, some excellent readers [*anagnostae*] and a great number [*plurimi*] of copyists [*librarii*]; in fact, there was not even a footman who was not expert in both these accomplishments.[6]

It's nice to know that beauty and brain can not only coexist in one person, but also were considered something worthy of comment in antiquity. Nepos, unfortunately, leaves out more of the kind of information we are interested in than he includes. For example, we would dearly like to know the numbers for who did what and when. The main import of the passage is that the members of Atticus's staff were versatile, although some, as is to be expected, did certain jobs better than others. The best ancient representation of copying I have found is not classical, but Egyptian. It is from the grave of Teji, secretary to Meneptah, the son of Ramses II (ca. 1232 BC).[7] In the left third of the picture are three stacked frames: two rows of seated scribes flank a scene of a single person writing on a roll. While each scribe is probably working on a different document, it is likely that 'mass' copying was done in this manner.

One of the few generalizations that holds true over the millennia is that authors are never satisfied with the reproduction of their work. Cicero implies that a stage existed equivalent to that of our page proofs, when the author has an opportunity to make corrections:

> My book for Varro will not be long. It is practically done, as you saw. It is now only a matter of correcting [*tolluntur*] copyists' errors [*librariorum menda*]. You know I had my doubts about this book [*libris*], but it's your responsibility. The clerks also have in hand the work I am presenting to Brutus.[8]

Cicero's word for removing mistakes ['*tolluntur*'] literally means 'lifting' or 'raising' with the 'ink' implied. It is an example of the ancient terminology accurately describing the actual process. Sometimes the author is too late with his corrections. In another letter, Cicero asks Atticus 'if you will get your clerks to substitute Aristophanes for Eupolis both in your copies and in other people's [the *Orator*].'[9] The Villa of the Papyri preserves:

> a 'coexistence of various and incomplete editions,' which are combined and integrated with each other. These are not just different editions or copies of the same 'book' but textually different ones. This is proved by several cases where we have double or triple copies of the same book of Epicurus' *On Nature*.[10]

Van Groningen stresses that our concept of an 'edition' didn't exist in antiquity. Instead he believes the Greek word, 'ἔκδοσις', which is generally translated as 'publish' or 'edition', merely indicates the stage at which the author lets the final draft out of his own hands.[11]

Publishing presented other hazards. Since copyrights did not exist and since 'publication' was almost always *ad hoc*, there was no control. Cicero complains to Atticus that Atticus has prematurely circulated one of Cicero's works and tells him that 'You will oblige me by keeping the others [remaining rolls of *On Ends*] back so that Balbus does not get them unrevised or Brutus stale.'[12] The way unauthorized copies were produced is interesting. Cicero, further on in the same letter, says:

> But how did it slip my mind to tell you? Caerellia, in her amazing ardour for philosophy no doubt, is copying from your people. She has this very work *On Ends*. Now I assure you (being human I may be wrong) that she did not get it from my men – it has never been out of my sight. Moreover, so far from making two copies they had difficulty in finishing one.[13]

The situation has analogies today with the circulation of manuscripts in draft, which get recirculated without the author's knowledge through re-xeroxing. Of even more serious concern now is the loss of the fixed text, because computerization allows changes that leave no traces.

Some copyists were so good that by the second century AD their texts were highly esteemed. M. Cornelius Fronto writes in his usual florid style to his pupil, Marcus Aurelius:

> What nobler fate could befall anyone save that alone, when in Heaven, as poets tell, the Muses sing, while Jove their sire is audience? Indeed, with what words could I express my delight at your sending me that speech of mine copied out with your own hand? . . . What fortune like this befell M. Porcius or Quintus Ennius, Gaius Gracchus, or the poet Titius? What Scipio or Numidicus? What M. Tullius, like this? Their books [*libri*] are valued more highly and have the greatest credit, if they are from the hand of Lampadio or Staberius, of Plautius or D. Aurelius, Autrico or Aelius, or have been revised by Tiro or transcribed by Domitius Balbus, or Atticus or Nepos. *My* speech will be extant in the handwriting of M. Caesar. He that thinks little of the speech will be in love with the very letters of it.[14]

Such texts were sometimes available for others to consult, as Suetonius in the previous century makes clear, when describing Augustus's handwriting quirks:

> I [Suetonius] have also observed this special peculiarity in his manner of writing: he does not divide words or carry superfluous letters from the end of one line to the beginning of the next, but writes them just below the rest of the word and draws a loop around them.[15]

Lucian (*The Ignorant Book-Collector*, 4), writing around the time of Marcus Aurelius, implies that such autograph copies have achieved the status of what we would today call collectibles. Over and above the pleasure of owning an 'original' autograph copy, that is a text written by the author himself, would be the knowledge that the text would be reasonably accurate. I qualify the 'accurate', because authors do make mistakes. Suetonius further relates about Augustus:

> Of course his frequent transposition or omission of syllables as well as of letters are slips common to all mankind. I should not have noted this, did it not seem to me surprising that some have written that he cashiered a consular governor, as an uncultivated and ignorant fellow, because he observed that he had written *ixi* for *ipsi*.[16]

'PROOFING'

The only means for assuring the accuracy of texts was through the comparison of copies. While proofing today is laborious and not totally error-free, in antiquity it was a herculean task, for each and every copy had to be checked individually. Moreover, as I have stressed, the arrangement of classical texts in unbroken blocks that varied from copy to copy increased the difficulties. Despite the differences between the display of their texts and ours, the two major ways of proofing a text haven't changed. Either you do it by visually comparing the two or by having one person read the original aloud, including punctuation today, as a second person checks the copy.[17]

Suetonius describes the process in his life of the grammarian Marcus Valerius Probus:

> After getting together a large number of copies [*exemplaria*], he gave his attention to correcting [*emendare*] and punctuating [*distinguere*] them and furnishing them with critical notes [*annotare*], devoting himself to this branch of grammar [*grammatices*] to the exclusion of all others.[18]

If you did not have access to multiple copies or, at least, a copy against which to compare the copy you bought, you could only hope for the best, especially if you were a doctor. T. W. Allen says:

> To such trouble was this encyclopaedic physician [Galen] put by the uncertainty of ancient books. He and others, it is well known, wrote out their prescriptions in full . . . and when that was useless, in verse (Galen in heroic hexameters!) in order to guarantee the proportions. His investigation of the Hippocratean text (vol. xv sq.) was not undertaken with a philological or antiquarian object, but to guarantee the correctness of the medical encyclopaedia.[19]

A number of papyri survive with corrections by the original scribe and some with corrections by a second person.[20]

The variable quality of texts was recognized at least as early as the sixth century BC, when Homer, according to tradition, received his first 'official' edition. The plays of the fifth-century Attic tragedians had become so corrupt by the following century that a special law was passed by Lycurgus to establish and maintain 'clean' copies.[21] Plutarch tells a story about Alcibiades in the fifth century:

> Once, as he [Alcibiades] was getting on past his boyhood, he accosted a school-teacher and asked him for a book of Homer. The teacher replied that he had nothing of Homer's, whereupon Alcibiades fetched him a blow with his fist, and went his way. Another teacher said he had a Homer which he had corrected [διωρθωμένον] himself. 'What!' said Alcibiades, 'are you teaching boys to read when you are competent to edit [ἐπανορθοῦν] Homer? You should be training young men.'[22]

The anecdote underlines the fact that the most likely place to find a book in classical Athens was in the possession of some reader. More important for the current discussion, it shows that individual readers felt the need to correct the texts they had. Today, when we see 'annotations' in a book, we view it as a desecration, even when mistakes are corrected. Not only were corrections considered essential then, but also the corrector was esteemed. What the account does not tell us is how that teacher made his emendations. Did he compare one copy of Homer with another? Did he decide on the basis of his own understanding of how Homer should read?

The first recorded instance we have of an historian recording a discrepancy between copies occurs in Polybius in the second century BC.[23] Strabo, a century later, complains about the quality of the texts of Aristotle:

> certain booksellers [βιβλιοπῶλαι] who used bad copyists [φαύλοις γραφεῦσι] and would not collate [ἀντιβάλλοντες] the texts – a thing that also takes place in the case of the other books that are copied for selling, both here [in Rome] and in Alexandria.[24]

'Collating' means comparing two texts against each other for agreement and disagreement and not merely ensuring that all the pages are in sequence. This usage of collating continues today for critical editions of texts like James Joyce's *Ulysses*, when the editor establishes the preferred reading word by word in the text with an '*apparatus criticus*' at the bottom that gives the variant readings from other 'editions' of the work.

Scribal errors were often so rife that it truly was '*caveat emptor*'.[25] Cicero writes to his brother: 'As for the Latin ones, I don't know where to turn, the copies are made and sold so full of errors.'[26] Varro limits his discussion of '*is*' ('*this*'): 'I have touched upon this classification more sparingly, because I am of opinion that the copyists will not take proper care in transferring these quite confusing matters.' The translator adds in a footnote: 'The condition of the manuscripts shows that Varro was right.'[27] Livy spares the writer and blames the scribe, when he says 'In the case of Lucius Scipio I would prefer indeed that there was an error [*mendum*] of the scribe [*librarii*] rather than a lie [*mendacium*] of the writers [*scriptores*] regarding the sum of gold and silver.'[28] Martial takes advantage of the relationship between author and scribe with the stock excuse:

> If any poems in these sheets [*chartis*], reader, seem to you either too obscure or not quite good Latin, not mine is the mistake: the copyist [*librarius*] spoiled them in his haste to complete for you his tale of verses. But if you think that not he, but I am at fault, then I will believe that you have no intelligence.[29]

The problems that accurate copies present lie behind Plutarch's praise for the library of Lucullus as having both 'many books and well written [γεγραμμένα καλῶς]'.[30]

A little flattery might get the author to personally go over your copies. So Pliny the Younger answers the request of Metilius Nepos:

> You want me to re-read and correct [*emendandos*] the copies of my speeches [*libellos*] which you have assembled with such care. Of course I

will, for there is nothing which I ought to do so gladly, especially at your request. When a man of your judgment, scholarship and eloquence (and moreover as busy as yourself and the future governor of an important province) thinks my writings worth carrying around with him, I should surely do my utmost to see that this item of luggage is not a useless encumbrance. My first care then shall be to make your present travelling companions as congenial as possible; and my second to provide you with more which you may like to add to them on your return. The fact that you are one of my readers is no small encouragement to new work.[31]

Authors in any age need little incentive to produce more.

The concern an author had for the accuracy of his text sometimes resulted in admonitions to readers and future copyists. According to Eusebius, Irenaeus (second century AD) ended his work, *The Octet*, with the following plea:

If, dear reader, you should transcribe this little book, I adjure you by the Lord Jesus Christ and by His glorious advent, when He comes to judge the living and the dead, to compare your transcript [ἀντιβάλῃς] and correct it carefully by this copy [ἀντίγραφον], from which you have made your transcript. This adjuration likewise you must transcribe and include in your copy.[32]

By the beginning of the fourth century AD not just authors, but scribes, collators, and correctors were sometimes acknowledged:

This volume has been transcribed from, and corrected by, the Hexapla of Origen, as corrected by his own hand. Antoninus, the confessor, collated [ἀντεβάλεν], and I, Pamphilus, corrected [διόρθωσα] the volume in prison, by the favour and enlargement of God. And if it be not presumptuous so to say, it would not be easy to find a copy equal to this copy.[33]

Sometimes the emenders were over-zealous. Aulus Gellius devotes a lengthy discussion as to whether Cicero used '*futurum*' or '*futuram*' in one of his speeches against Verres (2.5.167). Gellius remarks that he was using 'a copy of unimpeachable fidelity [*libro spectatae fidei*], since it was the result of Tiro's careful scholarship' with the result that 'there is no error in writing or grammar but those are wrong who do violence to good copies [*bonos libros*] by writing *futuram*.'[34] Quintilian sees the situation in more general terms: 'Unlearned readers are apt to alter such [archaic] forms when they come across them in old books, and in their desire to decry the ignorance of the scribes convict themselves of the same fault.'[35]

TITLES

Today, books automatically come with titles.[36] Yet their usefulness was not immediately apparent in antiquity, because the need for titles is a function of number. If you have only one written work, you can simply refer to it as 'the Book', as, indeed, the Bible (from *biblion*, book) is still known. When you have two works, you can refer to them in five basic ways: by number (one or two), by author, by subject, by the opening words, or a combination thereof. As soon as an author produces more than one work, then each work requires a further modifier, the content – hence the combination method of titling. We have Homer's *Iliad* and *Odyssey*. But, as I mentioned in Chapter 2, the names and the division into 'books' all postdate Homer. Homer's early readers would have probably said they were reading the 'book' about Achilles or the one about Odysseus. By the fifth century BC, the height of classical Greece, titles became common for the Attic plays, but remained rare for other writings. Herodotus opens his work (1.1): 'This is the exposition [ἀπόδεξις] of the history [ἱστορίης] of Herodotus of Halicarnassus. . . .'[37] Thucydides does the same thing (1.1): 'Thucydides the Athenian wrote down [ξυνέγραψε] the war of the Peloponnesians and Athenians. . . .' Both authors do two things to distinguish their works. First, they say who they are by giving their names and where they come from. Second, they give the subject of their works. In neither case is there a formal title. Instead, each author gives the pertinent information not in bullet style, as today, but in a sentence.

As with all of the tools related to literacy, titles become increasingly common as time passes. In the fourth century BC Plato names his dialogues after whoever is Socrates's main antagonist in the particular dialogue. His followers, however, often wanted more explicit information. So they retained his title, e.g. *Phaedo*, and added '*or about the Soul*'. The idea of compound titles continues today, as in the title of this book. But not everything had titles. One major group consisted of works, like speeches, that had no need for titles when originally composed. Sometimes several titles existed for the same work. Athenaeus makes the following reference:

> Archestratus of Syracuse (or was it Gela?) in a work which Chrysippus entitles 'Gastronomia,' but which Lynceus and Callimachus call 'The Art of High Living,' Clearchus, 'The Art of Dining,' and others, 'The Art of Fine Cookery' – the poem is in epic verse and begins, 'Of learning I offer proof to all Hellas.'[38]

Athenaeus in a later reference (7.278a) adds yet a fifth title ('Gastrology') for the same work. Even today fixed titles are not always the rule, especially when publishers think that the American and British markets differ. One of Agatha Christie's mysteries started out as *Ten Little Niggers* in Britain, became *Ten Little Indians* in the United States, and finally, *And Then There*

Were None. Both then and now the most conclusive way to tell whether the titles refer to the same work is to examine the originals. Descriptive summaries can sometimes be helpful. 'Cataloguing' information is today recorded directly in the book itself, generally on the back of the title page.

In antiquity they had one method that we never use. After Athenaeus has given the four alternate titles, he proves that they refer to the same work by quoting the opening line. The use of *incipits* ('*it begins*') to identify works was common. Callimachus, when he lacks a title and no obvious one is to hand, gives the incipit.[39] Incidentally, Callimachus often includes a count of the number of lines, even for non-metrical works. Poetry with its meter should have a consistent line count no matter what the handwriting or format; whereas prose could vary enormously in layout. None the less, the linecounts would give a general idea as to whether a work was very long or very short. As an example, according to Athenaeus:

> There is even a book by Chaerephon [a contemporary of Socrates] recorded by Callimachus in his *Table* [πίνακι] *of Miscellany*; he writes as follows: 'Writers on dinners: Chaerephon to Kurebion.' And then he subjoins the beginning of it, 'Since you have often bidden me' (and adds the size) 'in three hundred and seventy-five lines.'[40]

The titles themselves appeared on identifying tags and within the roll, often at the end, because that was the most protected portion of a roll, since it was innermost.[41] Not until late in antiquity do titles appear at the beginning of a roll.[42] This placement may have contributed to the use of incipits, since they would be the first part of any roll to be read. By the time of Cicero, titles were generally assigned by the authors themselves and not by scholars or librarians, as during the Hellenistic period, although, for example, Horace did not refer to his work as the *Ars Poetica*.[43] Pliny the Elder has a rather long and somewhat historical disquisition on the subject:

> There is a marvellous neatness in the titles [*inscriptionis*] given to books among the Greeks. One they entitled Κηρίον, meaning *Honeycomb* . . . and again *Violets, Muses, Hold-alls, Handbooks, Meadow, Tablet, Impromptu* – titles that might tempt a man to forfeit his bail. But when you get inside them, good heavens, what a void you will find in the middle! Our authors being more serious use the titles *Antiquities, Instances and Systems.* . . . Diodorus among the Greeks stopped playing with words and gave his history the title of *Library.* . . . For myself, I am not ashamed of not having invented any livelier title [than *Natural History*].[44]

Pliny the Younger advises that it is 'a writer's first duty . . . to read his title [*titulum*], to keep asking himself what he set out to say, and to realize that he will not say too much if he sticks to his theme [*materiae*], though he certainly will if he brings in extraneous matter.'[45] This statement is not so very different from a modern view of titles. Hazard Adams says that 'a true title must *always* be integral to the work.'[46]

Aulus Gellius takes a simple route:

> And since, as I have said I began to amuse myself by assembling these notes during the long winter nights which I spent on a country-place in the land of Attica, I have therefore given them the title [*inscripsimus*] of *Attic Nights*, making no attempt to imitate the witty captions [*inscriptionum*] which many other writers of both languages [Greek and Latin] have devised for works of th[is] kind . . . I thus fall as far short of all other writers in the dignity too even of my title [*inscriptionis*], as I do in care and in elegance of style.[47]

As with all textual aids in antiquity, titles were never quite standardized. Suetonius preserves my favorite example: 'The "Eunuch" [of Terence] was even acted twice in the same day and earned more money than any previous comedy of any writer, namely eight thousand sesterces; and for this reason the sum is included in the title-page [*titulo*].'[48] By the Middle Ages titles became essential, in part, according to Mary Carruthers, because they provided a mnemonic and, more importantly, the moral starting point for each work.[49] While we consider titles to be essential today, sometimes it is not very easy to decide what the title is; for example, Dickens went through at least fourteen titles before deciding on *David Copperfield*.[50] Scholars sometimes refer in print to a future project by a title that never makes it to print.

OTHER FORMS OF TRANSMISSION

In addition to physical replication of a text, one other major route of making one's work known was common: public readings or performances. The continuation of oral transmission is a natural development from an oral culture that only had public performances. Thomas Cole says: 'Until the term *poiêtês* (first attested in the mid-fifth century) gained currency, the language did not even have the means of distinguishing composer from performer.'[51] In an age without electricity and the marvels of communication that it allows, public performance before an audience physically in attendance remained a dominant form of transmission and not just for plays, which, both then and now, are almost invariably meant for performance. Like Shakespeare and opera, the best plays formed a standard repertory that would be performed regularly with the result that their texts needed to be preserved over time. I have already alluded to the corruption of the texts for the plays written by the fifth century BC Greek tragedians.

Most other kinds of texts, however, can be written either for performance or for reading or for both. Our earliest Greek 'literature' is Homer, whose works were originally circulated and made known orally. After his death, rhapsodes travelled from place to place performing Homer and other epic poets. When literacy became common, at least among the elite, the rhapsodes became the butt of the literate like Socrates in Plato's *Ion*. Simonides, whom you will meet at length in Chapter 7, is credited with the invention of pay for poetry, or as a scholiast (ancient commentator) put it: 'Simonides seems to have been the first to introduce money-grabbing into his songs and to write a song for pay. This is what Pindar says in riddling fashion in his *Isthmians* (2.1ff.).'[52]

Writers like Herodotus worked during a transitional period when the written word was becoming sufficiently common for individuals to begin to acquire texts. Lucian writes that:

> As soon as he [Herodotus] sailed from his home in Caria [Turkey] straight for Greece, he bethought himself of the quickest and least troublesome path to fame and a reputation for both himself and his works. To travel around reading his works, now in Athens, now in Corinth or Argos or Lacedaemon in turn, he thought a long and tedious undertaking that would waste much time. . . . The great Olympian games were at hand, and Herodotus thought this the opportunity he had been hoping for. He waited for a packed audience to assemble, one containing the most eminent men from all Greece; he appeared in the temple chamber, presenting himself as a competitor for an Olympic honour. . . . In a single meeting he won the universal approbation of all Greece and his name was proclaimed not indeed just by one herald but in every city that had sent spectators to the festival.
>
> The lesson was learnt. This was the short-cut to glory.[53]

Nielsen ratings may be a modern invention, but the principle on which they depend – the largest audience for the least cost – was established early. Some scholars, however, claim that because Lucian wrote so many centuries after the fact, he may not be an accurate source for the way Herodotus went about publicizing his works, especially since Lucian says that Herodotus 'so bewitched his audience that his books were called after the Muses, for they too were nine in number';[54] for we know that the names of the Muses were not attached to Herodotus's *Histories* until the Hellenistic period. Momigliano concludes that 'We simply do not know whether Thucydides, Xenophon and, for that matter, the other eminent historians of the fourth century BC (Ephorus, Theopompus) ever read their works in front of an audience.'[55] Yet we do know that, in addition to poets like Simonides and Pindar, various philosophers from the fifth century BC and later did go around Greece reading from their works.[56] Hence Lucian may be wrong about the originator of the practice, but not about the practice itself or its appearance in the fifth century BC.

By the fourth century BC, at least according to tradition, some audiences were less than captive. Diogenes Laertius records that 'when Plato read the dialogue *On the Soul*, Aristotle alone stayed to the end.'[57] Cicero repeats virtually the same story, but with different players:

> When reading that long and well-known poem of his [Antimachus] before an assembled audience, in the very midst of his reading all his listeners left him but Plato: 'I shall go on reading,' he said, 'just the same for me Plato alone is as good as a hundred thousand.' . . . If Demosthenes on the other hand had held only Plato as his auditor and was deserted by the rest, he could not have uttered a single word.[58]

As a result, Aristotle, in his work *On Rhetoric*, directly addressed what had become a common problem:

> Remarks aimed at the audience derive from an effort to make them well disposed and sometimes to make them attentive or the opposite; for it is not always useful to make them attentive, which is why many speakers try to induce laughter . . . as Prodicus [fifth century sophist] said, 'to throw in some of the fifty-drachma lecture when the hearers nod.'[59]

Conversely, there were lecture-groupies. Plato writes in the *Republic* about:

> Lecture-fanciers who love listening, the last persons in the world to be counted philosophers – they will never attend a discussion or any such serious study if they can help it, but their ears are for public hire; they run about to hear all the concerts at festival time, not leaving out one town or one village.[60]

Plutarch devotes an essay to the subject ('On Listening [to lectures]' = *Moralia,* 37c–48d). Some lecture-goers, like today, took extensive notes, and then circulated those notes much like the modern note-taking services that have sprung up around major universities. On the one hand, these notes are the basis of much of what has survived from the Hippocratic corpus and even of Aristotle; on the other hand, being notes, they are subject to all the problems of notes – contradictions, inaccuracies, lacunae. Quintilian explains the problems such notes present for an author:

> I have been all the more desirous of so doing [writing a work on teaching oratory] because two books on the art of rhetoric are at present circulating under my name, although never published by me or composed for such a purpose. One is a two days' lecture which was taken down by the boys who were my audience. The other consists of such notes as my good pupils succeeded in taking down from a course of lectures on a somewhat more extensive scale: I appreciate their kindness, but they showed an excess of enthusiasm and a certain

lack of discretion in doing my utterances the honour of publication. Consequently in the present work although some passages remain the same, you will find many alterations and still more additions, while the whole theme will be treated with greater system and with as great perfection as lies within my power.[61]

Quintilian is very aware of the differences between oral and written delivery, an issue to which I return later. The modern example *par excellence* for the publication of lecture notes by students is that of *The Course in General Linguistics* of Ferdinand de Saussure.

The Romans virtually institutionalized the practice of public performance.[62] According to Quinn, there were four different public venues in the first century BC:

[1] the traditional performance by the poet himself to a few friends; . . .
[2] some kind of contest in which more than one poet takes part; . . .
[3] non-dramatic performance by the poet himself; . . . [4] professional performance in the theatre as some kind of spectacle.[63]

The best known public performer today may have been Nero, who 'read his poems too, not only at home but in the theatre as well, so greatly to the delight of all that a thanksgiving was voted because of his recital, while that part of his poems [that had been read aloud] was inscribed in letters of gold and dedicated to Jupiter of the Capitol.'[64] Claudius, his predecessor, was not the performer Nero was:

When he gave his first reading to a large audience, he had difficulty in finishing, since he more than once threw cold water on his own performance. For at the beginning of the reading the breaking down of several benches by a fat man raised a laugh, and even after the disturbance was quieted, Claudius could not keep from recalling the incident and renewing his guffaws. Even while he was emperor he wrote a good deal and gave constant recitals through a professional reader [*lectorem*].[65]

Vergil, in contrast, was a master performer. According to Suetonius:

The success of the 'Bucolics' on their first appearance was such, that they were even frequently rendered by singers [*cantores*] on the stage [*in scena*]. When Augustus lingered at Atella to treat his throat, Vergil read the 'Georgics' to him for four days in succession, Maecenas taking his turn at the reading whenever the poet was interrupted by the failure of his voice. His own delivery, however, was sweet and wonderfully effective. In fact, Seneca has said that the poet Julius Montanus used to declare that he would have purloined some of Vergil's work, if he could also have stolen his voice, expression, and dramatic power; for

38

the same verses sounded well when Vergil read them, which on another's lips were flat and toneless.[66]

Vergil even found live performance an aid in composition in much the same way that I, at a much lower level, will notice some grammatical clanger when reading a formal lecture to an audience, but not to myself. Suetonius records:

> Eros, his amanuensis [*librarium*] and freedman, used to report, when he was an old man, that Vergil once completed two half-verses off-hand in the course of a reading . . . and he immediately ordered Eros to add both half-lines to his manuscript [*volumni*].[67]

Pliny the Younger performed well in certain situations and not in others. He wrote Suetonius a letter about his problems that I quote in full:

> Please settle my doubts. I am told that I read badly – I meant when I read verse, for I can manage speeches, though this seems to make my verse reading all the worse. So, as I am planning to give an informal reading to my personal friends, I am thinking of making use of one of my freedmen. This is certainly treating them informally, as the man I have chosen is not really a good reader, but I think he will do better than I can as long as he is not nervous. (He is in fact as inexperienced a reader as I am a poet.) Now, I don't know what I am to do myself while he is reading, whether I am to sit still and silent like a mere spectator, or do as some people and accompany his words with lips, eye and gesture. But I don't believe I am any better at mime than at reading aloud. Once more, then, settle my doubts and give me a straight answer whether it would be better to read myself, however badly, than to do or leave undone what I have just said.[68]

It is one thing to act out a poetic work, it is another to lip-synch the text. What is hard to comprehend is that Pliny could not have found himself a better reader – which would have made his decision much easier. No, we don't have the answer from Suetonius. We do have, however, three other letters of Pliny on the same subject. First, he mentions his devoted wife, who 'If I am giving a reading . . . sits behind a curtain near by and greedily drinks in every word of appreciation.'[69] Second, he writes to a friend about such entertainment:

> You [Julius Genitor] complain about a dinner party, a grand affair which filled you with disgust at the mimes and clowns and the male 'dancers' going the round of the tables. Please don't be for ever frowning – I have nothing of that kind in my own house, but I can put up with those who do . . . think how many people there are who dislike the entertainments which we find fascinating, and think them

either pointless or boring. How many take their leave at the entry of a reader, a musician, or an actor . . . . Let us then be tolerant.[70]

Third, Pliny has some astute observations about the average attender of poetic readings that still hold true:

> There was scarcely a day throughout the month of April when someone was not giving a public reading . . . in spite of the fact that people are slow to form an audience. Most of them sit about in public places, gossiping and wasting time when they could be giving their attention, and give orders that they are to be told at intervals whether the reader has come in and is reading the preface, or is coming to the end of the book. It is not till that moment – and even then very reluctantly – that they come dawdling in. Nor do they stay very long, but leave before the end, some of them trying to slip out unobserved and others marching boldly on.[71]

When public performance became more formal – that is, when the audience no longer was composed only of your friends and the larger public was invited, the logistics could be daunting. According to Tacitus:

> [A poet] finds himself obliged to run around into the bargain and beg people to be kind enough to come and form an audience. That too costs him something, for he has to get the loan of a house, to fit up a recitation-hall, to hire chairs, and to distribute programmes [libellos]. And even supposing his reading is a superlative success . . . what he gets out of it is never a friend, never a client, never any lasting gratitude for a service rendered, but only fitful applause, empty compliments, and a satisfaction that is fleeting.[72]

Hadrian, one of the more literate emperors, built an Athenaeum especially for such readings, and had a library attached to it.[73] According to some modern critics, 'That the *recitatio* [public reading] killed Roman literature is a familiar half-truth. One can argue that, on the contrary, it granted a patient who was already mortally ill an extended lease of life.'[74]

In summary, publication in antiquity is 'publication' only in quotes. Perhaps 'release' is a better term for a process over which the author and even his 'publisher' had so little control. Finally, publication throughout antiquity always had a large oral component. While authors today may give readings of their works, it is only of selections – except for children's books – and then only to entice you to buy them. It is inevitable that chaotic publication led to chaotic acquisition of books, which I discuss in Chapter 4.

4

THE ORGANIZATION OF COLLECTIONS OF WORDS

So far I have considered the book, or rather the roll, only as a single unit. Dealing with multiple works, as any highly literate person does, increases the problems of organization from that of the word within the text to the next level of texts within texts (multiple selections within the same unit), and finally to the highest level of separate texts that in sufficient numbers warrant a kind of storage developed specifically for them. This chapter focuses on the acquisition and arrangement of multiple texts, both literary and documentary, and the nature of access to them in antiquity.

OBTAINING BOOKS

The rich, as always, could afford to purchase what they wanted. They would get books in much the same way we do: buying directly from 'booksellers'; using public and private libraries; and borrowing and copying 'editions' owned by friends. Booksellers do not appear until the end of the fifth century BC. We don't know how they worked at the time and their role remains unclear even in later periods.[1] Did they keep a stock of basic texts to be copied on demand, much like the reproduction of American dissertations by *University Microfilms*? Did they have multiple copies of popular works? All major cities must have had bookshops of some sort. Pliny the Younger admits that:

> I didn't think there were any booksellers [*bibliopolas*] in Lugdunum [modern Lyons], so I was all the more pleased to learn from your letter that my efforts [*libellos*] are being sold. I'm glad they retain abroad [*peregre*] the popularity they won in Rome [*urbe*].[2]

In other words, Pliny has little idea what happens to his works once they leave his hands – a situation very similar to today. Most of the time we don't know where our books are going to be sold, especially outside our own country. It is uncertain what kind of payment, if any, authors received. It is extremely doubtful that they were paid anything like royalties. Horace ambiguously says 'That is the book to make money for the Sosii', who

41

were booksellers;[3] while Martial says: 'The whole collection of Mottoes in this slender little volume will cost you to buy four sesterces. Is four too much? it can cost you two, and bookseller [*bybliopola*] Tryphon would make his profit.'[4]

While books were neither great rarities nor terribly expensive in Rome, they still had a certain cachet, for Seneca the Younger asks:

> What is the use of having countless books and libraries, whose titles their owners can scarcely read through in a whole lifetime? . . . Let someone else praise this library [at Alexandria] as the most noble monument to the wealth of kings. . . . There was no 'good taste' or 'solicitude' about it, but only learned luxury – nay, not even 'learned,' since they had collected the books, not for the sake of learning, but to make a show, just as many who lack even a child's knowledge of letters use books, not as the tools of learning, but as decorations for the dining-room.[5]

Used books were available, and, along with them, opportunities for the shady to gull the innocent and the *nouveau riche*. Lucian in the second century AD devoted a dialogue to 'The Ignorant Book-Collector':

> Why, how can you tell what books are old and highly valuable, and what are worthless and simply in wretched repair – unless you judge them by the extent to which they are eaten into and cut up, calling the book-worms into counsel to settle the question? As to their correctness and freedom from mistakes, what judgement have you, and what is it worth? . . . What you would gain by it in the way of learning, even if you should put them under your pillow and sleep on them or should glue them together and walk about dressed in them? . . . I have never yet been able to discover why you have shown so much zeal in the purchase of books. . . . But perhaps you regard the matter as a display of wealth and wish to show everyone that out of your vast surplus you spend money even for things of no use to you?[6]

Learning by osmosis and the decorative use of books for home and office both have a long and venerable history.

LIBRARIES

The English word *library* dates back to the fourteenth century,[7] but in French its look-alike, *librairie,* means *bookstore* in English, while a totally different word *bibliothèque* is the equivalent of *library*. Both words go back to classical roots, when various words and phrases for 'repositories' for books were used with little consistency. *Library* and its relatives have Latin ante-cedents in '*librarius*', whose meanings ranged from '*record-clerk*' to '*scribe*' to '*bookseller*' and which itself is based on '*liber*', book.[8] *Bibliothèque*, however, depends on the Greek, βιβλιοθήκη (Latin = *bibliotheca*), which is literally a *'case for books'*. But this word had another, related, but somewhat disparate sense. When Diodorus Siculus needed a title for his forty-roll history that began 'with the most ancient times and . . . [went] down to his own day', he called it literally 'The Historical Library' [βιβλιοθήκη ἱστορική].[9] Pliny the Elder found the title apt: 'Diodorus among the Greeks stopped playing with words and gave his history the title of βιβλιοθήκη.'[10] More often, however, sizeable collections of books were called just that. So Xenophon, when writing about the pseudo-intellectual Euthydemus, said that he 'had formed a collection of works [γράμματα πολλὰ = literally 'many letters'] of celebrated poets and professors, and therefore supposed himself to be a prodigy of wisdom for his age.'[11] Athenaeus, some four to five centuries later, still refers to his own collection in a similar manner, as a 'possession of old Greek books [βιβλίων] [that] was so great that it surpassed all those marveled at for their collections.'[12]

Euripides was credited in antiquity with owning the first personal library. Eric Havelock, however, believes that this attribution was falsely made in the Hellenistic period through a misinterpretation of Aristophanes's *Frogs* (line 1409) where Euripides's bookishness was mocked.[13] In that case, which does seem likely to me, Aristotle's scholarly library in the Lyceum was the first; it was certainly the most famous, for it went from him through several hands before being acquired by Sulla and possibly Cicero after him.[14] Strabo's account of its history highlights many of the problems facing the literate:

Aristotle bequeathed his own library to Theophrastus . . . he is the first man, so far as I know, to have collected books and to have taught the kings [the Ptolemies] in Egypt how to arrange a library. Theophrastus bequeathed it to Neleus; and Neleus took it to Scepsis and bequeathed it to his heirs, ordinary people, who kept the books locked up and not even carefully stored. . . . But much later, when the books had been damaged by moisture and moths, their descendants sold them to Apellicon of Teos for a large sum of money, both the books of Aristotle and those of Theophrastus. But Apellicon was a bibliophile rather than a philosopher; and therefore, seeking a restoration of the parts that had been eaten through, he made new copies of the text, filling up the gaps incorrectly, and published the books full of errors . . . immediately after the death of Apellicon, Sulla, who had captured Athens, carried off Apellicon's Library to Rome, where Tyrannion the grammarian, who was fond of Aristotle, got it in his hands by paying court to the librarian, as did also certain booksellers who used bad copyists and would not collate the texts – a thing that also takes place in the case of the other books that are copied for selling, both here and in Alexandria.[15]

Athens itself did not get a 'public' library until the second century BC.[16] Public libraries did not exist in the modern sense of open access to anyone who walked in off the street. Instead the term 'public' in an ancient context refers to those libraries established either as part of a philosophical school, such as Aristotle's, or by various rulers.[17] Nor is it completely clear how access was controlled. Those studying at a particular school could use its library. For instance, Philostratus says that Proclus of Naucratis, in the second century AD, 'had a library [θήκη βιβλίων] at his own house which was open to his pupils and supplemented the teaching in his lectures.'[18] Famous 'scholars' might be invited or perhaps come on their own; otherwise, it was very probably a matter of whom you knew. A private library in antiquity by contrast would be similar to one today. It would be used by its owner and his friends.

The most notable library was the 'Museion' (Museum) established in Alexandria by Ptolemy I Euergetes, perhaps following an old Egyptian tradition, though Strabo in the passage just quoted implies that Theophrastus determined their 'arrangement'.[19] The way the library was stocked is instructive:

> Galen records (17a606 Kühn) that the early Ptolemies systematically sought out texts from all over the Greek world and even impounded books that arrived in Alexandria as cargo, had copies made of them and returned the copies, not the originals to their owners . . . (17a607) the texts of the great Attic tragedians, which were officially kept in the public record office at Athens as a guard against actors' interpolations, were borrowed by . . . Euergetes I . . . against an indemnity of fifteen talents; once safely at Alexandria the originals were kept for the Library, handsome new copies made for the Athenians, and the indemnity forfeited.[20]

Alexandria became a mecca for scholars, and the place where many of the cognitive innovations for reading began: the first critical examination of texts to establish what was genuine and what were later interpolations; the division of works into rolls of comparatively standard length; accenting of Greek; attempts at 'punctuation' (the obelus and asterisk date to this period); and the first glossaries.

It is still debated whether in the third century BC Callimachus made the first library 'catalogue'. According to Rudolf Blum, '[the] arrangement [of its contents] was intended to reflect as far as possible the arrangement of the scrolls on the shelves of bookcases.'[21] Yet P. M. Fraser rightly stresses that the title of the work, *'Tables of persons eminent in every branch of learning, together with a list of their writings'*, implies that it is not a list of the holdings of a library.[22] He believes that the work more likely resembled:

a sort of universal biography and bibliography, in which the authors and others were arranged according to subjects – 'Table of Lyric Poets', 'Table of Orators', 'Table of Philosophers', and so on – alphabetically under each heading. The amount of detail recorded is uncertain, but it appears that each entry normally contained a brief biography of the subject, followed by the titles of his works (or, where necessary, the opening lines), also listed alphabetically, and the total number of lines in the edition consulted by Callimachus.

The addition of biographies to the lists helps explain why it took up 120 rolls, four times the length of Pliny's *Natural History*. Again, the fact that it has the words 'table' and 'list' in its title does not mean that these tables and lists were displayed in columns. Instead it would have looked just like Pliny's 'Table of Contents'. Another curiosity is the way works with multiple books or rolls were listed. Diogenes Laertius, in the third century AD, instead of writing, for example, 'On Justice, four books', as the standard translation does,[23] begins his list of Aristotle's works with 'On Justice α β γ δ', with every single book recorded separately. Such a format is not only lengthy, but also in some ways less user-friendly, when works like Theophrastus' 'Refutative Arguments' take up eighteen books.[24]

That some kind of 'catalogue' existed in the library at Alexandria seems likely. We do know that the rolls that were impounded from the ships, as Galen recorded, were labeled 'from the ships'. Similarly, rolls from other places were likewise labeled. In addition, the 'editor' and/or 'corrector' of the copy and the original owner were noted, when known.[25] The scribe who produced the copy, however, was generally not recorded. All of this information pertains to the provenience of the particular copy and indirectly to its quality.[26] It says nothing about how the rolls were stored in the library or even about the existence of a catalogue in our sense.

Estimates for the holdings for the library in Alexandria range broadly from 100,000 to 700,000 'volumes'.[27] Nor do we know whether these figures refer to rolls or to works, though we do know that some rolls contained more than one work.[28] During the medieval period library collections were still very small by our standards: Papal 645, Avignon 2059, Sorbonne 1017 in 1290 and 1722 in 1388, etc. Alphabetic catalogues did not exist before the twelfth century and it was not until the fifteenth century that both shelf-lists and alphabetical listings were considered necessary.[29] The Rouses suggest that the medieval catalogues were originally made as inventories of property rather than as guides to the location of books. Unlike what we believe to be true for antiquity, the Rouses also say that medieval libraries were generally not physically arranged by subject matter until the thirteenth century. The precise arrangement of books in a classical library is virtually unascertainable.[30]

Even if a catalogue existed for Alexandria, and perhaps for other libraries, it does not mean that the catalogues themselves were reproduced. One never knew which library held which volumes, a situation that can still occur today, though vastly improved by national consortia of libraries and the recent advent of online catalogues. Diodorus Siculus in the first century BC writes that 'it is not easy for those who propose to go through the writings of so many historians to procure the books which come to be needed.'[31] Worse yet, Athenaeus implies that catalogues were selective in what they recorded:

> Alexis wrote a play called *The Teacher of Profligacy*, says Sotion of Alexandria in his book *On Timon's Satires*. I myself have not come across the play. Although I have read more than eight hundred plays of the so-called Middle Comedy . . . and I do not even know of anyone who thought it worth cataloguing [ἀναγραφῆς]. Certainly neither Callimachus nor Aristophanes has catalogued it, nor have even those who compiled the catalogues in Pergamum.[32]

The first 'union' catalogue that attempted to include all the holdings within a geographical region was organized by John Boston for Great Britain in the thirteenth century.[33]

As today, two types of libraries existed: circulating and non-circulating. Most were probably non-circulating. An inscription from the early second century AD library of Pantainos in the Agora of Athens says: 'Books shall not be taken out of the library and it shall be open from the first to the sixth hour.'[34] Gellius in the second century AD mentions using several libraries in Rome and one in Greece.[35] In the same period, Marcus Aurelius writes a somewhat ribbing letter to Fronto, his tutor:

> I read Cato's speech, 'On the Property of Pulchra,' and another in which he impeached a tribune. 'Hey,' you say to your slave, 'go as fast as you can and bring me those speeches from the library of Apollo.' You will be sending him in vain, for those volumes have followed me here! You must therefore ingratiate yourself with the librarian at the library of Tiberius. You might offer him a tip (which he and I will share equally when I come back to town).[36]

Making friends with the librarian is effective in any age. Though some libraries circulated their books, even these, however, probably limited that circulation to a select group, among which an heir-apparent to the rule of Rome clearly numbered. Often, the best, if not the simplest, way to obtain a book was either to borrow or to copy a friend's copy. For example, Cicero asks his friend Atticus to 'Please bring me Theophrastus on Ambition from Quintus' [Cicero's brother] library.'[37] Cicero writes to his brother:

> As regards filling the gaps in your Greek library and exchanging books and acquiring Latin ones, I should very much like all this done,

46

especially as I too stand to benefit. But I have nobody I can employ on such a business, not even for myself. Books, at least such as one would like to have, are not on the market and they can't be obtained except through an expert who is willing to take trouble. However, I'll give an order to Chrysippus and talk to Tyrannio.[38]

It should be mentioned that Cicero had not one but at least three separate libraries to stock, for each of his homes in Tusculum, Rome, and Antium.[39] On at least one occasion, he was fortunate enough to acquire a whole library.[40]

Nor was Cicero alone in his love of books. He writes about Cato:

So it may well be believed that when I found him taking a complete holiday, with a vast supply of books at command, he had the air of indulging in a literary debauch, if the term may be applied to so honourable an occupation.[41]

To balance this picture, consider that Seneca the Younger believed the exact opposite:

Accordingly, since you cannot read all the books which you may possess, it is enough to possess only as many books as you can read. 'But,' you reply, 'I wish to dip first into one book and then into another.' I tell you that it is the sign of an over-nice appetite to toy with many dishes; for when they are manifold and varied, they cloy but do not nourish.[42]

The contrast in approach between Cicero and Cato on the one hand, and Seneca on the other should make it clear that, like today, there was not a single, uniform attitude in antiquity towards literary matters. Elaine Fantham rightly wonders: 'Have we been too quick to assume that all educated Romans had libraries like those of Cicero, Lucullus, and Atticus?'[43]

When the libraries at Rome 'were destroyed by fire', Domitian, an emperor not known for his intellectual prowess, 'renewed [them] at very great expense, seeking everywhere for copies of the lost works, and sending scribes to Alexandria to transcribe and correct them.'[44] Remember that transcription is only half the process; collating or proofing, as we would call it, was a major task.

STORING BOOKS: OF PIGEONHOLES, SHELVES, AND JARS

As today, almost any container – baskets, jars, wooden boxes – could hold books.[45] If you had a lot of books, however, your methods of storage would more likely be directly suited for storing rolls. Libraries used two types of structures: pigeonholes and cabinets. Rather than small pigeonholes, which would hold just a single roll, the sections were large enough to accommodate a varying number of rolls, as an imperial relief from Neumagen shows.[46] When referring to the library at Alexandria, Vitruvius (7,Introduction,7) uses the word '*armaria*', which are wooden cabinets with doors to protect the rolls, as a relief of a doctor seated by his open armoire shows.[47] This example is particularly interesting, because the rolls take up only the top shelf with a bowl placed on the middle one. Seneca the Younger (*On Tranquillity of Mind*, 9.6) grumbles about elaborate armoires made 'of citrus-wood and ivory', when plain ones would do the job just as well. Personal libraries would clearly have fewer of these structures than 'public' libraries. The cabinets could line the exterior walls or be free-standing.[48] When the codex appeared, the same shelves of the cabinets could be used for stacking the codices, as an illumination from the Codex Amiatinus shows.[49]

In the fourth century AD, Flavius Vopiscus, one of the aliases of the author of the *Historia Augusta*, in the life of the Emperor Tacitus (*c.* AD 200–276; ruled AD 275–276) says:

> And now, lest any one consider that I have rashly put faith in some Greek or Latin writer, there is in the Ulpian Library in the sixth case [*armario sexto*], an ivory book, in which is written out this decree of the senate, signed by Tacitus himself with his own hand.[50]

Although it is generally held that virtually all the references to such documents in the *Historia Augusta* were made up to give a rhetorical air of authenticity, none the less, the way of referring to a book by its location in a numbered series of cases probably does reflect contemporary practice. It implies, first, that the cases themselves were probably numbered; otherwise I would think the author should have said something like 'the sixth case from the right, as you enter'. Second, the number of 'volumes' in any given case was sufficiently small that the case alone was a satisfactory reference. Today we would find a reference to one 'column' in a row of library stacks far too broad.

If you were particularly well organized, you might, like Zenon in the first half of the second century BC, have labeled each roll on the outside.[51] By the first century BC at the latest, the rolls were often identified by little tags hanging from the edges, somewhat like the tags for toes used in morgues today.[52] These tags may have been added by the owner and not the 'publisher' of the roll. So Cicero asks Atticus:

> to send me a couple of your library clerks [*librariolis*] to help Tyrannio with the gluing and other operations, and tell them to bring a bit of parchment [*membranulam*] for the labels [*indices*], σιττύβαι as I believe you Greeks call them.[53]

I know of one instance where a more elaborate container, a rectangular granite box, had the contents of its rolls inscribed on the outside: 'Dioskourides 3 Volumes.'[54] While comparatively heavy, it, too, could be placed on any kind of shelving arrangement.

The most popular containers, however, were jars. Perhaps the rounded form of the roll suggested round storage. The best known example may be the plain jars that held the Dead Sea Scrolls. In the Bible, Jeremiah (32.14) says: 'Take these deeds [*libri*], both this sealed deed of purchase and this open deed, and put them in an earthenware vessel [*in vase fictili*], that they may last for a long time.'[55] The narrow mouth of some jars would not just have limited the number of rolls stored, but also would have made removal of the rolls difficult.[56] Round containers with wider openings and covers were also used. In Latin they are known as '*scrinia*' ('*scrinium*' singular) and in smaller versions as '*capsae*' ('*capsa*' singular).[57] From Roman and medieval representations we know that the rolls were placed upright in the scrinia.[58] Both types usually had straps attached for carrying. An early second-century AD Roman relief shows a man carrying a number of tablets in a related kind of container.[59] It is without a lid and appears to be oblong in shape to hold two 'rows' of tablets.

The jars and scrinia that have survived either in actuality or in pictures do not have labels on the outside detailing their contents.[60] Only by taking out the roll and unrolling it would you know what you had. According to Tiziano Dorandi, a wall painting from Pompeii with the Muse Erato shows her seated by a *capsa* containing six rolls, all with tags.[61] I also know of two cases of scrinia with inscriptions, referring, not to their contents, however, but to the marble statues with which they appear as supports.[62] The inscriptions run across the tops of the rolls, that is, on the *cornua* of the dowels around which the rolls were wound, with each end carrying one to three letters. The inscriptions continue along the top band of the scrinium itself, and across its body in one case. In other words, the inscriptions are placed for ease of reading by the viewer of the statue. They refer to the offices held by the togate men portrayed standing next to them and thereby imply that the contents of the rolls, though not defined, probably related to that office.[63] In the late Roman Empire the term 'scrinia' by extension meant not just the container, but the various offices that needed those containers, such as the '*scrinium epistularum*' (Office of Correspondence) and the '*scrinium libellum*' (Office of Petitions).[64] The use of scrinia as a means to identify those associated with writing goes back to at least as early as the first century BC, for Suetonius describes a statue of Orbilius, who was 50 years old in 63 BC: 'His marble statue may be seen at Beneventum [his birthplace], on the left side of the capitol, representing him seated and clad in a Greek mantle [*palliati*], with two book-boxes [*scriniis*] by his side.'[65]

Because the scrinia were comparatively easy to carry, yet simple to store, they functioned as a cross between our bookcase within the home and our briefcase for toting documents outside.[66] The best modern equivalent would be the nineteenth-century traveling frontier libraries. *The American School Library* from 1839, for example, came in a wooden case with a handle that held approximately forty-five books on three shelves.[67] When Catullus (14.17–18) refers to the 'scrinia of the booksellers', he implies that the bookseller, when asked for a particular work, searches through the round boxes lined up on either the floor or shelves.[68] If your library was small, the chances are that you would remember what you had and which roll was which. If you had a large collection of rolls, you would probably have used shelves with pigeonholes and tags for the individual rolls, as already described.

Identification of the contents of codices by a label on the spine, as in the illumination from the Codex Amiatinus, was not the norm and did not become standard until print.[69] Instead, labels appeared on all possible surfaces: edges, covers, and spines. Paul Saenger and Michael Heinlen correlate the location of the label with the 'highly significant transition from horizontal to vertical shelving, which began to take place at the end of [AD 1501] or shortly after the incunable period.'[70] The word *bookcase* first occurs in the eighteenth century, though they appear earlier in pictures.[71] The advent of the printed book led to such an increase in production and lowering of cost that collections became larger, which in turn led to the need for more efficient storage containers. The form of the printed book, which was bound with stiff covers, strong enough to be stood on end, determined the design of the bookcase. At the same time, the handily exposed spine allowed for brief labels. Hence the 'carrier' of the writing affects the form of the storage, which, in turn, affects the ease of retrieval.

Finally, as we use cartons and boxes to store a variety of objects, so scrinia in antiquity also functioned as all-purpose containers. Pliny the Elder tells a moralizing story about Alexander the Great going through the booty of his defeated rival, the Persian King Darius:

> there was a scrinium of unguents made of gold and enriched with pearls and precious stones, and when Alexander's friends pointed out the various uses to which it could be put, since a warrior soiled with warfare had no use for perfume, he said, 'No, by Hercules, rather let it be assigned to keeping the books of Homer' – so that the most precious achievement of the mind might be preserved in the richest possible product of the craftsman's art.[72]

LETTERS

Letters form an interesting group from the point of view of retrieval. Cicero, in a number of letters, remarks about keeping copies of both the letters he sends and the ones he receives. For example, he writes to M.

Fabius Gallus: 'Don't distress yourself about the letter which you are so sorry you tore up. I have it safe at home. You can ask for it any time you like.'[73] None the less, he doesn't keep all his letters, because he writes to Atticus: 'There is no collection [συναγωγή] of my letters, but Tiro has about seventy and I shall have to get some from you.'[74] It is also possible that he keeps certain letters for only a limited period of time, the way we keep our personal income tax records for seven years.

In another letter to Atticus, Cicero writes:

> Having arrived at this point I unrolled the roll of your letters [*evolvi volumen epistularum tuarum*], which I keep under seal [*signo*] and preserve most carefully. Well, the one you dispatched on 21 January contains this passage. . . . You write this three days after our departure from Rome. Then on 23 January. . . .[75]

Five things are important. First, Cicero doesn't keep the original letters. Instead he makes fresh copies, which he stores not on tablets, but in rolls. Second, he doesn't make copies of everything he gets, for he writes to his slave, Tiro: 'I see your game! You want your letters too put into rolls.'[76] Third, presumably because of their delicate nature he keeps the letters from Atticus under seal and hence away from prying eyes. Fourth, the letters are generally dated to the day of the month, but not the year; the place where they were written is also sometimes included.[77] Augustus was more compulsive than most: 'He always attached to all letters the exact hour, not only of the day, but even of the night, to indicate precisely when they were written.'[78] If only an occasional letter is involved, neither date nor place is important. Their inclusion implies not just a heavy load of correspondence, but also that events are moving swiftly enough to make dates and places meaningful.

Fifth, in Cicero's case, major correspondents get separate rolls and within any roll the letters are recorded chronologically in order of receipt. Cicero, in the letter to Atticus, goes on to cite in order twelve letters received between 21 January and 9 March, 49 BC. Pliny the Younger may have been less organized than Cicero in his correspondence, because he begins his published collection with the comment that 'I . . . [am] not keeping to the original order . . . but taking them as they came to my hand.'[79] Conversely, Pliny may not have kept his own letters in chronological order, but in separate rolls for each addressee and within those rolls in chronological order. Actually, for all we know, Cicero may have done the same. It is, however, likely that neither Cicero nor Pliny followed the modern business practice of keeping two copies of each letter so that one could be filed by date and the other by subject. After you accumulate enough correspondence over enough years no matter what the order, it becomes cumbersome to search unless, of course, you are computerized. None the less,

Libanius, a Greek rhetorician in the fourth century AD, did have sufficient control over his own written production that, like Cicero, he could find both his previous speeches and particular letters for copying.[80] Rolls with letters would have been labeled and stored like other rolls.

5

RETRIEVAL:
DOCUMENTS AND TEXTS

DOCUMENTS AND RECORDS

If we leave the world of the 'book' and the individual reader for that of the 'governmental archive', the situation improves to a certain extent. From at least as early as the Hellenistic period, visual clues appear in documents that make it clear to the experienced in antiquity and the knowledgeable today what kind of document was involved. The classical scribes intuitively know what Donald Norman states directly: 'The most appropriate format depends upon the task, which means that no single format can ever be correct for all purposes.'[1] Classical scribes used a variety of means to indicate different kinds of documents, including hanging indents, large initial letters, different spacings between sections, and changes in scripts for different writers.[2] As Roger Bagnall puts it, '*Everything* has more articulation than prose literature.'[3] Turner says that 'Good layout is one aid which a practised scribe does not despise.'[4] Layout, however, is one thing; the text itself remains in the preferred format of *scriptio continua*. Moreover, that writing could be difficult to read, because it was often written in a rapid cursive which eschewed full articulation of individual letters.[5]

Inscriptions on public display were often designed to be pleasing to the eye rather than to the reader. From the latter part of the sixth century BC through most of the third century BC, Athens, for example, adopted the '*stoichedon*' style for its inscriptions.[6] Think of a rectangular grid like graph paper with each letter taking up the same amount of space and lining up directly with the letters above and below it. That arrangement resembles fixed-spaced type today, but the Greeks added a real challenge: the width of the text remains constant, which means that words wrap between lines, as in this example, using the next paragraph:

```
MOREIMPORTANTFORTHEPRESENTDISCUSSIONISTHEISSUEOFRETRI
EVINGRECORDSSCHOLARSHAVEGENERALLYASSUMEDTHATTHEPRIMEP
URPOSEFORWRITINGDOWNLAWSANDOFFICIALTRANSACTIONSLIKETR
EATIESISTOKEEPARECORDTHATCANBECONSULTEDNOTJUSTINTHEBU
```

53

TALSOINTHEFUTUREHENCEONCESOMETHINGISWRITTENITSHOULDBE
CAPABLEOFBEINGFOUNDEVENIFDOCUMENTSWEREOCCASIONALLYLOS
TASTHEYCANBETODAYRECENTLYSCHOLARSHAVEBEGUNTOREEXAMINE
THEEVIDENCEONHOWTHEGOVERNMENTARCHIVESOFTHETWOMAJORCLA
SSICALCITIESWEREUSEDATHENSSTOREDITSLAWSANDREGULATIONS
INTHEBOULEUTERIONANDMETROÖNANDROMEINTHEAERARIUMANDTAB
ULARIUM

This style of display was not something designed by engravers for the delight of engravers alone, but a format that was regulated by the government: 'The scribes must make their letters clear, engrave them deep enough to keep their color, and not overcrowd them on the stone surface.'[7] Achieving a balance between aesthetically arranged letters and easy visual comprehension took a long time to establish, as the title page from *The Boke Named the Gouernour* by Sir Thomas Elyot shows. Published in 1534, it puts 'THE' in the biggest letters at the top of the page, with 'BOKE' in smaller type on the line below, then on the third line in still smaller type, 'NA-' with the rest of the word 'med' in lower case on the fourth line with the rest of the title.[8] One aspect of stoichedon lingers today. Word processors allow us to justify, that is, align, our right margins, but the results are not always easy to read if the word processor is not capable of full micro-justification.[9]

More important for the present discussion is the issue of retrieving records. Scholars have generally assumed that the prime purpose for writing down laws and official transactions like treaties is to keep a record that can be consulted not just in the present, but also in the future. Hence once something is written it should be capable of being found, even if documents were occasionally lost, as they can be today. Recently scholars have begun to reexamine the evidence on how the government archives of the two major classical cities were used.[10] Athens stored its laws and regulations in the Bouleuterion and Metroön and Rome in the Aerarium and Tabularium.

Rosalind Thomas paints a very bleak picture for Athens at the height of its power in the fifth and fourth centuries BC.[11] No system controls whether a law is inscribed on stone with a copy in one of the two major 'archives' or whether the only copy or the original itself was displayed elsewhere within the city. She describes the situation:

In the *bouleuterion*, if the tablets and stelai were on the walls, reference was mostly a matter of knowing where to look . . . the use of jars as document containers was probably common. The written documents for cases which were to go before an arbitrator were put separately in jars, one jar for each side. The jars were sealed and handed over to members of the Forty: thus to 'file' a case was to put it in a jar and seal it (Arist. *Ath.Pol.* 53.2). The use of jars rather than shelves may have been more frequent than we would suppose. . . . It is after all comparatively easy to keep documents. It is a rather different step to use them again, find them and consult them. The archive's [the Metroön's] organization was simple, if not haphazard, without catalogues or important permanent keepers. With its combination of stelai, wooden tablets and large jars, it did in some ways continue the methods of keeping documents (including stelai) in the old *bouleuterion*. . . . Many records were not preserved at all. Certain types of document were destroyed as soon as the transaction they signified was over.[12]

Religious institutions did not do any better. The oracular responses of the Pythia at Delphi were kept in chests (κιβωτοί), and seem not to have been 'reconsulted' after their initial use.[13] Raffaella Cribiore adds that 'often documents were not written primarily to be read. They were presented on demand, saved for various amounts of time, and sometimes reused.'[14] Carol Lawton writes about the Attic document stelai with figured reliefs above the inscriptions:

> Although it is often assumed that documents were inscribed as a form of permanent record-keeping, only a small percentage of documents from any period were finally committed to stone. The documents that were inscribed were types for which an appeal to the public eye was important, documents of interstate relations and civil affairs, set up in public because they affected everyone and were expected to remain in force for some time, financial documents for public scrutiny of major official expenditures, and honorary decrees. . . . Most of the documents signalled [sic] out for decoration with relief concern the foreign and financial affairs of the Athenian Empire.[15]

As an archaeologist, I am, of course, delighted that the financial records for the construction of the Erechtheion on the Acropolis in Athens, among others, have been preserved; as someone living in the twentieth century, however, I find it very strange that financial records for what particular workmen were paid were carved in stone.[16]

Late Republican Rome shows little if any improvement on the Athenian system for finding documents.[17] Polybios, writing in the second century BC, paints a curious picture:

> Now since such treaties exist and are preserved on bronze tablets [χαλκώμασι] to this day in the treasury of the Aediles beside the temple of Jupiter Capitolinus, we can only read with astonishment what has been written by the historian Philinus on this subject. It is not the fact of his ignorance which is surprising, since even in our own day those Romans and Carthaginians whose age brought them nearest to the period in question and who were most versed in public affairs did not know of these records. What is extraordinary is how and on what authority he ventured to maintain the opposite.[18]

Significantly, Polybios does not fault the historian Philinus for not consulting records. He faults him only for not reporting the 'facts' as they were known; for elsewhere Polybios states that 'the study of documents is only one of the three elements which contribute to history, and stands only third in importance.'[19]

Because Polybios implies that the Romans relied on their memories for finding documents, it is remarkable that precise locations for some documents were recorded: 'Copied and verified from the bronze tablet posted on the Capitolium in Rome, by the altar of the Julian gens, on the outside left of the base: tablet I, column II, line 44.'[20] On the basis of the way Romans used records, Callie Williamson finds 'The precision of these directions . . . incredible.'[21] In a later article, she concludes that 'The entire formula is performative, rendering the action of law-making in words and anchoring the statute in a specific time, place and occasion.'[22] The Romans recognized the problem to a certain extent, for Julius Caesar, according to Suetonius, included among his projects one 'to reduce the civil code to fixed limits, and of the vast and prolix mass of statutes to include only the best and most essential in a limited number of volumes.'[23] The idea that some laws would fall by the wayside strikes me as noteworthy when American courts still cite British common law.

If the Romans were not using the information they took the time to engrave about the location of a document, why did they bother in the first place? Williamson believes that 'Bronze was used in order to create lasting memorials. Bronze tablets were eternal.'[24] Culham concludes that 'The reengraving shows that the Romans did not especially value reference to an original document; what they wanted was a bronze object dedicated at its original sacral site.'[25] If it is the object itself that matters, then we have an explanation for why Attic inscriptions would be written in *stoichedon* for so long. As Williamson puts it, 'Readability and visibility are two different things.'[26] What first impresses one, for example, about the Vietnam War Memorial in Washington DC is not who is listed but that so very many are listed. No one person reads the entire monument, though we do commemorate the dead with readings of all the names by a number of persons.

Unlike today when the written version of a law is paramount, then the reading of the law out loud constituted its 'publication' or 'being known'. Cicero remarks:

> Glaucia, that shrewd but unscrupulous man, used to warn the people, when some law was being read [*cum lex aliqua recitaretur*], carefully to mark the opening phrase. If it began, 'Dictator, Consul, Praetor, Master of the Horse,' they were to feel no concern; for they might know that it was nothing to them; but if it began 'Whosoever after the passing of this law,' then they were to see to it that they were not made liable to any new form of inquiry.[27]

Laws of a more immediate nature and concern were not engraved on bronze, but were painted with black letters on white-washed wooden tablets for posting where they would be accessible.[28] For example, Suetonius writes about Caligula:

> When taxes of this kind had been proclaimed, but not published in writing, inasmuch as many offences were committed through ignorance of the letter of the law, he [Caligula] at last, on the urgent demand of the people, had the law posted up, but in a very narrow place and in excessively small letters, to prevent the making of a copy.[29]

If the documents on public display were meant more for show than for use, then the situation for the documents that were kept in archives is even worse. Phyllis Culham bluntly says, 'A cynic could suggest that depositing *leges* or *consulta* at the *aerarium* might represent an effort to make such things inaccessible rather than the reverse.' Instead she believes that 'the old senatorial families could expect their need for information to be met by archival resources in their own households and in those of their friends.'[30] Culham has found information about 'only one man [Cato the Younger] who tried to consult documents in the *aerarium*; and his attempt demonstrates that it was next to impossible, even for a wealthy and powerful senator, to see documents in the *aerarium*.'[31] As Michael Clanchy puts it for the English royal archives during the Middle Ages: 'Historians today are better equipped to search the rolls than the king's clerks were in the thirteenth century.'[32] None the less, some did succeed in finding what they wanted. Cicero asks Atticus at least twice to find two different bits of recorded information, one a law (*lex*) and the other some item 'from that book [*ex eo libro*] with the senatorial decrees from the Consulship of Cn. Cornelius and L. Mummius.'[33]

With writing came a variation on the old problem of fraud: the falsification of records, especially in the late Roman Republic. Cicero bemoans that 'We have no guardianship of the laws, and therefore they are whatever our clerks want them to be; we get them from the State copyists, but have no official records.'[34] He also makes a point of his departure from the normal practice in one instance:

> Since I knew that the information had been entered in the public records, but that they would be retained, as was the traditional practice, in the safe-keeping of individuals, I did not conceal it or retain it at home, but immediately ordered it to be copied by all the clerks, distributed everywhere and given full publicity and made known to the Roman people.[35]

Writing has become *a* means of establishing the truth – even if it is only in certain cases and for contemporary events; this practice separates Rome from Athens of the high classical period. In most situations, however, witnesses counted more than written records. Plutarch reports that Cato the Younger:

> on one occasion when he was doubtful whether a certain decree had actually passed the senate, though many testified to the fact, he would not believe them, nor would he file the decree away until the consuls had come and taken oath to its validity.[36]

Cato the Younger employed his own copyists to document what actually transpired even after he had left the office of the quaestorship to prevent the production of fraudulent transactions. Cicero similarly remarks that:

> the audacity of the decemvirs is allowed considerable licence of tampering with the public registers and forging resolutions of the senate which have never been passed, since many of those who were consuls during those years are dead.[37]

In other words, if the original writers were dead, then the Romans believed that there was no way to check the accuracy of what had been written.[38] Such a standard differs dramatically from that of today when the validity of the Magna Charta or the Constitution of the United States is never questioned. None the less, a certain amount of trust in records must have existed, for 'he himself [Cato the Younger] paid five talents for books containing accounts of the public business from the times of Sulla down to his own quaestorship [approximately 30 years], and always had them in hand.'[39]

Cicero directly addresses the issue of accuracy for recording contemporary events – a situation one would think less prone to manipulation:

> your enemy's name was given, a crowded Senate and the memory of the event still fresh in their minds bore witness to it, and my clerks would even have shown the information to you, my friend and close companion, if you had wished, before recording it in the minutes; why, then, when you saw the record being falsified, did you remain silent?[40]

Sometimes the forgeries were quite elaborate, as when Antony posted false statutes, decrees, and edicts on bronze in public.[41] In the next century Suetonius remarked that Titus 'imitated whatever handwriting he had seen, and often declared that he could have been the greatest forger.'[42]

The problem was especially acute for wills. Suetonius says that it was during the reign of Nero:

> that a protection against forgers was first devised, by having no tablets [tabulae] signed that were not bored with holes through which a cord was thrice passed. In the case of wills it was provided that the first two leaves [cerae] should be presented to the signatories with only the name of the testator written upon them.[43]

Three safeguards were provided: the witnesses did not see the will itself; the holes could be lined up to deter the substitution of a different leaf; and the cord would have a seal.[44]

It is no wonder, then, that Livy in the late first century BC was ambivalent about the use of the written word. On the one hand, he recognizes that records for the early history of Rome are problematic:

> The history of the Romans from the founding of the City of Rome to the capture of the same . . . I have set forth in five books, dealing with matters which are obscure not only by reason of their great antiquity . . . but also because in those days there was but slight and scanty use of writing, the sole trustworthy guardian of the memory of past events, and because even such records as existed in the commentaries of the pontiffs and in other public and private documents, nearly all perished in the conflagration of the City.[45]

On the other hand, as Gary Miles points out, Livy does not trust more recent records, for Livy says about the Roman victory over the Samnites in 322 BC:

> It is not easy to choose between the accounts or the authorities. The records have been vitiated, I think, by funeral eulogies and by lying inscriptions under portraits, every family endeavouring mendaciously to appropriate victories and magistracies to itself – a practice which has certainly wrought confusion in the achievements of individuals and in the public memorials of events. Nor is there extant any writer contemporary with that period, on whose authority we may safely take our stand.[46]

Because written records were never trusted in antiquity the way they are today, they were never accorded the treatment necessary to truly keep them in order. As a result they were neither fully and easily retrievable, nor ever entirely reliable.

There was one area, however, where record-keeping seemed to work fairly well, at least, during the Roman imperial era: taxation. I use 'taxes' in the broadest sense to include the census, land-holdings, etc. which formed the bases for collecting revenues for the government. Money clearly focusses the bureaucracy of every age and culture. Most of our evidence comes from the detailed records preserved on papyri from Egypt.[47] An analysis of precisely how the Egyptian offices worked is beyond my scope, but two items are of interest. First, records were produced in multiple copies for filing in separate archives, and, in one case, six copies were required.[48] Second, the archives were sufficiently complicated that searchers were hired to find documents.[49]

Cicero mentions a curiosity among ancient literate practices in one of the passages just quoted. He describes the process of putting Senate discussions into written form: 'but men, I knew, whose memory, skill, and speed in writing enabled them to follow what was said with complete ease.'[50] In other words, the Romans had shorthand. According to F. G. Kenyon, the fact that Cicero used a Greek phrase (διὰ σημείων = 'by signs') rather than Latin indicated that 'he probably derived it [shorthand] from Greece.'[51] Possible support comes from an anecdote in Diogenes Laertius. He says that Xenophon, in the fourth century BC: 'was the first to take notes of [ὑποσημειωσάμενος], and to give to the world, the conversations [τὰ λεγόμενα] of Socrates, under the title *Memorabilia*.'[52] Unfortunately, the Greek is unclear whether Diogenes means that Xenophon 'took notes' in the sense of shorthand or in the sense of someone recording a lecture, whether in longhand or shorthand. Today, scholars (like Kenyon) tend to refer to the 'classical' shorthand by a 'Greek' word, 'tachygraphy'. Yet that word is not listed in LSJ; and its cognates, such as ταχυγραφέω, are late (Lydus from the sixth and Tzetzes from the twelfth centuries AD). Greek instead used terms based on the root σημει-, as Cicero indicates. In other words, unlike today, both the Greeks and Romans thought it more important that such writing consisted of 'signs' rather than that it was 'fast'. Incidentally, the English word 'stenography', again based on Greek roots (στενός = 'narrow' and γράφω = 'writing'), is a modern coinage dating back to the seventeenth century that stresses the amount of space such writing takes up rather than the speed at which it is written.[53]

In any event, according to tradition, shorthand was introduced to the Romans by Cicero.[54] Plutarch records:

> This is the only speech of Cato which has been preserved, we are told, and its preservation was due to Cicero the consul, who had previously given to those clerks who excelled in rapid writing instruction in the use of signs, which, in small and short figures, comprised the force of many letters; these clerks he distributed in various parts of the senate-house. For up to that time the Romans did not employ or even possess what are called short-hand writers [σημειογράφους], but then for the first time, we are told, the first steps toward the practice were taken.[55]

I find it interesting that Plutarch, three centuries after Cicero, feels the need to tell his readers what 'shorthand' is. Cicero himself used the 'system', because in one letter he apologizes to Atticus that 'You don't quite understand what I wrote to you about the ten Commissioners, no doubt because I used abbreviations.'[56] Cicero thereby implies that his abbreviations are not standard – a situation, which, in turn, supports the idea that such abbreviations had just been introduced and were not yet standardized. By the end of the medieval period there were over 14,000 abbreviations.[57] Tiro, a freedman of Cicero, was credited with introducing or inventing the Latin version, which consequently was sometimes called '*notae Tironianae*' or 'symbols of Tiro'.[58] According to Suetonius, the usefulness of such a skill was not

60

lost on the Emperor Titus: 'I have learned from many that he used also to take notes very quickly, competing with his secretaries as a game and joke.'[59] More typical, no doubt, is Seneca's view of the matter. He describes:

> our signs for whole words, which enable us to take down a speech, however rapidly uttered, matching speed of tongue by speed of hand. All this sort of thing has been devised by the lowest grade of slaves. Wisdom's seat is higher; she trains not the hands, but is mistress of our minds.[60]

A set of wax tablets with shorthand symbols in Greek concerning haulage have survived from the third century AD.[61]

THE PROBLEM OF RETRIEVAL: ALPHABETIZATION AND INDEXING

Seneca's dismissive attitude towards shorthand provides a partial explanation for the startling lack of organizational skills in classical antiquity. The idea that 'wisdom's seat is higher' means that the higher mind would turn not to the mundane production of words, literally, writing, but to their interpretation and classification. A Callimachus could be praised for organizing the Alexandrian library, a Zenodotus and Aristophanes of Byzantium for establishing accurate texts for that library, but the kinds of inventors we admire, like Edison or the Wright Brothers who work with 'mechanical' things, were often beneath notice. None the less, the very existence of shorthand in classical antiquity demonstrates that they, even if they were slaves, invented what they needed.[62]

What is remarkable is that they simply did not feel a need to make texts, as we would put it today, user-friendly. This phenomenon actually occurs fairly frequently. A notable modern example is the QWERTY keyboard for typewriters and computers. While many bemoan the amount of work the left hand, and particularly the left pinky, has to perform, most tests show that its nearest rival keyboard, the Dvorak arrangement, isn't sufficiently faster to make so many people switch. The layout is 'good enough', as Jerry Pournelle, a computer columnist, puts it.[63]

Similarly, although both the Greeks and Romans knew the alphabet and learned its letters in a fixed order in a highly arbitrary and rote fashion, they never realized the value of applying that same system to organizing their words. Again, the demand never arose. Petroski makes the very interesting point that:

> whereas the shortcomings of an existing thing may be expressed in terms of a *need* for improvement, it is really *want* rather than need that drives the process of technological evolution. . . . Luxury rather than necessity, is the mother of invention.[64]

I think it is difficult to imagine technical improvements in the absence of any existing models. Only use, and frequently inadvertent use, slowly led to the rich set of textual tools we have today. Again, Petroski puts it well, when he describes the process as 'form follows failure'.[65] Perhaps the best parallel is the invention of the fork, which appeared in the seventh century AD in the Middle East, reached Italy around 1100, but took until the seventeenth century to get to England. Yet its two basic elements existed in classical antiquity. The trident had the tines and was used for spearing and spoons had a curved contour to hold small pieces of food in place.[66]

Because the syllable remained the major operative unit for reading in antiquity, alphabetization, which depends on the letter and not the syllable, would not naturally spring to mind as a useful means of organization. In Greek, even the names for the letters of the alphabet work against alphabetization, because most of them are multi-syllabic in contrast to English with its predominately single-syllable names. Moreover, the names for letters in Greek do not always reflect the sound of the letters when pronounced in words the way the names for letters generally do in English. When Athenaeus (10.453c–d) quotes from a fifth-century BC play by Kallias with a chorus composed of letters of the alphabet, the letters are written out, as they would be pronounced. Latin, however, had primarily single-syllable names.[67] Again, it is an issue of the aural versus the visual. Alphabetization depends on a visual sorting of lists, for two reasons. First, sorting by sound in certain cases would lead to a different order. In English, for example, 'pneumonia' would be placed with words beginning with the letter 'n' rather than 'p'. Second, the maximum number of items that we can hold in short-term memory ranges between five and nine, which means that we would quickly lose our place.[68]

Plato in the fourth century sets up the issue nicely in a dialogue between Socrates and Theaetetus:

> SOCRATES: Suppose you are asked about the first syllable of 'Socrates.' Explain, Theaetetus, what is SO? How will you answer?
> THEAETETUS: S and O.
> SOCRATES: And you have there an account of the syllable?
> THEAETETUS: Yes.
> SOCRATES: Go on, then, give me a similar account of S.
> THEAETETUS: But how can one state the elements of an element? The fact is, of course, Socrates, that S is one of the consonants, nothing but a noise, like a hissing of the tongue, while B not only has no articulate sound but is not even a noise, and the same is true of most of the letters. So they may well be said to be inexplicable, when the clearest of them, the seven vowels themselves, have only a sound, and no sort of account can be given of them.[69]

Although in typical fashion Socrates leads Theaetetus to stumble, contradict, and retract this initial statement, none the less, it does reflect a commonly held view that the syllable counts in a way that the letter does not.[70] Hence whatever alphabetization occurs tends to be by the first or at the most the first three letters and not what we call 'absolute alphabetization' down to the very last letter. Even the simple form did not appear before the third century BC. Use of alphabetization was sufficiently erratic and distinctive that Michael Haslam has employed it as a means of analyzing the sources for the Homer Lexicon of Apollonius Sophista. He notes that as certain works are repeatedly copied over the centuries 'the alphabetization tends to get tidied up.'[71]

Pliny the Elder's use of alphabetization is instructive. According to Lloyd Daly, who has made the most extensive study of alphabetization in antiquity:

> Pliny, who is frequently hard put to it to find what he considers satisfactory ways of presenting his masses of information, generally resorts to alphabetic arrangement only when he has exhausted all other principles of organization, and even then is, at times, apologetic for what he apparently felt to be a rather unimaginative procedure.[72]

Nor does Pliny always allow for the differences between Greek and Latin alphabetical order when he uses a Greek source. In one case (*Natural History*, 37.138 and 37.151–156) he translated the Greek terms into Latin and rearranged the words by their first letter according to the Latin order, with the result that after 'Ca, Ce, Ci, Cr and Cy' come seven words beginning with 'Ch', the Greek 'chi', which is the third letter from the last in the Greek alphabet.[73] Photius (*Bibliotheca*, 145), writing in the ninth century AD, actually commented that Helladius, a fourth-century AD grammarian, had not followed alphabetic order 'for all the syllables, but only for the beginning one.' Photius significantly does not use the word 'alphabet', which he could have, since it was used as least as early as the second century AD.[74] Nor does he yet think in terms of ordering by letter (γράμμα or στοιχεῖον), but only by syllable (συλλαβή). It is not so much that the absence of a word means that the concept does not exist, but that in this case the circumlocutions used in antiquity indicate that the alphabet is not thought of as a distinct entity that would allow it to be used independently for organizational purposes.[75]

The case of Euripides's 'alphabet' plays is instructive for how both modern scholarship and antiquity work. In the nineteenth century Ulrich von Wilamowitz, a product of a highly alphabetical society, noticed that one medieval manuscript (L for Laurentine, the library where it is now) had all the surviving plays of Euripides except for the *Trojan Women*.[76] Moreover, it was the only manuscript to preserve the nine plays whose names started with letters between E and K. Wilamowitz believed that such a grouping indicated a conscious ordering of the plays into alphabetical order, which he dated to the second century AD. A relief-statuette of a seated Euripides supports this argument, because the names of Euripides's plays are listed in two columns, one on either side of him, in rough alphabetical order (for example, Alcestis, Archelaos, Aigeus).[77]

There are a number of problems with the theory. First, Wilamowitz assumes that lists and texts work the same way. For example, consider modern books with lists of the author's works given opposite the title page. These works are sometimes in alphabetical order, sometimes in chronological order. Only in rare cases would the actual works be stored in the same order in libraries as they are given in these lists. Non-fiction is ordered by subject. Second, the same manuscript is the sole source for the *Bacchae*, one of the plays outside the group of E-K. Third, L, as well as the other manuscripts with Euripides's plays, does not order any of the plays in alphabetical order, though Wilamowitz might claim that was the fault of the compiler of L itself and not the so-called original on which it ultimately depended.[78] Why, however, would later compilers change the order? It is always easier to slavishly copy than to reorganize. The alphabetical habit became more, not less, pronounced as time passed. Hence the Louvre list is 'more alphabetical' than an earlier list of Euripidean plays from the Piraeus.[79] The Piraeus list is far less complete and groups its entries roughly by letters but not in strict alphabetical order. Fourth, the alphabetical plays are mixed in with the others. Fifth, William Barrett believes that the intermediate codex which these plays would occupy would, unusually, have six rather than five plays.[80] Hence I believe that the 'alphabetical' plays belong not to Euripides but to Wilamowitz.

Some of the ancient reluctance to alphabetize may be due to the changes in what letters constituted the alphabet and their shifting order. Daly, none the less, contends that the alphabet was stable from almost the very beginning when it was first adopted by the Greeks and Romans, despite his acknowledgment that the Romans:

> inserted the newly devised G in the place of the Z for which they found no immediate use, so that the seventh letter was still the seventh and succeeding letters were still eighth, ninth, etc. By the first century BC when Y and Z were reintroduced at Rome they were, of course, added at the end of the alphabet, since their old places had by then been lost in the new convention as modified by omissions. Even the medieval J and W are not exceptions to the rule since they are only variant forms of the I and V which they follow.[81]

The presence or absence of qoppas, waus, and digammas in Greek alphabets is regional and chronological. Quintilian notes that:

Orthography, however, is also the servant of usage and therefore undergoes frequent change. I make no mention of the earliest times when our alphabet contained fewer letters and their shapes differed from those which we now use, while their values were different.[82]

Suetonius records that:

he [Claudius] invented three new letters . . . maintaining that they were greatly needed; he published [*edidisset*] a book [*volumen*] on their theory when he was still in private life, and when he became emperor had no difficulty in bringing about their general use. These characters may still be seen in numerous books, in the daily gazette [*diurnis* = 'dailies'], and in inscriptions on public buildings.[83]

Suetonius implies and Tacitus directly states (*Annals*, 11.14) that the three letters fell out of use when Claudius was no longer emperor.[84] In other words, while Claudius perceived a need for symbols for certain sounds, most did not. In some ways his attempt is akin to George Bernard Shaw's efforts to reform English spelling. The current systems were simply good enough.

Letters were, however, used individually in certain restricted situations: as numbers; as symbols for architects and artists; as symbols in mathematical and similar diagrams; and in acrostic texts. The Greeks had two different systems for numbers.[85] The East Greeks developed the idea of using the alphabet as numbers, a system still used today in numerology. In Athens in the fourth century BC, each tribe was identified by a letter as a part of the process of selecting members of the jury for trials.[86] Ancient examples of numerology occur by chance in an 'oral' poet like Homer and later by design. For instance, lines 264 and 265 in the seventh book of the *Iliad* both add up to 3498.[87] Suetonius quotes a Greek wisecrack about Nero: 'Nero, Orestes, Alcmeon their mothers slew./A calculation new. Nero his mother slew.' The 'calculation new' is that the numerical value of Nero in Greek (1005) equals the numerical value of the rest of the sentence in Greek.[88] Aulus Gellius was suitably skeptical of this kind of information. He called it 'merely a list of curiosities.'[89]

The other type of numbers used by the Greeks is known as the 'acrophonic' system in which the first letter of the numeral's name stood for that number. Hence P represents pente or 'five'. This second type of numbering is the only instance I know of where a single letter and not a syllable was commonly used in isolation the way we would today.[90] The Roman numerals were based on signs, even if we consider those signs to be letters today. The 'M' for a thousand is actually an abbreviation, which probably is related to the development of shorthand.[91] Not until the thirteenth century AD did Arabic numerals replace the cumbersome Roman system, except for certain vestigial appearances in copyright dates of movies, pagination of prefaces, and on timepieces.[92] Roman numerals, however, do have one advantage over Arabic numbers. They are easier to use for addition and subtraction. All you have to do is combine the two numbers by counting strokes for addition and deleting them for subtraction, as long as you do not use the 'short' method for representing numbers, such as 'XL' rather than 'XXXX' for '40'. For instance, to add 343 to 1186: CCCXXXXIIIMCLXXXVI = MCCCCLXXXXXXXVIIII = MCCCCCXXVIII = MDXXIX. To subtract 343 from 1186: MCLXXXVI = DCCCCCCXXXXXXXXXIIIIII = DCCCXXXXIII. No calculation is needed, only a lot of work space.[93] Division and multiplication, however, are a real pain with Roman numerals.

Masons often used individual letters as indicators for where blocks, tiles, and other parts of buildings should be placed.[94] For example, an alpha on a block indicated that that block would be positioned next to or over an alpha on the structure itself. Such markings were also employed by artisans for smaller-scale objects, like the sixth-century BC bronze krater from Vix, where letters indicate the location in the frieze for the figures, which had been separately cast.[95] Other related applications include the use of letters as symbols in technical discussions. Aristotle, for example, assigns letters to different parts of diagrams. He begins a discussion of the winds: 'Let A be the point where the sun sets at the equinox and B, the point opposite.'[96]

The last use of separate letters occurs in acrostics, an English word that is a transliteration of the Greek 'ἀκροστιχίς', which means the top or left-most of the line of verse (στιχός). As with the numerological examples, acrostics occur sometimes by chance, sometimes on purpose. Homer, as an oral poet, provides fertile ground for unintentional occurrences.[97] Eustathius, a twelfth-century AD commentator on Homer, said that the first letters of the first five lines of Book 24 of the *Iliad*, 'λεύκη' (literally 'white', metaphorically 'fortunate') refer to Hektor, who is ransomed by his father for burial at the end of the book. The earliest intentional uses of acrostics date to the Hellenistic period and come from Alexandria, a hotbed of scholarly erudition and pedantry. The back of one of the second-century AD Iliac Tablets has a nine-line poem in which each line begins with a letter from the name of the person dedicating the plaque.[98] The best-known example may be from the Old Testament in Proverbs 31.10–31 where the Hebrew and the Vulgate (the Latin translation made in the fourth century AD) versions precede each line with a letter from the Hebrew alphabet in alphabetical order. Acrostics appear elsewhere in the Bible as well as in other poems and ancient inscriptions.[99] They are developed to a high state of art during the medieval period with pictures that are themselves acrostics embedded within the overall acrostic.[100]

The most curious appearance of ancient acrostics occurs in oracles. Cicero writes about the Sibylline Books, the major collection of oracles for Rome:

[I]n the Sibylline books, throughout the entire work, each prophecy is embellished with an acrostic, so that the initial letters of each of the lines give the subject of that particular prophecy. Such a work comes from a writer who is not frenzied, who is painstaking, not crazy.[101]

Dionysius of Halicarnassus explains: 'Some of these [oracles] are found to be interpolations among the genuine Sibylline oracles, being recognized as such by means of the so-called acrostics.'[102] In other words, the acrostic serves as a means of authentication. While it may have been somewhat harder to fake an oracle using an acrostic, it would certainly have been easy enough. The real point is that they believed that this simple device for avoiding fraud worked.

Julius Caesar and Augustus developed crude ciphers, which were not only described by Suetonius ('substitute the fourth letter of the alphabet, namely D, for A, and so with the others') but were the subject of 'a commentary of the grammarian Probus, *On the Secret meaning of the Letters appearing in the Epistles of Gaius Caesar*, which is a very careful piece of work' according to Aulus Gellius.[103] Suetonius's key to the code may actually have come from the work described by Gellius, since Suetonius knew the works of Probus.[104] Herodotus (7.239) describes an even simpler device or mechanism:

> taking a double tablet [for writing], he [Demaratus] scraped away the wax from it, and then wrote the king's [Xerxes's] intent on the wood; which done, he melted the wax back again over the writing, so that the bearer of the tablet thus left blank might not be troubled by the way-wardens.[105]

And if you don't have wax tablets handy, you can always shave a slave's head, write your message on his now bald pate, wait some time for the hair to grow back in, and then send the slave with the instruction to have his head shaved on arrival.[106] Cicero, however, settles for 'call[ing] myself "Laelius" and you "Atticus", and I shall not write in my own hand [*chirographo*] or use my seal [*signo*], that is if the letter is such that I should not want it to get into strangers' hands.'[107]

These three uses of letters – as numbers, symbols, and acrostics – however, have little to do with the idea of sorting a list of words into a particular order. Not until the thirteenth century did the immediate ancestors of our modern retrieval tools appear. Richard H. Rouse and Mary A. Rouse make the point that:

> literate society certainly complicated things by inventing the subject index over two hundred years before inventing the [printing] press. The fact remains that indexes and other finding tools were invented because there was need for them – not because it was easy, or practical, to make them at a certain time.[108]

Again, the interesting point is that no one in antiquity felt that need with the one major exception of Eusebius. In his 'Canon Tables' he cross-referenced the passages in the *Gospels* to each other. Print, of course, made the whole process relatively easy, because it provided two crucial elements lacking in antiquity: uniformity between copies of the same text, and control over the format of that uniformity by one person, the printer.[109] In turn, print relied on the earlier innovation of the codex with its easily numbered pages. The Rouses further suggest that:

> [the] need for a system that permitted one to locate and refer to information in a text contributed materially to the introduction of arabic numerals in the West. . . . While historians of science may wax regretful that the West was so tardy in accepting the 'radically new [arabic] arithmetic' with its revolutionary concept of zero, we can observe to the contrary that the index-makers, indifferent to the ramifications of the arithmetic, adopted the numeral eagerly, for the down-to-earth reason that these provided an unmatched means of marking one's place.[110]

Even with print the idea of absolute alphabetization took a while to catch on. Walter J. Ong gives two nice examples:

> Indexing was long by first letter only – or, rather, by first sound: for example, in a Latin work published as late as 1506 in Rome, since in Italian and Latin as spoken by Italian-speakers the letter *h* is not pronounced, 'Halyzones' is listed under *a*. Here even visual retrieval functions aurally. Ioannes Ravisius Textor's *Specimen epithetorum* (Paris, 1518), alphabetizes 'Apollo' before all other entries under *a*, because Textor considers it fitting that in a work concerned with poetry, the god of poetry should get top billing.[111]

Absolute alphabetization remained a novelty as late as 1604, when Robert Cowdrey published his *Table Alphabetical* and still felt compelled to explain how to use his dictionary:

> If thou be desirous . . . rightly and readily to understand, and to profit by this Table, and such like, then thou must learne the alphabet, to wit the order of the letters as they stand, perfectly without booke, and where every letter standeth: as (b) nere the beginning, (n) about the middest, and (t) toward the end.[112]

Dictionaries, as compendia of day-to-day speech, did not exist in antiquity. What individual 'glossaries' there were did not appear until the time of Aristotle in the fourth century BC, and even then tended to be organized thematically around subjects, such as good Attic usage or obsolete words used by Homer.[113] It is difficult to imagine not being able to check the spelling or meaning of a word. In the second century AD Gellius decides

68

that 'the earlier writers called what we termed *narrationes*, or "tales", *insectiones* by older writers' and 'I *think* that both Marcus Cato and Quintus Ennius wrote *insecenda* and *insece* without *u*.'[114] He has no way of finding out. It is not so much that there were no rules, but that not all spelling follows the rules, much to the dismay of the Emperor Augustus, like Claudius an early-day George Bernard Shaw. According to Suetonius:

> He [Augustus] does not strictly comply with orthography, that is to say the theoretical rules of spelling laid down by the grammarians, seeming to be rather of the mind of those who believe that we should spell exactly as we pronounce.[115]

Quintilian sums up the situation:

> On all such subjects the teacher must use his own judgment. . . . For my own part, I think that, within the limits prescribed by usage, words should be spelt as they are pronounced. . . . I am however haunted by the thought that some readers will regard what I have said as trivial details. . . . I myself do not think that we should go so far as to lose our sleep of nights or quibble like fools over such minutiae; for such studies make mincemeat of the mind.[116]

Worse, imagine not knowing whether or not the word you are using is 'real'.[117] Actually that part might have been rather enjoyable, as Horace believed:

> [W]ords, though new and of recent make, will win acceptance, if they spring from a Greek fount and are drawn therefrom but sparingly. . . . And why should I be grudged the right of adding, if I can, my little fund, when the tongue of Cato and of Ennius has enriched our mother-speech and brought to light new terms for things? It has ever been, and ever will be, permitted to issue words stamped with the mint-mark of the day.[118]

So, for example, Horace (*Epistles*, 1.19.47) made up the word '*diludia*', 'a break in the *ludus* [game]'.[119] Varro is even stronger in his feeling about neologisms: 'And do they claim that there is such difference between the two senses [sight and hearing], that for their eyes that are always seeking some new shapes of their furniture, but they wish their ears to have no share in similar novelties?'[120] Nearly a century later Quintilian (1.5.70) noted the continuing Roman preference for new words of Greek rather than Latin origin, but then cautions:

> Current words are safest to use: there is a spice of danger in coining new. For if they are adopted, our style wins but small glory from them; while if they are rejected, they become a subject for jest. Still we must

make the venture; for as Cicero says, use softens even these words which at first seemed harsh.[121]

Julius Caesar, however, was very conservative in these matters and reminds us of modern teachers of writing: 'Avoid, as you would a rock, a strange and unfamiliar word.'[122] The concept of documenting *all* words is a very recent development, dating back to the nineteenth century and the beginning of the *Oxford English Dictionary*, and even then it was soon realized that the '*all*' is not possible to achieve.[123] Elaine Fantham rightly points out that the absence of dictionaries made learning foreign languages on one's own nigh impossible. Without dictionaries the only way to find out what a foreign word meant was by asking a foreigner or someone thoroughly trained in that language.[124]

The idea of an index never occurred. Nor could Pliny have conceived of using written keywords, as one scholar has claimed, because Pliny did not think in terms of isolated words, but in descriptive phrases as his 'Table of Contents' shows.[125] As Ong puts it, 'Alphabetic indexes show strikingly the disengagement of words from discourse and their embedding in typographic space.'[126] The closest equivalent to the modern habit of highlighting text does not occur until late in classical antiquity with a 'group of lawyers' aide-mémoires, all fourth century AD, in which the overlining of personal and geographical names and of key words picks out the essentials for quick study.'[127] In antiquity, the only types of text to consistently receive special marking to help the reader were legal ones with the headings in red.[128] The practice of using red to highlight information and especially opening words and beginnings of sections goes back to Egyptian practices in the Middle Kingdom, if not the Old Kingdom.[129]

As I mentioned in Chapter 2, punctuation and other markings were sometimes added by the reader. Since the production of every roll was totally individual, the width of the columns and the spaces between them likewise varied. In some cases, enough space remained for someone to put in personal annotations. While it is possible to tell from the handwriting whether the comments were added by the original scribe or someone else, they are often harder to pick out and separate from the text itself than handwritten notes today in the margins of a printed text.[130] In other cases, 'official' commentaries were often relegated to separate rolls,[131] in much the same way as they are sometimes produced today.[132] With the appearance of the codex came the possibility of more diverse arrangements of the physical page. Text could be placed within a 'frame' that could be surrounded by comments, with the result that comments could be physically and directly associated with the text to which they applied. Today we see remnants of the medieval display in the fixed positions for notes that can either be footnotes at the bottom of the page or end notes located at the end of each chapter or the entire text. Individual annotation of texts reaches its height in the eleventh and twelfth centuries AD. Print, however, made the page 'sacrosanct' until recent times,[133] when new technology, the highlighter, made the marking of text easier and bolder. Today marginalia, a word first used by Coleridge in the nineteenth century,[134] are considered permissible only if you become famous and will donate your library to some institution where your every scribble will be studied.

CONCLUSION

Three conclusions are plain. First, the written word in the beginning tended to be used like the oral word. Once written down for its original purpose, it ceased to be of importance. Gradually this attitude began to change, as discussed in Chapter 1. Ovid, for example, valued the durability of the word compared to the great ambivalence of Plato. Second, because the capabilities of writing were for the most part unknown, they could not be exploited, with the result that organization of the written word remained extraordinarily rudimentary. New techniques, and literacy is one of them, always have unanticipated side-effects that require still further new techniques.

Third, the Greeks and the Romans, none the less, did cope with the consequences of literacy. The way they did, however, differs dramatically from ours, for it rarely occurred to them to use written words to find other written words. Instead they used one of the tools they already had: memory. Memory became *the* classical means of cognitively organizing and, most significantly, retrieving words.[135] The increasing importance placed on memory in classical antiquity will be considered in three aspects. The Muses, instead of fading in importance, take on more specific functions and appear increasingly more frequently, especially in the pictorial arts, as writing becomes more established. At the same time techniques for improving memory were developed and continually refined. Finally, memory itself was one of the writer's most basic tools.

6

THE COGNITIVE DEVELOPMENT
OF THE MUSES

As Mnemosyne, the personification of Memory, becomes less important, her daughters, the Muses, take on an increasingly important role and appear more frequently in art. While Mnemosyne has her own cult in Greece, she has no equivalent among the Romans. Consequently it might seem that writing has indeed replaced memory as a storage medium, but that would be a false picture. Memory as a technique, as a tacit substratum of Roman life, flourishes.[1] In this chapter I concentrate on the daughters of Mnemosyne: why Memory is their mother and what their role is in Greek and Roman life.

WHO THE MUSES ARE

The number of Muses ranged from unspecified in Homer to the full nine, with every possibility in between except six. As early as Hesiod (seventh century BC) and early Attic black-figure vase painting (sixth century BC) they were nine and named, though without specific functions, which shifted over the centuries and even contemporaneously in different sources.[2] The Hellenistic period, notable for its scholarship, fixed the count firmly at nine and more or less (some drifting continued) defined their spheres. As we have 'inherited' the Muses, they are: Calliope, considered the most important, in charge of heroic poetry (epic); Clio of history; Melpomene of tragedy; Euterpe of flute music; Erato of lyric poetry and hymns; Terpsichore of the lyre, lyric poetry, and dance; Urania of astronomy; Thalia of comedy; and Polyhymnia of dance, pantomime, and geometry. String instruments of the lyre family often accompanied classical verse, as sometimes did the flutes, which became more popular from the second half of the fifth century onwards. The choruses in Greek plays added movement, that is, dance.[3] Astronomy and geometry, however, have seemed strange to scholars,[4] because the ties of the Muses to literacy have not been fully appreciated.[5] Astronomy and geometry fulfill two major requirements to come under the Muses' mantles: both are intellectual, scientific endeavors that depend on calculations that need writing and hence memory. Accordingly, St Augustine says, 'Likewise memory contains the reasons and innumerable laws of numbers and dimensions.'[6]

The one glaring omission in the list, seemingly so broadly defined by our standards, is the pictorial arts, which never in any ancient source had a Muse, not even part of one. Instead Athena was the patron of the artist.[7] It is not that pictorial imagery does not help memory for words; it does. What is more, the Greeks and Romans knew it did, although perhaps not until after the Muses themselves were pretty much established. It is more significant that what we consider intellectual endeavors that involve writing in a very global way were always kept separate from those that were considered to be craft or 'τέχνη' (technē), what we classify as the pictorial arts. A Cicero might write poetry, but he would not paint or sculpt.[8] Plutarch sums up the situation:

> a man who occupies himself with servile tasks proves by the very pains which he devotes to them that he is indifferent to higher things. No young man of good breeding and high ideals feels that he must be a Pheidias or a Polycleitus after seeing the statue of Zeus at Olympia or Hera at Argos.[9]

As always, there were occasional exceptions, but they were sufficiently rare to be noted as such by ancient writers.

The classical view of what constitutes art is reflected in what constitutes a classical liberal education. As today, reading, writing, and arithmetic formed the core subjects to which were added athletic activities and sometimes training in a musical instrument, either the lyre or the flute. In the fifth century BC Alcibiades, like many a schoolchild, rebelled against being forced to play a musical instrument:

> 'But we Athenians, as our fathers say, have Athene for foundress and Apollo for patron, one of whom cast the flute away in disgust, and the other flayed the presumptuous flute-player [Marsyas].' Thus, half in jest and half in earnest, Alcibiades emancipated himself from this discipline, and the rest of the boys as well. For word soon made its way to them that Alcibiades loathed the art of flute-playing and scoffed at its disciples, and rightly, too. Wherefore the flute was dropped entirely from the programme of a liberal education and was altogether despised.[10]

Training in painting and sculpture, however, was reserved for those who were going to practice a trade. Thus it would not be fitting for the same figures to be patrons of both word and picture. Further corroboration comes from the fact that the subjects of astronomy and geometry superintended by the two 'anomalous' Muses, Urania and Polyhymnia, were a part of a 'general education' from the Hellenistic period on.[11] Eratosthenes represents this combination, for he wrote a poem 'on the squaring of the

73

cube . . . in which he refers to the gift of [Ptolemy] Euergetes to [Ptolemy] Philopator of "things dear to the Muses and to Kings".[12]

While the Greeks and Romans believed that you needed a memory for words, never did they think that you might need a memory for pictures. The Muses only administer things that need memory and those things in classical antiquity involve only words and writing. According to Plutarch in the second century AD:

> Above all, the memory of children should be trained and exercised; for this is, as it were, a treasury of learning; and it is for this reason that the mythologists have made Memory the mother of the Muses, thereby intimating and hinting that there is nothing in the world like memory for creating and fostering.[13]

It might be thought that the ekphrastic tradition contradicts the separation of Muses from art and the absence of a need for a memory for pictures. From the Hellenistic period on, ekphrasis, the literary description of a work of art, became a part of rhetorical training and concomitantly a standard in literary works. For example, Aeneas describes the scenes decorating the Temple of Juno in Carthage in *Aeneid*, 1.453–493 and through Aeneas's eyes we see the scenes on the shield of Aeneas in 8.626–731.[14] While these descriptions are extremely effective at conjuring up mental images of the scenes, rarely can these scenes be re-created physically in a visual display with the exception of literary treatments that are specifically meant to be descriptions of works of art, such as the *Imagines* of Philostratus from the third century AD – though even here problems exist in re-creating the positions of each painting.[15] It is not just the separation of an ekphrasis from reality, however, that matters here. More importantly, the purpose of ekphrasis within a literary work is to *remind* the viewer and hence the reader. Such descriptions enable the reader to remember the words and the action, but not the reverse. This use of visual imagery for recalling memories is intimately connected with the artificial memory systems which are discussed at length in Chapter 8.

COGNITIVE STUDIES OF MEMORY FOR WORDS

Recent investigations into how memory works explain the association between the Muses and writing. Psychological experiments demonstrate that people remember better when more than one of their five senses is engaged simultaneously.[16] If you read a text silently to yourself, you are less likely to recall it than if you read it aloud, because then both your vision and your hearing are involved, as Quintilian already knew in the first century AD. Quintilian gives his own reasons, still valid today:

The question has been raised as to whether we should learn by heart in silence; it would be best to do so, save for the fact that under such circumstances the mind is apt to become indolent, with the result that other thoughts break in. For this reason the mind should be kept alert by the sound of the voice, so that the memory may derive assistance from the double effort of speaking and listening.[17]

On the same premise the addition of meter or beat to your words, as in poetry, makes them more memorable, again a well-known fact in antiquity. Aristotle explained:

It is easy to follow, because it can easily be remembered; and this because language when in periodic form can be numbered, and number is the easiest of all things to remember. That is why verse, which is measured, is always more easily remembered than prose, which is not: the measures of verse can be numbered.[18]

Combine that beat with melody and you, too, can sing snatches from Broadway shows or even the 'Star Spangled Banner' in all four of its verses.[19] It is the combination that counts. If you then add movement, as in dance, to the words set to music, you have yet another reinforcement for recall, because you associate a particular word or phrase with a particular action.[20] In other words, what you have are the Muses, the daughters of Memory.[21]

Modern psychological and cultural studies have documented the effect:

It is well-known that remembering the words to a song is greatly facilitated by singing the song – the tune and rhythm serve as mnemonics. Among the Kpelle in Liberia, Lancy (1975) has reported that 'my informants had great difficulty recalling the songs unless they were singing *and dancing* (p. 9; italics added [by Wagner]).' Thus we see a motoric or kinesthetic mnemonic that aids recall. Similar evidence was recently gathered in a study of memory in deaf children (Liben & Drury, 1977). In this study, deaf children created their own, apparently culture-specific or deaf-specific mnemonics for remembering. The authors observed the use of finger spelling and the use of mime representations as mnemonics.[22]

Part of the study of 'The Wreck of the Old 97' mentioned in Chapter 1 was a test of how well

undergraduates who were not familiar with the ballad tradition [were able] to learn and recall 'The Wreck of the Old 97' in order to determine if these recalls were also governed by similar constraints. . . . [The results were that l]ines with high imagery values or many poetic constraints were recalled more accurately. When the metrical agreement and the poetics were high, recall was more accurate. When poetic restraints were removed recalls had greater variability across subjects. Finally, when rhythmical information was emphasized in the stimulus, recalls were more accurate.[23]

Wallace in a later experiment adds:

> [T]he experiments indicate that the melody contributes more than just rhythmical information. Music is a rich structure that chunks words and phrases, identifies line lengths, identifies stress patterns, and adds emphasis as well as focuses listeners on surface characteristics.[24]

She adds one caveat: 'the text is better recalled when it is heard as a song rather than as speech, provided the music repeats so that it is easily learned.'

Charles Beye explains exactly how ancient Greek fits this pattern:

> As any singer will tell you, changing the pitch of a word slightly but inevitably changes the quality of the vowels. This helps explain the marked musicality of Greek. Since vowels are held either long or short and are sounded with either normal pitch or raised pitch, the range of variation is great. The chanting poet then would be using time, beat, and pitch, just as modern musicians do.[25]

In the most extensive study of Greek verse and how it works cognitively, A. M. Devine and Laurence D. Stephens rightly conclude that 'we need to bear in mind that verse is not the creation of patterns out of language but a regularization of the patterns in language.'[26]

THE DISPLAY OF THE MUSES

A history of the appearance of the Muses in the visual arts clearly marks the increasing association between the Muses and learning. While it can be hazardous to base arguments on the survival of ancient objects, none the less it must be significant that only a handful of examples exist today from the archaic period. The classical period signals the beginning of real popularity for the Muses in art,[27] because literacy finally reached a critical mass during the fifth century BC. For the first time school scenes appear on Attic vases. Boys make their way to the classroom carrying tablets and writing cases. Teachers sit reading lessons from rolls. The actual act of writing is depicted less often, and then only on tablets, not on rolls.

At the same time as the school scenes appear, the Muses become more frequently depicted and, significantly, often hold rolls.[28] They are associated with the written word, but, just as significantly, they are not seen writing words, only helping others to read and write, even though they do play instruments. For example, a white-ground Attic pyxis shows a cowherd, identified either as Hesiod or Archilochos, being inspired by six of the Muses, two of whom are playing their instruments, the auloi and kithara.[29]

76

On another Attic red-figure vase, a Muse stands reading the roll she holds, as Marsyas plays the auloi.[30] This conception of the Muses continues virtually unchanged through the late Antique period with only an occasional exception.[31]

That the separation of the Muses from actually writing themselves is conscious can be seen in the parallel iconographical development of the Fates (Moirai).[32] In Greek art the Fates appear traditionally spinning the thread of life, measuring, and then cutting it. In Roman art, however, they sometimes perform their job of controlling life through reading the fate from a roll and by examining the stars, indicated by a globe. For example, on a Roman sarcophagus, two of the Fates stand behind a mother and her new-born child.[33] Both are touching a globe and the figure on the right also holds a roll open in her left hand. The roll and globe are also attributes of the Muses. What sets the Roman Fates apart is that one of them is sometimes depicted as actually writing down the fate. In particular, I would note the Roman mosaic with the three Fates, all named.[34] On the left stands Clotho holding a spindle. Next to her Lachesis holds a roll in her left hand and a thread (?) in her right. Then comes Atropos reading from a roll. On a Roman sarcophagus portraying the death of Meleager one of the Fates stands on the far left writing his fate on a roll.[35]

Plato sets up one of the first, if not the first, 'mouseion' or museum.[36] According to Pausanias, within Plato's Academy 'There is an altar to the Muses, and another to Hermes, and one within to Athena, and they have one to Heracles.'[37] Plato feels the necessity of surrounding himself and his school with the reinforcers of memory and hence learning. Athena as goddess of wisdom is, of course, present. Hermes may seem less obvious, but among his many talents is the invention of the letters.[38] In the Middle Ages Hermes's association with memory becomes quite strong.[39] Herakles, generally the prototypical dumb muscleman, none the less appears in archaic Attic black-figure vase painting playing the lyre and was included with the Muses in the Sanctuary of Asklepios.[40]

The association between Hercules and the Muses was particularly favored by the Romans. According to Plutarch they had an altar together, because 'Hercules taught Evander's people [the Latins] the use of letters, as Juba has recorded. . . . And this action was held to be noble on the part of men who taught their friends and relatives.'[41] Marcus Fulvius Nobilior erected a temple to Hercules Musarum, 'Hercules of the Muses', in 187 BC in which he placed statues of the nine Muses and Hercules taken from Ambracia in Epirus after the Roman victory over the Aetolians. Q. Pomponius Musa commemorated them on his coins in the following century.[42] At least two other complete groups of Muses, but without Hercules, were on display in Rome in Pliny the Elder's time: one in the museum connected to the Atrium Libertatis, set up by Asinius Pollio, and another in the temple of Apollo Sosianus.[43] Hadrian also had a set at Tivoli.[44]

Cicero not only acquired books through the services of others, but also statuary for his villa at Tusculum. One of his agents clearly did him wrong:

> Not being acquainted with my regular practice you have taken these four or five pieces at a price I should consider excessive for all the statuary in creation. You compare these Bacchantes with Metellus' Muses. Where's the likeness? To begin with, I should never have reckoned the Muses themselves worth such a sum – and all Nine would have approved my judgement! Still, that would have made a suitable acquisition for a library, and one appropriate to my interests. But where am I going to put Bacchantes?[45]

Muses and libraries were clearly considered a natural association by the first century BC. This relationship was most fostered by the library at Alexandria, which had its own museum with its own statuary Muses. The dates are significant. Plato is fourth century BC. The first free-standing group of the Muses, according to Pausanias (9.30.1), was made in the same period by Kephisodotos, who was probably the father of Praxiteles. The library at Alexandria was established at the beginning of the third century BC. The union of Muses and learning continued throughout classical antiquity. By the second century AD the Muses were appropriated by private individuals as suitable symbols to decorate their eternal resting places. Well over 200 sarcophagi with the Muses have survived. They also appeared in numerous mosaics, sometimes joined by the Seven Sages.[46]

THE MUSES AND WRITING

This brief survey of the portrayal of the Muses in the pictorial arts has shown that they become more and more associated with the written word as time passes. While their mother, Mnemosyne, becomes less important in religious matters, her daughters become ever more popular in art.[47] For the first time it becomes clear why the Muses govern the domains they do. Astronomy and mathematics are both concerned with writing not just intellectually, but representationally, as the parallel history of the Fates in the pictorial tradition demonstrates. At the same time the ancient divisions make sense from a cognitive point of view. In order to write, the classical writer needed the skills that the Muses embody.[48]

Part II

THE HISTORICAL DEVELOPMENT OF ANCIENT MEMORY TECHNIQUES

7

THE GREEK METHODS

Thus far I have investigated the props of the highly literate in classical antiquity. I have considered what their writing looked like, how it was organized within a roll, and how, in turn, whole works were treated in public and in private. With this background I can now address the major issue: how did they find the written words they needed among the masses of written words that kept on growing and growing? Since their efforts at organizing their words for retrieval did not emphasize the development of major written aids external to the text itself, I believe that the highly literate concentrated on improving the one unwritten tool they already had: memory. Hence the Muses, the daughters of Memory, became more important as time passed. In this part of the book I focus on the ways they improved their natural memories through artificial memory systems. I consider the historical development of such systems, the way they worked then, and cognitive studies of their efficacy today.

'Mnemotechnics', despite its Greek roots, is a modern word, first used in the nineteenth century, for what was called in antiquity the 'art of memory', literally '*ars*' in Latin and 'τέχνη' (technē; technai plural) in Greek, but never as the compound word which classical scholars use today. From the fifth century BC on, a technē was considered to be 'an art or craft, i.e., a set of rules, system or method of making or doing, whether of the useful arts, or of the fine arts.'[1] Greek texts use the term 'mnemonic' to cover the range of memory devices in much the same way that the psychological literature does today.[2] The combination of the two words means, then, that particular skills could be taught for improving 'natural' memory, the memory we are born with. In classical antiquity any means of making our natural memory better was considered 'artificial'. Hence in the first century BC the Auctor ad Herennium says that memory is of 'two kinds . . . one natural, and the other the product of art. The natural memory is that memory which is imbedded in our minds, born simultaneously with thought.'[3] Here I am concerned only with the unnatural or 'artificial' sort, the 'memory which is strengthened by a kind of training and system of discipline.'[4] The discussion of classical mnemotechnics is divided into three major sections: the system of places – τόποι (*topoi*) in Greek (this chapter), and *loci* in Latin (Chapter 8) and its combination with mental imagery. Subsequently, other methods, ancient and modern, are considered in Chapter 9.

Aristotle, who wrote a short treatise on the subject, puts memory in strange company from a modern point of view, and even at the head of his list of the components of wisdom:

> Memory, experience, tact, good judgement, sagacity – each of these either arises from wisdom or accompanies it. Or possibly some of them are, as it were, subsidiary causes of wisdom (such as experience and memory), while others are, as it were, parts of it, e.g. good judgement and sagacity.[5]

The Auctor ad Herennium (pseudo-Cicero; 3.28) called memory 'the guardian of all the parts of rhetoric.' Cicero (*On Invention*, 2.160), following Aristotle, also made memory a part of wisdom along with intelligence and foresight. In the *Tusculan Disputations* (1.65) Cicero elevated memory even higher by making it one of the divine attributes along with activity, wisdom, and discovery. Pliny said it was 'the boon most necessary for life.'[6] Quintilian said that 'The surest indication in a child is his power of memory.'[7] Plutarch in his discussion of the 'education of children' adds that memory is a 'treasury of learning' in which 'children should be trained and exercised.'[8] As something no educated person could live without, the art of memory merited a noteworthy inventor.

THE INVENTION OF SIMONIDES

The various technai, like that of the letters of the alphabet discussed in Chapter 5, often had inventors. The account of the invention of mnemotechnics resembles one of Kipling's *Just So Stories*. I give the version in Cicero (*On the Orator*, 2.351–354), because it is the earliest and most complete to have survived, although all the ancient sources agree that Simonides of Keos (c. 556–468 BC) invented mnemotechnics in the early fifth century BC. Scopas, the winner of a boxing contest, had commissioned Simonides to write an ode in his honor.[9] When he learned that Simonides had devoted half the poem to Castor and Pollux, the divine twins famed for their own boxing skills, he paid Simonides only half the agreed sum and told him to get the rest from the two gods. Being a poet is never easy.[10] A little later, in the middle of the victory banquet, Simonides was called outside by two young men. Once outside, he saw no one:

> but in the interval of his absence the roof of the hall where Scopas was giving the banquet fell in, crushing Scopas himself and his relations underneath the ruins and killing them; and when their friends wanted

to bury them but were altogether unable to know them apart as they had been completely crushed, the story goes that Simonides was enabled by his recollection of the place [*loco*] in which each of them had been reclining at table to identify them for separate interment; and that prompted then by this circumstance he is said to have invented the order that especially brings light to memory. And so for those who would train this part of the mind, places [*locos*] must be selected and those things [*rerum*] which they want to hold in memory must be reproduced in the mind and put in those places: thus it would be that the order of the places would preserve the order of the things; moreover, the likeness [*effigies*] of the things would represent the things themselves, and so we use places instead of a wax tablet, images instead of letters.[11]

Quintilian, a rather practical sort who wrote a century after Cicero, said, 'For my own part, however, I regard the portion of the story which concerns Castor and Pollux [the two disappearing strangers] as being purely fictitious.' Quintilian's reason, however, may give us pause, 'since the poet himself [Simonides] has nowhere mentioned the occurrence; and he would scarcely have kept silence on an affair which was so much to his credit.'[12] Hence Quintilian implies that Simonides himself must have told about his invention in some writing now lost.

Two things happened in the early fifth century BC that affected the way the Greeks viewed memory. Because the number of written words had reached an unwieldy amount, changes in dealing with them had to occur. There were simply too many words with which to cope without some kind of improved retrieval system. Second, as discussed in Chapter 1, with writing comes the concept of a fixed text that must be repeated word for word – a phenomenon that made a poet a natural as an inventor of a system for memorization. He had to have a good memory, because he still recited his works orally. Yet, unlike the oral singers of earlier times, he did not compose anew for each performance, but delivered the text he had written ahead of time. The whole point of the performance depended on the exact words.[13] Freed from the constraints of memory for a totally oral creation, the new breed of poets no longer relied on stock phrases to complete lines. With greater variation within a poem came a greater need for remembering what those words were. The most highly educated people in antiquity learned mnemotechnics as part of their rhetorical training. Although no ancient text on rhetoric omitted reference to memory, memory itself did not become a formal division of rhetoric until sometime in the Hellenistic period, probably in the late second century BC.[14] This fact is crucial, because it has often been maintained by classical scholars that increasing literacy meant less rather than more reliance on memory. If that were the case, then training in mnemotechnics would have disappeared from the curriculum rather than being given a greater role in education.

The Muses would have slowly faded in importance. Instead, both the Greeks and the Romans continually refined and added to their techniques for improving memory.

In addition to aiding public performances by writers, mnemotechnics would help the orator remember the facts he needed to mention, their order, and the structure of his speech. Actors had lines to memorize. A government official would need to be able to remember contracts, correspondence, laws, treaties, etc. Everyone who has to deal with words can benefit from mnemotechnics. The art of memory applies to, first, sequential information, such as presenting a series of items in a specific order to lead to a particular conclusion, and, second, lists or groups of things, like members of the Senate, that need not have a particular order of recall. It is interesting that for both types of memorization, a sequential system works.

Take a modern example: if you want to learn the names of all the states, memorizing them in some kind of specific order will make the task easier. Hence you are likely to choose either an alphabetical or a geographical order. The alphabet itself is an arbitrary ordering of the letters that makes little conceptual sense, even if there are historical reasons for the positions of certain letters. A sequential order is forced upon the memorizer, because things are necessarily fed into memory one at a time. In other words, no matter what you do, you are likely to memorize a list in some kind of order, even if arbitrary like the alphabet. Moreover, if you have memorized a list of arbitrary items sequentially, then you will know far more quickly when you run through the list if you have omitted something.[15] Waiters and waitresses, when interrupted in their recitation of the day's specials, frequently have to start again at the top of the list.[16] How sequential and nonsequential information is actually stored in the brain is beyond the scope of this discussion.[17] Retrieval, however, can be either sequential or random. For example, if you are asked to name all the states, you will probably choose the order in which you memorized them. If you are asked whether a particular name is a name of a state, you will recall that information directly without going through the entire list – a skill still beyond most computers.

Simonides's method is simple. In order to remember who was present, he called up a mental image of the banquet to figure out where each person was sitting. Quintilian explains the value of mentally recreating a particular situation the way Simonides did:

> when we return to a place after considerable absence, we not merely recognise the place itself, but remember things that we did there, and recall the persons whom we met and even the unuttered thoughts which passed through our minds when we were there before. Thus, as in most cases, art originates in experience.[18]

Quintilian considers the original circumstances in which one has learned something so important that he recommends that:

There is one thing which will be of assistance to everyone, namely, to learn a passage by heart from the same tablets on which he has committed it to writing. For he will have certain tracks to guide him in his pursuit of memory, and the mind's eye will be fixed not merely on the pages on which the words were written, but on individual lines, and at times he will speak as though he were reading aloud.[19]

The phenomenon is known as 'state-dependent learning'.[20] Alan Baddeley, a psychologist, gives a wonderful, more recent example of the use of context for recall carried to an extreme. John Locke (1632–1704) tells the story of a young man who learned how to dance in a room with a large trunk: 'The idea of this remarkable piece of household stuff had so mixed itself with the turns and steps of all his dances, that though in that chamber he could dance excellently well, yet it was only while the trunk was there.'[21] Another similar story is told about a modern writer:

After getting writer's cramp midway through *What Maisie Knew*, Henry James engaged a shorthand typist. 'He became so used to the sound of the machine that if it broke down another would not do. The typewriter affected his style, making it exclusively Mandarin and identifiable as his "later manner".'[22]

The effect of physical context on recall has been established in experiments on the memories of divers. Because they are taught on land, when in the water they sometimes have difficulty recalling what they have learned.[23] Baddeley advises that:

This suggests a useful tip if you are trying to remember something, namely that it is worth taking time to try to recall the surroundings first, a procedure that not only provides a potentially useful mnemonic strategy, but also offers a useful technique for helping an eyewitness recall an incident. Indeed, it seems likely that some at least of the claims made for the usefulness of hypnosis in helping recall stems from the hypnotist's capacity to induce the subject to imagine the context in which the incident occurred before attempting detailed recall.[24]

Quintilian's explanation closely resembles Baddeley's tip, because the ancient technique is based on a very real effect.

Hypnotism, incidentally, is not ancient, but a discovery of the eighteenth century.[25] Baddeley's use of the word 'claims' is important, for hypnotism is a two-edged sword in that it can just as easily place ideas in your mental image, as well as helping you recall what you saw. As I am writing, a controversy is raging over 'recovered memory' on the side of the proponents and 'false memory syndrome' on the side of the opponents. Can adults suddenly recall memories of abuse in childhood? The dispute is not over the existence of child abuse or over the memories of those who have always remembered their past, but over the therapists who hypnotize and otherwise suggest to their patients that they have suffered from such abuse in the past. A number of benign experiments have been done and are continuing to be done that explore the incredible malleability of our memories. As Dr Marsel Mesulam says, 'the miracle is that anything we remember is true, not that there is distortion.'[26]

SOCRATES'S AND PLATO'S NON-CONTRIBUTIONS TO MNEMOTECHNICS

Three dialogues involving Socrates mention the art of memory and one of its fifth-century developers, Hippias, a Sophist from Elis. In Xenophon's *Symposium* Socrates says:

> I know also that you [Antisthenes] did the same [acted as a go-between] for Hippias, the Elean, from whom Callias got his memory system [τὸ μνημονικόν]; and as a result, Callias has become more amorous than ever, because he finds it impossible to forget any beauty he sees.[27]

When, a little more seriously, Plato pits Socrates and Hippias against each other, Socrates says, 'I have forgotten to mention your art of memory, which you regard as your special glory.'[28] In their other encounter, Socrates again makes reference to mnemotechnics and in a more directly disparaging way: 'I forgot you had the art of memory. So I understand: the Spartans enjoy you, predictably, because you know a lot of things, and they use you the way children use old ladies, to tell stories for pleasure.'[29]

Athenaeus refers to Plato as 'this devotee of the goddess of memory,'[30] and so it is no surprise that Plato whole-heartedly approves of memory. None the less, he is skeptical of any system that is not natural, that does not come from within. In the *Phaedo*, Socrates says:

> Coming to life again is a fact, and it is a fact that the living come from the dead, and a fact that the souls of the dead exist.
>
> Besides, Socrates, rejoined Cebes, there is that theory which you have often described to us – that what we call learning [μάθησις] is really just recollection [ἀνάμνησις]. If that is true, then surely what we recollect now we must have learned at some time before, which is impossible unless our souls existed somewhere before they entered this human shape. So in that way too it seems likely that the soul is immortal.[31]

Since we already know everything from before birth, all we should need is dialectic to bring out that knowledge or make it apparent to us. Plato disapproves of all artificial devices that might be subsumed under the name of memory or recollection. Hence he disdains external aids like the written word, as I discussed in Chapter 1, and does not condone the use of improvements like mnemotechnics for internal, natural systems. During antiquity, rhetoric, which came to encompass the artificial memory techniques, prevailed; in the Middle Ages dialectic again rose to the fore.[32]

ARISTOTLE AND THE *TOPOI*

Although Aristotle retains the connection between dialectic and memory, unlike Plato he believes in the value of mnemotechnics.[33] He speaks of:

persons who have seen such dreams, those, for example, who believe themselves to be mentally arranging a given list of subjects according to the mnemonic rule [κατὰ τὸ μνημονικὸν παράγγελμα]. They frequently find themselves to be mentally putting into its place some other image apart from the dream.[34]

Elsewhere he says that 'imagining lies within our own power whenever we wish (e.g. we can call up a picture, as in the practice of mnemonics by the use of mental images).'[35] These two quotes refer to mnemotechnics as a well-known technique that depends on order and mental images.

Aristotle wrote a separate treatise on memory that is the earliest surviving how-to manual on the subject. He makes no mention of Simonides or banquets, but recommends memorizing sequentially so that by remembering the flanking items, you will be able to remember what comes in between.[36] While Simonides could have presumably remembered the guests by thinking first of who dined across from him, then at the ends of the horseshoe – as the couches were frequently arranged – then in the center, it is far more likely that he recalled the banqueters in some kind of serial order, for two reasons: all the ancient accounts present only a sequential system, and, as just discussed, memorizing is a serial process. Aristotle describes the method:

But one should get a starting-point. And this is why people are thought sometimes to recollect starting from places. The reason is that people go quickly from one thing to another, e.g. from milk to white, from white to air, and from this to fluid, from which one remembers autumn, the season one is seeking.

In general in every case the middle also looks like a starting-point. For if no sooner, a person will remember when he comes to this, or else he will no longer remember from any position, as for example if someone were to think of the things denoted by A B Γ Δ E Z H Θ. For if he has not remembered at Θ, he will remember at Z for from here he can move in either direction to H or to E. But if he was not seeking one of these, after going to Γ he will remember, if he is searching for Δ or B, or if he is not, he will remember after going to A. And so in all cases.

> The reason why one sometimes remembers and sometimes does not, starting from the same position, is that it is possible to move to more than one point from the same starting-point, e.g. from Γ to Z or Δ.[37]

The example Aristotle gives at the beginning of the passage is not free association – one thing reminds me of another – but directed association with a definite starting point and a specific order to what follows, like the alphabet with its fixed sequence.[38] The way he divides the alphabet into a series of overlapping triplets reflects the method Simonides used in reconstructing the seating plan. His use of triplets for memorizing may be reflected in his development of the syllogism, a three-step argument. It may even broadly underlie such works as his *Nicomachean Ethics* where he advocates the mean between two extremes or the *Poetics* (1450b) where he proposes that a plot should have a beginning, a middle, and an end. One aspect of the system is unusual according to modern research on mnemotechnics. Aristotle has devised a system that enables you to go both backwards and forwards within the series, whereas most of the modern mnemonists only go forward. In fact, 'The memory span of a normal adult subject is halved when they are required to recall the digits in reverse order.'[39]

While on the surface Aristotle's kind of reasoning seems simple – at the most you are dealing with groups of three – it is actually more complicated, because both the seating plan and the alphabet are not meant to be used directly to represent what they are, that is the letters and a seating plan, but rather as containers for holding *any* sequence of things, thoughts, people, or whatever. Quintilian gives a simple example of the way the system worked, one that is still used today:

> For symbols are highly efficacious, and one idea suggests another: for example, if we change a ring from one finger to another or tie a thread round it, it will serve to remind us of our reason for so doing. Specially effective are those devices which lead the memory from one thing to another similar thing which we have got to remember.[40]

If 'bins' is substituted for 'places' in the passage from Cicero quoted at the beginning of the chapter, Aristotle's method becomes much clearer:

> And so for those who would train this part of the mind, [bins] must be selected and those things which they want to hold in memory must be reproduced in the mind and put in those [bins]: thus it would be that the order of the [bins] would preserve the order of the things; moreover, the likeness of the things would represent the things themselves.

I use the term 'bin' in a figurative, not a literal sense.[41] Since the basic concept is a mental construct, it has no physicality whatsoever. You can, for instance, substitute the idea of a template, like a database form, in which each field or slot in the same template can hold different pieces of information. This analogy, however, breaks down in that the same kinds of information have to go in particular slots – cities in the city field, states in the state field – whereas the system of places, as will be seen, can contain any kind of information within any particular place. Another analogy is a set of markers or indicators for the series of positions. Hence Aristotle chose the alphabet as his example; you could use numbers instead.

Combined with the placement of facts in the bins are the 'mental images' associated with those facts. The bins determine the order of the facts, but in order to remember which fact goes in which bin you need to think of some image to connect the two. Consider a modern variation on the ancient system:

One type of mnemonic operates by elaborating the material to be retained so as to make it more memorable, usually by linking it to something that is already known. A typical example is the pegword mnemonic whereby you first learn to associate the numbers one to ten with a rhyming concrete word as follows:

> One is a bun
> Two is a shoe
> Three is a tree
> Four is a door
> Five is a hive
> Six is sticks
> Seven is heaven
> Eight is a gate
> Nine is wine
> Ten is a hen

Having learnt these, they can then be used to learn lists of ten other items by taking each item and imagining it interacting with the item associated with the appropriate number. Let us assume, for example, that the first item is *submarine*, then you might imagine a submarine crashing into a huge floating bun. The second item might be a *duck* in which case you might imagine a duck sitting in a shoe and quacking. The third item might be *crocodile*, in which case you might imagine a crocodile with a tree growing out of it, and so forth.

When the time comes to recall you can go through the sequence, thinking first of number one and the bun which in turn will remind you of the submarine running into it and so forth. Alternatively, you can be cued by being given the number, for example three, which should evoke the keyword *tree*, which reminds you that it is growing out of a crocodile.[42]

The images described may seem far-fetched, but, as will be seen, they are no more so than the ancient examples. On the other hand, the idea of using a standard set of pegwords to mediate between the storage container and the thing to be remembered was not ancient. Instead, a different and very visual system was developed by the Romans and will be considered in Chapter 8.

Simonides and Aristotle recommend a permanent set of places or bins in which you store any number of different sets of information that must be remembered; each set of information has its own set of vivid images associated with your single set of bins. At this point a further complication occurs in the Greek and Roman system, because the words 'bin' and 'pegword' are not used, but 'τόπος' and '*locus*', the roots for the English 'topic', 'locality', and related words. Both classical words are usually translated as 'place', and like the English 'place' have a number of meanings ranging from the specific to the abstract. When referring to mnemotechnics, they mean both. In the passage from Cicero about Simonides, *place* refers literally to a seat or setting at a meal in the same way we use it today.[43] *Place* can more abstractly be considered a container or holder or marker, as I have been using *bin*. In a literal sense it may be a city that holds buildings; in a figurative sense, it may be a container to hold a particular 'fact'. The use of *topoi* provides the basis for our expressions 'in the first place', 'in the second place', etc., as each item is considered in sequence.

The idea of using the same set of places over and over again for different sets of information, I believe, led to the idea of the 'common places', now one word in English for the two words in Greek ('κοινοὶ τόποι') and Latin ('*communes loci*').[44] At the same time those things that were stored in those places came themselves to be called the 'commonplaces'. So Cicero says 'that Protagoras wrote out and furnished discussions of certain large general subjects such as we now call commonplaces; that Gorgias did the same.'[45] The modern use of 'commonplace' appears tacitly in our use of the term '*index*' for the list of items deemed significant and worthy of retrieval in non-fiction writing. The term '*index*' in this sense goes back to the medieval use as an '*index locorum communium*', 'list of common places'. In the medieval case it is a mental and not a written list of places that is meant – yet another reason, according to Michael Clanchy, for the length of time it took to use the alphabet as the standard for arranging information.[46] Classical Latin does not seem to link '*index*' and '*locus*'. Instead '*index*' refers to a list, whether it is sorted or unsorted.[47]

Aristotle's writings on the *topoi* and memory were in response to the Sophists, Protagoras (*c.* 485–415 BC) and Gorgias (*c.* 483–376 BC), whom Quintilian (3.1.12) credits with first treating the commonplaces. Their works on this subject are not extant.[48] Aristotle said:

90

Of the present inquiry [the *Sophistical Refutations*], on the other hand, it was not the case that part of the work had been thoroughly done before, while part had not. Nothing existed at all. For the training given by the paid professors of contentious arguments was like the practice of Gorgias. For he used to hand out rhetorical speeches to be learned by heart, and they handed out speeches in the form of question and answer, which each supposed would cover most of the arguments on either side. And therefore the teaching they gave their pupils was rapid but unsystematic. For they used to suppose that they trained people by imparting to them not the art but its products.[49]

Aristotle is arguing against the idea that canned responses are sufficient to answer specific questions. Quintilian, writing four centuries later, still complained about speakers using set pieces:

For how can such men find appropriate arguments in the course of actual cases which continually present new and different features? How can they answer the points that their opponents may bring up? how deal a rapid counterstroke in debate or cross-examine a witness? . . . And when they produce the same passage in a number of different cases, they must come to loathe it like food that has grown cold or stale, and they can hardly avoid a feeling of shame at displaying this miserable piece of furniture to an audience whose memory must have detected it so many times already.[50]

Good modern parallels are the campaign speeches, debates, and press conferences of politicians. The stump speeches of American presidential candidates become so familiar to the press corps that they repeat them along with the candidate. So also did a group of Athenians in the second century AD:

[A] rumour reached the pupils of Herodes [Atticus] that Philagrus, when a theme was proposed to him, used to improvise the first time, but did not do so on a second occasion, but would declaim stale arguments that he had used before. Accordingly they proposed to him this same theme 'The Uninvited,' and when he pretended to be improvising they retaliated by reading the declamation aloud. Then the lecture became the scene of uproar and laughter, with Philagrus shouting, and vociferating that it was an outrage on him not to be allowed to use what was his own.[51]

When politicians today reply with a general memorized answer to a specific question, they often demonstrate their lack of understanding of the topic. Hence Aristotle advocates a system that teaches you how to apply and combine individual arguments to answer specific needs. For a quick idea of how the system would work, consider Mark Twain's 'Patent Adjustable

Speech' that 'enable[d] him to carry in his head "a cut-and-dried and thoroughly glibly memorized speech that will fit every conceivable public occasion in this life."'[52] Twain describes a modern version of the classical method:

> *Any* lecture of mine ought to be a running narrative-plank, with square holes in it, six inches apart, all the length of it, & then in my mental shop I ought to have plugs (half marked 'serious' and the other marked 'humorous') to select from & jam into these holes according to the temper of the audience.[53]

As you read the examples from Aristotle that follow, keep in mind that he is providing a general and very flexible system with the result that he employs the term *topos* to cover a broad range of usages from the literal to the abstract. In the *Politics* he uses *topos* literally: 'the constitution is a community, and must at any rate have a common place – one city will be in one place, and the citizens are those who share in that one city.'[54] Here the city contains the citizens and a community. In the *Topics*, he extends the idea of the *topos* to contain 'rules' or 'principles':

> Moreover, it is well to alter a word into one more familiar, e.g. to substitute 'clear' for 'precise' in describing a conception, and 'meddling' for 'officious'; for when the expression is made more familiar, the thesis becomes easier to attack. This commonplace also is available for both purposes alike, both for establishing and for overthrowing a view.[55]

As with the pegword method, specific examples are put into your common or basic set of bins or places. Hence your bin in a sense has two levels: the literal one with 'clear' for 'precise', and the rule that governs that substitution. Since the rules are general, they can be applied by simple adaptation to either side of an argument.

In the next passage Aristotle combines the idea of commonplaces as arguments with the art of memory:

> It is best to know thoroughly arguments upon those problems which are of most frequent occurrence, and particularly in regard to those theses which are primary; for in discussing these answerers frequently give up in despair. Moreover, get a good stock of definitions; and have those of reputable and primary ideas at your fingertips; for it is through these that deductions are effected. You should try, moreover, to master the heads under which other arguments mostly tend to fall. For just as in geometry it is useful to be practised in the elements, and in arithmetic having the multiplication table up to ten at one's fingers' ends makes a great difference to one's knowledge of the multiples of other numbers too, likewise also in arguments it is a great advantage to be

well up in regard to first principles, and to have a thorough knowledge of propositions by heart. For just as in a person with a trained memory, a memory of things themselves is immediately caused by the mere mention of their 'places', so these habits too will make a man readier in reasoning, because he has his premisses classified before his mind's eye, each under its number. It is better to commit to memory a proposition of general application than an argument; for it is not very difficult to get a supply of first principles and hypotheses.[56]

The passage begins on a comparatively theoretical level with the recommendation that everyone have a basic set of arguments for recurring problems by having the primary features at his fingertips.[57] Anything that requires repetition requires memory, and the way to remember is through the *topoi*, which Aristotle approaches first with the concrete example, a *topos*, of the multiplication table where your fingertips literally are the containers or places for storing the multiples of numbers. As you move from one finger to another you are physically reminded of the next calculation, or, to take a previous example, the triplets of the alphabet. Then Aristotle makes the specific connection between knowing 'first principles by heart' and a 'trained memory'. All three examples – the multiplication tables, the first principles, the places – are versions of the same thing. Hence it makes perfectly good sense for the *Topics* to be basically a list of arguments, for the arguments are the bins that can be used to contain the specifics to counteract or support any particular cause or thesis.

Richard Sorabji says that Aristotle is not using the place system in the section of 'each under its number'.[58] None the less, by analogy with the pegword method, I think that it is the place system, but with the numbers as the containers. The number mediated by a mental image enables you to remember the argument. Otherwise why even bother with numbers at all? Because it reminds me of the old joke of giving jokes numbers that become so well known that a mere mention of a particular number can produce raucous laughter, I now have a mental image of Greek philosophers walking around the courtyard and calling out only numbers, as each in turn advances his argument in true dialectical fashion.

Aristotle next connects the *topoi* and dialectic:

> By in respect of the art, I mean in respect of its principles. Clearly, then, it is not of all refutations, but only of those that depend upon dialectic that we need to grasp the commonplace rules; for these are common to every art and faculty.[59]

Dialectic to Aristotle is the supreme method for argumentation and deductions. The road to the mastery of dialectic is through an understanding of those things – things in a very loose sense for argument, principle, strategy, what have you – that are common places. Thus a *topos* is a container or bin for whatever you want it to contain.[60] As Aristotle himself puts it:

> I mean that the proper subjects of dialectical and rhetorical deductions are the things with which we say the commonplaces are concerned, that is to say those that apply equally to questions of right conduct, natural science, politics, and many other things that have nothing to do with one another.[61]

In the same passage he defines commonplaces: 'By kinds I mean the propositions peculiar to each several class of things, by commonplaces those common to all classes alike.'[62] In other words, those bins or places that can be used over and over again become the commonplaces.

SUMMARY

Aristotle provides the first full description of the system of places invented by Simonides. Between the time of Simonides and that of Aristotle, the Sophists had developed the use of *topoi* to provide general arguments or discussions for a range of occasions and situations. Aristotle found the general method inadequate, but the underlying mechanism, the *topoi* themselves, remained central to his refinements. It becomes clear in tracing his usage and application of the *topoi* that he uses the term *topos* rather freely to apply both to the container and the contained. The system is called *topoi*, because it is based on the *topos*. By extension *topos* comes to refer to the actual rules or arguments or things stored in the *topoi*.[63] As a further twist to this usage, Aristotle tacitly recommends using the system of *topoi* on itself: to memorize various arguments or principles the best method is the system of *topoi*. Hence the *topoi* are numbered, because numbers in sequence, like the alphabet, enable you to recall both a heterogeneous *and* a sorted list of items, arguments, or principles. While I have used the terms 'storage' and 'container' or 'bin' to explain how the system works, keep in mind that as far as Aristotle and the Greeks are concerned, the system is purely a mental construct with no physical aspects.

8

THE ROMAN CONTRIBUTION

After Aristotle's treatise on memory no extended discussion of mnemo-technics has survived until the Romans in the first century BC, even though memory became a formal division of rhetoric in the intervening period. George Kennedy dates this elevation of memory to the generation before the Auctor ad Herennium, that is, to the late second century BC, a time when Rome is already of greater influence than Greece in the Mediterranean world.[1] Scholars, when studying Roman versions of Greek concepts, often attribute only the 'misunderstandings' to the Romans and none of the advances.[2] Hence the general assumption has been that the Greeks themselves extended the system of *topoi* from a purely mental construct into a physical embodiment where the places literally become buildings or settings. According to this view, it is mere happenstance that we have only Roman descriptions of the architectural version. It is foolish to think that ideas remain static and that the Romans would either slavishly mimic all that is Greek or would not adapt Greek tools for their own purposes. In adopting the art of memory from the Greeks, the Romans had to make adjustments to the system, because basic organizational skills were not increasing at the same pace as the quantities of written matter, with the result that the need for good memory skills had increased dramatically from the time of Plato and Aristotle. To get some idea of the quantity that a highly literate Roman could produce, consider that 914 of Cicero's letters have survived. It was imperative for the Romans to improve the Greek art of memory.

The survival of the literary sources reflects the reality of the situation. First, no Greek source speaks of the *topoi* as anything other than a mental construct. Second, only Romans could have developed such a system, because the Greeks have little sense of place, as is demonstrated most clearly by the virtual absence of setting in their pictorial arts.[3] Not only does a physical setting play a major role in Roman wall painting, but Pliny the Elder even attributes the idea of putting landscape paintings on walls to a Roman:

95

Spurius Tadius also, of the period of his late lamented Majesty Augustus . . . first introduced the most attractive fashion of painting walls with pictures of country houses and porticoes and landscape gardens, groves, woods, hills, fish-ponds, canals, rivers, coasts, and whatever anybody could desire.[4]

THE ARCHITECTURAL PLACES OR *LOCI*

Cicero explains why physical places are necessary for memory just after he has presented the Simonidean system of memory. The full passage is important for the context:

It has been skillfully discovered by Simonides or else discovered by some other person, that the most complete pictures are formed in our minds of the things that have been conveyed to them and imprinted on them by the senses, but that the keenest of all our senses is the sense of sight, and that consequently perceptions received by the ears or by reflexion can be most easily retained in the mind if they are also conveyed to our minds by the mediation of the eyes, with the result that things not seen and not lying in the field of visual discernment are marked by a sort of outline and image and shape so that we keep hold of as it were by an act of sight things that we can scarcely embrace by an act of thought. But these forms and bodies, like all the things that come under our view require a seat [*sede*], inasmuch as a material object without a place [*loco*] is inconceivable. Consequently (in order that I may not be prolix and tedious on a subject that is well known and familiar) one must use many places [*locis*] which must be clear, defined, and at moderate intervals, and images that are effective and sharply outlined and distinctive, with the capacity of encountering and speedily penetrating the mind.[5]

Before discussing the text proper, some comments on Cicero's choice of words are necessary. He uses '*sedes*' and then '*locus*', both of which can be translated as '*place*' in English. '*Sedes*' is sometimes used instead of '*locus*' in the Latin sources on mnemotechnics. The Roman usage resembles our use of '*place*', '*position*', and '*seat*'. '*Locus*' tends to be preferred, but here Cicero, having just mentioned Simonides, may want to keep the two kinds of places distinct, for Simonides's system was based on places at a banquet, which we phrase in English the same way Latin does – we take our places or our seats.

Cicero states that sight is more important than hearing, a belief maintained consistently throughout classical antiquity, although the things that were classified in antiquity as belonging to the two senses vary. For the immediate question what matters is that something perceived by sight has to be tangible, and something that is tangible takes up space, and therefore

96

cannot exist without a physical location. The Greeks, or at least some Greeks, saw the situation differently. Plato distrusts the senses.[6] According to his well-known parable of the cave in the *Republic* (7.514ff.), the senses give false impressions:

> when anyone by dialectic attempts through discourse of reason and apart from all perceptions of sense to find his way to the very essence of each thing and does not desist till he apprehends by thought itself the nature of the good itself, he arrives at the limit of the intelligible, as the other in our parable came to the goal of the visible.[7]

Since the Greek *topoi* are intimately connected with Greek argumentation and dialectic, it is no wonder that they work in a typically Greek abstract manner. Aristotle does say: 'So from perception there comes memory, as we call it, and from memory (when it occurs often in connection with the same thing), experience; for memories that are many in number from a single experience.'[8] Even though Aristotle believes you can trust your senses, he never even hints at the concrete imagery of the Roman *locus*. His *topoi* remain abstract constructs devoid of any physicality.

Lucretius, a contemporary of Cicero, states categorically that 'if there had been no substance of things nor place [*locus*] and space [*spatium*], in which all things are carried on, never would the flame have been fired by love through the beauty of Tyndaris.'[9] In other words, the Trojan War could never have occurred without Troy, or, to phrase it less poetically and more generally, anything whatsoever that happens in this world can only happen within a particular physical context. Cicero more directly says that 'an object cannot be understood without a place.'[10] This is another way of putting what Quintilian said in the following century and which I quoted in Chapter 7:

> when we return to a place after considerable absence, we not merely recognise the place itself, but remember things that we did there, and recall the persons whom we met and even the unuttered thoughts which passed through our minds when we were there before. Thus, as in most cases, art originates in experiment.[11]

Hence recall of thoughts and ideas inevitably means recall of the places where they occurred, as Cicero directly states:

> For my own part even the sight of our senate-house [Curia] at home (I mean the Curia Hostilia, not the present new building, which looks to my eyes smaller since its enlargement) used to call up to me thoughts of Scipio, Cato, Laelius, and chief of all, my grandfather; such powers of suggestion do places possess. No wonder the scientific training of the memory is based on these things.[12]

97

Between the Greek *topoi* and the full-blown, physical system of the Romans an intermediary stage might have occurred, though we have no surviving sources. Aristotle, when he suggests using your fingertips as *topoi* for storing thoughts, may have begun the process. The next stage would have been to use something physical, external to one's person as the 'place' of storage. An investigation of the memories of the Kpelle by Michael Cole and Sylvia Scribner is suggestive.[13] When their subjects could not remember well the various things that had been shown to them, Cole and Scribner decided to categorize and hold those things over four chairs. Though they never asked the subjects to recall the chair, none the less the physical association between objects led to a vastly improved recall. Cole and Scribner concluded that 'the fact of having a concrete reminder is more critical for good recall than the particular form the reminder takes.'[14]

With this background in mind, we can now consider precisely what the Roman contribution to mnemotechnics was. The earlier of the two major discussions was once thought to have been written by Cicero, but is now labeled either 'pseudo-Cicero' or the 'Auctor ad Herennium', that is, the author who wrote to C. Herennius. This work dates to *c.* 88–85 BC, and was quite influential in the Middle Ages.[15] A century later Quintilian in his major work on rhetoric takes a somewhat more skeptical view of the system. The two will be considered in chronological order.

THE AUCTOR AD HERENNIUM

Rather than splitting up the Auctor's remarks into bite-size chunks that give little sense of continuity and context, I start with his full instructions about how the system of *loci* works. In addition the reader should be aware that I am presenting my own quite literal translation of the passage, because earlier translations have made the Auctor's advice more opaque than it need be, at the same time as they have masked its position in the development of mnemotechnics by, for example, translating '*locus*' as 'background' and not 'place'.[16] The Auctor (3.16.29–3.19.32) recommends:

> We call places those things which by nature or by artifice are for a short distance, totally, and strikingly complete so that we can comprehend and embrace them easily with natural memory – like a house, an intercolumniation, a corner, an arch, and other things which are similar to these. Images are certain forms, both indications and likenesses of the things which we want to remember. For example, if we want to keep the memory of a horse, lion, and eagle, it will be necessary to locate the images of them in specific places. Now we shall show what kind of places to devise and by what means to invent the images and how to put them in the places.

98

Therefore, for example, those who know the letters are able to write what is dictated to them, and to read out what they have written. Likewise those who have learned mnemonics can locate in the places what they have heard and from these places can recite it. For the places are like wax tablets or papyrus, the images like letters, the disposition and arrangement of images like written characters, and the recitation like reading. Therefore, if we want to remember many things, it is necessary for us to prepare many places so that we can put many images in the many places. Likewise we think it is necessary to have those places in a sequence in case at some time by a disturbance of the sequence we are prevented from following the images from whatever place it is pleasing to any other place, whether from a previous or a subsequent part, and we are able to produce those things which had been assigned to the places. For example, if we should see a fair number of our acquaintances standing in a sequence, it will make no difference whether from the top or from the bottom or from the middle we begin to say their names. Likewise with the places arranged in sequence it will happen that reminded by the images, we can say what we shall have assigned to the places going from any place to whatever part it will be pleasing. Hence it seems best also to prepare the places in a sequence.

It will be necessary that those places which we have adopted be well studied in order that they can stick to us permanently; for the images, just like the letters, will be wiped out when we do not use them; the places, like a wax tablet, ought to remain. And in case by chance we can make a mistake in the number of places, it seems best that every fifth be marked. For example, if in the fifth place we put a golden hand, if in the tenth some well-known person whose first name is Decimus, then it will be easy to put similar marks in every fifth place in turn. Likewise it is more desirable to prepare places in an abandoned than in a crowded area, because the crowding and walking about of people disturbs and weakens the traces of the images. Isolation preserves the shapes of the likenesses whole. Furthermore, places must be prepared that are dissimilar in form and nature in order that they can be seen distinctly. For if someone will have adopted many intercolumniations, he will be confused by their resemblance so that he will not know what he will have placed where. And it is necessary to have medium-sized places of a moderate magnitude; for if excessively large they return vague images, and if too small often they do not seem to be able to take the placing of the images. Then it is necessary that the places have neither too much light nor be excessively dark in case the images be either hidden in darkness or blazingly shine with brilliance. It seems best that the spaces between the places be moderate, approximately a little more or less than thirty feet. For, like the range of vision, the mind is less powerful if you will have moved back too far or if you will have moved excessively close to that which needs to be seen.

Although it is easy for someone who knows very many things to prepare as many and as suitable places as he wants, nevertheless, if someone does not think that he can find enough suitable places, he is allowed to create as many places as he wants. For the mind can embrace any area whatsoever, and in that area the plan of a certain place can be arbitrarily constructed and a building can be designed. Therefore if we are not content with this available supply, we are allowed to create an area in our own mind, and to prepare the most suitable specification of the proper places.

Before beginning my analysis proper of how the art of memory works according to the Auctor, I draw your attention to the Auctor's analogy between words and mnemotechnics in the second paragraph. He sees a direct connection between how words preserve memory and how mnemotechnics preserve memory, for mnemotechnics is very much an art of literacy for the highly literate. The Auctor is very much indebted to his predecessors. He recaps the method of Simonides in his image of remembering acquaintances. He alludes to Aristotle's concept of a series like the alphabet that can be read in either direction, but uses people instead of letters. What most separates the Auctor from his predecessors is his literal interpretation of the term 'places' with its concomitant emphasis on visual perception. Since the ancient words *topos* and *locus* that describe the system mean 'place', it is a natural progression from purely mental places to 'real' physical ones. The places may be figments of your imagination, but they are architectural figments, and not linked, as with Aristotle, to another abstract anchor, like the alphabet or numbers.

Once the places take on a physical form, they become subject to the physical limits of human perception, for the Auctor believes that the external and the internal eye match in their abilities. Hence the places must be on a human scale: neither too big nor too small, neither too dim nor too bright, neither too crowded nor too far apart, neither too near nor too far away. This approach to mental images has its roots in Aristotle, who believed, contrary to Plato, that you could trust your senses.[17] Lucretius, a contemporary of the Auctor, displays little interest in memory and how it works, but in Book 4 is very much concerned with the senses.[18] He devotes considerable attention to observations on vision that parallel the Auctor's practical advice:

> The eyes avoid bright objects and refuse to gaze at them. The sun, indeed, actually blinds them if you persist in directing them towards it. . . . When we see the square towers of a city in the distance, they often appear round. . . . When we gaze from one end down the whole length of a colonnade, though its structure is perfectly symmetrical and it is

propped throughout on pillars of equal height, yet it contracts by slow degrees in a narrowing cone that draws roof to floor and left to right till it unites them in the imperceptible apex of the cone.[19]

Roman wall painters incorporated these perceptions in their illusionistic landscapes. Colonnades recede. Buildings in the distance take on rounder edges and become fuzzier than those in the foreground. Light rather than line defines figures and objects.[20]

Unlike the Auctor, Lucretius does not limit himself to practical observation, but explains why the Auctor is right in recommending that objects should not be too brightly lit and that an endless colonnade would confuse. While Lucretius's explanation of precisely how he thinks vision works is beyond the current topic, what is not is his belief, like the Auctor's, that visual and mental images work in the same way:

> The image of a Centaur, for instance, is certainly not formed from the life, since no living creature of this sort ever existed. But . . . as I have just explained, where surface films from a horse and a man accidentally come into contact, they may easily stick together on the spot, because of the delicacy and flimsiness of their texture. . . . The truth of this explanation may be easily inferred from the following facts. First, in so far as a vision beheld by the mind closely resembles one beheld by the eyes, the two must have been created in a similar fashion. It follows that something similar accounts for the motion of the mind, which also, no less than the eyes, beholds a lion or whatever it may be by means of films. The only difference is that the objects of its vision are flimsier.[21]

Whether mental and visual images function identically in the brain remains a contentious topic with the same basic division between proponents as in antiquity. The Platonists declare that mental images are totally distinct from visual images; the Aristotelians that they are related.[22] Two issues pertain directly to the Auctor's instructions: the case of a modern practitioner of mnemotechnics and recent experiments in neuropsychology.

S. the mnemonist

It might seem at first that it should make no difference whether you use the Grand Canyon or an atom for your setting for distributing the things you need to remember. Consider the mnemonist, Shereshevskii, or S., as he was called by the Soviet psychologist A. R. Luria in his classic study, *The Mind of a Mnemonist*:

> [H]e would 'distribute' [what he had to memorize] along some roadway or street he visualized in his mind. Sometimes this was a street in his home town. . . . On the other hand, he might also select a street in Moscow. Frequently he would take a mental walk along that street. . . .

[T]here was a simple explanation for the omissions [in his recall]. If S. had placed a particular image in a spot where it would be difficult for him to 'discern' – if he, for example, had placed it in an area that was poorly lit or in a spot where he would have trouble distinguishing the object from the background against which it had been set – he would omit this image when he 'read off' the series he had distributed along his mental route. He would simply walk on 'without noticing' the particular item, as he explained.

These omissions . . . clearly were not *defects of memory* but were, in fact, *defects of perception*. . . . The following is his [S.'s] explanation of how this happened [the omitted items are in italics]:

> I put the image of the *pencil* near a fence . . . the one down the street, you know. But what happened was that the image fused with that of the fence and I walked right on past without noticing it. The same thing happened with the word *egg*. I had put it up against a white wall and it blended in with the background. How could I possibly spot a white egg up against a white wall? . . . *Banner*, of course, means the Red Banner. But, you know, the building which houses the Moscow City Soviet of Workers' Deputies is also red, and since I'd put the banner close to one of the walls of the building I just walked on without seeing it. . . . Then there's the word *putamen*. I don't know what this means, but it's such a dark word that I couldn't see it . . . and, besides, the street lamp was quite a distance away.

Increasing the dimensions of his images, seeing to it that the images were clearly illuminated and suitably arranged . . . marked the first step in S.'s technique of eidetic images, which described the second phase of his memory development.[23]

Two points should be made at the outset. First, while Luria is aware of other people with extraordinary memories, he makes no mention of the classical system. Nor did S. know about it. Hence Luria performs the equivalent of a blind test or validation of the *loci*, as described by the Auctor. Most of the literature since Luria, whether it is humanistic or psychological, refers to both.[24] Second, S.'s system appeared in two stages. The first stage was totally intuitive or natural for S. When first questioned by his employer, a newspaper editor, about his memory, S., 'just under thirty' at the time:

> merely countered with amazement: Was there really anything unusual about his remembering everything he'd been told? Wasn't that the way other people operated? The idea that he possessed certain particular qualities of memory which distinguished him from others struck him as incomprehensible.[25]

So I would suggest that Simonides probably thought of his system in a totally natural way. Some people, as we might put it today, are already hard wired to remember by places.

The difference between Simonides and S. — and this difference is significant — lies in Simonides's recognition, at least according to the story, that others not only did not know the system, but also that others could be taught. Next, as with S., comes the realization that one can improve on nature with the result that by the time of the Auctor a number of principles had been formulated on how to best train the memory. Nor did it matter how good one's natural memory was, for, according to Quintilian, 'like everything else, memory may be improved by cultivation.'[26] Plutarch explained: 'This [memory], then, is to be trained in either case, whether one's children be naturally gifted with a good memory, or, on the contrary, forgetful. For we shall thus strengthen nature's generous endowment, and thus fill out her deficiency.'[27]

The ways in which S. differed from his ancient counterparts are rarely mentioned by scholars comparing the two.[28] Despite his prodigious memory feats, he was 'quite inept at logical organization.'[29] Luria explains that

> All this points to a distinct type of dissociation that S. and other people with highly developed capacities for figurative memory exhibit: a tendency to rely exclusively on images and to overlook any possibility of using logical means of recall. . . . [T]he psychologist L. S. Vygotsky gave him a series of words to recall among which were several names of birds. . . . When the experiments were over, S. was asked to enumerate the names of birds that had appeared in the first series. . . . He had failed to note that among the words for recall were some that were *related in meaning*, a fact he recognized only after he had 'read off' all the words in the series and had a chance to compare them.[30]

S.'s ability to remember details frequently overwhelmed his ability to recognize patterns and to think abstractly. For example, he was so taken by particulars that he became disconcerted when people changed their hairstyles. Furthermore:

> S. had often complained that he had a poor memory for faces: 'They're so changeable,' he had said. 'A person's expression depends on his mood and on the circumstances under which you happen to meet him. People's faces are constantly changing; it's the different shades of expression that confuse me and make it so hard to remember faces.' . . . S. saw faces as changing patterns of light and shade, much the same kind of impression a person would get if he were sitting by a window watching the ebb and flow of the sea's waves. Who, indeed, could possibly 'recall' all the fluctuations of the waves' movements?[31]

The mixing of the senses, 'synaesthesia', occurs fairly commonly among musicians, who will 'see' tones as colors. To a certain extent all of us experience this kind of sensation. Blues, for instance, are 'cool' colors, while reds are 'warm'. None the less, it would never occur to most people that 'If it's simply a matter of learning a phone number, though I can repeat it, I won't really know the number unless I've tasted it.'[32]

One of S.'s problems may be obvious: he simply could not forget. As he got older it became more and more of an issue, as he was unable to discard any previous information until finally after much trial and error he happened on a solution – in its own way quite remarkable. First he tried imagining that previous charts, for instance, were covered by some kind of opaque material, but what finally worked was his conscious decision that he would not see previous charts, simply because he did not want to![33] Cicero presents an amusing ancient parallel:

> [I]t is said that a certain learned and highly accomplished person went to him [Themistocles] and offered to impart to him the art of memory, which was then being introduced for the first time; and that when Themistocles asked what precise result that art was capable of achieving, the instructor asserted that it would enable him to remember everything; and Themistocles replied that he would be doing him a greater kindness if he taught him to forget what he wanted than if he taught him to remember.[34]

Cicero assumes that such a skill would be a splendid possession:

> Do you observe what mental force and penetration the man possessed, what power and range of intellect? inasmuch as his answer brings home to us that nothing that had once been introduced into his mind had ever been able to pass out of it, inasmuch as he would rather have been able to forget something that he did not wish to remember than to remember everything that he had once heard or seen.[35]

Cicero cannot conceive of the idea of never being able to forget as a problem, but then he may not have known the tale about Midas and the Golden Touch, which was first told later in the century after Cicero's death by Ovid (*Metamorphoses*, 11.90ff.). Cicero, however, should have known that Aristotle advised that 'a master of any art avoids excess and defect, but seeks the intermediate and chooses this – the intermediate not in the object but relatively to us.'[36] Colin Blakemore, already in 1977, saw the problem in modern terms:

> What we should be most afraid of, perhaps, is the fact that, since the invention of printing, magnetic tape and computer cards the Collective Mind has lost the vital ability to *forget*. . . . This problem is nowhere more acute than in science itself, where the sheer accumulation of facts

104

threatens to impede rather than to assist the progress of new ideas. . . .
[Man] might merely drown himself in a flood of information.[37]

The neuropsychological evidence on mental imagery

The case of S. has been helpful not just for pointing the moral of the
'Golden Mean', but also for demonstrating in modern terms how the
system of *loci* works. In particular, S. strikingly reinforces the advice of
the Auctor: images in the place system of memory are subject to all the
advantages and disadvantages of our physical vision. If we cannot see
something – the egg against the white wall – then we will not remember
it. If too many distractions occur in the setting, then whatever we are trying
to find physically or remember mentally will be lost in the crowd. In short,
practical experience implies that mental images obey the same rules as
visual images. Because proof that the two types of imagery use the same
visual apparatus of the brain has not been possible until recently, the
arguments between the two sides have depended more on philosophical
logic than on physical evidence that something different is happening, for
example, when someone looks at a football and when he or she merely
thinks of a football. How the two systems actually work – whether by
analog or digital storage, for example – is a separate issue.

The first inkling of proof for the unitary view came from experiments by
Roger Shepard in the 1970s. He discovered that when we are given an
object to rotate mentally 'there is a precise linear relationship between the
angle the mental image is rotated and the time required' to accomplish the
rotation.[38] Stephen M. Kosslyn and his colleagues tested people on their
recall of maps. The 'time taken to "see" the second [of two] object[s] was
directly related to the distance on the map between the two objects.'[39]
Kosslyn also found – and this conclusion relates directly to mnemotechnics
– that 'subjects took longer to "see" the parts of objects in small images
than in large.'[40] These and later experiments bolster the claims of the
mnemonists. On the other side, however, N. H. Kerr tried an experiment
similar to one of Kosslyn's:

[She] instructed her congenitally blind subjects to image a familiar
household object either next to a car or next to a paper clip, and
then measured how long it took them to search their image for a
particular named part, such as the dial on a radio. Just as Kosslyn had
found with sighted subjects, Kerr found slower response times to find
the named parts when the images were small. Her conclusion was that
the representations used in imagery do indeed have spatial properties,
like visual representations, but they need not be visual themselves; in
fact, with the congenitally blind subjects they were certainly not
visual.[41]

The distinction between visual and spatial representations is quite important, and is a subject which I will discuss below.

Neuropsychological testing breaks this 'theoretical stalemate' with evidence that 'expands qualitatively, as well as quantitatively, the support for visual perceptual mechanisms in visual mental imagery.'[42] Experimenters have run the same kinds of experiments as before with one exception: at the same time as the tasks are performed, they have examined regional cerebral blood flow and used electrophysiological techniques, electroencephalography and event-related potentials to see which parts of their subjects' brains are activated. According to Martha J. Farah:

> The most straightforward and parsimonious conclusion from this pattern of results is that mental images are visual representations, that is, they consist at least in part of some of the same representations used in vision. However, there does exist a logically correct alternative explanation according to which mental images are not visual representations, but are merely accompanied by activation in visual brain areas. . . . To distinguish between these alternatives, we must find out whether destruction of visual brain areas results in imagery impairments as well as visual impairments.[43]

The evidence again supports the linkage between visual and mental imagery:

> Specifically, imagery is not visual in the sense of necessarily representing information acquired through visual sensory channels. Rather, it is visual in the sense of using some of the same neural representational machinery as vision. That representational machinery places certain constraints on what can be represented in images and on the relative ease of accessing different kinds of information in images.[44]

Further proof for the linkage between what we see and what we imagine comes from John Hull, a man who went blind in his forties. He writes in his diary after five years of being blind:

> Today I could not remember which way the Arabic number three points. I had to trace it with my finger in the air, one, two, three. Now I remember. It points to the left. . . . Marilyn [his wife] was with me, and was surprised to find that such a deeply ingrained image could be partially lost.[45]

Oliver Sacks writes about an artist, whom he calls Jonathan I., who suffered a complete loss of color vision (achromatopsia) after a car accident:

> Jonathan I. did not lose just his perception of color, but imagery and even dreaming in color. Finally he seemed to lose even his memory of color, so that it ceased to be part of his mental knowledge, his mind.

106

Thus, as more and more time elapsed without color vision, he came to resemble someone with an amnesia for color – or, indeed, someone who had never known it at all.[46]

Hence it has taken two millennia to prove that the Auctor was absolutely correct in his recommendation that places for memory storage must comply with the constraints of our physical visual system.

In another article, Farah and her colleagues draw the distinction, alluded to earlier, between visual and spatial mental imagery.[47] First, I would like to clarify the two terms. This is one of the rare cases where the two disparate fields of cognitive psychology and art history directly conflict. I find the term *spatial* somewhat misleading in this context, because *spatial* sometimes in the usage of art historians implies a *sense of perspective*, a concept I would like to keep distinct. Instead, I will use the term *locational* to describe the ability that enables us to find something by its position in a particular place.[48] Hence the congenitally blind person has a locational sense. In simple terms, he or she gets around on both a micro and macro scale by going from place to place or, as in the example cited, by finding the right knob on the radio. Such locational information differs from information that can only be gained by sight, i.e. visually, such as what the object actually looks like, its colors, and other information that cannot come from the other four senses. The two types of visual information (sight and location) are served by two separate but parallel visual systems, which Farah and her colleagues find 'rather counterintuitive'.[49] They add: 'For present purposes, the anatomical separateness of these two systems is of less importance than their functional independence – the fact that each one can continue to function in the absence of the other.'[50]

This is one of those especially pleasing instances when humanists and scientists can be mutually enlightening, for art is basically a system of mental imagery made visual. It is well known to art historians that the representation of perspective, the location of objects in space, developed separately from the representation of objects. Linear perspective in art is the technical means by which three-dimensional objects are rendered in two dimensions and especially with respect to each other. That is, the rendering of individual three-dimensional objects individually must be distinguished from the way several three-dimensional objects are related to each other within a single representation. To use the terms from Farah's articles, I am distinguishing the *visual* – how an individual figure or object looks – from the *locational* (her *spatial*) – where that figure or object is located in space in relation to other figures or objects within that same space.

Naturalistic representations of individual figures occurred early, very early. Cave paintings, for example, show recognizable animals, but they float in space. By the end of the sixth century BC Greek art has figures that twist and turn in what we might call a realistic, three-dimensional manner.[51]

While each figure is in itself three-dimensional, together they do not quite work together the way figures interact with each other and their surroundings in representational art today, as anyone knows who has tried to disentangle who is located behind whom in many-figured scenes on Greek vases.

The Romans seem to do better in the sense that the viewer has an idea of figures in front, in the middle ground, and behind, in part because the Romans like to put their figures into physical settings both natural and manmade. A close analysis, however, reveals that the impression of a single, unified scene is incorrect. For example, in the painting from Pompeii of the riot of AD 59 at the amphitheater, a bird's eye view of the amphitheater is combined with people seen virtually head-on so that the viewer can see what is happening within the amphitheater.[52] Since the amphitheater has been excavated, we know that it was oval and not round in shape, as we 'read' the painting.[53] Even clearer and without the constraint of showing the interior of a building are the paintings from the *cubiculum* (bedroom) of a villa at Boscoreale.[54] In particular, the middle panel of the east wall shows a view of a city between columns in which each building aligns its vanishing points along a central axis, called the vanishing axis. What is perhaps most interesting about this painting is that the absence of our system of perspective does not jar our eyes and only close examination reveals its inconsistencies. Yet the Romans do have realistic depictions of individual objects. For example, fruit can be seen through the glass bowl that holds them.[55]

The history of art teaches us, then, that the visual representation of things develops separately from the representation of the location of these same things in space. Like the alphabet, our current system of perspective is a totally manmade invention. Like the alphabet it is both taken for granted and, perhaps more significantly, was invented only once. All systems of linear perspective with one or two vanishing points (the latter was a later development from the former) go back to the same invention in the fifteenth century.[56]

Thus Farah and her colleagues have explained why perspective developed separately from the representation of people, things, and landscape. We are hard wired with at least two separate visual systems: one for recognizing objects and the other for locating those same objects in space. Hence each form followed its own development in art. At the same time the neuropsychological evidence proves that the Auctor knew what he was talking about when he described how the system of *loci* worked. Ulric Neisser, following Herbert Simon, believes that

> the simple fact that the nervous system evolved through natural selection makes modular organization virtually inevitable. . . . My conjecture, then, is that the spatial module may be the principal vehicle of

personal memory. A system that originally evolved to deal only with movement through space now helps us to keep track of 'movement' through time as well.[57]

QUINTILIAN'S ELABORATION OF THE ARCHITECTURAL *LOCI*

A century after the Auctor, Quintilian continues to stress the need for an appropriate scale, clear images, and sequential order, which he describes with the lovely phrase 'linked one to the other like dancers hand in hand.'[58] His discussion, while briefer than the Auctor's, presents a more explicit description of how the system works:

> Some place is chosen of the largest possible extent and characterised by the utmost possible variety, such as a spacious house divided into a number of rooms. Everything of note therein is carefully committed to the memory, in order that the thought may be enabled to run through all the details without let or hindrance . . . let us suppose that the symbol is drawn from navigation, as, for example, an anchor; or from warfare, as, for example, some weapon. These symbols are then arranged as follows. The first image is placed, as it were, in the entrance; the second, let us say, in the atrium; the remainder are placed in due order all round the impluvium and entrusted not merely to bedrooms and bays, but even to the care of statues and the like. This done, as soon as the memory of the facts requires to be revived, all these places are visited in turn and the various deposits are demanded from their custodians, as the sight of each recalls the respective details. . . . What I have spoken of as being done in a house, can equally well be done in connexion with public buildings, a long journey, the ramparts of a city, or even pictures. Or we may even imagine such places to ourselves.[59]

Like S., Quintilian recommends a single but relatively complex path that would be taken naturally, as, for example, you would go from room to room in a house. Instead of S.'s street, he chooses an elaborate house of 'the largest possible extent' not in the sense of violating the physical constraints of our visual apparatus, but in the sense of a sufficient number of distinguishable nooks and crannies in which to 'deposit' the various things to remember. You do not want to be in the situation of having too many things to remember and not enough places to put them. You are not supposed to tack on another house when you run out of room in the first one, but are to choose one from the start that will suit your needs. In a way, it is like the planning needed before buying a real house: it should have enough space to hold all your possessions so that you will not have to store the towels at a neighbor's.

I find it remarkable that the system of *loci* not only works for some people, but also became even more elaborate and complex in the Renaissance.[60] Today it seems to be undergoing a visual resurgence on the computer. Xerox PARC has developed a 'search-and-retrieval' technology called 'The Information Theater'.[61] The latest 'advances' in computer programs are graphical representations of the 'world'. Robin Raskin gives a couple of examples: 'Apple's e*world and General Magic's Magic Cap are constructed like little shops on Main Street. You visit the bank when you want to do a financial transaction; the newsstand when you want the news.'[62] 'Managing Your Money for Windows' shows an office complete with two windows, a bookcase against the left wall holding such tomes as goals, tuition, and retirement, and a stand in the right corner with a calendar on top and a hefty catalog in the bottom. The desk has a register open on top and various drawers (accounts, categories, payee) on the front. The 'exit' is a mouse hole in the right wall.[63]

Quintilian, like myself and unlike the Auctor and S., however, is rather skeptical about the effectiveness of the system:

> I am far from denying that those devices may be useful for certain purposes, as, for example, if we have to reproduce a number of names in the order in which we heard them. . . . Such a practice may perhaps have been of use to those who, after an auction, have succeeded in stating what object they had sold to each buyer, their statements being checked by the books of the money-takers. . . . It will, however, be of less service in learning the various parts of a set speech. For thoughts do not call up the same images as material things, and a symbol requires to be specially invented for them, although even here a particular place may serve to remind us, as, for example, of some conversation that may have been held there. But how can such a method grasp a whole series of connected words? I pass over the fact that there are certain things which it is impossible to represent by symbols, as, for example, conjunctions. We may, it is true, like shorthand writers, have definite symbols for everything, and may select an infinite number of places to recall all the words contained in the five books of the second pleading against Verres, and we may even remember them all as if they were deposits placed in safe-keeping. But will not the flow of our speech inevitably be impeded by the double task imposed upon our memory? For how can our words be expected to flow in connected speech, if we have to look back at separate symbols for each individual word?[64]

Quintilian's criticisms seem, to me, to be perfectly justified, especially the idea that you have to remember not just the things but the places for the things. Vogl and Thompson compared the speed at which two different mnemonists, Rajan Mahadevan and Hideaki Tomoyori, recalled each digit of pi, which they had memorized to 31,811 and 40,000 places respectively. They concluded that 'Tomoyori used a mnemonic to retrieve the digits, thus slowing his rate of recitation in comparison to Rajan [who didn't].'[65] So Quintilian is right about the 'double task imposed upon the memory.' Memorizing by the system of *loci* will slow down recall, but you will at least recall what you have memorized.

Quintilian was not alone in his skeptical view about the art of memory in antiquity. Philostratus was even more dubious, though for a different reason:

> There is no such thing as an art of memory, nor could there be, for though memory gives us the arts [τέχνας], it cannot itself be taught, nor can it be acquired by any method or system, since it is a gift of nature or a part of the immortal soul. For never could human beings be regarded as endowed with immortality, nor could what we have learned be taught, did not Memory inhabit the minds of men.[66]

Plato would have approved. For people who have poor memories or who may on occasion have an exceptionally difficult passage to recall, Quintilian does suggest a modified version of the system of *loci*:

> [T]he following additional remedy . . . though drawn from the mnemonic system discussed above, is not without its uses: He will adapt his symbols to the nature of the thoughts which tend to slip from his memory, using an anchor . . . if he has to speak of a ship, or a spear, if he has to speak of a battle. For symbols are highly efficacious, and one idea suggests another.[67]

This part of Quintilian's advice brings us to the other major component of the ancient art of memory: mental images and their construction.

MENTAL IMAGERY

In order to show how the system of *topoi* developed from a mental construct to a physical, literal interpretation of the *loci*, I have left aside until now how the images are created that connect the thing to be remembered with its place. In technical terms, psychologists make a distinction between the encoding mnemonic, the mental image you create, and the organizational mnemonic, such as the *topoi* and *loci*, that puts the encoding mnemonics into a particular order.[68] Aristotle mentions the alphabet and numbers as examples of *topoi* or organizational mnemonics. Like the modern pegword system it has three components: the pegword or letter of the alphabet, the thing to be remembered, and the image that connects the first two items. Thus Baddeley suggested that, if you needed to remember the word 'crocodile' as the third item in a list, you would associate crocodile with the pegword 'three is a tree' by imagining 'a crocodile with a tree growing out of it'. In the psychological literature such imagery is called 'bizarre' for obvious reasons. Bizarre experiments have been devised to test just how bizarre the imagery should be, how long the retention span is for things memorized using this system, and, of course, whether it really works. Psychologists, however, face a major problem in testing the efficacy of mnemotechnics. Modern mnemonists claim that the imagery has to be created by the individual, whereas most psychological testing depends on giving groups of subjects the same material. Nor is it considered scientific to preselect the subjects for all or no mnemonists. At the same time the system, while teachable within thirty minutes, probably works better after practice, as the ancient sources imply.[69] What is of great interest is the striking agreement between the ancient and modern mnemonists on how the system works.

The Auctor presents the case for the mnemonists:

> I know that most of the Greeks who have written on the memory have taken the course of listing images that correspond to a great many words, so that persons who wished to learn these images by heart would have them ready without expending effort on a search for them. I disapprove of their method on several grounds. First, among the innumerable multitude of words it is ridiculous to collect images for a thousand. How meagre is the value these can have, when out of the infinite store of words we shall need to remember now one, and now another? Secondly, why do we wish to rob anybody of his initiative, so that to save him from making any search himself, we deliver to him everything searched out and ready? Then again, one person is more struck by one likeness, and another more by another. Often in fact when we declare that some one form resembles another, we fail to receive universal assent, because things seem different to different persons. The same is true with respect to images: one that is well-defined to us appears relatively inconspicuous to others. Everybody, therefore, should in equipping himself with images suit his own convenience.[70]

First, like Aristotle and modern mnemonists, the Auctor advises against prefabricated images. In a way, it is like teachers today telling students that they can do only so much spoon-feeding. Only the student can learn the vocabulary, the dates, the lesson. There are no shortcuts. Second, the Auctor clearly separates himself, a Roman, from the Greeks and their one-size-fits-all advice. In other words, the Auctor is directly stating that the Greeks did not always heed Aristotle and implies that the Romans made improvements on the system.[71] Third, since the Auctor did not have to adhere to the modern scientific method, he relied solely on practical experience. The effectiveness of his advice is best documented for the Middle Ages and the Renaissance, when his work was most popular.[72]

Finally, as a general rule, the harder you work to remember something the more likely you are to remember it within certain limits.[73] Because visual imagery for either the spoken or written word by its very nature involves more than one of the senses, the thing to be remembered will be more thoroughly recorded and hence more likely to be recalled. In Chapter 6 I discussed this issue with respect to the Muses. At the same time 'visual imagery essentially improves content organization, and thus recall, of microelements (sentences).'[74]

Creating mental images in antiquity applied to memory for words and memory for things.[75] This technique was first developed by the Greeks and is at least as early as *c.* 400 BC, the date of our earliest source, the *Dialexeis*. It advises:

> [W]hat you hear, place on what you know. For example, Χρύσιππος (Chrysippus) is to be remembered; we place it on χρυσός (gold) and ἵππος (horse). Another example: we place πυριλάμπης (glow-worm) on πύρ (fire) and λάμπειν (shine). So much for names. For things (do) thus: for courage (place it) on Mars and Achilles; for metal-working, on Vulcan; for cowardice, on Epeus.[76]

The description is somewhat cryptic if you do not know about the *topoi*. It simply advises you to divide words into their component parts and to think of something to which they are directly related. Psychologists call it the 'keyword mnemonic', although it has nothing to do with the layman's concept of a keyword as a summation of a text's contents. According to Desrochers and Begg keywords also differ from pegwords, as discussed in Chapter 7. They are specifically used 'to help people remember unfamiliar vocabulary items. The basic principle underlying this technique consists of associating the unfamiliar word with a familiar word that is physically similar to it.'[77] Unlike the pegword or *loci* method, keywords do not depend on a particular order in a list, just on knowing the linked words. In one study students using this method were quite successful in learning vocabulary over the short term – what I would call cramming – but, over the long term, which was only two days, recall was 'especially fragile'. Instead the old, familiar way of learning a word by 'studying it within a meaningful context' provided longer, lasting memories.[78]

By the time of the Auctor, who provides the fullest description, the 'keyword mnemonic' has become more elaborate in that it encompasses whole sentences and makes pictures of that whole. The Auctor suggests that:

> When we wish to represent by images the likenesses of words, we shall be undertaking a greater task and exercising our ingenuity the more. This we ought to effect in the following way: *Iam domum itionem reges Atridae parant.* [And now the kings, the sons of Atreus, prepare their

return home.] If we wish to remember this verse, in the first place we should put Domitius, raising hands to heaven while he is lashed by the Marcii Reges – that will represent 'Iam domum itionem reges'; in the second place, Aesopus and Cimber, being dressed for the roles of Agamemnon and Menelaus in *Iphigenia* – that will represent 'Atridae parant.' By this method all the words will be represented.[79]

As Quintilian (11.2.25) commented, this system omits certain kinds of words like conjunctions and, in this case, an adverb, '*iam*'. The Auctor refers to personalities well known to the Romans, like actors (Aesopus and Cimber) and the well born (the Marcii Reges). If we adopted this system and wished to remember 'Beauty is in the eye of the beholder', we might conjure up an image of some current beauty, like Brooke Shields or Madonna, reflected in the mirrored sunglasses of someone holding a bee. If the phrase were 'never say die', we might think of Prince Charles trying to tell someone not to discuss his ex-wife Diana. The system reminds me most of the modern game of charades. Words are broken down into syllables, much like a rebus, and the more bizarre the image enacted the more likely the side guessing is to win. In fact, around 1335 Thomas Bradwardine wrote a treatise 'On Artificial Memory' in which he called memory for words '*memoria sillabarum*' ('memory of syllables').[80]

Modern testing of the relationship between imagery and memory makes a distinction between bizarre imagery, as just described, and vivid imagery, which I treat next. The ancient texts imply that difference, but do not directly state it. Bizarre imagery tends to be of greater benefit today for remembering lists of things, memory for *res* as the Auctor would call it, as opposed to memory for words or prose, *verba* in the Auctor's terms. As with almost any technique, it is a matter of knowing when to use it, although tests so far remain unclear as to where those 'boundary conditions' lie.[81] Mnemonic strategies have been found to be particularly helpful in recall of content rather than of actual wording of texts.[82]

The Auctor recommends using mental imagery in one other way:

Often we encompass the memory of an entire act [*rei*] by one notation and a single image. For example, the prosecutor has said that the defendant killed a man by poison, has charged that the motive for the crime was an inheritance, and declared that there are many witnesses and accessories to this act. If in order to facilitate our defense we wish to remember this first point, we shall in the first place form an image of the entire act. We shall make the one about whom the case is being pled a sick man lying in bed, if we know what he looks like. If we do not know him, we shall yet take someone else to be our invalid, but not from the lowest class, so that he may come to mind at once. And we shall place the defendant at the bedside, with a cup in his right hand and writing tablets in his left, and a doctor holding a purse. In this way we can record the man who was poisoned, the inheritance, and the witnesses. Likewise then we shall put the other charges in sequence in the places, and whenever we want to remember a fact, if we use a proper arrangement of the forms and a careful notation of the images, we shall easily follow what we want in memory.[83]

The facts of the case suggest the images unlike the example for memorizing text, which stresses the superficial resemblances between the sounds of the words rather than their meanings. For the most part, the Auctor's image of the scene of the crime is easy to follow. Albertus Magnus (1193/1206–1280) explains the cup and the tablets as representing respectively 'the memory of the poison which he [the sick man] drank, and . . . the memory of the will which he signed.'[84] The purse contains the bribe for the doctor.

The recreation of the scene of the crime depends not on bizarre imagery, like memory for words, but on vivid description.[85] A series of full scenes is pictured with each stage of the argument of the case having its own scene, which includes all its elements. Together, the series of scenes resembles a continuous narrative much like a cartoon strip today or the late Roman Republican wall paintings of the Odyssey landscapes, from a building on the Esquiline in Rome dating some thirty years after the Auctor.[86] Seven episodes from one wall have survived that represent the three major adventures of Odysseus, which he relates to Alcinous in *Odyssey*, 10–12: his arrival in the land of the Laestrygonians, two attacks of the Laestrygonians, and the subsequent flight of Odysseus and his men; Odysseus in Circe's palace; and two scenes of Odysseus's trip to the Underworld.

While the figures are subordinated to the setting and not emphasized, as the Auctor has done for his description of a crime, the way the viewer sees each scene through pilasters painted over the landscape, which continues behind them, gives an idea of how the Auctor meant his system to work. If you recall, the Auctor recommends putting things to be remembered in intercolumniations. In both his scene of the crime and the Odyssey landscapes, the things in question are an ordered series of what we would call episodes or scenes. By demarcating more or less where one scene ends and the next begins, the pilasters in the painting make the scenes easier to 'read' and hence easier to remember by dividing the larger whole into more manageable-sized chunks, a practice which Quintilian recommends: 'If a speech of some length has to be committed to memory, it will be well to learn it piecemeal, since there is nothing so bad for the memory as being overburdened.'[87]

Approximately ten years earlier than the Odyssey landscapes is the fresco from the Villa of the Mysteries in Pompeii.[88] The villa gets its name from this frieze, which depicts an initiation of a woman into a Dionysiac cult. What concerns the current discussion is the repetition of the protagonist, the woman, in a series of episodes. Unlike the slightly later Odyssey landscapes, it is more difficult in this case to tell where one episode ends and the next begins, because the figures, instead of the dividers, are in the foreground. None the less, the background with its panels helps to punctuate the process of initiation: the arrival of the fully dressed woman, her preparation for the initiation, the initiation itself, and finally her return to normal attire. Both the Auctor and the painters are following similar principles, which in a certain sense is entirely to be expected, since they had the same audience. The Auctor has to give advice that is understandable; the painter has to produce art that is comprehensible.

I end with a modern endorsement of the system of successive images from Mark Twain. He described his memory as 'never loaded with anything but blank cartridges.'[89] Yet he was a frequent lecturer. He tried a number of systems that didn't work. One was quite Aristotelian in that he 'took the initial letter from each phrase and wrote one on each of his fingernails . . . [but] the audience came to believe he had more interest in his fingernails than in his subject matter or them.'[90] Finally, somewhat like S., he hit upon the following method in 1873:

> It was now that the idea of pictures occurred to me; then my troubles passed away. In two minutes I made six pictures with a pen, and they did the work of the eleven catch-sentences, and did it perfectly. I threw the pictures away as soon as they were made, for I was sure I could shut my eyes and see them at any time. That was a quarter of a century ago; that lecture vanished out of my head more than twenty years ago, but I could rewrite it from the pictures – for they remain.[91]

Twain implies one other point: the two lectures, though the same in content, would no doubt differ in words. As with the oral poets, verbatim recall is not the issue with this kind of memory.

9

OTHER ADVICE FOR
IMPROVING MEMORY

Most modern discussions of the ancient art of memory focus on the
systems of *topoi* and *loci*. Yet the variety of techniques and the number of
practical suggestions given by Quintilian demonstrate that training the
memory ˉin classical antiquity was a many-pronged process. What you
needed to memorize would determine which method should be employed.
As Baddeley puts it: 'Having a range of mnemonic strategies to hand can
therefore be rather useful, even though one only uses them from time-to-
time.'[1] Equally interesting are the methods that they did not use in antiquity
and why. Most important of all is what we call the 'bottom line': do these
techniques work?

QUINTILIAN'S RECOMMENDATIONS

Quintilian did not himself use the system of *loci* and mental imagery:

> the experts mentioned by Cicero as having trained their memory by
> methods of this kind, namely Charmadas, and Metrodorus of Scepsis
> . . . may keep their systems for their own use. My precepts on the
> subject shall be of a simpler kind.[2]

Neither Cicero nor the Auctor devote much attention to other, 'simpler'
kinds of advice. Much of what Quintilian recommends is just plain practical
and used today by many people without any realization of the long tradition. Foremost are practice, a daily regimen, graduated exercises, and divide
and conquer:

> all who, whatever their age, desire to cultivate the power of memory,
> should endeavour to swallow the initial tedium of reading and re-
> reading what they have written or read, a process which we may
> compare to chewing the cud. This task will be rendered less tiresome
> if we begin by confining ourselves to learning only a little at a time, in
> amounts not sufficient to create disgust. . . . We should begin with
> poetry and then go on to oratory, while finally we may attempt passages

still freer in rhythm and less akin to ordinary speech, such, for example, as passages from legal writers.[3]

He believes, as I quoted Chapter 8, that 'if a speech of some length has to be committed to memory, it will be well to learn it piecemeal, since there is nothing so bad for the memory as being overburdened.'[4] He is 'not, however, prepared to recommend any definite length; it will depend on the natural limits of the passage concerned, unless, indeed, it be so long as itself to require subdivision.'[5] Not only should you practice, but you should also test yourself to make sure you have got it right (Quintilian 11.2.34–35). Part of the reason for so much practice is that 'the abnormally rapid memory fails as a rule to last and takes its leave as though, its immediate task accomplished, it had no further duties to perform', as every student who has ever crammed for a test knows.[6] Modern psychological studies call practice 'rehearsal', and basically support Quintilian's advice, except for one major caveat with which Quintilian would entirely agree, but generally took for granted.[7] You must pay attention. For example, attempts to convert Americans from the fahrenheit to the centigrade scale for temperature at one time consisted in giving readings in both systems with the result that most listened for the fahrenheit and ignored the centigrade. Passive repetition is no help.[8]

Next after practice, 'the most powerful aid of all', comes the 'division and artistic structure' of whatever you are trying to memorize.[9] The necessity for organization or arrangement (τάξις in Greek, *dispositio* in Latin) was apparent from the time when the principles of rhetoric were first formulated.[10] The idea of order in a speech is related to the idea of order for the *topoi* and *loci*. Both depend on a particular sequence and both can hold different kinds of information. Aristotle uses the same word, τάξις, for both.[11] Different kinds of arrangement are needed for different situations. Aristotle says:

> The current division is absurd. For narration surely is part of a forensic speech only: how in a political speech or a speech of display can there be narration in the technical sense? or a reply to a forensic opponent? or an epilogue in closely-reasoned speeches? Again, introduction, comparison of conflicting arguments, and recapitulation are only found in political speeches when there is a struggle between two policies.[12]

Although different components, as we might call them, are preferred in different periods, having a set order makes a difference in ease of remembering.[13] Not only should your speech be well organized with clearly marked divisions, but also the subject of your speech should have its own internal logic. Quintilian advises that point should follow point in a natural development of the argument so that 'the connexion will be so perfect that nothing can be omitted or inserted without the fact of the

118

omission or insertion being obvious.'[14] One of the major benefits from such a tight organization goes unmentioned by Quintilian: your listeners and readers will also more easily understand and remember what you have written if it is presented in a clear and concise way.

Modern testing has established that when subjects are given lists of words with those separated that are normally associated with each other (for example, knife and fork), the subjects on their own make the association and recall the words together.[15] Our innate tendency to organize information makes it easier for us to cope with the incredible amount of information with which we are bombarded every day. We have to know what needs our attention and what we should ignore. Problems arise when either we come to a false conclusion or are dealing with complex material that admits to more than one arrangement.[16] What is important here is that in antiquity it was recognized that organization had to be treated separately from the memorization of images and words, a conclusion borne out in psychological tests. Michel Denis, for example, says that:

> The macrostructure, which contains the most important ideas of the whole text, mainly includes nonfigurative meaning components, based on knowledge about causal relationships, goals, motives, etc., all of which cannot be expressed easily in visual images.[17]

Quintilian has other suggestions that may seem curious today. For example: 'Both learning and writing have this feature in common: namely, that good health, sound digestion, and freedom from other preoccupations of mind contribute largely to the success of both.'[18] While we would agree that concentration on the matter at hand is more productive than letting the mind wander, good health and sound digestion are appreciated in their own right and in sports, but not always as an integral part of the literate life, as the lives of many scholars demonstrate.[19]

Quintilian also believes that you should not memorize silently, but 'our voice should be subdued, rising scarcely above a murmur', because in this way 'the mind should be kept alert by the sound of the voice, so that the memory may derive assistance from the double effort of speaking and listening.'[20] As I have already discussed in Chapter 6, engaging more than one of your senses in learning increases the likelihood of your remembering. In Chapter 2, I noted that in antiquity both ancient Greek and Latin were far easier to read, if read out loud, because of the format of the text, which runs all the words together with little or no punctuation.[21] The idea of murmuring rather than using a normal conversational voice or the louder volume necessary for conversation or delivery of a speech occurs most often among those reciting prayers, such as religious Jews.[22] I don't know any psychological studies of this specific practice, but it is related to 'shadowing', which is the repeating of speech aloud. Arthur Reber explains the 'technique' as it is used in psychological testing:

119

It is used extensively as a control procedure in experiments on attention, since shadowing a message commandeers one's attentional focus so thoroughly that little or no attention can be directed toward any other stimulus that may be present.[23]

Galotti summarizes one experiment in which subjects:

> heard prose in the attended message and a short list of simple words in the unattended message. Subjects failed to recognize the occurrence of most of the words in the unattended message, even though the list had been repeated 35 times![24]

I believe, then, that Quintilian's recommendation to murmur your text as you read forces you to focus directly on what you are memorizing and, at the same time, reduces your ability to notice distractions.

Furthermore, Baddeley stresses the importance of the 'phonological loop' for short-term memory. The phonological loop has two parts: the memory store that holds 'speech-based information and an articulatory control process based on inner speech.'[25] Since memory of speech fades rapidly, after about two seconds, the store can be refreshed by 'subvocal rehearsal'. Information from the articulatory control process returns it to the short-term memory store. Hence the murmuring would aid not just the process of construing the *scriptio continua*, but would provide its own feedback and reinforcement. At the same time the memorizer probably 'hears' what he or she is memorizing and compares it consciously or unconsciously with previous versions. Perhaps the best analogy for this process may be the way we learn the 'tunes' for telephone numbers we dial frequently on touchtone phones.[26] While I could never 'sing' the 'tunes', I am generally aware of when I have misdialed a frequently used number.

Next Quintilian turns to memorizing orally:

> On the other hand, if we attempt to learn by heart from another reading aloud, we shall find that there is both loss and gain; on the one hand, the process of learning will be slower, because the perception of the eye is sharper than that of the ear, while, on the other hand, when we have heard a passage once or twice, we shall be in a position to test our memory and match it against the voice of the reader.[27]

One of the reasons for the superiority of the eye is obviously the engaging of another sense, since, as already discussed, Quintilian advises murmuring while reading the text for memorizing.[28] At the same time the eye can distinguish homonyms that may take the ear longer to discern. Immediate testing and feedback are common sense. Modern testing makes one clarification: if only one sense, hearing or seeing, is involved, you will remember better if the thing to be remembered (like a telephone number) is spoken than if you read it.[29] *Pace* Quintilian, the ear alone is sharper than the eye alone for memory of words.

Perhaps most significant, although only implied by the last passage, is that Quintilian is fully literate and therefore prefers to memorize from a written text rather than orally. He says, as I quoted a little less fully in Chapter 7:

> There is one thing which will be of assistance to everyone, namely, to learn a passage by heart from the same tablets on which he has committed it to writing. For he will have certain tracks to guide him in his pursuit of memory, and the mind's eye will be fixed not merely on the pages on which the words were written, but on individual lines. . . . Further, if the writing should be interrupted by some erasure, addition or alteration, there are certain symbols available, the sight of which will prevent us from wandering from the track.[30]

This advice is an application of the idea already discussed that recall works best if you recreate the context in which you first experienced and, in this case, memorized something. When trying to track down some tidbit, I sometimes remember its source by its location in my files or on my shelves and the actual placement of the information on the page, whether it is on the left or right, close to the beginning or the end of the article or the book, etc. One of the challenges in designing computer displays has been to provide a context as rich as print is in newspapers and magazines. For this reason, among others, the World Wide Web has become increasingly popular.

Quintilian further suggests:

> If certain portions prove especially difficult to remember, it will be found advantageous to indicate them by certain marks, the remembrance of which will refresh and stimulate the memory. For there can be but few whose memory is so barren that they will fail to recognize the symbols with which they have marked different passages.[31]

Wax tablets are ideal for marking up, because texts could be easily obliterated by smoothing over the wax. While today we frown on marking the printed page, even permanent ancient texts, written on either rolls or codices, were supposed to be 'annotated' by the owner.[32] That the use of *scriptio continua* forced the reader to punctuate the text may not only have aided the reader in memorizing, in making the text truly his own, but also may have helped *scriptio continua* to survive for so long. If someone else punctuates the text, in effect does all the work for you, you will not be able to remember that text as easily. Mary Carruthers in her study of memory in the Middle Ages argues that in medieval manuscripts 'the basic function of all page decoration [is] to make each page memorable.'[33] That is, the decoration, which changes within each page and between pages, makes each part of the text distinctive and thereby easier to memorize. The result was the highly colorful, rubricated text of the Middle Ages. Recent psychological testing of writing supports the advice of Quintilian and medieval practice. When subjects are asked to write what they have read, their arrangement of the text takes the same format as the original input.[34]

Quintilian describes this final bit of advice as 'a curious fact':

> of which the reason is not obvious, that the interval of a single night will greatly increase the strength of the memory, whether this be due to the fact that it has rested from the labour, the fatigue of which constituted the obstacle to success, or whether it be that the power of recollection, which is the most important element of memory, undergoes a process of ripening and maturing during the time which intervenes. Whatever the cause, things which could not be recalled on the spot are easily co-ordinated the next day, and time itself, which is generally accounted one of the causes of forgetfulness, actually serves to strengthen the memory.[35]

An experiment conducted in 1924 seemed to have substantiated the phenomenon, but its findings were subsequently questioned.[36] I think the issue is twofold. First, we do not fully understand sleep, and especially dreaming, which remains one of the major unresolved issues. Second, the processes of learning and remembering are multiple and subject to multiple means of 'encoding'. Researchers have isolated some direct connections between sleep and learning. Negative effects on memory occur if subjects are awakened in the middle of rapid eye movement (REM) sleep. Waking subjects at other times does not affect recall the next day.[37] Related experiments on learning 'perceptual skills' have shown that practice alone does not make perfect, but that after learning something initially 'several hours of cerebral "consolidation"' occur. A similar 'consolidation' may happen when we 'sleep on it', but according to some experiments with rats such sleep must come within a certain time frame.[38] Furthermore, the amount of time spent in REM sleep is longer after learning sessions than when learning is not a factor. Moreover, it seems that such REM sleep matters only for certain kinds of learning and remembering, such as acquiring new motor and perceptual skills. Children learning a new language, for example, have longer periods of REM sleep.[39] Finally, experiments with fruit flies no less have shown that exposure to a stimulus every minute, that is, cramming, over a twenty-minute period was not effective in teaching the fruit flies to avoid a particular odor, but that single exposures followed by fifteen-minute rests in between were.[40] To remember, we need time to take in the stimulus.

OTHER RECOMMENDATIONS

The only ancient method that Quintilian and the others who wrote about mnemotechnics did not directly describe is the use of jingles and songs to learn things like the alphabet and arithmetic.[41] They probably did not mention them, because they did not consider them to be artificial devices for memorizing as we do today. Jingles and songs were used in teaching the young, while mnemotechnics was learned at the end of one's training and was used by only the most literate. Cicero in his discussion of the funerary regulations listed in the Twelve Tables says: 'You know what follows, for we learned the Law of the Twelve Tables in our boyhood as a required formula; though no one learns it nowadays.'[42] St Augustine remarks that 'in those days 'one and one are two, two and two are four' was a loathsome jingle [odiosa cantio].'[43] Today, we learn such things as 'In 1492 Columbus sailed the ocean blue' or 'Thirty days hath September/April, June and November'. What I particularly like about the second example is the lingering archaism of 'hath'. Baddeley notes that changing tastes affect what kind of mnemonics is permissible. For example, 'during certain historic periods, images were regarded as sinful and liable to predispose to lewd thoughts, with the results that in puritan times, visual imagery mnemonics were discouraged, and mnemonics based on meaningful associations regarded as more acceptable.'[44]

MODERN METHODS NOT USED IN ANTIQUITY

Today, we rely less on memory than in antiquity and more on external, written aids, like shopping lists and the refrigerator as bulletin board.[45] None the less, the mnemonic most commonly used today was never used in antiquity: the acronym or reduction coding mnemonics, as it is more formally called.[46] For instance, if you want to remember the Great Lakes, you need to memorize only one word, HOMES. Each letter stands for a lake: Huron, Ontario, Michigan, Erie, and Superior. Sentences can be used for more complicated examples. When I was a college freshman, we quickly learned the order of train stations on the Main Line from Philadelphia to Bryn Mawr with this sentence: Old Maids Never Wed And Have Babies. The stations are: Overbrook, Merion, Narberth, Wynnewood, Ardmore, Haverford, and Bryn Mawr. It was never clarified whether a comma should go between the 'Wed' and the 'And', if one is punctuating for sense and not grammar. Apparently some of us were either quite intrepid or overslept the station for Bryn Mawr, because one alumna reports that 'Rarely' was added at the end for Rosemont. What is perhaps more remarkable is that I have never forgotten the sentence and can still recall the order of stops. Despite my success with this tidbit of information, Joel Levin refers to this technique as 'the much ballyhooed *first-letter mnemonic*' which 'has turned out empirically to be a flop – likely as a result of the insufficient retrieval cues afforded by single letters.'[47]

As I discussed in Chapter 5 in the section on alphabetization, the idea of using individual letters to sort words never truly caught on, in part because the syllable was considered the more important unit. Athenaeus, who lived *c.* AD 200, however, does make attempts in various parts of the *Deipnoso-phistae* to alphabetize 'to make it easier for you to remember what was said.'[48] I am not sure how much easier his list of fish is to recall, because he alphabetizes only by the first letter, which means that you are quite likely to forget some of the members for a populous letter like 's', discussed in the following order: skaros, sparos, skorpios, skombros, sargoi, salpe, syno-dontes and synargis, sauros, skepinos, skiaina, syagrides, sphyrainai, sepia.[49] Aristotle's use of the alphabet as *topoi* is not an example of alphabetization, because each letter holds only one item in any given list of things and the things being stored are not in alphabetical order to begin with.

While abbreviations were common, they should not be considered mne-monic devices but rather as shorthand, time-saving devices for the writer. For example, '*AUC*' stands for the Latin '*ab urbe condita*' ('from the founding of the city') and is a quick way of referring to the foundation of Rome. The only ancient example of a spelling mnemonic is early Christian from the second century AD.[50] The first letters from the Greek phrase 'Ἰησοῦς Χριστὸς Θεοῦ Υἱὸς Σωτήρ' ('Jesus Christ Son of God and Savior') spells 'ἰχθύς' ('fish') with the result that a fish came symbolically to represent Christ and hence to identify early Christians to each other. Despite its resemblance to an acronym, I think that it was probably considered an acrostic similar to the one I mentioned in Chapter 5 from the first lines of Book 24 of the *Iliad.* Someone looking for hidden meanings realized that the phrase spelled fish.[51] If reduction coding mnemonics were known and used, one of the ancient discussions on memory would have mentioned them, since enough of them do survive. Incidentally, Douglas Coupland points out that today we have come full circle with acronyms: 'I'm realizing that three-letter acronyms are actually *words* now, and no longer simply acronyms: ram, rom, scuzzy, gooey, see-pee-you. . . . Words have to start somewhere.'[52]

In the fourth century AD St Augustine, however, does consciously use an acrostic as an aid to memory for the common people ('*vulgi*'):

> Since I also wanted the cause of the Donatists to reach the notice of very humble, entirely inexperienced and ignorant people, and since I wanted it as much as possible to cling to their memory, I composed a psalm which is sung by the Latin letters, but just to the letter V. Such things they call abecedaria . . . the refrain . . . and the prologue are not in the order of the letters, because that order begins after the prologue. . . . I did not want this to be composed as some kind of song lest

metric necessity would have compelled me to use some words which are less used by the common people.[53]

St Augustine says two curious things in this passage. His psalm is for the 'ignorant', yet he uses a mnemonic device that depends on literacy. Next he takes away the meter, which enables something to be memorized more easily – a fact known from the time of Aristotle – on the somewhat specious grounds that meter would force him to use abstruse vocabulary. Either St Augustine is rather ignorant himself of who uses letters and how, or his audience, as we would say today, are not the truly low and humble that he implies, but those between his own status and the truly low and humble.

The second device often used today is 'chunking', the division of a longer list into more manageable units. Today we especially use it to remember numbers and 'meaningless' groupings of letters that are used for telephone numbers, zip codes, social security numbers, and the like. For instance, to memorize a telephone number such as 18008727245, break the eleven digits into more manageable units, 1–800–872–7245. To make the task even easier, convert the number into words or even meaningless, but pronounceable syllables, 1–800–USA-RAIL (a real number for Amtrak). Because the '1–800' sequence is used for direct-dial, toll-free numbers in the United States, it does not require a conversion to syllables, but is automatically tacked on to the beginning of the crucial seven-digit sequence. Of course, there is the problem of coordinating the letters with the numbers on the telephone dial, especially since the numbers 1 and 0 do not have letters on American telephones. The British postal (zip) codes were explicitly designed with chunking in mind.[54] They may be easy to remember like words on American telephones, but like them they are also difficult to finger on a keyboard. Because there are trade-offs, you must decide ahead of time whether production or recall is most important. If you want to trip someone up when spelling a word aloud, all you have to do is to dictate incorrect chunks, as in CHO PHO USE, which presents no problem when seen as a whole ('chophouse').

Our brains control the number of chunks we are capable of remembering at one time. Memory is divided into short-term memory (STM), what you actively process with, and long-term memory (LTM), what is stored for later retrieval. STM is limited to holding 'seven plus or minus two' items, no matter what those items might be.[55] You actually cannot think of a zillion things at once, only seven plus or minus two. Those with superb STMs can consider nine items at once, while those with less stellar STMs can only think of about five things at once. If you treat the eleven-digit telephone number as eleven digits, chances are you will not be able to remember it. If you break it into four units, as is commonly done, you are well within your physical limitations. Using this method a British mathematician, Alexander

Craig Aitken, memorized pi to the first thousand decimal places. What is worse for those of us less 'gifted' in these areas, he described it as 'a reprehensibly useless feat, had it not been so easy.'[56]

More than one method can be used to achieve the same result. It may be of some comfort to learn that one psychologist (S. Slak) taught his subjects a mnemonic that equated each number with a letter so that the subjects could memorize longer numbers. Baddeley sums up the results:

> Unfortunately, however, Slak found that it took his subjects 20 hours to learn the digit-letter mapping system. Like many mnemonics, for most purposes, its potential advantages are outweighed by the effort needed to acquire and use it.[57]

Simple repetition does help. Too many income tax forms and its use as a general identification number have resulted in my learning my social security number without really trying.

Chunking is not quite the same as Aristotle's *topoi* with its triplets, although it is related to it. Aristotle bases his recommendations on a practical understanding of the capabilities of human memory that recognizes our limitation for actively being able to deal with large quantities of information. He, however, recommends an artificial system that works with groups of three alone no matter what the information, a kind of cognitive 'one size fits all'. Chunking more resembles Quintilian's advice that different kinds of text and different memorizers will need different size chunks. You tailor the chunks to fit both the information and the memorizer. As you become more adept, you can increase the size of the chunks. Rajan Mahadevan was able to increase the size of his chunks for remembering numbers, at which he excelled, but remained ordinary in his span for recalling letters. In other words, you have to consciously decide what you are going to do and then you have to work at it, that is, practice.[58] Mahadevan used a matrix system for memorizing pi to 31,811 places.[59] He placed the numbers in a table with rows and columns. As his ability improved, the number of items in a row (across) increased and formed a single chunk so to speak, generally ten. Finding a number in a particular spot in the grid depended on using primarily the first, and sometimes the last, column as a means of access to the row. That is, he memorized across by rows and not down by columns. As far as I know, this method was not used in antiquity.

DID IT WORK? ANCIENT FEATS OF MEMORY

It is memory which has brought oratory to its present position of glory. For it provides the orator not merely with the order of his thoughts, but even of his words, nor is its power limited to stringing merely a few words together; its capacity for endurance is inexhaustible, and even in the longest pleadings the patience of the audience flags long before the memory of the speaker.[60]

These words of Quintilian, which form part of his introductory remarks to his discussion of memory, have a certain ring of truth to them. While, as I noted, Quintilian is skeptical of the system of *loci*, he has no doubts whatsoever that memory can be trained, because he has improved his own memory which he believes to be 'of a very ordinary kind'.[61] Plutarch (*Moralia*, 9e (= 'On the Education of Children')), whom I quoted in Chapter 8, was a firm believer in such education and, as will be seen in Chapters 12 and 13, had an excellent memory himself. As far as people in the Roman era are concerned, memory training works and therefore forms an integral part of the education of the young. It is just as effective today. McDaniel and Pressley summarize some findings in much the same words as Plutarch: 'Mnemonic educational interventions are useful for very capable learners as well as for students who are considered academically impaired.'[62] Vogl and Thompson noticed the same results with the mnemonist, Rajan Mahadevan. Practice did improve his skill. Furthermore, they divide the mnemonists into two groups: those who simply have superb memories and those who have superb memories only for specific tasks, like memorizing the first 40,000 digits of pi. What is interesting is that one of the mnemonists with an exceptional general memory uses a variety of techniques depending on what he is memorizing. Perhaps even more important for my study, he 'developed exceptional memory performance around the age of 15 when he read a book that described different mnemonic techniques.'[63] The Auctor and Quintilian were right to devote so much space in their rhetorical handbooks to a variety of methods for memorization.

In Part III I discuss how the classical literate used memory when writing. Here I consider briefly some of the remarkable feats of memory reported in various ancient sources. All these feats belong to the ancient category of artificial, that is, trained as opposed to natural memory. In today's terms they depend on some kind of memorizing and consequently are to be distinguished from memory for experiences or past events, which is sometimes called episodic or autobiographical memory. As you read through the examples, keep in mind that most of the classical mnemonists are notable people. Would anyone today remark about a particular statesman's memory? While Tip O'Neill might say that 'all politics is local' and members of Congress often have elaborate files to keep track of their constituents, having a good memory is not among the characteristics that spin doctors use to sell their candidates. In contrast, in antiquity those with good memories are duly noted and lauded.

Seneca could reel off 2000 names he had just heard. He also said that 'when my assembled school-fellows each supplied a line of poetry, up to the number of more than two hundred, I would recite them in reverse.'[64] Pliny the Elder gives a typical list of memory feats:

> King Cyrus could give their names to all the soldiers in his army, Lucius Scipio knew the names of the Roman people, King Pyrrhus's envoy Cineas knew those of the senate and knighthood at Rome the day after his arrival. Mithridates who was king of twenty-two races gave judgements in as many languages, in an assembly addressing each race in turn without an interpreter. A person in Greece named Charmadas recited the contents of any volumes in libraries [*volumina in bibliothecis*] that anyone asked him to quote, just as if he were reading them.[65]

The importance of politicians remembering their constituents was clearly just as important then as it is now. To Pliny's list should be added the earliest example of such a politician. Plutarch said that '[Themistocles] was on good terms with the common folk, partly because he could call off-hand the name of every citizen.'[66] Quintilian, who cites some of the same examples as Pliny, remarks:

> I remember that it used to be alleged that there were persons still living who could do the same, though I never had the good fortune to be present at such a performance. Still, we shall do well to have faith in such miracles, if only that he who believes may also hope to achieve the like.[67]

William Harris agrees with Quintilian, although he would forgo the 'faith in such miracles': 'when Pliny asserts that L. Scipio (presumably the consul of 190) knew the names of the entire Roman people – which would have meant nearly a quarter of a million names – and that Charmadas recited by heart any book in "the libraries," something has gone wrong.'[68] I might share some of Quintilian's and Harris's skepticism except that Baddeley described the prodigious memory of Aitken. I also checked *The Guinness Book of Records* for memory feats, since it requires verification of the records it prints.[69] The 1991 edition lists three examples:

> Bhandanta Vicitsava recited 16,000 pages of Buddhist canonical texts in Yangon (formerly known as Rangoon), Myanmar (formerly Burma) in May 1974.

> Gon Yang-ling, 26, has memorized more than 15,000 telephone numbers in Harbin, China according to the Xinhua News Agency.

> George Uhrin of Houston, TX memorized a random sequence of thirty separate packs of cards (1,560) that had been all shuffled together on a single sighting with two errors at the Texas Commerce Tower, Houston, TX on 16 July 1989.[70]

Of the tasks, only the last matches Seneca repeating 2000 names instantly or Cineas so quickly and diplomatically learning the names of the Roman senators and knights. Harris may be right that if the Romans were some 250,000 strong in the early second century BC, the number of names is staggering to remember. Since Pliny does not qualify his term 'Roman people', he may have meant only those living in Rome. Even if Harris is right about the figure and Pliny has heard a tall tale,[71] enough other examples exist from then and now to support the idea that memory training works and enables mnemonists to accomplish astounding stunts that lesser souls cannot. The real question is whether you want to spend the time to learn how to memorize 1560 cards or 2000 names just to show off.

Vitruvius reports one case where someone's prodigious memory was actually checked against the 'original' source:

> A group of poets was first brought in to contend, and, as they recited their compositions, the whole audience by its applause showed the judges what it approved. . . . But Aristophanes, on being asked for his vote, urged that the poet who had least pleased the audience should be declared to be the first . . . he stated that only one of them – his man – was a poet, and the rest had recited things not their own. . . . The people were amazed, and the king hesitated, but Aristophanes, trusting to his memory, had a vast number of volumes [*volumina*] brought out from bookcases [*armaria*] which he specified, and, by comparing them with what had been recited, obliged the thieves themselves to make confession . . . [the king] honoured Aristophanes with the most gener-ous gifts, and put him in charge of the library.[72]

Knowing texts by heart had a distinctly practical value in at least two situations. While you might misplace a text or not have it with you when needed, your memory followed you wherever you went. So Antisthenes (*c.* 445–*c.* 360 BC) said: 'When a friend complained to him that he had lost his notes, "You should have inscribed them . . . on your mind [ψυχῇ] instead of on paper [χαρτίοις]".'[73] Several centuries later Seneca the Elder repeats the same advice, as I quoted earlier in this chapter. If books are not plentifully available outside of the big cities and if you were unfortunate enough to be either posted abroad or in exile like Ovid, knowing whole texts could prove a great boon. Although Ovid frequently laments his plight in the *Tristia* and the *Letters from Pontus*, he does not seem to have quite the 'memorial library' of the much later exile, William of Ockham in the fourteenth century.[74]

As a result, memorization of texts formed part of a classical education. Xenophon gives an example:

> 'My father was anxious to see me develop into a good man,' said Niceratus, 'and as a means to this end he compelled me to memorize all

of Homer; and so even now I can repeat the whole *Iliad* and the *Odyssey* by heart.'

'But have you failed to observe,' questioned Antisthenes, 'that the rhapsodes, too, all know these poems?'

'How could I,' he replied, 'when I listen to their recitations nearly every day?'

'Well, do you know any tribe of men,' went on the other, 'more stupid than the rhapsodes?'

'No, indeed,' answered Niceratus; 'not I, I am sure.'

'No,' said Socrates; 'and the reason is clear: they do not have the inner meaning of the poems.'[75]

The idea that knowing Homer would make Niceratus a good person is akin to the later idea that knowing the Bible would make someone a good person.[76] Carruthers explains it well: 'The choice to train one's memory or not for the ancients and medievals, was not a choice dictated by convenience: it was a matter of ethics. A person without a memory, if such a thing could be, would be a person without moral character and, in a basic sense, without humanity.'[77] Socrates, of course, rightly points out that understanding is necessary. On the other hand, all the understanding in the world will not help if you don't know the text in the first place. If you had a bad memory but were wealthy, you could remedy the situation, as Seneca the Younger describes:

I never saw a man [Calvisius Sabinus] whose good fortune was a greater offence against propriety. His memory was so faulty that he would sometimes forget the name of Ulysses, or Achilles, or Priam, – names which we know as well as we know those of our own attendants. . . . But none the less did he desire to appear learned. So he devised this short cut to learning: he paid fabulous prices for slaves, – one to know Homer by heart and another to know Hesiod; he also delegated a special slave to each of the nine lyric poets. You need not wonder that he paid high prices for these slaves; if he did not find them ready to hand he had them made to order. After collecting this retinue, he began to make life miserable for his guests; he would keep these fellows at the foot of his couch, and ask them from time to time for verses which he might repeat, and then frequently break down in the middle of a word. . . . Sabinus held to the opinion that what any member of his household knew, he himself knew also.[78]

These anecdotes of people with truly superb and frankly wretched memories reflect the extremes that continue to exist. Most of us fall somewhere in between. Nor is memory monolithic. Some people remember dates better than others, some texts, some images, some topography. Michel Denis divides people into naturally 'high' and 'low imagers', those who without special prompting or training use images, especially when reading.[79] The best documentation for the way memory works has come from modern studies of those with brain damage.[80] Some of the effects had already been noted in antiquity, as Pliny the Elder records:

> Also no other human faculty is equally fragile: injuries from, and even apprehensions of, diseases and accident may affect in some cases a single field of memory and in others the whole. A man has been known when struck by a stone to forget how to read and write but nothing else. One who fell from a very high roof forgot his mother and his relatives and friends, another when ill forgot his servants also; the orator Messala Corvinus forgot his own name.[81]

AN EXCURSUS ON WHY WE LEARN BY HEART IN ENGLISH AND FRENCH

Why do we 'learn by heart' and not by mind, as the Italians (*imparare a mente*) do? Why not skip the physical location and just describe the process like the Germans (*auswendig lernen*)? A consideration of bodily parts and the functions assigned to them in antiquity and the Middle Ages provides not just an explanation for where we got our expression, but also an intriguing glimpse of how different cultures believe the body and the mind work.[82]

Think about what determines death. Is it when someone stops breathing? Is it when the heart stops beating? Or is it when the brain no longer makes waves? Each means of verification has been decisive at different times and in different cultures. The Greeks and Romans consider life to be basically a matter of breath or spirit with the result that both breath and the seat of life reside in the lungs. Since our minds and thoughts are intimately connected with our spirit – once breath goes, so does our mind – thinking takes place generally in the chest and the lungs. Homer uses two terms, θυμός (*thumos*) generally as 'spirit' or 'soul' and sometimes as 'lungs' and φρένες (*phrenes*) as 'lungs'. Like our word 'lungs', *phrenes* is more often used in the plural for the same reason: each of us has a set of two. Homer even uses both words together: Achilles (*Iliad*, 1.193) literally 'pondered these things in his lungs and his breath' or, more poetically, in Richmond Lattimore's translation 'weighed in mind and spirit'. Because a concept of memorizing does not exist in Homer, his characters may recall or remember things, but they do not commit them to memory. Instead Homer has his figures 'store or put thoughts in their soul [*thumos*] or lungs [*phrenes*]', as does Hesiod (*Works and Days*, 107).[83]

In the early fifth century BC, writing sometimes becomes the means of placing items within the store.[84] Hence Aeschylus (*Prometheus Bound*, 789) does not just 'store thoughts in the lungs' like Homer, but now 'write[s them] on the memory tablets [δέλτοις] of [the] lungs [φρενῶν]' or more freely 'writes them on the wax tablets of the mind'. This expression and its variations last for most of the fifth century. In Plato in the fourth century BC, *phrenes* undergoes a shift in meaning from the lungs to the diaphragm or midriff. Plato describes its location in the *Timaeus*:

> And in the breast [στήθεσιν], and in what is termed the thorax [θώρακι], they incased the mortal soul [ψυχῆς], and as the one part of this was superior and the other inferior they divided the cavity of the thorax into two parts, as the women's and men's apartments are divided in houses, and placed the midriff [διάφραγμα] to be a wall of partition between them.[85]

When phrenes becomes the diaphragm, it ceases to serve as a place to store thoughts, be they learned orally or from written texts. That role is taken over by the ψυχή (psyche). Aristotle says that 'memory is always found in the psyche.'[86] Less literally, 'psyche' is translated as 'soul' or 'spirit'. While the words may have changed, psyche retains the Greek idea of 'breath'. The bodily parts involved and the functions they perform remain the same. 'Psyche' forms the basis of many of our words having to do with mental activities such as psychology, psychic, and psychedelic. The Latin equivalents to psyche are *animus* and *anima*. Seneca the Elder mentions Latro who 'had thus made books superfluous – he used to say he wrote in his mind (*animo*).'[87]

Plato does unite memory and heart in the *Theaetetus*:

> In some men, the wax in the soul [ψυχῇ] is deep and abundant, smooth and worked to the proper consistency; and when the things that come through the senses are imprinted upon this 'heart' of the soul – as Homer calls it, hinting at the likeness to the wax – the signs that are made in it are lasting, because they are clear and have sufficient depth. Men with such souls learn easily and remember what they learn.[88]

The word Homer uses for heart is 'κέαρ', which Burnyeat says has 'a superficial resemblance to the word for wax,' 'κηρός'.[89] Even if the two words were confused orthographically, they should not have been ambiguous when spoken, since their accents are different. Despite the enticing connection between heart and memory, Plato is not our source for 'learning by heart' for two reasons: first, he says the actual repository for memory is the soul and not the heart; and second, this image was never extended to apply directly to the heart without the soul in classical antiquity. Varro, however, does say that '*recordari* "to recall to mind," is *revocare* "to call back" again into the *cor* "heart".'[90] But 'recalling' is not the same thing as 'memorizing'. Similarly, when Latin authors sometimes exhort someone to 'remember and take something to heart',[91] they are not learning by heart, but are taking something seriously.

Cicero gives the Latin equivalent for φρένες in his translation of a passage from the *Iliad* (2.301). Where the Greek says, 'For they know this thing well in their phrenes,' Cicero (*On Divination*, 2.63) says, 'for all retain the portent in their remembering mind [*memori mente*].' Cicero uses '*mens*' rather than '*animus*', and explains why in another passage: 'Or do we think that like wax the soul [*animum*] has marks impressed upon it and that memory [*memoriam*] consists of the traces of things registered in the mind [*mente*]?'[92] While he goes on to argue that memory is divine, it is clear that memories are linked with minds, as Varro shows:

> Thus *reminisci* 'to recall,' when those things which have been held by mind [*mens*] and memory [*memoria*] are fetched back again by considering (*cogitando*). From this also *comminisci* 'to fabricate a story' is said, from *con* 'together' and *mens* 'mind,' when things which are not, are devised in the mind; and from that comes the word *eminisci* 'to use the imagination,' when the *commentum* 'fabrication' is uttered. From the same word *mens* 'mind' come *meminisse* 'to remember' and *amens* 'mad,' said of one who has departed *a mente* 'from his mind.'[93]

He adds: '*Meminisse* "to remember," from *memoria* "memory," when there is again a motion toward that which *remansit* "has remained" in the *mens* "mind".'[94] That this association between mind and memory continues is seen in two glosses to Vergil by Servius, who lived in the late fourth century AD: 'memory is in the mind' (on *Aeneid*, 2.224); and a simple equation of 'mind memory' (on *Aeneid*, 2.736).

Neither Greek nor Latin has quite the equivalent of our word 'memorize'. Both languages use a single word to convey the idea of 'learning thoroughly': ἐκμανθάνω and *edisco* respectively.[95] Both words depend on a root verb that means 'learn' and share cognate prefixes, *ek* and *e*, which give the sense of 'thoroughly'. In other words, you would learn something better, but not necessarily verbatim – the concept that underlies our idea of memorizing.[96] Although Latin does have several expressions – such as *ad verbum*, literally 'to the word' – that express accuracy in recording down to the level of the word,[97] the word 'verbatim' does not appear until the late fifteenth century according to the *OED²*. In any event, as Cicero's translation of Homer shows, the ancient idea of verbatim differs a great deal from ours.[98] In some ways it is analogous to the varying degrees of accuracy in measurements of time. Today, we expect the times for public transportation to basically (like within five minutes or so) match the times on our watches, but most of us do not require the precision of atomic clocks.

Greek uses one other expression to indicate 'by memory'. It takes two forms: 'ἀπὸ στόματος', literally 'from the mouth or lips', and those two words joined together to form a verb, 'ἀποστοματίζω'. The latter is defined in LSJ as 'teach by word of mouth, teach by dictation.' While

133

the prepositional phrase occurs before the fourth century BC, it is not in contexts associated with memory. It may refer to rivers and their mouths, as the phrase continues to be used throughout antiquity. Second, and more important for this discussion, it alludes to the spoken word. In the *Odyssey* (12.187) Homer speaks of 'the honey-sweet voice from the mouths' of the Sirens. Similarly a *Homeric Hymn* (25.5) says that 'sweet flows speech from his mouth', a phrasing that combines the two major usages: the flow of speech and rivers.

The fourth century BC marks a change in its use that parallels the shift from phrenes to psyche. As I quoted earlier in this chapter, Niceratus in Xenophon's *Symposium* says that his father 'compelled me to memorize all of Homer; and so even now I can repeat the whole *Iliad* and the *Odyssey* by heart.'[99] For 'memorize' the Greek uses the root word, 'μαθάνω', 'to learn', and for 'by heart', 'ἀπὸ στόματος'. The same phrasing occurs in Plato, who indirectly explains the usage when he uses the verb form in the *Euthydemus*: 'What happened, my dear Clinias, when the teacher dictated [ἀποστοματίζοι] to you? . . . And when a teacher dictates anything, does he not dictate letters.'[100] Here the idea is straightforward: the student learns what is spoken orally and obviously speech comes from the mouth or the lips. In the *Theaetetus* (143a), when Euclides is asked to repeat a conversation he had heard, he responds: 'No by Zeus, certainly not just from the mouth. But I wrote down notes then immediately on coming home.' While it might seem that in this case the phrase resembles our 'off the top of my head', based on the other examples it has been translated more freely as 'Certainly not, just from memory'.[101]

The Greek use of 'from the mouth or the lips' continues through the rest of antiquity.[102] It makes sense as the equivalent for our 'learning by heart', for it captures two concepts. Much of learning and education then, far more so than now, was oral. Second, it accords with the Greek belief in the connection between lungs, breath, and thought. If memories are stored in the lungs, when they are produced they will naturally come out with the breath through the lips or mouth. It is interesting that the expression is introduced only when literacy is fairly well established in the fourth century BC and not earlier. Latin does not seem to have an equivalent expression.

Since in English and French we do not learn by lips or mouth but by heart, and that expression is clearly not classical, it is now time to expand the search for its origin. The expression does occur in two other ancient cultures, the Egyptian and Hebrew, and the latter got it from the former. The Egyptians believed that the heart was 'the organ which conceives thought, and the tongue is the organ which creates the conceived thought as a phenomenal actuality.'[103] According to the Memphite theology of creation in a text from *c.* 700 BC:

There came into being as the heart and there came into being as the tongue (something) in the form of Atum. The mighty Great One is Ptah, who transmitted [*life* to all gods], as well (as) their *ka*'s, through this heart, by which Horus became Ptah, and through this tongue, by which Thoth became Ptah.

(Thus) it happened that the heart and tongue gained control over [every] (other) member of the body, by teaching that he is in every body and in every mouth of all gods, all men, [all] cattle, all creeping things, and (everything) that lives, by thinking and commanding everything that he wishes. . . . The sight of the eyes, the hearing of the ears, and the smelling the air by the nose, they report to the heart. It is this which causes every complete (concept) to come forth, and it is the tongue which announces what the heart thinks.[104]

I note only in passing that the last line confirms in a certain sense the Greek use of learning 'by the mouth'. The heart, according to the Egyptians, is central not just to thought, but to creation itself. Such an explanation is known as a 'folk model of the mind' because 'it is a statement of the common-sense understandings that people use in ordinary life and because it contrasts with various "specialized" and "scientific" models of the mind.'[105] When we have the opportunity to question people about their beliefs and not just the silent pages of antiquity, as Plato might put it, we can learn the reasoning behind the functions attributed to particular organs:

According to the Aguaruna of the Amazon: 'The people who say that we think with our heads are wrong because we think with our hearts. The heart is connected to the veins, which carry the thoughts in the blood through the entire body. The brain is only connected to the spinal column, isn't it? So if we thought with our brains, we would only be able to move the thought as far as our anus?'[106]

While the Egyptian association with creation was dropped, the heart remained the central organ and retained its function as the seat of thought for the Hebrews according to the Old Testament. Proverbs (3.1–3) says:

My son, do not forget my teaching,
  but let your heart keep my commandments. . . .
Let not loyalty and faithfulness forsake you;
  bind them about your neck,
  write them on the tablet of your heart.[107]

The last line recurs in Proverbs 7.3 and 2 Corinthians 3.3.[108] It very much resembles the line from Aeschylus exhorting Io to 'write on the tablets of the lungs' except, of course, for the change in the organ of storage. Jeremiah 31.33 omits the tablets and says 'I will write it upon their hearts' directly. Both the phrasing and underlying concept can be seen in the Egyptian

'Instruction of Amen-em-Opet', written sometime between the tenth and sixth centuries BC and generally considered to have one of the most 'direct literary relation[s]' to the Bible and specifically Proverbs.[109] The 'Instruction' begins:

> Give thy ears, hear what is said,
> Give thy heart to understand them.
> To put them in thy heart is worth while,
> (But) it is damaging to him who neglects them.
> Let them rest in the casket of thy belly,
> That they may be a *key* in thy heart.[110]

The Bible was translated into Greek during the Hellenistic period and into Latin towards the end of the fourth century AD by St Jerome. His version, known as the *Vulgate*, became the most commonly read translation of the Bible during the Middle Ages and later and must have been the source of our own expression of 'learning by heart'. When something is written in your heart, you know it forever and hence in a less elegant modern phrasing 'you know it by heart'.[111]

Because the idea of memory as an independent place of storage within a person's thinking apparatus is not fully developed until after classical antiquity, people did not directly 'memorize' in the way we do today, but tended to 'commit' things to be remembered to various organs of the body. To some extent our own phrase 'commit to memory' resembles 'storing thoughts in the soul'. This particular phrasing according to the *OED*[2] first appears as 'commend to memory' in the middle of the sixteenth century and was later replaced by 'commit to memory' in the nineteenth century.[112] Before the sixteenth century and at least as early as Middle English, we 'learned by heart' as in the Bible and according to Egyptian practices.[113]

CONCLUSION

This chapter completes my examination of the panoply of techniques used in antiquity to enhance natural memory. The methods themselves are not as important as the fact that training in memory was an integral part of the educational curriculum by the time of the Romans. Today, we get virtually no schooling in how to memorize other than what we find on our own in the self-help section in the bookshop. I want to stress that the techniques did not spring like Athena fully developed from the mind of some Greek, whether it was Simonides, a Sophist, or Aristotle. The practices were continually refined to meet the changing requirements of contemporaries until by the time of Quintilian's 'codification' they were quite extensive. Nor were they frozen from that time on, for in both the Middle Ages and the Renaissance mnemotechnics underwent substantial changes and development. The need for better memory techniques increased in step with the increase in written texts. How precisely the art of memory was used by the literate in classical antiquity is considered in Part III, where I focus first on the production of written words and then on indirect examples of the art of memory.

Part III

WRITING HABITS OF
THE LITERATE

10

TOOLS OF THE TRADE

INTRODUCTION

It is difficult today to realize that the common, everyday office filing cabinet represented a major revolution in handling information when it was first introduced in the early twentieth century. It allowed large amounts of material to be organized in an efficient, well-structured manner.[1]

Some 2700 years after writing came to Greece, major advances in its storage and retrieval continue to occur. I am not talking about anything major like the invention of print or the computer, but merely a lowly container. The vertical filing cabinet had an incredible ripple effect. Just having several drawers stacked one on top of the other was no advance over stuffing things in boxes, although it did provide direct and immediate access to each drawer. The real innovation came with the reorganization of knowledge, which, in turn, entailed major changes in a number of existing tools. The vertical file permitted a hierarchical system of organization that was immediately evident to the user via the labels on drawers, on groups of folders, and on the folders themselves in addition to the original piece of paper. Even those pieces of paper became standardized in two sizes, 'regular' and legal, in order to fit neatly within the folders. Despite the efficiency and, indeed, elegance of the system, we still can't find things, because the vertical file was too successful. It enabled us to retrieve far more papers than before and, as always seems to be the case, thereby created far more papers for us to store, with the result that another major invention was needed. The computer enables us to retrieve even more information in far less space even more easily, but the increase in the amount of information now available is simply staggering. What is perhaps most interesting here is that each tool or technology makes it possible to deal more efficiently with the current accumulation of words, but by virtue of its success propagates yet more words that need yet more techniques to control them.

The proliferation of texts in classical antiquity was every bit as dramatic

141

and startling as the multiplication of words today. As I discussed in Parts I and II, the search for a means of organizing the growing store of words resulted in the creation of techniques to improve our natural memory. In Part III I consider how those techniques were actually used by the highly literate in combination with their cognitive artifacts, the ancient equivalents of the vertical file with its folders, labels, and papers.[2] Donald Norman, who has carried out a number of studies of ergonomics and principles of design for everyday things, says that:

> There are two views of a cognitive artifact: the *personal* point of view (the impact the artifact has for the individual person) and the *system* point of view (how the artifact + person, as a system, is different from the cognitive abilities of the person alone). From a person's *personal* point of view, artifacts don't make us smarter or make us have better memories; they change the task. From the *system* point of view, the person + artifact is more powerful than either alone.[3]

Hence I believe that a kind of Sapir-Whorf hypothesis applies to the relationship between the tools available and the products produced, because the tools you have *may* influence what you can produce. Edward Sapir and Benjamin Lee Whorf maintained that the language you spoke affected your thought and behavior. Or, as Marshall McLuhan would have put it: the medium is the message. Most computer people would disagree. The message, the digital stream of data, is totally separate from the medium, which just happens to be whatever hardware and software you have.[4] Librarians would, in turn, disagree with the computer people, because if you don't have the right machine and the right software, you may never be able to read the message. If that is the case – and I think it is – then the medium affects at the very minimum whether you can get your message across.

The Sapir-Whorf hypothesis itself, as it was originally proposed, has come under strong attack. Today 'it seems likely that habitual thought follows along the lines laid down by language, but that people are adaptable and can transcend their linguistic boundaries if they pause to reflect.'[5] A good example from another field would be the invention of the computer. Charles Babbage in the nineteenth century figured out how a digital computer would work, but, despite generous funding from his patron, Ada Lovelace, the daughter of Byron, no one was able to make the parts for such a machine from the equipment then available. For a current example, consider that my use of the CD-ROMs with Greek and Latin have made my research for this book enormously easier, but they have not necessarily affected the result. On the other hand, the fact that I can read the Greek and Latin on the CD-ROMs has dramatically affected this book. Otherwise I would concentrate on other kinds of studies, such as problems of style in the pictorial arts, that can be done well without such knowledge.[6]

142

The real issue, however, is that without promptings from outside of one's own world there is often no reason to 'pause to reflect' and there is every likelihood that the existing tools will affect, if not actually shape the results.[7] It is important to know that in antiquity some noticed this connection, as Quintilian's advice about one of the tools, wax tablets, shows:

> The wax tablets should not be unduly wide; for I have known a young and over-zealous student write his compositions at undue length, because he measured them by the number of lines, a fault which persisted, in spite of frequent admonition, until his tablets were changed, when it disappeared.[8]

The reverse effect occurred in the early days of portable computers. Some reporters who used the Radio Shack portable with its scant four-line display found themselves writing very short sentences in very short paragraphs. College students using early Macintoshes with their tiny screens were judged less able in English composition than those writing on IBM PCs, and clones. Conversely, 'students wrote markedly longer pieces when using a small-type, single-spaced format than a large-type, double-spaced format.'[9] Donald Norman remarks that 'corrections tend to be made locally, on what is visible. Large-scale restructuring of the material is more difficult to do, and therefore seldom gets done.'[10]

Christina Haas baldly states the 'Technology Question', as she calls it, for writing:

> Technology and writing are not distinct phenomena; that is, writing has never been and cannot be separate from technology. . . . To go further, writing *is* technology, for without the crayon or the stylus or the Powerbook, writing simply is not writing. Technology has always been implicated in writing: In a very real way, verbal behavior without technological tools is not, and cannot be, writing. . . . [T]heories of writing implicitly claim that writing is writing is writing, regardless of the technologies used. No one would claim that writing with a stick in the sand is the same as writing on a modern word processor, yet theories of writing, in ignoring the Technology Question, are making just such a claim, albeit implicitly.[11]

None the less, Haas recognizes that:

> A technology is not an object but rather a vital system that is bound to the world of time and space; that is, a technology is always inextricably tied both to a particular moment in human history and to the practical action of the human life world in which it is embedded.[12]

Colette Sirat agrees: 'one cannot detach a writing-system from a whole set of intellectual, social, and technical conceptions.'[13]

Marvin Powell believes that the bulkiness of clay tablets limited the length of Near Eastern works. He calculates that the longest known cunei-form work, a bilingual dictionary, which comprises forty-two tablets, would hold *'no more than half* of Herodotus' *Histories*.'[14] At the same time, he says that because 'cuneiform is a three-dimensional script[, i]t began on clay, and there it ended – probably for that reason.' In more recent times at least one author allowed the printed format to affect his story. When Alexandre Dumas Père was paid by the line for *The Three Musketeers*, which came out in serial fashion, he invented a monosyllabic character, Grimaud the servant. When the publisher declared that the line had to extend beyond half of the column in order to be counted, Dumas killed off the character.[15] Hugh Kenner has devoted a book, *The Mechanic Muse*, to studying just this phenomenon in modern writers.[16]

Extraordinarily little information exists today about the mechanics of reading and writing in classical antiquity. Authors don't talk much about it; artists rarely represent the activities. Work habits by their very nature tend to be unmentioned. I found it somewhat disheartening to learn, when discussing work habits informally with a colleague, that when he says 'at my desk' he means it metaphorically and not literally. He prefers to work in an armchair or on a sofa. I, however, am quite literal when I use the phrase 'at my desk'. How will some latter-day archaeologist know that my colleague eschews the desk for the couch? Psychologists, spurred on in part by the advent of a new means of writing, word processing, have been studying the process of writing, but primarily in controlled environments on short-term assignments. As with memory, studies in and out of the laboratory are necessary.[17]

Today, an author might thank a secretary, a research assistant, and even a few years ago a word processor in a preface, but generally scholars give no further details on how they conduct research.[18] Did the author cogitate at home? on walks? at the office? in the library? at the research laboratory? at a café? or a combination? Did the author take notes? Shuffle the notes before writing? Make an outline? Write several drafts changing through various colored papers like Jacqueline Susann until the manuscript was all white?[19] Circulate the manuscript to friends and colleagues, some of whom might be both? Did the author write a draft or drafts in longhand, on the typewriter, or directly online? Was the author seated at a desk, lying in bed, or on a couch, or did a secretary type a draft into the computer? At least secretaries sit at desks, because touch typing requires a steady surface for the keyboard.

One professor I know keeps notes in blue books by the year. Would anyone know what blue books are if they hadn't attended an American college? How does that professor, now retired, sift through those notes? Unlike me, can she remember what year she noted something down? Does an author, who like me in this work, refers to a number of sources, textual and visual, have them open in a kind of jury-rig fashion on the desk? Does it matter how long it takes a scholar to collect the data? What difference does it make in the final written version, if the data comes from experiments or if it comes from reproductions of objects in books and selections from literary sources? Does anyone ever talk about the process of gathering that data? Certainly, I have never mentioned in print the inordinate amount of time it can take me to find a photograph of a particular object that was referred to in not quite enough detail for me to know whether or not it is important until I see it in some obscure nineteenth- or early twentieth-century source owned by only five libraries in the United States, and missing, damaged, or checked out in at least two of them.

Does any aspect of modern work habits make any difference in the final product? Can a reader tell whether the work was composed in bed or at the screen? Does having the actual references and photographs before me, as I write, make my citations more accurate? Do xeroxing and having access to computerized data increase the number of citations? Does writing directly online affect how and what I write? This last question I can answer. Because I have been part of the transition from the typewriter to the computer, some of the writing tasks I perform I no longer take for granted. My first crisis online was trying to figure out how what went on the screen converted to an 8½ x 11 inch piece of paper with pica, not elite, type. When I realized that a single-spaced screenful was roughly equivalent to a single double-spaced typewritten page, I underwent an almost instantaneous adjustment to the screen. I had to make this equivalency in order to know when to paragraph, which meant in turn that, to me, paragraphing is to a great extent visual and not intellectual. In other words, the medium does affect my message, or rather the medium which I learned first affects all my subsequent messages no matter what their media are, with one exception. Writing online produces different errors from those of my typewriter days. Gone are blatant misspellings. Instead, words repeat repeat themselves or a sentence starts out one way, gets some changes, and the remnants remained remain. I almost always caught those errors when using a typewriter. I never had two words repeating unless I had fully intended to write something like Bora Bora.[20]

With these thoughts in mind I turn to classical antiquity. I have already discussed some of the mechanics in Part I. Here I am going to examine how an individual ancient writer physically went about the process of reading, researching, and writing.

WRITING TOOLS

First, the tools of the trade were much more limited compared to the variety available today. Two basic choices of writing instruments were available for the two major media: metal or ivory styli (stylus, singular) for inscribing in the wax on wooden tablets and reed pens for writing with ink on papyrus, parchment, and plain wooden tablets.[21] Herodotus comments that 'the Ionians have from ancient times called papyrus-sheets [βύβλους] skins [διφθέρας], because formerly for lack of papyrus they used the skins of sheep and goats; and even to this day there are many foreigners who write on such skins.'[22] Especially fine, thin leather is, of course, vellum, the finest of parchments, which did not become widespread until the Middle Ages. When neither of these paper-like materials were available, a writer could use 'palm-leaves . . . the bark of certain trees, folding sheets of lead . . . and sheets of linen.'[23] In addition, and perhaps implied by the 'bark', plain wooden tablets, frequently coated with white paint, were quite common.[24]

The wax on the tablets was generally colored, usually in black but sometimes red, so that the marks would appear as white. The white color results from the way the broken surface of the wax refracts light. One of the rare examples of a tablet with the wax still intact is a writing exercise with the teacher's model on top and the student's attempt between lines below.[25] Lucian in the second century AD writes purportedly about himself that: 'I had played with wax [as a child]; for whenever my teachers dismissed me I would scrape the wax from my tablets and model cattle or horses or even men. . . . I used to get thrashings from my teachers on account of them.'[26] Thus the same wax that sculptors would use for modeling was used for wax tablets.

Quintilian advises that:

> It is best to write on wax owing to the facility which it offers for erasure, though weak sight may make it desirable to employ parchment [*membranarum*] by preference. The latter, however, although of assistance to the eye, delays the hand and interrupts the stream of thought owing to the frequency with which the pen has to be supplied with ink.[27]

Erasing on wax was accomplished by inverting one's stylus to use its blunt end to smooth over the wax. So Horace advises that 'Often must you turn your stylus to erase, if you hope to write something worth a second reading.'[28] Like today, it was also possible to fiddle the books, and so Cicero tells how Verres when 'he was at last thoroughly frightened and upset . . . then applied the blunt end of his stylus to his records.'[29]

In the Fall of 1993 for a graduate seminar, 'From Papyrus to Book: From Representation to Illustration', I did a number of informal experiments with writing and writing materials that were suggestive. Among them, I made my own wax tablets with certain anachronistic details like a shallow aluminum foil tray to hold the wax. Beeswax is not an easy medium to work with. First, melting beeswax attracts bees, even in New York City on the ninth floor in early October. Second, I was able to get the wax smooth only by melting it down. The ancient wax, however, was not pure beeswax, and may have been easier to 'erase'.[30] In addition, Michelle Brown says that the triangular end of the stylus was heated in order to erase – something not mentioned, to my knowledge, in a classical source.[31] When I used the back of a heated spoon I was successful in removing 'mistakes', though the spoon, like Goldilocks's porridge, must be neither too hot – the wax melts and then oozes – nor too cold – nothing happens. You also obviously need to have a source of heat nearby to warm the stylus.[32] Third, and this part was reassuring, whether I used black beeswax (a colored candle – since coloring wax is not a simple matter) or its natural tawny color, I was able to see my marks. I was not convinced to give up paper and pen, much less the wonderful magic slate of the word processor.

I did find clay tablets more malleable and easier to erase, if, of course, done before the clay had dried. The clay is basically a one-shot deal, while the wax on the tablet is more economical in that it can be reused, or at least in my case re-melted, a number of times. What was interesting about the clay, however, was the difficulty I had in finding a modern 'instrument' to make the wedge-shaped marks of cuneiform.[33] I finally happened on a container for pencil leads that was trapezoidal in section with acute angles. Writing on the clay in English with a pointed instrument, like a stylus, was less successful than writing in English on the wax tablets, because too much of the clay tended to be 'picked up' at the ends of strokes.[34] From this brief foray I realized that your tools must work together as a set. The ones that don't are either adapted or replaced. Not only must the writing instrument fit the medium, but so must the written form of the language fit the tools to create that written form. Hence the wedge-shaped reed, clay tablets, and cuneiform die virtually simultaneously after continuous use from 3100 BC through AD 74/75.[35] Following a similar line of reason, Saenger believes that 'The use of the tablet had inhibited the development of a flowing and looped cursive script', which comes in only with the smoother surface of 'membrane codices'.[36]

One curious use of pens in classical antiquity and the Middle Ages should be mentioned, because it demonstrates that the pen was literally as mighty as the sword. Julius Caesar, as he was being stabbed to death, at first tried to defend himself. According to Suetonius: 'Caesar caught Casca's arm and ran it through with his stylus, but as he tried to leap to his feet, he was stopped by another wound.'[37] Since there are at least two other classical examples of styli being used as impromptu weapons in the Forum, it seems likely that they were part of the normal equipment of those doing business there, especially for use in the Curia for recording discussions and speeches, and for taking notes.[38] More disturbing to me personally, as a professor, is the idea that pens were sometimes used by irate students to stab their teachers to death, though the earliest example seems to be post-classical, from the fifth century AD.[39] Then again, it might have been deserved, since whipping students – not just the more

147

modern rapping on the knuckles – was allowed.[40] We also know of a case where a pen was used to hide poison, and which, coincidentally, shows that biting on the end of the pen or pencil has a long history. According to one version Demosthenes ended his life (322 BC) in the following way:

> [H]e retired into the temple, and taking a scroll, as if about to write, he put his pen [κάλαμον] to his mouth and bit it, as he was wont to do when thinking what he should write, and kept it there some time, then covered and bent his head. The spearmen, then, who stood at the door, laughed at him for playing the coward, and called him weak and unmanly, but Archias came up and urged him to rise. ... But Demosthenes, now conscious that the poison was affecting and over-powering him, uncovered his head . . . he had no sooner gone forth and passed by the altar than he fell, and with a groan gave up the ghost.[41]

A Paestan vase, more or less contemporary with Demosthenes, shows a seated woman biting on the end of her stylus, which, unlike the reed pen of Demosthenes, could not hold poison.[42]

Mistakes in ink on 'whitewashed' wooden tablets, papyrus or parchment could be 'washed' away, though parchment was better for that purpose than papyrus. In some cases a complete text was removed and the surface totally reused.[43] Martial, in describing his prototypical version of the codex, 'pugillares membranei' ('small tablets made of parchment') asks the reader to: 'Imagine these tablets are waxen, although they are called parchment. You will rub out as often as you wish to write afresh.'[44] Hence a sponge was part of a writer's equipment.[45] A 'penknife' was used to sharpen the reed pens. The use of compasses would depend on whether one needed to draw. Rulers and inkpots or inkhorns, literally a horn in many medieval illuminations, would be common, as also was pumice used for rubbing off the rough bits from the surface of both parchment and papyrus.[46] Several Pompeiian wall paintings picture the various tools needed: tablets and rolls, pens and double inkpots for red and black ink, as well as a scrinium with rolls.[47] It is important to keep in mind that these tools are not displayed on tables, but are shown on shelves.

Medieval illuminations illustrate every stage of writing and illuminating a manuscript from the preparation of skins for making parchment or vellum to the actual writing and illustrating. Moreover, a number of incomplete manuscripts physically demonstrate the various stages.[48] While many of the practices remained the same from antiquity through the Middle Ages, others had to change to adapt to the shifts from roll to codex and from water soluble to metallic inks in the Middle Ages. Because metallic ink could not be washed away, it could only be 'erased' with the knife, preferably before the ink had a chance to settle into the parchment. Hence sponges were no longer an essential part of the equipment of medieval scribes, though they could be used for wiping ink off the pens.[49] Knives also held the parchment down as the scribe wrote on his slanting desk – a function that was not necessary for the Greeks and Romans, as will be discussed shortly.[50] The slanting desk meant that the dominant direction of writing had changed on rolls, because the roll, instead of running horizontally was positioned vertically so that one end would fall over the top of the desk and the other on to the lap of the scribe or to the floor.[51] I mention these differences, because it is important to keep in mind that, although medieval illuminations can corroborate ancient practices, they must still be used with caution as evidence for antiquity.

On a third century AD relief from Neumagen with a school scene, a boy on the right can be seen arriving late for the lesson, since two other students are already seated and reading from open rolls.[52] This boy holds what looks very much like an attaché case in his left hand, which in a sense it is, for it contains his writing equipment: pens, ink, and knife.[53] This particular representation does not include the slave who often accompanied schoolchildren, as the following excerpt from a medieval glossary, based on practices that go back at least as early as classical Greece, describes: 'I went to school. I entered and said, "Hello, teacher," and he kissed me and greeted me in return. My slave who carries my books handed me my waxed tablets, my writing box, and my writing instruments.'[54] It would seem likely that anyone doing research in a library, public or private, would carry such a writing case as well as tablets or papyri for taking notes. Perhaps Julius Caesar carried such a case on the Ides of March, when he was killed. Tablets came in various sizes from the very tiny ('Vitellian' according to Martial 2.6.6 and 14.8) to enormous ones that contained government records like taxes, as shown on the Anaglypha Traiani.[55] More often, mid-size tablets would have been used. They are called '*pugillares*', because they fit in one's hand.[56]

Since neither papyrus nor parchment was particularly cheap or sufficiently plentiful, the reverses were often reused for literary texts and letters, as well as our equivalent of scrap paper for drafts of texts or the temporary recording of business and government transactions.[57] Fragmentary pottery (sherds) served as scratch paper both for temporary use by adults and as practice material for children learning to write.[58] Their best known use today was as the ostraka used in ostracism in classical Athens. Each Athenian with a vote would scratch on the sherd the name of the person he wished to be exiled. Four joining ostraka, that is, four fragments from the same pot, were inscribed by different hands with the names of Hippokrates Anaxileo, Megakles (twice), and Themistokles.[59] Clearly, pieces from a broken pot were handed out to the voters in just the same way that today someone in a meeting tears up a piece of paper and distributes the scraps for people to write their votes on. Plutarch tells a story about Aristides:

149

as the voters were inscribing their *ostraka*, it is said that an unlettered and utterly boorish fellow handed his *ostrakon* to Aristides, whom he took to be one of the ordinary crowd, and asked him to write *Aristides* on it. He, astonished, asked the man what possible wrong Aristides had done him. 'None whatever,' was the answer, 'I don't even know the fellow, but I am tired of hearing him everywhere called "The Just".' On hearing this, Aristides made no answer, but wrote his name on the *ostrakon* and handed it back.[60]

Being literate was not a requirement for either Athenian citizenship or voting. And, yes, Aristides was ostracized. In the second half of the second century AD a sherd was used for a business letter.[61] I even know of a case where a contract for a sale of houses in Greece, dated *c.* 375–350 BC, was recorded on a piece of unworked limestone.[62] The inscription is arranged to fit the irregular, roughly triangular shape.

Wooden and wax tablets were the preferred temporary repositories for almost every kind of written transaction, which would be transferred later to the more permanent medium of the roll. When Cicero talks about his court stenographers, they were taking notes on wax tablets. When Quintilian (I, Preface, 7–8) mentions the lecture notes made by his students, those notes were probably taken down on tablets. This practice may go back to at least as early as Aristotle and explains some of the roughness and contradictions in his works, as we have them.[63] When Pliny the Younger (*Letters*, 3.5) writes about how his uncle, Pliny the Elder, made excerpts from everything he read, he most likely means that either his uncle or a secretary took the notes on tablets for later transference to rolls. The representation of the simultaneous use of tablets and rolls appears only in business scenes. On a second-century AD relief from Kostolac one man is seated at a table counting money with his right hand as he glances at the diptych in his left.[64] Before him stands a second man reading from a roll. They are probably comparing what someone was supposed to have paid (the roll) with what was paid at the time (the diptych) with the total amount collected on the table. One of the best known examples of counting money appears on the Arch of Constantine (AD 312–315) in Rome in the four scenes with the distribution of largesse.[65]

'DESKS'

So far the Greek and Roman tools and their use are straightforward and understandable. What is not – and what seems especially strange today – is that they never wrote on desks or tables.[66] The tables present in many financial scenes, like the tax-relief from Kostolac, are there not for recording the transaction, but for counting the money. Without a table the money would fall to the ground and be harder to divide into different denominations. In fact, the modern Greek word for bank, 'trapeza', means table and goes back to its use for banking transactions in antiquity.[67] The very idea that trapeza came to mean bank and not desk underlines its use for just that purpose. Why tables were not used for writing, when they were plentiful enough and even used in a related area that required writing, may best be explained by Petroski's theory that 'want' not 'necessity' is the mother of invention.[68] It simply did not occur to anyone to use desks or tables as a support for writing. In part the nature of the media made the idea of desks less obvious. Because tablets were stiff to begin with, they provided their own support. Rolls are awkward no matter what the system of support.

How then did the Greeks and Romans write? The visual evidence for classical antiquity is quite sparse compared to that from the Middle Ages, because the layout of the text and the roles of scribe and artist have changed. When text is an undifferentiated block and, for the most part, without pictures, then artists do not have to deal with rolls. With the highly illuminated manuscripts of the medieval period artists were actively engaged with text, and had a natural arena where they could depict what they did. Furthermore, one person could be both scribe and illuminator, a combination not likely to occur in classical antiquity, since the two tasks dealt with different media and had different functions.[69]

At the same time the status of scribes underwent changes throughout antiquity. Among the Etruscans, for example, scribes were regarded so highly that Mucius Scaevola was unable to distinguish his target for assassination, Lars Porsenna the ruler, from the scribe, with the result that Scaevola killed the scribe.[70] A fair number of representations of scribes occur in Egyptian and Near Eastern art.[71] Greek and Roman scribes, however, seem never to have attained quite the exalted position of either the Etruscan or Near Eastern scribes.[72] While Greek artists of the fifth century delighted in representing writing on tablets, the novelty of the process wore off with the result that later representations concentrate on the symbol – roll, tablet, and stylus – rather than on the production of that symbol.[73] The literary evidence is barely more plentiful than the visual. What is helpful, however, is that the evidence from both sources is consistent: in classical antiquity they wrote with the papyrus flopping across their thighs, as it unwound horizontally from left to right. Ovid, says: 'My right hand holds the pen [*calamum*], a drawn blade [*strictum . . . ferrum*] the other holds, and the paper [*charta*] lies unrolled in my lap [*gremio*].'[74] No table is mentioned.

Hence many Greek and Roman papyri are under 12 inches high in order to fit on an average thigh. Moreover, rolls held by figures in representations, be they paintings, reliefs, or statues, match that height.[75] The granite box with the three rolls that I mentioned in Chapter 4 has interior measurements of 8 inches by 10 inches and, according to its inscription, held three rolls.[76] Horizontal lengths varied according to the work from 10 to 50 feet. Smaller lengths could be pasted together to form longer ones. The reverse also occurred with longer rolls being cut into smaller ones. Average rolls were between 20 and 30 feet long. At the same time columns for literary texts are often narrow, seemingly to fit a thigh's width, and sometimes they lean like the Tower of Pisa.[77] Egyptian papyri tend to have wider columns than Greek ones, because Egyptian scribes wrote seated, cross-legged on the ground, which naturally gave them a wider expanse, that of the lap, on which to write.

Yet Greek papyri, especially documents, do have wide columns frequently enough that the phenomenon needs to be explained.[78] Most of our surviving documents come from Egypt, and they could have been written in the Egyptian manner with the scribe seated on the ground. More likely, however, is that scribes automatically adjusted widths to match the needs of the 'text' or document. In my writing experiment in the Fall of 1993, I had students write in the Greek manner across the thigh on brown wrapping paper cut in 10-foot lengths, the size of a 'modest' Greek roll.[79] All but one student had columns wider than their thighs – a result I had not expected. When I asked them how they did it, the answer was quite simple: without even thinking about it, they just shifted the roll from side to side as they wrote each line.[80] Presumably, shifting papyrus was no more difficult in antiquity. I also had some students experiment with writing in the Egyptian manner to see whether the Egyptians placed a board under the papyrus for support or merely relied on their kilts being pulled taut, as is debated today.[81] The students found that a stretched 'skirt' without a board underneath was, indeed, a satisfactory surface. Pliny the Elder comments on how the tools, in this case pen and papyrus, have to work together:

> Other points looked at in paper [*chartis*] are fineness, stoutness, whiteness and smoothness. The status of best quality was altered by the emperor Claudius. The reason was that the thin paper of the period of Augustus was not strong enough to stand the friction of the pen [*calamis*], and moreover as it let the writing show through there was a fear of a smudge being caused by what was written on the back, and the great transparency of the paper had an unattractive look in other respects.[82]

It is, of course, interesting that the emperor controls the quality of papyrus. We also know that in AD 301 Diocletian regulated the pay of scribes.[83] Sometimes, Egyptian scribes sat on chairs or stools with the papyrus still running across their laps; sometimes, they would stand or even kneel with the papyrus rolled up and balanced against their left forearms as they took notes in extremely narrow columns the width of their forearms.[84] These practices continued virtually unchanged from the Old Kingdom through the New Kingdom, a period of over 1000 years. The New Kingdom statue of Horemheb shows the position: he sits cross-legged with part of the roll rolled up on the ground and his 'inkpot' balanced on his left thigh.[85] Though the Egyptian methods of writing were certainly time tested and available to the Greeks and Romans, they were not adopted by classical writers for at least two reasons. First, the Greeks and Romans were sufficiently satisfied with their own methods. Second, their pens differed.[86] The Egyptians used a rush pen whose 'point' worked more like a brush in contrast to the sharp point on the end of the Greek reed pen. With a more brush-like instrument it would be easier to write across the 'skirt' without a support underneath; with a more pointed instrument the support of the thigh would be helpful. Since the strokes each pen makes differ, the Egyptian and Greek 'letters' differ in form to fit the kind of strokes most easily made by their tools.

Unlike the Egyptians, the Greeks sat on chairs or stools most of the time.[87] The clearest representation appears on a Roman funerary relief from the early third century AD from Strasbourg where a man sits in a high-backed chair with the end of the papyrus hanging over his right thigh and with the rest of the roll held in his left hand.[88] Somewhat later, around the turn of the century, is a funerary relief from Thessaloniki that shows a scribe from the side view with his left thigh slightly raised as he writes.[89] The position is corroborated in a contemporary colophon (signature of the scribe) on a papyrus of the *Iliad*, which says, 'the reed pen wrote me, right hand and knee.'[90] The absence of desks and tables and the need to refresh the ink in one's reed pen, as Quintilian mentions, meant that either the ink was awkward to reach because it was on the ground or, more likely, as in the case of the Strasbourg relief, held ready and, I assume, steady, by a slave. Although the ancient representations are few, medieval ones with this pose are quite plentiful, because a figure writing became a popular motif for the representation of evangelists and prophets. A late fifteenth-century illumination, for instance, shows St John recording the last book in the Bible, *Revelation*, as the Devil attempts to steal his inkpot and pen case which lie on the ground not beside his right and writing hand, but on the left behind his rather voluminous cloak.[91]

Colette Sirat believes that no early Greek representations of writing on rolls exist for three interconnected reasons.[92] First, she believes that Greek scribes, like the Egyptians, sat on the ground to write.[93] Second, she maintains that the upper class would not sit on the ground. Therefore, third, because the vase paintings depict the upper class and its activities, they do not show anyone writing on rolls, only on tablets. Her theory accounts for the visual evidence, as it has survived. We do not have any representations of Greeks writing on rolls until the time of the Strasbourg relief. We do, however, have plentiful representations of figures holding rolls in Attic vase paintings. So we know that Greeks had rolls in the fifth century BC. In addition, three statues of 'scribes', dated to *c.* 500 BC, were

153

among the dedications on the Acropolis in Athens. All three figures are seated and hold open diptychs. Ismene Trianti believes that these are officials connected with the Cleisthenic reforms.[94] The tablets and pose identify the office. That statues were dedicated indicates a certain degree of wealth. Hence these figures are not likely to portray the lower classes. We also know that Plato wrote on tablets, because of the story I mentioned in Chapter 1 about the problems he had with the opening words to the *Republic*. According to Diogenes Laertius, writing in the first half of the third century AD: 'Some say that Philippus of Opus copied out the *Laws* [of Plato], which were left upon waxen tablets [ἐν κηρῷ].'[95] Lucian, in the second century AD, writes similarly about a contemporary of Plato, Dionysius the Elder (431–367 BC), tyrant of Syracuse. When he had difficulties writing, he 'took great pains to procure the wax-tablets on which Aeschylus used to write, thinking that he too would be inspired and possessed with divine frenzy in virtue of the tablets.'[96]

On the other side, however, Quintilian recommended, as quoted earlier in this chapter, writing on parchment, if you have poor eyesight. Papyrus would work in a similar way. Also remember the story from Plutarch about Demosthenes's suicide, which I quoted earlier in this chapter (see p. 148). Demosthenes 'retired into the temple, and taking a scroll [βιβλίον], as if about to write, he put his pen [κάλαμον] to his mouth and bit it, as he was wont to do when thinking what he should write.'[97] Elsewhere Plutarch (*Moralia*, 847a/b) not only repeats the story, but also gives his source as Satyrus, a third-century BC biographer, who had a good chance of knowing about the writing habits of the previous century. Lucian in the same essay just quoted records a related anecdote: 'collect and keep all those manuscripts [συλλαβών] of Demosthenes that the orator wrote with his own hand, and those of Thucydides that were found to have been copied, likewise by Demosthenes, eight times over.'[98] Whether or not Demosthenes copied Thucydides eight times is debatable. The anecdote, however, indicates that Lucian finds the idea reasonable, I would think, because the process would certainly have helped Demosthenes to memorize Thucydides and may well have been a method for memorizing used in Lucian's own time.

So, it seems likely that highborn Greeks were writing on papyrus by the fourth century BC at the latest. The evidence, both literary and pictorial, from later periods is consistent with the idea that they would have sat on a chair or stool to write. Hence whether or not the highborn would sit on the ground does not affect the argument one way or another. The only question, which is not answerable from the current evidence, is whether or not it was the scribes or the authors themselves who wrote the texts in the high classical era. Because Attic vase paintings show slaves and servants, *pace* Sirat, as well as the highborn, it may be mere happenstance that no Greek representations of writing on rolls have survived.

Tablets, which were stiff, were less of a problem for the process of writing. They were most often balanced on the knees, as shown in representations from the fifth century BC and after.[99] Kallimachos in the Hellenistic period says that 'the very first thing I put the writing-tablet on my knees.'[100] Less frequently a scribe might stand, as a schoolboy does on one of the reliefs from Neumagen.[101] When Christ appears before Pilate in the sixth-century AD Rossano Gospels, a court reporter, standing on the right, notes down the proceedings in a diptych.[102] The colors clearly show the wooden frame surrounding the dark wax. It is likely that the clerks whom Cicero mentions as taking down the proceedings of the Senate also stood.[103] A relief from the third century AD provides the earliest extant representation of using a table for support for taking notes, as a lecturer stands on a podium holding forth.[104]

Writing desks and tables to hold tools and ink do not become common until the eighth to ninth centuries AD, when their increased use must have been driven by the increased use of the codex. The codex, at first, probably seemed to suffer from the disadvantages of both tablets and rolls. Because it originally lacked the stiff backing of the tablets, it would flop across the thigh, but the unused pages could not be gathered in a neat roll to be held by the non-writing hand.[105] Hence a purely practical reason may account for some of the slowness in the adoption of the codex.[106] With the medieval desk both problems were solved. The form of the desk, however, is not like ours with a large, flat surface and drawers below, on either side of the knee-hole. Instead it generally had a highly slanted top that was placed on top of a stand much like a lectern today. And like the modern lectern there was often no room for writing supplies. Illuminations often show scribes with separate writing desks and stands for their supplies.[107]

Skeat mentions one other possible advantage of the roll over the codex: you can not only view several columns at once, but you can also choose which set of columns you want.[108] With a codex you are locked into what is on the obverse and reverse of each page. I think, however, that the usefulness of this kind of display was not as great as Skeat thinks. He rightly points out its usefulness for looking at pictures and charts today, but classical papyri rarely had any kind of illustration. Moreover, with their block-like texts I think that the advantage in antiquity, if any, was quite small.

READING STANDS

It seems likely that the sloping, medieval desks were not developed specifically to ease writing but were based on ancient reading stands, the evidence for which is slightly less sparse than that for the process of writing. The earliest extant information comes from a Roman relief from the first half of the first century AD.[109] On the left sits a half-draped man, commonly identified as Menander, contemplating a mask held in his left hand. On the right stands a woman, perhaps a Muse, with her left hand on her hip and gesturing with her right hand. Between them is a table on which are two more masks and a narrow roll dangling partially open over the side of the table by Menander. That this table was most likely not used for writing is implied, if not proven, by the fact that it seems to serve more for holding things, such as the two additional masks which sit upon it. Above the left mask is a reading stand with a vertical shaft supporting a horizontal frame that holds an open roll, whose left half can be seen. Its right half is not preserved; nor can its base be seen behind the mask. Without the frame the roll might easily fall off the stand. Some scholars believe that the relief copies an earlier Greek original, which they would date to the third to second century BC and which would place the earliest use of reading stands in the same period as the height of the Library at Alexandria.[110] Plato in one passage writes: '[the boys] put down beside them on the benches [βάθρων] the poems of excellent poets to read . . . and learn by heart [ἐκμανθάνειν].'[111] All this anecdote proves is that at least some students did not have desks or tables or even reading stands in the fourth century BC. It does not really help us to decide whether the Alexandrians had reading stands.[112]

An imperial relief from Athens with a young girl, Abeita, shows a reading stand on which a roll lies open at a middle section, as can be seen by the two rolled portions on either side.[113] The whole sits within a kind of shallow, open box. A stand that is transitional between the classical and medieval types appears in the author portrait of the *Vergilius Romanus* from the late fourth century to the early fifth century AD.[114] Vergil sits in the center with a closed scrinium or capsa on the right and a reading stand with a slanted top on the left. In an early fourteenth-century AD Armenian manuscript, Christ reads from a codex on top of a high, portable, folding reading stand, which resembles an elongated, vertical camp stool.[115]

Martial in the first century AD wrote a couplet about a reading stand: 'To prevent your toga or cloak making your books frayed, this fir-wood will give long life to your paper [*chartis*].'[116] Two points are significant about the passage. First, the stand is to protect the paper from becoming frayed or, in Martial's terms, more literally 'bearded'.[117] The abrading of the edges, especially as the papyrus dried out, must have been common, because Johnson remarks that 'relatively few papyri preserve the upper and lower margins intact.'[118] From Martial's poem it seems that the stand is not to make it easier for the reader to read or, as I shall next discuss, to copy. Second, Martial called the poem '*manuale*', that is, something that could be held in the hands. Hence he is not referring to the stands just considered, but to a portable version.

Elfriede Knauer has astutely identified these 'scroll holders', as she calls them, in representations from the time of Augustus and later.[119] The earliest examples occur in wall paintings from Boscotrecase dating to *c.* 10 BC and Pompeii. Also extremely clear is the example on a second-century AD relief from Como, as well as the partially preserved holder on the relief of the schoolroom from Neumagen, already mentioned. There, the boy seated in a high-backed chair on the left clearly has his roll set within a holder, whose edge can be seen on the left. The holders are boxes without a top member and no lid. They must have been awkward to use, because it is not a matter of turning a single page from right to left, but of taking out the whole roll, unwinding it to the desired section, rewinding the part already read, and then reinserting the roll into the holder. The frame, however, would protect the bottom edge and also the rolled up portions from being overly handled, at the same time as it would keep the roll open to the place you wanted.

The earlier examples have cut-outs on both sides of the frame about a third of the way up from the bottom. Knauer suggests that they would enable the *umbilicus*, the dowel around which the roll was wound, to be held in place for carrying. I would add from the Como relief that they also provided a handy grip for the 'living lectern', as Knauer elegantly calls the Muse holding the roll holder on the Como relief. Its seated poet follows the text with a stylus held in his right hand. The use of living holders instead of specialized pieces of furniture is common in other tasks, for which we have objects today that are either free-standing or fixed in place. For example, an Eros holds up a box mirror for the initiate as she fixes her hair in the fresco from the Villa of the Mysteries in Pompeii.[120] Of the three paintings from Pompeii that I know of with panel painters, only one uses an easel, while the other two have assistants to balance the picture on the floor or on a table.[121]

'*Manuale*' is not a distinctive term for a reading stand in that it captures more the idea of portability than the object of that portability. It is possible that another Latin word '*pluteus*' may refer in certain contexts to reading stands.[122] The word occurs most often in descriptions of military maneuvers as either a 'movable screen . . . for protection in siege warfare' or a 'protective parapet'. It also refers to 'the upright board forming the back, or far side, of a couch.'[123] None of these definitions, however, makes sense, when Persius (*Satires*, 1.106) recommends that one should write in a style that 'neither strikes the *pluteum* nor bites the nails to the quick.' Most translators equate '*pluteus*' with desk, but, as I have just shown, desks did not exist in the first century AD.[124] Nor does it makes sense here as shelf, as it is sometimes translated in other contexts.[125] Instead I suggest that '*pluteus*' refers to a reading stand, an object that captures the two qualities of uprightness and movability present in its basic definition. At the same time, the full-height ancient reading stands do resemble our modern movable lecterns, which one can well imagine a speaker pounding for emphasis. Indirect corroboration for the use of '*pluteus*' as 'reading stand' may come from the later medieval use of the term for a wonderful device that is, unfortunately, no longer made: a revolving reading stand that sits on the table and allows several books to be open upon it simultaneously. This contraption is known as either a *'rota'* ('wheel') or *'pluteus versatilis'* ('turning reading stand'). An example can be seen in a medieval illumination of Livy at work.[126]

READING WITHOUT SUPPORTS

Skeat describes the mechanics of reading a roll:

> the right hand merely *supports* the bulk of the roll while the left pulls out a stretch for reading. When this had been read, the left hand does not roll it up – it rolls itself up, the left hand merely preventing it from rolling up too far. The left hand then pulls out another stretch of papyrus, and the reading proceeds. With practice these operations would have become as automatic as turning the leaves of a codex.[127]

Reading a codex would be like reading a book today – simply a matter of turning the pages, with the exception that without the stiff modern binding, the codex might be somewhat more difficult to control.

With either format the situation in antiquity in a certain sense resembles that today. Books can be read anywhere: not just in the library or the professor's office, not just in the school or the playground, but in the park, on the train or the plane.[128] Reading while in transit goes back to antiquity. Pliny the Elder 'used to be carried about Rome in a chair' so that he could continue to read. Pliny the Younger adds that 'I can remember how he scolded me for walking; for he thought any time wasted which was not devoted to work.'[129] This is the same person who during the eruption of Mt Vesuvius:

> called for a volume of Livy and went on reading as if I had nothing else to do. I even went on with the extracts I had been making. Up came a friend of my uncle's. . . . When he saw us [Pliny the Younger and his mother] sitting there and me actually reading, he scolded us both. . . . Nevertheless, I remained absorbed in my book.[130]

Pliny the Younger does say that he was only seventeen at the time. In any event, Pliny the Elder was not the only busy Roman to snatch bits of time in which to read. Cicero says that:

> [Marcus Cato] possessed, as you are aware a voracious appetite for reading, and could never have enough of it; indeed it was often his practice actually to brave the idle censure of the mob by reading in the senate-house itself, while waiting for the senate to assemble.[131]

SUMMARY

When considering ancient writing habits, as well as modern ones, the art of composing must not be treated in isolation from the tools available. The author and his or her tools work together to produce particular products, as will be seen in the following chapters. Here I have outlined what the writing tools were like in antiquity. Instead of using flat desks for writing, as we do, they used their thighs. This system worked admirably with both rolls and tablets, but not codices, with the result that when the switch was fully made to the codex the writing surface also changed to a sloping desk. Finally, reading stands were common and came in two varieties, 'manual' and full height.

11

RESEARCH TECHNIQUES

Now that the classical writer has been equipped, let us send him to the library to do research. As I have already discussed in Chapter 4, both 'public' and private libraries were available. Since I am considering only the very highly literate, let us assume that our typical writer has access to one of the superb private libraries, such as those owned by Lucullus or Cicero, or one of the twenty-eight public libraries in Rome that were created from the end of the Roman Republic onwards.[1] Next, let us generously assume that the writer has found the text he wants, since I have already discussed the issues of retrieval, as well as the storage and arrangement of books in libraries, in Chapters 4 and 5. In all likelihood, at least some of the time, the writer will use a multi-rolled work, since any given roll contained relatively little (a book of the *Iliad* or of Livy's *History of Rome*). Where does the writer put the rolls? What happens when the writer wants to take notes? How are the libraries physically set up? In short, how does the writer work?

LIBRARIES: THEIR PHYSICAL SET-UP

We have almost no evidence. None of the great libraries has survived, and even those libraries that have are either tentatively identified or mere shells without the 'stacks' and, certainly, the movable furniture such as chairs. The one possible exception is the Villa of the Papyri at Herculaneum, which I discuss later in this chapter. Early large libraries were associated with either gymnasia (palaestrae), such as Aristotle's in the Lyceum, or temples, such as the library at Pergamon in the sanctuary of Athena. Libraries in these settings tended to be rooms off porticoes, and hence were not distinctive architecturally. Major Roman libraries had some or all of the following characteristics, depending on the library: separate rooms for Greek and Latin works in major Roman libraries like the one on the Palatine, the library of Trajan in the Basilica Ulpia, and the library in Hadrian's Villa at Tivoli;[2] some kind of arrangement to close off the books for protection; niches on podia with steps, which could be used for either books or statuary; sometimes a second floor gallery with storage for more books; and walkways. Natalie Kampen questions whether the niches were for storing books. She finds their depth too shallow for the storage of rolls, but appropriate for decorative reliefs like the Spada reliefs with their mythological scenes.[3] Vitruvius, our major written source on classical architecture, adds little information about the structure and furnishings, because he is primarily concerned with books *vis-à-vis* the weather:

> Bedrooms and libraries ought to have an eastern exposure, because their purposes require the morning light, and also because books in such libraries will not decay. In libraries with southern exposures the books are ruined by worms and dampness, because damp winds come up, which breed and nourish the worms, and destroy the books with mould, by spreading their damp breath over them.[4]

Not only does Vitruvius not mention any details about the physical arrangement of libraries, he also speaks only of private, not public libraries, though an eastern exposure makes sense in either case. Cicero writes in a number of letters about his use of libraries, but does not give any architectural details.

Plutarch in his description of the library of Lucullus, which Cicero used, adds a little more information:

> His libraries [βιβλιοθηκῶν] were thrown open to all, and the porticoes [περιπάτων] around them, and scholasteria [σχολαστηρίων], were accessible without restriction to the Greeks, who constantly repaired there as to an inn of the Muses . . . Lucullus himself also often spent his leisure hours there with them, walking about in the walkways with their scholars.[5]

The Greek word 'scholasterion' is rare, and related to 'schole' [σχολή], which means 'leisure' and, by extension, those who have leisure become 'scholars'. Hence a scholasterion indicates some kind of room for study. From Moschion, a third-century BC tragic poet, we learn:

> Adjoining the Aphrodite room was a scholasterion large enough for five couches, the walls and doors of which were made of boxwood; it contained a library [βιβλιοθήκη], and on the ceiling was a concave dial made in imitation of the sun-dial on Achradina.[6]

In this case, the library forms a part of the scholasterion which, I should add, was just one room on an extravagant ship built for Hieron of Syracuse (Athenaeus 5.206d). Seneca the Younger (*Dialogues*, 9.9.7) decries the use of libraries that had become 'an ornament now between the baths and warm baths and necessary even for the home.' Pliny the Younger in his country villa has 'a room built round in an apse to let in the sun as it moves round and shines in each window in turn, and like a library [*bibliothecae speciem*] with a storage-cabinet [*armarium*] attached to one wall to hold the books which I read and read again.'[7]

Because books have always been portable and their actual use depends on other items that are also portable, ancient libraries tended not to have a distinctive architecture. Even today that situation holds true. A personal library primarily needs walls against which to place movable bookcases. A public library has the opposite requirement: interior space in which to place rows of movable shelving. None the less, the actual shells for both types of libraries are not unique to their function. This rather short survey demonstrates that Lora Lee Johnson's conclusion about public libraries applies equally to private ones: 'Libraries during the Roman period attained an important public status which makes it difficult to distinguish between monumental construction and features assigned library functions.'[8]

LIBRARIES: HOW THEY WERE USED

No classical representations have survived of libraries. Our best evidence for an idea of actual use comes only indirectly from medieval manuscript illuminations of evangelists and prophets writing within apses. Such backgrounds are identified as the *scaenae frons* of a stage, because stage 'backgrounds' also had niches with statuary, as in Roman wall paintings from Pompeii. Stages, however, seem to me to be less likely a place for writing and inspiration than a library, especially since the Roman examples that are cited never show the writers actually writing.[9] Remember the paucity of representations I was able to cite in Chapter 10 to illustrate the way Romans wrote. There is a big difference between attending a performance of one's work and actually producing the work itself. Moreover, the medieval examples are actually a different type, in that their meaning depends on the act of writing itself and hence depicts a different moment from the classical representations. Instead of figures sitting within niches holding texts, like the Roman 'models', the figures are in the process of writing. Therefore the motif of the writing evangelist is a medieval creation and only very indirectly based on a classical prototype.

For instance, one illumination shows Dioscurides, seated on the right, as he writes in a codex with a painter on the left, and in between them a personification of Epinoia ('Power of Thought') standing like a statue within an apsidal niche.[10] This representation might reflect a Greek library such as the Museum at Alexandria, which had statues of the Muses, or a Roman library such as that founded by Asinius Pollio with portraits of distinguished writers. Pliny puts it more poetically:

> We must not pass over a novelty that has also been invented, in that likenesses made, if not of gold or silver, yet at all events of bronze are set up in the libraries in honour of those whose immortal spirits speak

162

to us in the same places, nay more, even imaginary likenesses are modelled and sense of loss gives birth to countenances that have not been handed down to us, as occurs in the case of Homer.[11]

Other medieval illuminations reduce the setting to just the apse with its writing evangelist, as in the Canon Table with Matthew and John in the Rabbula Gospels.[12] No matter whether the setting for the writer is complex or simple, flat tables are not shown.

If desks and tables were not used for writing and if reading stands were occasionally used for reading, as discussed in Chapter 10, they may not have had tables in libraries. By 'table' I mean a flat top supported by legs, generally four, to distinguish it from the sloping top of writing desks and reading surfaces in medieval libraries.[13] To my knowledge, neither of these forms existed in antiquity.

Consider modern reconstructions of Roman libraries. Hadrian's library at Tivoli has been reconstructed in the Museo della Civiltà in Rome as a large open room with niches for wooden armaria (cupboards) for the books, a statue of Athena in a niche on one of the short walls and a marble table in the center.[14] James Packer, in a study of the library of Trajan in Rome, makes a similar reconstruction of niches, statue, and large open central area, in which he has placed two rows of long marble tables. A number of men sit at these tables with writing tools and rolls laid out in front of them.[15] In a personal communication he said that he had two reasons for his reconstruction:

> I base those tables on the fact that the Bibliotheca Ulpia did not lend scrolls (hence, readers needed to consult the books in situ) and on the patterns in the colored slabs in the marble pavement. There are two rows of smaller slabs aligned with the columns of the tabernacle at the west end of the room and with the columns in antis at the entrance. These, I assumed, marked the position of the conjectural tables just as changes in pavements marked the position of tables in triclinia in Pompeii and other Roman sites.

His comment about borrowing books has no real bearing on the matter, since, as we have seen, they don't seem to have used tables for reading and writing at home. His other reason is more intriguing, but not compelling. First, tables for dining were not marble but wooden, because they had to be light enough to carry from the kitchen to the dining-room. That is, they served as the equivalent of our trays with the result that courses, as we would say today, were called 'tables', as in the 'first table'.[16] Second, while wear and design patterns on the floor can sometimes be an indication of furnishings, they need not be.[17] They can be merely decorative. Third, to quote Packer, 'no fragments of marble tables actually turned up in the Forum of Trajan.' Hence I believe that the tables in modern reconstructions reflect modern practices rather than ancient ones. Let us now turn to the ancient evidence for how one read.

A Roman mosaic from a villa near Pompeii and dated to the first century AD adds some information, but does not entirely resolve the question of the table. It shows a group of seven bearded men, identified today as philosophers in Plato's Academy because of the setting.[18] When Plutarch uses the Greek word 'peripatoi' to describe the walkways of Lucullus's library, he uses the same word that gives its name to the philosophers called the 'Peripatetics', who got their name from their habit of discussing things while strolling. Porticoes are typical features of much of Graeco-Roman construction because of the shade they offered from the sun and because of the shelter they provided from rain. On the mosaic the two columns on the left indicate the portico. A third column, topped by a sundial (recall Moschion's passage about the library on the ship quoted above), and the acropolis on the right complete the setting.[19] The mosaic is in keeping with Vitruvius's advice for the construction of palaestrae, which also had libraries: 'In the three colonnades construct roomy recesses with seats in them, where philosophers, rhetoricians, and others who delight in learning may sit and converse.'[20]

In the mosaic, the two end figures stand; the rest are seated on a semi-circular bench in various attitudes of concentration as they discuss the large sphere in the center, which is interpreted as a globe with the paths of heavenly bodies. Three of the men hold wound-up rolls ready for consulting to prove this or that point. What may be significant for the present inquiry is that the rolls have been taken outside and that, while seating is provided, no table is present. The sphere in its box, for example, need not have sat on the ground, but could just have well have been placed at eye level on a table, as we would today. This subject enjoys a minor but continuing popularity, and iconographically forms the basis for depictions of Christ and his Apostles. In none of the representations do tables appear.[21]

While no tables have survived from those areas and buildings identified as libraries, marble tables have been found *in situ* in the atria of villas at Pompeii.[22] These tables could have been used for working with rolls. Yet it seems more likely that they were not, for Varro says:

A second kind of table [*mensa*] for vessels was of stone, an oblong rectangle with one pedestal; it was called a *cartibulum*. When I was a boy this used to be placed in many persons' houses near the opening in the roof of the court, and on and around it were set bronze vessels.[23]

When a roll was being read by more than one person, as might happen with the philosophers in the mosaics, it is possible that a greater width was unrolled and the two ends were held by two people, as medieval representations of the 'communal scroll' show.[24] Xenophon writes jokingly about

Socrates's penchant for youths, when he has Charmides describe Socrates reading 'the same book-roll at the school, sitting head to head, with your nude shoulder pressing against Critobulus's nude shoulder.'[25] A two-figure terracotta statuette almost captures the scene, except for the fact that it is a boy not a youth.[26] An old, bearded, and very Socratic-looking teacher sits on the right with his right arm about the boy, who leans his head on his shoulder as he reads from the roll he holds.

Cicero implies that tables were not used when multiple rolls were being consulted, for he writes in a letter (2.2) to Atticus: 'I was holding in my hands the *Pellenaioi* and by Hercules I had built up a great pile of Dicaearchus before my feet.' In another passage he says:

> I was down at my place at Tusculum, and wanted to consult some books from the library of the young Lucullus; so I went to his country-house, as I was in the habit of doing, to help myself to the volumes I needed. On my arrival, seated in the library I found Marcus Cato; I had not known he was there. He was surrounded by piles of books on Stoicism.[27]

No mention is made here as to whether Cato, like Cicero, had the rolls at his feet or on a table. Nor does Cicero mention using a table for reading or writing in any of his letters. The only corroboration for a table and rolls appears in the relief with Menander discussed in Chapter 10. Since the roll appears with the two masks, it is not conclusive. Lastly, the room in the Villa of the Papyri at Herculaneum that has been identified as the library did not have a table in the room. According to a description by Winckelmann, written at the time of its discovery: 'Around the walls were cupboards, as customarily in archives, to a man's height, and in the middle of the room is another such rack for texts on both sides so that one could freely walk around it.'[28] The size of the room is approximately 3 meters (*c.* 10 feet) square. The aisles surrounding the central cupboard, and the space neces-sary for the cupboards along the wall allow no room for chairs, much less a table for regular reading. The nub of the problem, however, is that this room may not be *the* library, but only a room for excess storage or just the Greek library, because only one *capsa* of Latin rolls has been found and all the other papyri are Greek. It is assumed that the Latin (if not the main) library must still remain buried within the lava.[29]

Cicero in the quotation from Plutarch states directly that Cato was seated. Representations of seated, single readers go back to the fifth century BC. They may sit on 'blocks', stools, or chairs.[30] Figures writing on tablets are not represented seated on chairs but on stools, perhaps because classical chairs are made for sinking back in a gentle slouch; whereas it is necessary to sit upright or to lean forward when writing with tablets balanced on one's knees.[31] Aulus Gellius implies that libraries had multiple chairs or benches: 'As I chanced to be sitting in the library of

Trajan's temple, looking for something else, the edicts of the early praetors fell into my hands. . . . Then a friend of mine who was sitting with us. . . .'[32] It is almost impossible to tell what the number and arrangement of the chairs and/or benches were like, since chairs, being made generally of wood, have not survived *in situ*. Most would have certainly been easily portable. Two Hellenistic Etruscan sarcophagi show two readers with separate rolls. One shows two winged demons facing each other and holding open rolls: the left one sits on a stool and the right one on a diphros or campstool.[33] In the other relief a man with a roll held open stands on the right facing a man with a second roll held open.[34] This figure sits on a high-backed chair with his feet on a footstool. Between them stands a woman. In addition, as the mosaic with philosophers shows, there could also be permanent stone seating, frequently arranged in a semi-circle, presumably to foster discussion.

When at home, readers, like today, sometimes read on couches or in bed. Marcus Aurelius writes to his tutor, Fronto: 'I returned to my books. After pulling off my boots and taking off my cape, I stayed on my couch for nearly two hours. I read Cato's speech, "On the Property of Pulchra," and another in which he impeached a tribune.'[35] An early second-century BC Etruscan sarcophagus gives an idea of how they read on a couch.[36] Laris Pulena half-reclines with a roll held between both hands and opened to a section in the middle of the roll. The inscription about his career as a magistrate is written to be read by the viewer, from right to left, as Etruscan is written, and from top to bottom, rather than by Laris himself. Also remember the mention of couches in the floating library described by Moschion, though it is possible that the number of couches refers instead to the size of the room.[37]

The only literary references I have come across that combine reading and tables refer to the Greek and Roman custom of being read to while eating. So, Aulus Gellius says, 'At Favorinus' table [*apud mensam*], when he dined [*in convivio*] with friends, there was usually read either an old song of one of the lyric poets, or something from history, now in Greek and now in Latin.'[38] He uses the common phrase for dining, as we might do today. Moreover, the diners were not the readers, for in another passage about Favorinus, Gellius says: 'after the guests had taken their places and the serving of the viands began, a slave commonly stood by his table [*assistens mensae eius*] and began to read something.'[39] Cornelius Nepos comments that hearing something read while eating 'is the most agreeable form of entertainment' and that Atticus 'never served at his house without reading of some kind.'[40] One other passage is of interest. Pliny the Younger describes his habits of reading his writings before 'publication' to his friends, in this case for two days(!): 'in the dining-room [*triclinio*] I gathered my friends together in the month of July (which is usually a quiet time in the law courts) and settled them with chairs [*cathedris*] in front of the couches [*lectos*].'[41] Pliny uses the dining-room the way we would a living room.

I have one last argument in favor of the absence of flat-topped tables for reading and writing in both the library and the home. They are not a component of medieval libraries.[42] Various, and sometimes quite remarkable, arrangements for displaying books were adopted, from the 'wheel' arrangement cited in Chapter 10 to chaining books to their 'stacks', with the result, intended or unintended, that one could only read certain books in conjunction with certain other books. Saenger makes the very astute connection between the shift from reading aloud to reading silently and the associated changes in libraries.[43] You cannot have a number of people reading different texts aloud simultaneously if they are sitting side by side, as most of us are well aware today from the annoyances of noisy laptops in libraries.

Nor are flat tables a component of Renaissance libraries. The time of the switch between the 'portable' sloping writing/reading desk and flat-topped tables for individuals can be documented in the portrayals of St Augustine and St Jerome. Not until Carpaccio's painting in 1502 of *Saint Augustine Visited by the Soul of Saint Jerome* does St Augustine work on a flat-topped table.[44] Even a late eighteenth-century drawing of the ideal library shows only one table in a vast empty hall.[45] Multiple tables for the literate are a recent innovation. In short, the evidence for the use of tables for reading remains slim, ambiguous, and, in the final analysis, doubtful. The evidence for chairs, however, is clear.

THE USE OF MULTIPLE TEXTS

The use or non-use of tables and reading stands affects how the researcher who uses written sources writes. For example, if I quote a particular source, I have it open on my desk or I have already excerpted the section I want and copy it into my text. If I have a number of sources that pertain to a particular discussion, I am likely to have the full works or the excerpts laid out in some fashion on my desk. Remember that we are physically limited to retaining, at most, six to eight items in short-term memory. Having the actual texts available all at once circumvents that problem. We do know from Cicero's letter and his encounter with Cato that multiple rolls were used at least serially, if not simultaneously. Even with tables multiple rolls are cumbersome, because they would not necessarily lie flat to stay open at the appropriate section. Furthermore, keeping track of where multiple references are within blocks of text written in *scriptio continua* would be no easy matter.

There are no representations of multiple reading stands; nor are there any ancient representations of multiple texts open simultaneously. As discussed in Chapter 4, depictions do show scrinia or *capsae* containing multiple rolls – but containers for rolls clearly are not the same thing as displays of rolls. Multiple texts, however, are not shown open while scribes write until *c.* AD 1200 and, even then, do not become common until after AD 1400. Let us look at some of these representations.

In the first group a scribe, Jean Miélot (died 1472), sits at a table with a slanting stand for the text and with various codices, at least some of which are open, scattered around him on all available flat surfaces, including a couple of volumes at his feet *à la* Cicero.[46] In another example with Miélot his bed can be seen through partially opened curtains behind him.[47] If it is a matter not of composing but of copying, the writing stand sometimes has an addition of a second, similarly sloped portion that holds the exemplar, as appears in both of the illuminations with Miélot. In a third representation of Miélot, his 'day couch' can be seen standing against the rear wall and this time a lamp hangs above his writing stand.[48] One of my favorite illuminations shows William of Tournai, *c.* AD 1200, in bed, with a blanket covering his lower body because of the cold. He writes on a set of wax tablets with three codices balanced open on his legs and with three more open codices on a trestle table to the right.[49] The work illustrated is important: it is a manuscript of extracts or a florilegium, and the illumination shows the actual process of excerpting. William makes his excerpts on wax tablets and not in another codex, to which the extracts will eventually be transferred for 'publication'.

The second and earlier group of illuminations depicts the evangelists writing the Gospels. Because they are divinely inspired, they have no need of a text to copy. Instead a woman (later labeled 'Sophia' or Wisdom) might be present to 'direct' the writing, as in the Rossano Gospels from the sixth century AD where St Mark sits in a high-backed wicker chair writing on a roll laid across his thigh.[50] Sometimes the personification is omitted. In the Pericopes of Henry II (AD 1007–1012) St Mark cants his head heavenward as he dips his pen into an inkpot, placed on a separate stand, before writing on the roll that is elegantly draped over his left hand and across his thigh.[51] A companion portrait shows St Matthew writing on tablets with a closed codex held between his thighs – one method of dealing with two texts and no tables or stands.[52] It is interesting that Matthew does not use the stand that is present to support the tablets, but instead holds them in his left hand as he writes with his right. The portrait of Ezra from the Codex Amiatinus, *c.* AD 700 and discussed in Chapter 4, shows him sitting on a stool with his feet resting on a footstool and his right thigh slightly raised to support the codex he is writing in.[53] Despite the presence of a table which holds his double inkpot, an open codex lies on the floor in front of the stool. Behind him stands an open armarium or bookcase with more closed codices displayed on its shelves. Last of this group is the early fourth-century AD relief of a physician seated on a high-backed chair, also mentioned in Chapter 4. The doctor reads from a scroll in front of an open armarium that holds a pile of rolls on the top shelf and a bowl on the middle shelf.[54] Above the armarium is an open case containing his surgical instruments.

TAKING NOTES

If a classical writer wanted to take notes and he had no table, how did he do it? One way would be to annotate the text either in the margins or between the lines, as we sometimes do today. Some examples of this practice exist.[55] More often, they sometimes put 'conventional signs . . . into the margin of the text to indicate that the passage was interesting in some way, for instance corrupt or spurious, and that the reader would find comment on the point in the explanatory monograph.'[56] These explanations or commentaries were on separate rolls until the sixth century AD, though, as with the coexistence of the roll and codex, both formats for commentaries overlapped.[57] The format of the codex made a big difference, because it allowed a wider variety of layouts for text than did the roll. The 'main' text could float in the center with marginalia surrounding it. The evidence, then, indicates that notes would have been either on separate tablets or rolls. Remember two hands are needed to hold a roll open and tables don't seem to be used. Three methods are possible for taking notes when writing: (1) visually copying an exemplar, (2) memorizing the exemplar before writing it down, and (3) writing from dictation.

Today we primarily use the first method. In antiquity some used reading stands with the exemplar on it and the roll or tablets in their lap, as shown on the relief with Abeita discussed in Chapter 10. Evidence for a second person, who functions as a human reading stand, appears in one of the two Como reliefs, also discussed there, and in medieval illuminations where classical authors, unlike the evangelists, had to obey the physical laws of mortals. Hence the first-century AD historian Josephus, dressed like a worthy twelfth-century author, stands holding his text open before his scribe, the monk Samuel.[58] Each figure is neatly labeled with his name. The codex the scribe is working on is on a stand, which also holds his ink.

Quintilian describes this process from the point of view of the scribe:

> There is, therefore, a certain mechanical knack, which the Greeks call ἄλογος τριβή, which enables the hand to go on scribbling, while the eye takes in whole lines [versus] at once as it reads, observes the intonations [flexus] and the stops [transitus], and sees what is coming before the reader has articulated to himself what precedes. It is a similar knack which makes possible those miraculous tricks which we see jugglers and masters of sleight of hand perform upon the stage.[59]

Notice how Quintilian describes the active parsing of the block-like text into intonations (words) and stops (punctuation). You do, however, need training in reading for Quintilian also recommends:

169

Reading . . . must be kept slow for a considerable time, until practice brings speed unaccompanied by error. For to look to the right, which is regularly taught, and to look ahead depends not so much on precept as on practice; since it is necessary to keep the eyes on what follows while reading out what recedes, with the resulting difficulty that the attention of the mind must be divided, the eyes and voice being differently engaged.[60]

The practice of looking ahead when reading aloud is called the 'eye–voice span' and some evidence exists for a related 'eye–inner-voice span' for reading silently and presumably also for copying a text. According to Crowder and Wagner:

the eye is typically about four words ahead of the voice. To measure the eye–voice span yourself, get someone to read aloud from a sheet of paper in front of you. Then, suddenly and without warning, snatch the paper away and see how many words more can be reported accurately.[61]

The Roman scribe could, then, memorize small chunks in short-term memory just for the transfer of the text from the source on a reading stand to that on his knee. It is also possible that the scribe would memorize the passage from the roll or tablets he held, put down that set, pick up the new roll or tablets, write the text, put down the second writing medium, and begin the process all over again. The last possibility for the second method would have the scribe memorize whole passages permanently in long-term memory before recording them.

In a psychological study of 'copytyping' it was found that eye–hand coordination was dependent on the 'lexical representation' of the text.[62] That is, typists work at the level of the word rather than at the level of individual letters. I would add an exception. When typing something written in a language totally foreign to me, I am forced to go letter by letter, because I have no idea how to group the letters in a meaningful and helpful manner. Presumably the Greek and Latin scribes worked in a similar manner. They would 'parse' the exemplar, as they copied it either silently or more likely out loud, and so could work at a fair rate of speed. When I tested copying a text visually or aurally through dictation with my graduate students, I found that they preferred, contrary to my expectations, the dictation, though they did grumble about the accent of the person (not me) dictating. Shifting your eyes back and forth between the original and the copy is tiring and increases the number of errors. Just think of the modern aids for typists that indicate which line they are on so that they don't lose their place. In the case of classical texts with their block-like displays, I would think the task would be even more difficult than with our texts. One other advantage occurs with the combination of dictation and writing. As discussed in Chapter 6, because two different senses are involved, eye and ear, you are more likely to remember what you have written.[63] In other words, Rose Mary Woods, when transcribing the Watergate tapes, would have had a greater likelihood of remembering what she typed than if she copied only visually, although, as a rather good typist, I can tell you that I am always aware of what I am typing.

The third method, dictation, is probably the most common method for copying anything written in antiquity, as the written sources testify. To some extent it is easier to write dictated Latin or Greek than dictated English, because, like Italian, they are more regular in their orthography.[64] English allows incredible scope for errors. It is not that any clerk today would write 'ghoti' for 'fish', as George Bernard Shaw might have claimed, but that someone could very well write 'sun and air' when referring to the last will and testament of a wealthy old man who wanted to leave his worldly goods to his 'son and heir'.[65] Skeat maintains that dictation was used to make copies of an original, because one class of scribal errors, phonetic mistakes, could occur only under conditions of oral delivery.[66] Others claim, however, that if a scribe were visually copying and repeated the phrase or section to himself, then the same kind of phonetic error would occur.[67] A papyrus fragment with a commentary on Pindar's *Pythians* probably demonstrates visual copying. Three different scribes (you can tell by the handwriting) wrote a column and a half of text, and '[o]ne of them, who finished it off, also added a comment at the foot of the previous column on a passage passed over by the first scribe.'[68] While it is possible that the person dictating could have omitted the passage, it seems more likely that visual copying was involved. Even when visual copying *is* involved, it does not mean that 'exact replicas' were produced in the sense that a scribe would have the same number of words per line as in the exemplar.[69]

While Skeat was concerned with 'publication', I am focussing on the individual writer and his working methods. Here Skeat rightly points out that 'authors dictating their own literary works . . . is, of course, a common-place of every age and civilization.'[70] Consider the habits of Pliny the Elder. I have already quoted in Chapter 10 one passage from his nephew's letter about him reading while traveling. What is instructive is that every time Pliny the Younger mentions his uncle reading, he mentions his uncle extracting passages:

(1) After something to eat . . . in summer when he was not too busy he would often lie in the sun, and a book was read aloud while he made notes and extracts. He made extracts of everything he read, and always said that there was no book so bad that some good could not be got out of it. . . . (2) A book was read aloud during the meal and he took rapid notes. . . . (3) In the country, the only time he took from his work

was for his bath, and by bath I mean his actual immersion, for while he was being rubbed down and dried he had a book read to him or dictated notes. (4) When traveling he felt free from other responsibilities to give every minute to work; he kept a secretary at his side with book and notebook.[71]

I have added numbers to my own extracts to indicate that in one short section Pliny the Elder is described reading four times and at all four of those times two people are involved. Either Pliny dictates the passages he wishes to excerpt to his secretary or the secretary reads to him and Pliny takes down the passage. The combination of reading and note-taking is a joint activity.[72] Clearly, if someone wanted to take notes in the library, he could have his slave come along and either read aloud to the slave or vice versa.

According to psychological studies of reading, being read to has certain advantages:

> [It allows the listener] to process text at a higher level and at a more rapid rate than one could process the text alone in oral or silent reading. The experiences of listening to another orally read free one up somewhat from decoding responsibilities (although it depends upon how the listening is done) that may permit space for greater imagination and reflecting than having to decode *and* comprehend.[73]

It seems likely to me that this description fits the situation in antiquity. Pliny, for example, would listen until he heard something he wanted to note down. Once it was, the reading would continue.

Pliny the Elder describes Julius Caesar as a quintessential example of an efficient statesman:

> The most outstanding instance of innate mental vigour I take to be the dictator Caesar. . . . We are told that he used to write or read and dictate or listen simultaneously, and to dictate to his secretaries four letters at once on his important affairs – or, if otherwise unoccupied, seven letters at once.[74]

While the idea of dictating four letters simultaneously is clearly what Pliny the Elder wishes to stress, it is also evident that Caesar, like Pliny himself, practices the two-person method of taking notes from reading. Caesar's method of working was common for politicians. Cicero describes the work habits of Galba:

> [He was] surrounded by lettered slaves, to whom after his habit he was dictating memoranda now to one and now to another at one and the same time. . . . Rutilius added as a relevant circumstance, that the scribes who came out with him [Galba] were badly used up, an indica-

tion he thought of the vehemence and temper of Galba in preparation as well as action.[75]

The only comfort those scribes may have derived is that, according to Seneca, the pace of dictating was slower than that of actually speaking: 'You can expect to be interrupted by persons with as little taste as the one who, when Vinicius was jerking the words out one by one, as if he were dictating rather than speaking, exclaimed, "I call on the speaker to speak."'[76] In the third century AD Ambrose generously funded the following secretarial help for Origen: '[A]s he dictated there were ready at hand more than seven shorthand-writers, who relieved each other at fixed times, and as many copyists, as well as girls skilled in penmanship [ἐπὶ τὸ καλλιγραφεῖν].'[77] The papyrus fragment with the commentary on Pindar (mentioned above) gives a good idea of what such a text would look like. The idea of simultaneously dictating different texts to several scribes seems to be a commonplace for prolific writers that continues into the Middle Ages, when Thomas Aquinas in the thirteenth century:

> used to dictate in his cell to three secretaries, and even occasionally to four, on different subjects at the same time. . . . No one could dictate simultaneously so much various material without a special grace. Nor did he seem to be searching for things as yet unknown to him; he seemed simply to let his memory pour out its treasures.[78]

I would imagine that this skill is somewhat akin to playing several games of chess at once and, as such, requires someone with a particular talent for not losing the thread of thought. To some extent, it would have been easier then than today, because not only was dictation commonly practiced in adult literate life, but it was also part of the standard Roman school curriculum. Horace, like an earlier George Bernard Shaw, asks 'What, would you be so foolish as to want your poems dictated in common schools? Not so I.'[79] Even so, modern cases exist: 'He [Joseph Hirschhorn] occasionally held a telephone to each ear and shouted buy and sell orders to his associates while a manicurist worked on his nails, a barber cut his hair, and a waiter from the Savarin restaurant served him lunch.'[80]

Horace finds the talent to dictate rapidly less than praiseworthy:

> Herein lay his [Lucilius's] great fault: often in an hour, as though a great exploit he would dictate two hundred lines while standing, as they say, on one foot. In his muddy stream there was much that you would like to remove. He was wordy, and too lazy to put up with the trouble of writing – of writing correctly, I mean; for as to quantity, I let that pass.[81]

I am reminded of Pascal's famous apology: 'I have made this letter longer only because I have not had the time to make it shorter.'[82] Similarly, it seems that the etiquette of writing personal letters by hand stems from antiquity. Cicero, when pressed for time, apologizes to Atticus for using a scribe:

> I believe you have never before read a letter of mine not in my own handwriting. You may gather from that how desperately busy I am. Not having a minute to spare and being obliged to take a walk to refresh my poor voice, I am dictating this while walking.[83]

Another time in a letter to his brother (2.2) Cicero said that he was forced to dictate the letter because he was suffering from an eye inflammation (*lippitudo*). As in any era, however, most people did not have secretaries, and therefore wrote their own letters.[84]

'RESEARCH ASSISTANTS'

Generally slaves or freedmen took the dictation, and every writer of note seems to have had access to one or more such scribe. The image of the poor, struggling writer trying to make ends meet in some garret was not common in antiquity. To write you were either rich to start with or you had a rich patron. Horace employs a scribe: 'Go, lad, and quickly add these lines to my little book.'[85] The literate slaves and freedmen would qualify for the modern term 'research assistants' in that they did more than a stenographer might do today. They could translate from Greek to Latin or vice versa. Pliny the Elder mentions that 'Pompeius however on getting possession of all the royal booty [of Mithridates] ordered his freedman Lenaeus, a man of letters, to translate these [Greek treatises on medicine] into Latin. This great victory therefore was as beneficent to life as it was to the state.'[86] Christopher Jones believes that Plutarch relied on such 'bilingual scribes' for his Roman lives, since '[w]hen his citations can be checked, they sometimes correspond so exactly with the original as to give a strong impression of first-hand knowledge.' Jones adds that 'acknowledgement [of the scribes and assistants] was not the rule.'[87]

Aulus Gellius writes that 'Tullius Tiro was the pupil and freedman of Marcus Cicero and an assistant in his literary work [*adiutor in litteris studiorum*].'[88] This is the same Tiro who is credited with the invention of Latin shorthand discussed in Chapter 5. Gellius's high respect for 'Tironian care and learning' (1.7.1) leads to the following remark:

> In Cicero's second book *On Glory* there is an evident mistake, of no great importance – a mistake which it does not require a man of learning to detect, but merely one who has read the seventh book of Homer. Therefore I am not so much surprised that Marcus Tullius erred in that matter, as that it was not noticed later and corrected either by Cicero himself or by Tiro, his freedman, a most careful man, who gave great attention to his patron's books.[89]

Cicero had substituted Ajax for Hector in a quotation from the *Iliad* (7.89). Every writer appreciates the assistant who catches the 'obvious' mistakes. Even more appreciated is the assistant who can read your handwriting better than you can. So Cicero writes to Atticus: 'If the copyists up there can't make out my handwriting, you will put them right. There *is* a rather difficult insertion [*interpositio*] which I don't find easy to read myself.'[90]

Sometimes, like us, the Romans were not so fortunate in their aides. Cicero writes to P. Sulpicius Rufus that:

My library [*bibliothecen*], worth a considerable sum, was in the charge of a slave of mine called Dionysius. Having pilfered a large number of books and anticipating a day of reckoning, he ran away. He's now in your province. . . . If you see to it that he is returned to me, I cannot tell you how much it will oblige me.[91]

Quintilian tell us about Seneca who:

had many excellent qualities, a quick and fertile intelligence with great industry and wide knowledge, though as regards the last quality he was often led into error by those whom he had entrusted with the task of investigating certain subjects on his behalf.[92]

Quintilian also warns about other problems with scribes:

[I]f the amanuensis is a slow writer, or lacking in intelligence, he becomes a stumbling-block, our speed is checked, and the thread of our ideas is interrupted by the delay or even perhaps by the loss of temper to which it gives rise. . . . Finally, we come to the most important consideration of all, that the advantages of privacy are lost when we dictate.[93]

Such assistants would be used for a variety of tasks, including keeping their master's research collection in order. Cicero writes to Atticus:

You will find that Tyrannio has made a wonderful job of arranging my books. . . . And I shall be grateful if you would send me a couple of your library clerks to help Tyrannio with the gluing and other operations.[94]

Cicero's son, while studying in Athens, writes a very warm letter to Tiro, which he concludes by saying: 'Thank you for attending to my commissions. But do please get a clerk sent out to me, preferably a Greek. I waste a lot of time copying out my notes.'[95]

SUMMARY

In this chapter I have considered the mechanics of the classical researcher. Not only did they not write on tables, they did not have tables in libraries.

As a result, taking notes was generally a two-person process with one person dictating to the one taking the notes. The absence of tables, both in 'public' and private libraries, also means that multiple sources were not likely to be laid out in front of the writer. The implications of this arrangement are the subject of Chapter 12.

12

COMPOSING THE WORK

Now that our classical writer is equipped with his tools and seated in his chair or reclining on his couch, he can begin composing his work.[1] This chapter focusses on the process of creation rather than on the types or genres of writing, with one exception. In order to understand how the classical writer composed, it is necessary to use particular examples as illustrations. I have drawn on the historians and compilers of information like Pliny the Elder and Aulus Gellius, for they often speak directly to the reader about what they are doing and why. 'Literary' works like the *Aeneid* generally do not contain descriptions of the problems the author faced when writing.

Lucian advises the would-be historian:

> As to the facts themselves, he should not assemble them at random, but only after much laborious painstaking investigation. . . . When he has collected all or most of the facts let him first make them into a series of notes, a body of material as yet with no beauty or continuity. Then, after arranging them into order, let him give it beauty and enhance it with the charms of expression, figure, and rhythm.[2]

I am not going to discuss interviewing techniques, on-site visits, etc., because they are not dependent primarily on writing skills, although both investigations in the field and research in libraries and archives are reduced to notes in memory and on tablets and rolls. This chapter opens at the next stage recommended by Lucian: the selecting and ordering of the material that has been collected.[3]

SELECTING AND ORDERING EXCERPTS

There are two major types of reductions of text: (1) abridgments; and (2) notes, excerpts, and quotations. Cicero preserves our earliest mention of the ancient equivalent of *The Reader's Digest Condensed Books*, when he refers to abridgments of whole Latin works by Brutus.[4] The practice became quite popular during the Middle Ages.[5] I am not concerned here with

177

abridgments, because they depend mainly on excising and summarizing an existing text in sequential order rather than on the creation of a new text from excerpts and notes.

Reducing a work to snippets, whether, as today, on note cards and in the computer or, as then, on tablets and in rolls, begins at least as early as the late fifth century BC, when the quantity of existing texts must have been sufficiently unwieldy as to make selections desirable. According to Xenophon, Socrates said:

> And the treasures [θησαυρούς] that the wise men of old have left us in their writings I open and explore with my friends. If we come on any good thing, we extract it, and we set much store on being useful to one another.[6]

By the first century BC the practice was so pervasive that the Auctor ad Herennium wryly comments that 'if the ancient orators and poets should take the books of these rhetoricians and each remove therefrom what belongs to himself, the rhetoricians would have nothing left to claim as their own.'[7] In the next century, Pliny the Elder, as we have seen, was a voracious reader and extractor. By the time of his death he left his nephew, Pliny the Younger, '160 notebooks [*volumina*] of selected passages, written in a minute hand on both sides of the page [*opistographos*], so that their number is really doubled.'[8] Incidentally, note the use of both sides of the papyrus. Pliny the Elder himself in his Preface to the *Natural History* informs Titus, to whom the work is dedicated:

> As Domitius Piso says, it is not books but store-houses [*thesauros*] that are needed; consequently by perusing about 2000 volumes, very few of which, owing to the abstruseness of their contents, are ever handled by students, we have collected in 36 volumes 20,000 noteworthy facts obtained from one hundred authors.[9]

The English word 'treasury' comes from the Greek (θησαυρός) and Latin (*thesaurus*) words and, like them, applies not just to money but also to treasuries of reading and in particular anthologies.

This long-lived image, uniting words and treasuries, had a third and even more important link in antiquity to memory, an association that continued into the Middle Ages and that has been revived in cognitive studies of memory.[10] Cicero says (*On the Orator*, 1.18): 'What shall I say about the treasure-house of all things, memory?' The Auctor ad Herennium introduces his extended discussion of mnemotechnics with: 'Now let me turn to the treasure-house of the ideas supplied by Invention, to the guardian of all the parts of rhetoric, the Memory.'[11] Quintilian makes it clear that the image is a commonplace:

Indeed it is not without good reason that memory has been called the treasure-house of eloquence . . . whatever it [the mind] discovers, it deposits by some mysterious process in the safe-keeping of memory, which acts as a transmitting agent and hands on to the delivery what it has received from the imagination.[12]

Seneca speaks of 'things I have deposited with it [memory].'[13] The idea behind the image is straightforward. One extracts some thought, idea, or fact from a larger work and deposits it in one's own storehouse, that is, memory, from which it can be recalled whenever needed, like withdrawing money from a treasury. The equation of treasury directly with memory and only indirectly with writing depends on the fact that it is memory and not a superior filing technique that allows the classical writer to retrieve the appropriate excerpt.

Little scholarly attention has been paid to the frequent mention of memory in the prefaces of classical writers. Such acknowledgments occur more rather than less frequently as time passes. Consider how the classical writer went about the organization of those extracts from his treasury. Aulus Gellius in his Preface says:

But in the arrangement of my material I have adopted the same haphazard order that I had previously followed in collecting it. For whenever I had taken in hand any Greek or Latin book, or had heard anything worth remembering, I used to jot down whatever took my fancy, of any and every kind, without any definite plan or order; and such notes I would lay away as an aid to my memory, like a kind of literary storehouse, so that when the need arose of a word or a subject which I chanced for the moment to have forgotten, and the books from which I had taken it were not at hand, I could readily find and produce it.[14]

First, Gellius stresses the role of memory in a way that a modern writer would not. He expresses a naiveté in how writing aids memory that resembles the delight of early users of word processors. Such acknowledgments are quite common in ancient prefaces and introductions.[15] Second, while Gellius has simplified his task by merely including all his notes in whatever order he originally took them, he does claim later in the Preface to have been selective in what notes he took:

For all of them [his predecessors], and in particular the Greeks, after wide and varied reading . . . with no effort to discriminate, swept together whatever they had found, aiming at mere quantity. The perusal of such collections will exhaust the mind through weariness or disgust, before it finds one or two notes which it is a pleasure to read, or inspiring to have read, or helpful to remember. I myself, on the contrary, having at heart that well-known saying of the famous

Ephesian [Herakleitos], 'Much learning does not make a scholar,' did it is true busy and even weary myself in unrolling and running through many a scroll. . . . I took few items from them.[16]

Plutarch says in the Preface to the second 'book' (βιβλίον) of his *Table-Talk* or *Dinner Conversations*: 'The conversations which follow have been written in a haphazard manner, not systematically but as each came to memory [μνήμην].'[17] We might have discounted Plutarch's 'random' order of topics, if it were not for the Preface of Gellius. Instead, his explanation told the ancient reader that what was to follow fitted a well-known genre of collections of discussions on diverting topics. Pliny the Younger in his dedicatory letter to the first roll of his *Letters* writes similarly:

> You [Septicius Clarus] have often urged me to collect and publish any letters of mine which were composed with some care. I have now made a collection, not keeping to the original order as I was not writing history, but taking them as they came to my hand [*in manus*].[18]

Pliny, like Gellius and Plutarch, 'publishes' his letters in a haphazard order, because he felt it made no difference to either their individual worth or, perhaps more surprisingly to us, to their understanding to have the original order. I discuss below what he means by 'some care' in their composition.

Certain genres like history, however, even in antiquity, required a particular sequence of topics. When an author had to arrange his excerpts according to some system or another, Cicero advises:

> [W]hen the inclination arose in my mind to write a text-book of rhetoric, I did not set before myself one model which I thought necessary to reproduce in all details, of whatever sort they might be, but after collecting all the works on the subject I excerpted what seemed the most suitable precepts from each, and so culled the flower of many minds.[19]

The likening of excerpting to picking flowers is common during antiquity; and during the Renaissance the word '*florilegium*', 'a selection of flowers', is applied to collections of such extracts.[20] Seneca advises:

> We should follow, men say, the example of the bees, who flit about and cull the flowers that are suitable for producing honey, and then arrange and assort in their cells all that they have brought in. . . . We also, I say, ought to copy these bees, and sift whatever we have gathered from a varied course of reading, for such things are better preserved if they are kept separate; then, by applying the supervising care with which our nature has endowed us . . . we should so blend those several flavours into one delicious compound that, even though it betrays its origin, yet it nevertheless is clearly a different thing from that whence it came.[21]

From these two passages, two major points stand out: first, before writing yourself, go over all the relevant sources; second, when you combine those sources into your new whole, keep your items separate. The latter is essential for retrieval, since according to the art of memory each item is stored in its own place and, as Mary Carruthers puts it, 'composition starts in memorized reading.'[22]

Diodorus Siculus remarks on the difficulties of keeping numerous sources straight. He says:

> [S]ince both the dates of the events and the events themselves lie scattered about in numerous treatises and in divers authors, the knowledge of them becomes difficult for the mind to encompass and for the memory to retain.[23]

Diodorus makes it very clear that writers in antiquity did not organize their excerpts by sorting them on the ground or on the table as we do with note cards today, but by arranging them in their heads.[24] This method of writing has wide implications for our understanding of historical, biographical, and synthetic works like Pliny's *Natural History*. Modern scholars, however, in their discussions of excerpting have given little attention to the paramount role that memory, both natural and artificial, plays in the actual process of composing in antiquity.

'ORAL COMPOSITION' IN SHORT-TERM MEMORY

Pliny the Younger gives one of the fullest descriptions of how a Roman writes:

> [When I wake] my shutters stay closed, for in the stillness and darkness I feel myself surprisingly detached from any distractions and left to myself in freedom; my eyes do not determine the direction of my thinking, but, being unable to see anything, they are guided to visualize my thoughts. If I have anything on hand I work it out in my head, choosing and correcting the wording, and the amount I achieve depends on the ease or difficulty with which my thoughts can be marshalled and kept in my head. Then I call my secretary, the shutters are opened, and I dictate what I have put into shape; he goes out, is recalled, and again dismissed. Three or four hours after I first wake (but I don't keep to fixed times) I betake myself according to the weather either to the terrace or the covered arcade, work out the rest of my subject, and dictate it.[25]

Pliny the Younger composes in his head in short snatches that match our limitations on short-term memory. He is following the advice of his teacher, Quintilian:

181

The mind cannot devote its undivided and sincere attention to a number of things at the same time, and wherever it turns its gaze it must cease to contemplate its appointed task. . . . Demosthenes took a wiser view; for he would retire to a place where no voice was to be heard, and no prospect greeted the sight, for fear that his eyes might force his mind to neglect his duty.[26]

Two centuries later Plotinus the philosopher uses the same method:

He worked out his train of thought from beginning to end in his own mind, and then, when he wrote it down, since he had set it all in order in his mind, he wrote as continuously as if he was copying from a book.[27]

Dictating to a scribe what one has composed in one's head continued as the norm until the fourteenth century AD, when the author became the one to write down his text first.[28] This generalization does not mean that some did not write first on wax tablets or papyrus. It means merely that most composed this way most of the time.[29] Horace (*Epistles*, 2.1.112–113), for instance, implies that at least his first drafts were written directly by him since, as noted in Chapter 11, he has an assistant: 'Awake before the sun has risen I ask for pen, paper, and case [*scrinia*].' I have also already mentioned that Plato struggled with the opening words to the *Republic*.[30] Finally, Rosalind Thomas notes that in the fifth century BC 'the poet did not necessarily write down the poem until fairly late in the process of composition – the image of the poet in the throes of composition given in Aristophanes does not include pen and paper.'[31]

The procedure of working out the text first in memory and then setting it down was taught as a part of rhetoric. Quintilian (10.6.1) calls it '*cogitatio*', that is, 'reflection', 'thought' or 'premeditation'. He says:

For there are places and occasions where writing is impossible, while both are available in abundance for premeditation . . . this practice will not merely secure the proper arrangement of our matter without any recourse to writing, which in itself is no small achievement, but will also set the words which we are going to use in their proper order, and bring the general texture of our speech to such a stage of completion that nothing further is required beyond the finishing touches. And as a rule the memory is more retentive of thoughts when the attention has not been relaxed by the fancied security which results from committing them to writing.[32]

Quintilian warns:

We need judgement as well. So long as we do not lie back with eyes turned up to the ceiling, trying to fire our imagination by muttering to ourselves, in the hope that something will present itself, but turn our thoughts to consider what the circumstances of the case demand.[33]

Quintilian would have approved the results of Augustus's attempts to compose in the 'tub', somewhat like singing in the shower today:

> There is another [book], equally brief, of 'Epigrams,' which he composed for the most part at the time of the bath. Though he began a tragedy with much enthusiasm, he destroyed it because his style did not satisfy him, and when some of his friends asked him what in the world had become of Ajax, he answered that 'his Ajax had fallen on his sponge.'[34]

In case this method of composition seems a backward way to go about writing, I quote at length a fascinating account by John Hull of his adjustment to writing lectures in his head when he went blind during his forties. He was in a rare position of knowing how both the sighted and the blind compose. I am omitting the various methods, like recording notes on tape, that he discarded as awkward and unmanageable in practice. This is the system that worked:

> I now seem to have developed a way of scanning ahead in my mind, to work out what I am going to say. Everybody does this in ordinary speech; otherwise we couldn't complete a sentence. Somehow or other, and without effort, I have developed a longer perspective, and now when I am speaking I can see paragraphs coming up from the recesses of my mind. It is a bit like reading them off a scanner. While I am speaking, another part of my mind is sorting out into paragraphs what I am going to be saying in the next few minutes, and a yet more remote part is selecting alternative lines of argument from a sort of bank of material. This seems to give my lecturing style a greater sense of order than I had before, and people seem to be able to follow me more easily.[35]

Hull's lecture material is more complicated than business letters, which are frequently dictated. He keeps two basic things in short-term memory: what he is saying currently and what he wishes to say next. Note his use of visual (scanning, perspective, recesses) and memory (bank of material) terminology.

Cicero writes about the casting of sentences in terms very similar to Hull's:

> I would not have the structure obtrude itself in such trivialities; but a practised pen will nevertheless easily find the method of composition. For as the eye looks ahead in reading, so in speaking the mind will foresee what is to follow.[36]

This method is akin to that used by oral poets like Homer. Instead of paragraphs, episodes are organized using a 'ring composition'. Think of a set of successively smaller horseshoes with each successive horseshoe set within the previous one and with never more than the six that a good short-term memory can hold at one time.[37] The oral poet starts with the 'leg' of horseshoe 1, leaves it dangling, goes to the 'leg' of horseshoe 2, then 3, and then in reverse order (3,2,1) picks up the other 'legs'. His listeners do the same thing as they follow the story.[38]

Hull also reflects on the physical organization of his material with conclusions analogous to mine about my adjustment to online writing:

> A sighted author tends to paragraph his or her work retrospectively. You see the stuff unrolling on the typewriter or screen, and you think that it is about time you started a new paragraph. A person listening to books on cassettes, where the actual paragraphs in the printed page are not normally indicated, does his own paragraphing, and when composing tends to project this into the future of the composition. I think that this also helps me to organize my material in advance when I am speaking in public. A sighted lecturer reading from a typescript concentrates mainly upon what he has said, that is, the paragraphs slip away behind him as he 'swims' forward through his speech. A blind speaker has to concentrate entirely upon what he is about to say, or what he will be saying fifteen minutes from now, because otherwise he will lose direction.[39]

Hull's mental structuring of his own work resembles the way classical and medieval readers would mentally punctuate their block-like written texts.

The method Hull uses to understand something he hears from a tape is directly comparable to the way someone in antiquity would have heard a speech. Hull says that 'I have not put any particular effort into learning how to [remember structure in a written work read to me]. . . . You tend to make unconscious mental notes of the structure so that you can go back again if necessary.'[40] In other words, the process works in both directions: it helps one compose in the mind and it helps one follow an oral 'reading'. What is especially remarkable is that composing mentally has improved rather than destroyed his ability to lecture. It may not be accidental, however, that what he has published is not one, long connected work, but rather excerpts, each ordered within the excerpt itself, but, none the less, a series of separate episodes and thoughts; for his work is a diary which he kept during the first years of his total blindness to help him accept and understand his condition. He dictated this diary into a tape recorder, the modern-day equivalent of the ancient scribe.

The most famous case of a blind writer is, of course, John Milton, who composed *Paradise Lost* after he had gone blind. I exclude Homer, who most likely suffered an 'ethical' rather than a real blindness. In antiquity the

184

blind were considered to have a different kind of sight and hence it seemed appropriate and in character for the greatest Greek poet to be blind. *Paradise Lost* is of considerable length (10,565 lines) and took him a considerable period (six years) to compose.[41] According to Ian Hunter:

> Milton planned the overall structure and then composed the detailed wording in sections of up to 40 lines which he held in his head while, as he put it, waiting to be milked; that is, until he could dictate the section to a scribe. Subsequently, he had people read portions of the text to him so that he could make amendments.[42]

Incidentally, the English word 'dictate' and its relatives go directly back to the Latin *'dicto'* which meant either our 'dictate' or – and this is significant – 'compose', because the common way of composing something was through dictation.[43] In the Middle Ages the meaning 'compose' was the more common usage.[44]

COMPOSING IN MEMORY AND THE ANCIENT HISTORIAN

Composing in memory works. If we pull together our information so far, our average ancient historian should first read through his notes, then order them in his memory, and finally write down the ordered contents of his memory. It does have certain effects on the results that are particularly apparent in works of history and biography, when conflicting accounts of the same event need to be reconciled.

Consider a specific example. T. J. Luce has made an excellent analysis of Livy's method of composing his history. According to Luce:

> Take as an example what Livy conceived his chief task to be in appraising his sources for the Trials of the Scipios [in Book 38]. It is indeed true that he compares and at times evaluates parts of the story in isolation from one another: e.g. the site of Scipio's tomb, the date of his death, and so forth. But he does so not in order to select the best *parts* from each to use, but to identify the best account overall. The thought that he might or should fashion the separate pieces into a version essentially of his own making did not occur to him. One reason, of course, is that such a proceeding would to him doubtless have smacked of the irresponsible and the willful.[45]

In his discussion Luce expands on that reason, which goes to the heart of what Romans thought history was, but does not mention the factor that I would add. It simply was not possible physically for ancient historians with their work methods to dissect in memory contradictory variants into separate elements in order to produce a single, more logical version.

A similar process may have happened when the Etruscans took over the

Phoenician alphabet. Although Etruscan does not use all the Phoenician letters, none the less, when the Etruscans first made model alphabets, they included even the letters not used in Etruscan.[46] Wholes are not dissected. For a modern example, remember the waiter from Chapter 7 who can only remember the whole menu and not extract an item from the middle. Imagine having to keep ten such menus in working memory.[47] Instead, like the modern waiter, the ancient historian could deal only in wholes each of which came with its own indivisible set of elements. At the same time, memory techniques emphasized, as I quoted earlier from Seneca (*Epistles*, 84.3, 5), that items should be kept separate. As in the work of John Hull, within any particular variant, the organization, style, and so on of the writing could be indistinguishable from a writer relying solely on written methods of composition.

C. B. R. Pelling is one of the few modern historians to consider the limitations that ancient literary tools imposed. He even recognizes that Plutarch, his main concern, relies on memory, when he explains Plutarch's method of composing the *Lives*:

> The curious fidelity to a single source for individual episodes is most easily understood if we make a simple assumption: that, following this initial wide reading, an author would generally choose just one work to have before his eyes when he composed, and this work would provide the basis of his narrative. . . . Items from the earlier reading would more widely be combined with the principal source, but a writer would not normally refer back to that reading to verify individual references, and would instead rely on his memory, or on the briefest of notes. Alternatively, it may be that an author, immediately before narrating an episode would *re*read one account, and compose with that version fresh in mind. . . . Stray facts and additions would be recalled from the preliminary reading, but it would be a very different matter to recall the detail of an episode's presentation, and combine versions independently and evenly.[48]

Pelling expands his examination of Plutarch to other ancient writers to note that the use of a single source is a common trait:

> Time and again, we find Greek and Roman historians claiming a wide range of reading, and deserving to be believed; yet, time and again, we find them demonstrably basing their narrative of individual episodes on a single source. Cassius Dio [*Fragment*, 1.2] is one example: he claims to have read 'nearly every book' on Roman history – but, as he goes on to say, he 'did not write up all his material, but only a selection' . . . he is generally content to draw his material from a single source at a time. . . . Dionysius quotes widely among his authorities (some thirty names in the first few books) – but he, too, seems generally to be faithful to a

single source in narrating an episode. And even Tacitus seems to be similar.[49]

So C. H. Oldfather says that 'while Diodorus probably leaned very strongly upon a single author for one or another section of his work, he used at the same time other writers as well.'[50] Diodorus himself admits the problem: 'because the works [his sources] vary so widely and are so numerous, the recovery of past events becomes extremely difficult of comprehension and of attainment.'[51] Andrew Dyck in his analysis of the Homer Lexicon of Apollonius Sophista has concluded that

'Apollonius' method of composition . . . [is] based on successive use of a fixed number of sources, and . . . determination of an entry's specific reference is often enabled by the fact that 'the glosses tend to fall into series by the order of the occurrence of the lemmata in *Iliad* and *Odyssey.*'[52]

First, it should by now be obvious that even easier than ordering whole variants in memory and presenting each in turn would be to mentally run through all the possibilities and choose only one for your new text. Remember also that *scriptio continua* means that no external physical order is imposed on the text, with the result that its seamlessness makes it harder to divide mentally into logical segments. The layout of the ancient text virtually forces the reader to rely on memory for cues to content rather than on the visual display, as today. For example, think about how you might have checked my reference to the quotation from Seneca a few pages back. If you looked for the actual text, you probably focussed on the sections that were indented as quotes.

Aristotle had already noted the same problem of following an oral narrative, and gives an explanation that is quite similar to my modern one:

Why do we feel more pleasure in listening [ἀκούομεν] to narratives [ἱστοριῶν] in which the attention is concentrated on a single point than in hearing those which are concerned with many subjects? Is it because we pay more attention to and feel more pleasure in listening to things which are more easily comprehended, and that which is definite is more easily comprehended than that which is indefinite?[53]

It is interesting that Aristotle uses the Greek word 'ἀκούω', 'hear' or 'listen', rather than 'ἀναγιγνώσκω', generally 'read'. Since there was virtually no silent reading in antiquity, 'ἀκούω' came by obvious extension to mean 'read'.[54] Works were judged on how well a listener rather than a viewer understood them, with the result that Dionysius of Halicarnassus reverses the modern assessment of the relative standings of Thucydides and Herodotus. Dionysius concludes that 'whereas Thucydides has taken a single subject and divided the whole body into many parts, Herodotus has chosen

187

a number of subjects which are in no way alike and has made them into one harmonious whole.'[55] Elaine Fantham suggests that 'The normal practice of listening to, rather than looking at, texts helps to explain the extraordinary importance attached by Roman critics to the rhythmic and periodic qualities of a composition.'[56]

THE ACCURACY OF THEIR EXCERPTS

That the classical writer did not always retrieve the right extract demonstrates not necessarily sloppy research or writing but poor organizational tools, as I discussed in Chapters 4 and 5. While Pliny the Elder boasts that his roll-long list of contents to the *Natural History* will facilitate finding information in its thirty-six rolls, we have seen that the actual likelihood of success was exceedingly low. Consequently there is no reason to think that Pliny himself would have been any better at retrieving selections from his own notes. A. Locher, however, believes that Pliny or one of his scribes made extensive marginal notations. Then Pliny went through 'a stage of mechanical separation [of the bits of information]. Here I [Locher] imagine a pile of little tablets, of scraps of papyrus, each of which contained one passage taken from the *commentarii*, be it *res, observatio* or *historia*.'[57] The idea of an ancient equivalent of modern note cards is totally misguided for four reasons.

First, while they did use scraps of papyrus, small tablets, and even sherds to scribble on, the formats are such that they don't easily sort into stacks. Think of piling up sherds or bulky tablets. Second, remember that Pliny has 160 rolls of notes. Or rather, since they are written on both sides and in crabbed handwriting, he has at least 320 rolls. It is not likely that he would use one roll until it was filled up and then proceed to the next, because then he would have no need to take notes on wax tablets, but would merely write directly on to the day's roll – the method that Aulus Gellius probably adopted. Since Pliny has the equivalent of 320 rolls of notes, but uses only thirty-six rolls for the *Natural History* (the first with the 'table of contents' doesn't count), he has to boil down his information considerably. Some of the 320 rolls are probably on totally extraneous topics like oratory and problems in grammar.[58] Some were probably not yet written when he undertook the *Natural History*. So let us be generous and assume he has only half of the 320 rolls of information to sift through. To give Pliny his due, it is extraordinarily difficult to separate knowledge into neat little cubby-holes or, in his case, rolls. If he originally allocated one roll for this topic, one roll for that topic, certain topics would, none the less, overflow. Other notes would have been miscategorized, especially if recorded early on, as most of us know from personal experience of taking notes on paper. Even with a rough allocation of different topics to different rolls, it is likely that within those gross categories the information was in the order of his having noted it down. Suppose, for example, he decided to leave generous spaces between topics on individual rolls, somewhat like the method used by British libraries when they used to paste cataloguing slips into large folios. We have no reason to believe that Pliny's allocations of empty spaces within rolls was any better than that of the British libraries, which used periodically to have to lift and repaste slips. Third, marginal notations on some 160 rolls would have been difficult to control. Only the computer enables me to find my notes and even then I all too often discover that I 'remember' some tidbit that I did not record.[59] I simply cannot believe that Pliny the Elder always got his note.[60]

Fourth and most important, our evidence about how people dealt with text in classical antiquity indicates that they would have used their memories instead. Pliny wrote a work called *The Scholar* which was 'three volumes divided into six sections on account of their length, in which he trains the orator from his cradle and brings him to perfection.'[61] He also said that 'Memory [was] the boon most necessary for life.'[62] Hence we are safe in concluding that Pliny thoroughly knew how mnemotechnics worked and himself must have relied heavily on it. A psychologist has suggested that scanning sources to find the part you want depends on silent, not oral, reading and that the increase in silent reading goes hand in hand with 'the increased use of reading to locate information, compare opinions, reference cases and so forth.'[63]

Because of the classical training in mnemotechnics, Greeks and Romans trusted their memories to an extent that we would never trust ours today. Seneca the Elder, for example, laments that:

> I do not deny that my own memory was at one time so powerful as to be positively prodigious, quite apart from its efficiency in ordinary use. . . . My memory used to be swift to pick up what I wanted it to; but it was also reliable in retaining what it had taken in. Now it has been undermined by age, and by a long period of idleness – which can play havoc with young minds too. . . . But I must ask you not to insist on any strict order [*certum aliquem ordinem*] in the assembling of my memories; I must stray at large through all my studies, and grab at random whatever comes my way.[64]

Seneca believes that his retrieval of memories was accurate unless a specific reason, like old age, existed for doubt. He tacitly assumes that everyone writing knows that one is supposed to 'assemble' their memories in 'strict order'. Cicero in his essay *On Old Age*, written when he himself was in his sixties, has Cato at the age of 84 remark:

> in order to exercise my memory, I follow the practice of the Pythagoreans and run over in my mind every evening all that I have said, heard, or done during the day. These employments are my intellectual

189

gymnastics; these the race-courses of my mind; and while I sweat and toil with them I do not greatly feel the loss of bodily strength.[65]

Thomas Macaulay had a similar esteem for his own memory, and a similar concern about its effectiveness as he aged: 'I have now, the whole of our University Fasti by heart; all I mean, that is worth remembering. An idle thing, but I wish to try whether my memory is as strong as it used to be, and I perceive no decay.'[66] Macaulay's attitude must be balanced by that of Charles Darwin, his contemporary, who 'found verbatim memorisation irksome'.[67] A cross-cultural study of memory of the old found that one's cultural expectations may affect the accuracy of one's memory. If you grow up being told that your memory will get worse as you get older, it will. Conversely, if you are Chinese and believe that being old is not something negative, then your memory will remain strong.[68]

In antiquity Seneca may be contrasted to Augustus, who would have appreciated the modern teleprompter; for, after the war at Mutina:

> [H]e never afterwards spoke in the senate, or to the people or the soldiers, except in a studied and written address, although he did not lack the gift of speaking offhand without preparation. Moreover, to avoid the danger of forgetting what he was to say, or wasting time in committing it to memory, he adopted the practice of reading every-thing.[69]

Just because every literate person in classical antiquity received special training in mnemotechnics does not mean that their retrieval was invariably accurate. Nor is it just that the probability of anyone checking for accuracy was low. Sometimes they did, as Aulus Gellius remarks:

> The expression that I quoted above [9.13.11] from Quintus Claudius, 'On account of his great size and savage aspect [*facies*],' I have inquired into by examining several old manuscripts [*libris*], and have found it to be as I wrote it.[70]

What they check, however, differs from what we would check. They seem, to me, to be extraordinarily interested in variations of spelling and word usage, or, at least, their comments that have survived are frequently on those subjects; and yet they did not have dictionaries, as I mentioned in Chapter 5. Gellius might also single out Cicero's making Ajax rather than Hector the speaker, as I quoted in Chapter 11.

Polybios had harsh words for the 'armchair' historian:

> Inquiries from books may be made without any danger or hardship, provided only that one takes care to have access to a town rich in documents or to have a library near at hand. After that one has only to pursue one's researches in perfect repose and compare the accounts of different writers without exposing oneself to any hardship. Personal

inquiry, on the contrary, requires severe labour and great expense, but is exceedingly valuable and is the most important part of history.[71]

This picture of the intrepid ancient historian seeking out eyewitnesses at the time of the event must be tempered by Polybios's description of how the historian should question those eyewitnesses:

> For the inquirer contributes to the narrative [ἐξήγησιν] as much as his informant, since the suggestions of the person who follows the narrative guide the memory of the narrator to each incident, and these are matters in which a man of no experience is neither competent to question those who were present at an action, nor when present himself to understand what is going on, but even if present he is in a sense not present.[72]

We would call this method leading the witness, and would not allow it. They did, because their standard of truth and accuracy necessarily differs from ours.

Truth and accuracy are loaded terms in any age, but through the ages they are even more difficult to deal with, since their meanings vary so much over time and across cultures. So, before delving into their meaning and role in antiquity, I want to stress that I am well aware that other explanations exist or, better, coexist. Not only are the reasons multiple, but they also change throughout antiquity and even contemporaneously. The problem with analysis is that the dissection is always too neat. People are complex. Their products are complex. Here, literally for the sake of argument, I restrict myself to a consideration of only one class of explanation – the cognitive – that has been little explored in classical scholarship.[73]

The most famous and earliest discussion of the yin and yang of truth vs. accuracy occurs in the 'archaeology' of Thucydides. He says:

> As to the speeches that were made by different men . . . it has been difficult to recall with strict accuracy [ἀκρίβειαν] the words actually spoken. . . . Therefore the speeches are given in the language in which, as it seemed to me, the several speakers would express, on the subjects under consideration, the sentiments most befitting the occasion, though at the same time I have adhered as closely as possible to the general sense of what was actually [ἀληθῶς] said. But as to the facts of the occurrences [ἔργα] of the war, I have thought it my duty to give them, not as ascertained from any chance informant nor as seemed to me probable, but only after investigating with the greatest possible accuracy [ἀκριβείᾳ] each detail.[74]

When Thucydides says that in certain cases, such as the speeches, accuracy is not possible, we would tend to agree, since he lived before the invention of shorthand. Even then, the shorthand writers were not always accurate, for Suetonius records that Julius Caesar:

> left several speeches, including some which are attributed to him on insufficient evidence. Augustus had good reason to think that the speech 'For Quintus Metellus' was rather taken down by shorthand writers who could not keep pace with his delivery, than published by Caesar himself . . . [75]

In fact, without tape recorders of some sort it would have been impossible, although Michael Agar points out that making accurate transcripts is no easy matter. He says it takes him eight hours to transcribe one hour of tape, and that is just for the first run-through.[76] When Thucydides makes the further distinction that giving not the gist, as we might say, but what the 'speakers would express' is sufficient to portray the truth, then we know that different criteria are being applied.[77]

Moreover, that gist, according to Aristotle, can be more telling than accuracy. While we would consider mimetic fidelity better – either it happened this way or it did not – Aristotle in the *Poetics* (1460b 8–11) reverses our judgment by putting 'as they ought to be' at the top of his three levels of imitation with 'as they were or are' at the bottom.[78] He also says (*Poetics*, 1451b) that:

> The real difference [between history and poetry] is this, that one tells what happened and the other what might happen. For this reason poetry is something more philosophical and serious than history, because poetry tends to give general truths while history gives particular facts.[79]

Once we understand that the ancient standard of 'accuracy' is 'gist', we can also understand why they would so willingly rely on their memories for retrieval. Most remarkable to me, however, is that research today on autobiographical, or what we might call personal, memory uses precisely the same terms without any reference to the ancient tradition or Thucydides. Craig Barclay writes that:

> Our claim is that overconfidence in the accuracy of autobiographical memories is due to the fact that many 'events' could have happened as remembered because such events are consistent with the theme or gist of one's life – they are truthful but inaccurate recollections. This gist tends to remain fairly stable over time because it is derived from a relatively stable sense of self.[80]

Studies of natural memory have demonstrated that we are incredibly good at remembering gist and just as incredibly bad at remembering verbatim. Ulric Neisser made the landmark study of this issue, when he compared John Dean's testimony before the Senate in the Watergate Hearings with the actual tapes of White House conversations made by Nixon. Neisser concluded that:

> Given the numerous errors in his reports of conversations, what did he [John Dean] tell the truth about? . . . John Dean did not misrepresent this theme [Nixon's own view of Watergate] in his testimony; he just dramatized it. In memory experiments, subjects often recall the gist of a sentence but express it in different words. Dean's consistency was deeper; he recalled the theme of a whole series of conversations and expressed it in different events. Nixon hoped that the transcripts would undermine Dean's testimony by showing that he had been wrong. They did not have this effect because he was wrong only in terms of isolated episodes. Episodes are not the only kinds of facts.[81]

Incidentally, the idea that a head of state wants to preserve his every action for posterity, or at least be able to prove what he said when, must be a symptom of the office. Suetonius wrote about Augustus that: 'Even his conversations with individuals and the more important of those with his own wife Livia, he always wrote out and read from a note-book, for fear of saying too much or too little if he spoke offhand.'[82]

Now let us combine the three strands of my discussion – first, the physical problems of writing in antiquity; second, the classical training in mnemotechnics; and third, the ancient concept of accuracy as gist – when considering how one specific ancient writer, Plutarch, worked. I have chosen Plutarch because of the detailed and acute analysis of his techniques made by C. B. R. Pelling. Pelling says that 'the literary devices which Plutarch employed in streamlining his material . . . [were] conflation of similar items, chronological compression and dislocation, fabrication of circumstantial detail, and the like.'[83] It is remarkable how much Pelling's conclusions about Plutarch's *Lives* match Neisser's conclusions about John Dean's testimony, particularly when considering that John Dean relates events that happened to him and Plutarch relates events that happened to others. One might think that John Dean should have got it right, since he was not just an eyewitness but a participant.

On the other hand, Plutarch could have checked his sources or could have remembered during that space of time between rereading his notes and the actual writing of his *Lives*. Pelling's response would be that the problem is less one of memory and more one of 'literary devices'. I would contend that some instances are, some are not, and some are combinations. In fact, Neisser in a later article distinguishes between two types of auto-biographical memory: 'any actual instance of remembering falls somewhere on a continuum between two extremes: utility (using the past to accomplish some present end) and verity (using memory to recapture what really happened in the past).'[84] Neisser's utility would match Pelling's literary devices. Here, however, I am concerned only with the issue of verity.

193

Consider just one trait, *'abridging* the narrative'.[85] Like John Dean, Plutarch conflates similar events. In his life of Caesar, the Senate exposed and sentenced the Catilinarian conspirators in one session. In reality we know it took three sessions; more to the point, Plutarch knew that it took three sessions, because he wrote about all three in other *Lives*.[86] Did he, then, reduce the events to one session in his life of Caesar because he found 'it tedious to distinguish' among them? That is, is it a literary device to keep the narrative moving? Or was it a failure of memory? Was it both? Can we even decide? In answer to the easiest question, the last, not enough information survives for a certain conclusion.

I think that we try to hold ancient writers to a standard far higher than we ourselves could achieve. How many of us can remember what we wrote last week, much less over a period of several years? To some extent it depends on the passage. You will remember a particularly well-turned phrase. With luck you will remember the gist. More likely, if you are like me, you will find it remarkable how little you remember of actual content. In Flannery O'Connor's words, 'Total non-retention has kept my education from being a burden to me.'[87] We, at least, can easily check our previous works, even the long ones such as books, if we have made a good index or now have the work in digital form. The nub of the problem is that Pelling and other scholars interpret misinformation in Plutarch and other ancient historians as willful reworkings of sources rather than as accidental results caused by lapses in accurate recall. The real point is that memory for what we have read is subject to the same limitations as our basic memory for what we have done.

This area has begun to receive increasing attention by psychologists. Marcia Johnson with others has proposed a framework for 'source monitoring', which is 'the set of processes involved in making attributions about the origins of memories, knowledge, and beliefs.'[88] In other words, can you tell whether something you remember was something you imagined or from reading about it, seeing it on television, or hearing about it from a friend? What are the processes that you go through in order to decide what your source is? What are the kinds of failures or successes you have in doing so? The processes are complex and dependent on the particular person, the particular thing to be remembered, the way that thing was initially encoded or stored, and the situation at the time that the thing is recalled. Steen Larsen distinguishes between memory for events personally experienced and for events experienced only indirectly through, for example, the news media. He calls the first 'experienced events' and the second 'reported events'. His article is more a call for further research than a study of the phenomenon. He does, however, discuss the common-sense idea that reported events would be remembered less well.[89]

Neisser with others suggests that personal involvement in an event, such as the California earthquake in 1989 at Loma Prieta, improves recall, because those who experienced the quake probably talked about the experience more than those who merely heard about it via the news media.[90] Rehearsal, as the phenomenon is termed, makes for better recall. This kind of rehearsal differs little, if at all, from Quintilian's suggestion to practice or rehearse one's speech in order to remember it, as I discussed in Chapter 9. At the same time, something that one experiences directly is likely to have more perceptual and contextual information recorded than something merely read, with the result that the experienced event will be more easily and more accurately recalled.[91] Mark Sadoski and Zeba Quast obtained results similar to those of Neisser in their test of college students' memory for journalistic text: 'readers may be more likely to remember content that is subjectively important (reflected in imagery and affect ratings) than a content viewed as objectively important (reflected in importance ratings).'[92]

A psychological study of good and bad readers, or in technical terms 'high and low comprehenders', may clarify one of the problems involved with memory of written matter:

> [S]ubjects heard short stories and subsequently attempted to recognize sentences as having appeared in those stories or not. If a sentence had in fact occurred, then both groups were equally likely to detect it, but the errors they made were different. The high comprehenders tended to accept falsely sentences that were valid inferences from the passage, even though they had not actually occurred, whereas the low comprehenders were more likely than the high to falsely accept sentences that described invalid inferences from the passage. In short, the high comprehenders appeared to have a much better memory for the gist, although they were not found to be any better at verbatim memory.[93]

Therefore it is likely that a good reader or high comprehender, such as a highly literate classical writer like Plutarch, would make inferences based on 'gist', on what should have happened, even if it did not. If the episode rings true for the theme under discussion, then that is sufficient.[94] In Plutarch's case, it simply does not matter that a different version was given in another place. The second version, if narrated 'correctly', would have been true within its own context – an achievement that Aristotle would have approved of as representing the highest accuracy.

We can see the same process happening on the Ara Pacis where Agrippa is included prominently among the Julio-Claudians, even though we know that he couldn't possibly have been in Rome at the time of the procession.[95] Yet if he had been in Rome, he certainly would have been there. More important, even though he wasn't in Rome physically, surely he was there in spirit. As Barclay and Wellman put it, when writing about autobiographical memory: 'What one remembers then is, at least in part, what could have happened or should have happened in one's life.'[96] Valuing gist over accuracy sometimes affects the classical attitude of who said or did what. *Bons mots*, for example, can be attracted to the most prominent personage. According to Seneca the Elder: 'With them [the Epicureans] . . . whatever Hermarchus says, or Metrodorus, is ascribed to one source. In that brotherhood, everything that any man utters is spoken under the leadership and commanding authority of one alone [Epicurus].'[97]

Schemas, scripts, gist, and natural memory

The idea that actions and speeches should be appropriate to their contexts reflects a basic way people deal with everyday situations. To understand why, some background on research into memory, judgment under uncertainty, and problems with creating intelligent computers are helpful.

In 1978 Ulric Neisser called for a major change in the way psychologists examined memory.[98] Instead of testing memory in the laboratory under exceedingly unnatural conditions, psychologists should investigate it in real, live human beings in real, live settings. An enormous amount of current study focusses on natural memory, which is somewhat awkwardly termed 'ecological' memory, with its subset autobiographical memory.[99] Just how accurate is your own memory? As you grow older, do you mix events? conflate people and things? forget dates? Can you remember where you were on the day John F. Kennedy was assassinated? Most people believe they can. Memories of such momentous events are called flashbulb memories, akin to the flash lighting the scene as one takes a picture. A study of undergraduates' memories of the start of the Gulf War proved such flashbulb memories to be no more accurate three months later than any other memories. Instead, such memories serve as 'benchmarks in our lives that connect personal histories to cultural history.'[100]

What about events that we personally saw or were part of? How accurate are eyewitness accounts? Alas, not very. One of the most striking examples is the horrible story of the woman who was raped while her television set was on, and who, as a result, superimposed the image of the man on the television over that of her assailant. Yes, it was a live broadcast. And, perhaps even more poignant, the man on the television, Donald Thompson, is a psychologist who studies memory.[101] This kind of error in recall is generally attributed to a breakdown in one's ability to monitor the sources for memories, which I mentioned in the previous section. Ronald Reagan provides a more benign example. On an episode of the television news magazine, *60 Minutes*, he told:

> about an act of heroism that he attributed to a real U.S. pilot but that bore an uncanny resemblance to a scene from a Dana Andrews movie released in the 1940s. According to the report of this incident, no record of a similar, real act of heroism could be found.[102]

As a result I now trust certain kinds of circumstantial evidence far more than eyewitness accounts. Clearly such findings have profound implications for our assessment of ancient historians, although my focus here on the role of memory and writing precludes a full discussion.

If our memories of remarkable events are fallible, then our memories of everyday occurrences cannot be any better and most likely must be far worse. Here the work of psychologists and computer scientists is important. In 1932 F. C. Bartlett proposed the idea of 'schemas' as one of the major ways we remember. His concept was extended in the 1970s by Ulric Neisser on the cognitive psychology side and 'narrowed' by Roger Schank and R. Abelson on the computer end in their idea of 'scripts'.[103] Schemas apply to patterns, whether they are recognition of letters, grumpy people, or embarrassing situations. Scripts are subsets that apply more specifically to situations and sequences of actions, such as what you do in a restaurant. For example, we know that something is wrong in a story if a writer sends someone to a McDonald's for roast suckling pig. We know that no Civil War battle could have been fought with jet planes. When we are on a jury, we make similar assessments as to the likelihood that a particular action is in character for the defendant in a particular situation. That we are sometimes misled matters less than that we have in cognitive terms all sorts of scripts and schemas which help us conduct our lives.

Amos Tversky and Daniel Kahneman have done landmark studies on how we actually make decisions compared to how probability theory says we should 'objectively' make decisions. The classic case involves a fictitious person called Linda:

> Linda is 31 years old, single, outspoken and very bright. She majored in philosophy. As a student, she was deeply concerned with issues of discrimination and social justice, and also participated in anti-nuclear demonstrations. . . .
> Linda is a bank teller.
> Linda is a bank teller and is active in the feminist movement.[104]

Which statement is more likely? If you are like 85 per cent of the 142 undergraduates who took this test, you would say the second, because the description of Linda presents the image of a concerned liberal. The idea of her being a bank teller is atypical of liberals and hence excluded unless it tags along with the feminist clause, even though the second statement violates what is called the 'conjunction rule'. We simply do not analyze the components on the basis of logic. 'As one of the subjects said after acknowledging the validity of the conjunction rule, "I thought you only asked for my opinion."'[105] Yet, if you think about it, the probability of two events occurring is much less likely than that of one event. Thus the first statement is more likely than the second. Tversky and Kahneman in test after test, even with experts tested within their fields of expertise, found that we more often than not violate the conjunction rule.[106] We do not follow principles of logic, even when some of us know better, but instead we use heuristic rules to guide us. These 'rules of thumb' work well enough that we apply them in most situations.[107]

In other words, the fact that a Livy or a Plutarch does not deconstruct conflicting accounts into their basic components has a reason beyond literary devices and an explanation that underlies short-term memory. We are more likely to remember something that we can slot into a pre-existing schema.[108] In daily life we rely on those schemas and scripts to decide, for example, what to eat in which restaurant and to understand what feminists do. We tend to notice only the exceptions and the contradictions. Otherwise we would be caught in the same warp as S., the mnemonist, who noticed so much detail that he found it disconcerting when people changed their hair-styles. Hence it makes sense that in antiquity, visual portraits were created of even those long dead like Homer. 'Imaginary likenesses' merely had to be in character, which was far more important than any physical resemblance.[109] So, Plutarch explains in the beginning of his life of Alexander the importance of the telling incident:

> in the most illustrious deeds there is not always a manifestation of virtue or vice, nay, a slight thing like a phrase or a jest often makes a greater revelation of character than battles where thousands fall, or the greatest armaments, or sieges of cities. Accordingly, just as painters get the likenesses in their portraits from the face and the expression of the eyes, wherein the character shows itself, but make very little account of the other parts of the body.[110]

Today we would probably disagree that the 'other parts of the body' are not important for portraits. It would depend, among other things, on who the person was, what they were like, and how they moved.

If the telling incident is contradicted by 'facts', 'honest' historians today would feel compelled to omit that incident.[111] Plutarch, however, resembles John Dean. In his life of Solon, he writes:

> As for his interview with Croesus, some think to prove by chronology that it is fictitious. But when a story is so famous and so well-attested, and, what is more to the point, when it comports so well with the character of Solon, and is so worthy of his magnanimity and wisdom, I do not propose to reject it out of deference to any chronological canons [χρονικοῖς κανόσιν], so called, which thousands are to this day revising, without being able to bring their contradictions into any general agreement.[112]

In this case he *realizes* that the meeting could not have occurred. The truth according to Plutarch, however, is that it doesn't matter whether the meeting occurred, because it if it could have, it would have gone as he reports it.[113]

Another of Plutarch's compositional devices is, according to Pelling, 'the *expansion* of inadequate material, normally by the fabrication of circumstantial detail.'[114] Filling out the details of an incident makes it both more memorable and more believable. Ephorus (405–330 BC), a Greek historian, states the case well:

> On contemporary events, we regard as most believable those who give the most detailed account; on events in the distant past, however, we consider such an account wholly implausible, on the grounds that it is unlikely that all actions and most speeches would be remembered over so long a period of time.[115]

In other words, a schema existed in antiquity to be wary of too much detail, which the source couldn't possibly have known. Yet even today we are likely to fall for that kind of argument in certain situations. Tversky and Kahneman address this failing in their analysis of scenarios, especially those presented by attorneys in criminal cases:

> A detailed scenario consisting of causally linked and representative events may appear more probable than a subset of these events. . . . The attorney who fills in guesses regarding unknown facts, such as motive or mode of operation, may strengthen a case by improving its coherence, although such additions can only lower probability. . . . As Pooh-Bah in the *Mikado* explains, such additions provide 'corroborative details intended to give artistic verisimilitude to an otherwise bald and unconvincing narrative.'[116]

Nor do we remember whole events. Two processes occur: first, we break any given event into little pieces and store them all over the place, so to speak, with the result that one event can have multiple labels.[117] There is no such thing as static memory; it is always in flux. According to Steven Rose, a neurobiologist: 'each time we remember, we in some sense do work on and transform our memories; they are not simply being called up from store and, once consulted, replaced unmodified. Our memories are recreated each time we remember.'[118] Rose's last sentence strikingly recalls and helps explain what Alfred Lord said about oral singers: 'They [the oral singers] create the text anew each time they tell the story.'[119] Results from positron emission tomography (PET), a technique for taking images of the brain as it performs different tasks, are beginning to prove that we do, indeed, store our information, whatever it may be, in different parts of the brain. Moreover, we use different parts of the brain for the same information at different stages of our knowledge from naive to practiced.[120]

Second, Schank says that:

199

The process of story creation, of condensing an experience into a story-size chunk that can be told in a reasonable amount of time, is a process that tends to converge. Subsequent iterations of the same story tend to get smaller rather than larger, and, after a while, all versions of the story are very similar. We leave out more details, more quickly get to the essence. In the end, we are left with exactly the details of the story that we have chosen to remember. In short, story creation is a memory process.[121]

Worse yet similar stories get mixed up with each other. Like John Dean, 'people tend[ed] to confuse stories with similar scripts, misremembering an event that took place in one script and imagining that it might have taken place in another similar script that they had also heard a story about.'[122] Psychologists have tested Schank and Abelson's theory about scripts and, significantly for my study, found that:

> Subjects tended to confuse in memory actions that were stated with unstated actions implied by the script. This tendency increased as more related script instances were studied. Subjects also preferred to recall script actions in their familiar order; a scrambled text that presented some script actions out of order tended to be recalled in canonical order.[123]

Thus it is perfectly reasonable that Plutarch occasionally got mixed up about which actions occurred when or were carried out by whom.

The more I learn about memory the more miraculous it seems that we get anything 'right'. None the less, that does not mean we should assume that all misinformation in ancient writers is due only to lapses in memory. Nor am I claiming that all historians are always 'accurate' even by ancient standards. Some did manipulate what facts they had and sometimes for less than benign purposes. Polybios separates himself from the 'plausible liars', who became stock types.[124] My point is that certain kinds of 'errors' in facts can be explained by the nexus of different standards, different schemas, and their research techniques.

Indeed, Pliny the Elder says that 'It is astounding to what lengths Greek credulity will go; there is no lie so shameless as to lack a supporter.'[125] Elsewhere he revels in revealing their lies: 'Here is an opportunity for exposing the falsehoods of the Greeks. I only ask my readers to endure these with patience since it is important for mankind just to know that not all that the Greeks have recounted deserves to be admired.'[126] Yet Pliny himself is quoted by Aulus Gellius as saying 'that the change of women into men is not a fiction.'[127] Gellius accepts Pliny's account, because Pliny was 'a man of high authority in his day and generation by reason of his talent and his position.'[128] If Gellius's reasons for trusting Pliny seem less than compelling today, consider Pliny's own more extended explanation for false information:

> persons of high position, although not inclined to search for the truth, are ashamed of ignorance and consequently are not reluctant to tell falsehoods, as credulity is never more easily let down than when a false statement is attested by an authority of weight. For my own part I am less surprised that some things are outside the knowledge of gentlemen of the equestrian order . . . than that anything should be unknown to luxury, which acts as an extremely great and powerful stimulus.[129]

One could ask for no better analysis of many an action by government or big business today. James Hankins succinctly summarizes the ancient approach, which he believes held to *c.* AD 1600:

> Implausible overgrowths are cut back on the principle of 'current things' – whatever is considered possible at the current moment. . . . The idea that it [the story about Medusa] is false *simpliciter* does not occur. The truth of tales is judged by all sorts of criteria besides the ability to verify it on the basis of authentic sources or experience: it should be true if edifying, morally sound, or (in the Christian period) theologically correct.[130]

SUMMARY

In this chapter I have discussed how the classical writer went about his task of composing a work. The process of creating a text subtly depends on the tools you have and the cultural context in which you live. While it is the nature of a work such as mine to dissect and examine the individual parts, I hope that it is clear that these parts all work together and do in the aggregate affect the product. If you can physically line up all of your sources, you will combine them differently than if you have to sort them in memory. If checking sources is difficult, you can depend on it that few readers will catch your errors. Today, however, there is 'the legendary figure . . . a Norwegian lighthouse keeper who has nothing to do on long nights throughout the winter but read our books, searching for mistakes.'[131] Mistakes in 'facts' are the least of our problems. As Pogo put it, 'the enemy is us.' First we remember patterns or schemas. Next we remember the anomalies in those patterns. Then we mix them all up. The fallibility of our memories is equaled only by our confidence in them. The fewer Norwegian lighthouse keepers who exist, the more highly we regard the accuracy of our memories. *Caveat lector!*

13

TYPES OF WORKS OR GENRES

In Chapter 12 I considered the process of writing what we might call non-fiction with a focus on history. Here I consider specific components that comprise ancient non-fiction. As throughout this book, I am interested primarily in the memory–literacy axis and the way the ancient tools mediated the results. What precisely is the role of memory, natural and artificial, in the creation and recording of conversations, speeches, translations, and quotations? How does memory affect revisions and digressions?

CONVERSATIONS OR DIALOGUES

The high regard for gist over verbatim accuracy affects the ancient record of conversations and dialogues. Thucydides, as we saw in Chapter 12, admits right from the start that he isn't going to be able to give the precise words of the speeches he heard. Despite that fact, scholars generally treat the speeches, especially Pericles's funeral oration, as if they were recorded verbatim. A. J. Woodman is one of the few historians who believes that 'the majority of each speech in his [Thucydides's] work is the creation of the historian himself.' Despite this appropriate skepticism and even his use of Neisser's study of John Dean, Woodman also maintains 'that through living in an oral culture Thucydides no doubt possessed powers of memory superior to our own.'[1]

Ian Hunter, a psychologist, knew that 'in experiments where people listen to stories and try to recall them . . . there is not much word-for-word recall.' As a result he became 'curious about the popular belief, with its implication that some nonliterate people are gifted with a verbatim, tape-recorder-like ability to assimilate and reproduce lengthy speeches.' Unlike other researchers, he did not stop at examining the evidence for verbatim accuracy, but considered the further and more intriguing problem of 'how did the belief arise and gain currency?'[2] First, as is to be expected, he found no examples whatsoever of 'lengthy verbatim recall', which he defined as a word-for-word correspondence for fifty words or more between text and recall. His survey included not only the Slavic material studied by Parry and

Lord, but also studies of oral African history, the Icelandic sagas, and even, like me, feats from the *Guinness Book of Records*.[3] Two of his conclusions are very important.

First, in his consideration of Thomas Macaulay, renowned for his memory, he found that 'at the level of LVR [lengthy verbatim recall], it is not true that Macaulay had only to read something once in order to be able to recall it word for word. . . . This claim is, by the criterion of LVR, a myth.' He has an excellent source to back up his statement – Macaulay's own account in his diary:

> I walked in the portico, and learned by heart the noble Fourth Act of the Merchant of Venice. There are four hundred lines, of which I knew a hundred and fifty. I made myself perfect master of the whole, the prose letter included, in two hours.[4]

In other words, an expert memorizer like Macaulay took two hours to learn 250 lines – no mean feat in itself. He had to decide specifically to memorize a particular text, and he had to have the text itself.[5]

Second, Hunter concluded that literate people have a textual bias which they project on nonliterate cultures.[6] They, like Woodman, impute accomplishments that simply could not occur without literacy. I realize that Thucydides is literate, but he, unlike Cicero, is not living at a time when court stenography existed. Nor, as far as we know, was such stenography used outside of settings where disputes might arise as to precise wording. Obviously, only the advent of sound recording at the beginning of the twentieth century has enabled us to check both the nonliterate's memory and our own.[7]

Consider what Plato says in the introductory section of the *Theaetetus*:

EUCLIDES: When I visited Athens he [Socrates] repeated to me their [Socrates and Theaetetus] conversation, which was well worth the hearing . . .

TERPSION: . . . But what was this conversation? Could you repeat it?

EUCLIDES: Certainly not, just from memory [ἀπὸ στόματος]. But I made some notes [ὑπομνήματα] at the time, as soon as I got home, and later on I wrote out what I could recall at my leisure. Then, every time I went to Athens, I questioned Socrates upon any point where my memory had failed and made corrections on my return. In this way I have pretty well the whole conversation [πᾶς ὁ λόγος] written down.[8]

Plato recognizes that one hearing is simply not enough to learn a conversation by heart. Instead, Euclides first jots down some notes, then realizes that there are gaps, and keeps going back to Socrates not once, but a number of times, to check what had actually been said. Now I don't think that even with all that toing and froing either Euclides or Socrates would claim verbatim accuracy in the modern sense. The clue lies in the fact that

203

the translator felt compelled to use 'conversation' and not 'word' for λόγος (*logos*).[9] Hence the dialogues of Plato and the 'conversations' of Xenophon all record *logoi*, that is, the gist or the argument of what was said by Socrates and his friends, and not the actual words. It would never have even occurred to them in the late fifth/early fourth centuries BC that they had to use the exact words. It is probably St Jerome in the late fourth century AD in his Vulgate translation of the *Bible* who most popularized the equation of '*logos*' with 'word', when he 'translated' John 1 as, 'In the beginning there was the Word and the Word was with God, and the Word was God', using the Latin '*verbum*' for the Greek '*logos*'.[10]

The *Theaetetus* continues:

EUCLIDES: Let us go indoors, and, while we are resting, my servant [παῖς] shall read to us.

TERPSION: Very well.

EUCLIDES: This is the book [βιβλίον], Terpsion. You see how I wrote the conversation [λόγον] – not in narrative [διηγούμενον] form, as I heard it from Socrates, but as a dialogue [διαλεγόμενον] between him and the other persons he told me had taken part. These were Theodorus the geometer and Theaetetus. I wanted to avoid in the written account the tiresome effect of bits of narrative interrupting the dialogue, such as 'and I said' or 'and I remarked' wherever Socrates was speaking of himself, and 'he assented' or 'he did not agree,' where he reported the answer. So I left out everything of that sort, and wrote it as a direct conversation [διαλεγόμενον] between the actual speakers.[11]

Notice that the work is read to them so that they can more freely mull over the text together. Next, Plato astutely realized that real conversation is saturated with all sorts of filler that is quite distracting in a written work. Donald Norman maintains that:

Written and spoken speech are so different that we are ill-served by artifacts that too readily attempt to convert one into the other. The difference becomes dramatically apparent if you ever read a transcript of a spoken interchange. What appeared to be fluent, graceful, profound speech in reality turns out to be clumsy, repetitive, and ill-formed in the reading.[12]

In fact, I had a curious experience a few years ago, when I assigned students oral reports which were to be converted into written form. While the papers did not have to be written at the time of delivery, several were. I thought the oral reports went well, but when I read the exact same words I found various phrasings jarring and in some instances grammatically incorrect. It is not just that I obviously have different criteria for oral and written words, it is also that speech with its intonations and pauses makes words comprehensible in the way the silent page does not. Last, it is just a mirage of the translation that Plato seems to be saying that he is reporting the 'direct conversation'. Instead, he presents the course of the argument as it went back and forth between the speakers.

Plato used a similar opening, the recounting of a discussion, in five other dialogues (*Phaedo, Symposium, Phaedrus, Parmenides,* and *Timaeus*). Of these the *Phaedrus* is the most interesting for my purposes. Socrates teases Phaedrus (227b–228e) as to whether he has memorized a 'discourse' or 'amusement' (διατριβή) of Lysias on the 'beautiful'. In the course of their bantering, or rather Socrates's, since no one really, except for Alcibiades, challenged Socrates, Phaedrus admits that he 'has taken the book [βιβλίον]' with the text 'to learn the argument [λόγον] thoroughly [ἐξεπιστάμενος]' and is about 'to practice outside the walls'. Phaedrus modestly says that he 'hasn't learned the phrases thoroughly [ῥήματα οὐκ ἐξέμαθον]', but that he can 'go through the thought [διάνοιαν] more or less in summary in order beginning from the first [ἐν κεφαλαίοις ἐφεξῆς δίειμι, ἀρξάμενος ἀπὸ τοῦ πρώτου].' I have given the Greek for my very literal translation to make it clear that in no way do Phaedrus or Socrates imply a verbatim rendition of Lysias's 'amusement', even though Phaedrus is attempting to 'learn the arguments thoroughly'. At the same time Phaedrus uses terminology that reflects the union of rhetorical argument with mnemotechnics, for he begins at the beginning and proceeds in serial order.

By the time of Cicero the literary genre of a conversation or dialogue was so well established that Cicero made up a number of dialogues in which various famous Romans discussed philosophical matters in words that Cicero felt logically fit their personalities or schemas, as we might say. Cicero fully realizes that that is what he is doing, for he tells Atticus:

> The conversation is supposed to have taken place when I was a boy, so that I could not take part. . . . In the five volumes which I composed *On Ends* I gave the Epicurean case to L. Torquatus, the Stoic to M. Cato, and the Peripatetic to M. Piso. I thought that it would excite no jealousy, since none of them was still living. This treatise on the Academy I had given, as you know, to Catulus, Lucullus, and Hortensius. It must be confessed that the matter did not fit the persons, who could not be supposed ever to have dreamed of such abstrusities. So when I read your letter about Varro I seized upon it as a godsend. No name could have been better suited to that brand of philosophy, in which he seems to me to take particular pleasure; and his role is such that I have not succeeded in making my own case appear the stronger. For Antiochus' arguments are very persuasive and I have set them out faithfully; they have the acuteness of their originator with my elegance of style, that is if I can claim such a quality.[13]

While Cicero believes that what he has written rings true for the different schools of philosophy, he none the less finds the discussion out of character for some of his discussants. When Atticus presents him with a more likely participant, he gladly accepts the suggestion. At the same time Cicero feels that his presentation remains faithful to the thoughts of Antiochus, but has been appropriately enhanced by his own more elegant wording. Cicero separates substance from form, and considers the substance and not the words themselves to most represent a particular person. Yet, curiously, he will not violate a certain 'factual' truth: he could not have taken part in reality and so he does not in his dialogue.

The dialogue or conversation obeys certain literary requirements. So Cicero introduces the dialogue 'On Friendship' in words that recall the Theaetetus just quoted. Cicero says:

> I committed the main points of that discussion to memory, and have set them out in the present book in my own way; for I have, so to speak, brought the actors themselves on the stage in order to avoid the too frequent repetition of 'said I' and 'said he,' and to create the impression that they are present and speaking in person.[14]

In the Tusculan Disputations, Cicero similarly says: 'a discussion took place which I do not present in narrative form, but as nearly as I can in the exact words [eisdem fere verbis] of our actual discussion.'[15] Whether or not any Roman writer ever meant the same degree of precision we mean by 'verbatim' is debatable. Mary Beard, for example, notes that in the Arval Acta that 'When the verbatim account is included, the words recorded are not always identical.'[16]

SPEECHES

Openly attributing invented dialogues to dead people is one thing. Revising one's speeches from the text actually delivered is another, especially since the speeches often do not come with a warning that they are not those that were actually spoken at the time. The fact that oral and written works have different requirements, as Plato knew for his dialogues, was also recognized. Aristotle says:

> One should not forget that a different lexis is appropriate for each genus [of rhetoric]. For the written and agonistic [style] are not the same. . . . [Debate] consists in knowing how to speak good Greek; [writing] avoids the necessity of silence if one wishes to communicate to others [who are not present], which is the condition of those who do not know how to write. Written style is most exact; the agonistic is very much a matter of delivery. . . . On comparison, some written works seem thin when spoken, while some speeches of [successful] orators seem amateurish when examined in written form.[17]

Aristotle is able to make the distinction between written and oral rhetoric, because by his time in the fourth century BC speeches were being 'published'. In fact, the earliest ghostwriters (*'logographoi'*) go back to that period. Antiphon and Lysias would write speeches for their clients to deliver in court.[18] Socrates says, 'But why, my friend, should he not have plenty to say? Every rhetorician has speeches ready-made.'[19] Rosalind Thomas makes the excellent point that the speeches were written down precisely so that they could be memorized, because 'orators and litigants wished to give the appearance of speaking extempore.'[20] Demosthenes claimed that 'his speeches were neither altogether unwritten, nor yet fully written out.'[21] Quintilian, however, cautions:

> For my own part I think that we should never write out anything which we do not intend to commit to memory. For if we do, our thoughts will run back to what we have elaborated in writing and will not permit us to try the fortune of the moment. Consequently, the mind will waver in doubt between the two alternatives, having forgotten what was committed to writing and being unable to think of anything fresh to say.[22]

If better speakers did deviate from their prepared texts, then a text written before a speech was delivered would not necessarily reflect the one that was given. The tradition that Pericles is supposed to have been the first to have written his speeches out beforehand does not mean, if Thucydides had had access to those texts, that those texts would have been accurate.[23] Even today, when the custom of the fully prepared speech dominates, much to the dismay of their 'handlers' politicians still say things off the cuff. Moreover, classical historians often felt free to revise the speeches of others. According to Polybios:

> But what is quite untrue to the facts, besides being full of affectation and pedantry, is to expand a speech without point or occasion so as to include every possible argument, and this is what Timaeus with his trick of inventing arguments does to every subject. This practice has indeed caused many statesmen to fail and be brought into contempt, whereas the essential principle, on the contrary, is to select those arguments which are relevant and suitable to the occasion.[24]

It is notable that Polybios does not condemn Timaeus for not reporting speeches precisely as they were given, but only for adding to them. If, however, Timaeus had made a judicious selection, even if it made a rambling, long-winded speaker into a model of logic and conciseness, then by Polybios's standard Timaeus would have been a decent historian.

Among the first to extensively revise his speeches was Demosthenes in the fourth century BC, who, according to Plutarch, did not feel it necessary to limit himself to his own works:

[W]hatever speeches he [Demosthenes] chanced to hear delivered he would take up by himself . . . and he would introduce all sorts of corrections and changes of expression into the speeches made by others against himself, or, contrariwise, by himself against others.[25]

By the time of Quintilian it was such an established custom to rework speeches for publication that he advises:

> Well, you ask, is an orator then always to speak as he writes? If possible, always. If, however, the time allowed by the judge is too short for this to be possible, he will have to cut out much that he should have said, but the published speech will contain the omitted passages. On the other hand, such passages as were uttered merely to suit the character of the judges will not be published for the benefit of posterity, for fear that they should seem to indicate the author's deliberate judgement instead of being a mere concession to the needs of the moment.[26]

The Aristotelian approach holds sway. The speech as delivered is one thing, the speech as published is another. Each form should meet the requirements of its own schema, but significantly not for the reasons that Donald Norman postulates. It is not that oral and written words have different requirements – that is a technical issue of lesser concern here – but rather that the gist or schema for the courtroom is not the same as the gist or schema for the reader.

Revision would be used not just to embellish and improve the text, but also to change the record or the gist of what had occurred. It surely matters that Cicero published his speeches against Catiline three years after they were given, with the explicit desire that they show him like 'Demosthenes . . . in his so-called *Philippics* . . . turned away from this argumentative, forensic type of oratory to appear in the more elevated role of statesman.'[27] Even so, according to George Kennedy, 'we cannot say with certainty of any passage in the *Catilinarians* that it *must* have been added or revised later.'[28] Cicero would most likely have written his introduction (*exordium*) out in full and followed an outline for delivering the rest of the speech. He even mentions one case in which he actually presented a speech from a written draft and refers to it in the midst of another speech: 'Let this speech be read to the court, for, in view of the importance of the occasion, it was delivered from manuscript [*dicta de scripto est*].'[29] Quintilian comments that:

> It is, however, a common practice with those who have many cases to plead to write out the most necessary portions, more especially the beginnings of their speeches, to cover the remainder of that which they are able to prepare by careful premeditation [*cogitatione*] and to trust to improvisation in emergency, a practice regularly adopted by Cicero, as is clear from his note-books [*commentariis*]. But the notes of other orators are also in circulation [*quoque*]; some have been discovered by chance,

just as they were jotted down previous to a speech, while others have been edited in book form [*in libros digesti*], as in the case of the speeches delivered in the courts by Servius Sulpicius, of whose works only three speeches survive. These memoranda, however, of which I am speaking are so carefully drawn up that they seem to me to have been composed by himself for the benefit of posterity. But Cicero's notes were originally intended merely to meet the requirements of the moment, and were afterwards collected by Tiro.[30]

Cicero would have had notes to use as a basis for expanding the gist of what he actually said for publication.[31] For others to obtain copies of the notes could not have been easy, for Quintilian does not say who has them, but merely that they are 'here and there' (*quoque*). Not all orators, however, wanted to publish their speeches. Marcus Antonius, the grandfather of *the* Mark Antony, felt that the absence of a circulating text meant 'that if taxed, as some orators were, with inconsistency, he could flatly deny the charge whatever its truth.'[32] Today we are so accustomed, especially during election campaigns, to the news media juxtaposing what was said that day with what was said sometime in the candidate's past that it is somewhat surprising to me that the *Congressional Record* still remains 'open' for a certain period to allow members of both Houses to edit their remarks before the *Record* is printed.[33]

REVISIONS

By now it should be no surprise that most of the ancient speeches we have are not verbatim texts of the ones given, but were reworked after the fact. Pliny the Younger describes the process. He begins with an explanation for why he reads his speeches to an audience *after* they had been given:

> But it is unnecessary to read a speech already delivered. It would be if the audience and the speech were exactly the same, and you read the speech immediately after delivery; but if you make certain additions and alterations, if you invite new people along with those who heard you before, and after a certain interval, why should it be less suitable to read a speech than to publish it?[34]

He goes on to explain his method of revision:

> Personally, I do not seek praise for my speech when it is read aloud, but when the text can be read after publication, and consequently I employ every possible method of correction. First of all, I go through my work myself; next, I read it to two or three friends and send it to others for comment. If I have any doubts about their criticisms, I go over them again with one or two people, and finally I read the work to a larger audience; and that is the moment, believe me, when I

209

make my severest corrections, for my anxiety makes me concentrate all the more carefully.[35]

His process of several rounds of correction cannot be bettered today, although we tend to circulate drafts rather than hold formal readings. Our circulation of drafts makes sense in one other respect, because English, when written, is much more a visual language than either Greek or Latin. Hence our expository style often seems awkward when read aloud. Pliny the Younger takes such great pains with his writing, because:

> Nothing can satisfy my desire for perfection; I can never forget the importance of putting anything into the hands of the public, and I am positive that any work must be revised more than once and read to a number of people if it is intended to give permanent and universal satisfaction.[36]

Despite or because of all the effort Pliny expends, he found the process of revision a 'disagreeable task I detest and . . . more like one of the hardships of country life [where he was at the time] than its pleasures.'[37]

Drafts could be either on papyrus or on tablets. Cicero used both.[38] Quintilian recommends:

> But whichever we employ, we must leave blank pages [vacuae tabellae] that we may be free to make additions when we will. For lack of space at times gives rise to a reluctance to make corrections, or, at any rate, is liable to cause confusion when new matter is inserted.[39]

Quintilian would have loved the computer with its continuously scrolling display that can be broken at any point for insertions or, even better, that allows for cut-and-paste of any and everything written. For the record, in the process of writing this chapter and juggling all my excerpts, I have relied heavily on the computer's ability to find things and to move them around in order to circumvent the limitations of my short-term memory.[40] It must be added, however, that Quintilian advised against those:

> [who] with the utmost speed of which their pen is capable . . . write in the heat and impulse of the moment. They call this their rough copy [silvam]. They then revise what they have written. . . . But while the words and the rhythm may be corrected, the matter is still marked by the superficiality resulting from the speed with which it was thrown together. The more correct method is, therefore, to exercise care from the very beginning . . . in such a manner that it merely requires to be chiselled into shape, not fashioned anew.[41]

Whether or not Pliny the Younger followed Quintilian's advice is not known, but we do know that Pliny and Tacitus swapped drafts, for Pliny writes to Tacitus:

I have read your book, and marked [*adnotavi*] as carefully as I could the passages which I think should be altered or removed, for if it is my custom to tell the truth, you are always willing to hear it; no one accepts criticism so readily as those who best deserve praise. Now I am awaiting the return of my book from you, with your comments: a fair exchange which we both enjoy. I am delighted to think that if posterity takes any interest in us the tale will everywhere be told of the harmony, frankness, and loyalty of our lifelong relationship. It will seem both rare and remarkable that two men of much the same age and position, and both enjoying a certain amount of literary reputation (I can't say much about you when it refers to me too), should have encouraged each other's literary work.[42]

Knowing that Pliny was deeply concerned about posterity in the publication of his speeches, I cannot help but wonder whether he revised his letters accordingly. He does say in the opening letter that his letters 'were composed with some care.'[43] Otherwise it seems to me that the passage implies that he had some potentially unwelcome suggestions for Tacitus to correct and that he was trying to ease the pain, for pain it is to correct.

I have already mentioned several times how Plato was supposed to have worked on the opening lines of the *Republic*. Dionysius of Halicarnassus adds that 'Plato, even at the age of eighty, never let off combing and curling his dialogues and re-plaiting them in every way.'[44] Suetonius provides an interesting glimpse into the writing habits of Vergil:

> When he [Vergil] was writing the 'Georgics,' it is said to have been his custom to dictate each day a large number of verses which he had composed in the morning, and then to spend the rest of the day in reducing them to a very small number, wittily remarking that he fashioned his poem after the manner of a she-bear, and gradually licked it into shape. In the case of the 'Aeneid,' after writing a first draft in prose and dividing it into twelve books, he proceeded to turn into verse one part after another, taking them up just as he fancied, in no particular order. And that he might not check the flow of his thought, he left some things unfinished, and, so to speak, bolstered others up with very slight words, which, as he jocosely used to say, were put in like props, to support the structure until the columns should arrive.[45]

Vergil uses the same method as Pliny the Younger in composing. First, write in your head, then dictate to a scribe what you have written. Next, Vergil becomes more like Plato agonizing over each and every word. Two things are striking about the writing of the *Aeneid*: Vergil had an outline in prose and, as customary, by the first century BC, the author and not some later commentator divided the work into 'books'. The average length of a roll had begun to affect and shape the composition. Vergil's further polishing of individual parts, as the fancy struck him, resembles the common advice today of 'just get it down' and then revise. Unfinished, or at least short, lines remain to this day in the *Aeneid*. Great writers, however, were not the only ones to take pains with their compositions. Suetonius writes that Nero followed the Quintilian method of writing:

> I have had in my possession note-books [*pugillares*] and papers [*libelli*] with some well-known verses of his [Nero's], written with his own hand and in such wise that it was perfectly evident that they were not copied or taken down from dictation, but worked out exactly as one writes when thinking and creating; so many instances were there of words erased or struck through and written above the lines.[46]

Cicero, who often sent his drafts to Atticus, writes to Atticus: 'I fear you will run your red 'pencil' [*miniata cerula*] under many passages in it [my treatise].'[47] He later tells Atticus: 'I am glad you like my book, from which you quoted the very gems; and they seemed to me all the more sparkling for your judgment on them. For I was afraid of those red "pencils" of yours [*cerulas tuas miniatulas illas*].'[48] Strictly speaking, the *miniata cerula* most resembles a red crayon today, for it was red wax.[49] A crayon-like mark or line could be made at a troublesome part, which would then be explained in the accompanying letter. This method would resemble that used for ancient commentaries on texts, as discussed in Chapter 12. It seems less likely that the red marker was used for writing, since we have no mention of that kind of use. Another time Cicero responds to Atticus's corrections by returning the same copy on which Atticus had commented with his own corrections and insertions. He then asks Atticus to 'read this, after it has been transferred to good papyrus, privately to your dinner guests.'[50] Cicero's request implies that between his and Atticus's markings the text is difficult to read and that Atticus has the staff to copy it on to better papyrus.

The staff must have been numerous, because in another letter to Atticus Cicero says:

> Brutus has sent me word from T. Ligarius that the mention of L. Corfidius in my defence of Ligarius is an error on my part. It was a mere *lapsus memoriae* [slip of the memory], as they say. I knew that Corfidius was a close friend of the Ligarii, but I find that he died before the case. So pray commission Pharnaces, Antaeus, and Salvius to delete his name in all the copies.[51]

This letter is interesting also because it corrects a matter of content, not just of infelicity of style or phrase, as more frequently happened.

212

'Corrections in stride'

Much the same processes of correction apply to the revision of other kinds of texts. They, too, would be circulated to small groups of friends, read aloud, revised, and recirculated, until the author, like Pliny the Younger, was satisfied that he had done the best he could. In this section I want to focus on a characteristic of oral composition that carries over into literate composition in antiquity in part because of the logistical limitations of their writing tools.

Richmond Lattimore noticed that when Herodotus either forgot a particular piece of information or made a mistake, he merely broke his narrative at the point of his realization to make the addition or the correction.[52] This phenomenon Lattimore called a 'forward, or point to point, or progressive style . . . [c]orrection-in-stride.' Lattimore believes that 'the whole History is, substantially at least, a first draft which was never revised, nor meant to be, because the first draft was always meant to be the final draft.'[53] He particularly remarks on the logistics:

> To insert the Athenian and Lacedaemonian excursuses (1.59–69 or whatever you think the insert is) *into* an *already written* sequence would have been no simple process but a bitterly difficult one. What has been gained to justify the labor and time spent? It was hard enough to write the History anyway.[54]

He also notes that early Greek 'conspicuously lacks the terminology for such stages and processes as successive drafts, revision, editing, etc.,' all of which he places in the first half of the fourth century BC.[55]

Herodotus's habits make sense, because he was writing at a time when composition was predominately oral. The habit continues, though to a lesser extent, into later Roman writings despite Quintilian's warnings:

> Space must also be left for jotting down the thoughts which occur to the writer out of due order, that is to say, which refer to subjects other than those in hand. For sometimes the most admirable thoughts break in upon us which cannot be inserted in what we are writing, but which, on the other hand, it is unsafe to put by, since they are at times forgotten, and at times cling to the memory so persistently as to divert us from some other line of thought.[56]

I have already quoted Cicero's remark to Atticus about a manuscript so encumbered with corrections that it needed to be transferred to fresh papyrus. Sometimes, however, it simply wasn't worth the effort to make an adjustment. So Plutarch in his life of Pericles breaks the narrative to tell a variety of things about Aspasia. He, unlike Herodotus, is fully aware that he might have integrated the information more gracefully, so he excuses himself to the reader: 'These things [about Aspasia] coming to my

213

recollection, as I write, it were perhaps unnatural to reject and pass them by. But to return to the war against the Samians.'[57] What is significant is that Plutarch admits that he is writing off the top of his head, as we might say, because in his day it would, indeed, have been unnatural not to.

DIGRESSIONS

Pliny the Elder calls his *Natural History*: 'a work of a lighter nature, as it does not admit of talent, of which in any case I possessed only quite a moderate amount, nor does it allow of digressions [*excessus*], nor of speeches or dialogues, nor marvellous accidents or unusual occurrences.'[58] To be sure, there are no speeches and dialogues. The absence of 'marvellous accidents or unusual occurrences' can be understood in the light of the ancient view of accuracy discussed in Chapter 12. It is the denial of digressions that I find marvelous and unusual in equal amounts, for the *Natural History* seems like one enormous digression with little discernible order to it. It is almost as if Pliny had poured out the contents of his mind in thirty-six rolls. Unlike Aulus Gellius, who, as already mentioned, 'adopted the same haphazard order that [he] had previously followed in collecting it', Pliny has ordered his information or, as he calls it, his 'facts, histories, and observations'. In his Table of Contents in Book 1, he includes an overall count of '*res et historiae et observationes*' for all the succeeding books. Since those numbers – for example, Pliny says 100 authorities, but cites 473 – do not match what modern scholars have counted, Ferraro must be right that they are used as '*numeri infiniti*' in much the same way I might say that I have consulted hundreds of works for this book.[59]

Francesco Della Corte provides an analytical chart to the *Natural History* that is topped by the 'world', which is divided into three major spheres: the heavens, the air, and the earth.[60] Remnants of these divisions can still be seen in Roget's *Thesaurus*. The last of Pliny's major categories, the earth, is, in turn, divided into the most numerous topics: land and water, fire, man, animals, trees, medicine, and metals. His text seems more a jumble of oddities than a reasoned work on natural history, perhaps because we consider 'natural history' to be a science rather than a subject of humanities. We find it strange that Pliny discusses Julius Caesar's method of dictating to several secretaries simultaneously. Yet our problem with Pliny is more than his subject matter. It is the very ordering of his contents, for he discusses what we consider to be art history in his books on precious metals, rather than in Book 7, which is on man.

Our confusion with Pliny is twofold. What is a digression and how should one organize facts, histories, and observations? Herodotus believes that digressing is an integral part of his work, for he says things like 'But I wonder – for my *logos* from the beginning has always required additions.'[61] As a result, he feels quite free to break into his narrative with some tidbit or another. It is an element of oral style. By the time of Pliny the Elder digressions were not quite the same thing. They had become a formal part of a speech during the Hellenistic period, according to Cicero, who attributes their inclusion to Hermagoras.[62] One of the best definitions of a digression comes from Quintilian:

> In the natural order of things the *statement of fact* is followed by the *verification*. . . . But before I enter on this portion, I have a few words to say on the opinions held by certain rhetoricians. Most of them are in the habit, as soon as they have completed the *statement of facts*, of digressing to some pleasant and attractive topic with a view to securing the utmost amount of favour from their audience. . . . Such passages may also serve as a kind of peroration after the main question. The Greeks call this παρέκβασις, the Romans *egressus* or *egressio* (digression). They may however, as I have said, be of various kinds and may deal with different themes in any portion of the speech. For instance we may extol persons or places, describe regions, record historical or even legendary occurrences. . . . Παρέκβασις may, I think, be defined as the handling of some theme, which must however have some bearing on the case, in a passage that involves digression from the logical order of our speech. . . . For whatever we say that falls outside the five divisions of the speech already laid down is a digression, whether it express indignation, pity, hatred, rebuke, excuse, conciliation or be designed to rebut invective.[63]

Quintilian himself begins the topic and then makes what we would call a 'digression', but which, since it does not seek to arouse any particular emotion, does not qualify in his terms as a digression. It is the emotional appeal that makes a Latin digression a digression. Otherwise, it is a useful piece of information, even if it is only tangentially associated with the subject. So Livy prefaces his excursus on 'how the Roman State would have fared in a war with Alexander [the Great]' with an explanation:

> Nothing can be thought to have been more remote from my intention, since I first set about this task, than to depart unduly from the order of events, and to aim, by the introduction of ornamental digressions, at providing as it were agreeable bypaths for the reader, and mental relaxation for myself. Nevertheless the mention of so great a prince and captain evokes certain thoughts which I have often silently pondered in my mind.[64]

Pliny gives us lots of digressions, but makes no attempt to arouse anything other than wonder and delight at 'natural history'. The real problem with Pliny is that he seems like a combination of a modern almanac and Ripley's *Believe It or Not*. Let us look at his organization in more detail. For example, if he thinks of each roll as a room in a thirty-six-room villa, then all he has to remember is the order in which he walks through those rooms and what he has distributed where according to the *loci*-form of mnemo-technics. The more order he can impose on what he has to remember the more he will remember. Hence he generally proceeds from what he con-siders to be the most important to the least important.

In the overall arrangement of rolls he treats the heavens and air first, then the earth. Within, for example, the metals, he starts with gold, then *minium*, silver, bronze, iron, lead, painting, stones, and gems. The only categories that seem odd in the listing are *minium* and painting. According to the *Oxford Latin Dictionary*, '*minium*' is cinnabar, a sulphide of mercury. Pliny in the ordering of metals, as with the Ages, should naturally discuss silver next, but he also has to discuss *minium*. It is easiest for him to remember if he recalls that it is a sulphide and hence puts it right after 'lead sulphide', but before silver because it, and this is equally important (33.36.111), 'is also found in silver mines'. Painting (*pictura*) comes where it does, because:

> We have now practically indicated the nature of metals, in which wealth consists, and of the substances related to them, connecting the facts in such a way as to indicate at the same time the enormous topic of medicine and the mysteries of the manufactories and the fastidious subtlety of the processes of carving and modelling and dyeing. There remain the various kinds of earth and of stones, forming an even more extensive series, each of which has been treated in many whole volumes, especially by Greeks. For our part in these topics, we shall adhere to the brevity suitable to our plan, yet omitting nothing that is necessary or follows a law of Nature. And first we shall say what remains to be said about painting.[65]

He uses as 'the point of departure . . . stones and soils from which the pigments are extracted' which he considered in Book 34.[66] In other words, each item discussed has a good and, significantly, memorable reason for its location in the overall scheme.

When Pliny has to order information within the individual topics, he also proceeds the same way and, as Isager shows, consistently.[67] Within a particular category Pliny proceeds in a hierarchical order from most to least important in a manner that resembles newspaper reporting today. For example, he says, 'After thus defining the periods of the most famous artists, I will hastily run through those of outstanding distinction, throw-ing in the rest of the throng here and there.'[68] As Daly pointed out, Pliny uses rough alphabetical order only as a last resort.[69] It is as if he walks through his Villa Memoriae, looking first at the most important furniture in each room, of what those pieces are constituted, and then at whatever remains to be seen in a sorted order, whether it is seemingly tangential like the *minium* or alphabetical. The art of memory also accounts for his proceeding from named and titled works to those without either, but with specific locations.

TRANSLATIONS

Consider the *Topica* (*Topics*) of Cicero. I quote fairly extensively from its Preface, because Cicero gives a full description of its genesis with a number of details of interest:

> When we [Cicero and his friend, Gaius Trebatius Testa] were together in my Tusculan villa and were in the library, each of us according to his fancy unrolling the volumes which he wished, you hit upon certain Topics of Aristotle which were expounded by him in several books. Excited by the title, you immediately asked me what the subject of the work was. And when I had made clear to you that these books contained a system developed by Aristotle for inventing arguments so that we might come upon them by a rational system without wandering about, you begged me to teach you the subject. . . . Not so much to avoid labour as because I thought it would be for your good, I urged you to read the books yourself, or acquire the whole system from a very learned teacher of oratory whom I named. You had tried both, as you told me. But you were repelled from reading the books by their obscurity; and that great teacher replied that he was not acquainted with these works, which are, as I think, by Aristotle. I am not indeed astonished in the slightest degree that the philosopher was unknown to the teacher of oratory, for he is ignored by all except a few of the professed philosophers. . . . When you repeated your request again and again . . . I was afraid that my hesitation might be thought to be ingratitude or discourtesy. But you yourself can best testify how busy I was when we were together; and when I left you, and set out on my way to Greece . . . on reaching Velia I saw your family and your home, I was reminded of this debt. . . . Therefore, since I had no books with me, from memory recalled I wrote down these things on the voyage itself.[70]

First, as we do today, Cicero and his friend are browsing by title. When they see something interesting, they look inside. Second, Trebatius, who practiced civil law (Cicero, *Topica*, 19.72) and who could read Greek, found Aristotle's *Topics* hard going – a fact that should be of some consolation to those of us today who find it equally obscure. Third, Aristotle at the time Cicero is writing, *c.* 44 BC, is not well known at all, though that situation was in the process of being remedied, in part by Cicero himself. Fourth, Cicero puts off writing his translation, mainly because he doesn't have the time, but also because he fittingly needs a prod to his memory and, we might say today, his conscience. I say 'fittingly' because Cicero, as an accomplished

217

practitioner of mnemotechnics, would see a great significance in a place, Velia, that is a *locus*, jogging his memory. Remember his feelings about the sight of the Curia (*On Ends*, 5.1.2), which I quoted in Chapter 8. Fifth and finally, the whole work is produced from memory, but is supposed to be 'Aristotle's'.[71]

The last point has been the most worrisome to scholars. Cicero's *Topica* bears only a superficial resemblance to Aristotle's *Topics*. Various explanations have been offered. Some translate '*conscribo*' as 'writing a summary' rather than as 'writing down', as I adapted the LCL translation. Like a condensed book today, only a passing likeness to the original would be necessary. Eleanor Stump has suggested that the title of the original work, '*Aristotelis Topica*', means not *the* Topics of Aristotle, but 'Aristotelian Topics', and therefore Cicero's version is neither a translation nor a summary, but merely about the subject of Aristotelian topics.[72] Yet Cicero, in two different places – a letter to Trebatius and the Preface to the actual work – has said that he is presenting Aristotle's *Topics*. The crux of the matter is that writers in his period simply did not have our concept of verbatim.[73]

Aristotle, however, would judge Cicero's version of his *Topics* not on the basis of whether an exact translation was made, as we would, but on the basis of whether Cicero had understood his treatise and made an accurate representation of its arguments. Aristotle had himself done something quite similar, as Cicero records:

> Aristotle collected the early books on rhetoric . . . he made a careful examination of the rules of each author and wrote them out in plain language, giving the author's name, and finally gave a painstaking explanation of the difficult parts. And he so surpassed the original authorities in charm and brevity that no one becomes acquainted with their ideas [*praecepta*] from their own books, but everyone who wishes to know what their doctrines are, turns to Aristotle, believing him to give a much more convenient exposition. He, then, published his own works and those of his predecessors, and as a result we became acquainted with him and the others as well through his work.[74]

The first half of the quotation tells what Aristotle did. He paraphrased and explained the works of his predecessors. The last sentence, however, is the crucial one. If you can say it better than in the original, then you have not done an injustice to the original, but instead have made the original more available. It is, to use the Greek, the *logos* and not the *word* that counts. In that respect Cicero was well within his rights in his version of Aristotle's *Topics*.

In fact, verbatim is not the only kind of verbal accuracy, for, as everyone knows, literal translations often fail to capture the 'flavor' of the original text and sometimes make it downright incomprehensible. For example, in English we say 'it's raining cats and dogs', but the French say 'il tombe des cordes'. I am not going to comment on either expression. From my own occasional adaptations of modern translations here, it should be clear that my idea of an accurate translation differs from many of the translators of our 'standard' editions, in part because I have a particular purpose: to understand the Greeks and Romans from their point of view. I am not trying to bridge the gap between our culture and theirs, but rather I am trying to figure out the characteristics of that gap. Hence I need to know what they said literally, not figuratively.

Sometimes, of course, no equivalent expression exists. Either the original word has to be used or a cumbersome paraphrase. Pliny the Elder (*Natural History*, 34.65), in a passage well known to classical art historians, says that 'Latin has no word for "*symmetria*" [symmetry].' Vitruvius speaks directly to his reader: 'Harmonics [*Harmonice*] is an obscure and difficult branch of musical science, especially for those who do not know Greek. If we desire to treat of it, we must use Greek words, because some of them have no Latin equivalents.'[75] Then there are the words that mean one thing in one language and something else in another. Vitruvius noted a whole group of such terms for parts of buildings. For example, he says: 'As a Greek term, ξυστός means a colonnade of large dimensions in which athletes exercise in the winter time. But our people apply the term "*xysta*" to uncovered walks which the Greeks call παραδρομίδες.'[76] Cicero recognizes these facets of translation. He says:

> I translated [*converti*] the most famous orations of the two most eloquent Attic orators, Aeschines and Demosthenes, orations which they delivered against each other. And I did not translate them as an interpreter [*interpres*], but as an orator [*orator*], keeping the same ideas and forms, or as one might say, the 'figures' of thought, but in language which conforms to our usage. And in so doing, I did not hold it necessary to render word for word [*verbum pro verbo*], but I preserved the general style and force of the language [*genus omne verborum vimque*]. For I did not think I ought to count them out to the reader like coins, but to pay them by weight, as it were.[77]

In the *Brutus*, Cicero explains that he became proficient in Greek in part out of necessity:

> This exercise [preparing and delivering declamations] I practised much in Latin, but more often in Greek . . . partly too because the foremost teachers, knowing only Greek, could not unless I used Greek, correct my faults nor convey their instruction.[78]

QUOTATIONS AND CITATIONS

Quotations suffer from the same problems as lengthier translations. Classical authors generally do not check them for accuracy for the three reasons already discussed: the logistical problems of using ancient texts; the wide-spread belief in the excellence of their memories; and a lack of any real concern for verbatim accuracy. I know one major class of exceptions. Cicero, in a letter to Atticus (9.10), which I quoted in Chapter 3, cites passages from twelve letters he had received from Atticus between 21 January and 9 March, 49 BC. Presumably these citations are precisely what Atticus had written. In fact, unlike the case with literary or philosophical works, Cicero never felt the need to memorize letters in the first place. When he wished to cite them he knew he had to go back to the source. Frank Frost similarly concluded that Plutarch:

> where his Latin sources can be checked . . . is quite accurate. This would seem to suggest a general rule: that the more familiar Plutarch was with his source, or story, the more likely he was to be a bit casual with his data; when on unfamiliar ground, he is more careful and has perhaps made more precise notes. This is by no means an unknown tendency in scholarship.[79]

Plutarch is one of the great believers in a trained memory, as I have quoted him in Chapter 7, and naturally believes that his is infallible.

The entire gamut of errors occurs in ancient quotations. The words are wrong. The author cited is wrong. The speakers are incorrect. The passage is from another work.[80] These kinds of mistakes are often due to various errors in source monitoring. For example, one psychological study 'found that subjects were more likely to misattribute statements made by one speaker to another when the two speakers had described the same events than when they had described different events.'[81] One of the problems is that, as I mentioned in the previous chapter, we do not store our memories whole, but in pieces so to speak. The result is that 'recognition and identification of origin [of a particular memory] may be based on different aspects of memory or different relative contributions of heuristic and systematic processes.'[82]

Mistakes in quotations in classical texts may be at an even more basic level: that of the word. Sometimes words are misinterpreted, often with hilarious results. Livy misreads Polybios's 'θυρεούς' (shields) as 'θύρας' (doors), with the result that he has miners using doors to fight off attackers.[83] More serious are the times when the meaning is changed. Livy takes the Greek 'τοῖς μὲν οὖν ὅλοις' ('*general* satisfaction') to mean '*ad unum*' ('unanimously').[84] Jacqueline de Romilly has done a fascinating study of the word-by-word differences between Thucydides and Plutarch to demonstrate that 'what an author leaves out in a quotation or an imitation is generally what was most intimately linked with the personal views of the writer he takes after.'[85] More remarkable to me are the numerous occasions when the ancient authors are right. For example W. C. Hembold and E. N. O'Neill say that 'His [Plutarch's] memory was prodigious, and his confidence in it no less so, as when he asserts that such-and-such does *not* occur in Plato (*Moralia*, 1115C–D); and sure enough it does not.'[86]

The real problem is that we have to assume that Plutarch is correct, because not all of Plato has survived against which to check Plutarch's accuracy. Even more troublesome is that we often do not know which is the 'original' version of a statement if more than one version has survived. The situation is especially acute for the Pre-Socratic philosophers, none of whom has survived intact. Instead, scholars reconstruct both their works and thoughts by using the summaries and quotations embedded in other classical works. Margaret Williamson eloquently lays out the problem of reconstructing a writer like Sappho who has survived primarily by quotation in others. She, like me, presents 'modern' versions of the problem. In a witty illustration she reduces Hamlet's soliloquy ('To be or not to be' in Act 3, Scene 1) to the kind of fragmentary snippets we have for Sappho and then shows how a scholar today would reconstruct it . . . erroneously, of course.[87] Likewise, the major Athenian dramatists (Aeschylus, Sophocles, and Euripides) have not survived in the original, in part because actors made so many changes – probably in ways quite similar to that of some performers of Gilbert and Sullivan today – that the texts had become corrupt, as was recognized a century later, when Lycurgus in 330 BC, according to Plutarch, passed a law that:

> their tragedies be written out and kept in a public depository [ἐν κοινῷ . . . φυλάττειν], and that the clerk of the State [τὸν τῆς πόλεως γραμματέα] read them to the actors who were to perform their plays for comparison of the texts and that it be unlawful to depart from the authorized text in acting.[88]

Bernard Knox believes that 'This official copy is presumably the one which Ptolemy Euergetes I borrowed (and kept) for the Alexandrian library.'[89]

Now consider the fact that the majority of the texts we have are transmitted through medieval intermediaries. Eric Turner remarks that 'it has not yet proved possible to trace the derivation of one papyrus manuscript from another, let alone the descent of a medieval manuscript from a papyrus one.'[90] To my knowledge, no one has made a study of the ancient uses of classical sources for whole periods and not limited to individual authors or genres like the Pre-Socratics or Greek lyric poets. It is somewhat daunting to learn that quotation marks are modern with their first attestation in the 1880s.[91] Yet in the end, despite our heightened skepticism about truth and accuracy, we are just as trusting and naive as writers were in antiquity. The worse case is probably Homer, who remains an active battleground for classicists.[92] If Homer was a fully oral poet, how were the *Iliad* and the *Odyssey* transmitted to us? Was he written down immediately? If not, when? And, of course, how? All we know is that there was some kind of 'edition' in the sixth century BC, possibly at the instigation of Peisistratos.

We also know that the scholars working in Alexandria in the Hellenistic period decided that the texts they had were terribly corrupt and that they made their own emendations. After 150 BC the text appears to stabilize and the 'wild', divergent readings disappear.[93] How in the world do we know that the Alexandrians got it 'right', especially when we know that matters of style are exceedingly hard to define?

We don't even know if 'our' Homer follows the Alexandrian 'edition'. Eric Turner describes the situation:

> The Homeric papyri have in common the characteristic of adding extra lines, leaving out lines known to us, and containing substantial variant phrases or formulas. One such papyrus, of *Iliad* viii, preserves 93 lines all told: of these 21 (i.e. one in four) are extra lines, and the manuscript has also 27 peculiar variants of its own.[94]

Consequently, if a quotation of Homer does not match the text we have, is it because the quoter, for example Plato, had a different text from ours, since Plato lived before the Alexandrian edition was made? Or did Plato merely botch the quote?[95] For instance, we do know that Quintilian 'misquoted' Vergil, even though he should have had access to a decent text, since he was born only fifty years later than Vergil. The assumption here is not that Quintilian's memory failed him, but that 'the MSS of Quintilian were influenced by an already corrupt Virgilian tradition.'[96] In other words, an older manuscript is not necessarily more reliable than a more recent one.[97] What may be noteworthy is how quickly scholars slide over the problem, and that includes me, for I have given a large number of quotations as examples without ever saying anything about this issue. I hope and assume that the ancient sources, as they have survived, have preserved the gist, if not the accuracy.

Similar issues arise with ancient citations of sources where the author has paraphrased or summarized his source. If you recall, Pliny the Elder indulges in an ancient form of overkill. Book One of the *Natural History* is an extended list of the contents of each of the succeeding books. Pliny first gives the topics, then the count of things mentioned, and finally all the authorities (literally 'from the authors') he has consulted. He sees no necessity to directly unite the individual titbit of information with its source. Nor does he give the names in the order in which he cites them, but first lists the Romans, then the foreigners (*externis*). Sometimes he groups professions together, such as doctors; sometimes he helpfully identifies individuals by their profession; at other times he omits that information.[98]

Pliny shows one other idiosyncrasy in his citations. He frequently refers to his sources not in the format of author and work, but rather in the formula of 'so-and-so who wrote on such-and-such,' as in 1.35: 'Metrodorus who wrote on architecture.'[99] In other words, Pliny considers sources to be not the works, but the people who wrote those works; and the way to identify those people, if they are not sufficiently well known just by their name, is to say what they wrote about. Hence, even within the text itself, Pliny, if he gives a source, follows the same system. Famous people are cited by name only, the not so famous with a qualifying description.[100] Nor does Pliny always say directly who his source was. Nineteenth- and early twentieth-century scholars were particularly fond of imputing earlier sources for various authors.[101] Today, philologists are more circumspect in much the same way that archaeologists are less inclined to 'restore' fragmentary ancient art. Despite our difficulties in pinning down Pliny's sources, he is quite pleased with his scholarship: 'You will deem it a proof of this pride of mine that I have prefaced these volumes with the names of my authorities.'[102]

CONCLUSION

Your tools work together. Change one and the results change.[103] In this chapter I have considered how memory, which I consider a tool, forms the glue that holds together the written word in classical antiquity. If sources are not easy to check, then you rely more on your memory. If you rely more on your memory, then your standards of accuracy will of necessity differ from those who will actually check statements against a text or even a videotape today. Because the classical tools did not allow great precision in verbatim accuracy, no one even thought about being accurate in that way. Instead you concentrated on making sure you got the argument absolutely right. *How* Socrates or Aristotle said something mattered far less than *what* either said. Hence you can, of course, revise your speeches after they were given. It only matters that you get the gist right.

If correction of your drafts is difficult, you will more carefully choose your words before setting them down. The only way you can do that is by working out what you want to say in memory first. You will also be less inclined to make changes and, when you do, you will be more 'conversational' in those corrections by leaving your mistake intact, and saying, as if in an informal discussion, 'No, what I really meant was . . . '.

I have not considered the entire gamut of classical writings, although many of my points can be broadly applied. Nor, as should be quite clear, have I been at all exhaustive within my chosen categories. Instead I hope that this chapter has made clear the general *modus operandi* for classical writers.

223

14

INDIRECT APPLICATIONS OF THE ART OF MEMORY

The art of memory was more than a technique for memorizing. Because it was a basic component of rhetoric and education, its effects permeated classical life. I have already discussed how it affected the work habits of the highly literate. Here I consider some indirect examples, mainly literary and many of which can be and have been understood and interpreted without a knowledge of mnemotechnics, although that knowledge deepens our understanding of classical culture.

First, some clarifications. Varro in his discussion of words related to '*meminisse*' ('to remember') says that:

> From the same [root] is *monere* 'to remind', because he who *monet* 'reminds', is just like a memory. So also the *monimenta* 'memorials' which are on tombs, and in fact alongside the highway, that they may *admonere* 'admonish' the passers-by that they themselves were mortal and that those passers-by are too. From this, the other things that are written and done to preserve their *memoria* 'memory' are called *monimenta* 'monuments'.[1]

According to this passage, all funerary markers, whether simple burials or elaborate structures like the Mausoleum of Halicarnassus, are artificial reminders. The category includes monuments erected by the 'state' to commemorate events or glorify the state, such as the Column of Trajan after the Dacian Wars or the city treasuries at major sanctuaries like Delphi and Olympia.[2] While all these things record and preserve the past for those living in the present and the future, they do not all do so in the same way. It is important to understand the differences, because they reflect different attitudes to memory, different technologies, and different cultural contexts. Hence the treasuries are not good illustrations of the system of *loci*, but the Column of Trajan is, not because it commemorates a historical event, but because of the way in which it does so.

As the passage from Varro makes clear, any object can provoke memories. For Proust, it was madeleines. Such objects do not concern me here, because they are not constructed to be reminders, but rather they are memorable just by their very being. A reminder, however, that is specifically created for recalling specific memories is of interest. Here I can only survey some representative examples of the various types of triggers for memory.

LITERARY SHIELDS

Consider two contrasting verbal descriptions of visual decorations: the shield of Achilles in the *Iliad* (18.483–608) and the shield of Aeneas in the *Aeneid* (8.626–728). Both heroes need new armor. Both have doting mothers who get Hephaistos to make a special set. Both shields are decorated with a number of scenes that have great import for the heroes and the readers of the two epics, yet the decoration on neither shield can be visually reconstructed, although attempts have been made; for the decoration of both is a literary device and, in the case of Aeneas, modeled on that of Achilles.[3] After briefly describing the physical aspects of the shield ('huge and heavy . . . a shining triple rim'), Homer leaps directly into describing the scenes. The first-time listener or reader has no idea of what order Homer is following intellectually or physically in the location of a particular subject on the shield. Homer generally introduces a new subject with 'He [Hephaistos] made upon it . . . ' and puts everything in general terms:

> He made the earth upon it, and the sky, and the sea's water . . .
> He made upon it a soft field, the pride of the tilled land,
> wide and triple-ploughed, with many ploughmen upon it
> who wheeled their teams at the turn and drove them in either direction.[4]

While Homer refers to gods by name (Ares and Pallas Athene) and occasionally to a specific story (Daedalus and Ariadne), most of his topics are generic actions performed by unnamed figures. For example, in lines 490–494:

> On it he wrought in all their beauty two cities of mortal
> men. And there were marriages in one, and festivals.
> They were leading the brides along the city from their maiden
>   chambers
> under the flaring of torches, and the loud bride song was arising.

Or in lines 550–553:

> He made on it the precinct of a king, where the labourers
> were reaping, with the sharp reaping hooks in their hands. Of the cut
>   swathes
> some fell along the lines of reaping, one after another,
> while the sheaf-binders caught up others and tied them with
>   bind-ropes.

225

Some scholars after repeated readings believe that Homer used a ring composition in which each scene has a complement that enables the poet and the audience to remember their place in the narrative.[5] Ring composition is like a set of nesting horseshoes, each smaller and placed within a larger, and obviously differs from the fixed, serial sequence of the *topoi* and *loci*. I discussed this method briefly in Chapter 10, when I considered how John Hull writes now that he is blind.

Vergil's description (8.626–629) of Aeneas's shield begins very differently from Homer's:

> For there the Lord of Fire had wrought the story
> of Italy, the Roman's victories,
> since he was not unskilled in prophecy
> or one who cannot tell the times to come.
> There he had set the generations of
> Ascanius, and all their wars, in order.

At the start of the description Vergil informs the reader of the organizing principle that governs what follows: a specific story, the history of Italy, significantly described 'in order' (*'in ordine'*), by which Vergil means chronologically. This phrasing is the same as that used by the Auctor in his instructions, except that time functions for Vergil as the equivalent of the *loci* with named hero following upon named hero from the first glimmerings of Rome until the present.[6] Although the physical location of every scene on the shield cannot be reconstructed, Vergil places the most important events in prime, memorable positions in the same way as the Auctor (3.18.31) recommends that every fifth column be marked. 'Carved in the upper part [*in summo*] was Manlius' (line 652), while the center of the shield (line 675, *'in medio'*) is reserved for the battle of Actium, Rome's and Augustus's greatest achievement. Even Vergil's general descriptions, though recalling Homer, depend on specific events and people. Antony's fleet sailing from Egypt to Actium provides an opportunity for a description of a typical fleet at sea (8.687–693):

> . . . and – shamefully –
> behind him follows his [Antony's] Egyptian wife [Cleopatra].
> The squadrons close headlong; and all the waters
> foam, torn by drawn-back oars and by the prows
> with triple prongs. They seek the open seas;
> you could believe the Cyclades, uprooted,
> now swam upon the waters or steep mountains
> had clashed with mountains as the crewmen thrust
> in their great galleys at the towering sterns.

Vergil, as a literate poet, is not precluded from using oral techniques like Homer's ring composition. Rather he tends to use both oral *and* literate

226

techniques. In the case of the two shields, Homer's may be memorable because of its ring composition, Vergil's because of its serial composition. Either method will work, but the second method depends very much on literacy and the art of memory. Vergil's attempt at giving more precise physical locations for the events may also be due to mnemotechnics. I would not, however, want to press too far Aeneas's reaction to the shield (8.730): 'he marvels, and ignorant of the events [*rerum*] rejoices in their picture [*imagine*].' While Vergil again uses a phrase ('the image of things') that occurs in the Auctor (3.20.33), it also fits Vergil's context so well that it may have little to do with the art of memory.

PERCEPTION OF ORDER AND MAGNITUDE AND THE *TOPOI*

At this point let us backtrack in time to consider another and different kind of indirect example. In the fourth century BC Xenophon wrote a dialogue, the *Oeconomicus*, on estate management, a sensible enough subject. Socrates, not noted for his ability as a provider or for his skills in running a household, leads the discussion with Ischomachus. Moreover, Socrates says in the *Phaedrus* that 'I'm a lover of learning, and trees and open country won't teach me anything, whereas men in the town do.'[7] Ischomachus and Socrates discuss at length the need for and the way to instill order in Ischomachus's new wife. I quote fairly extensively, because the number and kinds of examples Ischomachus presents show that some of the concepts underlying the *topoi* had broad, philosophical underpinnings.

As a parenthetical comment, the opening and closing portions of this part of the dialogue are interesting for what they say about women in antiquity.[8] Ischomachus describes his wife's problem: 'I recollect that she was vexed and blushed crimson, because she could not give me something from the stores when I asked for it. And seeing that she was annoyed, I said: "Don't worry, dear. . . ."'[9] After appropriate training of the little woman by Ischomachus, Socrates accords her the highest accolade possible:

'Upon my word, Ischomachus, your wife has a truly masculine mind by your showing!'

'Yes,' said Ischomachus, 'and I am prepared to give you other examples of high-mindedness on her part, when a word from me was enough to secure her instant obedience.'[10]

The wife's problem was that she could not remember where things were kept, which is precisely the problem that the art of memory addresses; for finding actual objects differs little from remembering arguments or facts in a legal case. Now for Ischomachus's examples and instructions, with the parts that directly reflect the art of memory in italics:

My dear, there is nothing so convenient or so good for human beings as order. Thus a chorus is a combination of human beings . . . an army in orderly array is a noble sight . . . a man-of-war laden with men . . . a goodly sight to friends. . . .

And so, my dear, if you do not want this confusion, and wish to know exactly how to manage our goods and *to find with ease* whatever is wanted and to satisfy me by giving me anything I ask for, *let us choose the place that each portion should occupy; and, having put the things in their place, let us instruct the maid to take them from it and put them back again. Thus we shall know what is safe and sound and what is not; for the place itself will miss whatever is not in it, and a glance will reveal anything that wants attention, and the knowledge where each thing is will quickly bring it to hand, so that we can use it without trouble* . . . .

How good it is to keep one's stock of utensils in order, and how easy to find a suitable place in a house to put each set in. . . . Yes, no serious man will smile when I claim that there is beauty in the order even of pots and pans set out in neat array, however much it may move the laughter of a wit. *There is nothing, in short, that does not gain in beauty when set out in order.* For each set looks like a troop of utensils, and the space between the sets is beautiful to see, when each set is kept clear of it, just as a troop of dancers about the altar is a beautiful spectacle in itself, and even the free space looks beautiful and unencumbered. . . .

[T]here is no ground for any misgiving that it is hard to find someone who will get to know the various places and remember to put each set in its proper place. For we know, I take it, that the city as a whole has ten thousand times as much of everything as we have; and yet you may order any sort of servant to buy something in the market and to bring it home, and he will bring it home, and he will be at no loss: every one of them is bound to know where he should go to get each article. Now *the only reason for this is that everything is kept in a fixed place.* . . .

I decided to show her the possibilities of our house . . . the rooms are designed simply with the object of providing as convenient recep-tacles as possible for the things that are to fill them, and thus each room invited just what was suited to it. Thus the store-room by the security of its position called for the most valuable blankets and utensils, the dry covered rooms for the corn, [etc.]. . . .

[A]fter showing her [the housekeeper] their places and counting and making a written list of all the items, we told her to give them out to the right servants, to remember what she gave to each of them, and when receiving them back to put everything in the place from which she took it.

In appointing the housekeeper, we chose the woman whom on consideration we judged to be the most temperate in eating and wine drinking and sleeping and the most modest with men, the one, too,

228

who seemed *to have the best memory,* to be most careful not to offend us by neglecting her duties, and to think most how she could earn some reward by obliging us.[11]

As with the art of memory, an appropriate distribution of items can be recalled, while an empty space indicates that something is missing. Such order is part of the very fabric of life: from choruses and the army to the man-of-war to the Phoenician ship to one's own household to the city itself. So Aristotle also applied the *topoi* to a wide variety of items, ranging from the alphabet to a city. Similarly, Aristotle used the alphabet as a container, because of the alphabet's fixed order of letters.[12] It is particularly interesting that the housekeeper must have a good memory despite the written list she is given, since she is expected to remember, not refer to the list, when she manages the servants. Unlike our use of lists today where they serve as a substitute for memory, here the list serves only as a means to fix the items in her memory, after which it is no longer needed. At the same time definite differences distinguish the art of memory and the order presented by Xenophon. English obscures one of them, since it uses 'place' for both τόπος and χῶρος, the word Xenophon used. χῶρος, the older of the two words, occurs in Homer, while τόπος appears first in Aeschylus in the fifth century BC.[13] This chronology may reflect a later need for a more abstract kind of 'place', for χῶρος generally applies to physical places, such as a place in the countryside, a region, or as Xenophon uses it here, a place for storage; it is never used instead of τόπος in discussions of memory.

Another difference between the art of memory and Xenophon's passage lies in the meaning of 'order'. Although the art of memory depends on order, it is an order of sequence and certainly not of the right thing in the right place. As far as the art of memory is concerned, if you were using it to keep track of your shopping list, you could store the paper towels in the foyer, the olive oil in the living-room, and the milk in the bedroom, as long as you remembered the sequence of that storage. Xenophon describes a direct system with a one-to-one relationship between the place and the item it holds. The *loci*, however, are a 'mediated' system in which an intermediary image connects the place with the item to be remembered. Hence it is appropriate that Xenophon uses κόσμος (*kosmos*), which means 'order' in the sense of a 'harmonious arrangement' rather than in the sense of 'sequence'. Since Xenophon was well trained in rhetoric and was obviously by this passage very interested in having a good memory, the fact that he does not describe the system of *loci* I think makes it clear that that system was not known to the Greeks of the late fifth to fourth centuries BC.[14] Instead, what we have is a precursor where the viewing, physically or mentally, of a physical setting prompts your memory of what is missing or not as the case may be.

229

A memorable order has nothing to do with beauty even though, according to Aristotle, it does share one aspect of beauty: magnitude. In the *Poetics* Aristotle describes the beautiful:

> [T]o be beautiful, a living creature, and every whole made up of parts, must not only present a certain order in its arrangement of parts, but also be of a certain definite magnitude. Beauty is a matter of size and order, and therefore impossible either in a very minute creature, since our perception becomes indistinct as it approaches instantaneity; or in a creature of vast size – one, say, 1,000 miles long – as in that case, instead of the object being seen all at once, the unity and wholeness of it is lost to the beholder. Just in the same way, then, as a beautiful whole made up of parts, or a beautiful living creature, must be of some size, but a size to be taken in by the eye, so a story or plot must be of some length, but of a length to be taken in by the memory.[15]

Like Xenophon, Aristotle here speaks of a different kind of order from that prescribed for mnemotechnics. The description of size, however, very much fits the Auctor's recommendations on the construction of one's imaginary *loci*, for both are based on human perception and its physical limitations. The Auctor (3.19.31) is the first text we have which explicitly prescribes that 'it is necessary to have medium-sized places of a moderate magnitude; for if excessively large they return vague images, and if too small often they do not seem to be able to take the placing of the images.' Differing times of composition may explain why the passage from the *Poetics* but not Aristotle's treatise on memory, written earlier, shows the connections between magnitude, perception, and memory. For Aristotle, memory depends on perception and hence is subject to the same laws. In the *Metaphysics* he says:

> By nature animals are born with a faculty of sensation, and from sensation memory is produced in some of them, though not in others. . . . And from memory experience is produced in man; for many memories of the same thing produce finally the capacity for a single experience.[16]

The linking of memory and perception has already been discussed in Chapter 6. The connection between memory, order, and beauty continues into the late Roman Republican period with the ties between the three growing stronger and more apparent.

THE ROMAN SENSE OF PLACE, ONCE AGAIN

Defining what is beautiful is not a simple matter, because ideas of what is beautiful change so much over time and from place to place. It may seem strange that Aristotle equates beauty with 'size and order', two characteristics which we rarely think of first in terms of beauty. It certainly has seemed sufficiently odd to some scholars that they have claimed that Cicero, among others, had no sense of 'natural beauty'. J. C. Davies, however, shows that for Cicero, like Aristotle, beauty meant '*order* on a large, often cosmic, or smaller, agricultural, scale . . . fulfilling a *function*; and . . . a certain easily recognized *organic unity* or *identity*.'[17] When Cicero decides to decorate his villa at Tusculum, his sense of beauty and his beliefs about how memory works together determine his choice of sculpture.

For background, recall what I quoted from Cicero's *On Ends* in Chapter 6 about how actual places and buildings activate one's memories:

> For my own part even the sight of our senate-house . . . used to call up to me thoughts of Scipio, Cato, Laelius, and chief of all, my grandfather; such powers of suggestion do places possess. No wonder the, scientific training of the memory is based on these things.[18]

In Chapter 6 I referred to Cicero's problems in obtaining appropriate statuary for his villa in Tusculum.[19] He wanted Muses, not Bacchantes, to decorate his library. Here I would add a further reason for his request beyond what is thematically appropriate for a library. He specifically wanted to recall the time he had spent in Athens, something to which he refers in the section introducing the quotation above, when he sets the scene of the dialogue: 'We arrange to take our afternoon stroll in the Academy.'[20] Because of his love for Athens, he names two parts of his villa after the Academy and the Lyceum where Plato and Aristotle respectively taught. He writes to Atticus about decorating his Academy:

> I am eagerly expecting the Megarian statues and the herms you wrote to me about. Anything you may have of the same sort which you think suitable for the Academy [*Academia*], don't hesitate to send it and trust my purse. . . . Things that are especially suitable for a lecture hall [γυμνασιώδη] are what I want.[21]

Elsewhere he says, 'For the sake of a stroll we had gone to the Lyceum, which is the name of my upper gymnasium.'[22] Cicero's purchases would be displayed within these peristyles with their walkways. Thus Cicero not only uses his rhetorical training in the art of memory to remember his speeches and arguments in law courts, but also has so absorbed the system that it affects the way he designs and arranges the decoration of his villas. John Moffitt, without mentioning the villas of Cicero, makes the connection between the system of *loci*, ancient topography, and Vitruvius's recommendations for scene-painting: 'for walkways with lengthy walls the decoration was a variety of landscape settings [*varietatibus topiorum*] which copied the most characteristic features of specific places [*a certis locorum proprietatibus*].'[23]

While Cicero's villas have not been found, others that are similar in conception have. Hadrian followed Cicero in naming parts of his villa at Tivoli after places he had been:

> His villa at Tibur was marvellously constructed, and he actually gave to parts of it the names of provinces and places of the greatest renown, calling them, for instance, Lyceum, Academia, Prytaneum, Canopus, Poecile and Tempe. And in order not to omit anything, he even made a Hades.[24]

The area called the 'Canopus' still exists and statuary stands between columns around the artificial canal. The decorative programs of villas at Pompeii and Herculaneum work in a similar way. In particular, the Villa of the Papyri at Herculaneum fits much of what Cicero describes in his letters. Again, one of the major criteria for purchase is subject matter rather than style or artist. Again, sculpture is displayed in the peristyles, of which there are also two. Again, there is a significant library with primarily philosophical holdings. Unlike Cicero, however, the owner of this villa did not mind having Dionysiac pieces associated with more intellectual subjects, such as busts of various notables including famous military and political leaders as well as writers and philosophers.[25]

The Romans had a very deep regard for their ancestors, which was particularly apparent in their attitude toward portraits. Pliny the Elder says:

> We must not pass over a novelty that has also been invented, in that likenesses made, if not of gold or silver, yet at all events of bronze are set up in the libraries in honour of those whose immortal spirits speak to us in the same places. . . . At Rome this practice originated with Asinius Pollio, who first by founding a library made works of genius the property of the public. Whether this practice began earlier, with the Kings of Alexandria and of Pergamum, between whom there had been such a keen competition in founding libraries, I cannot readily say.[26]

Thus not only do the memories of the people who once lived and worked in particular places linger on in one's imagination, but they are also physically represented in portraits to recall the person in the same kind of place they might visit in the present.[27]

The same conception lies behind the display of statuary in the city of Rome. The Forum Augustum, dedicated in 2 BC, was built by Augustus in fulfillment of a vow made at Philippi in 42 BC.[28] The Temple of Mars Ultor stands against the back wall with two colonnades, beginning in *exedrae*, defining the sides of the Forum. In niches along the back wall of the *exedrae* and the colonnades were statues of the ancestors and relatives of Augustus and Rome's most important historical figures, a kind of ancient Hall of Fame, as Luce puts it.[29] Ovid describes them:

Mars Ultor himself comes down from Heaven to see the honours paid him, and his splendid temple in the Forum of Augustus. Huge the god and huge the temple . . . on one side he sees Aeneas with his dear burden [Anchises], and many an ancestor of the Julian house; on the other Romulus carrying the arms of the conquered leader [Titus Tatius], and all the statues ranged in order, with their famous deeds inscribed.[30]

Each statue came with a *titulus* identifying the figure, as well as a separate, lengthy inscription, an *elogium*, detailing his deeds. Sallust explains how such images work:

I have often heard that Quintus Maximus, Publius Scipio, and other eminent men of our country, were in the habit of declaring that their hearts were set mightily aflame for the pursuit of virtue whenever they gazed upon the masks of their ancestors. Of course they did not mean to imply that the wax or the effigy had any such power over them, but rather that it is the memory of great deeds that kindles in the breasts of noble men this flame that cannot be quelled until they by their own prowess have equalled the fame and glory of their forefathers.[31]

Copies of the statues from the Forum Augustum were set up in other Roman cities like Pompeii to similarly recall Rome and the Romans. As a Roman walked in the Forum, he would see each figure between columns in a manner similar to that described by the Auctor ad Herennium who suggested adopting a colonnade as the *locus* for memorizing. The only major difference between the two was that presumably every fifth inter-columniation was not distinctively marked in the Forum's colonnades. Thus the colonnade with its statues served at least two memorial purposes: it directly prompted memory of the men most notable in Rome's past; and it served, whether directly or indirectly, as a model *locus*.

Some scholars believe that Vergil's description of the descendants of Aeneas in Book 6 of the *Aeneid* (756–853) inspired the arrangement in the Forum Augustum.[32] Unfortunately, not all the figures have survived either from the Forum itself or in sets of replicas from elsewhere to be able to correlate the two. The general conception certainly predates both Vergil and the Forum Augustum. Polybios in the second century BC described a parade of Roman ancestors, which was based on actual Roman funerary practices that continued well into the Empire.[33] The setting of the parade of descendants in the Underworld makes it obvious that Vergil was thinking about that common Roman practice. At the same time not just all those colonnaded buildings in late Republican Rome with all those people ordinarily standing between those columns, but also actual statuary appearing between columns must have been a common sight in late Republican Rome. For example, Cicero, in one of his speeches against the light-fingered Verres, asks: 'Where are those statues now Verres? I mean those we saw in your house the other day, standing by all the columns, and in all the spaces between the columns too, yes, and even yet about your shrubbery in the open air.'[34] Hence it is more likely that the idea of unifying the selection of all the statuary under one theme is what is significant about the Forum Augustum rather than the arrangement itself.

Before leaving portraits entirely, I would like to briefly mention the Roman practice of *damnatio memoriae*, the removal of all mention, verbal and visual, of a particular person, as punishment for treason. It should be clear by now that the Romans' reverence for portraits as reminders of their ancestry was great. Hence a *damnatio memoriae* is stern punishment: the removal of all traces of the person. In a way it is a physical embodiment of the Greek word for truth, '*alētheia*' (ἀλήθεια), which literally means 'that which is not forgotten', as in the river Lethe (Forgetfulness) in the Under-world. In other words, whatever is remembered is 'true': a very sobering thought for historians.[35] Suetonius describes the process in his account of the events that immediately followed the death of Domitian:

> The senators . . . were so overjoyed, that they raced to fill the House, where they did not refrain from assailing the dead emperor with the most insulting and stinging kind of outcries. They even had ladders brought and his shields [which had portraits of Domitian on them] and images [*imagines*] torn down before their eyes and dashed upon the ground; finally they passed a decree that his inscriptions [*titulos*] should everywhere be erased, and all record [*memoriam*] of him obliterated.[36]

In the case of the written word the logistics were not terribly difficult, since it is a relatively easy task to remove letters from an inscription in a public place.[37] It is much harder to remove the features from a sculpted image and for the piece still to be an effective work of art. None the less, the Romans became fairly adept at doing so. One of the two Cancelleria reliefs, dated AD 93–95, shows a departure scene with Domitian the first figure on the left after Minerva.[38] His head has been recarved to look like that of his successor, Nerva, with the result that he looks like a modern model with a long, willowy body topped by a small head.

My third and last example from Vergil occurs in Book 8 (306–369) of the *Aeneid*, when Evander takes Aeneas on a walk through Rome. The use of the word *locus* is not sufficient to identify a passage dependent on the system of *loci*. The conversation between Aeneas and Evander, however, does work in a mnemonic way. As the two physically walk through Rome, various monuments (*monimenta* in line 312) prompt Evander's memory in much the same way that a person memorizing according to the *loci* would recall his list by mentally strolling in order through his set of places. This example works on a direct level – what you see prompts a direct image – and not in the indirect way of the system of *loci* – what you see is linked by an intermediary to what you want to memorize. As Cicero in the *On Ends* put it:

> It is a common experience that places do strongly stimulate the imagination and vivify our ideas of famous men. . . . All over Athens, I know, there are many reminders of eminent men in the actual place where they lived; but at the present moment it is that alcove over there which appeals to me, for not long ago it belonged to Carneades. I fancy I see him now (for his portrait is familiar).[39]

This walk directly anticipates the ones taken by S., the Russian mnemonist whom Luria studied. I repeat the salient section here from Chapter 8:

> [H]e would 'distribute' [what he had to memorize] along some roadway or street he visualized in his mind. Sometimes this was a street in his home town. . . . On the other hand, he might also select a street in Moscow. Frequently he would take a mental walk along that street.[40]

SOME CAUTIONARY WORDS ABOUT OBJECTS

Not all objects and literary texts are examples of the *topoi* and *loci*, although almost any object can be a memento, as I said earlier.[41] For example, the 'Mourning Women' sarcophagus from Sidon shows six women in various positions of grieving on each of the long sides and three more on each of the ends for a total of eighteen women.[42] At first glance the sarcophagus seems to represent the Auctor's recommendation that intercolumniations be used to separate people one wants to remember, because each woman stands isolated between columns. Two reasons, however, preclude such an interpretation. Most obvious is that the sarcophagus is fourth century BC, and therefore made before the development of the architectural *loci* by the Romans. Second, the women, like Homer's scenes on the shield of Achilles, are too generic. Only their poses have major differences. Their faces, their hair-styles, their dress, their physiques all look too much alike. Mnemotechnics depends on clear and unambiguous elements, as S. made clear when he didn't see the pencil against the fence.

In contrast, Roman column sarcophagi from the late second century AD and later use columns as separators but sometimes with distinctive figures and action. A number of sarcophagi portray the labors of Herakles between columns, generally in the same order.[43] Because the same deeds appear on other contemporary sarcophagi without the dividing columns, columns alone are not a sufficient indicator of the *loci*.[44] Even specific details have to be arranged in a serial order to qualify. Roman sarcophagi with weddings tend not to belong to this class, although they meet the other requirements of columns and the representation of particular people. The married couples stand in the middle intercolumniation.[45] Their heads are portraits, while their bodies share the same physique, with neither the scrawny nor the obese being depicted. They are frequently shown surrounded by scenes, often generic, with flanking Dioskouroi enclosing the whole. The sequence of events, however, is not serial, as on the sarcophagi with Herakles, but, like Homer, follows a ring composition. Moreover, the weddings, like Herakles, also appear on sarcophagi without columns.[46]

Agnès Rouveret makes the compelling suggestion that the Iliac Tablets served as mnemonic devices for their stories, though clearly the memories for stories based on the tablets would differ from the memories based on the texts.[47] In the main picture on the Capitoline Tablet a walled city is depicted with basically three 'registers' or areas within the gates.[48] Outside the walls are four sections. Each part gets the action that occurred there. The trio of figures, which is repeated, indicates that the tablet shows 'continuous' narrative or a succession of episodes within one story. At the city gates is Aeneas carrying his father Anchises and holding the arm of his son, Ascanius. In the lower right the same three figures in the same order appear boarding a ship. One physical setting encompasses a number of different moments within the fall of Troy in what is known technically as a synoptic picture. Furthermore, the tablet could serve as an independent set of *loci* that could be used to store anything to be memorized. Each figure, each segment, could be memorized in order with the items to be memorized distributed in the sequence supplied by the parts of the tablet. We have no literary source which says that pictures were used in this manner, though we do know that the Zodiac did supply *loci*. By analogy then, Rouveret's idea is certainly plausible and possible, if not provable.

Next, let us look at the Column of Trajan.[49] It commemorates the two wars Rome fought with Dacia between AD 101 and 106. In a continuous band that spirals around the column it contains 155 scenes with over 2500 figures. The first scene starts at the bottom in the same manner as the scenes from the *Iliad* on the Iliac Tablets. It shows the Roman frontier settlement on the Danube from which the Roman army will depart with Trajan as the leader. What is remarkable for a classical representation is that every single action occurs against a specific backdrop, although we can't identify them all today. Even if some of the settings are more 'typical' than 'actual', the important point is the use of place. One Roman frontier settlement could well resemble another frontier settlement in the same terrain, since the Romans tried to construct their forts to follow the same plan. Certain actions, such as sacrifices and the address of the troops, are repeated throughout the column in a manner that punctuates the flow which the Auctor ad Herennium would have approved with his recommendation that every fifth column be marked. At the same time these actions are good examples of the common places (*communes loci*) recommended in the treatises on rhetoric. Like the 'literary' commonplaces for arguments in a law court, they are typical and recurring actions that happen in every war campaign and actually occurred during the Dacian Wars.

A BRIEF COMMENT ON ILLUSTRATIONS
AND THE ART OF MEMORY

Today, we take it so much for granted that illustrations are important for textbooks and children's books that it is difficult to imagine either without pictures.[50] Books for adults, however, tend not to have pictures, and, if they do, they are often an afterthought, clumped together and stuck in the middle or the back of the book. At the same time, psychological research on the role of illustrations in text has only recently begun to grapple with how illustrations do or do not enhance text and under what conditions.[51] We all too easily assume that the old saw is right: a picture is worth a thousand words.[52] Yet the idea of coordinating picture and text was not obvious and the degree of linkage between the two has varied dramatically between cultures and over time. Furthermore, the variety of illustrations that exists today were a very, very long time in development. While pictures can make a text more memorable and certainly were used in that manner during the Middle Ages, they rarely accompanied texts in classical antiquity. Since thousands of papyri have survived, the paucity of extant examples is significant.[53] I think you have to understand how each medium works in order to understand how to coordinate them. Not only do you have to have the appropriate set of tools (codex, parchment, desk, etc.), you also need the desire for such illustrations. Thus technical drawings which directly explain and enhance the text appear relatively early. In this category are maps, plans, diagrams, and scientific illustrations, but even they were not common.

The really startling fact is that the Romans have a visual system, the *loci*, for remembering words, but do not use a visual system to make those words clearer and more understandable or to even find those words within a mass of text. Not until the Middle Ages do such visual finding aids appear. At that time illuminations helped to make each page easier to memorize in much the same way that today we often remember that this or that fact appeared in conjunction with a particular picture on the lower left of a page approximately one-third of the way through the text.[54] At the same time the system of *loci* works like the modern pegword system for memorizing. As a result, the memorizer could make up an image that connects picture and word to make both more memorable than either independently. Yet it still took nearly the entire Middle Ages to learn how to make picture and text fit. All too often, scribe and artist worked independently, with the result that the artist had to fit his illuminations willy-nilly in the space left to him (or sometimes her) by the scribe.[55]

THE ART OF MEMORY AND THE ART OF THINKING

Today, we think of memory primarily in terms of retrieval. It remains, as it was in antiquity, a storehouse. If we are of a cognitive bent, we might also think of memory as a space for organizing our thoughts. In antiquity, however, memory was considered to be more than a passive receptacle: it was intimately connected to thinking. For this association we need to look at another strand of ancient thought about memory. Plato in the *Meno* (81e) said that 'learning [μάθησιν] is recollection [ἀνάμνησις].'[56] (I am not going to get into any of the rather complex issues of Plato's and Socrates's belief in reincarnation and the theory of forms with which this statement is connected.) Next, in Chapter 5 I quoted Aristotle (1250a35) who put memory at the beginning of his list of the components of wisdom. Cicero similarly considered memory to be a part of wisdom (*prudentia*), though he reduces the parts to three. The other two are intelligence (*intellegentia*) and foresight (*providentia*).[57] While I have not concentrated on this aspect of the ancient view of memory, I do want to note here that it was combined with the system of the *loci* in the Middle Ages and Renaissance to become a means of thinking.[58]

One curious passage from Philo Judaeus, a philosopher who lived during the early Roman Empire, does link memory, in terms very like those of the artificial memory systems, to God and creation:

> When a city is being founded . . . there comes forward now and again some trained architect who . . . first sketches in his own mind well nigh all the parts of the city that is to be wrought out, temples, gymnasia, town-halls, market-places, harbours, [etc.]. . . . Thus after having received in his own soul, as it were in wax, the figures of these objects severally, he carries about the image of a city which is the creation of his mind. Then by his innate power of memory, he recalls the images of the various parts of this city, and imprints their types yet more distinctly in it. . . . Just such must be our thoughts about God. . . . As, then, the city which was fashioned beforehand within the mind of the architect held no place in the outer world, but had been engraved in the soul of the artificer as by a seal; even so the universe that consisted of ideas would have no other location than the Divine Reason, which was the Author of this ordered frame.[59]

In the Middle Ages, pictures are specifically constructed as physical *loci*. I've already mentioned the possible use of the Iliac Tablets in this way. A woodcut from 1505 illustrates the *Gospel According to John* in a mnemonic way. It encapsulates Chapters 7–12 of the *Gospel According to John* in one complex 'monster'.[60] The main figure is an eagle (John himself) with an eye (the healed blind man) at the beginning of its tail and the upper torsos of a woman (the adulteress) kissing a man. A skull (antithesis of the Resurrection of Lazarus) sits atop one wing and a jar of ointment (Mary Magdalene) on another. Moreover, the positions are numbered so that you can remember them in proper order. This 'synoptic' was designed by someone familiar with the Roman memory systems. Other medieval and Renaissance pictures are less absurd and provide both the slots for storage, as well as a method of organizing one's thought that is both ethical and religious. Lina Bolzoni has the best illustrated overview of their development. Here I only note that Trees of Life and Towers of Wisdom were common where memory is used to guide thought. They reached their apogee with Ramon Lull in the fourteenth century, who based his system on 'the names and attributes of God, on concepts such as goodness, greatness, eternity, power, wisdom, will, virtue, truth, and glory.'[61] Other followers such as Giordano Bruno in the sixteenth century lie totally beyond my scope, except for Robert Fludd in the seventeenth century, who brings us full circle. Frances Yates has convincingly demonstrated that he used the Globe Theater as his major *locus*. Because of the incredible accuracy of his description of his memory theater, we are able to reconstruct the real theater from the system.[62]

CONCLUSION

A few guidelines can be established for indirect applications of the art of memory. Since the system of the *topoi* did not exist before the fifth century BC, all applications of it must come from that period or later. Since mnemotechnics changed over time both in its importance and in its very nature, its manifestations are also subject to the same chronological restrictions. As a result, the number of Greek examples is fewer than the Roman, because the art of memory was neither a formal part of rhetoric until the Hellenistic period nor had the architectural system of *loci* been developed until the late Roman Republican period. Furthermore, because the art of memory was a technique for remembering words, its appearance in pictorial narratives is often both difficult to discern and open to other interpretations. It is very important to keep in mind that the systems of *topoi* and *loci* involve the recall of specifics (things, facts, words, whatever) in a particular fixed serial order. I have not considered single pictorial or literary scenes that exhibit 'vivid' imagery, because the vividness is too much in the eye or the ear of the beholder.

CONCLUSION

Costume designers maintain that when actors wear period costumes, not only the outer, but even the inner garments must be accurate or the actors will not move in the right way. You cannot wear a bustle with a half slip. A similar situation faces anyone trying to interpret classical antiquity. We have a pretty good idea of the surface – how things looked – but when we try to animate the scene the people all walk with a modern stride. I have tried to build a consistent portrait in which both the inner and outer characteristics of the classical literate form a consistent whole, for culture is in the details.

I began with an archaeological approach. Look at what was produced and try to figure out why it is the way it is and what that implies for tasks that it was used for. The artifacts in this case are related to literacy. How does a culture cope with new technology? For I believe that literacy is among other things a technology. It is also communication. It is also external memory. The problem has been disentangling the whole to examine the parts and how they fit together, for fit they do. Moreover, the nature of that fit changes from person to person, from period to period, from culture to culture. Even if the pace of technological change was slower in antiquity than now, none the less, it is a pace. At no time did development stop, as is often assumed by the classical scholars who are followers of Pliny the Elder, who said that 'art ceased' after the fourth century BC.[1] Instead, cultural phenomena are like Heraclitus's stream, constantly in flux. We cannot attribute all that is creative and inventive to the Greeks and all that is derivative to the Romans. I have emphasized the patterns of change and adaptation. The exceptions that exist are like those which exist in any age. It is not that they prove the rule; it is that they are merely exceptions.

I have emphasized two major and related aspects of literacy which have received little attention among classicists: display and retrieval, since the display affects how you retrieve. Literacy is not merely the ability to write or to read. *How* you write and read matters. If your text is all run together in *scriptio continua*, then you will very likely read out loud and not be able to easily find a piece of information once you have passed it by. If you can't easily find what you once read, then it is likely that your methods of citation, not to speak of your standards of reference, will differ from someone who has a well-indexed book at hand. If you write with the papyrus across your knee, then the format of the codex will not seem nearly as attractive as it does to those of us weaned on books. What is interesting is that the balance between the tools constantly shifts. If you change one, then chances are the others will also need changes. Hence the advent of the codex fosters the shift of the writing surface from knee to desk. Once you start writing on parchment you change your pen and your inks. With parchment and its new inks comes the highly illuminated page with a highly colored text. With print the page blackened and fonts were developed. Today we have come full circle or rather spiraled round on the computer: we retain the fonts with a soupçon of color. At no time, including now, are such changes instantaneous.

In Donald Norman's terms both your tools and you yourself work together to form a cognitive artifact, which reminds me of the old adage that if all you have is a hammer, then everything looks like a nail.[2] So, when the number of words to sort through became too much to cope with, classical man – it was not classical woman – refined one of the tools he already knew how to use well: memory. The idea that writing is an external store that substitutes for internal memory is a very modern phrasing of the issue, even though the connection between writing and memory was apparent early, as Plato's writings demonstrate. It is more that if you think of writing as a means of storage outside of yourself, then you are more likely to think of a means of retrieval outside of yourself.

The art of rhetoric develops to tame the oral words with written ones. No longer does paratactic organization dominate. Instead, elaborate advice is given for arrangement (*taxis*) of your speech. Still, merely having an order was not sufficient; tricks for remembering precisely what went into that order, the content, were developed in tandem. Not until the Hellenistic period, however, was it clear that memory was such an essential hammer that it had to be included among the standard tools of rhetoric, because, as I have stressed repeatedly, the number of words was growing astronomically. The art of memory continued to be refined and to grow more complex over the centuries. Nor was the classical art of memory just the systems of *topoi* and *loci*. It was a whole panoply of techniques, though the *loci* particularly prospered in the Middle Ages and the Renaissance, when their use was extended to ethics and epistemology. They continued to thrive in the nineteenth century, when over one hundred works were published in English alone.[3] They persist even today in memory prodigies such as S. The reason for their incredible ability to survive is not difficult to find. Put simply, they work.[4]

What has been different about my investigation from most studies of classical antiquity is that I have made a detailed analysis of modern cognitive theories about memory and especially mnemonic devices, and used that

241

analysis to assess classical mnemotechnics and its relationship to literacy. The modern studies have helped me to explain exactly how the systems worked and in some instances even why they work. I hope that the value of applying a cognitive approach to classical antiquity is evident. What I have not emphasized is that the benefits work in both directions. I mentioned in the Introduction that the work of Milman Parry and Alfred Lord has influenced cognitive psychology in its studies of how memory works. I also said that virtually every modern study of mnemotechnics refers to the ancient systems, especially that described by the Auctor ad Herennium. An understanding of classical antiquity can make other contributions. I showed how what neuropsychologists found curious – separate visual systems for recognizing objects and their locations – really wasn't, if you knew the development of Western art; for the rendering of objects developed separately from depicting their relationships to each other in linear perspective.

Other examples can also be adduced. My two commentaries in *Psycoloquy*, an electronic journal, were in response to a computer scientist who wanted to develop a computer model for reading. I came to three conclusions:

> First, in alphabetic cultures there has been a slow development towards an increasing visualization of written language. Second, as the way language is displayed changes, so does the way it must be processed. Third, because of the second conclusion, I do not think the study of reading can be divorced from the way language is written, which means that if a computer model is to be of significant help in understanding human processing, it will have to closely model the input that humans use.[5]

One of the people who responded informally to me said that the history I had traced for the display of alphabetic languages matched the way children learn how to write, because initially they write in *scriptio continua* and only later learn to divide the letters into words.[6] In other words, when dealing with a manmade system today, it behooves us to study its genesis and development in order to understand why it is the way it is. In a sense this approach is related to that of the psychobiologists. Why we act the way we do today has very deep roots in our evolutionary history.[7] If you want to know why we like a room with a view, then you need to know where our ancestors first grew up and how they adapted to that environment.

If you want to know where the computer revolution is headed, then you have to know where it came from. The reception of technologies follows patterns. I emphasize the plural. One pattern involves the dewy-eyed optimists who see only nirvana in their future. Martial fit that type. Plato, however, was the reverse: the Luddite pessimist who uses the tool, but only grudgingly, as he foresees the utter fall of mankind. This reaction is well known. What people today focus less on is the day-to-day nitty-gritty of coping with a new technology. First, you start out treating it like the hammer you already have. The first cars were buggies without the horses in front, though we still think of cars in terms of horsepower, as we think of lights in terms of candlepower. The first word processors were glorified typewriters, an automated delete key. New technology inevitably builds on the old. And sometimes that old lingers for a very long time indeed. In fact, today we are responding to the computer and its incredible proliferation of words in precisely the same manner as the Greeks and Romans did to their own increase in words. Instead of improving retrieval then by using the word to find the word, they used their well-known and proven technique of memory. Today, instead of depending solely on the computer to produce, find, display, and keep computerized words, we consume staggering amounts of paper to print everything out, because in the depths of our souls we cannot fully trust what we feel we cannot fully control.

I have written about the syllogism and how it was displayed in antiquity, horizontally rather than vertically as today. But even more important is how much the type of thinking that Aristotle fostered has lingered on today. It is not just that logic goes back to him, for logic is now a somewhat arcane branch of philosophy. Rather it is that the pioneers of artificial intelligence were mathematicians and firmly convinced that all reasoning was logical. Today we are witnessing the logical end of the logical syllogism, for much of the early views on thinking and artificial intelligence never panned out. Man does not reason only logically. In fact, almost the last way we do reason is logically.[8] In investigating precisely how we think, the new field of cognitive science has arisen. If the Greek Revolution, as it is often called, has provided the blueprint for literacy and memory for the past two millennia in the Western world, so it also makes the way clear for the next revolution. As writing enabled thought to become more sequential, less paratactic, so the computer enables thought to be more threadlike within its hypertext environment. You will no longer have to doggedly follow an author's arguments in his or her order. You will be able to pursue each point and its related points in the order you like until you have all the threads that compose the work.[9] At the same time sequential thought will not die, even if it will no longer be the prime tool in a writer's arsenal. Those who are pessimists should merely think of modern plotless literature and the explosion in popularity of that sequential standby, the mystery.[10]

The computer revolution resembles the Greek Revolution in that it too has as one of its major elements the intertwined issues of memory and literacy. I stress the 'one of its elements', because I think the idea that a 'revolution' per se depends on a single idea or impetus is simplistic. A number of things are always happening simultaneously and these things feed each other and reinfluence each other so that intellectual revolutions never follow a simple, straight line. A better image comes from the new field of emergent systems or complexity, an offspring so to speak of chaos theory.[11] Everything in the pot works together in various ways to simultaneously influence each other and in turn be influenced. Out of the primordial stew of everyday life emerges the new.

Nor is any revolution in thinking ever finished. It is, even in today's fast-moving times, a slowly evolving phenomenon. So, Eric Havelock really didn't go far enough when he said literacy begins with Plato. Literacy is always beginning. It never ceases to change. Its practitioners are forever on the verge of something new and different. That process of change is fascinating to us, because so much of it reflects our own history of knowledge. Perhaps one of the most enduring traits of the interconnectedness between literacy, memory, and technology is that together they so often supply the images for the way people think about their minds. Today if we want to find something, we search our personal memory banks, for we are hardwired and run software in our wet ware. Then you wrote it on the wax tablets of your mind.

NOTES

PREFACE

1 Merton, *OTSOG*, 23–25. 'Anticipatory plagiarism' refers to those situations where a scholar thought of something totally independently, only to discover later that someone else had already thought of the same thing. It is not my fault that Aristotle though of the idea first. Hence I deserve similar credit. In Merton's case, it was someone equally illustrious who was the culprit (Isaac Newton).

2 One of my readers responded that, in Pliny the Younger's words, 'I have read your book, and marked as carefully as I could the passages which I think should be altered or removed, for it is my custom to tell the truth, you are always willing to hear it; no one accepts criticism so readily as those who best deserve praise.' Pliny the Younger, *Letters*, 7.20. Translation from Radice, *Pliny Y.* I quote this passage more fully in Chapter 13.

INTRODUCTION

1 Yates, *Memory*, xii.

2 Dorr 1995a, 136.

3 Harris, *Literacy* and multiple responses in the *Journal of Roman Archaeology*, Supplementary Series 3 (1991).

4 I am referring to Harry Caplan's translation of 3.16.29–3.19.32 in the LCL edition. Unfortunately, people who do not know Latin are led very much astray by this translation.

5 *Nicomachean Ethics*, 1111a8–11. Translation from Aristotle, Bollingen. I remembered the misquotation, because I am intrigued by the metaphors used for 'mind'. For an illustration of the variety over the millennia with discussion, see Shipley, *OriginMind*, 1995 frontispiece and Chapter 10.

6 Bergmann 1994a, especially 254. Bolter (1993a, 109–110), in contrast, recognizes the serial nature of mnemotechnics, which he sees distinguishes from hypertext, which allows for 'a network of relationships'.

7 I am concerned only with how the different ways of thinking of the psychologist and the classicist are made evident in their work habits and written productions. For some studies of the larger matter of 'truth' or 'science' vs. 'relativism', see: Laudan, *SciRel*, from the point of view of a philosopher; Cromer, *Uncommon*, 1–22 from the point of view of a scientist; and Bagnall, *ReadPap*, 1–9 from the point of view of a classicist.

8 Galotti, *CogPsych* is a college textbook that is an excellent introduction to cognitive psychology because it is clearly written, presents the various topics without smoothing over the controversies, and has a superb bibliography. For specific studies of memory, I suggest: Baddeley, *HumMem*; Rubin, *MemOral*; and Schachter, *Searching*. Schachter is probably the most accessible. Rubin directly addresses questions of interest to classicists in his study of the oral transmission of 'stories'. Because he treats many of the same topics that I do, though from the point of view of orality rather than literacy, he is a good counterpoint to this book. For classical antiquity, I recommend as a start: *CHCL-1* and *CHCL-2* for literary matters; *OHCA* for art history; *OHCW* for classical history; and for general reference, *OCD*^{2}, which is due out in a third edition by the end of 1996. The best single work on papyri with the most illustrations is Turner, *GrMss*.

9 I give as an example, Capasso, *Volumen*, a group of articles on various aspects of classical rolls.

10 Quintilian 1, Preface, 25. Translation from the LCL.

1 MEMORY FOR WORDS

1 Norman, *Things*, 78.

2 *Odyssey*, 1.1 and 10. In *Odyssey*, 8.488, Homer refers to 'the Muse, child of Zeus' and in the *Iliad*, 2.484 places the Muses on Olympus. That they 'know all things' explains their usefulness to Homer. Thomas (*LitOral*, 115 with references in n. 41) remarks that 'it has been noted that both Homer and Hesiod call on the Muses not for inspiration, as later Hellenistic poets do, but for the *facts* of what happened.'

3 Lucian, 'A Conversation with Hesiod', 4. Typically for Lucian, the dialogue ends (9): 'it was some divine inspiration filled you with your verses, and not so very reliable at that, or it would not have kept part of what it promised and left the rest unfulfilled.' Translation from the LCL. On poetic inspiration, see Murray 1981a.

4 Nagy, *Best*, 17. He bases this conclusion on Detienne, *Vérité*, 9–27, a chapter devoted to the 'Memory of the Poet' and the Muses. Murray (1981a) has a very interesting discussion on the interrelated subjects of the Muses, memory, and poetic inspiration. In particular, she stresses (especially pp. 90–92) that the Muses in early Greek poetry impart knowledge. The best discussion I have read of the transmission of Homer and the exceedingly complex issues of orality and literacy in Homer is Nagy, *PoetPerf*.

5 Lord 1985a, 37.

6 Lord 1985a, 50.

7 For today, Harris, *Literacy*, 30–33. For antiquity, Caesar, *Gallic Wars*, 6.14.

8 Diamond, *Chimp*, 51.

9 Neisser, *MemObs*, 241. Earlier in the same work (pp. 16–17), he makes some cogent observations: 'In general, the relation between literacy and memory is poorly understood. It is one of those issues where every possible position can be and has been plausibly argued. . . . In my own view, it may be a mistake to treat culture and literacy as overriding variables: individual differences and individual experience are more important. If the experimental task is remembering oral stories, then experience in listening to stories will make a big difference.' Recent experiments, however, support the view that reading enhances memory, for which see Baddeley, *HumMem*, 88.

10 Norman, *Things*, 78.

NOTES

11 Cole/Scribner, *CT*, 138.
12 Lord, *Singer*, 27.
13 Lord, *Singer*, 28. Compare also Lord 1985a. I. Hunter (*apud* Ellis/Beattie, 249), commenting on this passage, puts it well: 'For them, a "word" means nothing more than an "utterance".'
14 Havelock, *LitRev*, 8 and 32 n. 5 respectively. Compare his discussion in *Muse*, 113: 'There is probably no attestable instance in Greek of the term *logos* as denoting a single "word," though it is often translated as though it did. The first "word for a word" in the early philosophers seems to have been *onoma* a "name."'
15 Scholes/Willis 1991a, 224.
16 Adams, *BegRead*, 296–299 with the quotation on pp. 298–299. Also see Gleitman *et al.* 1989a, 97–101 with other references. In agreement with Adams, David Olson (*Paper*, 126–127) says that children do not distinguish between paraphrase and verbatim until aged 5–6.
17 Roberts 1992a, 135.
18 McArthur, *EngLng*, 1119–1120, s.v. 'Word. Literacy and the Word'.
19 *CEL*, 132–137 ('The Acoustics of Speech'), especially p. 136.
20 Negroponte, *Being*, 141.
21 Negroponte, *Being*, 92.
22 Olson 1993a, 2 and 15 respectively.
23 Olson 1993a, 14.
24 DeFrancis 1996a, 30. DeFrancis discusses the implications of the Chinese confusion of character for word.
25 Wallace/Rubin 1988a, 292 and 303.
26 Finnegan 1985a and Lord, *apud* Finnegan 1985a, 156–157 in response in 'Discussion'. Similarly, Nagy (1992a, 318) notes that 'To show, as Finnegan does, that literacy is not incompatible with oral poetics in some societies is not to prove that written poetry cannot be distinguished from oral poetry.' He discusses at length (pp. 328–329 n. 54) her misunderstanding of Parry's thesis.
27 Pliny, *Natural History*, 28.11. Translation from the LCL. Compare Cicero, *On the Responses of the Soothsayers*, 12.23: 'if an aedile made a mistake by a word . . . then the games had not been conducted appropriately . . .' (Beard 1985a, 136–137 with discussion and references).
28 Paris, Louvre MA 1096 (9830383 AGR). The precise date depends on who the sacrificer is. Kleiner (*RomSculp*, 141, 142 fig. 117, 164 for references) believes the relief shows Augustus and Tiberius and hence was made in AD 14. Koeppel (1983a, 80–81, 124–129, figs. 34–35, and with references), on the other hand, consider the two protagonists to be Claudius and L. Vitellius, and hence dates it after AD 48. He also says (p. 126) that the four letters on the diptych are probably modern. Tortorella (1992a, 82 with n. 5, and 81 fig. 1 for a good photograph) believes that the object is not a diptych, but an *acerra* or incense box. Incense boxes, however, tend to be squarer than the object represented.
29 Hunter 1985a. For full discussion of this issue, see Chapter 13.
30 For the existence of official oral remembrancers in Greece, see Evans, *Herodotus*, 129–132; against that idea, see Thomas, 198 and Thomas 1993a, 225. Aristotle's description of the later '*mnemones*', the Greek term for 'remembrancers', clearly differs from the oral ones just described. He says (*Politics*, 1321b 34–40): 'Another magistracy is the one that has to receive a *written* return of private contracts and of the verdicts of the lawcourts; and with these same officials the registration of legal proceedings and their institution have also to take place. In some states this office also is divided into several, but there are places where one magistracy controls all these matters; and these officials are

247

called Sacred Recorders, Superintendents, Recorders, and other names akin to these' (Translation from the LCL; my emphasis). For a full study of history in 'oral' societies, see Vansina, *OralTrad*.

31 Donald, Chapter 8, 'Third Transition: External Symbolic Storage and Theoretic Culture', 269–360. Compare also the multiple book review of Donald with his response in *Behavioral and Brain Sciences* 16 (1993): 737–791.

32 Williams 1972a, 216 quoting from P. Ch. Beatty IV, vol. 2/5–3/11. He dates the document as 'Ramesside', i.e. in the New Kingdom between *c.* 1300 and 1085 BC.

33 Plato, *Phaedrus*, 274e–275d. Translation adapted from Plato, Bollingen. I have translated φάρμακον as 'drug' rather than 'recipe', since Plato clearly means the stronger word. φάρμακον also has the connotation of 'poison', on which see LSJ 1917, *s.v.* φάρμακον. For a discussion of this aspect, see Derrida's commentary ('Plato's Pharmacy' in Derrida, *Dissem*, 61–172) and Neel's (*Plato*, 79–99) commentary on Derrida. Donald Norman (*Things*, 259) has an interesting response to Plato and the value of oral give-and-take, as Plato portrays it: 'Phaedrus seems to be a wimp as a debating partner. It isn't clear why having a debating partner who responds "very true" or "Once again you are perfectly right" after each interchange adds anything to the words that have just been spoken – they might just as well have been read.' For a more traditional examination of this passage and especially the '*pharmakon*', see Steiner, *Tyrant*, 212–216.

34 Julius Caesar, *Gallic Wars*, 6.14. Translation from the LCL.

35 Seneca the Younger, *Letters*, 88.33. Translation from Campbell, *Seneca*.

36 Vitruvius 7, Introduction, 9. Translation by Morgan.

37 Ovid, *Pontic Epistles*, 4.8.50–52. Translation from the LCL. Ovid's argument was recognized at least as early as the fourth century BC when Alcidamas, a rhetorician and contemporary of Plato, wrote a defense of extemporaneous speaking. The last of his four reasons for writing down his speech was that 'we are eager to leave behind also memorials of ourselves and to gratify our love of honor, we are putting our hand to writing speeches' ('On Those Who Write Written *Logoi* or On Sophists' 32. Translation from Matsen *et al.*, 42).

38 Seneca the Elder, *Suasoriae*, 7.2 and 7.4. Translations from the LCL.

39 Quintilian 1.8.64. Translation from the LCL. The same story is also told by Dionysius of Halicarnassus, *On Literary Composition*, 25. It is possible that this story is just that, a story. It would none the less reflect the idea of writing drafts on wax tablets from at least as early as the first century BC (the time of Dionysius) and after.

40 *Republic*, 327a. Translation from Plato, Bollingen. On Plato's concerns about the openings of his dialogues, see Clay 1992a. On Plato and writing in general, see two essays in Part IV, 'Platon en mal d'écriture', of Detienne, *Savoirs* (Vegetti 1988a and Loraux 1988a).

41 Plato, of course, was not alone in this attitude, but became the best known exponent. Alcidamas, according to Thomas Cole (1996a, 147) was 'the single most important source . . . for the Greek exaltation of the spoken against the written word.' Harris (1989a, 105) cites an unpublished paper by Julius Tomin that Plato's 'conflicting attitudes towards writing . . . are explicable chronologically by reference to the failure of the philosopher's political experiment in Sicily. . . . Plato eventually ends up in the *Laws* as a convert to the new technology.' If today we change our minds, so did they then in antiquity. There is little reason to expect total consistency in anyone's thoughts over a lifetime. Gamble (*Books*, 259 n. 111), however, believes that Plato in the *Phaedrus* was

not condemning writing *per se*, but rather teaching by writing, on which compare Alexander 1990a. Cole (*OrigRhet*, 123) suggests that Plato is attacking written *technē*, that is, 'canned' texts used in teaching. None the less, Plato was considered to be anti-writing in antiquity, as 'his' second letter, an ancient forgery, shows: 'It is a very great safeguard to learn by heart instead of writing. It is impossible for what is written not to be disclosed. That is the reason why I have never written anything about these things, and why there is not and will not be any written work of Plato's own. What are now called his are the work of a Socrates embellished and modernized. Farewell and believe. Read this letter now at once many times and burn it. So much for these matters.' (Plato, *Letters 2*, 314b–c. Translation from Plato, Bollingen.) Compare Stirewalt, *Epistolography*, 38–39.

42 Roediger (1980a, 238) cites research on 'knowing not': 'people should take longer to respond that they do not know something than that they do. In general, this is true, but several experiments have shown that people can reject false information with high confidence faster than they can respond to true facts.' One of the best examples I know is to ask someone the capital of a 'lesser known' country like Zanzibar or Madagascar.

2 ANCIENT BOOKS

1 Transferring the book to the computer presents a different set of organizational problems. For example, this particular one is solved by a 'visual thumb', a 'scroll bar' that runs vertically along one edge (generally the right) of the text. Either the bar increases in length or a small box, called the 'scroll box', moves downward as you read through the text and decreases or moves upward as you 'flip' or page back to the beginning.

2 A very useful summary of what ancient books looked like, including the tools to make them, their layout, handwriting, etc. is Bischoff, *LatPal*. Kenney (1982a, 15–17) is helpful for the Latin terms.

3 'Scroll' and 'roll' are interchangeable in English according to the *RHUD*, but 'roll' is the term preferred by classical scholars. Torahs are one of the few scrolls still produced. They differ from the classical ones in having two 'rolling pins' ('trees of life'), one for each end, which makes a difference in ease of use. Sometimes classical rolls were wound around dowels, called ὀμφαλοί in Greek and *umbilici* in Latin. Expensive models might have the ends of the dowels (*cornua*) capped with ivory (Gamble, *Books*, 48). According to Černý (*Paper*, 11), the *umbilicus* was not used for ancient Egyptian rolls. Černý's work remains an excellent summary and description of Egyptian practices.

4 Roberts/Skeat, *Codex*, 11.

5 Plain wooden tablets were also common. A speech of Isocrates appears on such a set, dating back to the fourth or fifth century AD and found in Egypt at Ismet-el-Ghareb near Dakhleh (Blanck, *Buch*, 47–48 with photograph on p. 47).

6 *Scrivere Etrusco*, especially the reconstruction on pp. 24–25 and the three illustrations on p. 23, of which the top left, an Etruscan cinerary statue from Chiusi, with a *liber linteus* on the left under the hat of a haruspex, is the earliest. This object is in Berlin, Staatliche Museen, inv. E 33. Livy (4.7.12) mentions that such 'linen books' were in the Temple of Juno Moneta on the Capitoline in Rome and implies that at least some of them contained lists of magistrates. See Ogilvie, *Comm*, 544. Piccaluga (1994a) discusses the sacral nature of linen compared to either parchment or papyrus for the Romans.

7 Roberts/Skeat, *Codex*, 12, 29 ['still-born' in reference to Martial's experiment] and 75 respectively.

8 For the history of the codex in early Christianity, see Gamble (*Books*, 46–66). The earliest extant codex dates to the beginning of the second century AD and is a Latin work, *De bellis Macedonicis* (P. Oxyrhynchus 30), on which see Gamble (*Books*, 52). He says (p. 65) that seventeen Greek codices have survived from the second century AD, of which 'six are what may appropriately be called professional manuals – grammatical, lexical, and medical handbooks. It may well be that several of the literary texts [the other eleven codices] were working copies for educational use and so also fall into the category of professional manuals. Thus, the early non-Christian evidence suggest an essentially utilitarian attitude toward the codex.'

9 Carruthers, 29. For a study of the terminology used for the various forms of ancient books, see Holtz 1989a, especially for the time of St Augustine. For a history of wax tablets from their beginnings in the Near East until modern times, see Lalou, *Tablettes*.

10 As Frank Abate pointed out to me, poets and readers would be aware of the meter no matter what the display. Understanding of the meter, however, does not necessarily entail awareness of the unit of the line, if one takes the lack of awareness of the word on the part of the Guslar singers as an analogy. Williamson (*Sappho*, 45) remarks that in the first printed editions of Sappho in the sixteenth century: 'The most striking feature of these late additions [to the existing printed text] is the fact that they are quoted as if they were prose. Neither Estienne nor anyone else has yet established the correct metrical divisions.'

11 This problem is especially acute for Propertius and Ovid. See William A. Johnson, 'When Is a Poem a Poem? The Augustan Poetry Book and Problems of Poem Division in Propertius and Ovid', lecture given at Rutgers University, February 1996. I especially thank Johnson for letting me read the typescript for this lecture.

12 Pritchett, *DionHal*, 68 n. 8 with bibliography.

13 Suetonius, *On Grammarians*, 2. Translation from the LCL.

14 Bower *et al.* 1979a, 185 for the quotation. The experiment is described on pp. 184–188.

15 Aristotle, *Sophistical Refutations*, 20 = 177b. Translation from Aristotle, Bollingen.

16 Reynolds/Wilson, 9.

17 Nagy, *PoetPerf*, 125. Nagy's whole discussion of accents (pp. 125–128) is of interest.

18 *OCD*^{2}, 174, s.v. 'Books, Greek and Latin' (F. G. Kenyon and C. H. Roberts). Turner, *GrMss*, 8 with examples illustrated. He notes that Isocrates (*Antidosis*, 59) in the fourth century BC already uses the term *paragraphe* and that such marks appear in the earliest papyri. For an example of the *paragraphus* used to indicate a change in speaker, see Turner, *GrMss*, 58–59 No. 28 = Sophocles?, Cambridge University Library Ms. Add. 5895, P. Oxy. viii. 1083; dated to the second century AD.

19 Turner, *GrMss*, 8 and 10, with examples cited in n. 41. For an example of a comparatively well marked up ancient text, consider a papyrus with the *Hypsipyle* of Euripides from AD 175–225. The scribe not only uses the *paragraphus* to mark changes in speakers, but also hanging indents. He has also added indications of 'high stops, accents, tremata, rough breathings . . . apostrophes . . . and marks of long quantity' (Turner, *GrMss*, 62–63 No. 31. Oxford, Bodleian, MS. Gr. Class. b. 13 (P) = P. Oxy. vi 852).

20 According to Reynolds/Wilson (245), 'The use and gradual refinement of punctuation are still debated.' They add (pp. 247–248) that recent scholarship questions whether classical Latin really provided 'more in the way of punctuation and aids to the reader' than classical Greek (ibid., 4). Perhaps even more telling, they (p. 253) remark about Nicanor, who lived during the time of Hadrian and who wrote about the punctuation of the *Iliad*, that 'His system was sophisticated and no doubt partly for that reason there is no sign that it ever came to be more widely adopted.' The best and fullest treatment of the history of punctuation is Parkes, *Pause*, and for antiquity, especially pp. 9–19. For a review of the scholarship of the past fifty years on punctuation, see Rafti 1988a. Fantham (*RLC*, xiii) mentions that with respect to literature and rhetoric 'for at least part of the second century of our era Greek seems to have renewed its hegemony over Latin.' Clearly, the demise of the interpunct reflects that change.

21 Saenger/Heinlen 1991a, 235.

22 Today we face a similar problem: the death of the footnote. Many publishers seem to fear that using those incredibly nice little numbers will scare some readers into thinking that the book is too difficult. Instead, whole phrases are used to key the notes, with the result that only the truly masochistic read them. See Geoffrey Pullum's (62–63) wonderful description of the twelve steps it takes to read certain arrangements of footnotes.

23 Diogenes Laertius 3.65–66. Translation from the LCL. The translation gives an example in parentheses for each of the marks, though they are not present in the text. On such marks, see Kaster, *Suetonius*, 246–247 with bibliography and brief discussion of the *Anecdoton Parisinum* (extract from the codex, Paris. lat. 7530 (s. viii)), which comprises two lists of such *notae*.

24 Starr 1981a and Rubincam 1989a. Frakes (1995a, 241–242) discusses the category of 'unfulfilled cross-references', which an author uses to refer to something he intends to write about later, but then forgets to do. Frakes cites examples from not just Ammianus Marcellinus, but also Herodotus and Diodorus Siculus. The one major exception to the vague cross-reference is early Christian. Eusebius (*c.* AD 260–340) developed a system, the 'Canon Tables', for 'locating parallel passages in the Gospels', on which see Metzger, *TextNT*, 24–25.

25 'quam te, conspicuae divina Philippica famae,/volveris a prima quae proxima' (Juvenal, *Satires*, 10.124–126).

26 Turner, *GrMss*, 16.

27 Turner (*GrMss*, 12) defines the *coronis* as 'essentially a paragraphus with an elaborate structure of decorative curly lines above and below.' For an actual example, see: papyrus fragment of Homer, *Iliad*, 2 ('The Harris Homer'), later third century AD; London, British Museum, Pap. 126; from Ma'abdeh near Assiut (Turner, *GrMss*, 40–41 No. 14).

28 For example, on a papyrus fragment with Pindar, *Paeans*, Nos. 14 and 15. Poem No. 14 ends evenly spaced above No. 15, but the title of the next poem (15) is written to the left (Turner, *GrMss*, 50–51 No. 22 = P. Oxy. xxvi 2441, II c. AD) Turner notes that 'Critical signs . . . and lectional signs were probably added later', that is not by the original scribe, but probably by the owner.

29 Turner (*GrMss*, 1) cites two examples: *Edict of Diocletian: de pretiis rerum venalium*, col. 7.39–41, from AD 301; and *B.M. Papyrus 2110*, Oxyrhynchus, II c. AD. The first says: 'To a scribe for best writing, 100 lines, 25 denarii; For second quality writing. 100 lines, 20 denarii; To a notary for writing a petition or legal document, 100 lines, 10 denarii.' The second example is similar, but without

mention of quality. I thank William Johnson for bringing these passages to my attention. He also suggested that this use of stichometry, as it is called, began early. For a papyrus with the totals for both the column and the entire roll, see the 'Harris Homer' mentioned in note 27 above.

30 Johnson 1994a.

31 For example, Turner, *GrMss*, 100–101 No. 59 'Abstracts of Contracts', now in Ann Arbor, P. Mich. Inv. 622; recto col. iv., AD 42.

32 Saenger/Heinlen 1991a, 251–252.

33 Hadas, 13–14. Reynolds/Wilson, 4. Saenger/Heinlen 1991a, 252.

34 Saenger/Heinlen 1991a, 251, 253.

35 See Connors 1993a for a discussion of the various fonts and papers available today and how they affect the message.

36 Scisco 1994a, 477. The program is produced by Microsoft Corporation.

37 Miller 1994b, 80.

38 Lanham, *ElecWord*, 7. Unfortunately, because my word processor fails at San Francisco and Gothic, I have substituted Braggadocio Regular (a wonderful name – what is Braggadocio Irregular?) and Algerian Regular. Also see Lanham, *ElecWord*, 30–52 = Chapter 3 ('Digital Rhetoric and the Digital Arts') on more possibilities and the historical background.

39 'The Effect of Color on Memory', *Resolution* 1 No. 2 (May 1994): 5. The article, without named author, does cite four studies from, naturally, the advertising world. *Resolution* is a 'newsletter' produced by Hewlett-Packard to sell their products, in this case clearly a color printer.

40 The program is put out by FontShop USA and was reviewed by Edward Mendelson, 'Beowolf Fonts Mimic the Look of Metal Typography', *PC Magazine* vol. 14 no. 15 (12 September 1994), 49.

41 Legal documents are an exception, but they tend to be considerably shorter than literary texts. They are discussed in Chapter 5.

42 Aulus Gellius, *Attic Nights*, 9.4.13. Translation from the LCL 2.166 with n. 2. The modern system of citation began in the thirteenth century. See Rouse/Rouse 1991a, 235.

43 For an example of a reference to the very beginning of a work, consider Gellius, *Attic Nights*, 18.9.5: 'a manuscript of Livius Andronicus of undoubted antiquity, entitled "Odusseia", in which the first line contained this word [*insece*] without the letter "*u*"' (translation from the LCL). The ends of texts, '*explicits*', do not seem to be cited with any great frequency. According to the OED^2, '*explicit*' in this sense comes in with medieval Latin and is not formally used as a term to indicate the last words of a work until 1658.

44 Fraser (*Alexandria*, I: 327 and IIa: 485 n. 174) believes that the Library at Alexandria, because of the large number of works with which it had to deal, fostered a certain amount of standardization to ease both production and storage. Van Sickle (1980a) presents the idea of some 'standardization' for certain kinds of poetic works. See also OCD^2, 173 s.v. 'Books, Greek and Latin': 'The number of lines varies with the height of the column and the size of the writing; but numbers less than 25 or more than 45 are exceptional. Neither in the roll nor later in the codex, where reference was easy, as it could never have been with the roll, was the ancient scribe concerned to keep the same number of lines to a column. The number of letters to a line similarly varied.' Morrison (1987a, 244 and elsewhere) relates the development of the increasing refinements of layout to the development of certain kinds of logical argumentation.

45 Pliny the Elder, *Natural History*, Preface, 33. Translation from the LCL.

46 'quid singulis contineretur libris huic epistulae subiunxi. . . .'

47 Only the fact that everything was written by hand matters for my argument. The precise 'hands' used do not. The writers range from children learning to write to scribes, who write a fast cursive, with letters often run together, for documents, and other scribes, who produce the slow, but beautiful and quite readable 'bookhand'. Not until the medieval period do distinct 'upper' and 'lower case' letters appear. On students' hands, see Cribiore, *WTS*, Chapter 4 with summary p. 240. For Greek hands, see Turner, *GrMss*, 1–4. For an example of a cursive hand, see note 27 above. For a bookhand see papyrus with Homer, *Iliad*, 2.755–775, illustrated in Turner, *GrMss*, 38–39 No. 13 = Oxford, Bodleian Ms. Gr. Class. a. I (P); middle second century AD. For Latin script in Antiquity and the Middle Ages see Bischoff, *LatPal*, 54–82 and 83–149 respectively.

48 Stout, *Scribe*, 82. For an illustration of the problem, see *CEL*, 187.

49 Gellius, *Attic Nights*, Preface 25. Translation from the LCL.

50 Translation from the LCL. The chapter divisions are, of course, not ancient.

51 Saenger (1991a) presents an excellent summary and discussion of these issues. He is also the source for my information on the distinction between alphabets with and without vowels, as well as the reference to Seneca. The implications are my own.

52 Crowder/Wagner, 13–14.

53 Sampson (*Writing*, 89) implies that very early Hebrew did not have spaces.

54 Eyre/Baines 1989a, especially 100–105, provide a very interesting discussion of ancient Egyptian and how it works from a cognitive point of view, though they do not use the term 'cognitive'.

55 Savage-Rumbaugh/Lewin, *Kanzi*, 232–233.

56 Sampson (*Writing*, 92–98) has a good discussion of information theory and redundancy in a comparison between Hebrew (written without vowels) and English and the efforts needed to decode both. Compare also Shimron/Sivan 1994a. Campbell (*GramMan*, especially 67–74) presents one of the clearest accounts of information theory in far more detail than I can go into here. He puts information theory into a very broad context that includes how the genetic code (DNA), thermodynamics, and language work. He is also a pleasure to read.

57 Shimron/Sivan 1994a, 20. Beginning texts in Hebrew generally use pointed Hebrew. So, in classical antiquity children similarly had texts that marked the syllables and words either by spaces or oblique strokes (Cribiore, *WTS*, 67).

58 New Kingdom Egypt had a proverb – 'Write with your hand, read with your mouth, and seek advice' – that indicates that they, too, must have read aloud. For the proverb in two different texts (P. Anast. III, 3/10–4/4 and P. Anast. V, 22/6–23/6), see Williams 1972a, 218.

59 Compare Schenkeveld 1992a and Johnson 1994c, especially 238–239. So Cassiodorus (*c.* AD 490–583) remarks on 'copying the precepts of the Lord. . . . What happy application, what praiseworthy industry, to preach unto men by means of the hand, to untie the tongue by means of the fingers.' In other words, writing is meant to be spoken. See Cassiodorus, *Senatoris Institutiones*, 1.30.1. Translation from Metzger, *TextNT*, 18.

60 Bruthiaux 1993a.

61 Bruthiaux 1993a, 28. He gives a good summary of the history of punctuation from the point of view of its function. He also rightly concludes (p. 35) that 'the nature of punctuation did not shift smoothly from prosody toward syntax.'

62 Seneca the Younger, *Letters*, 40.11–12. Translation from Campbell, *Seneca*. One

of the earliest comparisons between Greek and Latin was made by Cato the Elder two centuries earlier (191 BC): 'Moreover, he [Cato] says the Athenians were astonished at the speed and pungency of his discourse. For what he himself set forth with brevity, the interpreter would repeat to them at great length and with many words' (Plutarch, *Life of Cato the Elder*, 12.5. Translation from the LCL). See also Astin, *Cato*, 160–161 on Cato and the Greeks.

63 Morrison 1987a, 244 (the quote), 258, 263. He presents a fascinating interpretation of how the layout of the written word affects what the written words are.

64 Quintilian 1.1.31. Latin does not really have a word for 'sentence'. Their word, '*sententia*', on which ours is based, means an opinion, thought, or sense rather than our idea of a particular grammatical unit that contains a subject and verb ending, in print, with a period. The Latin definitions are from the *OLD*, s.v. '*sententia*'.

65 Quintilian 1.8.1–2. Translation from the LCL.

66 Ellis/Beattie, 227. So also Crowder/Wagner (161), who devote an entire chapter to 'The Role of Speech in Reading', pp. 156–188. When Saenger (1982a, 383) claims the opposite effect, he probably means that the visual display remains as a prompt and reminder of the difficult text. In any case, he adds (pp. 383–384) that in the seventh century Isidore of Seville was already recommending 'that the tongue and lips be moved quietly' to aid comprehension.

67 Quoted in Saenger/Heinlen 1991a, 255 n. 59 from: Erasmus, *De recta graeci et latini sermonis pronunciatione*, ed. M. Cytowska, in *Opera omnia Desiderii Erasmi Rotterdami recognita et adnotatione critica notisque illustrata*, ser. I, vol. 4 (Amsterdam 1973), 38. Translation by A. S. Osley, *Scribes and Sources: Handbook of the Chancery Hand in the Sixteenth Century: Texts from the Writing Masters* (London 1980), 34.

68 Metzger, *TextNT,* 13 with examples from the New Testament in n. 2.

69 Paul Saenger (1982a, 1990a, 1991a) has·written a number of excellent articles on the subject, and is currently working on a book.

70 Knox 1968a, 432.

71 Plutarch, *On the Fortune of Alexander,* 340a. Translation from the LCL.

72 Schenkeveld 1992a, 130 n. 2 (in *de judicandi facultate et animi principatu*, 5.2).

73 Knox 1968a, 422.

74 Horowitz 1991a, 135.

75 For example, compare not only Knox 1968a, but Schenkeveld 1992a and Starr 1991a, all of which give citations to previous scholarship as well as a variety of ancient sources.

76 Svenbro 1989a, 236.

77 Saenger 1990a, 54–55. Compare his fuller discussion of word separation in Saenger 1982a, 377–379.

78 Bruthiaux (1995a, 1) says that the semi-colon was most popular in the seventeenth and eighteenth centuries; he now considers it a 'marginal component of the English punctuation system.'

79 Crowder/Wagner, 23–24. For a review of recent studies, see Hartley 1992a and 1993a, and Jandreau/Bever 1992a. Hartley notes that putting individual words, each on their own line, does not aid comprehension. For an interesting study of the kinds of errors one makes because of visual displays, 'slips of the eye', including those from chunked arrangements, such as in my text, see Cowie 1985a.

80 Gamble, *Books*, 229–230. Technically this practice is known as '*per cola et commata*', that is 'by phrase and clause'. Metzger (*TextNT,* 29) says that this

practice began with classical orations of Demosthenes and Cicero, but gives no references to actual papyri. The idea of composing speeches in a 'periodic' style, however, goes back to the fourth century BC, on which see Aristotle, *Rhetoric*, 3.9 (compare Kennedy, *AristRhet*, 239–243); and Dionysius of Halicarnassus, *Demosthenes*, 39 and 43.

81 Dionysius of Halicarnassus, *On Literary Composition*, 25. Translation from the LCL. Quintilian (1.1.30–31) in the next century offers the same advice. See Ahl, *Meta*, 36. The idea may go back to the fifth century BC, when Kallias wrote a play about the letters: 'The chorus of women is composed by him [Kallias] with the collocation of letters in pairs, set to metre and accompanied by tunes in the following manner: "Beta alpha ba, beta ei [epsilon] be, beta eta bê, beta iota bi . . . "' (Athenaeus 10.453e. Translation from the LCL). What was first considered a performance worthy of entertaining adults becomes a model, even if only indirectly, for the way children are taught to read later. On primary education in general, see Marrou, *HistEduc*, 150–153. Plutarch (*Life of Cato the Elder*, 20.5) preserves an interesting tidbit about Cato the Elder: 'His History of Rome, as he tells us himself, he wrote out with his own hand and in large characters [μεγάλοις γράμμασιν]' for his son. Translation from the LCL. Cribiore, *WTS*, discusses the mechanics of learning to write in detail. She provides a complete catalog of extant school exercises (pp. 292–439), which she divides into eleven categories (p. 12), including syllabaries. One of her major conclusions (p. 242) is that 'students, after learning the alphabet and before being introduced to the study of syllables (that is before reading), copied sentences and verses from models in order to improve the quality of their hand.' She discusses the literary passages on teaching writing on pp. 242–249 and carefully distinguishes between discussions of learning to read (Dionysius of Halicarnassus's passage) and learning to write. In other words, (abstract to thesis) 'writing preceded reading and . . . copying from a model was introduced at the beginning of the curriculum.' For an example of a syllabary with separate lists of syllables and words divided by syllables see Cairo Museum, Ms 65445, third century BC, papyrus with photographs in Bonner, *Education*, 170–171 figs 18–19 respectively.

82 For a discussion of the role of song in aiding memorization, see Chapters 6 and 9, the section 'Other Recommendations'. For spelling and learning to read, see Shankweiler/Lundquist 1992a.

83 For the major study, see Marilyn Adams, *BegRead*. For the reaction, see Bower 1992a and Adams *et al.* 1991a.

84 Henderson 1992a, 19 and 17 respectively.

85 I took this sentence from a book on linguistics, which used it for quite a different purpose: to illustrate the problem of not knowing where the pauses are when learning a foreign language. Unfortunately, this is one of the references that got away; I do not remember the source.

86 Sirat (1994a, 425) claims that the situation for Latin is actually worse: 'the writing units can indeed be letters but mostly they are strokes, chunks of strokes, parts of words, whole words . . . reading is not the pronunciation of a string of letters. The image of the word has to be interpreted, decoded by means of former knowledge and by use of the context.'

87 See Ahl, *Meta*, especially 35–44 . Ahl's Introduction (17–63) is a fascinating and convincing account of different types of word play in Latin. In particular, Ahl stresses (p. 45) that 'meaning evolves at the level of the syllable' and that 'it evolves at the alphabetic level' in remarkable anagrams that relate, e.g. *flumina* (rivers) and *fulmina* (thunderbolts). Ahl does not consider the idea that some of

the classical focus on the syllable derives from their visual display of text. On classical grammarians and their linguistic knowledge, see Atherton 1996a.
88 Frost 1994a and Chitiri/Willows 1994a, both with references to the extensive bibliography on the subject. The Frost article is particularly interesting for using Hebrew in its pointed (shallow) and unpointed (deep) orthographies to test reading processes. It should be noted that a controversy still exists as to whether the distinction between 'shallow' and 'deep' orthographies is valid, on which see Frost/Katz, *OPMM* with articles on both sides. For the negative, especially see Besner/Smith 1992a.
89 Crowder/Wagner, 143.
90 Shimron/Sivan 1994a, 22.

3 'PUBLICATION'

1 Gigante, *Philodemus*, 17. Especially helpful is Dorandi 1993a.
2 Marital, *Epigrams*, 2.1. Translation from the LCL.
3 Clanchy (*Memory*, 63) describes a medieval example of the process of making multiple copies in which one poor scribe couldn't fit at the table with the others, and so he 'was therefore given a place higher up, where he could make his copy over the treasurer's scribe's shoulder.'
4 Petitmengin/Flusin 1984a, especially 252–255.
5 Gigante, *Philodemus*, 29–30.
6 Cornelius Nepos, *On Famous Lives*, 25, Atticus 13.3. Translation from the LCL. See also Phillips 1986a. Horsfall (*Nepos*, 89, *ad Atticus* 13.3), contra Phillips, rightly says: 'Numerous expert slaves could clearly produce many copies for a close friend (i.e. Cicero); that does not make Atticus what we may properly call a publisher, and there is no evidence at all that he made money thereby. His activity in the world of books is to be seen, as elsewhere, in terms of friendship and the return of favors.'
7 Posner, 87 figs. 20–21. Parkinson/Quirke, 61 fig. 41.
8 Cicero, *Letters to Atticus*, 13.23. Translation from Shackleton Bailey, *Atticus*, No. 331. The translator uses the singular 'book' for the Latin 'books', implying a multi-rolled work.
9 *Letters to Atticus*, 12.6a. Translation from Shackleton Bailey, *Atticus*, No. 243.
10 Gigante, *Philodemus*, 18. The words in quotes are from G. Cavallo, but without any further attribution.
11 Van Groningen 1963a, especially 4.
12 *Letters to Atticus*, 13.21a (Shackleton Bailey, *Atticus*, 327), 13.22.3 (Shackleton Bailey, *Atticus*, 329); and 13.23.2 (Shackleton Bailey, *Atticus*, 331). See also Phillips 1986a.
13 Cicero, *Letters to Atticus*, 13.21a.2. Translation from Shackleton Bailey, *Atticus*, No. 327.
14 M. Cornelius Fronto, *Correspondence*, Ambr. 62 (Naber, p. 17) 3–4. Translation from the LCL.
15 Suetonius, *Life of Augustus*, 87. Translation from the LCL.
16 Suetonius, *Life of Augustus*, 88. Translation from the LCL.
17 McArthur, *EngLang*, 811–812, s.v. 'Proof-reading' (William W. Barker). This entry gives a brief history of proofing from the time of print and explains the difficulties that proofing presents today, though without any mention of the kinds of errors that computerized typescripts cause. For an interesting study of a medieval, eleventh-century scriptorium with sixty-four scribes, see Cohen-Mushlin 1992a, with a summary of the process of proofing on p. 198.

NOTES

18 Suetonius, *On Grammarians*, 24. Translation from the LCL. For an excellent discussion of the terms, see Kaster, *Suetonius*, 260–266.

19 Allen 1910a, 80.

20 For an example of the original scribe correcting his own mistakes see P. Teb. I. 4, coll. iv–v; middle of the second century BC papyrus fragment of Homer, *Iliad*, 2; Turner, *GrMss*, 38–39 No. 12. There, according to Turner, 'the word κατω indicates that the following verse, omitted in error, was supplied in the lower margin.' For an example of a second person correcting someone else's mistakes see a third-century AD papyrus of Hesiod, *Catalogue*. P. Oxy. xvii 2075. Turner, *GrMss*, 34, 36–37 No. 11.

21 See my discussion on both Homer and the Tragedians in Chapter 13 with full references.

22 Plutarch, *Life of Alcibiades*, 7.1–2. Translation from the LCL.

23 Allen 1910a, 77 n. 2. Much of my discussion on errors and how they were corrected in antiquity comes from this article, pp. 76–80.

24 Strabo 13.1.54. Translation from Hadas, 21–22. The rest of this passage is discussed in Chapter 4.

25 For a discussion of the gamut of possibilities, as they occur within just one set of manuscripts, the *Letters* of Pliny the Younger, see Stout, *Scribe*, 81–113.

26 Cicero, *Letters to His Brother Quintus*, 3.5. Translation from Shackleton Bailey, *Friends*, No. 25.

27 Varro, *On the Latin Language*, 8.51. Translation from the LCL, with note 'e' on p. 411.

28 Livy 38.55.8. My translation.

29 Martial, *Epigrams*, 2.8.1–6. Translation from the LCL.

30 Plutarch, *Life of Lucullus*, 42.1.

31 Pliny the Younger, *Letters*, 4.26. Translation from Radice, *PlinyY.*

32 Eusebius, *The History of the Church*, 5.20.2. Translation from Williamson, *Euseb.*

33 Codex Sinaiticus, *c.* AD 309, translation from Skeat 1956a, 194.

34 Aulus Gellius, *Attic Nights*, 1.7 summary and 1.7.1. Translation from the LCL.

35 Quintilian 9.4.39. Translation from the LCL.

36 One of the fuller discussions of ancient titles appears in Blum, *Kallimachos*, especially 146–148, 156–157. See also Horsfall 1981a.

37 I have not translated ἀπόδεξις as 'publication', as it frequently is, because I think the English word has implications beyond what Herodotus would have meant.

38 Athenaeus 1.4e. Translation from the LCL. According to the *OCD²* (97, s.v. 'Archestratus' (J. D. Denniston)), Archestratus was a contemporary of Aristotle.

39 Blum, *Kallimachos*, 156. The use of an *'explicit'* ('unrolled'), that is, the last words, is medieval. *'Colophon',* as the term for the identifying information at the end of a work, is seventeenth century, according to the *RHUD.* Sometimes the word *'subscription'* is used, as in Reynolds/Wilson, 31 and 39–43. The earliest Greek colophon is third century BC according to Parássoglou 1979a, 17.

40 Athenaeus 6.244a. Translation adapted from the LCL. 'Kurebion' was a nickname for Epicrates, a Middle Comedy playwright who lived before 347 BC. *OCD²*, 390 s.v. 'Epicrates'; and LSJ 1012, s.v. κυρηβίων.

41 Bischoff, *LatPal*, 188 on this custom passing from the roll to the codex. He also notes (p. 79) that running titles begin with the earliest codices. I discuss the tags in Chapter 4.

42 Turner, *GrMss*, 13–14. Gamble, *Books*, 48. One of the papyri from the Villa of the Papyri in Herculaneum (late first century BC) shows the title in large letters

at the end of the roll. *P. Herc.* 1424, after col. 28 = Philodemus, *On Household Management*, photograph in Gigante, *Philodemus*, fig. 14.

43 Quintilian (8.3.60), approximately a century later, is the first such reference, but his wording is interesting: 'such as Horace describes in the first part of his book on the poetic art [*in prima parte libri de arte poetica*].' Because of the absence of any means of distinguishing titles from the rest of the text, it is not possible to tell whether Quintilian is describing the content or labeling the text. Compare Fantham, *RLC*, 85 and 265 n. 1 and 279 n. 67.

44 Pliny the Elder, *Natural History*, Preface, 24–26. Translation adapted from the LCL.

45 Pliny the Younger, *Letters*, 5.6.42. Translation from Radice, *PlinyY*. Naturally this comment comes at the end of one of Pliny's longest letters.

46 Adams 1987a, 10.

47 Aulus Gellius, *Attic Nights*, Preface, 4, 10. Translation from the LCL.

48 Suetonius, *On Poets – Terence*, 2. Translation from the LCL.

49 Carruthers, 86.

50 Adams 1987a, 7.

51 Cole, *OrigRhet*, 41. Compare Thomas, *LitOral*, 113–127.

52 Translation from the LCL, *Lyra Graeca*, 2nd edition, 3.348. Pindar says, 'the Muse was not in love with money then – /she didn't work for hire,/nor would wanton songs with silvered faces saunter/from melodious Terpsichora's shop into the market place.' Translation by Nisetich, *Pindar*, 300. According to Nisetich (298), Pindar is being 'ironical' here. On Simonides's reputation as a tightwad, see Carson 1993a.

53 Lucian, *Herodotus or Aëtion*, 1–2. Translation from the LCL.

54 Lucian, *Herodotus or Aëtion*, 2. Translation from the LCL.

55 Momigliano 1978a, 368. Johnson (1994c) is similarly skeptical (especially p. 245). He discusses the division of Herodotus into books on p. 241. When Johnson, however, says (p. 246) of the opening of the *Histories* that 'Herodotus standing before the crowd would hardly refer to himself in the third person', it makes me think that he has never watched American politicians of a certain age, like Bob Dole, who almost never refer to themselves in the first person. During the period of time I have been writing this book, Bob Dole has become the presidential candidate for the Republican Party and with his new position has adopted a new style. He now occasionally speaks of himself in the first person. Thomas (1993a) considers Herodotus and his similarities to the early Hippocratic writers. She rightly notes (p. 226) that 'We are not dealing with either oral transmission or written, as alternatives, but a complex combination of both.' She strongly believes that Herodotus did do public 'readings' and that the real issue is the nature of those readings.

56 For example, Hippias of Elis who lived *c.* 485–415 BC. *OCD²* 517, s.v. 'Hippias (2)' (W. D. Ross). Hippias was the subject of two of Plato's dialogues.

57 Diogenes Laertius 3.37. Translation from the LCL. Diogenes attributes this factoid to Favorinus, who lived in the second century AD.

58 Cicero, *Brutus*, 51.191. Translation from the LCL.

59 Aristotle, *Rhetoric*, 3.1415b. Translation from Kennedy, *AristRhet*. On public speaking and written texts, see Cole, *OrigRhet*, 71–74 ('Technê and Text').

60 Plato, *Republic*, 5.475d. Translation from Rouse, *Plato*.

61 Quintilian, 1, Preface 7–8. Translation from the LCL. Fantham (*RLC*, 15) suggests that 'the existence of such pirated publications surely suggests that there was profit . . . in the reproduction of such works.' This profit probably accrued to the reproducer, that is the bookseller, rather than either the author

or the students in Quintilian's case. Alexander (1990a) discusses the importance in the ancient world of oral teaching over written learning. Writing, he concludes, is to remind and prod the memory of what it already knows. Compare the extensive discussion of Gamble (*Books*, 203–231) on public reading of Christian books.

62 Our sources disagree on who was the first to make a regular practice of performing in public among the Romans. Suetonius (*On Grammarians*, 2) more or less attributes its introduction to Crates of Mallos (*c.* 169 BC), while Seneca the Elder (*Controversies*, 4, Preface, 2) says it was Asinius Pollio in the first century BC. Dalzell (1955a) suggests that Seneca really means that Pollio organized formal recitations in the Atrium Libertatis to which the public at large could come. I think small 'public' readings must have always occurred, but that open invitations even to those not personally known by the author were later. In general, see Quinn 1982a, 140–165 ('IV. The Poet's Audience'); Salles, *Lire*, 93–110. Fantham (*RLC*, 2) baldly states that 'The author at Rome was in many genres and most periods both composer and performer.' Not all writers, however, were happy about performing, as Horace makes clear in *Epistles*, 1.19.35–49, on which see Fantham, *RLC*, 86–87. Howell (*Martial*, 104 *ad* 1.4) notes that Martial was an exception who regularly addressed his readers rather than his listeners, whom he refers to only twice (9.81 and 12, Preface, 9–10).

63 Quinn 1982a, 154 with discussion following.

64 Suetonius, *Life of Nero*, 10.2. Translation from the LCL. Fantham (*RLC*, 153–158) discusses Nero's literary oeuvre.

65 Suetonius, *Life of Claudius*, 41.1. Translation from the LCL.

66 Suetonius, *On Poets – Vergil*, 26–29. Translation from the LCL.

67 Suetonius, *On Poets – Vergil*, 34. Translation from the LCL.

68 Pliny the Younger, *Letters*, 9.34. Translation from Radice, *PlinyY.*

69 Pliny the Younger, *Letters*, 4.19. Translation from Radice, *PlinyY.*

70 Pliny the Younger, *Letters*, 9.17. Translation from Radice, *PlinyY.*

71 Pliny the Younger, *Letters*, 1.13. Translation from Radice, *PlinyY.*

72 Tacitus, *A Dialogue on Oratory*, 9.4. Translation from the LCL. For a consideration of such recitations during the time of Pliny the Younger and Tacitus, see Fantham, *RLC*, 211–221.

73 Richardson, *NDTAR*, 40–41, s.v. 'Athenaeum'. *LTUR* 1, 131–132 s.v. 'Athenaeum' (F. Coarelli). The building has not been found. On earlier places for recital, especially the Temple of Apollo Palatinus, see Fantham, *RLC*, 88–90.

74 Quinn 1982a, 162.

4 THE ORGANIZATION OF COLLECTIONS OF WORDS

1 Kenney 1982a, Knox 1985a, Starr 1987a and 1990a. On fourth-century AD Antioch, see Norman 1960a. For the possibility of book auctions, see Kleberg 1973a.

2 Pliny the Younger, *Letters*, 9.11. Translation from Radice, *PlinyY.*

3 Horace, *The Art of Poetry*, 345. Translation from the LCL. Also see discussion in Kenney 1982a, 20–22. Blanck (*Buch*, 126 with fig. 82) suggests that the end of a papyrus roll with a 'signature', 'of Sosius' (<u>C</u>WCYOY) in Greek, after the author and title of the work ('Apollodoros the Athenian, Grammatical Questions on Book 14 of the *Iliad*') refers to the book dealer Sosius and not to the scribe. Milan, R. Università di Milano I, Nr. 19.

4 Martial, *Epigrams*, 12.3. Translation from the LCL. A number of booksellers in Rome were located in the Argiletum, a road that ran into the Forum Romanum between the Curia and the Basilica Aemilia, and connected the Forum with Subura, a valley between the Viminal and Esquiline hills. Martial refers to them in 1.3.1. Richardson, *NTDAR*, 39 s.v. '*Argiletum*'.

5 Seneca the Younger, *On Tranquillity of Mind*, 9.5. Translation from the LCL.

6 Lucian 1, 4, and 19. Translation from the LCL. For a discussion of other forgeries, especially for stocking the library at Alexandria, see Fraser, *Alexandria*, 325–326. For a discussion of the antiquarian trade in Rome, especially in the second century AD, see Zetzel 1973a and Reynolds/Wilson, 30–31.

7 Onions, *ODEE*, 526 s.v. 'library'. On classical libraries in general, see: Clark, *Libraries*; Dix, *Libraries*; Johnson, *Library*, and Strocka 1981a. For bibliography, see Bruce 1985a.

8 For the Latin words, see *OLD*, 1027, s.v. *librarius* nos. 2 and 3.

9 Diodorus Siculus 1.3.6. Translation from the LCL.

10 Pliny the Elder, *Natural History*, Preface 25. Translation from the LCL.

11 Xenophon, *Memorabilia*, 4.2.1. Translation from the LCL.

12 Athenaeus 1.3a.

13 Havelock, *Preface*, 55 n. 14. For a summary of the evidence, see Woodbury 1976a, 354–355 n. 15. Rawson (*IntellLife*, 51) believes that Varro's lost work, *On Libraries*, would have filled in many of our gaps in knowledge, for she says that in it 'he described materials and manufacture of books, and almost certainly the history of great libraries in the Greek world and in Rome, with perhaps discussion of the best way to organise them.' I think she is overly optimistic.

14 Cicero, *Letters to Atticus*, 4.10 = Shackleton Bailey, *Atticus*, 84. Shackleton Bailey (*Cicero*, 90) interprets the crucial passage as being ambiguous. Either Cicero is working at the library of Faustus, the son of Sulla, or he has purchased the library and refers to it by its previous owner. Dix (*Libraries*, 16–71) discusses this 'library' extensively. He concludes (p. 25) that 'After Faustus Sulla [the son of Sulla], then, we do not know the fate of the library.'

15 Strabo 13.1.54. Translation from Hadas, 21–22. Grayeff (*Aristotle*, 74–75) disagrees with the part of Strabo's account about the rolls being 'moth-eaten'. He (p. 76) also attributes a major reappraisal of Aristotle as a philosopher to Cicero as a result of his acquisition of Aristotle's works. Compare the arch description by Horsfall (1993a) on stocking the library in the temple of Apollo Palatinus set up by Augustus. Dix (*Libraries*, 2–7) remarks that Aemilius Paullus and Lucullus, in addition to Sulla, acquired libraries as war booty.

16 Even then, it was a gift of a Ptolemy. Gellius (*Attic Nights*, 7.17) incorrectly claimed that in the sixth century BC Peisistratos had already established a public library at Athens. Compare Reynolds/Wilson, 5. See also *OCD²*, 607–608, s.v. 'Libraries' (F. G. Kenyon and C. H. Roberts).

17 Van Groningen (1963a) presents a fairly compelling case for extremely limited access to the various major libraries, such as the Museum in Alexandria.

18 Philostratus, *Lives of the Sophists*, 21.604. Translation from the LCL. It is unclear whether the phrase for 'library' should be taken more literally as a 'case for books'. That is, Proclus has a single *scrinium* or *capsa* to hold the pertinent rolls rather than that he has a number of such containers.

19 On the Egyptian library and Herodotus, see Evans, *Herodotus*, 136. On both Egyptian and Near Eastern antecedents, see Shubert 1993a and Parkinson/ Quirke, 57–64. Delia (1992a) gives a useful overview of the history of the

library through the Islamic period with good bibliography. For a cautious and well-documented treatment, see Fraser, *Alexandria*, I: 320–335 and notes in II: 473–494; for a more speculative view, see Canfora. For the members of the Museum, see Bagnall, *Reading*, 62–64.

20 Knox 1985a, 31.

21 Blum, *Kallimachos*, 191.

22 Fraser, *Alexandria*, I: 452. Fraser's discussion is excellent. He cites most of the literary sources in the original: I: 452–453 with notes in II: 654–656. I have also used Fraser's translation (p. 452) for the title. Fraser (331), incidentally, does not believe that Callimachus was one of the librarians.

23 Diogenes Laertius 5.22 (Aristotle). Translation from the LCL.

24 Diogenes Laertius 5.43 (Theophrastus). Translation from the LCL.

25 Fraser, *Alexandria*, 326–328. Fraser's discussion is, again, excellent with full bibliography, but I do question, as will be seen in Chapter 5, his belief that eventually everything was alphabetized.

26 An interesting parallel for the kind of information recorded occurs on early accession cards for the Smithsonian collections. In the nineteenth century the Smithsonian received numerous donations of classical objects from Americans who traveled abroad. The cataloguers at the time clearly knew little about the objects, had little time or interest in ascertaining more, and so all they recorded was who had donated the object – a very important item of information for a public museum – when, and sometimes where they had bought it. Of course, this kind of information was easily ascertainable and the other not.

27 *OCD²*, 607, s.v. 'Libraries' (F. G. Kenyon and C. H. Roberts). They add that the ancient figures are notoriously unreliable.

28 Fraser, *Alexandria*, 329.

29 Daly, 77.

30 Rouse/Rouse 1991a, 236 and 239. The Villa of the Papyri at Herculaneum is not an exception. I discuss the Villa of the Papyri in more detail in Chapter 11.

31 Diodorus Siculus 1.3.8. Translation from the LCL.

32 Athenaeus 8.336d–e. Translation from the LCL.

33 Rouse/Rouse 1991a, 237.

34 Athens, Agora Museum, I 2729. Travlos, *PDAA*, 432 and 435 fig. 553. Blanck, *Buch*, 215 fig. 121. Camp, *Agora*, 191 fig. 161 with discussion of the library, 187–193.

35 Gellius, *Attic Nights*: Trajan's Library = 11.17, Palace of Tiberius = 13.20, Library of Peace = 16.8.2, and Library of Tibur = 19.5.4 all in Rome; and the Library at Patras in Greece = 18.9.5.

36 Marcus Aurelius, *Fronto: Correspondence*, 4.5. Translation from Shelton, *Romans*, 325 No. 322. Fantham (*RLC*, 239–246) discusses the education of Marcus Aurelius.

37 Cicero, *Letters to Atticus*, 2.3. Translation from Shackleton Bailey, *Atticus*, 84 No. 23.

38 *Letters to His Brother Quintus*, 3.4.5. Translation from Shackleton Bailey, *Friends*, No. 24. On Cicero's acquisition of books, see Dix, *Libraries*, 98–107.

39 Dix, *Libraries*, 108–120.

40 *Letters to Atticus*, 2.1 = Shackleton Bailey, *Atticus*, 21. This library was received as a gift upon the death of its owner.

41 Cicero, *On Ends*, 3.2.7. Translation from the LCL.

42 Seneca the Younger, *Letters*, 2.4. Translation from the LCL.

43 Fantham, *RLC*, 202.

44 Suetonius, *Life of Domitian*, 20. Translation from the LCL. For an optimistic

view of libraries and the availability of books in Rome, see Marshall 1976a. For a clear account of libraries in the first century BC in Rome, see Quinn 1982a, 125–128 and for a more detailed account of Roman libraries, both public and private, Fedeli 1988a.

45 See Richter, *Furniture*, 114–116, and Johnson, *Library*, 152–156 for a discussion of the ancient terms with bibliography. Richter groups the words together as follows: chest = *arca, arcula, cista, capsa, scrinium, loculus*; shelf = *pegma, loculamentum, pluteus*; and cupboard = *armarium*. I tend to refer to the last as 'cabinet' or 'armoire'. Johnson adds *forulus* ('pigeonhole arrangement') and *nidus* (the pigeonhole itself). I discuss *pluteus* in Chapter 10. The lack of distinction between the words for 'chest' and 'shelf' I believe reflects our lack of knowledge rather than that all these terms were used interchangeably and generically like our 'chest'. See Also Delia 1992a, 1455 with n. 21 for references on *armaria* and *loculamenta*. The same problem exists for the Greek words (such as κάμπτρα, κάμψα, and κάψα) that are generally translated as 'bookcase'.

46. Blanck, *Buch*, 181 fig. 90. The relief is now lost.

47. New York, Metropolitan Museum of Art 1948.48.76.1, sarcophagus from Portus (near Ostia). Weitzmann, *Spirit*, 279–280 No. 256, with detail on p. 280. Amedick, *SarkMensch*, 135 No. 81 (with full bibliography) and pl. 114 figs. 1–2.

48 For a reconstruction of the Library of Trajan in the Forum in Rome, see Packer 1993a, 420. For a physical reconstruction of the Library of Hadrian at Tivoli, see Blanck, *Buch*, 204 fig. 111. Compare also the free-standing cabinet in the Villa of the Papyri, for which see Chapter 11.

49 For example, the Codex Amiatinus (fol. Vr), *c.* AD 700 with Ezra writing in front of such a cabinet. Florence, Biblioteca Medicea Laurenziana, Amiatino 1. Marsden (1995a) discusses the arrangement of the codices in the *armarium* with an illustration (p. 9 fig. 1) in which the 'titles' are restored along their spines. Marsden (p. 13) notes that 'The artist . . . has made no attempt to show the relative sizes of the volumes in the *armarium*, where the largest volume would in practice be some five times bigger than the smallest.' For a good color illustration, see Weitzmann, *LateAnt*, pl. 48. An earlier example of an armarium (AD 424–450) appears in a representation of St Lawrence in the Mausoleum of Galla Placidia, Ravenna, for which see Kitzinger, fig. 95.

50 *Scriptores Historiae Augustae*, 'Tacitus', 8.1. Translation from the LCL. David Magie, the translator, says that 'the "ivory book" is doubtless as fictitious as the "libri lintei" [mentioned earlier in *Scriptores Historiae Augustae*, "Aurelian," 1.10].' Either the work is a codex with ivory covers or the ivory refers to the ivory added as 'caps' to the end of fancy *umbilici* (the dowels that sometimes held rolls). It is now believed that one author wrote under six pseudonyms. This particular passage was 'attributed' to one Flavius Vopiscus. On the 'forgery' or, if you like, scholarly *tour de force*, see Wiseman 1993a, 124–125.

51 Posner 155–156. Zenon, the son of Agreophon, was the manager of a very large estate belonging to Apollonios, the finance minister of Ptolemy II Philadelphus. Unfortunately it is not known how Zenon actually stored his rolls. *KP* 5, 1497 s.v. 'Zenon No. 1' (Hans Volkmann). On such labeling of rolls, which tended to be lengthwise and at right angles to the text, see Luppe 1977a.

52 For three examples from Oxyrhynchus, see Turner, *GrMss*, 34–35 Nos. 6–8.

53 Cicero, *Letters to Atticus*, 4.4a. Translation from Shackleton Bailey, *Atticus*, No. 78. On what the library clerks did and how they did it, see Turner 1983a. On why Cicero needed the clerks and what they did, see Dix, *Libraries*, 135–137. For the best discussion of the *sittybai* and its synonyms (*sillyboi, index*, and

titulus), see Dorandi 1984a with actual examples illustrated. See also Gamble, *Books*, 48 and Turner, *GrMss*, 34–35 Nos. 6–8.

54 Delia 1992a, 1454–1455, with fig. 2. Delia believes that the findspot of this container may indicate the location of the library at Alexandria.

55 Translation from the Revised Standard Version.

56 Reggiani, 67 fig. 55 for an example in the Museo Egizio, Torino.

57 Latin used other variations on *capsa*, such as *capsella* and *capsula*, for which see the *OLD*. Gamble (*Books*, 48) says that *capsa* was the 'protective parchment wrapper', but the *OLD* does not list that usage. Instead Gamble's other word, '*membrana*', is the appropriate one for the 'cover for manuscripts' (*OLD*, 1095 s.v. '*membrana*' no. 3). Greek had a transliteration for 'scrinium' (σκρίνιον), which was late. In addition it also used several different words for chests or boxes that could carry rolls: ζύγαστρον, κιβωτός, and κίστη (Georgoudi 1988a, 235–236).

58 For example, a Roman wall painting of a schoolteacher from Herculaneum, no longer extant, but often reproduced from a nineteenth-century engraving (Bonner, *Education*, 29). In San Vitale, Ravenna (*c.* AD 540–547) two evangelists appear with open scrinia with the tops of the rolls showing and the covers tilted behind. See Kitzinger, pl. V in color and pls. 154, 157. A closed scrinium with a metal clasp and a leather strap for carrying appears beside a seated Vergil in the *Vergilius Romanus* manuscript in the Vatican Library, Cod. lat. 3867, fol. 14r. See Weitzmann (*Studies*, 114 fig. 91, and 115) for the date to the first half of the fifth century AD.

59 Chatsworth Relief, from Rome (Chatsworth, Collection of the Duke of Devonshire. Hadrianic). This relief is generally discussed in relation to the Anaglypha Traiani (AD 118–119) which depicted the burning of the debt records by Hadrian. Because the tablets themselves are very large on the Anaglypha, they are carried in small groups of approximately three at a time. The Chatsworth Relief, however, shows smaller tablets carried in greater numbers. Some scholars (e.g. Kleiner) call the container on the first man's shoulder a bag or sack, but a sack with such a weight should flop over the man's shoulders and not be flat with stiff, upright sides. Furthermore, a narrow fillet forms a base molding for the container, which would not appear on a sack (Kleiner, *RomSculp*, 251 with fig. 218 for the Chatsworth Relief; and 248–250 with figs. 216–217 and 265 for references for the Anaglypha Traiani. Koeppel 1985a, 148–149, 171 No. 8, and 172 figs. 10–12).

60 One of the jars from Qumran, the findspot of the Dead Sea Scrolls, has 'John' painted in Hebrew on the outside, which probably indicates its owner and not its contents, since the Dead Sea Scrolls could not refer to the 'Gospel according to John', which is part of the New Testament. The jar dates to the first century AD. For a picture, see Laymon, *InterpComm*, 947. Small containers with labels for the medicine they held have been found in Gaul. I thank Ann Hanson for this information. The term *instrumentum domesticum* refers to writing on such portable objects, on which see Harris 1995a and Harris, *Inscribed*. Curtis (1984/1986a, 210) discusses the labeling (*tituli picti*) of transport amphorae with 'various types of information, such as the name of the person to whom the vessel was sent, the shipper transporting the container, and certain numbers which might record the weight of the container or of the product itself.' Curtis focuses on containers of fish sauce, especially those from Pompeii.

Avrin (*Scribes*, 91) says that the Egyptians stored 'Scrolls . . . in ceramic jars, wicker baskets, wooden boxes, and chests. A few of these had labels; one chest had an illustration on it that may have reflected the subject the scroll that once was inside. Another had a title on it, *Book of the Sycamore and the Olive*, and an *ex libris* on a faience tag. Cylindrical book containers seen in Theban tomb paintings of the Eighteenth Dynasty resemble the later *tik*, the Torah case used by Jews living in Near Eastern countries.'

Even today unmarked containers present a problem. During the Gulf War, 'Of the 40,000 intermodal containers ferried to the Persian Gulf, two-thirds had to be opened and inspected to determine what was inside. . . . To avoid a repeat of this snafu, the Pentagon is installing a $70 million logistics-management system' (*Business Week*, 6 February 1995, 149).

61 Dorandi 1984a, 190. Reinach, *RP*, 155 fig. 5. From Pompeii, Praedia Iuliae Felicis, Regio II 4, 3 (= Helbig 859), now in Paris, Louvre. The detail of the labels can be seen in *LIMC* 7, 1020 Musae No. 71 with pl. 733 bottom, second from the left.

62 Both date from the third century AD and are in the Museo Nazionale Romano, Rome: Inv. 124472 and 2001539. For the first: Giuliano, *MNR*, vol. 1, pt. 2, 41–42 No. 30; Helbig⁴ No. 2374. For the second: Giuliano, *MNR*, vol. 1, pt. 8/2, 396–397 No. VIII.32; Reggiani 66 fig. 54. On statues of grammarians, also depicted with scrinia, see Kaster, *Suetonius*, 136–137.

63 Both say '*constitutiones corporis munimenta*' (see *CIL* 6.29814).

64 Seeck, *RE*, 2nd series, vol. 11 pt. 1, 893–904, s.v. 'Scrinium'. Posner, 207–209.

65 Suetonius, *On Grammarians*, 9 (L. Orbilius Pupillus). Translation from the LCL.

66 These uses are reflected in the English translations of *scrinium*, because English has a separate word for each differently shaped 'holder': 'portfolio' (Sallust, *The War with Catiline*, 46.6 *apud* LCL); 'despatch cases' (Pliny, *Natural History*, 7.94 *apud* LCL); 'round bookcases' (Ovid, *Tristia*, 1.1.106 *apud* LCL); and 'files' (ibid., 10.65.3, p. 283). I find the concept of a 'round book-case' incongruous and somewhat misleading, except literally as a 'case for books', although not as much as 'desk': 'desk' (Pliny the Younger, *Letters*, 5.5.5 *apud* Radice, *PlinyY*, 138); and 'writing-desk' (Suetonius, *Life of Nero*, 47.2 *apud* LCL). The only way you could use a *scrinium* as a desk would be analogous to holding a large drum between your legs. Likewise it is a mistranslation to call a *scrinium* a 'writing-case' (Horace, *Epistles*, 2.1.113 *apud* LCL), because the Romans used either '*graphiarium*' or the Greek word '*theca*' for writing-case (Suetonius, *Life of Claudius*, 35.2). I discuss 'desks' and other writing tools in Chapter 10.

67 Washington, DC, The National Museum of American History with an illustration in Olmert, *Books*, 212.

68 I know of no representations of multiple *scrinia* together.

69 Pollard 1962a, 17. I thank Elizabeth McLachlan for this reference and for discussing the minutiae of medieval books with me. For the Codex Amiatinus, see note 49 above.

70 Saenger/Heinlen 1991a, 237.

71 According to the *OED²*, the earliest citation is from 1742 on a sign for a maker of them, while the *RHUD* claims the word dates to 1720–1730.

72 Pliny the Elder, *Natural History*, 7.108. Translation adapted from the LCL.

73 Cicero, *Letters to Atticus*, 7.25.1. Translation from Shackleton Bailey, *Atticus*, No. 261.

74 Cicero, *Letters to Atticus*, 16.5.5. Translation adapted from Shackleton Bailey, *Atticus*, No. 410.

75 Cicero, *Letters to Atticus*, 9.10.4. Translation from Shackleton Bailey, *Atticus*, No. 177.

76 Cicero, *Letters to His Friends*, 16.17. Translation from Shackleton Bailey, *Friends*, No. 186.
77 For example, Cicero, *Letters to His Friends*, 7.18: '8 April, Pomptine Marshes.' Translation from Shackleton Bailey, *Friends*, No. 38.
78 Suetonius, *Life of Augustus*, 50. Translation from the LCL.
79 Pliny the Younger, *Letters*, 1.1. Translation from Radice, *Pliny Y.*
80 Norman 1960a, 125.

5 RETRIEVAL: DOCUMENTS AND TEXTS

1 Norman, *Things*, 60.
2 For hanging indents and large initial letters: Turner, *GrMss*, 100–101 No. 59, abstracts of contracts from AD 42. Ann Arbor, P. Mich. Inv. 622. For different spacings between sections and different hands: Turner, *GrMss*, 114–115 No. 68 = letter about books, Egypt Exploration Society, P. Oxy. xviii 2192, AD 170. In this example, the body of the letter was written by the scribe, the sender added the closing greeting, and a third person, possibly the recipient, added notes about the books. Likewise, documents that required either witnesses or endorsements would come with those signatures at the end of the document. For example, two officials endorsed the sale of a slave: Egypt Exploration Society; P. Oxy. 1 3593; found in Oxyrhynchus, but written in Rhodes; AD 238–44; Turner, *GrMss*, 144–145 No. 85. Some documents, such as tax records, might arrange their information in a list: Julio-Claudian tax archive from Philadelphia (Egypt), A.P. Mich. inv. 876 recto, col. ii: year ledger for AD 39/40; Hanson 1991a, 187–193 with picture on 193.
3 Letter, March 6, 1996.
4 Turner, *GrMss*, 8.
5 Cribiore, *WTS*, 2.
6 Woodhead, 29–34. Immerwahr (*Script*, 176) 'suspect[s it] was an indigenous Athenian development occurring first about 540 BC.' Osborne (1973a, with bibliography) notes that there were occasional lapses in the regularity of the 'checkerboards'.
7 Steiner, *Tyrant*, 103, summarizing *SIG* II 921.121–126, 61–64.
8 Ong, *Orality*, 120 fig. 1.
9 Connors 1993a, 73–75 with references. Back in the early days of micro-computers and clumsy dot-matrix printers, a lawyer said that he always right justified anything he didn't want people to understand. I personally became aware of the problems when I tried to read something I had written out loud and all the emph*á*ses were wrong.
10 I thank both Rosalind Thomas and Phyllis Culham for discussing these matters with me. For a 'review' article on Greek practices with copious references, see Boffo 1995a. Demougin, *MémPerdu* contains a number of articles on Roman archival practices, not all of which share my pessimistic view of the efficiency of Roman bureaucracy. Bowman/Woolf likewise contains a set of studies that focuses on the relations between writing and power, and hence frequently of documents and bureaucracy.
11 Thomas, especially 68ff.
12 Thomas, 78, 80, 82. According to Athenaeus (5.214e) the same Apellicon, who had acquired Aristotle's library and 'restored' the missing sections, also 'began surreptitiously to acquire the original copies of the ancient decrees in the Metroön, as well as anything else in other cities which was old and rare' (translation from the LCL). Note that Apellicon died in 84 BC, several centuries

after the period about which Thomas writes. For further discussion of copies, see Lawton, *ADR*, 15–16.

13 Steiner, *Tyrant*, 81 n. 75 with further information about other oracles.

14 Cribiore, *WTS*, 2.

15 Lawton, *ADR*, 27.

16 Lawton, *ADR*, 9–10. Burford, *Craftsmen*, 24–25. In addition to the inscribed building records from Athens, she discusses those from Delos, Delphi, and Epidauros.

17 One of the best accounts of how Roman documents worked from a traditional scholarly point of view is Sherk, *RDGE*, 4–19. For the other side, see Beard 1985a, Culham 1989a and 1991a, and Williamson 1987a and 1995a.

18 Polybios, *History*, 3.26.1. Translation by Scott-Kilvert, *Polybius*.

19 Polybios, *History*, 12.25i. Translation by Scott-Kilvert, *Polybius*.

20 Quoted and translated by Williamson 1987a, 166 = Bruns[7] no. 98, lines 16–19, which is a military certificate of release from service dated to AD 71. Compare Williamson 1995a, 244.

21 Williamson 1987a, 166 n. 20. Lawton (*ADR*, 5 and 14–15) says that classical Athenian practice was similar in that the decrees ended with a 'publication formula' which included information as to where the stele was to be erected.

22 Williamson 1995a, 249.

23 Suetonius, *Life of Julius Caesar*, 44.2. Translation from the LCL.

24 Williamson 1987a, 169. Mary Beard (1985a, 115) comes to a similar conclusion about the 'Arval Acta' during the three centuries that they were recorded: 'The principal function of the writing was "symbolic".'

25 Culham 1991a, 123.

26 Williamson 1987a, 172 n. 49.

27 Cicero, *For Rabirius*, 6.14. Translation from the LCL.

28 Williamson 1987a, 163 with bibliography in n. 10.

29 Suetonius, *Life of Caligula*, 41.1. Translation from the LCL.

30 Culham 1989a, 103, 105. So also Williamson 1995a, 247.

31 Culham 1989a, 113, based on Plutarch, *Life of Cato the Younger*, 16.

32 Clanchy, *Memory*, 70.

33 Cicero, *Letters to Atticus*, 13.26 = Shackleton Bailey, *Atticus*, No. 275 regarding a sumptuary law and a shrine which Cicero wished to build. The second reference is to 13.33 = Shackleton Bailey, *Atticus*, No. 309. Williamson (1995a, 242) uses the first letter as a springboard for her consideration of how the process worked and comes to conclusions (p. 247) similar to those of Culham, just cited.

34 Cicero, *On Laws*, 3.20.46. Translation from the LCL. There is, of course, the simple, time immemorial, oral deceit of merely lying, for which see, among others: Cicero, *Letters to Atticus*, 4.17 (Shackleton Bailey, *Atticus*, No. 91) where Cicero says that 'The Consuls are in the thick of a tremendous scandal' with three Augurs and three Consuls all willing to bear false witness.

35 Cicero, *For Sulla*, 42. Translation from the LCL.

36 Plutarch, *Life of Cato the Younger*, 16.3. Translation from the LCL.

37 Cicero, *On the Agrarian Law*, 2.14.37. Translation from the LCL.

38 Williamson 1987a, 168 n. 30; and Williamson 1995a, 248. Today, electronic transactions have reopened the issue of verification and witnesses, on which see Raloff/Lipkin 1995a, 138.

39 Plutarch, *Life of Cato the Younger*, 18.5. Translation from the LCL.

40 Cicero, *For Sulla*, 44. Translation from the LCL.

NOTES

41 Williamson 1987a, 168. She cites Cicero, *Philippics*, 1.26, 2.97, 3.30, 5.11, and 12.12.
42 Suetonius, *Life of Titus*, 3.2. Translation from the LCL.
43 Suetonius, *Life of Nero*, 17. Translation from the LCL.
44 Jolowicz/Nicholas, 414–420 consider the changes that are made with the 'increased use of writing'. A related method was used to 'secure' documentary papyri, which were written across the height in a single column (see further discussion of this format in Chapter 10). The same text or summary thereof would be written twice with the first section rolled up and sealed. For example, the Latin Slave Sale (London, British Library 229) from Seleucia in Pieria from AD 166 comes with a rolled up section at the top of the papyrus that has seven seals in a line across its width (Turner 1978a, 30–31 with schematic drawing on p. 30). Turner discusses wills, with examples on pp. 43–44.
45 Livy 6.1–2. Translation from the LCL.
46 Livy 8.40.4–5. Translation from the LCL. Miles (*Livy*, 57–62) discusses this passage and the previous one.
47 Cockle (1984a) gives a good overview.
48 Cockle 1984a, 116–117 and 119–120 (referring to P. Oxy. XVII, 2116, dated to AD 229).
49 Cockle 1984a, 118 (citing P. Oxy. XIV, 1654, dated to AD 150). This searcher was paid 10 obols, whereas the cost of two memoranda was 16 obols.
50 *For Sulla*, 42. Translation from the LCL.
51 *OCD²*, 1033, s.v. *Tachygraphy.*
52 Diogenes Laertius 2.48 (Life of Xenophon). Translation from the LCL.
53 Onions, *ODEE*, 867 s.v. 'stenography'.
54 For an example of abbreviations in a Greek document, see Turner, *GrMss*, 100–101 No. 59, abstracts of contracts from AD 42. Ann Arbor, P. Mich. Inv. 622. Turner notes that the scribe uses 'a great deal of abbreviation, which often gives an illusion of dividing the letters into word groups. Words are normally abbreviated by suspension.'
55 Plutarch, *Life of Cato the Younger*, 23.3. Translation from the LCL.
56 Cicero, *Letters to Atticus*, 13.32. Translation from Shackleton Bailey, *Atticus*, No. 305.
57 Cappelli, *DizAbbrev.* For bibliography, see Reynolds/Wilson, 291–292. Compare Sirat 1994a, 413: 'there were then two kinds of writing: one for the eye assuming the function of communication of the written text and one for the hand, this one being the tool of the intellectual activity and for narrower circulation.'
58 *KP* 5, 357–358 s.v. 'Stenographie'. Boge, *GrTach.* Teitler, *Notarii.* Ganz, *TirNoten.*
59 Suetonius, *Life of Titus*, 3.2. Translation from the LCL.
60 Seneca the Younger, *Letters*, 90.25–26. Translation from the LCL.
61 London, British Library, Add. MS. 33270. Brown 1994a, 4 fig. 3.
62 Lee (1973a, 70–73) presents a convincing case against the argument that (p. 70) 'slavery was a cause of technological backwardness'.
63 Despite the relative recentness of the invention of the typewriter, its history is not clear. Compare Gould, *Bully*, Chapter 4: 'The Panda's Thumb of Technology', 59–75; and Norman, *PsychEv*, 145–151.
64 Petroski, *Evolution*, 22.
65 Title of Chapter 2 in Petroski, *Evolution*, 22–33.
66 On the history of the fork, see Petroski, *Evolution*, 3–21, and p. 8 for the dates.
67 Allen & Greenough, 1, section 1 note 1 and Gordon, *LetNames.* Gordon

theorizes that the switch from multiple to single syllables may have come to Latin via Etruscan. For a quote from Kallias's play, see Chapter 2.

68 Baddeley, *HumMem*, 41–42. For a full discussion, see Chapter 6, this volume.

69 Plato, *Theaetetus*, 203b. Translation from Plato, Bollingen. For discussions of this part of the Theaetetus (201c–206b), see: Ryle 1960a; Gallop 1963a, who responds to Ryle; and Benardete, *Theaet*, I.169–175. For a good brief summary of the history of 'words' and 'syllables' in philosophical thought through the time of Lucretius, see Long, *HellPhil*, 131–139.

70 Xenophon (*Memorabilia*, 4.2.13) recounts another Socratic encounter where Socrates says: 'I propose, then, that we write delta in this column and alpha in that, and then proceed to place under these letters, delta and alpha, what we take to be works of δικαιοσύνης [justice] and ἀδικίας [injustice] respectively' (translation adapted from the LCL). This example does use letters independently, but note that the words to be sorted into the two columns have nothing to do with alphabetical order.

71 Haslam 1994a, especially 10 and 13; and Haslam 1994b, 114 for the quote.

72 Daly, 36.

73 This example is from Daly, 38, who discusses it in more detail than I do. From a search of the PHI Latin CD-ROM 5.3, containing all Latin texts in machine readable form through AD 200 with some later writers, I had the following results. Variations on 'order of the letters' ('*ordo litterarum*') appear from the first century AD and on. Suetonius uses the phrase when discussing Julius Caesar's cipher (*Life of Julius Caesar*, 56.6). Pliny the Elder (*Natural History*, 37.138) does so in the passage just cited by Daly. From a similar search of the *TLG*, Greek through the first century BC uses the phrase 'κατὰ στοιχεῖον' to mean more generally 'according to the element' for discussions of things like 'atoms'.

74 The earliest reference I have found to 'alphabet' as a whole word is in the *Adversus haereses* (1.8.12, 1.8.15–16, and 1.13.1) of Irenaeus, a Christian theologian who came from Asia Minor and wrote in Greek. He even speaks of 'learning the alphabet' in the last reference. Tertullian, who lived a little later than Irenaeus, is the first to use the term in Latin in the *De praescriptione haereticorum* (50) according to Lewis and Short, s.v. '*alphabetum*'. In the first century AD, Juvenal (*Satires*, 14.209) refers to the 'alpha and beta' which 'all girls learn' a phrase similar to our 'learning the ABCs'. It may be a happenstance of survival that the Greeks in our extant sources first used the word 'alphabet' so late, because they had the word 'ἀναλφάβητος', 'not knowing one's a b c' according to LSJ, as early as the fourth century BC. For a consideration of the Greek terms used for 'letter', see Steiner, *Tyrant*, 106 and 117–120.

75 Two partial exceptions exist. According to Keaney (1973a, 416) Harpocration's *Lexicon of the Ten Orators* 'contains 1247 glosses, of which slightly less than ten percent break the alphabetic order.' He also mentions that Galen in his *Interpretation of Hippocratic Glosses* said that he had ordered the work 'κατὰ τὴν τῶν γραμμάτων τάξιν' (= 19.63 Kuhn)', that is, 'according to the arrangement of the letters'. (Keaney 1973a, 415 with n. 2). The question is whether this order, as Keaney (415) puts it, was 'imposed by the author . . . [or] due to a later . . . revision.' For Harpocration Keaney feels certain that it is the author's arrangement. Both Daly (85–90) and I disagree with Keaney (422) that file cards were used to assist in alphabetization.

76 Wilamowitz-Moellendorff, *AnalEur*, 131–143.

77 Paris, Louvre Ma 343. Found in Rome on the Esquiline *c.* 1704. Richter, *Portraits*, 137 'Euripides II a' with bibliography and figs. 760–761. The inscription is *CIG* 6047.

78 The order of the plays within L is: *Suppliants, Bacchae, Cyclops, Heraklidei, Hercules, Helen, Rhesus, Ion, Iphigenia at Taurus, Iphigenia at Aulis, Hippolytos, Medea, Alcestis, Andromache, Electra, Hecuba, Orestes,* and *Phoenician Women.* No matter whether the plays are spelled in Greek, Latin, or English, the list of plays is not alphabetical. The manuscripts and their order are given in the unpaginated prefatory material (*'Codicum Catalogus'*) to the *Oxford Classical Texts* edition of *Euripidis Fabulae,* Vol. 1 (1902).

79 *IG* II² 2363 II.11–25, a library catalogue dated to the end of the second/ beginning of the first century BC. Platthy, *Sources,* 133 No. 90 and 135–136.

80 Barrett, *EurHipp,* 50–53. Barrett has one of the clearest discussions of this scholarly red herring with full references.

81 Daly, 11–12.

82 Quintilian 1.7.11. Translation from the LCL. Quintilian has a lengthy discussion of spelling in Chapter 1.7.

83 Suetonius, *Life of Augustus,* 41.3. Translation from the LCL. So also Tacitus, 'influenced by the discovery that even the Greek alphabet was a gradual creation, . . . introduced and popularized new Latin characters.' Tacitus, *Annals,* 11.13. Translation from Grant, *Annals,* 231.

84 The three letters were '[a capital H without the right vertical bar], to represent the sound between *u* and *i* in *maxumus, maximus,* etc.; [a backwards "C"], for the sound of *bs* as *ps*; [a capital E without the top horizontal bar] for consonant *u.*' LCL 76 n. *a* to translation of quoted passage. For surviving examples and discussion, see Gordon, *LatEpig,* 116–118 Nos. 41 and 43 with illustrations.

85 Woodhead (107–111) gives a good summary and tables for all the numbers.

86 For a full description and pictures of the allotment machine, see Camp, *Agora,* 110–112.

87 This information comes from n. 7 to Aulus Gellius, *Attic Nights,* 14.6.4, in the LCL translation. That certain lines were equal in this sense to others was 'discovered' in antiquity, as Gellius (ibid.) indicates.

88 For the translation and information about the numerical value of the verse, see the LCL for Suetonius, *Nero,* 34.2. Technically this kind of word play is called 'isopsepha'. See Cameron 1995a, 478 and Ahl, *Meta,* 62–63 with further references to Greek, Latin, and Hebrew examples. The idea of assigning numbers to letters and thereby deriving significance from the numerical values of words has been carried to new depths. Ian Stewart (1994a) describes artificial systems ('new merology') that enable the values of the letters to equal the number of the word they spell. Hence if o=-7, n=5, and e=3, the total for 'one' would be '1'. Since the system depends on negative numbers, the idea of such equivalencies would never have occurred in antiquity.

89 Aulus Gellius, *Attic Nights,* 14.6.3. Translation from the LCL. A useful modern application of this type of curiosity occurs in computer 'signatures' for individual files. An algorithm calculates a number from the content of a file and that number is either the 'Checksum' or the 'CRC' (for Cyclic Redundancy Check or Code) depending on which system was used. This number changes only if the file changes, and hence is a major means of checking for computer viruses.

90 The Greek use of the alphabet as numbers remains murky for the earlier periods. See *OCD²,* 741 s.v. 'Numbers, Greek'; Wyatt/Edmonson 1984a, 163–164; and Dilke, *Math,* 13–16.

91 *OCD²,* 741–742 s.v. 'Numbers, Roman'.

92 Arabic numerals are themselves derived from India. Barrow (*Pi,* 92) says that 'The Indian system of counting has been the most successful intellectual

innovation ever made on our planet. It has spread and been adopted almost universally, far more extensively even than the letters of the Phoenician alphabet which we now employ. It constitutes the nearest thing we have to a universal language.' According to the *RHUD*, the 'plus sign' dates to 1645–1655, the 'minus sign' to 1660–1670, and the 'equal sign' to 1905–1910. The amount of time it took to develop these symbols is sobering.

93 Norman, *Things*, 66–69.

94 See, for example, Wyatt/Edmonson 1984a on the use of letters in the fifth century BC on the coffers of the Hephaisteion in the Agora, Athens.

95 Bloch/Joffroy 1953a.

96 Aristotle, *Meteorology*, 2.6 (363a34). Translation from Aristotle, Bollingen. Since Aristotle's works were not preserved in good order from his lifetime, as discussed in Chapters 4 and 10, it is possible that this particular wording, which implies an accompanying diagram, was added after Aristotle.

97 Cameron (1995a) in a discussion of other kinds of word play, primarily anagrams, points out (pp. 480–481) that ancient anagrams were always clearly signaled in the text.

98 Like ancient acrostics, this one repeats the beginning letter vertically to make the acrostic more obvious. Rouveret, *HistImag*, 354–369, 363 n. 175 with bibliography and 364 fig. 21 for the acrostic with the name of Moschion. Since the poem signifies ownership, it uses the genitive, Moschionos, to make the nine lines. The plaque also has on its back a separate word square with letters written in the squares of a graph that read the same up and down and across in both directions.

99 A brief but excellent discussion is given by Pease, *CicDiv*, 529–531. See also *KP* 1.222–223, s.v. 'Akrostichon'. Discussions of the biblical examples are scattered throughout the *JerBibComm*, but note especially 203 section 10 and 559 section 4. The first edition of the *JerBibComm* (1968) gives a complete list on 505 *ad* Proverbs 31.10–31.

100 On the prime practitioner of this arcane art, Venantius Fortunatus in the sixth century AD, see Graver 1993a. An unusual modern variant is the telestich where the last letters of the words spell something. One particular example by B. Gordon Dickey is both a conventional acrostic and telestich, as well as having all eight-letter answers. It is printed in Thomas M. Middleton, editor, *Super Crostics Book. Series No. 2* (New York 1993), No. 164.

101 Cicero, *On Divination*, 2.54.112. Translation from the LCL. See also *ad loc.* Pease, *CicDiv.*

102 Dionysius of Halicarnassus 4.62.6. Translation from the LCL.

103 Suetonius, *Life of Julius Caesar*, 56.6. Translation from the LCL. Note that Suetonius uses the word '*elementa*' for 'alphabet'. The other quote in the text is from Aulus Gellius, *Attic Nights*, 17.9.5. Translation from the LCL.

104 *Life of Augustus*, 88. Suetonius discusses Probus in *On Grammarians*, 24, although he does not actually mention this particular text.

105 Herodotus 7.239. Translation from the LCL.

106 This story is told in both Herodotus 5.35 and Gellius, *Attic Nights*, 17.9.18–27. Ovid (*Art of Love*, 3.619–630) provides a number of suggestions for secret communication between two lovers, including writing your message on your servant's back and in invisible 'ink'.

107 Cicero, *Letters to Atticus*, 2.20. Translation from Shackleton Bailey, *Atticus*, No. 41.

108 Rouse/Rouse 1991a, 255. This article is an excellent study of retrieval aids, their nature, and their evolution.

NOTES

109 Saenger/Heinlen 1991a, 255.
110 Rouse/Rouse 1991a, 242–243. The quote is from George Sarton, *Introduction to the History of Science*, 2.1 (Baltimore 1931), 5.
111 Ong, *Orality*, 124–125. Clanchy (*Memory*, pl. XIX) illustrates the rudimentary indexing in a lawbook from the 1290s, with commentary and references in the caption, and further discussion on pp. 180–181.
112 Quoted by Daly, 91 from M. M. Matthews, *A Survey of English Dictionaries* (Oxford 1933), 18. For the idea of alphabetical order as an 'organizing principle', see Rouse/Rouse 1991a, 226–235 and 240–241. Compare also the discussion in Clanchy, *Memory*, 177–184.
113 DeFrancis (1996a) provides a fascinating account of how Chinese dictionaries work. Their organization around 'radicals', which are supposed to be based on meaning, very much resembles the concept behind 'glossaries' in antiquity. They also have a rather interesting resemblance to Roget's *Thesaurus* and its organizational principles.
114 *Attic Nights*, 18.9.4–5. Translation from the LCL. My emphasis. Compare Quintilian's (1.7) similar discussion on changes in orthography.
115 *Life of Augustus*, 88. Translation from the LCL.
116 Quintilian 1.7.30 and 33. Translation from the LCL.
117 Nock 1972a, especially 642–643. For more information on the later development of our common research tools, see Tom McArthur, *Worlds*, a delightful book on dictionaries and encyclopedias from their origins to modern times. Linguists see the issue of 'words' differently. Robin Tolmach Lakoff (*Talking*, 27) says: 'What is a word? Is *glasnost* a full-fledged word of English in 1989? Is *archiphoneme*, a linguistic technical term, a word with the same status, as, say, *word*? Is *fuck* a word, and if so, why isn't it in my dictionary, and if it's not a word, why not? How about compounds? When, if ever, do they become words in their own right? *Cost-effective*? *Junk bond*?'
118 Horace, *Art of Poetry*, 52–59. Translation from the LCL. Pliny the Elder (*Natural History*, 33.49), however, views Latin coinages from the Greek differently: 'One is ashamed to see the new-fangled names that are invented every now and then from the Greek to denote silver vessels filigreed or inlaid with gold.' Translation from the LCL.
119 Quinn 1982a, 149.
120 Varro, *On the Latin Language*, 9.16.21. Translation from the LCL.
121 Quintilian 1.5.71–72. Translation from the LCL. Quintilian returns to the topic in Book 8.3.30–37. Two things are of interest. First, he makes a general backwards reference to his previous discussion ('as I said in the first book' at 8.3.30). Second, he notes (8.3.19) that Vergil invented the word *porca* (sow), as the feminine for *porcus* (pig) in *Aeneid* 8.641. Coining new words is generally frowned upon today, but kudos should go to Jack Hitt (*Word*) for producing a dictionary of 'words that don't exist but ought to'. For example, 'xerlusion' is: '[Xerox + delusion]: The seductive, lulling belief that you've read an article because you've photocopied it . . . (Ellen Gruber Garvey, writer).' 'Sniglets' are a less formal, but illustrated version of Hitt's dictionary.
122 *Apud* Aulus Gellius, *Attic Nights*, 1.10. Translation from the LCL.
123 Willinsky, *Empire*, 13 and especially Chapter 11, 'The Sense of Omission', 176–189.
124 Fantham, *RLC*, 29. She has an interesting discussion of bilingualism among the Romans (pp. 24–29).
125 Rottländer (1986a, 19): 'personally I am convinced that Pliny wrote his keywords at the top of his *tabulae ceratae*.' For a view against such an idea, see

271

Dorandi (1991a, 14). Today, in one of those weird twists that only the computer era manages, key words are 'for hire' either to the entity they identify or to the enemy of the entity they identify. If you want to advertise your product on the Internet and it competes with Windows 95, you buy the privilege of flashing your message every time someone searches for Windows 95 (Eisenberg 1996a).

126 Ong, *Orality*, 124.

127 Turner, *GrMss*, 8 n. 29 with a reference to P. Col. vii 174 Introduction.

128 For references see *OLD*, 1664 s.v. *rubrica* and *rubricatus*. Compare Petronius, *Satyricon*, 46.

129 Černý, *Paper*, 24. Parkinson/Quirke, 44–46.

130 For two obviously different handwritings, consider the papyrus from the end of the first century BC to early first century AD with a fragment from Alcman, *Partheneia*. It has a comment in the top margin of fragment *a* in a hand later than the original text. P. Oxy. xxiv 2387 frr. 1 and 3; Turner, *GrMss*, 42–43 No. 15. Another papyrus with the same work again has two clearly discernible hands, but here lengthy comments are squeezed between the columns. Paris, Louvre, E. 3320; dated to the first century AD. Turner, *GrMss*, 41–42 No. 44.

131 For an example, a papyrus with commentary on Homer, *Iliad* 2. P. Oxy. viii 1086; London, British Museum Pap. 2055; dated to the first century BC Turner, *GrMss*, 98–99 No. 58. This papyrus is also interesting, because on the back of it are medical prescriptions (P. Oxy. 1088) dating to the following century. Compare Barrett, *EurHipp*, 49.

132 For example, Ogilvie, *Comm*, a stand-alone commentary to the first five books of Livy.

133 Saenger/Heinlen (1991a, 254) use this word, and discuss the steps leading to this development (pp. 249–256).

134 Onions, *ODEE*, 555 s.v. 'marginalia'.

135 The importance of memory for retrieval has been apparent to medievalists for quite some time; by comparison their classical brethren have devoted little attention to the topic. An exception is Corbier 1991a, 113. In particular, for full treatments see Yates, *Memory;* more recently, Carruthers; Rouse/Rouse 1982a; Coleman, *Memories;* and Corsi, *Loom*.

6 THE COGNITIVE DEVELOPMENT OF THE MUSES

1 My view is diametrically opposed to that of James Notopoulos (1938a, especially 466), who sees Mnemosyne as becoming less and less important as 'the written word triumphed over memory and the spoken word'.

2 Hesiod (*Theogony*, 1–113) presents one of the earliest and fullest accounts of the Muses. He both names them and counts them at nine. For an extended discussion of the Muses and Hesiod, see especially Pucci, *Hesiod*, 29–33. Pucci also considers the nexus between the Muses, writing, and, as I will discuss later, truth.

3 On memory and dance, see Kaeppler 1991a. On the performance of Greek 'texts' with both music and dance, see Thomas, *LitOral*, 117–123.

4 This information and that above from *KP* 3.1475–1479, s.v. 'Musen'.

5 So also Alastair Fowler in his review of Carruthers in the *TLS*, No. 4578 (December 28, 1990 to January 3, 1991), 1391: 'the Muses themselves were daughters of Mnemosyne (Memory), a genealogy utterly cryptic in modern terms.'

6 St Augustine, *Confessions*, 10.12.

7 Compare Kristeller (1990a, 166–174) who notes that there is no Muse for the arts and discusses its implication. Similarly, Murray (1989a, 24) says that 'it is symptomatic of ancient attitudes to art that there is no tradition associating artists with inspiration.' Neither offer the explanation I do here. I thank the anonymous reader for Routledge for bringing the reference to Murray to my attention. This article provides an excellent introduction to the ancient view of creativity.

8 Murray 1989a, 22–25.

9 Plutarch, *Life of Pericles*, 2. Translation from Scott-Kilvert, *Plutarch*.

10 Plutarch, *Life of Alcibiades*, 2.5–6. Translation from the LCL. Aulus Gellius (*Attic Nights*, 15.17.1) gives the real reason for Alcibiades's hatred of the flutes: 'when the pipes were handed to him and he had put them to his lips and blown, disgusted at the ugly distortion of his face, he threw them away and broke them in two.' Translation from the LCL.

11 Marrou, *HistEduc*, 176–185 (for the Greek ἐγκύκλιος παιδεία, from which comes our word '*encyclopedia*') and 281–282 (for the Roman equivalent, *artes liberales*, which are still taught today). Robb, *LitPaid*, 159–251, especially on the role of reading in Greek education.

12 Fraser, *Alexandria*, IIa: 477 n. 127.

13 Plutarch, *Moralia*, 9e (= 'On the Education of Children'). Translation adapted from the LCL.

14 See Fowler 1991a, 25 n. 1 for bibliography. The subject is particularly popular now. See also Goldhill 1994a, Zeitlin 1994a, Heffernan, *Museum*, and the essays in Elsner, *Art*, a companion volume to Goldhill/Osborne. I discuss the shield of Aeneas in Chapter 14.

15 Karl Lehmann-Hartleben (1941a) wrote the classic article on the subject. Two things are notable about his reconstruction. First, he is absolutely sure that he knows more than the author. Second, any time he comes upon a 'problem' he posits another architectural form, such as a window, new room, etc. For the second item and a very interesting analysis of Lehmann-Hartleben's methodology, see Bryson 1994a.

16 Conway/Gathercole 1990a.

17 Quintilian 11.2.33. Translation from the LCL.

18 Aristotle, *Rhetoric*, 3.1409b 1ff. Translation from Bollingen edition. Plutarch (*Moralia*, 407f = 'The Oracles at Delphi', 27) in the second century AD basically repeats the same thought: 'the ideas communicated, by being bound up and interwoven with verse, are better remembered and kept firmly in mind.' Translation from the LCL.

19 Baddeley, *HumMem*, 34 on musicians and memory, and ordinary people and tunes. Vansina (*OralTrad*, 46) notes that: 'In Rwanda the dynastic poets first learned a melody and afterwards the words of the poem they wished to remember. One of the poets actually explained that the melody serves as a means to remember the words.'

20 Baddeley, *HumMem*, 169, with citations of studies 169–170. Ernest (1987a, 233) notes that 'the dominance of the visual modality [sense] in the sighted may limit their access to the mnemonic [memory] potential of other sensory modalities, such as the auditory and tactual-kinaesthetic. Indeed, research on the mnemonic effectiveness of kinaesthetic or motor imagery in the sighted is rather sparse.' Rubin (*MemOral*, 90–121) discusses 'combining constraints'. He concludes (p. 119) that 'Multiple constraints decrease choices and increase cues, thereby increasing stability in transmission. But this does not occur without

cost. Each constraint cannot be optimized if a combination of constraints needs to be met.'

21 That their father was Zeus matters little for the current discussion other than giving them a very powerful father. The genealogy appears in Homer (*Odyssey*, 1.10 and 8.488).

22 Wagner 1978a, 186. His citations are to: D. F. Lancy, *Studies in Memory in Culture*, paper presented at the Conference on Issues in Cross-cultural Research, New York Academy of Sciences (1975); and L. S. Liben and A. M. Drury, 'Short-term memory in deaf and hearing children in relation to stimulus character-istics', *Journal of Experimental Child Psychology* 24 (1977), 60–73.

23 Wallace/Rubin 1988a, 293 and 303.

24 Wallace 1994a, 1471. See also Rubin, *MemOral*, 85–88 on meter and rhythm, and 282–284 and 286–287 on the 'Wreck of the Old 97'. Rubin (*MemOral*, 257–298) devotes a chapter to modern ballads from North Carolina.

25 Beye, *Epic*, 26.

26 Devine/Stephens 1993a, 400. They present an excellent summary of the psychological literature that pertains specifically to rhythm and meter. See also Devine/Stephens, *Prosody*.

27 The earliest is a fragment from a seventh-century Corinthian kotyle with an inscription that labels both Apollo and the Muses. (Stavros (?), from Ithaca: Amyx, *CVP*, 2.566 Inscription 36 and p. 618.) Most famously, all nine appear together and fully labeled on the François Vase by Kleitias, dated *c.* 560 BC (Florence 4209: *ABV* 76 No. 1; *LIMC* s.v. Mousa, Mousai No. 121.) Two archaic objects, the Chest of Cypselus (Pausanias 5.18.4, *LIMC* 6 s.v. Mousa, Mousai No. 53) and the Altar at Amyklai (Pausanias 3.19.5; *LIMC* 6 s.v. Mousa, Mousai No. 148), are mentioned in later literary sources as having representa-tions of Muses, but neither has survived; nor are they described in useful detail. In general, see the full discussion in *LIMC* 6 and 7, s.v. Mousa, Mousai, Musae.

28 The two best sources for these representations are Beck, *Album*, 17–20 for the list of examples and pls. 9–15 for illustrations; and *LIMC* 6, s.v. Mousa, Mousai, *passim*.

29 Boston, Museum of Fine Arts 98.887: *ARV²* 774 No. 1 (Hesiod Painter); *Addenda²* 287; *LIMC* 6 s.v. Mousa, Mousai No. 77 (dated to *c.* 460–450 BC) with photograph.

30 Bell-krater, Paris, Louvre G 490: *ARV²* 1190 No. 21 (Pothos Painter); *Addenda²* 342; *LIMC* 6 s.v. Mousa, Mousai No. 103 (dated to *c.* 420–410 BC) with photograph.

31 For example, on a late third-century AD sarcophagus, the Muse standing on the far left is writing on tablets. London, British Museum 2305: Wegner, *Musen-Sark*, pl. 101a No. 42. *LIMC* 7, 1040 Musae No.119, with photograph.

32 Stefano de Angeli, *LIMC* 6, s.v. Moirai, with full discussion, references, and illustrations.

33 Florence, Uffizi 82. *c.* AD 150–170/80, *LIMC* 6, s.v. Moirai No. 39.

34 Kato Paphos (Cyprus), 'Villa of Theseus', main room. End of fourth to beginning of fifth century AD. *LIMC* 6, s.v. Moirai No. 45 with photograph.

35 Paris, Louvre MA 539. *c.* AD 180–190. *LIMC* 6, s.v. Moirai No. 51 and, for photograph, s.v. *LIMC* 6, s.v. Meleagros No. 138.

36 Possibly the Pythagoreans did so first (*KP*, 3.1482, s.v. 'Mouseion'). In any case, places with Muses, such as Mt Helicon (Athenaeus 14.629a) where the manu-scripts of Hesiod were kept or where they were worshipped, were all known as Museia. Harrison/Verrall, 596–600. Murray (1981a) in her examination of Muses and early Greek poetry emphasizes the fact that the Muses impart

knowledge. Clearly that idea continues later, when the Muses come to 'administer' the knowledge stored in books and not just that which they directly impart to the poet.

37 Pausanias 1.30.2. Translation from the LCL. Compare Cicero, *Letters to Atticus*, 1.4.

38 Gnaeus Gellius *apud* Pliny, *Natural History*, 7.192. Pliny also lists other contenders for the honor, who numbered at least twelve according to the scholia to Dionysius Thrax. Bekker, *AnecGr* II. 774, 781–786. This last reference, including the count, comes from Svenbro 1989a, 229 n. 1. Hermes was also the inventor of the lyre and, as the messenger of the gods, came to be associated with oratory. *OCD²*, 503, s.v. 'Hermes'.

39 As the god of money, Hermes is associated with treasuries, and treasuries are repositories of memory. For a full discussion of the image of treasuries, wisdom, and memory, see Chapter 12.

40 Pausanias 4.31.6. *LIMC* 4, 810–817, s.v. 'G. Herakles "mousikos"'.

41 Plutarch, *Roman Questions*, 59 (278 E). Translation from the LCL. Aeschylus somewhat cryptically seems to imply an association between Muses and writing in the *Prometheus Bound* (460–461): 'I invented for them [people] the putting together of letters, the memory of all things, the work of the mother of the muses.'

42 Pliny the Elder, *Natural History*, 35.66. For the coins, see Crawford, *RRC* I, 437–439 No. 410, in 66 BC. For the Ambracia group, see Ridgway, *HelSculp I*, 246–252 and 268 n. 1 with bibliography. Nash, *PDAR* I, 471, s.v. 'Hercules Musarum' with bibliography.

43 Pliny the Elder, *Natural History*, 36.33 where the Muses are referred to as 'Thespiades' and 36.34 (in the temple of Apollo near the portico of Octavia) respectively. See Isager, 162–167.

44 Ridgway, *HelSculp I*, 252 and 269–270 n. 12 with bibliography.

45 Cicero, *Letters to Friends*, 7.23. Translation from Shackleton Bailey, *Friends*, No. 209.

46 Theophilidou 1984a.

47 For the pictorial tradition surrounding Mnemosyne, see *LIMC* 6, s.v. Mnemosyne.

48 I have purposely not discussed the representations of the Muses in detail for two reasons. First, a number of studies already exist that more than adequately cover the topic. Second, my argument rests on the intellectual association between Muses and memory and not on what they looked like. It is the increasing frequency of their association with writing that counts, not whether this Muse held a roll and that one a globe. For more information on the representations, in addition to the major entries in *LIMC* 6 and 7, see: Ridgway, *HelSculp I*, 246–274; *EAA* 5 (1963) 286ff., s.v. 'Muse' (Max Wegner); Cohon 1991/1992a; Shelton 1983a (an excellent article on late Antique examples); and Koch/Sichtermann, 197–203 (for the Roman sarcophagi only).

7 THE GREEK METHODS

1 LSJ, s.v. τέχνη. In Homer the word had a connotation of cunning or art in a pejorative sense which it had lost by the fifth century BC, except for the fact that the wealthy would spurn the practice of technē. Greene 1994a, 29–30. Compare discussion in Chapter 6 on the idea that a Cicero would not be a sculptor. For a broader treatment of the relationship between technē, creativity, and genius, see Murray 1989a, especially 22–25.

2 The third-century BC *Parian Chronicle* (54) calls Simonides's memory system 'τὸ μνημονικόν', but adds no further information. In the tenth century AD, the *Suda*, s.v. Σιμωνίδης, refers to it as 'ἡ μνημονικὴ τέχνη'.

3 Auctor ad Herennium 3.16.28. Translation from the LCL.

4 Auctor ad Herennium 3.16.28. Translation from the LCL. I do not consider natural memory other than how it works with artificial memory. It is not that the 'emotional' or 'affective' aspects of natural memory are not important. They are. But this book would be twice the length.

5 Aristotle, *On Virtues and Vices*, 1250a 35. Translation from Aristotle, Bollingen.

6 Pliny the Elder, *Natural History*, 7.88. Translation from the LCL.

7 Quintilian 1.3.1. Translation from the LCL.

8 Plutarch, *Moralia*, 9 e (= 'On the Education of Children'). Translation adapted from the LCL.

9 The fullest accounts are Cicero, *On the Orator*, 2.353–354 and Quintilian 11.2.11–17. Certain details, like the name of the winner of the contest, vary from telling to telling. Quintilian (11.2.14) says 'There is, however, great disagreement among our authorities as to whether this ode was written in honour of Glaucus of Carystus, Leocrates, Agatharcus or Scopas, and whether the house was at Pharsalus . . . or at Crannon.' Translation from the LCL.

10 I discussed the other great 'invention' of Simonides, pay for poetry, in Chapter 3.

11 Cicero, *On the Orator*, 2.353–354. Translation adapted from the LCL.

12 Both Quintilian quotes are from 11.2.16. Translation from the LCL.

13 Pratt (1995a) presents a cogent interpretation of 'the seal of Theognis' in which she makes the point that Theognis is writing during a transitional period between orality and literacy. His intent is that (p. 179) 'writing seal these words', for (p. 175) he is creating a written text from which other performers can memorize elegies for performance. . . . Indeed, the primary function of many early texts of Greek poetry . . . is surely precisely this: to serve as mnemonics for performance rather than as texts to be read.'

14 Kennedy, *RhetRom*, 124. Compare Quintilian 3.3.1: 'The art of oratory, as taught by most authorities, and those the best, consists of five parts: invention, arrangement, expression, memory, and delivery or action.' Translation from the LCL. In contrast, Blum (*Mnemo*, 80–104) claims that Theodectes, *c*. 400 BC, made memory a fully-fledged part of rhetorical training. This date is too early. See also Cole, *OrigRhet*, 170 n. 23.

15 Baddeley, *HumMem*, 185–186: '[T]here is no doubt that serial order does have one crucial advantage, it ensures that every item is produced, whereas free recall tends to be very effective for producing most of the items, but has the drawback that some items will almost always be forgotten.'

16 A waiter with a superlative memory has been studied by psychologists. This man could remember up to twenty dinner orders at one time 'by breaking them down into their various components. He would begin by grouping together all of the salad dressings by their first letter. . . . Next, he would list the starches. . . . Lastly, he would group together the meat items by temperature (e.g., rare, well done).' Vogl/Thompson 1995a, 337, a summary of Ericsson/Polson 1988a. Vogl and Thompson note that the waiter's great skill in memory did not transfer in a significant way to other memory tasks.

17 Great progress is being made with new methods that 'map' responses of the brain to various stimuli. An exhibit (Corsi, *Loom*) with sumptuous catalogue and excellent essays traces the history of the study of memory with a chapter on 'Biological Memory', 338–346. Posner/Raichle, *Images*, is devoted solely to

the subject of how the brain reacts to the gamut of inputs, again with beautiful color photographs.

18 Quintilian 11.2.17. Translation adapted from the LCL.

19 Quintilian 11.2.32. Translation from the LCL.

20 For a discussion of the importance of one's surroundings, both physical and mental, see Gallagher, *Power*, 127–138, and especially 131–132.

21 Baddeley, *HumMem*, 268. Marcel Proust's madeleine in *Remembrance of Things Past* may be the best-known example of such a trigger for memory, but, as part of a work of literature, overly subject to authorial embellishment.

22 Jack Hodges, *The Maker of the Omnibus: The Lives of English Writers Compared*, quoted by Foden 1993a, 5.

23 Baddeley, *HumMem*, 268–271.

24 Baddeley, *HumMem*, 270. Compare Ulric Neisser 1988a, 553: 'According to the doctrine of "encoding specificity," for example, retrieval works best when those circumstances reinstate the situation that prevailed during learning. . . . We must take into account not only the stimuli present at retrieval but the reason for retrieval.'

25 Gregory, *Mind*, 330–333. The term 'hypnotism', however, is a nineteenth-century coinage.

26 The quotation is from Goleman 1994a, C8. The study of false memory syndrome is burgeoning. A few selected works that will lead to the rest are: Bower 1993a and 1994a, Gardner 1993a, Nelson/Roediger, and Schacter, *Searching*, chapters 4 and 9, for a balanced account with good references. Ofshe/Watters may be of particular interest, because it examines the accusations that combine child abuse with satanism and witchcraft. The latter have a startling and rather horrifying resemblance to the Salem Witch Trials.

27 Xenophon, *Symposium*, 4.62. Translation from the LCL.

28 Plato, *Hippias Minor*, 368d. Translation from Plato, Bollingen.

29 Plato, *Hippias Major*, 285e–286a. Translation from Woodruff, *Plato*.

30 Athenaeus 5.216b. Translation from the LCL.

31 Plato, *Phaedo*, 72d–e. Translation from Plato, Bollingen. The full 'proof' that learning is recollecting follows through section 76e.

32 Here I am not interested in all that Plato has said about memory, but only that which applies to *artificial* memory and writing. For 'learning as recollection', see Moravcsik 1971a. For a summary of Plato on memory in general, see Coleman, *Memories*, 5–14. She also presents a lengthy investigation into the medieval tradition. The best introduction to the memory systems of the Renaissance remains Yates, *Memory*. In particular in her Chapter 8, note how Ramon Lull extends the idea of artificial memory from being a technique for recall to being a technique for thought.

33 Both Carruthers (153) and Yates (*Memory*, 57) discuss the importance of the revival of the connection between dialectic and memory in medieval and Renaissance times; whereas memory in classical antiquity becomes less a part of philosophy, as we would put it, and very much a part of rhetoric.

34 Aristotle, *On Dreams*, 458b20–25. Translation from Aristotle, Bollingen.

35 Aristotle, *On the Soul*, 427b15–20. Translation from Aristotle, Bollingen.

36 The ancient approach does not resemble the children's or the psychologists' game of seeing how much you can recall in any order of items in a picture, but resembles the memorization of the alphabet then and now. Compare Baddeley, *HumMem*, 185–186 on recall of the states of the Union vs. serial recall of the presidents.

37 Aristotle, *On Memory*, 452a12–452a25. Translation by Sorabji, *Memory*, 56.

38 Aristotle's use of the alphabet as his pegs does not contradict what I said in Chapter 5 about alphabetization. The two processes are separate issues mentally and in antiquity.

39 Thompson *et al.*, *MemSearch*, 130–131.

40 Quintilian 11.2.30. Translation from the LCL.

41 Carruthers (33) also uses the image of 'bin'.

42 Baddeley, *HumMem*, 188–189.

43 Thomas Cole (*OrigRhet*, 88–89) suggests a different origin. He thinks that the use of *topos* for 'rhetorical commonplaces' may be due to 'the physical layout of such collections. ... Students would have been constantly unrolling the papyrus on which a *techné* was written to the spot [*topos*] containing a model piece hence, by a natural metonymy, the substitution of the name of the container for that of the contained.' This usage resembles English usage, such as 'find the place in the text'. The earliest citation in LSJ for this meaning, however, is third century BC (*PCair.Zen*, 327.83), which postdates the use of *topos* in passages on memory. Moreover, the layout of ancient Greek papyri with block-like texts and the absence of any numbering or lettering system for 'columns' or 'pages' make Cole's suggestion unlikely from a practical point of view.

44 According to Sorabji (*Memory*, 30), the modern realization that the rhetorical *topoi* were related to the mnemonic *topoi* goes back to at least as early as Solmsen in 1929. Here I extend that connection to the use of *commonplace*.

45 Cicero, *Brutus*, 11.46–47. Translation from the LCL.

46 Clanchy, *Memory*, 177–184. Compare also Ong, *Orality*, 125, according to whom 'The alphabetic index is actually a crossroads between auditory and visualist cultures.'

47 For the use of '*index*' as 'list' in Latin, see among others: Seneca the Younger, *Letters*, 39.2; Aulus Gellius, *Attic Nights*, 3.3.1; and Quintilian 10.1.57.

48 Similarly, Cicero, *Brutus*, 12.46–47, where the same information is given somewhat indirectly. Kennedy (*AristRhet*, 45) says that Isocrates, early in the fourth century BC, had used the term *topos* 'in the sense of "topic" . . . and probably others did before him.' He adds that 'neither in *Topics* nor in *Rhetoric* does Aristotle give a definition of *topos*, another sign that he assumed the word would be easily understood.' I am interested here *only* in the *topoi* as a mnemonic system; the nature of the arguments they contained, their broader role in dialectic and philosophy in general, etc. are subjects beyond my scope. On this distinction, see also Huby 1989a, 74 n. 10. For an overview with bibliography on the 'philosophical' aspects of the *topoi*, see van Ophuijsen 1994a.

49 Aristotle, *Sophistical Refutations*, 183b35–185a4. Translation from Aristotle, Bollingen.

50 Quintilian 2.4.28–29. Translation from the LCL.

51 Philostratus, *Lives of the Sophists*, 580. Translation from the LCL. This passage is also interesting, for implying the informal circulation of notes taken at lectures over a wide area, since earlier in the same passage (579) Philostratus says that the original speech was given 'in Asia'.

52 Walsh/Zlatic 1981a, 228. The quote from Twain is from 'Post-Prandial Oratory,' *Mark Twain Speaking*, edited by Paul Fatout (Ames, IA 1976), 230–235.

53 From *The Love Letters of Mark Twain*, edited by Dixon Wecter (New York 1949), 165–166 quoted by Walsh/Zlatic 1981a, 227.

54 *Politics*, 1260b40. Translation from Aristotle, Bollingen. Christina Kraus (1994a, 270) views Livy in terms very similar to those of Aristotle: 'Like the city it describes and constitutes, then, the *Ab urbe condita* [*From the Foundation of the*

City, the name of Livy's work] is a growing physical object through which the writer and the reader move together. Like that city, too, it is constructed of places – that is, of commonplaces . . . the typical scenes of which much ancient literature is composed.'

55 *Topics*, 111a12ff. Translation adapted from Aristotle, Bollingen. Robin Lakoff (*Talking*, 146) comments on the opposite extreme in academe today: 'The idea is, if more than three people can understand it, it can't be worth much. . . . It's not that there's no need to be intelligible. It's that there is a need not to. . . . We write and speak, but we do not communicate. That is our art.'

56 *Topics*, 163b17–33. Translation from Aristotle, Bollingen.

57 According to the *OED²*, the expression 'at our fingertips' is late and not based on the Greek, though both have the related meaning of 'being near at hand'.

58 Carruthers (29) follows Sorabji, *Memory*, 29, 31.

59 *Sophistical Refutations*,170a33–170b11. Translation from Aristotle, Bollingen.

60 Compare Stump, *Boethius*, 166–167. She does not think that a *topos* can be so flexible as to contain virtually anything that needs to be remembered sequentially.

61 Aristotle, *Rhetoric*, 1357a10. Translation from Aristotle, Bollingen. Stump (*Boethius*, 16) has an excellent discussion of the relationship between *topos* as a mnemonic and as a dialectical and rhetorical construct. She (165–166) rightly believes that the mnemonic usage preceded the rhetorical. For a more extended discussion of dialectic and mnemonics, see Sorabji, *Memory*, 26–31.

62 Aristotle, *Rhetoric*, 1358a31. Translation from Aristotle, Bollingen.

63 This kind of semantic change in meaning happens quite often, and is known as 'generalization' when the meaning becomes broader as opposed to 'specialization' when the meaning narrows. See Hughes, *Words*, 9, 11–12; and McArthur, *EngLang*, 433 s.v. 'Generalization' and 965, s.v. 'Specialization'. In Chapter 4 I discussed two other examples of the broadening of meaning: '*scrinium*' from a container for rolls to the bureau in charge of rolls; and '*liber*' from the material, which a book is made of, to the actual object. For an analysis of '*liber*' see Holtz 1989a, 107.

8 THE ROMAN CONTRIBUTION

1 Kennedy, *RhetRom*, 124.

2 This attitude pervades the study of ancient art. Greek art, even when preserved only in Roman 'copies', is more highly rated than Roman art. Greene (1994a) gives the Romans their due in an article on technology, which, to a certain extent, is what mnemotechnics is. See especially n. 24–25 on 'Stereotypes' and (23): 'praise for the achievements of the Greeks is tempered by disappointment at the Romans.'

3 Compare Ann Kuttner (1993a, 347): 'Roman art and literature in the Republic and early Empire demonstrate an interest in architectural subjects not matched elsewhere in the Hellenistic world. On coins and reliefs and paintings, in the poetry of Lucretius and Vergil, we find a sustained attention to architectural subjects and architectonic imagery without Greek parallels.'

4 Pliny the Elder, *Natural History*, 35.37.116. Translation from the LCL.

5 Cicero, *On the Orator*, 2.87.357–358. Translation adapted from the LCL.

6 Among others, Lloyd, *EGS*, 79.

7 Plato, *Republic*, 7.532b. Translation from Plato, Bollingen.

8 Aristotle, *Posterior Analytics*, 100a5ff. Translation from Aristotle, Bollingen.

9 Lucretius 1.471–474. Translation from Bailey, *Lucretius*.

10 Cicero, *On the Orator*, 2.358. The Latin is interesting: '*corpus intellegi sine loco non potest.*' Cicero uses '*corpus*' which ranges in meaning from 'body' to 'corpse' to the solid object I have used in my translation. '*Intellego*' means not just 'to understand' or 'grasp mentally' but also 'to discern, recognize (form, colour, taste, or other physical characteristics.' The definitions are from the *OLD*.

11 Quintilian 11.2.17. Translation from the LCL.

12 Cicero, *On Ends*, 5.1.2. Translation adapted from the LCL. Cicero gives these words to Marcus Piso.

13 Cole/Scribner, *CT*, 123–140 (Chapter 6: 'Culture, Learning, and Memory'), especially 130–131.

14 Cole/Scribner, *CT*, 131.

15 *KP* I, 728–729, s.v. 'Auctor ad Herennium'. Carruthers, especially Chapter 4, 122–155. She refers to him as 'Tully' after Cicero's 'middle name' of Tullius. I prefer to use the Latin 'Auctor'.

16 The example given in the text is from the LCL edition, translated by Harry Caplan. I have found his translation very misleading on many points.

17 Among others, Lloyd, *EGS*, 115.

18 For more information on ancient theories of perception, see Everson, *Psych*, 240 (references) with discussion *passim*. On Hellenistic theories, see Annas, *Mind*, especially Chapter 3 (71–88) on the Stoics and Chapter 7 (157–174) on the Epicureans, of whom Lucretius was one.

19 Lucretius 4.324, 354–355, 427–431. Translation by Latham.

20 For example, one of the landscapes from the Villa of Agrippa Postumus at Boscotrecase, now Naples, Museo Archeologico Nazionale, No. 147502. Bianchi Bandinelli, *RomeCenter*, 140 fig. 148.

21 Lucretius 4.739–756. Translation by Latham.

22 Gregory, *Mind*, 353–355, s.v. 'Imaging'. For both sides of the debate, see Block 1983a (Aristotelian) and Sterelny 1986a (Platonist). Block (p. 581) refers to the sides in modern terms as 'pictorialism' and 'descriptionalism'. See also Rollins, *Imagery*. The best summary appears in Tye, *Imagery*.

23 Luria, *Mnemonist*, 32, 35–36, 41.

24 Thompson *et al.*, *MemSearch*, provide an excellent summary of previous scientific investigations of mnemonists or memorists, as they call them, in Chapter 8, 125–134. They review the evidence for S. on pp. 128–129. It should be stressed that not all mnemonists use the same methods, much less the system of *loci*. Moreover, as it makes perfectly good sense, 'retrieval strategies [of the subject of the Thompson study, Rajan Mahadevan] depend on the task he is given' (ibid., 137). Mahadevan is also interesting because he does not use visual imagery for remembering, but something more akin to Aristotle's serial *topoi* that enables him to go not only forwards in his recall of numbers, but also backwards (130–131).

25 Luria, *Mnemonist*, 8.

26 Quintilian 11.2.1. Translation from the LCL.

27 Plutarch, *Moralia*, 9 e (= 'On the Education of Children'). Translation from the LCL.

28 Carruthers gives an excellent summary (pp. 75–79) of S.'s method, but says (p. 79) that he was treated like a freak and 'a vaudeville act'. Yet it was his choice to capitalize on his skill by becoming a 'vaudeville act' or entertainer, for a less pejorative term. She implies that he was absolutely normal. He was not. On the problems S. had, see Rose, *Memory*, 100–106.

29 Luria, *Mnemonist*, 57.

30 Luria, *Mnemonist*, 58–59.

31 Luria, *Mnemonist*, 64.

32 S. *apud* Luria, *Mnemonist*, 134. Thompson *et al.* (*MemSearch*, 129) note that S.'s synaesthesia is 'unique among the memorists who have been investigated.' For a 'popular' study of synaesthesia, see Cytowic, *Tasted*.

33 Luria, *Mnemonist*, 66–73. Jorge Luis Borge tells the story of 'Funes the Memorious' who could never forget and becomes caught almost in a time warp as he *fully* relives his memories.

34 Cicero, *On the Orator*, 2.84.299. Translation adapted from the LCL.

35 Cicero, *On the Orator*, 2.74.300. Translation from the LCL.

36 Aristotle, *Nicomachean Ethics*, 1106b4–5. Translation from Aristotle, Bollingen.

37 Blakemore (*Mechanics of the Mind* (Cambridge 1977), 118–119) quoted in Coleman, *Memories*, 12 n. 20.

38 Gregory, *Mind*, 347, s.v. 'Image, Rotation'. For an especially clear summary of the history of the study of mental imagery, see Baddeley, *HumMem*, 98–116. On imagery and memory, see Rubin, *MemOral*, 39–64 (= Chapter 3: 'Imagery').

39 Block 1983a, 581. Kosslyn (*Image*) devotes an entire book to the debate and his findings. This is the best single source for the scientific experiments.

40 Farah 1988a, 309. She presents an excellent summary of the experimental evidence.

41 Farah 1988a, 309. For a review of the evidence on imagery, memory, and the blind, see Ernest 1987a. She (p. 232) makes the interesting point that 'research relevant to the processes involved in coding spatial position suggests that the frame of reference of the blind is egocentric or self-referent; it tends to be externally based for the sighted or for those who have had the experience of sight.'

42 Farah 1988a, 309. See also Farah *et al.* 1988a. For a good summation of the 'neural substrate of two systems of imagery', see Rubin, *MemOral*, 57–59 with references.

43 Farah 1988a, 312.

44 Farah 1988a, 315.

45 Hull, *Touching*, 157 (entry for 25 February 1985).

46 Sacks, *Mars*, 40. The entire essay, 'The Case of the Colorblind Painter', is fascinating.

47 Farah *et al.* 1988a, with definitions on pp. 442–443.

48 I am not alone in finding Farah's terminology awkward. Rubin (*MemOral*, 57) finds the word 'visual' confusing and prefers the term *object*.

49 Farah *et al.* 1988a, 444.

50 Farah *et al.* 1988a, 445.

51 For example, the 'ballplayer base', from Athens, *c.* 500 BC, now Athens, National Museum 3476. Stewart, *GrSculp*, vol. 2, pl. 138–140.

52 Now in Naples, Museo Nazionale, from Pompeii Regio I 3, 23. Kraus, *Pompeii*, 51, fig. 50.

53 For a plan and a photograph of the amphitheater, see Kraus, *Pompeii*, 51, figs. 51–52 respectively.

54 Now New York, Metropolitan Museum of Art 03.14.13. For the vanishing points drawn in, see Richter, *Perspective*, fig. 210.

55 A number of examples have survived, of which perhaps the best known is the still life from Pompeii (Regio II 4, 3), now in the Museo Archeologico, Naples, Inv. 8611. Croisille, *NatM*, pl. 19, fig. 36. For a color photograph, see Ward-Perkins/Claridge, *Pompeii*, vol. 1, 74 No. 241 and vol. 2, 197. For still lifes in general, see Croisille, *NatM*.

56 White, *Birth, passim*. He discusses classical antiquity on pp. 236–273. The scholarship on this subject is enormous.

57 Neisser 1988b, 368–370.

58 Quintilian 11.2.21. Translation from the LCL.

59 Quintilian 11.2.18–21. Translation adapted from the LCL.

60 Still the best source for the later use of the *loci* is Yates, *Memory*. The best collection of pictures of medieval and Renaissance examples of memory theaters is in Corsi, *Loom*. Bower (1970a) is an accessible, critical description of the system written by a psychologist.

61 Curiously the article (Clarkson 1992a) makes no mention of its Renaissance antecedents which are surely reflected in its name.

62 Raskin 1994a. Incidentally, Raskin takes a rather dim view of these interfaces: 'Their rich inconsistencies make me long for the days of a uniform C:\.'

63 'Managing Your Money for Windows' is produced by MECA Software.

64 Quintilian 11.2.23–25. Translation adapted from the LCL.

65 Vogl/Thompson 1995a, 322. Tomoyori set the record on 9 March 1987.

66 Philostratus, *Lives of the Sophists*, 22 (523). Translation from the LCL.

67 Quintilian 11.2.29–30. Translation from the LCL.

68 Bellezza 1987a, 35–36.

69 For example, Zoller *et al.* (1989a) gave their subjects specific images in an attempt to test whether what seems more bizarre to the testers will also be more bizarre and hence more memorable to the tested – an approach answered by the Auctor in the next quote in my text. Other psychologists accept the lack of controls, for which see, for example, Wollen/Margres 1987a. The time needed to teach the system comes from Higbee *et al.* 1991a, 69. McDaniel/Pressley provide the best and most complete survey of modern mnemotechnics with review articles of virtually all aspects. See also Cook 1989a. McDaniel *et al.* (1995a, 433) suggest that 'the distinctiveness, and hence the memorability, of a particular item depend on the constitution of items in the retrieval set.' This last article also has an extensive bibliography.

70 Auctor ad Herennium 3.23.38–39. Translation from the LCL.

71 According to Grayeff (*Aristotle*, 75–76) a 'complete reappraisal of Aristotle as a philosopher' occurred when Tyrannio, a first-century BC grammarian and 'a client or friend of Cicero' spoke to Cicero about Aristotle's works, which he had seen. From being merely a 'leading Platonist and author of fine popular works' he became 'admired as a great philosopher in his own right'. This reversal in Aristotle's worth may help explain why his precepts on memory were not being followed.

72 For example, Albertus Magnus (*de bono*, Tractatus IV, Quaestio II 'De Partibus Prudentia', Article 2, Solutio) says 'We say that art of memory is best which the Auctor teaches.' Translation adapted from Carruthers, 275. Carruthers has a number of extensive discussions about the Auctor and his influence in the Middle Ages.

73 Einstein *et al.* (1990a) summarize research on the relationship between effort and recall: 'Although there was initially a good deal of support for this 'Protestant work ethic' theory of memory, more recent research indicates that the relationship between difficulty and memory is not as straightforward as initially proposed.' The quote is on p. 56.

74 Denis 1987a, 206.

75 The Auctor (3.20.33) uses the terms '*res*' and '*verbum*'. While *verbum* is simply enough translated as 'word', *res* has a wide range of meanings, including the English 'thing', as I have translated it, but also 'fact' and 'deed'.

76 *Dialexeis*, frag. 9. Translation from Yates, *Memory*, 29–30.
77 Desrochers and Begg 1987a, with quote on p. 56. For a review of studies of the efficacy of 'verbal mnemonics', see Cook 1989c.
78 Wang/Thomas 1995a, 468 for the quotes and 473 for the time-span.
79 Auctor ad Herennium 3.21.34. Translation adapted from the LCL.
80 Carruthers, 135–136. Carruthers (281–288) provides an English translation of the full treatise, which she (p. 113) dates to 1335. Compare also my discussion in Chapter 5 on alphabetization.
81 Einstein/McDaniel 1987a, 99. Einstein *et al.* 1990a.
82 See McCormick/Levin 1987a. A later study (Cornoldi/De Beni 1991a, 511) found that '*Loci* mnemonics facilitated memory of passages, the increase being greater for oral presentation of text than after private study of a written text.'
83 Auctor ad Herennium 3.20.33–34. Translation adapted from the LCL. I have made one major change in the translation that affects the interpretation of the text. I have revived the reading of Albertus Magnus (1193/1206–1280) by translating '*medico*' as 'doctor' rather than 'finger'. The reasons for choosing 'doctor' are complex in that they depend not only on the Latin, but also on the history of the terminology for fingers in Greek and Latin. The 'purse' is literally 'ram's testicles' ('*testiculi arietini*'). Festus, a late second-century AD epitomizer of *On the Significance of Words* by the Augustan freedman Verrius Flaccus, explains: '*Suffiscus* [ram's scrotum] is said to be the skin of a ram's testicles which are used instead of a pouch, so called from its resemblance to a purse.' Modern commentators have assumed that the ram's testicles are the purse that contains money for bribing witnesses. I discuss these matters fully in Small, Forthcoming a. For the text of Albertus Magnus, see Carruthers, 139 and 321 n. 22 for the Latin text = *Objection*, 16.
84 *Objection*, 16. Translation after Carruthers, 139 and 321 n. 22 for the Latin text.
85 Compare Quintilian 6.2.29, 31–32 on *enargeia*. This topic is of great interest to literary critics, but is beyond my scope. Leach, *RhetSpace*, 10–18. Vasaly (*Rep* (89–104)) is of particular interest as background to my discussion, because Vasaly directly addresses the issue of *enargeia* and the art of memory.
86 Now in Rome, Vatican. Helbig[4] 1.355–360. Ling, *RomPaint*, 107–111 and 229 n. 4 for bibliography. For a two-page spread of all the scenes, see Schefold, *SB* 5, 350–351 fig. 313.
87 Quintilian 11.2.27. Translation from the LCL. I said 'more or less' when I described the use of the pilasters in the Odyssey landscapes, because they were added after the scenes were painted with the result that in some cases the separation is more artificial and arbitrary than it should be in order to maintain an even spacing of the pilasters.
88 Ling, *RomPaint*, 101–104 and 229 n. 1 for bibliography.
89 Quoted from *Life on the Mississippi* (New York 1903), 59 by Walsh/Zlatic 1981a, 225.
90 Walsh/Zlatic 1981a, 225.
91 Quoted from *The Complete Essays of Mark Twain*, edited by Charles Neider (Garden City, NY 1963), 500 by Walsh/Zlatic 1981a, 225. Walsh and Zlatic give other examples, including the games Twain invented for memorization and profit.

9 OTHER ADVICE FOR IMPROVING MEMORY

1 Baddeley, *HumMem*, 196.
2 Quintilian 11.2.26. Translation from the LCL. He presents his own advice in 11.2.26–11.2.49.

NOTES

3 Quintilian 11.2.41. Translation from the LCL.
4 Quintilian 11.2.27. Translation from the LCL.
5 Quintilian 11.2.28. Translation from the LCL.
6 The quote is from Quintilian 11.2.44. Translation from the LCL. Philostratus, the skeptic about memory systems whom I quoted in the previous chapter, agrees with Quintilian's advice, because he accounts for those with superlative memories as people who 'engrave them [the declamations of Dionysius of Miletus] on their minds, and when, by long practice rather than by sheer memory . . . they came to be called "the memory-artists", and men who made it into an art.' *Lives of the Sophists*, 22 (Dionysius of Miletus), 523. Translation from the LCL.
7 Thompson *et al.* (*MemSearch*, 140) stress that 'Our data demonstrates that Rajan does not remember unless he rehearses.'
8 Baddeley (*HumMem*, 159–160) uses a British example: the change in frequency for a radio station of the BBC. He (pp. 143–173) also devotes an entire chapter, 'When Practice Makes Perfect', to the subject.
9 Quintilian 11.2.36. Translation from the LCL.
10 Our earliest extant reference to arrangement and rhetoric occurs in Plato, *Phaedrus*, 266 and 277b–c. Aristotle (*Rhetoric*, 1403b5–7 and 1414a30ff.) gives the first full discussion.
11 Aristotle, *On Memory*, 451b29 with regard to the *topoi* and *Rhetoric*, 1403b5 for the order of a speech.
12 Aristotle, *Rhetoric*, 1414a36–1414b3. Translation from Aristotle, Bollingen.
13 What those components were and when they were popular are topics beyond the current discussion.
14 Quintilian 11.2.36–37. Translation from the LCL.
15 Baddeley, *HumMem*, 182. Compare S.'s inability to make associations, which was discussed in Chapter 8.
16 Baddeley, *HumMem*, 182–186. Such skills were clearly necessary for our survival as a species, on which see Barkow *et al.*, *Mind*, for excellent essays on 'evolutionary psychology' and culture. For an amusing exposition of 'people as explanatory creatures' or our mental models, see Norman, *PsychEv*, 38–53.
17 Denis 1987a, 206.
18 Quintilian 11.2.35. Translation from the LCL.
19 Baddeley (*HumMem*, 197) lists concentration among the strategies to improve memory in the elderly, but clearly anyone can benefit from concentrating. As for a sound mind in a sound body, consider the massive physical preparations undertaken by championship chess players and the reasons behind school lunch programs. I thank Dr Deborah Goldstein for these examples.
20 Quintilian 11.2.33. Translation from the LCL.
21 James Tatum in a personal comment says: 'Curiously, *I* think they *still are*. I note in both myself and the students I teach that construing, sense, style, etc. all come much more easily if one *reads aloud* the passage in question.'
22 A Rabbinical commentary on 1 Samuel 1.13 says that 'it is forbidden to raise one's voice loudly in prayer' (*apud* Horowitz 1991a, 162 n. 7). The explanation does not address the issue of the efficacy of remembering the prayer through a kind of chanting.
23 Reber, *DictPsych*, 694 s.v. *shadowing*.
24 Galotti, *CogPsych*, 75. She is describing an experiment from Moray 1959a. She discusses other 'dichotic listening tasks', that is, hearing two messages, one in each ear, and shadowing, that is, repeating, only one, on pp. 74–75 and 244.
25 Baddeley, *HumMem*, 72. The information I present in the text is based on his

full discussion of the subject on pp. 71–95. See also Baddeley 1992a, 284–285. For a good overview of the broader topic, attention, see Galotti, *CogPsych*, 70–96 (Chapter 3, 'Attention and Automaticity').

26 One of my readers points out that 'dial' is a 'technological fossil' for pressing the buttons on a touchtone telephone. These 'fossils' abound. We 'board' an airplane because we 'board' a boat. The power of a car engine is still measured by the power of a horse. Computerese accelerates such 'obsolescence'. The 'floppy disk' no longer 'flops' – a fact which led a friend of mine, who is less than computer literate, to refer to it as the 'hard disk', which everyone who is computer literate knows resides within and not outside the machine.

27 Quintilian 11.2.34. Translation adapted from the LCL.

28 Compare Conway/Gathercole 1990a and their 'translation hypothesis' between two senses (modalities).

29 Baddeley, *HumMem*, 31–33.

30 Quintilian 11.2.32. Translation from the LCL.

31 Quintilian 11.2.28–29. Translation from the LCL.

32 Quintilian in the passage quoted uses the phrase *'apponere notas'*, literally 'to place notes'. Seneca the Younger (*Oedipus*, 821) uses the term *'nota'* in a more general sense as a 'sign' that 'can jog to life/A distant memory long lost and buried.' Translation from Watling, *Seneca*.

33 Carruthers, 247. Chapter 7 'Memory and the Book' is a fascinating account of how illuminations, text, and memory worked together. Art historians have been actively pursuing these connections, especially since the appearance of Carruthers's book.

34 Hartley 1992a, 5.0.

35 Quintilian 11.2.43. Translation from the LCL.

36 Baddeley, *HumMem*, 244–246. Baddeley is skeptical that learning before going to bed is effective.

37 Experiments linking REM sleep and memory have been carried out by Dr Avi Karni at the National Institute for Mental Health and reported in the *New York Times* (11 November 1992) p. C3, and *Science News* 142 (14 November 1992), 333.

38 Bower 1993b. This article also refers to the experiments of Avi Karni.

39 Lavie, *Sleep*, 137–142 with citations of the various experiments.

40 Pennisi 1994a, 244 on the experiments of Tim Tully.

41 My examples come from Bonner, *Education*, 165–166.

42 Cicero, *On Laws*, 2.23.59. Translation from the LCL. Bonner (*Education*, 166) translates *'carmen necessarium'* as 'obligatory chant'. This method of teaching also appears among the Egyptians, for which see Williams 1972a, 216 ('recited the lesson in a singsong fashion').

43 St Augustine, *Confessions*, 1.13. Translation by Pine-Coffin, *Conf.*

44 Baddeley (*HumMem*, 186–188). Hunter (1979a, 3–4) has an interesting discussion on how various peoples keep track of the days of the month.

45 For a cross-cultural study of the refrigerator as bulletin board, see Norman, *TurnSig*, 48–58. The use of the refrigerator for this purpose seems to be restricted to the US and those who have lived for a sufficient length of time in the US. I am not discussing all possible methods of enhancing memory, only the more common and effective ones that could have been used in antiquity but were not.

46 Baddeley, *HumMem*, 190–193.

47 Levin 1993a, 242. This is a good review of the success of various methods in actual classrooms.

48 Athenaeus 7.277c. Translation from the LCL. The quote precedes a discussion of fish. Daly (37–38) has performed the noble service of counting the number of fish (p. 81) mentioned.
49 Athenaeus 7.319e–323c. I have transliterated the Greek names in order and followed Athenaeus in including the 'and' for synodontes and synargis, which he treats together.
50 *KP* 1.2, s.v. 'Akrostichon' and *KP* 2.1335, s.v. 'Ichthys'.
51 It is probably for this reason that this example is cited as an acrostic in *KP* 1.222, s.v. 'Akrostichon'. Of course, both the words and the symbol have religious resonances from the story of the loaves and the fishes, etc.
52 Douglas Coupland, *Microserfs* (New York 1995), 53.
53 St Augustine, *Retractiones*, 1.20. The opening of the chapter describes St Augustine's audience (as we would call it today) as: *'ipsius humillimi vulgi et omnino imperitorum atque idiotarum.'*
54 Baddeley, *HumMem*, 180–181.
55 This oft-repeated phrase was part of the title of an article by George Miller (1956a) that has become a classic. It was 'partially' reprinted (Miller 1994a) with two commentaries: Baddeley 1994a and Shiffrin/Nosofsky 1994a. The idea of chunking first occurred in the nineteenth century to Sir William Hamilton (1788–1856). See Baddeley, *HumMem*, 40–42; and Gregory, *Mind*, 148 s.v. 'Chunking'.
56 Hunter 1962a, 257 for the quote. The article is devoted to an analysis of Profesor Aitken's method. For 'chunking' and the recitation of Greek verse, see Devine/Stephens 1993a, 388–391.
57 Baddeley, *HumMem*, 41. Compare its recent application for recalling dates in Carney/Levin 1994a. I agree with Baddeley's assessment.
58 Thompson *et al.*, *MemSearch*, 142.
59 Thompson *et al.*, *MemSearch*, 125. All the information in this paragraph comes from this work, especially p. 139 (on size of chunks) and p. 143 (matrix-learning).
60 Quintilian 11.2.7–8. Translation from the LCL.
61 Quintilian 11.2.39. Translation from the LCL.
62 McDaniel/Pressley, 300. See also Snowman 1987a, who specifically used 'loci mnemonics' and McCormick/Levin 1987a.
63 Vogl/Thompson 1995a and p. 339 for the quotation.
64 For both examples: Seneca the Elder, *Controversies*, 1, Preface, 2. Translation from the LCL.
65 Pliny the Elder, *Natural History*, 7.24.88–89. Translation from the LCL. For a list of such ancient achievers, see Caplan, *Eloquence*, 216–219. I separate the ability to speak a variety of languages from mnemotechnics, and merely note that Pope John Paul II is a good modern example of such a skill.
66 Plutarch, *Life of Themistocles*, 5.4. Translation from the LCL. I quoted Cicero's praise of Themistocles's memory in Chapter 8.
67 Quintilian 11.2.51. Translation from the LCL.
68 Harris, *Literacy*, 31–32. Horsfall (1991a, 61–64) finds 'his scepticism . . . unnecessarily severe.'
69 The publication does not include the rules it uses for verifying the various stunts, because different stunts require different rulings. If you wish to get into the book and are not an athlete whose records are maintained by a recognized athletic organization, they suggest that you contact them first. To get an idea of the process, you might read *Road Fever* by Tim Cahill (*Road Fever*), which describes a Guinness record of the 'longest drive south to north . . . from the southern tip

of South America to the northern edge of Alaska' (p. 278). He describes his consultation with Guinness on pp. 19–27.

70 Donald McFarlan, Editor, *The Guinness Book of Records 1991* (New York and Oxford 1990), 16. No information is given about their methods of memorizing.

71 Even the *Guinness Book of Records* has occasional cheaters: "'I [Alan Russell, then editor] suppose the biggest group of fakes are people claiming to own old cats.' . . . Those who cheat are so few and far between that Mr Russell remembers them well. There was, for instance, an individual in Spain who claimed to be 120 years old, which would make him the world's oldest man. In an attempt to authenticate the record, Russell discovered that the man was using his father's birth certificate: an eighty-five-year-old geezer who, to his shame, thought he could put one over on the world' (Cahill, *Road Fever*, 23).

72 Vitruvius 7. Introduction, 6–7. Translation from Morgan. Note that the Aristophanes mentioned in the passage is not the fifth-century BC playwright, but lived *c.* 257–180 BC according to the *OCD²*, 114, s.v. Aristophanes (2).

73 Diogenes Laertius 6.5. Translation from the LCL.

74 Carruthers (158–160) presents a very interesting analysis of how such memorial libraries worked in practice and how scholars have frequently misinterpreted the medieval use of sources.

75 Xenophon, *Symposium*, 3.5–6. Translation from the LCL. Compare also Plato, *Ion*, a comic dialogue which focusses on the rhapsodes and their wholesale memorization of Homer. The best translation and commentary are by Woodruff, *Plato*, 5–39.

76 The Koran, the Talmud, and other sacred texts are often memorized whole. For a very interesting discussion, see Neusner, *MemTorah*. Jousse (*Oral*, 167) notes: 'If there are, for example, Jews able to recite by heart, starting from a given word, the entire Talmud, which constitutes a library in itself, such persons are a phenomenon nowadays [*in our milieux*, at least]; but *before* the invention of printing, and above all before that of writing, such powers of memory *would not have seemed astonishing* . . . to-day it is something extraordinary to encounter a person who knows the *Aeneid* by heart.'

77 Carruthers, 13.

78 Seneca the Younger, *Letters*, 27.6–7. Translation from the LCL.

79 Denis 1987a. One of his interesting conclusions (p. 215) was that: 'there is a widespread agreement among individuals that imagery is useful in learning and memory, and this is true for people having either high- or low-imagery abilities. This gives support to the idea that subjects' statements about the usefulness of imagery should not be taken as reliable indicators of the likelihood of their making actual use of imagery in cognitive processing.'

80 This is a topic far beyond a study of mnemotechnics in classical antiquity. Baddeley (*HumMem*, *passim*) with his historical overview and extensive bibliography provides an excellent starting point. Oliver Sacks has written a number of extremely readable essays about various losses in his patients; these have been published in several books.

81 Pliny the Elder, *Natural History*, 7.90. Translation from the LCL. For an introduction to the various memory deficits that strike people today, see Schachter, *Searching*. On problems with visual memory, visual agnosia, see Farah, *Visual*.

82 I have retained a somewhat stripped down, but updated version of Small 1994b, because the topic pertains directly to the Greek and Roman views of what is the mind and where memories are stored. Since that publication,

Professor Tran tam Tinh has informed me that the Vietnamese also 'learn by heart'. The Hungarians, according to Helen Nagy, learn 'from the outside in'.

83 The use of φρένες and θυμός in Homer are the subject of book-length studies: Sullivan, *Phren*, and Caswell, *Thumos*. See also Sullivan 1994a and Pelliccia, *Mind*, especially 15–27. One of the best discussions of the various Greek and Latin words, which we translate as 'mind' or 'brain', remains Onians, *Origins*, 1–173. For fuller discussions of the literary references, see Bremmer, *Soul*, especially 53–63, and Nieddu 1984a. Padel (*Mind*, especially 18–48) believes (29 n. 65) that Onians, among others, strives for definitions that are more precise than the evidence allows. She also believes that the Greeks did not view such terms as metaphorical, but instead that they 'refer to concrete and abstract phenomena simultaneously' (review of Padel by B. Goff, *Classical Philology* 89 (1994): 177). Steiner (*Tyrant*, 101–116) analyzes the Greek sources in greater depth than I do here, especially the image of making impressions on the 'soul'. Her discussion complements mine. The only place where we might disagree is that she translates 'στῆθος' (Diogenes Laertius, 6.5) as 'heart' rather than as '*breast*, of both sexes, being the front part of the θώραξ' as in LSJ, 1643 s.v. στῆθος.

84 Steiner (*Tyrant*, 21–22, 30) makes the connection between writing on one's innards, so to speak, and 'reading' the entrails of animals in divination.

85 Plato, *Timaeus*, 69e–70a. Translation from Plato, Bollingen.

86 Aristotle, *Topics*, 125b10. Translation adapted from Aristotle, Bollingen.

87 *Controversies*, 1, Preface, 18. Translation from the LCL.

88 *Theaetetus*, 194c. Translation from Burnyeat, *Theaetetus*.

89 Burnyeat, *Theaetetus*, 329 n. 46. Riding (1985a) considers this passage in comparison with some cognitive theories of imagery and memory.

90 Varro, *On the Latin Language*, 6.46. Translation from the LCL. This passage is cited by Carruthers (48–49) as proof that the expression 'learn by heart' is classical in origin. She does not mention the reference in Plato.

91 '*Habe semper in memoria atque in pectore*' from Aulus Gellius, *Attic Nights*, 1.10.4. Translation from the LCL.

92 Cicero, *Tusculan Disputations*, 1.61. Translation from the LCL. According to Onians (*Origins*, p. 172) the mind [*mens*] is a part of the *animus* or soul. Pliny the Elder (*Natural History*, 11.251), however, is an exception who believes that 'the memory is seated in the lobe of the ear, the place that we touch in calling a person to witness . . . .' Translation from the LCL.

93 Varro, *On the Latin Language*, 6.44. Translation from the LCL.

94 Varro, *On the Latin Language*, 6.49. Translation from the LCL.

95 For the Greek, see LSJ. For the Latin, see *OLD*.

96 The one major exception was texts used in the performance of certain rituals, although here someone generally followed the text rather than relying on memory, as in Pliny the Elder, *Natural History*, 28.11. I discussed this passage in Chapter 1.

97 *OLD*, s.v. *verbum* no. 8 with citations.

98 The longest, preserved translation of Homer by Cicero is *On Divination*, 2.30 (63–64) of Homer (*Iliad*, 2.278–330). Among other things Cicero mistakenly says the passage is about Agamemnon rather than Odysseus. The Greek takes thirty-two lines, his translation twenty-nine. See Pease, *CicDiv*, 454–456 for commentary; and, in general, Jones 1959a.

99 Xenophon, *Symposium*, 3.5–6. Translation from the LCL.

100 Plato, *Euthydemus*, 276d–277a. Translation adapted from Plato, Bollingen. Bonner (*Education*, 177) interprets ἀποστοματίζω in this passage to mean

'oral repetition', which is obviously related to, but not quite the same as, the concepts of 'dictation' and 'memorization'. Because that meaning does not really work for Plato, I wonder whether the usage of ἀποστοματίζω as 'repeat' is not considerably later than Plato, since a passage in Plutarch (*Life of Theseus*, 24.5) uses it unambiguously in that sense: 'And this oracle they say the Sibyl afterwards repeated to the city. . . .' Translation from the LCL.

101 Translation from Plato, Bollingen.

102 A variant occurs in medieval Greek with the expression ἐπὶ στόματος, a switch in the preposition from ἀπὸ, and where the verb is sometimes ἐκστηθίζω or ἀποστηθίζω, both of which are based on the Greek for 'chest' (στῆθος). Eustathius *ad Iliad* 7.974 and Scholiast *ad* Dionysius Thrax (= *AnecGr*, Bekker II 672.25) respectively. Both passages refer to a portrait of Aristarchus with Tragedy depicted on his chest, because he knew all tragedy by heart. Reinach, *Textes*, 406–406 Nos. 544a and 544b.

103 Frankfort, *Before Phil*, 66. Discussion of the Memphite text of creation is on pp. 65–69, which I quote next in the text. I thank Dr Robert Bianchi for confirming that the use of 'heart' in Egyptian texts is not a figment of the translator's art. He also directed me to the following two references: Böhlig 1983a and Shupak 1985a.

104 Pritchard, *ANET-A*, 1–2.

105 D'Andrade 1987a, 113. Compare also in the same volume, Keesing 1987a. The Greek and Roman views presented in the first half of this excursus also represent folk models.

106 Howes/Classen 1991a, 284. While the heart is a common repository for the soul, according to Howes and Classen (pp. 283–284), 'the Mehinaku of Brazil place the soul in the eye, the Zinacanteco of Mexico, in the blood. In the West, we think of the mind as residing in the head; the Uduk of the Sudan locate it in the stomach.' Makes our minds reel!

107 The translation is from the *The Holy Bible. Revised Standard Version* (Cleveland and New York 1946–1952), as are all other translations from the Bible. The last line quoted does not appear in the standard *Septuagint* text, but may have existed in one of the alternate versions. The line is, however, crucially in the Masoretic version of Proverbs, and the Latin is a literal translation of the Hebrew. William McKane (*Proverbs*, 291) believes that the presence of this line 'may be a later expansion. It makes the line unusually long.' In any case, since the same phrasing appears elsewhere, as noted in my discussion to follow, and since it appeared in the *Vulgate* translation made *c.* AD 400, its presence or absence in the *Septuagint* does not matter for my argument. I thank Professor Robert Kraft of the University of Pennsylvania for discussing the *Septuagint* and Hebrew texts with me. Carruthers (28–29) discusses this passage, but does not make the connection with 'learning by heart'.

108 The *Septuagint* uses neither 'δέλτος' nor 'πίναξ' for 'tablet', but 'πλάτος' and 'πλάξ' respectively. 'καρδία' is the Greek word used for 'heart'.

109 Pritchard, *ANET-A*, 237. On the interconnections between the Hebrew and Egyptian 'heart' and 'mind', but without citing the passages I have discussed, see North 1995a, with bibliography.

110 Translation from Pritchard, *ANET-A*, 437.

111 Michael Sperberg-McQueen (personal communication) said he was taught that 'learn by heart' comes from a confusion in French between *choeur* (choir) and *coeur* (heart), that is, choirs would sing their songs by heart. I obviously do not think that is the correct explanation. However, it, does make me wonder whether the Norman conquest of England in the eleventh century brought

the expression to England and hence down to us, though English could have also derived it directly from the *Vulgate*. For the later history of the components of the image – 'chest', 'breast', speech, and heart – in the Middle Ages, see Jager 1990a and 1996a.

112 The *OED²* says that 'memorise' is 'chiefly US' and nineteenth century, but the *RHUD* makes it late seventeenth century.

113 For a brief history of the expression during the Middle Ages, see also Carruthers, 48–49.

10 TOOLS OF THE TRADE

1 Norman, *Things*, 159–160.

2 The term 'cognitive artifact' comes from Norman, *Things*, especially 47–53. In his introduction (p. 4) he says 'my studies caused me to question the manner by which our cognitive abilities are, in turn, manipulated by the tools cognition has helped to create.'

3 Norman, *Things*, 78. See also his *PsychEv* for how various modern devices work and don't work.

4 'We're very anti-McLuhan here [the MIT Media Lab],' says Walter Bender, the project's principal [News in the Future] research scientist. 'We believe the *message* is the message. The challenge is to extract it from the medium, to transcode it from one medium to another' (*PC Magazine* Vol. 12 No. 15 (14 September 1993), 29).

5 McArthur, *EngLang*, 886, s.v. 'Sapir-Whorf Hypothesis'. For a very clear, but informal exposition, see Agar, *LangShock*, 61–72. His book is an investigation of cultural boundaries and their absence. For the interplay between or rather the inextricable melding of language and culture, he suggests the word 'languaculture'.

6 A related and ongoing debate involves the effects of literacy. Does it make any difference to how one thinks if one is literate? Is it a question of quality or quantity? For the most part, such questions are not germane to my discussion, because I am concerned only with how the highly literate functions and not the differences between various degrees of skill of literacy and orality. The debate finds Eric Havelock, Jack Goody, Walter J. Ong, and David R. Olson saying that literacy makes a difference in how one thinks, with Ruth Finnegan and John Halverson saying that it does not. A number of other players are involved, but these are the most persuasive and vociferous for each side. The second/third fascicle of *Language & Communication* 9 (1989) is devoted to this topic. See also Olson/Astington 1990a, the series of articles by John Halverson (1991a, 1992a, 1992b), and the various works in the *Select Bibliography* under the names of the scholars cited.

7 Hunt/Banaji (1988a, 60–61) stress the difference between 'constrained' and 'dictated'. 'Whorf was a linguistic relativist, not a linguistic determinist. He did not believe that thought was dictated by language, but he did believe that language predisposed thoughts to take certain shapes.' The Hunt/Banaji article is an excellent discussion of Whorfian principles, culture, and cognitive science. Compare also Hunt/Agnoli 1991a where they cite (p. 377), among other examples, bilingual speakers who 'have maintained that they do think differently in different languages.'

8 Quintilian 10.3.32. Translation from the LCL.

9 'When Quantity Means Quality,' *Science News* 145 (19 March 1994), 188. The article reviews the work of Robert A. Josephs, a psychologist studying

'complex judgment based on ambiguous standards.' The best overall study of the effects of writing on a computer is Haas, *WritTech*.

10 Norman, *PsychEv*, 211.

11 Haas, *WritTech*, x–xii. 'The Technology Question' is the title of her first chapter, in which she surveys the scholarship on the question going back to Plato.

12 Haas, *WritTech*, xii.

13 Sirat 1994a, 387.

14 Powell 1981a, 435.

15 Maurois, *Titans*, 176–177.

16 'Kenner presents Pound's "The Return" (1912) as a poem that "could only have been composed on a typewriter"' (Foden 1993a, 5).

17 See especially Haas, *WritTech*. One of the rare detailed descriptions of a modern office at home is that of Witold Rybczynski in *Home*, 16–20. For a review of research, see Hartley 1991a.

18 Schmitt, *Object* is a study of the research methods of art historians. It is the advent of the computer and its tools that has prompted such examinations today.

19 This anecdote is a memory from past years – in this instance, way past, back to high school, a time before I realized that trivia needed to be documented.

20 For a very brief consideration of 'how writing method affects style', see Norman, *PsychEv*, 210–213. Norman takes it as obvious that one's tools affect one's products.

21 The Greek term for pen is γραφίς or γραφεῖον, which was sometimes used in Latin (*'graphium'*). For pictures of examples of both kinds of writing instruments, see Reggiani, 70 figs. 63–66; she also illustrates inkpots on p. 71 figs. 67–70. Much of the discussion that follows is based on Turner, *GrMss*, 4–7, who goes into detail on certain aspects, such as handwriting and ruling of lines on wax and papyrus. Černý, *Paper*, despite its date of publication and concentration on Egypt, is an excellent discussion of the mechanics of writing. Harris (*Literacy*, 193–196) focuses on availability and cost of the tools. Johnson (1980a) discusses the early use of parchment in the classical world. He concludes that parchment was not invented by the Pergamenes, but rather that they developed a particular type, *bicolor*, in which one side was dyed yellow. He makes the excellent point (p. 138) that any comparison of costs between parchment and papyrus must take into account the quality or grades of both.

22 Herodotus 5.58. Translation from the LCL. See Avrin, *Scribes*, 68–69. Walter Burkert (1987a, 44 and 58 n. 3) believes that the first written *Iliad* was made on leather rolls in the first half of the seventh century BC.

23 All these examples are from Pliny the Elder, *Natural History*, 13.22.69. Translation from the LCL. Pliny then goes on to discuss papyrus in detail and preserves the fullest explanation (13.23–27 (74–89)) for how 'paper' was made from papyrus. See Menci 1985a (especially 261 nn. 2–3) and Dimarogonas 1995a, both with references to previous scholarship. For surviving letters on wood, see Bowman/Thomas.

24 Cribiore, *WTS*, Chapter 1 discusses the various writing materials available, their relative advantages, and their relative costs, especially with regard to school exercises. Perhaps her most important conclusion is that, contrary to what might be expected, papyrus was the preferred material (p. 19), because wax tablets, in particular, were more expensive (p. 46). She also found 'plain' wooden tablets to be as popular as waxed, wooden tablets (p. 48).

25 The tablet, found in Egypt and dating to the second century AD, is now in the British Library, Add. MS. 34186(1). It is widely reproduced, but for a good

picture see Turner, *GrMss*, 32–33 No. 4. Shelton (*Romans*, 114 No. 132) translates the exercise: 'From a wise man seek advice. Do not blindly trust all your friends.' Compare Shelton's previous selection (113 No. 131; *Corpus Glossariorum Latinorum* III, pp. 645–647 (*Colloquia Monacensia*)) where a schoolboy says: 'I printed the assigned sentence. When I had finished it, I showed it to the teacher. He corrected it, wrote over my errors, and bid me to read it aloud.' Seneca the Younger, *Epistle*, 94.51 preserves one of the rare mentions of the actual training: 'Their [boys'] fingers are held and guided by others so that they may follow the outlines of the letters; next, they are ordered to imitate a copy and base thereon a style of penmanship (*chirographum*).' Translation from LCL. For how children were taught to write, see Cribiore, *WTS.*

26 Lucian, *The Dream*, 2. Translation from the LCL. For a broader consideration of this passage *vis-à-vis* technē, see Murray 1989a, 23.
27 Quintilian 10.3.31. Translation from the LCL. On the problems of poor eyesight in ancient Rome, see Horsfall 1995a.
28 Horace, *Satires*, 1.10.72–73. Translation adapted from the LCL.
29 Cicero, *Against Verres*, 2.2.41 (101). Translation adapted from the LCL.
30 The chemical analysis of the wax on a late eighth-century tablet from Nimrud, the earliest extant example, showed that it was 75 per cent beeswax and 25 per cent orpiment (arsenic trisulfide, a mineral). Bass *et al.* 1989a, 11. The Greeks often used a separate term, μάλθα or μάλθη, for wax mixed with pitch. LSJ, s.v., 1077 'μάλθα'. According to Brown (1994a, 7), medieval tablets sometimes 'were tempered with resin, turps or linseed oil.'
31 Brown 1994a, 4.
32 A Roman sarcophagus with the Muses may illustrate this action. It shows Clio standing with an open diptych held in her left hand and with her right hand holding a stylus that rests on or in a small bowl placed on top of a stand. Rome, Museo Nazionale Romano Inv. No. 125353, from Rome, Via Prenestina near the Tor de' Schiavi. Giuliano, *MNR*, Vol. I Pt. 8, 31–34 No. I,7 (Maria Elisa Micheli) with picture on p. 34.
33 See Powell 1981a, 424–431 for an excellent discussion of the tools used to write cuneiform, especially for the type of marks reeds could make, and step-by-step illustrations of how it was done.
34 Sirat (1994a, 410) comments that writing on wax leads to 'disjointed strokes' which make reading more difficult.
35 Matthews 1995a, 312. A clay tablet from the fourth century AD with an account of receipts in grain has been discovered at Ismant el-Kharab (Kellis, in the Dakhleh Oasis in Egypt), but it is written in Greek not cuneiform. I thank Roger Bagnall for this information.
36 Saenger 1982a, 386.
37 Suetonius, *Life of Julius Caesar*, 82. Translation from the LCL.
38 See also discussion in Chapter 5 about Cicero's use of 'court reporters'. 'Seneca (*De Clementia*, 1.15) relates the tale of a certain Tricho, who had his son flogged to death for some unnamed crime (was it adultery?) after which "populus graphiis in foro confodit"' (David Meadows, e-mail on the Classics Listserv, 1/3/93). The other example involves Caligula (Suetonius, *Life of Caligula*, 28) arranging for a senator to be stabbed by styli at the Curia's entrance. In view of the discussion of work habits, it should be noted that I am indebted to the people on the Classics Listserv during January 1993 for my information about 'death by pen'. I know of one other case where the hazards of a literate life caused death, though not by the pen but by the book. Pliny the Younger (*Letters*, 2.1) says that Verginius Rufus in old age had picked up too heavy a

tome, dropped it, and broke his hip when, bending to pick it up, he slipped on the polished floor. He never recovered.

39 Death by pen seems to be a relatively common fate for 'schoolmaster saints', since it is recorded for Cassian of Imola and three other martyrs, according to Attwater, *Saints*, 81 s.v. Cassian of Imola.

40 For a drawing of a now lost Pompeiian wall painting see Bonner, *Education*, 118 fig. 11. It shows a school scene in the Forum at Pompeii where a student is being thrashed 'in the catomus ("over the shoulders") position'. A Hebrew manuscript of the *Pentateuch* with the five *Megilloth, c.* AD 1395 shows a teacher brandishing a whip as his pupil reads. British Library, Oriental Collections, Add. 19776, f. 72v. Gaur, *Writing*, 153 fig. 93.

41 Plutarch, *Life of Demosthenes*, 29.4–7. Translation from the LCL.

42 St Petersburg, Hermitage 1779, from Ruvo. Bieber, *Theater*, 141 fig. 514 and 295 n. 59 with bibliography. Bieber says that the woman 'digs with the stylus . . . at her teeth', which implies, to me, that it is being used more like a toothpick today. While the representation is not clear one way or the other, biting seems a more likely action.

43 Turner, *GrMss*, 7 with illustrations on 75 No. 40 and 83 No. 46 for 'erasure' on a pot sherd. The 'new' texts written over the 'old' are called 'palimpsests'. Cribiore (*WTS*, 46–47) comments that plain wooden tablets with white paint were also used for school exercises, because the paint made the surface smoother and easier to write on.

44 Martial, *Epigrams*, 14.7. Translation from the LCL. Compare also Martial, *Epigrams*, 4.10, where he sends a sponge along with his work, just in case the content is not pleasing to the recipient. On the ability to 'erase' on parchment, see Roberts/Skeat, *Codex*, 20. Störmer *et al.* 1990a present the results of a chemical analysis of papyri from Herculaneum. They conclude that the ink was indeed carbon-based (gum arabic, carbon, and water), as Pliny the Elder *(Natural History*, 35.25.41–43) and Vitruvius (7.10.2) recommend.

45 Egyptian practice provides an interesting sidelight. If the mistake was noticed immediately, it would be washed away, but Černý (*Paper*, 24) adds that the scribe 'probably often simply licked away the ink, since the word *ftt* for "obliterate (an inscription)" is determined by the image of a tongue and a man with his hand on his mouth.' Extensive mistakes would be corrected by cutting out the bad part of the text and re-pasting the papyrus.

46 Turner, *GrMss*, 7. See also discussion in Williams 1992a, 184 on Ovid's description of the various tools of the writer in the *Tristia*, 1.1.3–14.

47 All Naples, Museo Nazionale. Blanck (*Buch*, 68 fig. 42) conveniently, but somewhat misleadingly, repeats without comment the old conglomeration of six examples together as if they were originally painted this way, when, however, they are drawn from several paintings, from top to bottom, left to right, as follows: Inv. 4676, 8598 and 8598; 4675, 9822, 9819. Also see Croisille, *NatM*, pls. CIV–CX. A poem of Phanias, a Hellenistic poet, preserved in the *Greek Anthology* (6.295), may allude to a 'paperweight' and 'blue spectacles (?) that give sweet light.' Unfortunately both objects are mentioned only in this poem and not plainly enough for us to understand. The translation is from the LCL. See also discussion in Turner, *GrMss*, 5 n. 10.

48 One of the best discussions, accompanied by color photographs, is De Hamel, *Scribes*. See also Alexander, *MedIll*.

49 Hildebert may be about to throw a sponge at the mouse running off with the cheese in the well-known illumination of him with his assistant, Everwinus. Prague, Metropolitan Library, A. XXI/1, folio 153v, of Augustine, *City of God*.

Alexander, *MedIll*, 15 fig. 19. I thank Elizabeth McLachlan for telling me about the sponge. One of the best descriptions of a medieval scribe at work is by De Hamel, *Scribes*: for making corrections, see p. 39; for pictures of scribes see the cover, frontispiece, etc. and for sharpening a pen, see p. 30 fig. 23. According to Bischoff (*LatPal*, 18–19), the full medieval scribal equipment consisted of chalk, two pumice stones, two inkhorns (for red and black inks), a sharp knife, two razors also for erasing, a 'punctorium', an awl, lead, straight edge, and a ruling stick.

50 St Dunstan is portrayed with curved penknife and pen in the frontispiece to a commentary on the Rule of St Benedict, made for the Cathedral Priory of Christ Church, Canterbury, about AD 1170. Now London, British Library, MS Royal 10.A.xiii, f.2v. Laurence, prior of Durham AD 1149–1154, uses a straight penknife to hold down the page as he writes. Durham, University Library, MS Cosin V.III.1, f.22v. Both in De Hamel, *Scribes*, title page and 37 fig. 29 respectively.

51 Writing '*transversa charta*', 'across the papyrus', occurred in Pharaonic Egypt from the second half of the eighteenth Dynasty onward for documents (Černý, *Paper*, 21–22). This practice also occurs in limited situations on Greek and Roman papyri. Suetonius (*Life of Julius Caesar*, 56.6) preserves our only citation of '*transversa charta*': 'previously [to Julius Caesar] consuls and generals sent their reports written right across the sheet.' Translation from the LCL. For a full discussion of its use, see Turner 1978a, 26–53 ('Transversa Charta: Sorting out the Confusion'). Turner calls such a roll a 'rotulus', always in quotes. According to him, this format remained documentary in antiquity and was never used for any work of literature (p. 31). My point is that when the 'rotulus' style became dominant, it entailed a change in the writing support. Nor do I mean to imply that the other method totally died.

52 Trier, Landesmuseum. Blanck, *Buch*, 66 fig. 40.

53 For a full discussion of such cases, see Small 1991a, 252–256. The earliest extant versions appear on Etruscan reliefs.

54 *Corpus Glossariorum Latinorum* III, pp. 645–647 (*Colloquia Monacensia*). Translation from Shelton, *Romans*, 113 No. 131.

55 The relief, AD 118, shows men with tablets large enough to be balanced on their shoulders. The tablets contained debt records, and the representation therefore portrays the ultimate cancellation of a debt. Nash, *PDAR* 2, 177 fig. 905, with references on 176, s.v. 'Plutei Traiani'. Kleiner, *RomSculp*, 248–250 and 249 fig. 217 and Bibliography on 265. Compare Chapter 4 n. 61. The idea of the public destruction of written records for debt occurs at least as early as Hammurabi, King of Babylonia *c.* 1760 BC. See Steiner, *Tyrant*, 71 n. 38.

56 On writing tablets from their origins in the Near East until today, see Lalou, *Tablettes*. For terminology, especially in the Middle Ages, see Rouse/Rouse 1989b. The earliest extant date to the Bronze Age, for which see n. 30 above, and confirm Homer's mention in the *Iliad*, on which see Chapter 2. For a photograph of the earliest tablets, see Bass *et al.* 1989a, 10 fig. 19. For a short but excellent overview through the Middle Ages, see Brown 1994a.

57 Turner (1978a) is devoted to the problem of distinguishing the 'front' ('*recto*') from the back ('*verso*'), when both sides of the papyrus have been used and no clear indication of date appears on either side. He traces both the modern usage and misusage of '*recto*' and adopts the definition proposed by Ulrich Wilcken at the beginning of this century: 'it is that side on which it is possible to see the pasted joins between the sheets of which the roll is composed' (Turner 1978a, 13). In other words, *recto* means the inside of a roll.

58 Millard 1994a, 52 for two photographs of sherds with texts. Cribiore (*WTS*, 63) notes that 'Their durability made them particularly ideal for model alphabets', even though their rough surfaces often meant that writing on them was not all that easy.

59 Brenne 1994a, 20 fig. 25. This article is a very nice introduction to the extant ostraka, of which there are now over 10,000, with copious illustrations.

60 Plutarch, *Life of Aristides*, 7.5–6. Translation from the LCL.

61 Hoogendijk 1985a.

62 From Vrasta, Chalkidike. The object was item 11 in the exhibition, 'Macedonia: The Northern Greeks and the Era of Alexander the Great' (Copenhagen, National Museum, from 16 September 1994 to 8 January 1995).

63 Grayeff (1956a, 119) in his study of the 'genesis' of Aristotle's text concludes: 'It is likely that Tyrannion and Andronicus gathered and collected peripatetic lecture versions from wherever they could.'

64 Now in Belgrade, Narodni Muzej. Bianchi Bandinelli, *RomeLate*, 127 fig. 117 and 429.

65 For a good photograph, see Bianchi Bandinelli, *RomeLate*, 77–78 fig. 70.

66 Despite the fact that there have been several articles on the subject, which will be discussed here and in Chapter 11, and that the medieval evidence is very well known to medievalists, classical scholars persist in assuming the presence of tables. For example, Cornell University Press uses an eighteenth–nineteenth-century engraving of Horace in its book catalogue from 1993 (p. 39) for W. R. Johnson, *Horace and the Dialectic of Freedom. Readings in Epistle 1*. There Horace sits, presumably in the first century BC, writing on a marble table with a roll in front of him, and, even more anachronistically, an Attic red-figure vase from the fifth century BC at the side. Possibly on the basis of this illustration, Daniel M. Hooley in his review of the book (*Bryn Mawr Classical Review* 2 No. 21 (1994)) says that Horace is 'the friendly, fat and beery poet, perched at his desk writing familiar things as we at ours dash off another. . . .' Continuous use of such illustrations does a great disservice to our understanding of antiquity.

67 Similarly the word 'bank' in English and its cognates in French ('banque') and Italian ('banca') originally meant 'bench' and by extension 'bank' for money. See the *OED*², s.v. 'bank²'. I thank Elizabeth McLachlan for bringing this derivation to my attention.

68 Petroski, *Evolution*, 22.

69 Alexander, *MedIll*, 6.

70 For more information on the role of scribes in Italy (Etruscan and Roman) see Small 1991a, especially 254–256.

71 See *Naissance, passim*. On Egyptian scribal practices, see Schlott, *Schrift*, with a discussion of their tools in Chapter 1.2 (52–85).

72 For the status of Egyptian scribes, see Williams 1972a, 218. He quotes a nineteenth-dynasty text (P. Ch. Beatty IV, Vol. 4/3–6): 'Be a scribe . . . that you may go out dressed in white, being exalted so that the courtiers salute you.'

73 For representations of scribes in Roman art, see Wrede 1981a, who lists only twelve examples.

74 Ovid, *Heroides*, 11.3–4. Translation from the LCL. On the use of '*charta*' as 'papyrus roll', see Turner 1978a, 32.

75 For measurements, see Johnson 1993a, especially 47 where he notes that a height of '25–32 cm., will be the rule', that is, 10–13 inches high, with further comments by Dimarogonas (1995a). For a statue, see Kraus, *Pompeii*, 129 fig. 146 = Marcus Nonius Balbus the Elder, probably from the Theater at Herculaneum, now in Naples, Museo Nazionale. A well-known example of reading

occurs in the fresco from the Villa of the Mysteries (Pompeii) where a mother sits holding a scroll in her left hand and resting her right hand on her son's shoulder as he stands reading beside her. See Kraus, *Pompeii*, pl. 120.

76 Delia 1992a, 1454.

77 Johnson (1993b) finds that Greek papyri for history, philosophy, and oratory have similar widths for their texts, which generally have columns between 4 and 8 centimeters (*c.* 1½ and 3¼ inches) in width. While his article shows equal distribution of widths between genres, the maximum width he notes is 9 centimeters (*c.* 3½ inches), which is by modern standards narrow. Johnson (1993c) makes the interesting suggestion that the slant of the columns was not due to writing on the thigh, but was done to achieve 'a deliberate aesthetic effect' (p. 212), because he has noted that scribes used rulings and dots to keep their columns in slanting alignment. So, Cribiore (*WTS*, 278) similarly says about school exercises that 'layout mattered at every level' for organizational and aesthetic purposes. Luxury book rolls tended to be the same height as regular rolls, but had a higher quality script and shorter columns with wider margins all around, on which see Johnson Forthcoming a. I thank Johnson for allowing me to see this article in manuscript.

78 One of the widest documentary papyri I have come across has a width of *c.* 21 inches. It contains abstracts of contracts from AD 42. Ann Arbor, P. Mich. Inv. 622. Turner, *GrMss*, 100–101 No. 59. I mentioned this papyrus in my discussion of shorthand in Chapter 5.

79. The term 'modest', as well as these measurements, comes from Van Sickle 1980a, 6–7. According to Pliny the Elder (*Natural History*, 13.23.77) standard rolls 'never' contained more than twenty sheets, on which see Skeat 1982a.

80 Since the paper differed significantly in its tensile strength from papyrus, the students were allowed to use the modern writing tool of their choice. Felt-tipped markers were preferred. I re-ran this experiment in the Spring of 1996 and had similar results. Unfortunately, because of the size of the group, I was not able to test whether writing a poetic line affected the width of the column. That is, did the student feel compelled to keep to the poetic line no matter the width it implied for a line? Turner (*GrMss*, 12) says that the 'verse unit . . . coincide[d] with the written line' by the middle of the third century BC, though he notes exceptions from as late as the third century AD.

81 A number of statues of Egyptian scribes have survived, dating back to at least the Old Kingdom (fourth and fifth dynasties, *c.* 2500 BC). See, for example, a painted limestone statue in Cairo, Egyptian Museum, Inv. JE 30272 = CG 36, from Sakkhara, early V dynasty, *c.* 2475 BC: Turner, *GrMss*, supplement pl. I and Avrin, *Scribes*, 97 pl. 93. Another well-known painted limestone statue is in Paris, Louvre AE/N 2290 = E 3023 = IM 2902: *Naissance*, 16 (color photograph), 340 No. 285. For discussion, see Parkinson/Quirke, 35–36 with illustrations. Also see Parkinson/Quirke, 9–16 on the manufacture of papyrus, and 16–19 on its 'size and format'.

82 Pliny the Elder, *Natural History*, 13.24.79. Translation from the LCL.

83 See Chapter 2 n. 25 for references and discussion.

84 For seated scribes, see the representation of a records office, from the tomb of Teji (Tjay), a vizier under Ramses II, *c.* 1225 BC at Thebes (Posner, 87 fig. 20; and Parkinson/Quirke, 61 fig. 41). Parkinson/Quirke, 36–37 illustrate a scene of 'assessment by the board of the estate' where a number of scribes are shown in various actions of using and recording on papyri. This scene is from the tomb of Ti, fifth dynasty, *c.* 2400 BC. Sometimes, instead of both thighs providing a flat platform for writing while seated, one leg would be

raised to provide a sloping surface, for which see: Egyptian scribe, New Kingdom, *c.* 1370 BC, now in Berlin, Ägyptisches Museum, inv. 22621; Sirat 1994a, 392 fig. 9.

85 New York, Metropolitan Museum of Art 23.10.1. Diorite. Eighteenth dynasty, *c.* 1355 BC. Avrin, *Scribes*, 13 pl. 18 (three-quarters view).

86 My information about the two pens comes from Tait 1988a, although the conclusions about the positions for writing are mine. Dorothy Thompson (1994a, 74–75) uses this fact when discussing scribal practices in Ptolemaic Egypt to distinguish native Egyptian writers from the Greek. Clarysse (1993a) traces the Hellenization of Egypt and the process of Greek eventually supplanting Egyptian for written communication for administrative purposes. For good discussion and illustrations, see Parkinson/Quirke, 30–37.

87 See especially, Parássoglou 1979a, 14 n. 15 where he responds to Skeat (1956a, 183–185) who claims that the classical scribe commonly sat on the ground.

88 Esperandieu 7, 151 No. 5503. Parássoglou 1979a, 10 and pl. 2. Parássoglou there and in 1985a presents all the evidence, both literary and visual. Elisabeth Alföldi-Rosenbaum (1995a) publishes a funerary relief from Trier that is quite similar in pose to the Strasbourg relief, but the Trier example dates nearly two centuries later, to the late fifth century AD. Metzger (*HistLit*, 123–137 = Chapter 12: 'When Did Scribes Begin to Use Writing Desks'), who also discusses the practices of Christian and Jewish scribes.

89 Thessaloniki, Archaeological Museum, Inv. no. 10105, from Thessaloniki, Odos Filikis Etaireias. Parássoglou 1979a, 12–14 and pl. 6. Turner 1978a, 46.

90 'κάλαμος μ' ἔγραψε, δεξιὰ χεὶρ καὶ γόνυ.' Turner, *GrMss*, 5 n. 13 (P. Lit. Lond. 11).

91 De Hamel, *Scribes*, 31 fig. 24. From a Rouen Book of Hours.

92 Sirat 1994a, 399–407, especially 406.

93 Sirat 1994a, 391 and 399, despite the fact that she cites Parássoglou 1979a.

94 Trianti 1994a, with pictures and full documentation, and Trianti 1994b. The statues are Athens, Acropolis Museum 144, 146, and 629.

95 Diogenes Laertius 3.37 (Life of Plato). Translation from the LCL. I thank Walter Burkert for this reference.

96 Lucian, *The Ignorant Book-Collector*, 15. Translation from the LCL. Lucian uses the word πυξίον for the tablets, which is a term for tablets made of boxwood.

97 Plutarch, *Life of Demosthenes*, 29.4. Translation from the LCL.

98 Lucian, *The Ignorant Book-Collector*, 4. Translation from the LCL.

99 Perhaps the best known Greek example occurs on the Attic red-figure kylix by Douris of a school scene: Berlin, Charlottenburg F2285; from Cerveteri, *c.* 480 BC; *ARV²* 431 No. 48; *Addenda²*, 237; Blanck, *Buch*, 24 fig. 9 bottom. For an Etruscan example, see the relief from Chiusi with a scribe recording results of athletic events: Palermo 8385, from Chiusi, *c.* 480–470 BC; Small 1991a, 255 with n. 33; Sprenger/Bartoloni, pl. 166; and Jannot, *RelChiusi*, 48–49 fig. 171.

100 Callimachus, *Aetia apud Papyrus Oxyrhynchos* 2079, lines 21f. The Greek is given in Metzger, *HistLit*, 126 n. 2 with other literary references for comparison.

101 Trier, Landesmuseum. Blanck, *Buch*, 66 fig. 40.

102 Weitzmann, *LateAnt*, 91 pl. 31, with caption on p. 92. Rossano Gospels, fol. 8r.

103 Cicero, *For Sulla*, 42. Compare discussion in Chapter 5.

104 In the museum at Ostia. Blanck, *Buch*, 70 fig. 44. Metzger (*HistLit*, 135–137) rightly argues that the 'table' from the scriptorium at Qumran was not used

for writing because it was too low (less than 20 inches high), concave on top, and 'the shape of the under part of the "table" is such as to make it impossible for a scribe to sit close enough in to write comfortably on its top.'

105 Gamble (*Books*, 69) describes the bindings and/or covers that were used for the early codices. Two points are of especial interest. First, 'No codex of the first three centuries has been preserved with its cover.' Second, 'Like covers for rolls, covers were probably not always provided for codices.' Gamble describes in detail the covers for the codices from Nag Hammadi which are dated to the mid-fourth century AD. These covers were made of leather strengthened by papyrus glued to the inside. It would seem likely that the utility of hard covers was one of those modifications that became known over time through experience.

106 Compare Roberts/Skeat, *Codex*, especially 6–7 and 61, and the review by McCormick (1985a). Roberts and Skeat unequivocally state that papyrus was durable and not too brittle to be folded, and hence neither of these characteristics prevented papyrus from being used in codices. Pliny the Elder (*Natural History*, 13.26.83; translation from the LCL) says that he had 'seen documents in the hand of Tiberius and Gaius Gracchus written nearly two hundred years ago.' Parkinson/Quirke (17) cite a modern curator who actively demonstrated using a roll 3000 years old. Skeat (1994a, 265) calculates no real difference in the cost of production, including materials, for either format. He suggests (1994a, *passim*) that the attractiveness of being able to fit all four Gospels in one codex (it would take four rolls) was paramount to the Christians adopting the codex. Gamble (*Books*, 49–66) presents a summary of previous theories including the last one, but believes that it was the Pauline letters and not the Gospels that determined the success of the codex. In particular (p. 63), he believes that the codex enabled random access (compared to the sequential access of the roll) that was especially helpful for a non-continuous text like letters. One of the major arguments against this idea is that compilations of excerpts were quite popular from the Hellenistic period on and would have presumably benefitted from the format of a codex. Similarly, texts like the letters of Cicero or the *Attic Nights* of Aulus Gellius would work better in a codex. Harris (1991a, 80) believes that the codex aided consultation, because it was possible to put 'markers between the pages of a codex'. If, however, those markers are as effective as my loose ones, then the advantage is not as great as Harris thinks. I am primarily concerned with why the codex took so long to supplant the roll. I also doubt that a single text was the determining factor for its popularity, despite the modern analogy of the 'killer app[lication]' that is supposed to sell particular computers. Instead, I think it was a combination of factors, among which were learning how the codex really worked as a tool and then making the appropriate adaptations.

107 London, British Library, Harley 3011, folio 69v; Dialogues of Pope Gregory the Great. Alexander, *MedIll*, 16 fig. 22.

108 Skeat 1990a.

109 Rome, Lateran Inv. 9985. Helga von Heintze in Helbig[4], vol. 1, 770 no. 1069 with bibliography. For a decent photograph, see Bieber, *Theater*, 89 fig. 317a. She also has (p. 89 fig. 316) a picture of a fragmentary copy of the same scene, now in Princeton Art Museum 51–1, for which see Ridgway, *Princeton*, 100–106 (Anne-Marie Knoblauch) with extensive bibliography. Knauer 1993a, 26 fig. 31.

110 See previous note with references to Heintze, Bieber, and Knauer. It is possible that a reading stand appears on another theatrical relief, also existing

NOTES

in a number of copies and dating to the second century BC. In this case, the stand has a high, rectangular base, a vertical shaft, square not round in section, and a horizontal rest for the roll. See Bieber, *Theater*, 85 fig. 308 (Naples) and 286 n. 33 with references. Two examples exist in Rome: Conservatori Inv. 2011 and Capitoline Inv. 622 for which see Helbig[4] I nos. 1517 (with bibliography) and 1379 respectively.

111 Plato, *Protagoras*, 325e. Translation from Knox 1985a, 11.

112 Allen and Dix *(BegUnd*, 61 No. 45 with 36 fig. 6) identify a wooden 'table' from Karanis (Egypt), broadly dating from the first century BC to the fourth century AD, as a 'reading table'. Its small dimensions of 33.3 cm. (*c.* 13 inches) in length and 17.5 cm. (*c.* 7 inches) in height with the 'back' half of the top (measurement not provided) tilted at a slight angle make me wonder how it would be of use in reading a roll. It is narrower than the average lap with the result that the papyrus would still flop off at either end. More importantly, the tilt makes it likely that the roll would have had to bend horizontally across the middle. I don't think the tilted section is sufficiently high to hold the roll, while the flat part was used for taking notes on either papyrus (awfully unwieldy) or on tablets. It is so low that it would either have to be placed on a table or a bench, or one would have to sit on the ground to use it. If it were found with other writing materials, as in the illustration, then it is possible that it was a table or stand for holding ink pots, pens, etc.

113 London, British Museum Inv. 1805.7–3.187, unknown provenience. Avrin, *Scribes*, 152 pl. 136. Turner, *GrMss*, frontispiece, with discussion on p. 6. Binsfeld 1973a, 201 and 203 fig. 2. Knauer 1993a, 25 fig. 30.

114 Manuscript in the Vatican Library, Cod. lat. 3225. See Weitzmann, *LateAnt*, 11 fig. III. For a color photograph, see Olmert, *Books*, 40. A nearly identical example, but with the *capsa* and reading stand reversed, appears in the *Vergilius Vaticanus*, 3867 fol. 14r: Weitzmann, *Studies*, 114 fig. 91. Weitzmann (ibid., 115) dates this codex to the first half of the fifth century AD.

115 Los Angeles, University of California, Glajor Gospel p. 327. The Armenian term for this contraption is *grakal*. Mathews/Sanjian, 138–139 No. 39 with color photograph.

116 Martial, *Epigrams*, 14.84. Translation from the LCL. '*Charta*' is another term used for papyrus. See *OLD*, s.v. 'charta'.

117 The 'bearding' of the papyrus should be distinguished from the original 'hirsute' or 'hairy' state before the rough edges of the individual strips of papyrus were made even and smoothed, generally with pumice. Ovid uses the word '*hirsutus*' in the *Tristia*, 1.12, on which see Williams 1992a, 186.

118 Johnson 1993a, 47 n. 6. Turner (1978a, 15–17) discusses precisely how a roll was manufactured and the way the problem of the fraying of the 'vertical' edges of the first and last sheets was solved by adding protective sheets, whose fibers ran vertically, not horizontally.

119 Knauer 1993a, 18–28 with illustrations of all the major examples. Note the examples from Boscotrecase (19 figs 16–17) and Como (Civico Museo Archeologico Paolo Giovio, 23 fig. 26 for the portable holder and 23 fig. 25 for the 'lectern' type; p. 40 n. 53 for bibliography). Knauer does not illustrate the school scene from Neumagen, now in Trier, Rheinisches Landesmuseum. For pictures of that see: Binsfeld 1973a, 202 fig. 1 (with excellent discussion); Wightman, *Trier*, 150 and pl. 14 fig. a; and Bonner, *Education*, 56 fig. 9. Note that Turner, *GrMss*, supplementary pl. IIIb has printed the photograph in reverse.

120 This frieze is often reproduced. Among other places, see Kraus, *Pompeii*, 92 fig. 114.

121 For a line drawing of a pygmy as portraitist using an easel: Pompeii, Regio VIII 3, 13bis 16, now destroyed; Reinach, *RP*, 161 fig. 6 = Helbig 1537, and Schefold, *WP*, 221. For a woman painter with the panel held by a youth and balanced on the floor: now Naples, Museo Archeologico 9018, from Pompeii, Regio VI 1, 10, *c.* AD 50; Ling, *RomPaint*, 211 fig. 232; Reinach, *RP*, 262 fig. 8; Schefold, *WP*, 92–93. For the panel balanced on a table: Reinach, *RP*, 262 fig. 9 = Helbig 1443.

122 The Greek words, ἀναλογεῖον and ἀναγνωστήριον, have later attestations in Hesychius (fifth century AD), and Pollux (second century AD), for which see LSJ, 111 s.v. *ʼἀναλογεῖον*.

123 All definitions are from the *OLD*, 1394 s.v. *ʼpluteus'*.

124 For example, G. G. Ramsay in the LCL translation for Persius and H. E. Butler in the LCL translation for Quintilian 10.3.21, when Quintilian quotes Persius.

125 Richter, *Furniture*, 115. In the last paragraph of the entry on 'Libraries' in the *OCD²* (p. 608), *ʼpluteus'* along with *ʼarmaria'* is translated as 'presses . . . of such libraries'.

126 Paris, Bibliothèque Nationale, Ms. fr. 273, f.7. Radding/Clark, frontispiece. For the term, see Genest 1989a, 149–151. Clark (*Libraries*, 57–58) comments that the 'revolving desk . . . can be raised or lowered by a screw.' The American mail order firm, Levenger's, now offers a version based on a folding desk designed by Thomas Jefferson.

127 Skeat 1994a, 265. Skeat (1981a, 373–376) also found that re-rolling was not 'an irksome and time-consuming task' (p. 373) from experiments with re-rolling a roll of wallpaper, though I think that wallpaper and papyrus are not that close in texture and hence 'rewindability'. Moreover, he found that a dowel for the roll did little to speed up the process, which (p. 376) 'may explain why so few traces of *umbilici* have been found in papyri from Egypt.'

128 Horowitz (1991a, 136 fig. 1) gives a complex chart of possibilities for reading (orally, listening to oral reading, and silently), by whom, where, mode (e.g. radio, text), etc.

129 Pliny the Younger, *Letters*, 3.5. Translation from Radice, *PlinyY*.

130 Pliny the Younger, *Letters*, 6.20.5. Translation from Radice, *PlinyY*.

131 Cicero, *On Ends*, 3.2.7. Translation from the LCL.

11 RESEARCH TECHNIQUES

1 The number of libraries comes from the Constantinian *Notitia*, for the text of which and a commentary, see Richter, *TopRom*, 370–376 and 376–377 respectively.

2 For the Palatine library, see: Blanck, *Buch*, 192 figs 98–99; *LTUR* 1, s.v. 'Apollo Palatinus', 55 (P. Gros). For the library of Trajan, see: Blanck, *Buch*, 196–197 figs 100–101; Packer 1993a; *LTUR* 1, 133–135 s.v. 'atrium Libertatis' (F. Coarelli); *LTUR* 2, 353–354 s.v. 'Forum Traiani. 7' with bibliography on pp. 355–356 (J. Packer). For other libraries in Rome, see: *LTUR* 1, s.v. 'Bibliotheca . . .', 195–197. For plans of the library at Tivoli, see: Blanck, *Buch*, 202–204 figs 108–111. Marina de Franceschini (*Adriana*, 399 and 463–477) questions the last identification and, instead places the library in the section of the villa known as the Piazza d'Oro. In general on the architecture of classical libraries, see Johnson, *Library*, and Chapter 9 in Blanck, *Buch*. On early

bilingual libraries oriental and not Greek – see Shubert 1993a. Compare also my discussion in Chapter 4.

3 Kampen 1979a, 597. In particular, she notes the use of free-standing *armaria*. The libraries with niches, to which she specifically refers, are the southwest room of the Library of Trajan in the Basilica Ulpia, the one in the Baths of Trajan in Rome, and the one at Tivoli.

4 Vitruvius 6.5.1. Translation by Morgan. He merely repeats his advice about an eastern orientation in 6.7.3.

5 Plutarch, *Life of Lucullus*, 42.1–2. Translation adapted from the LCL. Compare Dix, *Libraries*, 76–77.

6 Moschion *apud* Athenaeus 5.207e. Translation adapted from the LCL. On couches as a unit of measurement, see Pomeroy, *Xenophon*, 288 *ad* Xenophon, *Oeconomicus*, 8.13.

7 Pliny the Younger, *Letters*, 2.17. Translation adapted from Radice, *PlinyY*. Fantham (*RLC*, 202–203) is of the view that 'Pliny had little use for literature in the sense we privilege' and that this small collection of books was basically all that Pliny owned. She bases her conclusion on the fact that Pliny 'does not speak of reading any book; nor does he ask any friend to lend him or seek out a text. . . . His emphasis is almost entirely on writing, not on reading.' I think her conclusion is too strong, especially in light of the fact that she notes (p. 201) that his letters differ markedly from Cicero's in that they did not 'contain the actual news and inquiries.' Rather they are more like set pieces and resemble prose versions of Horace's poetic epistles. Hence daily minutiae like requests for books would not survive Pliny's editing for 'publication'.

8 Johnson, *Library*, 9. See also the summary on pp. 4–9. Dix (*Libraries*, 131) comes to similar conclusions about the private libraries he examines: 'A panel in a mosaic floor cannot tell us whether a bed or a cupboard stood in a room, or what a cupboard held; shelves cannot tell us what was stored on them; a niche cannot tell us what it displayed. One of the hallmarks of Roman architecture is the adaptability of interior spaces.'

9 I plan to discuss the medieval tradition of the writing evangelist at length in an article, 'Strike the Set: Evangelist Portraits, Writing, and the *Scaenae Frons*.' The idea of the *scaenae frons* goes back to Friend 1927a and especially 1929a. For bibliography, etc., see Kouymjian 1981.

10 Vienna Dioscurides fol. 5v, dated to *c.* AD 512 and from Constantinople. Weitzmann, *LateAnt*, 64–65 pl. 17.

11 Pliny the Elder, *Natural History*, 35.2.10. Translation from the LCL. Likewise Pliny the Younger (*Letters*, 4.28) mentions that 'The well-known scholar Herennius Severus is very anxious to hang in his library portraits of your fellow-townsmen, Cornelius Nepos and Titus Catius' (translation from Radice, *PlinyY*).

12 Rabbula Gospels, fol. 9v. Weitzmann, *LateAnt*, 99–100 pl. 35.

13 See Clark, *Libraries*.

14 For photographs, see Blanck, *Buch*, 203–204 figs 110–111.

15 Packer 1993a, 420 and 422. He discusses the furnishings of the library on p. 427. The personal communication referred to in my text is an e-mail response on 6 April 1994 to my written request for further information. Other than my disagreement with his assumption of the presence of the tables, the article is an excellent summary of what has been found and how it can be reconstructed. I also thank Professor Lawrence Richardson, Jr, for writing to me about the evidence about dining-tables and floors from Pompeii.

16 Small 1994a, 90 n. 15.

17 For example, Roger Ling (1991a, 250), in discussing the small library in the House of Menander at Pompeii, says that 'the room had originally been a bedchamber . . . with the places for the beds reserved in the mosaic pavement against the south and east walls.' As for the identification of this room as a library, he says: 'Whatever the correctness of this theory (there is no hard and fast evidence one way or the other). . . .' August Mau (*Pompeii*, 264) says: 'The inner part of the dining room, designed for the table and couches, was *often* distinguished from the free space in the same way that the place for the bed was indicated in bedrooms, sometimes by a difference in the design of the mosaic floor, *more frequently* by the division of the wall decoration and the arrangement of the ceiling.' I have emphasized in the quotation the phrases that demonstrate that the floor design need not indicate function one way or the other.

18 From Torre Annunziata, now in Naples, Museo Nazionale Inv. 124545. Gaiser, *PhilMos*, with full discussion of both the mosaic and related examples (pp. 13–23). Sometimes the motif is called the 'Seven Wise Men'. For an excellent color reproduction, see Kraus, *Pompeii*, pl. 215 with description on p. 166.

19 On sundials and philosophers, see Shelton 1983a, 18.

20 Vitruvius 5.11.2. Translation by Morgan.

21 Mathews (*Clash*, 109–114) discusses the later development and also illustrates two fourth-century AD examples. The first (fig. 83) is a partially preserved mosaic from Apamea, Syria with the Seven Wise Men, and the second consists of four seated statues of philosophers from Dion (fig. 84). In the latter case, note the tiny rolls (thigh-lengths in height) that they hold. While Mathews dates this group to the fourth century, the Archaeological Museum at Dion says they are *c.* AD 200, as does Harrington (1996a, 32) with good color photograph.

22 Richter, *Furniture*, 113 on the table from the atrium of the House of Cornelius Rufus. See also her general discussion on Roman tables (pp. 110–113). She rightly does not mention their use in libraries. Also see Kraus, *Pompeii*, 66.

23 Varro, *On the Latin Language*, 5.125. Translation from the LCL. Peter White (letter of 2/24/96) brings to my attention Juvenal 7.11, which lists items auctioned off by impoverished poets: 'vases [*oenophorum*], tripods [*tripedes*], armaria, and cistae.' The last two items are two different kinds of containers for rolls, as I discussed in Chapter 4. The first item is either a container for the wine necessary to get the poetic juices flowing or else was won as a prize. The second item is the crucial one. Three-legged tables were common in antiquity, but so also were tripods, which were awarded as prizes. I believe that this is such a tripod. The *OLD* (s.v. '*tripes*') also says that it could be a 'three-legged stool', in which case the poet would sit on it while reading or writing.

24 For example, a depiction of a dialogue between two ecclesiastics from MS. B. III. 32, fol. 56v, Durham Cathedral, and the giving of the Regularis Concordia where three people hold the same roll from Cotton MS. Tiberius A. III, fol. 2v, in the British Museum. Both are from the tenth to eleventh century AD and appear in Wormald, *EngDraw*, pls 29 and 23 respectively.

25 Xenophon, *Symposium*, 4.27. Translation from the LCL.

26 London, British Museum, Life Collection 31. Third century BC. Beck, *Album*, pl. 15 No. 83 and p. 20. Bonner, *Education*, 26 fig. 5 (right).

27 Cicero, *On Ends*, 3.2.7 and 3.3.10. Translation from the LCL. The crucial words in Latin are: '*M. Catonem quem ibi esse nescieram vidi in bibliotheca sedentem, multis circumfusum Stoicorum libris.*'

28 My translation of the German quoted by Blanck (*Buch*, 158): '*Rundherum an der Mauer waren Schränke, wie in den Archiven zu sein pflegen, in Manneshöhe, und in der*

NOTES

Mitte im Zimmer stand ein anderes solches Gestelle für Schriften auf beiden Seiten, so daß man frei herumgehen konnte.' Blanck (pp. 158–160) gives a good summary of the Villa's discovery in the eighteenth century and its contents. The *OCD²* (608, s.v. Libraries) says that there was a table in the center of the room, but, if that were true, I would have thought Winckelmann would have used the standard German word for table, '*Tisch*'. In addition, Winckelmann says that the central 'object' was 'another such' referring back to the cupboards. For reviews of publications on the Villa, see: Dorandi 1995a, more on the papyri themselves; and Sider 1990a, more on the architecture.

29 The best article on the papyri, where they were found and what they were, is Auricchio/Capasso 1987a with a plan on p. 47. An attempt was made by the residents of the Villa to save some of the rolls from the eruption of Mt Vesuvius, because they were found scattered in five different locations. In addition to the 'library', rolls were found in the rooms and corridors just to the west of the large peristyle. In one instance, they were in a cabinet (*armarium*) with doors. The other rolls were in packing cases (two) and scattered by the lava. The majority come from the room that Winckelmann described. Gigante, *Philodemus*, fig. 1 opposite p. 58. Kleve *et al.* (1991a) is a 'how-to' article on unrolling the papyri and exposing each layer. McIlwaine (1990a, 88 and 117–118) gives a bibliography on the recent excavations that began in 1986. They have reopened the mid-eighteenth-century tunnels, for the villa has never been exposed to light since it was covered by lava in AD 79. All the excavation was done by tunneling some 60–70 feet below the surface. The combination of noxious gases and the complaints of those who owned houses above the tunnels stopped the excavations at that time. For a vivid description of the earlier excavations, see Kraus, *Pompeii*, 13, 123–124 and 149. The current excavations are still in a preliminary stage and have not reached any of the areas where papyri were found. Compare Gigante, *Philodemus*, 1–2. For a picture of an unrolled papyrus, see Turner, *GrMss*, 134–135 No. 78 = Philodemus, *On Poems (?)*; P. Herc. 1676 cr. 4 (cols. xvi–xviii); first century BC.

30 Beck (*Album*, Chapter 2) has the most complete list of Greek representations of literate activities, with many of the examples illustrated. Here I note a single example for each 'seat'. Youth reading on a 'block': Washington DC, Smithsonian, Museum of Natural History 136373; Attic red-figure kylix, Akestorides Painter, *c.* 460 BC; Beck, *Album*, pl. 14 No. 76; *ARV²* 781 No. 4. Woman reading on a chair: London, British Museum E 190; Attic red-figure hydria, Manner of the Niobid Painter, 475–450 BC; Beck, *Album*, pl. 69 No. 351; *ARV²* 611 No. 36. Woman reading on a stool: London, British Museum E 209; Attic red-figure hydria, Manner of the Shuvalov Painter, 450–420 BC; Beck, *Album*, pl. 69 No. 352; *ARV²* 1212 No. 4.

31 For example, on the frequently reproduced Attic red-figure kylix by Douris with a school scene: Berlin, Charlottenburg 2285; *ARV²* 431 No. 48; Beck, *Album*, pl. 10 No. 53b; Blanck, *Buch*, 24 fig. 9.

32 Aulus Gellius, *Attic Nights*, 11.17.1 and 4. Translation from the LCL. Latin authors commonly use the 'editorial we' for 'I' and so the first mention of Gellius actually says '*nobis*' ['us'], as does the second reference, '*nobiscum sedens amicus meus*'. Compare also Cicero, *On Divination*, 2.3.8: 'we then sat in the library [*in bibliotheca . . . assedimus*], which is in the Lyceaum.' The plural 'we' refers here to Cicero and his brother.

33 Copenhagen, Ny Carlsberg Glyptothek H 278, from Tarquinia. A good photograph appears in Herbig, *Götter*, pl. 44 fig. 2 with caption on p. 48. See also Messerschmidt 1931a, pl. 3 fig. 5.

303

34 Volterra, Museo Guarnacci 270. *CUE* 2.2, 32–33 No. 32 with bibliography. BrK 2 pl. 65 No. 7c.

35 Marcus Aurelius, *Fronto: Correspondence*, 4.5. Translation from Shelton, *Romans*, 325 No. 322.

36 Tarquinia, Museo Nazionale inv. 9804. *Civiltà* 350 No. 15.1 *6*, with photograph on p. 352. Blanck, *Buch*, 32 fig. 14. Two excellent photographs are in Sprenger/ Bartoloni, pls 250–251 with text on pp. 149–150.

37 Translator's note to Athenaeus 5.207e in the LCL edition.

38 Aulus Gellius, *Attic Nights*, 2.22.1. Translation from the LCL.

39 Aulus Gellius, *Attic Nights*, 3.19.1. Translation from the LCL. Booth (1979a, 11–14) convincingly interprets the '*mensa*' in Martial, *Epigrams*, 10.62.3 ('*et delicatae diligat chorus mensae*') as referring to the banquet/dining table and hence to the slaves who wait on such tables.

40 Cornelius Nepos, *On Famous Men*, 25. Translation from the LCL.

41 Pliny the Younger, *Letters*, 8.21.1. Translation from the LCL.

42 The best work on the furnishings of medieval and Renaissance libraries remains Clark, *Libraries*. Genest (1989a) in his study of the vocabulary for libraries makes no mention of words for 'table'. See also Vezin 1989a. I thank Eric Garberson for discussing the furnishings of libraries with me.

43 Saenger 1982a, 396.

44 Venice, Scuola di S. Giorgio degli Schiavoni. Stapleford 1994a, 72 fig. 4. Stapleford also illustrates a number of the predecessors. It is instructive to flip through the first two volumes of the *Histoire des bibliothèques françaises* (here = Vernet, *HBF* and Jolly, *HBF*) to see the table tops change. Long, flat tables appear in libraries only in the second volume, though one must be careful to check whether such tables are modern additions.

45 The drawing is by Etienne-Louis Boullée, *Deuxième projet pour la Bibliothèque du Roi* (Paris 1785) and reprinted in Balayé 1988a, 230, and in Chartier, *Order*, fifth plate, where it is captioned 'Boullée imagines the King's Library as a gigantic basilica containing the entire memory of the world.' Not until recently with the advent of the computer has this idea recurred. Douglas Lenat leads a project to capture all knowledge on the computer, for which see Freedman, *Brainmakers*, 33–34, 48–61.

46 De Hamel, *Scribes*, 36 fig. 28. Paris, Bibliothèque Nationale, MS fr. 9198, f. 19.

47 De Hamel, *Scribes*, front cover. Brussels, Bibliothèque Royale Albert Ier, Mss 9278–80, f. 10.

48 Delaissé *et al.*, No. 32. Brussels, Bibliothèque Royale Albert Ier, Mss 9095, fol. 1. Delaissé's claim that the scattered books reflect more an artistic *horror vacui* than reality misses the point – it is a *topos*, because studies were like that.

49 Paris, Bibliothèque Mazarine, MS. 753. Pernoud/Vigne, 74 (color photograph) and Rouse/Rouse 1989a, 180 and 181 fig. 2. That the cold affected one's choice of writing tools comes from a remark of Orderic Vitalis that he wrote on wax during the winter and transferred the text to parchment when it was warmer. Brown 1994a, 8.

50 Rossano, Archiepiscopal Treasury, fol. 121r. Weitzmann, *LateAnt*, 95 pl. 33 and with discussion on p. 96. Calkins, *IllBks*, 25–29 with pl. 5 on p. 28.

51 Munich, Bayerische Staatsbibliothek, Clm 4452, Pericopes of Henry II, fol. 4r. Calkins, *IllBks*, 153 pl. 78 and discussion on 150.

52 Munich, Bayerische Staatsbibliothek, Clm 4452, Pericopes of Henry II, fol. 3v. Calkins, *IllBks*, 152 pl. 77 and discussion on p. 150.

53 Originally written and decorated at Monkwearmouth or Jarrow; now Florence,

Laurentian Library, fol. Vr. Calkins, *IllBks*, 69. Weitzmann, *LateAnt*, 126–127 pl. 48. Compare discussion in Chapter 4 on *armaria*, with further references.

54 New York, Metropolitan Museum of Art 1948.48.76.1, sarcophagus from Portus (near Ostia). Weitzmann, *Spirit*, 279–280 No. 256, with detail on p. 280. Amedick, *SarkMensch*, 135 No. 81 (with full bibliography) and pl. 114 figs 1–2. Again, compare Chapter 4 n. 47.

55 For an example, see Chapter 2 n. 24.

56 Reynolds/Wilson, 10. Their discussion runs from pp. 10–18, and p. 52 for my next bit of information. We tend to refer to these comments as 'scholia'. Turner (*GrPap*, 121–123) also has a good discussion. For the varied history of different sets of scholia, see Zetzel 1975a. 'Glosses' in antiquity referred to comments on words rather than to marginalia. For glossing in the Middle Ages as part and parcel of the process of reading itself, see Dagenais, *Ethics*.

57 Turner, *GrPap*, 123. He presents a somewhat more detailed picture than Reynolds/Wilson on this topic. For what a papyrus with commentary would look like, see Turner, *GrMss*, 98–99 No. 58 = B.M. Pap. 2055, first century BC. This commentary is on Homer, *Iliad*, 2.781ff. with spaces between the comments.

58 Cambridge, St John's College, ms. A.8, f.103v. De Hamel, *Scribes*, 4 fig. 1 where dated to *c.* 1130.

59 Quintilian 10.7.11. Translation from the LCL. The Latin, '*usus quidam irrationalis*', and the Greek, 'ἄλογος τριβή', are interesting phrases in that both stress the 'unreasoning' or 'irrational' aspects of practicing a skill. Compare Lucian, *The Ignorant Book-Collector*, 2: 'you read some of them aloud with great fluency, keeping your eyes in advance of your lips [στόμα].' Translation from the LCL.

60 Quintilian 1.1.33. Translation from the LCL.

61 Crowder/Wagner, 184.

62 Inhoff *et al.* 1992a.

63 Conway/Gathercole 1990a, 515.

64 I have already mentioned in Chapter 5 that Augustus complains that Latin was not spelled 'exactly as we pronounce' it (Suetonius, *Life of Augustus*, 88). None the less, it is still more regular than English.

65 This delightful example comes from a mystery by Sarah Caudwell.

66 Skeat 1956a. It is an interesting and general principle that only the errors enable us to figure out how certain processes work. For example, students cheating in exams can be caught if the mistakes are the same, but not if both papers are perfect. In analyzing how the brain works, more has been learned from people with problems such as strokes or epilepsy than those who are normal in their responses.

67 I thank Roger Bagnall for making this point. He also thinks that 'the wide belief in the dominance of dictation is of doubtful correctness.' Letter, 6 March 1996. To my knowledge, no one has compiled a statistical analysis of the mistakes, etc. to determine what the percentages actually are. The literary sources support dictation – a view that may reflect the fact that the highly literate, whose texts are preserved, could afford or had access to personal scribes.

68 Turner, *GrPap*, 120. The papyrus is P. Oxy. xxxi. 2536.

69 Johnson 1993b, 424.

70 Skeat 1956a, 185.

71 Pliny the Younger, *Letters*, 3.5.10–15 *passim*. Translation from the LCL.

72 Compare Kenney 1982a, 16 and Bonner, *Education*, 127, both of whom recognize the limitations imposed by the lack of tables.

73 Horowitz 1991a, 141.

74 Pliny the Elder, *Natural History*, 7.25.91. Translation from the LCL.

75 Cicero, *Brutus*, 23.87. Translation from the LCL.

76 Seneca the Younger, *Letters*, 40.10. Translation from Campbell, *Seneca*.

77 Eusebius, *Ecclesiastical History*, 6.23.2. Translation from the LCL.

78 'The Life of St Thomas Aquinas' by Bernardo Gui quoted by Carruthers, 3.

79 Horace, *Satires*, 1.10.74–76. Translation from the LCL. See also Bonner, *Education*, 177.

80 Freund, *Objects*, 99.

81 Horace, *Satires*, 1.4.9–13. Translation from the LCL.

82 *Lettres Provinciales*, 14 December 1656.

83 Cicero, *Letters to Atticus*, 2.23. Translation from Shackleton Bailey, *Atticus*, No. 43. Compare also Harris, *Literacy*, 220–231 on ancient letter writing, with the use of scribes discussed on p. 231. For an example of a letter with the body written by a scribe, but with closing greetings from the sender, see Turner, *GrMss*, 114–115 No. 68 = Egypt Exploration Society, P. Oxy. xviii 2192, AD 170.

84 The correspondence from Vindolanda, the Roman imperial fort near Hadrian's wall in England, is especially interesting. See Bowman/Thomas.

85 Horace, *Satires*, 1.10.92. Translation from the LCL.

86 Pliny the Elder, *Natural History*, 25.3.7. Translation from the LCL. For Plutarch's use of Greek translations of the Latin, see Jones, *Plutarch*, 84–87. This reference and some of those that follow are drawn from his footnotes.

87 Jones, *Plutarch*, 83–84.

88 Aulus Gellius, *Attic Nights*, 13.9.1. Translation from the LCL.

89 Aulus Gellius, *Attic Nights*, 15.6.1–2. Translation from the LCL. Holford-Strevens (139–141) discusses Gellius's skills in assessing variant readings. Gellius, for example, comes to the logical conclusion that the older the roll the more likely it is to be accurate. The principle is sound, but in practice in antiquity it was problematic, because it meant trusting the bookseller, who was as likely to be honest as a modern-day antiquities dealer. Holford-Strevens finds that some of the readings Gellius accepts contain 'crass errors'.

90 Cicero, *Letters to His Friends*, 16.22. Translation adapted from Shackleton Bailey, *Friends*, No. 185.

91 Cicero, *Letters to His Friends*, 13.77.3. Translation from Shackleton Bailey, *Friends*, No. 212. Compare the follow-up letter from Vatinius (*Letters to His Friends*, 5.9 = Shackleton Bailey, *Friends* No. 255) who is a general and a friend of Cicero who promises to find the runaway slave, whom he specifically calls a reader ('*anagnostes*').

92 Quintilian 10.1.128. Translation from the LCL.

93 Quintilian 10.3.20–21. Translation from the LCL.

94 Cicero, *Letters to Atticus*, 4.4a. Translation from Shackleton Bailey, *Atticus*, No. 78. The successful completion of the tasks is recorded in 4.8 (No. 79) and 4.5 (No. 80). Compare discussion of this passage in Chapter 3.

95 Cicero, *Letters to Friends*, 16.21. Translation from Shackleton Bailey, *Friends*, No. 337.

12 COMPOSING THE WORK

1 This chapter contains an updated version of a portion of a short article (Small 1995a), which, in turn, was based on my contribution to a panel I co-organized

with Professor James Tatum, 'New Approaches to Memory', American Philological Association, Annual Meetings, December 1993.

2 Lucian, *How to Write History*, 47–48. Translation from the LCL.

3 I am not following the sequence of processes recommended in ancient rhetoric, since my purpose is to analyze the cognitive aspects of composition, not the 'stylistic' ones. Compare discussion in Chapter 7 on the divisions of rhetoric.

4 *Letters to Atticus*, 12.5b and 13.8.

5 *OCD²*, 402, s.v. *epitome*. See also: LSJ, 667 s.v. ἐπιτομή; and *OLD*, 613 s.v. *epitome*.

6 Xenophon, *Memorabilia*, 1.6.14. Translation from the LCL.

7 Auctor ad Herennium 4.3.5. Translation from the LCL.

8 Pliny the Younger, *Letters*, 3.5.17. Translation from Radice, *PlinyY.* For a close analysis of Pliny the Elder's method of taking notes, especially the meanings of *legere*, *adnotare*, and *excerpere*, see Dorandi 1991a, 14–15 with summary on pp. 32–33.

9 Pliny the Elder, *Natural History*, Preface, 17. Translation from the LCL. The numbers Pliny gives are all guesstimates, except for the number of rolls, which may be accurate.

10 Carruthers, especially 33–45. The earliest instance I have found uniting memory and treasury dates to the third century BC and the Stoic philosopher, Chrysippos, a follower of Zeno. Sextus Empiricus, *Against the Mathematicians*, 7.373 preserves the reference. For a modern example, see Koriat/Goldsmith 1996a. In Roediger's (1980a, 235–236) review of modern cognitive metaphors for memory he says 'In a delightful spoof of these types of two-store views, Hintzman (1974) compared memory to a cow's stomach.' Little does either Roediger or Hintzman realize that this comparison also has a long *and* serious history, going back to antiquity. Remember the quote from Quintilian (11.2.41) I cited at the beginning of Chapter 9 where he refers to 'chewing the cud'. On its development in the Middle Ages, see Carruthers, 164–169. Roediger refers to: D. L. Hintzman, 'Psychology and the Cow's Belly,' *The Worm Runner's Digest* 16 (1974), 84–85.

11 Auctor ad Herennium 3.16.28. Translation from the LCL.

12 Quintilian 11.2.1 and 3. Translation from the LCL.

13 Seneca, *Controversies*, 1, Preface, 3. Translation from the LCL.

14 Aulus Gellius, *Attic Nights*, Preface, 1. Translation from the LCL. Note that Gellius uses '*penus*' rather than '*thesaurus*' for 'storehouse'. The difference is not significant for the current discussion. He also makes a very similar statement about his work methods at 9.4.5.

15 Janson (*Prefaces*) does not include 'memory' in his discussion of literary commonplaces in Latin prefaces. He does, however, remark briefly (pp. 152–153) on bees and flowers, a subject that Carruthers (191–192) identifies as a common motif in the Middle Ages for the gathering of memories, on which see my discussion immediately below. Compare also the Preface of Seneca the Elder to his *Controversies*, 1, Preface, 2–5.

16 Aulus Gellius, *Attic Nights*, Preface, 11–12. Translation from the LCL.

17 Plutarch, *Moralia*, 629D. Translation adapted from the LCL.

18 Pliny the Younger, *Letters*, 1.1. Translation from the LCL. Fantham, *RLC*, 200–203.

19 Cicero, *On Invention*, 2.4. Translation from the LCL.

20 On florilegia during the Middle Ages, see Carruthers, 174–185. The word *florilegium* is modern Latin according to the *OED²* (s.v. 'florilegium') and its

first recorded usage dates to 1647. The Latin word was originally *summarium* (summary) and later *breviarium* (breviary) according to Seneca the Younger (*Letters*, 39.1). When Pliny the Elder (*Natural History*, 21.9.13) uses a related Greek word, *anthologicon*, he explicitly says that it refers to flowers, since *anthos* is the Greek word for flower. According to the *OCD²* (67, s.v. *anthology*), the word was not used to mean 'a collection of poems . . . until the Byzantine period.' The English word 'anthology' derives from the Greek.

21 Seneca the Younger, *Letters*, 84.3, 5. Translation from the LCL.

22 Carruthers, 191. She then goes on to discuss the passage from Seneca.

23 Diodorus Siculus, 1.3.4. Translation from the LCL.

24 Mejer (*DiogLaert*, 27) in an excellent study of excerpting techniques (16–29) points out the additional problem of reading one's handwriting, especially when ambiguous abbreviations are used. He does not consider the role of memory. For more on handwriting, see my various discussions in Part I.

25 Pliny the Younger, *Letters*, 9.36. Translation from Radice, *PlinyY.*

26 Quintilian 10.3.23 and 25. Translation from the LCL. Pliny says he was taught by Quintilian in *Letters*, 2.14.9.

27 Porphyry, *Life of Plotinus*, 8. Translation from the LCL. It may be of interest that Plotinus was forced to use this method because of poor eyesight.

28 Saenger 1982a, 387–391. Saenger also discusses the evidence from medieval illuminations there. Carruthers discusses composing in memory during the Middle Ages in Chapter 6, and especially for St Augustine (p. 207).

29 For example, Harris (*Literacy*, 173 n. 115) believes that this is the case for Cato's composition of *On Agriculture*.

30 For further analysis of dictation in general by the Romans, see Herescu 1956a, and Quinn 1982a, 167–169.

31 Thomas, *LitOral*, 124 with references to Aristophanes's *Acharnians*, pp. 383–479 and *Thesmophoriazusae*, pp. 95–265.

32 Quintilian 10.6.1–2. Translation from the LCL. Compare also Carruthers (especially 196–203) for an extensive discussion of this practice in the Middle Ages with frequent references back to antiquity.

33 Quintilian 10.3.15. Translation from the LCL. Compare also Carruthers, 197, 201.

34 Suetonius, *Life of Augustus*, 85.2. Translation from the LCL. Johnson (1980a, 141 n. 48) interprets the 'sponge' as referring to the removal or washing away of the ink from papyrus. Both senses might be true. Fantham (*RLC*, 148–149) comments that young aristocrats often tried their hands at writing poetry and plays during the late Republic, but that the practice virtually ceased from the time of Tiberius on.

35 Hull, *Touching*, 123–124, entry for 19 August 1984.

36 Cicero, *Orator*, 44.150. Translation from the LCL.

37 See, among many others, Beye, *Epic*, 110–112, 114–115, and 268–269 (brief history of scholarship with references). Thalmann (*Form*, 1–32 with notes on 187–196) devotes a chapter to this topic. I disagree with his statement (p. 16) that 'more complex structures [more than 2 horseshoes in my terminology] are possible, with *any* number of framing elements grouped concentrically.' Oral poets are constrained by their short-term memories. Compare Rubin, *MemOral*, 274–278, an analysis of ring composition in North Carolina ballads.

38 Compare my discussion in Chapter 14 on Homer's description of the shield of Achilles.

39 Hull, *Touching*, 124, entry for 19 August 1984.

40 Hull, *Touching*, 124, entry for 19 August 1984.

NOTES

41 Murray 1989a, 10–11.
42 Hunter 1985a, 227.
43 *OLD*, 538, s.v. *dicto* 2b. Compare Kenney 1982a, 12.
44 Bischoff, *LatPal*, 41. Carruthers, 196. Clanchy, *Memory*, 270–271.
45 Luce, *Livy*, 144. So Sir J. G. Frazer in his introduction to the LCL edition of
   Apollodorus, *The Library*, written in the first century AD, says (p. xvii): 'he
   [Apollodorus] used excellent authorities and followed them faithfully, reporting, but seldom or never attempting to explain or reconcile, their discrepancies
   and contradictions.'
46 The best known model Etruscan alphabet is on the ivory writing tablet from
   Marsiliana d'Albegna, now in Florence, Museo Archeologico, dated *c.* 650 BC. It
   is very tiny: 88 x 51 mm. For a colour photograph, much enlarged, see *Civiltà*,
   98 top = 96 No. 3.14.17. For other examples, including this one (No. 1), see
   Bonfante, *EtrLang*, 106–109.
47 The problem was particularly difficult when dealing with the conflicting versions for the foundation of Rome. For example, Dionysius of Halicarnassus
   (1.72–73) gives eight Greek versions with a ninth as 'others unmentioned' and
   then adds four Roman variants.
48 Pelling 1979a, 92.
49 Pelling 1979a, 91–92.
50 Introduction to the LCL edition of Diodorus Siculus, Vol. 1, p. xvii.
51 Diodorus Siculus 1.3.8. Translation from the LCL.
52 Quote from Haslam 1994a, 2. Dyck's article, 'The Fragments of Heliodorus
   Homericus', was in press at the time.
53 Aristotle, *Problems*, 18.9 = 917b. Translation from Aristotle, Bollingen.
54 Schenkeveld 1992a. See also my discussion in Chapter 2. On ἀναγιγνώσκω and
   why it means 'read' in Greek, see Steiner, *Tyrant*, 26–29. Compare Allan 1980a.
   For other words meaning 'read' in Greek, see Chantraine 1950a.
55 *Letter to Gnaeus Pompeius*, 3. Translation from *Critical Essays*, LCL 2, 381.
   Compare the essay 'On Thucydides' where Dionysius says, 'the thought has
   occurred to me that I shall seem like a lone pioneer breaking new and
   unexpected ground if I take it upon myself to discredit any part of Thucydides's work . . . and yet the principles on which his methods were based are not
   irrefragable' (ibid., LCL 1, 465, 467).
56 Fantham, *RLC*, 42.
57 Locher 1986a, 26–27 with quote on p. 27.
58 Pliny the Younger (*Letters*, 3.5) lists his major works.
59 My citation of the sentence, 'It is difficult to wreck a nice beach' (Chapter 2) is
   an example. On the other hand, I am extraordinarily proud of having found the
   reference to Maurois's biography of the Dumas, because I had read it in high
   school before I knew the value of precise references.
60 Compare discussion in Skydsgaard, *Varro*, 103. Skydsgaard devotes a chapter to
   the 'Roman Scholar' (pp. 101–124). He mentions mnemotechnics only once in
   passing (p. 115).
61 Pliny the Younger, *Letters*, 3.5. Translation from Radice, *PlinyY*.
62 Pliny the Elder, *Natural History*, 7.34.88. Translation from the LCL.
63 Horowitz 1991a, 140.
64 Seneca the Elder, *Controversies*, 1, Preface, 3–4. Translation from the LCL.
   Seneca's memory feats are discussed in Chapter 7.
65 Cicero, *On Old Age*, 11.38. Translation from the LCL. Among the 'employ-
   ments' mentioned are publishing his speeches, investigating law, and studying
   Greek literature.

66 Quoted by Hunter 1985a, 228. Hunter has an excellent discussion of the literate view of memory.

67 Hunter 1985a, 228–229.

68 'Memory of Elderly Takes Cultural Turns', *Science News* 146 No. 1 (2 July 1994), p. 13. This is a summary of work by Becca Levy and Ellen Langer of thirty residents of Beijing, thirty deaf people in the United States, and thirty hearing US volunteers.

69 Suetonius, *Life of Augustus*, 84.1. Translation from the LCL.

70 Aulus Gellius, *Attic Nights*, 9.14.1. Translation from the LCL.

71 Polybios 12.27.4–6. Translation from the LCL. Some 300 years later, Pliny the Elder (*Natural History*, 2.45.117) would claim the reverse: 'Now-a-days a person may learn some facts about his own region from the notebooks of people who have never been there more truly than from the knowledge of the natives.' Translation from the LCL. Scholars today would naturally agree.

72 Polybios 12.28a.9–10. Translation from the LCL.

73 Gill/Wiseman, *Lies* is a set of essays on the ancient concepts of truth, falsehood, and fiction. Of particular interest for my discussion are the articles by Wiseman (1993a) and Moles (1993a). I have also found helpful Woodman, *RhetHist*; Gabba 1981a; and Luce 1989a. From the cognitive point of view, consider Kurt W. Back (1994a, 46), who says about 'autobiographical' memory: 'in different societies, the audience is socialized to expect different autobiographical communications and has its own definitions of truth and its importance.'

74 Thucydides, 1.22. Translation from the LCL. See Pollitt, *AncView*, 122 especially and in general 117–125. This is among the most discussed passages in modern scholarship. See, for example, Gentili/Cerri 1978a, 139. For discussion of truth and accuracy, compare Schultze 1986a, 126. For the translation of *ergon* as 'fact' rather than 'deed', see Immerwahr 1960a, 276. See also Woodman, *RhetHist*, 9–28; Moles 1993a, 104–107.

75 Suetonius, *Life of Julius Caesar*, 55.3. Translation from the LCL.

76 Agar, *LangShock*, 188–189. He says these problems of transcription explain why the Watergate tapes provided such a field-day for the lawyers.

77 See especially Woodman, *RhetHist*, 10–15.

78 In between is 'as they are said to be or seem' (Pollitt, *AncView*, 136). Compare also Pollitt's discussion of *aletheia* (125–138) and *diligentia* (351–357), the Latin equivalent of *akribeia*; and Fornara, *NatHist*, 93–96 on the earlier passage, 1459a, with its description of the historian's brief. Each generation of historians questions what is 'truth' and 'accuracy' – a topic that engages just as much today as it did in Thucydides's and Aristotle's times.

79 Translation adapted from the LCL 35. Moles (1993a, 107–108) discusses this passage in relation to Thucydides.

80 Barclay 1988a, 291. Even the title of Barclay's article 'Truth and Accuracy in Autobiographical Memory' has a Thucydidean ring. Compare also Back 1994a.

81 Neisser 1981a, 159.

82 Suetonius, *Life of Augustus*, 84.2. Translation from the LCL.

83 Pelling 1980a, 127. I am deeply indebted to his two articles. Reactions to his articles and a similar analysis of Plutarch's literary techniques applied to other works of Plutarch may be found in Larmour 1992a, especially 4160–4162 and 4165–4174; and Podlecki/Duane 1992a, 4067.

84 Neisser 1988a, 557.

85 Pelling 1980a, 127. All quotes from Pelling, unless otherwise specified, are from 1980a. I simply give the exact page reference in parentheses in my text.

86 Plutarch mentions the three debates in his lives of *Cicero* (19.1–4 and 20.4–21.5) and *Crassus* (13.3), but not *Caesar.*

87 O'Connor, *Letters*, 93.

88 Johnson *et al.* 1993a, 3. This article is a review of the field with an extensive bibliography.

89 Larsen 1988a, 326 and especially 224–226.

90 Neisser *et al.* 1996a.

91 Compare Johnson *et al.* 1993a, 6.

92 Sadoski/Quast 1990a, 256.

93 Baddeley, *HumMem*, 138–139.

94 C. B. R. Pelling (1990a, 36) calls this a 'concept along the lines of "true *enough*", more true than false.'

95 Kleiner, *RomSculp*, 90–99 with photograph on p. 94 (fig. 74) and bibliography on p. 119. For Agrippa's actual absence, see Billows 1993a, 91.

96 Barclay/Wellman 1986a, 101. This article reports on a test of memory in adults over a four-month period by adding 'foil items' that never occurred to the events which had actually occurred. They found that (p. 93) 'the false recognition of nonevent, foil items increased after a 1- to 3-month delay. Confidence ratings of recognition accuracy remained consistently high over all tests, even though recognition accuracy deteriorated.' In short, there was 'an overconfidence in the "facts" of one's life.'

97 Seneca the Younger, *Letters*, 33.4. Translation from the LCL. On this passage, see Alexander 1990a, 235.

98 Neisser 1982a = reprint of a paper given in 1978. Studying natural memory in natural surroundings has not met with uniform acceptance by psychologists. For arguments on both sides see Loftus 1991a in response to Banaji/Crowder 1989a; and Koriat/Goldsmith 1996a.

99 For studies on this topic, see Rubin, *AutobioMem* and *Remembering*; Neisser/Fivush; and Schwarz/Sudman.

100 *Science News* 143 (13 March 1993), pp. 166–167. Winograd/Neisser. Schachter, *Remembering*, 195–201.

101 Bower 1990a, 312. Schachter, *Remembering*, 114–118 with references. Johnson *et al.* 1993a, 11–12 on eyewitness testimony and source monitoring. The work of Elizabeth Loftus is extremely important here; I recommend the popularization Loftus, *Witness*, as a start. Compare also my discussion in Chapter 7 on 'false memory syndrome'.

102 Johnson *et al.* 1993a, 13 with discussion. This episode occurred while Reagan was still president and presumably before he had Alzheimer's Disease. On amnesia and source monitoring, see the Johnson article, pp. 15–16.

103 Schank has written a number of popularizations of his work, of which perhaps the most revealing title for the current discussion is *Tell Me a Story*. In order to get the computer to understand events reported in the newspaper he has had to learn how we ourselves extract and remember information. Not everyone believes that the idea of schemas or scripts works. Whether or not they do in computer applications is a different question from whether or not they do for people. For a brief history of the idea and a critical summary, see Baddeley, *HumMem*, 335–347. For a short history of the topic, see Gregory, *Mind*, 695–697 s.v. '*Schemas*'. From an anthropological point of view, see Casson 1983a. Rubin, *MemOral*, 15–38 (Chapter 2, 'The Representation of Themes in Memory') is one of the best discussions, since Rubin melds the psychological with the literary in a consideration of the oral transmission of stories. Classicists are beginning to become aware of the value of the

approach. See, for example, Minchin 1992a, who also explains more of the background on scripts than I do here. For an excellent discussion of the cultural effects of schemas, see Hunt/Banaji 1988a.

104 Tversky/Kahneman 1983a, 297 and for the 'conclusions', 299.

105 Tversky/Kahneman 1983a, 300.

106 Tversky and Kahneman (1983a, 297) started off with eight statements about Linda, but when they found that the majority of responses violated the conjunction rule, they adopted 'a series of increasingly desperate manipulations to induce subjects to obey the conjunction rule' to no avail. In my quotation, I have taken the description of Linda and joined it with the last of their 'desperate manipulations'.

107 Tversky/Kahneman (1974a) present a clear summary of the types of errors we make, which they group under three heads: representativeness, availability, and adjustment and anchoring. I believe that most, if not all, of these errors occur in our ancient sources (and naturally in our modern ones too). A full study of them is beyond the scope of this work. Their conclusions are not without controversy, for which see Bower (1996a) on the work of Gerd Gigerenzer and Daniel G. Goldstein, who maintain that people use the general heuristic of 'take the best'. See Kruglanski (1989a both quotes, p. 407) for a discussion of such judgements from a 'situationally specific approach' that defines accuracy as 'relative to the situation and to the standard setter's perceptions rather than being absolute in any strong sense of the term.'

108 For a discussion of schemas and memory, see Baddeley, *HumMem*, 335–347. For schemas and personal memories, see Barclay 1986a.

109 The phrase 'imaginary likenesses' is from Pliny the Elder, *Natural History*, 35.2.10, quoted at greater length in Chapter 11. Murray (1989a, 26) notes 'their [ancient biographies'] curious inversion of the biographical fallacy: rather than seeking to interpret the work of art in terms of the artist's life, the life was invented out of the work.'

110 Plutarch, *Life of Alexander*, 1. Translation from the LCL.

111 Moles (1993a) is very good at discussing the slipperiness of truth. He does not touch on the cognitive aspects I have been stressing.

112 Plutarch, *Life of Solon*, 27.1. Translation from the LCL. Compare Moles 1993a, 120.

113 Roger Bagnall (letter, 3 June 1996) points out that the ancient chronographers were not very reliable, and Plutarch is therefore making a critical assessment of their worth. While that might indeed be true, I still think that Plutarch would value gist over accuracy. This attitude hasn't changed. Harry Stein (1994a, 53), in *TV Guide* no less, writes, 'Perhaps no one over 10 ever believed the tale of George Washington and the cherry tree, but it still served to illustrate vital truths about the man's character.'

114 Pelling 1980a, 129–30 (quote on p. 129). So Walker (1993a, 371) says of Dionysius of Halicarnassus that 'He undertook a dramatic elaboration of material that his readers knew only from *annales* and as legends from the distant past . . . [H]is is an imaginative reconstruction of the "events."' Walker also notes (p. 374) that 'a likeness to reality, and not . . . a fidelity to "the facts"' was important without mentioning scripts or schemas. The manufacturing of evidence had a long history in Roman history. As Badian (1966a, 11) terms it 'the expansion of the past' (p. 12): 'it is difficult to avoid the conclusion that there was simply not as much information to be had as [Gnaeus] Gellius produced. He must have used to the full the freedom that Hellenistic

historians allowed themselves of inventing the verisimilar to eke out the meagre truth.' Similarly, see Wiseman, *Clio*, Chapter 2 'Annals and History'. Wiseman (ibid., 22 n. 81) quotes Peter Gay (*Style in History*, 1975, 206): 'It has all too often been the historian's assignment to assist his culture in remembering events that did not happen.'

115 *FGrH* 70 F 9, quoted in Harpocration's lexicon. This information and the translation are from Wiseman 1993a, 142.
116 Tversky/Kahneman 1983a, 308.
117 Schank, *Connoisseur*, 75, 124–125.
118 Rose, *Memory*, 91.
119 Lord 1985a, 50. Compare my discussion in Chapter 1.
120 Ezzell 1991a. Posner/Raichle, *Images*, 105–129 (Chapter 5, 'Interpreting Words'), especially pp. 125–129 on the effects of practice.
121 Schank, *Connoisseur*, 223.
122 Schank, *Connoisseur*, 90.
123 Bower *et al.* 1979a, 177. See especially Experiment 2, 188–193.
124 The translation is from Wiseman 1993a, 142 for Polybios 3.33.17 = 'τοῖς ἀξιοπίστως ψευδομένοις'. Compare also Seneca the Younger, *Natural Questions*, 4b 3.1 (also in Wiseman 122–123), and Lucian's Preface to his *True History*.
125 Pliny the Elder, *Natural History*, 8.39.82. Translation from the LCL. On Pliny's reliability, see Coulson 1976a, especially 368.
126 Pliny the Elder, *Natural History*, 37.11.31. Translation from the LCL.
127 Aulus Gellius, *Attic Nights*, 9.4.15. Translation from the LCL. Gellius is referring to Pliny the Elder, *Natural History*, 7.4.36–37. This assessment occurred, of course, in the days before operations to change one's sex were possible.
128 Aulus Gellius, *Attic Nights*, 9.4.13. Translation from the LCL.
129 Pliny the Elder, *Natural History*, 5.1.12. Translation from the LCL. Grundy Steiner (1955a, 143) remarks that from Pliny's 'rather numerous, but always highly unsteady attempts at skepticism we get a vivid impression of how exhausting the task must have been to sift through the almost unlimited fund of conflicting sources.' Recall the quotation in Chapter 5 from Petroski, *Evolution*, 22: 'Luxury, rather than necessity, is the mother of invention.'
130 Hankins 1991a, 514. Hankins reviews four books by historians that all touch in one way or another on 'truth', history, and 'proof'. In the passage quoted, he presents his own view. Wiseman (for example, 1993a, 130) discusses at length the ancient views of the mythological, the legendary, and the 'real' in a very similar vein.
131 Gell-Mann, *Quark*, xvi.

13 TYPES OF WORKS OR GENRES

1 Woodman, *RhetHist*, 12–13 for both quotes. An account of Neisser's study precedes the two quotes I have chosen.
2 Hunter 1985a, 209 for all quotes.
3 Compare my discussion in Chapter 1 on the fact that knowledge of words comes only with literacy – something which Hunter also considers. On exactly how oral transmission works, see Rubin, *MemOral*, 122–145 and 304–307.
4 Hunter 1985a, 228.
5 Hunter (1985a) also discusses cases where a nonliterate, to use his term, is

'fed' a text orally bit by bit so that in the end, like with the Lord's Prayer, the person knows the whole verbatim, though without being able to read.

6 Compare Cole/Scribner, *CT* (123): 'A great deal of cross-cultural psychological research is based on notions and theories about non-Western thinking that are centered about a *deficiency hypothesis*. . . . "In respect to such-and-such a cognitive skill, X tribe fails to perform as well as (American) (Genevan) (English) groups." But when we turn to the area of memory, the picture is reversed. The severest critics of "primitive mentality" unite in extolling the superlative quality of primitive *memory*, and find Europeans wanting in comparison.'

7 Compare my discussion in Chapter 1 and, for an additional reason, see the quotation from Cole/Scribner, *CT,* 138 about the !Kung.

8 Plato, *Theaetetus,* 142d–143a. Translation from Plato, Bollingen.

9 Bernadete (*Theaet*), for example, uses 'speech' instead of 'conversation'. That translation makes no difference to my argument, whose point rests on the fact that 'word' is not used.

10 For commentary, see *JerBibComm,* 1291. Gamble (*Books,* 12–20 and 79) implies that the Jewish religion far more than Christianity valued the written word. For example, he says (277 n. 130) that 'Promoting careful inscription [of a text] was the rule [B. T. Megillah 29b] that any sheet of parchment that contained as many as four errors was not to be corrected but discarded (and buried).'

11 Plato, *Theaetetus,* 143b–c. Translation from Plato, Bollingen.

12 Norman, *TurnSig,* 11. Norman's (pp. 1–15) discussion of modern reproductions of live events is noteworthy and amusing.

13 Cicero, *Letters to Atticus,* 13.19. Translation from Shackleton Bailey, *Atticus,* No. 326. For an explanation of the presence of Varro as 'reflect[ing] the social complications of the literary scene', see Fantham, *RLC,* 48–50.

14 Cicero, *On Friendship,* 1.3. Translation from the LCL.

15 Cicero, *Tusculan Disputations,* 2.3.9. Translation from the LCL.

16 Beard 1985a, 131.

17 Aristotle, *Rhetoric,* 3.12.1–2. Everything within square brackets is verbatim from the translation in Kennedy, *AristRhet,* 255, and not my additions. Kennedy (*AristRhet,* 253–254) also discusses other Greeks writing on this subject, including Plato, Alcidamas, and Isocrates. According to Cole (1996a, 147), Isocrates was 'the earliest author to distinguish between 'oral' and 'written' styles and to compare their advantages and disadvantages'. Alcidamas, a fourth-century rhetorician and sophist, wrote a diatribe 'On Those Who Write Written *Logoi* or On Sophists'. He concentrates primarily on the loss of spontaneity and inflexibility of a written speech compared to total, oral delivery. For a translation of Alcidamas, see Matsen *et al.,* 38–42. On Aristotle and Isocrates's speeches, see Bons 1993a.

18 Kennedy, *AristRhet,* 254 for both the information and use of the term 'ghost-writing'.

19 Plato, *Menexenus,* 235d. Translation from Plato, Bollingen.

20 Thomas, *LitOral,* 92.

21 Plutarch, *Life of Demosthenes,* 8.5. Translation from the LCL. Thomas Cole (*OrigRhet,* 117) believes that such incomplete speeches allowed the speaker to customize with pertinent details, as necessary.

22 Quintilian 10.7.32. Translation from the LCL.

23 The tradition seems to be late, since our earliest record is from the Suda Lexicon (end of the tenth century AD). See Thomas, *LitOral,* 13. Plutarch (*Life of Pericles,* 8.4–5) says that 'Pericles, with all his gifts, was cautious in his

discourse [λóγον]. . . . In writing he left nothing behind him except the decrees which he proposed.' Translation from the LCL.

24 Polybios, *History*, 12.25i. Translation from Scott-Kilvert, *Polybius.*
25 Plutarch, *Life of Demosthenes*, 8.2. Translation from the LCL. Thomas, *LitOral*, 124–125.
26 Quintilian 12.10.55. Translation from the LCL. Compare my discussion on his reaction to the circulation of lecture notes by his students in Chapter 3.
27 Cicero, *Letters to Atticus*, 2.1.3. Translation from Shackleton Bailey, *Atticus*, No. 21.
28 Kennedy, *RhetRom*, 177 with bibliography in note 45. Compare also ibid., 126.
29 Cicero, *For Gnaeus Plancius*, 30.74. Translation from the LCL.
30 Quintilian 10.7.30–31. Translation from the LCL. See also Kennedy, *RhetRom*, 276–277.
31 The meaning of the Latin '*commentarius*' has been subject to much discussion, since it seems to range from finished essay to our concept of notes. In addition, its Greek 'equivalent', ὑπόμνημα (*hypomnema*), has its own, different range of meanings. See Fornara, *NatHist*, 180–185 for a discussion of both terms. For just the Latin terms see Skydsgaard, *Varro*, 104–105; and Nicolet, *Space*, 101.
32 Kennedy, *RhetRom*, 81 on Cicero, *For Cluentius*, 140.
33 I thank Dr Deborah Goldstein for bringing this lingering archaism to my attention.
34 Pliny the Younger, *Letters*, 7.17. Translation from Radice, *PlinyY.*
35 Pliny the Younger, *Letters*, 7.17. Translation from Radice, *PlinyY.*
36 Pliny the Younger, *Letters*, 7.17. Translation from Radice, *PlinyY.* Pliny makes similar remarks in another letter (5.3) to Titius Aristo. There he also defends his writing of 'verse which is far from serious' because 'there are besides times when I laugh, make jokes, and enjoy my fun, in fact I can sum up all these innocent relaxations in a word "I am human"' (translation from Radice, *PlinyY*). Pliny's quote is from Terence, *Heauton Timorumenos*, 77.
37 Pliny the Younger, *Letters*, 9.10. Translation from Radice, *PlinyY.*
38 Cicero, *Letters to Atticus*, 13.8: 'I really have nothing to write about, as you have just left and sent me back my tablets [*triplicis*] soon after' (translation from Shackleton Bailey, *Atticus*, No. 313). Cicero here interestingly enough refers to a set of three tablets strung together. For papyrus, see discussion below on Cicero, *Letters to Atticus*, 16.3 = Shackleton Bailey, No. 413.
39 Quintilian 10.3.32. Translation from the LCL. On revisions, see also Herescu 1956a, 141–142.
40 Haas (*WritTech*) makes an extensive analysis and comparison of how writers write on paper and online, especially in Chapters 3 and 4. The two major differences in writing online are that corrections tend to be local and the writer often loses a 'sense' of the text and how it coheres as a whole. For the record, I have discovered this finding to be all too true and eventually decided that interim printouts, which I had stopped making, were an absolute necessity. As for keeping track of the various snippets that I quote and the sources that I cite, I use a 'personal information manager' (*InfoSelect*) that allows me to put free-form notes of any size into 'stacks', but then has the wonderful ability to search through all of the stacks when I can't remember where I put what.
41 Quintilian 10.3.17–18. Translation from the LCL. Quintilian discusses the topic of composition/revision at length in 10.3.
42 Pliny the Younger, *Letters*, 7.20. Translation from Radice, *PlinyY.* See also Dorandi 1991a.

43 Pliny the Younger, *Letters*, 1.1. Translation from Radice, *PlinyY.*
44 Dionysius of Halicarnassus, *On Literary Composition*. Translation from the LCL, 2.225.
45 Suetonius, *On Poets – Life of Vergil*, 22–25. Translation from the LCL.
46 Suetonius, *Life of Nero*, 52. Translation from the LCL. Compare also my discussion in Chapter 10 on erasing mistakes on wax tablets.
47 Cicero, *Letters to Atticus*, 15.14. Translation from the LCL.
48 Cicero, *Letters to Atticus*, 16.11. Translation from the LCL.
49 Shackleton Bailey's translation of the two words as 'red wafers' is unlikely. How would they be stuck to the papyrus? Wouldn't they shift when the papyrus was rolled and unrolled? Carruthers (318–319 n. 142) similarly doubts that Robert Grosseteste used parchment slips. The earliest example I know occurs in Albrecht Dürer's 'Portrait of Erasmus', dated 1526, where Erasmus is writing on a portable sloping desk-top at the side of which are a few creased markers. For an illustration and interesting discussion of them as the predecessor to today's Post-it notes, see Petroski, *Evolution*, 85.
50 '*sed tamen idem* σύνταγμα *misi ad te retractatius, et quidem* ἀρχέτυπον *ipsum crebris locis inculcatum et refectum. hunc tu tralatum in macrocollum lege arcano convivis tuis.*' Note that Cicero uses the Greek for 'treatise' and 'original' respectively. Cicero, *Letters to Atticus*, 16.3 (my translation). Johnson (1994b, 64) defines a *macrocollum* as 'a roll with wide – not tall – sheets.'
51 Cicero, *Letters to Atticus*, 13.44. Translation from Shackleton Bailey, *Atticus*, No. 336.
52 Lattimore 1958a, with a number of examples cited to prove his point. The quotation that follows is on p. 10.
53 Lattimore 1958a, 9.
54 Lattimore 1958a, 10. I am reminded of Charles Greville's astute comment about Marguerite, Countess of Blessington (1789–1849): 'The fact of her existence as an authoress is an enigma, poor as her pretensions are; for while it is very difficult to write good books, it is not easy to compose even bad ones' (Hibbert, *Greville*, 166 (from the entry for 17 February 1839)).
55 Lattimore 1958a, 20 n. 18. Johnson (1994c, especially 229–230 n. 4) believes that Lattimore is 'not likely to be right. His assertions on the difficulties of writing are overstated.' Johnson believes that the logistics (material on which to write and staff to transcribe) make drafts likely, but I believe that just because the materials were there does not mean that they were used in the same way we would use them. Again, think of the tables that were not used for writing. Johnson believes that the phenomenon that Lattimore has noticed is instead part of the 'archaic style' and used 'for some artistic effect'.
56 Quintilian 10.3.33. Translation from the LCL.
57 Plutarch, *Life of Pericles*, 24.7–25.1. Translation from the LCL.
58 Pliny the Elder, *Natural History*, Preface 12. Translation from the LCL.
59 Ferraro 1975a and Isager, 28 n. 81. For a bibliographical overview on all aspects of Pliny the Elder, see Serbat 1986a.
60 Della Corte 1982a, 37. For an analysis of Pliny's late Roman Republican predecessors and how they organized works, especially of agriculture, see Rawson, *IntellLife*, 132–142 (Chapter 9, '*Dialectica*'). For a study of the entire tradition of ordering knowledge from before Pliny till today, see McArthur, *Worlds.*
61 Herodotus 4.30. My translation.
62 Cicero, *On Invention*, 1.97. Hermagoras lived *c.* 150 BC. See discussion in Kennedy, *RhetRom*, 116–117.

63 Quintilian 4.3.1, 12, 14–15. Translation from the LCL. Compare Quintilian
3.9.4 on the same topic where he gives an additional synonym for 'digression',
'*excessus*'.

64 Livy 9.17.1–2. Translation from the LCL.

65 Pliny the Elder, *Natural History*, 35.1.1–2. Translation from the LCL. Note that
Pliny does not use the word '*loci*' for topics here, but merely '*iis*', 'these things'.

66 Isager, 114. Isager thoroughly treats Pliny's organization of the books that deal
with art. The main reason for their inclusion is that Pliny is interested in what
man does to nature. Isager does not discuss the role of memory.

67 Compare Isager, 59 and 75.

68 Pliny the Elder, *Natural History*, 34.19 (53). Translation from the LCL.

69 Daly, 36. Full quote is in Chapter 5.

70 Cicero, *Topica*, 1.1–5. Translation adapted from the LCL. Two curiosities about
the LCL translation should be noted, because they are common errors. First,
H. M. Hubbell, the translator, has Cicero and Trebatius 'sitting' in the library,
although no word for 'sitting' appears in the Latin. They may have been
standing and pulling out various rolls, as we might before a modern bookcase.
Second, in the last sentence quoted the translator says 'I wrote up what I could
remember' when Cicero never uses 'could', for Cicero believes he has remembered everything. A letter (*Letters to Friends*, 7.19) that Cicero wrote to Trebatius
after he sent off the manuscript to him has also survived. It repeats more
briefly the information quoted in the text. I am not interested here in the topics
of the *Topica*, but only in how it was written and the role of memory in that
process. On the work itself, see Huby 1989a, with bibliography.

71 Carruthers (296 n. 52) says that the idea of writing something up from memory
like Cicero became an 'authorial trope'.

72 Stump, *Boethius*, 20–21. The two crucial Latin terms, '*conscribo*' and '*Topica
Aristotelea*', appear also in Cicero's letter to Trebatius (Cicero, *Letters to Friends*,
7.19). On Cicero's translations in general, but not on his *Topica* in particular, see
Jones 1959a.

73 Turner (*GrPap*, 108–111) comes to a similar conclusion (p. 108): 'they did not
regard the exact expression (especially the order of words) of the author as
sacred. It is a sobering explanation.' His analysis, especially the comparison to
printed editions of musical works today, which are full of errors ignored by and
unknown to the public, is very useful. He believes that (p. 108) 'in the Roman
period . . . there is a steady respect for the authority of the text.' I would add,
mainly in comparison to the 'Greek' period, but not in comparison to today.
On translation in classical antiquity with extensive references, see Rochette
(1995a), who does not mention the *Topica* in his discussions of Cicero (pp.
249–250 and 252–253).

74 Cicero, *On Invention*, 2.2.6–7. Translation from the LCL. The Latin for the last
sentence is important: '*Atque hic quidem ipse et sese ipsum nobis et eos, qui ante fuerunt,
in medio posuit, ut ceteros et se ipsum per se cognosceremus.*' The Latin does not quite
say 'published' but literally 'put in the middle' or more freely 'made accessible'.

75 Vitruvius 5.4.1. Translation from Morgan.

76 Vitruvius 6.7.5. Translation from Morgan.

77 Cicero, *On the Best Kind of Orators*, 5.14. Translation from the LCL. Cicero
strongly believes that Greek works should be available in Latin translations, as
he says at length in *On Ends*, 1.2–3 (4–10). He does not say what makes a
translation good, although he does mention poor translations (p. 5).

78 Cicero, *Brutus*, 90.310. Translation from the LCL. On bilingual education in
Rome, see Fantham, *RLC*, 24–31. She notes (p. 30) that the situation changed

in the time after Cicero to an education primarily in Latin. St Augustine (*Confessions*, 1.13–14; translation adapted from the LCL) remarks on his difficulties in learning Greek compared to Latin (1.14): 'The time was also (when I was an infant) that I knew not a word of Latin; yet by marking I got that without any fear or tormenting.' He concludes: 'a free curiosity has more force in children's learning of languages, than a frightful enforcement can have.' His conclusion applies to learning in general, but is not at all specific to learning a foreign language. On learning second languages, see Bialystok/Hakuta.

79 Frost 1980a, 165.

80 I give just a single example of each error, though many more could be found. Wrong words: Aristotle, *Rhetoric*, 3.7 = 1410a. According to Kennedy (*Arist-Rhet*, 242 n. 102), 'The quotes in this section are all from Isocrates' *Panegyricus* (1, 35, 41, 48, 72, 89, 105, 149, 181, and 186, respectively) but apparently from memory, since they are not very accurate.' I thank Hardy Hansen for this reference.

    Wrong author: as an instructive example, consider the one that did not get away. Cicero wrote to Atticus (12.6a, quoted here in Chapter 3) to ask him to change a mistake he had made in the *Orator* (9.29), where he had mistakenly claimed that Eupolis, a fifth-century BC Attic playwright, was the author of a quotation, rather than Aristophanes (*Acharnians*, 530–531).

    Wrong speaker: Cicero (*On Divination*, 2.30 (63)) says that Agamemnon is speaking when it is Odysseus in the passage from Homer, *Iliad*, 2.278–283. Compare also Aulus Gellius, *Attic Nights*, 15.6.1–2, which I quoted in Chapter 11 on another similar error of Cicero.

    Wrong work: Aristophanes in the *Frogs*, 1124ff., attributes the lines of Aeschylus to the *Choephoroi* (*Libation Bearers*) rather than the *Agamemnon*, though scholars account for the wrong play by saying, for example, that the second play of the trilogy is the first about Orestes. I thank Cynthia Shelmerdine for this reference.

81 Johnson *et al.* 1993a, 7.

82 Johnson *et al.* 1993a, 12.

83 Polybios 21.28.11. Livy 38.7.10. The example comes from Walsh 1958a, 84. This kind of mistake continues throughout the ages. There was the Renaissance printer who substituted '*porcos*' (pigs) for '*procos*' (suitors) (Grafton 1980a, 277). Then there was the story a friend told me about a friend of hers, who had a book typeset in Korea in which all the references to the *Koran* were changed to *Korean*. And so it goes.

84 Polybios 21.30.7. Livy 38.9.12. Again the example and translation comes from Walsh 1958a, 85.

85 De Romilly 1988a, 23.

86 Hembold/O'Neill, ix with brief discussion of Plutarch's use of quotation. For example, Plutarch makes the following references: 221 to Homer, 41 to Aeschylus, 34 to Sophocles, 137 to Euripides, and over 600 to Plato. Nor are those all the sources he quotes. These numbers are from Frost 1980a, 161. The major collection of Plutarch's quotes is Helmbold/O'Neill. For recent works on Plutarch's use of his sources, see the various essays in *ANRW* Pt. II, Vol. 33.6, among which see especially Podlecki/Duane 1992a, 4060–4063.

87 Williamson (*Sappho*, 34–59 = Chapter 2, 'Papyrus into Print'). She rightly reminds us that (p. 41) 'It is not so much the loss of a classical author's work that requires explanation as its survival.'

88 Plutarch, *Moralia*, 841F. Translation from the LCL.

89 Knox 1985a, 15.

90 Turner, *GrPap*, 126. One of the major issues is the dearth of 'autograph' copies, or at the least, copies that we *know* the author approved or oversaw in production. According to Dorandi (1993a, 73), we have about eighteen possible examples from the first century BC through the sixth/seventh century AD. The autograph papyri that we do have tend to be either letters or the works of 'bad poets' (Dorandi 1993a, 78–79) like Dioskoros of Aphrodito in Upper Egypt. In this case, since Dioskoros was also an official, we have samples of his handwriting.

91 McArthur, *EngLang*, 838, s.v. 'Quotation Marks'. Both this entry (pp. 838–839) and the previous one on 'Quotation' (pp. 836–837) are quite interesting for the history of quoting, both accurately and inaccurately, both inadvertently and in plagiarism. The twentieth century is notable for 'live' quotations taken not from print but from interviews and speeches.

92 Four works to consult are: Janko 1990a; Powell, *Homer* with collected reviews in the *Cambridge Archaeological Journal* 2 (1992), 115–126; Nagy 1992b and *PoetPerf*; and Boyd 1995a for an excellent discussion and a skepticism closest to mine. Also compare my discussion in Chapter 1.

93 Boyd 1995a, 44.

94 Turner, *GrPap*, 107. Compare also the discussion in Reynolds/Wilson, 8–14.

95 Compare Mitscherling 1982a. He suggests that Plato (*Meno*, 95d–96a) deliberately misquoted Theognis 35, substituting διδάξεαι for μαθήσεαι. Mitscherling assumes that Plato must have come up with this reading, even if 'from faulty memory', because all extant manuscripts of Theognis have the second word. That our manuscript tradition could be at fault is not mentioned. In turn, Mitscherling therefore assumes that Xenophon (*Memorabilia*, 1.2.20) followed Plato rather than a divergent reading from a separate source. The situation may be worse. Diogenes Laertius (3.57 and 3.62; translation from the LCL) writes that 'Now, says Thrasylus, the genuine dialogues are fifty-six in all. . . . The following dialogues are acknowledged to be spurious . . . .' Since Thrasylus lived in the first century AD, it means that already the transmission of Plato's works was questionable. On the 'edition' of Homer, which Plato had, see Nagy, *PoetPerf*, 142–143.

96 Luck 1981a, 172. The two passages are Vergil, *Eclogues*, 4.62 and Quintilian 9.3.8.

97 Much has been written about textual criticism, which is perhaps best described as an art. I would suggest starting with Luck (1981a), which gives a nice historical overview, and Reynolds/Wilson. An interesting article that approaches the problem from a slightly different angle – that of ancient additions to the 'original text' – is Tarrant (1987a), who sees three kinds of interpolations: emendation, annotation (gloss, comment, and citation), and imitation-collaboration.

98 I give one example of each type from the *Natural History*:
Professions grouped: 'doctors' in 1.29 (with Botrys listed)
Name without modifier: 'Botrys' in 1.34
Individual by profession: 'Marsus the poet' in 1.34
Author with many works and none specified: 'Euripides' (1.37 and 37.32).

99 The LCL translates the Latin by our conventional system of author/title, hence as 'Metrodorus's *Science of Architecture*'. If Pliny had wanted to use a title he would have, because in the Preface (pp. 24–27) he demonstrates that he knows all about how works are titled by both the Greeks and the Romans.

100 Examples abound, but just two are from Book 34: 'L. Piso handed down that . . . ' (30) and 'Varro says . . . ' (56).

101 The endeavor, which is valuable when not carried to extremes, is known by its German name of '*Quellenforschung*', on which see, among others, Miles, *Livy*, 1–7.
102 Pliny the Elder, *Natural History*, Preface, 21. Translation from the LCL.
103 Compare Rouse/Rouse 1991a, 249 on the same issue for medieval writers: 'There was a reciprocity between tools and the materials they served, which affected the transformations in both.'

14 INDIRECT APPLICATIONS OF THE ART OF MEMORY

1 Varro, *On the Latin Language*, 6.49. Translation adapted from the LCL. Similarly, in the fourth century AD, Servius (on *Aeneid*, 3.486) continued to equate 'monuments' and 'memory': 'monuments' however are so called from the reminding [*admonitione*] of the mind.' That the word '*monumentum*' actually depends on an Indo-European root, **men-* ('to think') does not affect my argument, which deals with what the Romans thought, not with what we know. Miles, *Livy*, 17.
2 Evans (*Herodotus*, 116, 123–130) discusses the range of such monuments and how they would serve as mnemonic devices. He also notes (p. 130): 'Local traditions that centered around monuments . . . could be purely fictional. An isolated monument without a legible inscription is a mythopoeic catalyst. . . . But not every monument was an unreliable commemorative.'
3 The translations of Homer are from Lattimore, *Iliad*. The translations of Vergil are from Mandelbaum, *Aeneid*. The two shields have been much studied. For a recent work, see Becker, *Shield*. I published an abbreviated version of this section in Small 1995a.
4 Homer begins each section with 'on it' ('ἐν δέ') followed by some word for 'place' ('ἐτίθει') or 'made' ('ποίησε'). Compare also Beye, *Epic*, 45: 'Homer's Trojan War is really a generic war, the kind that must have been fought over and over again throughout the second millennium. More to the point, it is the stock war for a poet of stereotypes.'
5 Thalmann, *Form*, 190 n. 32 with references.
6 In this particular instance it is not important that Vergil uses the preposition 'in' and the Auctor (3.17.30) 'ex', because Vergil (1.456) introduces the serial description of the decoration of the Temple of Juno in Carthage with 'ex ordine'.
7 Plato, *Phaedrus*, 230d. Translation from Plato, Bollingen.
8 This aspect has been much studied in recent years. See, among others, Pomeroy, *Xenophon*, 87–90.
9 Xenophon, *Oeconomicus*, 8.1. Translation from the LCL.
10 Xenophon, *Oeconomicus*, 10.1. Translation from the LCL.
11 Xenophon, *Oeconomicus*, 8–9. Translation from the LCL. Pomeroy (*Xenophon*, 285–303) provides a lengthy and very interesting commentary to the text without mentioning memory training.
12 Socrates plays with the spelling of names, his own and that of Theaetetus, in the *Theaetetus* (Plato, 203ff.).
13 This information comes from LSJ, for which see under τόπος and χῶρος.
14 On Xenophon's training in rhetoric, see Pomeroy, *Xenophon*, 15–17.
15 Aristotle, *Poetics*, 1450b34–1451a7. Translation from Aristotle, Bollingen. Compare the *Metaphysics* where Aristotle briefly refers to '[t]he chief forms of beauty' as 'order and symmetry and definiteness' (Aristotle, *Metaphysics*, 1078b1. Translation from Aristotle, Bollingen).

16 Aristotle, *Metaphysics*, 980a25ff. Translation from Aristotle, Bollingen. The quoted passage is a fuller account of a similar passage from the *Posterior Analytics* (100a5ff.) which I quoted in Chapter 8. The Greek concept of magnitude also maintains that there is an appropriate size for each situation, something that is neither too much nor too little: in short, the 'Golden Mean', as Horace (*Odes*, 2.10.5) called it. (In Latin the term is '*aurea mediocritas*'. How words do change!) While Aeschylus (*Eumenides*, 530) was among the earliest to refer to the 'mean', Aristotle in the *Nicomachean Ethics* uses it as an ethical principle around which to organize one's life.

17 Davies 1971a, 155.

18 Cicero, *On Ends*, 5.1.2. Translation adapted from the LCL. Cicero gives these words to Marcus Piso. For another example, well and extensively analyzed, see Ann Vasaly (*Reps*, 104–130) on Cicero's second speech *Against Verres* (2.4), with its laundry list of precious objects stolen by Verres. She concludes (p. 127): 'The image created through this combination of *topographia* (description of place) and *enargeia* or *evidentia* (vivid description) is then tied by the orator to various associations and ideas, for in each case Cicero has attempted to create a binding link in the minds of the audience between the visually imagined object [the item stolen by Verres] and the meaning he has assigned to it.'

19 Marvin (1989a) discusses Cicero's acquisition of sculpture in detail, with all of the pertinent letters given in an Appendix. She rightly stresses (p. 32) that Cicero 'did not ask for replicas of specific works, only for the "generic brand" of gymnasium statuary. He sought to create not a literal copy of Plato's Academy but what he saw as its essential character as a place of philosophic discussion – what he remembered from his student days . . . by awakening the associations Cicero thought proper.' Rouveret (*HistImag*, 323–325) also discusses Cicero's acquisitions, but solely from the point of view of the art of memory and its relation to *topographia*, which she defines (p. 323) as a 'description of a real place'.

20 Cicero, *On Ends*, 5.1.1. Translation from the LCL.

21 Cicero, *Letters to Atticus*, 1.9. Translation from Shackleton Bailey, *Atticus*, No. 5.

22 Cicero, *On Divination*, 1.5. (8). Translation from the LCL.

23 Translation from Moffitt 1993a, 61 with discussion there and on p. 66 n. 11.

24 *Scriptores Historiae Augustae*, 'Hadrian', 26.5. Translation from the LCL.

25 Warden/Romano 1994a, 232–235 with a plan of the distribution of the sculpture for the large peristyle on p. 233. Gigante, *Philodemus*, 8–13, 47–48. The J. Paul Getty Museum in Malibu, California is a reconstruction of this villa. It reproduces not just the physical plan of the building itself, but also has replicas of the statuary in the large peristyle.

26 Pliny the Elder, *Natural History*, 35.2.9–10. Translation from the LCL.

27 Interpretations other than 'memorious' ones are generally given for the choice of sculpture in the Villa of the Papyri. It is not that I wish to argue against those, but that I want to add mine to them, for the choice of decoration worked in more than one way and on more than one level for the Romans. See, among others, Warden (1991a), for a review and summary article of Neudecker, *Skulp*. Rouveret (1987a) discusses the notion of Roman collections and how they worked. She considers some of the same passages that I have here and also from the point of view of the art of memory. Our treatments are complementary.

28 Richardson, *NTDAR*, 160–162, s.v. Forum Augustum. Nash, *PDAR* 1, 401–410, s.v. Forum Augustum. *LTUR* 2, 289–295 s.v. '*Forum Augustum*' (V. Kockel). Hofter, *Kaiser*, 149–199. Luce 1990a. Zanker, *Power*, 210–215 with

plan on p. 194 fig. 149. The literary, as well as inscriptional sources, are collected in Dudley, *Urbs*, 123–129.

29 Luce 1990a, 123. For the remains of the statues themselves, see Tufi 1981a.
30 Ovid, *Fasti*, 5.551–553, 563–566. Translation from Dudley, *Urbs*, 125.
31 Sallust, *The Jugurthine War*, 5.5–6. Translation from the LCL.
32 For example, Zanker, *Power*, 213. Against Vergil's influence: Luce 1990a, 123.
33 Polybios 6.53. Compare the related discussion by Pliny the Elder, *Natural History*, 35.6–7, on which see Isager, 116 with n. 372 for bibliography.
34 Cicero, *Against Verres*, 2.1.19.51. Translation adapted from the LCL.
35 It may be significant that Socrates, in Plato (*Cratylus* 421b), derives *alētheia* from '*theia alē*', 'divine wandering'. Neither the Greeks nor the Romans were particularly good at etymologies. Nor are we much better today, when 'reworkings' of Greek words, as if they were English roots, result in such abominations as 'herstory' and 'shero'.
36 Suetonius, *Life of Domitian*, 23.1. Translation from the LCL.
37 Kajava (1995a) gives examples where the *damnatio memoriae* was symbolic rather than actual. He has a good summary of the practice *vis-à-vis* inscriptions on pp. 208–209.
38 Rome, Vatican Museums inv. 13389–13391 (= Frieze A). Helbig⁴ 8–12 No. 12. Kleiner, *RomSculp*, 191–192 with Bibliography on pp. 203–204 and photograph on p. 190 fig. 159. Pollini (1984a, 547–548) has a decent introduction to the practice in Roman art.
39 Cicero, *On Ends*, 5.2.4. Translation from the LCL.
40 Luria, *Mnemonist*, 32.
41 Tatum 1995a.
42 Lullies/Hirmer, pl. 207–209.
43 On a sarcophagus in Rome appear six deeds of Herakles, each separated from the next by a column; from left to right: the Nemean lion, the Hydra, the Boar, the Stag, the Stymphalian Birds, and, somewhat unusually, a dead Amazon. The last is not generally included among the Labors, but belongs to the category of 'parerga' or deeds accomplished by Herakles, while performing the Labors proper. Rome, National Museum 15492. Koch/Sichtermann, 148–149 and fig. 168. *LIMC* 5, Herakles 1724 and pl. 20; dated there to the late second century AD.
44 *LIMC* 5, Herakles 1716–1723.
45 For two specific examples: Pisa, Camposanto – Koch/Sichtermann, 104 and fig. 98; Kampen 1981a, 56–57 and pl. 12 figs 24–25; and Florence, Museo dell'Opera – Koch/Sichtermann, 104 and fig. 99.
46 Kampen 1981a, 57 with n. 63 and pl. 12 fig. 28 (Rome, Museo Nazionale Romano 40799). Koch/Sichtermann (97–196) on marriage sarcophagi in general.
47 Rouveret, *HistImag*, 354–369.
48 Sadurska, *Tables*, 37 (for date of manufacture); 24–37 and pl. 1 (Tabula Capitolina = Rome, Capitoline Museum, Inv. 316). Helbig⁴ 2, 116–119 No. 1266 (with bibliography). Weitzmann, *Roll*, 34ff., pl. 24 fig. 56. Rouveret, *HistImag*, 354–369 with fig. 20 on p. 361. Horsfall 1979a. I have discussed the 'acrostics' on the back of one of them in Chapter 5.
49 Brilliant, *VisNar*, 90–123. He focusses on how it would have been viewed in antiquity, since the figures are small, the relief a continuous spiral, and the column blocked by buildings. For complete photographic documentation and excellent commentary, see Settis, *ColTraiana*.
50 I cannot do justice to the topic of illustrated texts within a book devoted

primarily to memory and literacy, even though I well recognize that artists are
affected by both memory and literacy. I am also well aware that pictures
independently of texts can serve as mnemonic devices, especially for those
who are not literate. These are topics I plan to return to at length in another
work.

51 For excellent surveys of research on illustrations, see Williams/Houghton, 1
and 2. For diagrams, see the collection of articles in Glasgow *et al.*, *Diag.*
Cognitive studies of pictures and imagery as independent topics are far more
advanced than studies of how picture and text work together.

52 According to James Rogers (*Cliches*, 235) it was a Chinese proverb 'long ago',
though with a worth of 10,000 words rather than the frugal 1000 I grew up
with. Rogers adds that Ivan Turgenev in *Fathers and Sons* (1862) said that 'A
picture shows me at a glance what it takes dozens of pages of a book to
expound.' Mieder (*AmerProv*, 463 s.v. *picture* no. 4) dates its arrival in the US to
the 8 December 1921 issue of *Printers' Ink.*

53 For a list of illustrated papyri, see Bartoletti 1963a. The situation has not
changed much since that date. For discussion of the significance of that
number, see Turner, *GrMss*, 136–137. For technical illustration in classical
antiquity, see Stückelberger, *Bild.*

54 Carruthers, Chapter 7, 'Memory and the Book', pp. 221–257. Numerous
articles have been written on this subject both before and after the appearance
of Carruthers's book. To cite two: Gibson-Wood 1987a and Huot 1992a.

55 Broderick (1983a) is a good study of this situation for a manuscript dated to *c.*
AD 1000. It is Oxford, Bodleian Library, SC 5123 = MS Junius 11, also known
as the 'Caedmaon Manuscript'. For studies of how the medieval illuminator
worked, see Alexander, *MedIll* and De Hamel, *Scribes.*

56 Compare Coleman, *Memories*, 9–12; Everson, *Psych*, 225–226 for bibliography.

57 Cicero, *On Invention*, 2.52.160. The Auctor ad Herennium (3.2.3) likewise says:
'a well-furnished memory, or experience in diverse matters, is termed Wisdom
(*prudentia*).' Translation from the LCL.

58 So also Coleman, *Memories*, 13. The number of studies on this subject has been
rapidly increasing in recent years. I would suggest starting with Yates, *Memory*;
Carruthers; Coleman, *Memories*; and Bolzoni 1991a.

59 Philo Judaeus, *On the Creation*, 17–20. Translation from the LCL.

60 Thomas Anshelm, *Rationarium evangelistarum omnia in se evangelia prosa, versu,
imaginibusque quam mirifice complectens*, Pforzheim (1st ed. 1505), M.D.X. Small
4 Fol. a iiir. Biblioteca Nazionale Centrale, Florence. Bolzoni 1991a, 36–37
No. I, 12 with illustration on p. 37. She says that the type originated in the
Upper Rhineland *c.* 1470. My description in the text is based on Bolzoni.

61 Bolzoni 1991a, 48 with fig. I.29. Her commentary is to 'Ramon Lull with the
ladders of his Art' from Thomas Le Myésier (?-1336), *Parvum Electorium seu
Breviculum*, fol. 5r, Arras, *c.* 1321–1336; now Badische Landesbibliothek, Karls-
ruhe Cod. St Peter 92. For the 'Tree of Life', ibid., 27–28 with fig. I.2: Pacino
di Buonaguida, *c.* 1310, painting on wood; now in Florence, Galleria dell'Ac-
cademia Inv. no. 8459 (from the Clarisse di Monticelli Convent near Florence).
For the 'Tower of Wisdom', ibid., 27 with fig. I.1: *Thebit de scientia imaginum,
sive variorum opera, partim Astronimca, partim etiam moralia*, fol. 1r, manuscript,
fourteenth to fifteenth century; now Florence, Biblioteca Medicea Laurenziana, Cod. Pluteo 30.24. To give an idea of the variety of pictures used for
memorial purposes, Bolzoni also illustrates plans (pp. 32–34), playing cards
(pp. 38–44), the multilingual *Orbis Pictus* of Comenius (pp. 51–56), and
Noah's ark (pp. 56–59).

62 Yates, *Memory*, Chapter XVI, 'Fludd's Memory Theatre and the Globe Theatre', 342–367.

CONCLUSION

1 Pliny the Elder, *Natural History*, 34.19.52. Pliny does add that art 'revived in the 156th Olympiad [156–153BC], when there were the following [artists], far inferior it is true to those mentioned above.' Translation from the LCL.

2 Norman, *Things*, 78. He also says (p. 4) that 'my studies have caused me to question the manner by which our cognitive abilities are, in turn, manipulated by the tools cognition has helped to create.' This is a thought echoed by Freeman Dyson, the physicist, who said 'Scientific revolutions are more often driven by new tools than by new concepts' (*Apud Skeptical Inquirer* 18 (Winter 1994), 169). Such technological determination generally meets with less favour among humanists, on which see the set of essays in Smith/Marx. The arguments for and against in many ways resemble those that are put forth regarding the Sapir-Whorf hypothesis, which I discussed in Chapter 10.

3 Walsh/Zlatic 1981a, 218.

4 Reynolds, *RhetMem* is a collection of essays on the topic of reinstating memory in modern rhetoric.

5 Small 1992a, 2.1. Compare Small 1993a.

6 E-mail communication from Marilyn Jager Adams, 3 November 1992.

7 For example, Barkow *et al.*, *Mind*.

8 Compare Tversky/Kahneman 1983a, 313: 'we do not share Dennis Lindley's optimistic opinion that "inside every incoherent person there is a coherent one trying to get out," and we suspect that incoherence is more than skin deep.'

9 The best exposition on hypertext is Bolter, *Writing*. For hypertext and how it differs from Aristotle's topic, see Bolter 1993a. For other possibilities in a computerized world, see Lanham, *ElecWord*. For a critical review of their writings and others, see Haas, *WritTech*, especially Chapter 2. One of Haas's major concerns is that (p. 32): 'As long as "the computer" remains unspecified, under specified, or too variously specified, attempts to understand the complex, symbiotic relationship between writing and technology will remain disjoint, or even contradictory.' Once of the things I have tried to do in this book is to pin down precisely what the writing tools were and how they worked in specific situations.

10 For example, Birkerts, *Gutenberg*. Birkerts rightly recognizes that writing on a computer will dramatically affect future writing, but his lack of knowledge as to how computers work vitiates much of his discussion. He still writes masochistically on an IBM Selectric typewriter (p. 28). If God had meant us to have computers, he would never have invented the Selectric.

11 For accessible, general introductions to complexity and its various offshoots, see Lewin, *Life*, Waldrop, *Complexity*, and Gell-Mann, *Quark*.

SELECT BIBLIOGRAPHY AND
ABBREVIATIONS

ABV	J. D. Beazley, *Attic Black-Figure Vase-Painters* (Oxford 1956).
ACEL	Heiki Solin, Olli Salomies, and Uta-Maria Liertz, eds, *Acta Colloquii Epigraphici Latini*, Helsinki 3–6 September 1991, *Commentationes Humanarum Litterarum* 104 (Helsinki 1995).
Adams 1987a	Hazard Adams, 'Titles, Titling, and Entitlement To,' *Journal of Aesthetics and Art Criticism* 46 (1987): 7–21.
Adams, *BegRead*	Marilyn Jager Adams, *Beginning To Read: Thinking and Learning about Print* (Cambridge and London 1990).
Adams *et al.* 1991a	Marilyn Jager Adams and various commentators, '*Beginning to Read*: A Critique by Literacy Professionals and a Response by Marilyn Jager Adams,' *The Reading Teacher* 44 (1991): 370–395.
Addenda[2]	Thomas H. Carpenter, *Beazley Addenda. Additional References to ABV, ARV[2], and Paralipomena*, 2nd edn (Oxford 1989).
Agar, *LangShock*	Michael Agar, *Language Shock. Understanding the Culture of Conversation* (New York 1994).
Ahl, *Meta*	Frederick Ahl, *Metaformations. Soundplay and Wordplay in Ovid and Other Classical Poets* (Ithaca and London 1985).
Alexander, *MedIll*	J. J. G. Alexander, *Medieval Illuminators and Their Methods of Work* (New Haven 1992).
Alexander 1990a	Loveday Alexander, 'The Living Voice: Scepticism towards the Written Word in Early Christian and in Graeco-Roman Texts,' in David J. A. Clines, Stephen E. Fowl, and Stanley E. Porter, eds, *The Bible in Three Dimensions* (Sheffield 1990), 221–247.
Alföldi-Rosenbaum 1995a	Elisabeth Alföldi-Rosenbaum, 'A Funerary Relief from Trier, the Diptych of Probianus, and an Evangelist Type of Charlemagne's Court School,' in Christopher Moss and Katherine Kiefer, eds, *Byzantine East, Latin West. Art-Historical Studies in Honor of Kurt Weitzmann* (Princeton 1995), 115–118.
Allan 1980a	D. J. Allan, ''Αναγιγνώσκω and Some Cognate Words,' *Classical Quarterly* n.s. 30 (1980): 244–251.

Allen 1910a — T. W. Allen, 'The Text of the *Odyssey*,' *Papers of the British School at Rome* 5 (1910): 1–85.

Allen & Greenough — J. B. Greenough, G. L. Kittredge, A. A. Howard, and Benjamin L. D'Ooge, *Allen and Greenough's New Latin Grammar* (Boston 1931).

Allen/Dix, *BegUnd* — Marti Lu Allen and T. Keith Dix, eds, *The Beginning of Understanding. Writing in the Ancient World* (Ann Arbor 1991).

Amasis Papers — *Papers on the Amasis Painter and His World* (Malibu 1987).

Amedick, *SarkMensch* — Rita Amedick, *Die Sarkophage mit Darstellungen aus dem Menschenleben, Die antiken Sarkophagreliefs*, vol. 1 pt. 4 (Berlin 1991).

Amyx, *CVP* — D. A. Amyx, *Corinthian Vase-Painting of the Archaic Period* (Berkeley, Los Angeles, and London 1988).

Annas, *Mind* — Julia Annas, *Hellenistic Philosophy of Mind* (Berkeley and Los Angeles 1992).

ANRW — Hildegard Temporini and Wolfgang Hase, eds, *Aufstieg und Niedergang der römischen Welt* (New York 1972–present).

Aristotle, Bollingen — Jonathan Barnes, ed., *The Complete Works of Aristotle. The Revised Oxford Translation*, Bollingen series 71.2 (Princeton 1984).

ARV^2 — J. D. Beazley, *Attic Red-figure Vase-Painters*, 2nd edn (Oxford 1963).

Astin, *Cato* — Alan E. Astin, *Cato the Censor* (Oxford 1978).

Atherton 1996a — Catherine Atherton, 'What Every Grammarian Knows?,' *Classical Quarterly* n.s. 46 (90) (1996): 239–260.

Attwater, *Saints* — David Attwater, *The Penguin Dictionary of Saints* (Middlesex 1965).

Auricchio/Capasso 1987a — Francesca Longo Auricchio and Mario Capasso, 'I rotoli della Villa Ercolanese: Dislocazione e ritrovamento,' *Cronache Ercolanesi* 17 (1987): 37–47.

Avrin, *Scribes* — L. Avrin, *Scribes, Script and Books. The Book Arts from Antiquity to the Renaissance* (Chicago and London 1991).

Back 1994a — Kurt W. Back, 'Accuracy, Truth, and Meaning in Autobiographical Reports,' in Schwarz/Sudman, pp. 39–53.

Baddeley 1992a — Alan Baddeley, 'Working Memory: The Interface between Memory and Cognition,' *Journal of Cognitive Neuroscience* 4 (1992): 281–288.

Baddeley 1994a — Alan Baddeley, 'The Magical Number Seven: Still Magic after All These Years?,' *Psychological Review* 101 (1994): 353–356.

Baddeley, *HumMem* — Alan Baddeley, *Human Memory. Theory and Practice* (Boston 1990).

Badian 1966a — E. Badian, 'The Early Historians,' in T. A. Dorey, ed., *The Latin Historians* (London 1966): 1–38.

Bagnall, *Reading* — Roger S. Bagnall, *Reading Papyri, Writing Ancient History* (London and New York 1995).

Bailey, *Lucretius*	Cyril Bailey, *Titi Lucreti Cari de Rerum Natura Libri Sex* (Oxford 1949).
Balayé 1988a	Simone Balayé, 'La Bibliothèque du Roi, première bibliothèque du monde 1664–1789,' in Jolly, *HBF*, pp. 209–233.
Banaji/Crowder 1989a	Mahzarin R. Banaji and Robert G. Crowder, 'The Bankruptcy of Everyday Memory,' *American Psychologist* 44 (1989): 1185–1193.
Barclay 1986a	Craig R. Barclay, 'Schematization of Autobiographical Memory,' in Rubin, *AutobioMem*, pp. 82–99.
Barclay 1988a	Craig R. Barclay, 'Truth and Accuracy in Autobiographical Memory,' in Gruneberg *et al.* 1988a, pp. 289–293.
Barclay/Wellman 1986a	Craig R. Barclay and Henry M. Wellman, 'Accuracies and Inaccuracies in Autobiographical Memories,' *Journal of Memory and Language* 25 (1986): 93–103.
Barkow *et al.*, *Mind*	Jerome H. Barkow, Leda Cosmides, and John Tooby, eds, *The Adapted Mind. Evolutionary Psychology and the Generation of Culture* (New York and Oxford 1992).
Barrett, *EurHipp*	W. S. Barrett, ed., *Euripides. Hippolytos* (Oxford 1964).
Barrow, *Pi*	John D. Barrow, *Pi in the Sky. Counting, Thinking, and Being* (Oxford 1992).
Bartlett	F. C. Bartlett, *Remembering: A Study in Experimental and Social Psychology* (Cambridge 1932).
Bartoletti 1963a	V. Bartoletti, 'Papiro,' *EAA* 5 (1963): 943–947.
Bass *et al.* 1989a	G. F. Bass, G. Pulak, D. Collon, and J. Weinstein, 'The Bronze Age Shipwreck at Ulu Burun: 1986 Campaign,' *American Journal of Archaeology* 93 (1989): 1–29.
Beard 1985a	Mary Beard, 'Writing and Ritual. A Study of Diversity and Expansion in the Arval Acta,' *Papers of the British School at Rome* 53 n.s. 40 (1985): 114–160.
Beck, *Album*	F. A. G. Beck, *Album of Greek Education* (Sydney 1975).
Becker, *Shield*	Andrew S. Becker, *The Shield of Achilles and the Poetics of Ekphrasis* (Lanham, MD 1995).
Bekker, *AnecGr*	Immanuel Bekker, *Anecdota Graeca* (Berlin 1816, rpt Graz 1965).
Bellezza 1987a	Francis S. Bellezza, 'Mnemonic Devices and Memory Schemas,' in McDaniel/Pressley, pp. 34–55.
Benardete, *Theaet*	Seth Benardete, *Plato's Theaetetus* (Chicago and London 1986).
Benson/Constable	Robert L. Benson, Giles Constable, and Carol D. Lanham, eds, *Renaissance and Renewal in the Twelfth Century* (Cambridge, MA 1982).
Bergmann 1994a	Bettina Bergmann, 'The Roman House as Memory Theater,' *Art Bulletin* 76 (1994): 225–256.
Berry *et al.*	Berry, J. W., Irvine, S. H., and Hunt, E. B., eds, *Indigenous Cognition: Functioning in Cultural Context* (Dordrecht, Boston, and Lancaster 1988).
Besner/Smith 1992a	Derek Besner and Marilyn Chapnik Smith, 'Basic Processes in Reading: Is the Orthographic Depth Hypothesis Sinking?,' in Frost/Katz, *OPMM*, pp. 45–65.

Beye, *Epic* Charles Rowan Beye, *Ancient Epic Poetry. Homer, Apollonius, Virgil* (Ithaca and London 1993).

Bialystok/Hakuta Ellen Bialystok and Kenji Hakuta, *In Other Words. The Science and Psychology of Second-Language Acquisition* (New York 1994).

Bianchi Bandinelli, *RomeCenter* R. Bianchi Bandinelli, *Rome: The Center of Power* translated by P. Green (New York 1970).

Bianchi Bandinelli, *RomeLate* R. Bianchi Bandinelli, *Rome: The Late Empire*, translated by P. Green (New York 1971).

Bieber, *Theater* Margarete Bieber, *The History of the Greek and Roman Theater*, 2nd edn (Princeton 1961).

Billows 1993a Richard Billows, 'The Religious Procession of the Ara Pacis Augustae: Augustus' *supplicatio* in 13 BC,' *Journal of Roman Archaeology* 6 (1993): 80–92.

Binsfeld 1973a W. Binsfeld, 'Lesepulte auf Neumagener Reliefs,' *Bonner Jahrbücher* 173 (1973): 201–206.

Birkets, *Gutenberg* Sven Birkerts, *The Gutenberg Elegies. The Fate of Reading in an Electronic Age* (New York 1994).

Bischoff, *LatPal* Bernhard Bischoff, *Latin Paleography. Antiquity and the Middle Ages*, translated by Dáibhí O Cróinín and David Ganz (Cambridge 1990).

Blanchard, *Codex* Alain Blanchard, ed., *Les débuts du codex, Bibliologia 9* (Turnhout 1989).

Blanck, *Buch* H. Blanck, *Das Buch in der Antike* (Munich 1992).

Bloch/Joffroy 1953a Raymond Bloch and René Joffroy, 'L'alphabet du cratère de Vix,' *Revue Philologique* 27 (1953): 175–191.

Block 1983a Ned Block, 'Mental Pictures and Cognitive Science,' *Philosophical Review* 92 (1983): 499–542, reprinted in Lycan, *Mind*, pp. 577–607.

Blum, *Kallimachos* Rudolf Blum, *Kallimachos. The Alexandrian Library and the Origins of Bibliography*, translated by Hans H. Wellisch (Madison 1991).

Blum, *Mnemo* Herwig Blum, *Die antike Mnemotechnik, Spudasmata 15* (Hildesheim and New York 1969).

Boffo 1995a Laura Boffo, 'Ancora una volta sugli "archivi" nel mondo greco: conservazione e "pubblicazione" epigrafica,' *Athenaeum* 83 (1995): 91–130.

Boge, *GrTach* H. Boge, *Griechische Tachygraphie und Tironische Noten. Ein Handbuch der Schnellschrift der Antike und des Mittelalters* (Berlin 1973).

Böhlig 1983a Alexander Böhlig, '"Herz" in der Übersetzung des koptischen Neuen Testaments,' in Manfred Görg, ed., *Ägypten und Altes Testament. Studien zu Geschichte, Kultur und Religion Ägyptens und des Alten Testaments, Fontes atque Pontes 5* (Wiesbaden 1983), pp. 47–61.

Bolter 1993a Jay David Bolter, 'Hypertext and the Rhetorical Canons,' in Reynolds, *RhetMem*, pp. 97–111.

Bolter, *Writing* Jay David Bolter, *Writing Space. The Computer, Hypertext, and the History of Writing* (Hillsdale, NJ 1991).

Bolzoni 1991a Lina Bolzoni, 'The Play of Images. The Art of Memory from Its Origins to the Seventeenth Century,' in Corsi, *Loom*, pp. 16–65.

Bonfante, *EtrLang* Giuliano Bonfante and Larissa Bonfante, *The Etruscan Language* (New York and London 1983).

Bonner, *Education* Stanley F. Bonner, *Education in Ancient Rome* (Berkeley and Los Angeles 1977).

Bons 1993a J. A. Bons, 'Ἀμφιβολία: Isocrates and Written Composition,' *Mnemosyne* 46 (1993): 160–171.

Booth 1979a Alan D. Booth, 'The Schooling of Slaves in First-Century Rome,' *Transactions of the American Philological Association* 109 (1979): 11–19.

Bower 1970a Gordon H. Bower, 'Analysis of a Mnemonic Device,' *American Scientist* 58 (1970): 496–510.

Bower 1990a Bruce Bower, 'Gone But Not Forgotten. Scientists Uncover Pervasive, Unconscious Influences on Memory,' *Science News* 138 (17 November 1990): 312–314.

Bower 1992a Bruce Bower, 'Reading the Code, Reading the Whole,' *Science News* 141 (29 February 1992): 138–140.

Bower 1993a Bruce Bower, 'Sudden Recall. Adult Memories of Child Abuse Spark a Heated Debate,' *Science News* 144 (18 September 1993): 184–186.

Bower 1993b Bruce Bower, 'Visual Skills Show Two-Pronged Development,' *Science News* 144 (18 September 1993): 181.

Bower 1994a Bruce Bower, 'Child Sexual Abuse: Sensory Recall . . . ,' *Science News* 145 (4 June 1994): 365.

Bower 1996a Bruce Bower, 'Rational Mind Designs. Research into the Ecology of Thought Treads on Contested Terrain,' *Science News* 150 (13 July 1996): 24–25.

Bower *et al.* 1979a Gordon H. Bower, John B. Black, and Terrence J. Turner, 'Scripts in Memory for Text,' *Cognitive Psychology* 11 (1979): 177–220.

Bowman/Thomas A. K. Bowman and J. D. Thomas, *Vindolanda: The Latin Writing-Tablets, Britannia Monograph Series* 4 (London 1983).

Bowman/Woolf Alan K. Bowman and Greg Woolf, eds, *Literacy and Power in the Ancient World* (Cambridge 1994).

Boyd 1995a 'Libri Confusi,' *The Classical Journal* 91 (1995): 35–45.

Bremmer, *Soul* Jan Bremmer, *The Early Greek Concept of the Soul* (Princeton 1983).

Brenne 1994a Stefan Brenne, 'Ostraka and the Process of Ostrakophoria,' in Coulson *et al.*, *AAADem*, pp. 13–24.

Brilliant, *VisNar* Richard Brilliant, *Visual Narratives. Storytelling in Etruscan and Roman Art* (Ithaca and London 1984).

BrK H. Brunn and G. Koerte, *I rilievi delle urne etrusche* (Berlin 1870–1916).

Broderick 1983a Herbert R. Broderick, 'Observations on the Method of Illustration in MS Junius 11 and the Relationship of the Drawings to the Text,' *Scriptorium* 37 (1983): 161–177.

Brown 1994a Michelle P. Brown, 'The Role of the Wax Tablet in Medieval Literacy: A Reconsideration in Light of a

329

Recent Find from York,' *The British Library Journal* 20 (1994): 1–16.

Bruce 1985a — Lorne Bruce, 'Roman Libraries: A Review Bibliography,' *Libri* 35 (1985): 89–106.

Bruthiaux 1993a — Paul Bruthiaux, 'Knowing When to Stop: Investigating the Nature of Punctuation,' *Language and Communication* 13 (1993): 27–43.

Bruthiaux 1995a — Paul Bruthiaux, 'The Rise and Fall of the Semicolon: English Punctuation Theory and English Teaching Practice,' *Applied Linguistics* 16 (1995): 1–14.

Bryson 1994a — Norman Bryson, 'Philostratus and the Imaginary Museum,' in Goldhill/Osborne, 255–283.

Burford, *Craftsmen* — Alison Burford, *Craftsmen in Greek and Roman Society* (Ithaca 1972).

Burkert 1987a — Walter Burkert, 'The Making of Homer in the Sixth Century B.C.: Rhapsodes versus Stesichoros,' in *Amasis Papers*, pp. 43–62.

Burnyeat, *Theaetetus* — Myles Burnyeat, *The Theaetetus of Plato* (Indianapolis and Cambridge 1990).

Burstein/Okin — Stanley M. Burstein and Louis A. Okin, eds, *Panhellenica. Essays in Ancient History and Historiography in Honor of Truesdell S. Brown* (Lawrence, Kansas 1980).

Cahill, *Road Fever* — Tim Cahill, *Road Fever* (New York 1991).

Calkins, *IllBks* — R. G. Calkins, *Illuminated Books of the Middle Ages* (Ithaca 1983).

Cameron 1995a — Alan Cameron, 'Ancient Anagrams,' *American Journal of Philology* 116 (1995): 477–484.

Camp, *Agora* — John M. Camp, *The Athenian Agora. Excavations in the Heart of Classical Athens* (London 1986).

Campbell, *GramMan* — Jeremy Campbell, *Grammatical Man. Information, Entropy, Language, and Life* (New York 1982).

Campbell, *Seneca* — Robin Campbell, translator, *Seneca. Letters from a Stoic* (Harmondsworth 1969).

Canfora — Luciano Canfora, *The Vanished Library. A Wonder of the Ancient World*, translated by Martin Ryle (Berkeley and Los Angeles 1989).

Capasso, *Volumen* — Mario Capasso, *Volumen. Aspetti della tipologia del rotolo librario antico* (Naples 1995).

Caplan, *Eloquence* — Harry Caplan, *Of Eloquence. Studies in Ancient and Medieval Rhetoric* (Ithaca and London 1970).

Cappelli, *DizAbbrev* — Adriano Cappelli, *Dizionario di abbreviature latine ed italiane* (Milan 1954).

Carney/Levin 1994a — Russell N. Carney and Joel R. Levin, 'Combining Mnemonic Strategies to Remember Who Painted What When,' *Contemporary Educational Psychology* 19 (1994): 323–339.

Carruthers — Mary Carruthers, *The Book of Memory* (Cambridge 1990).

Carson 1993a — Anne Carson, 'Your Money or Your Life,' *The Yale Journal of Criticism* 6 (1993): 75–92.

Casson 1983a — Ronald W. Casson, 'Schemata in Cognitive Anthropology,' *Annual Review of Anthropology* 12 (1983): 429–462.

Caswell, *Thumos*	Caroline P. Caswell, *A Study of Thumos in Early Greek Epic*, Mnemosyne Supplement 114 (Leiden 1990).
Cavallo, *Biblio*	Guglielmo Cavallo, editor, *Le biblioteche nel mondo antico e medievale* (Rome 1988).
Cavallo, *Ercolano*	Guglielmo Cavallo, *Libri scritture scribi a Ercolano*, Cronache Ercolanesi 13 Supplement 1 (1983).
CEL	David Crystal, *The Cambridge Encyclopedia of Language* (Cambridge 1987).
Černý, *Paper*	Jaroslav Černý, *Paper and Books in Ancient Egypt* (London 1952).
Chantraine 1950a	P. Chantraine, 'Les verbes grecs signifiant "lire" (ἀναγιγνώσκω, ἐπιλέγομαι, ἐντυγχάνω, ἀναλέγομαι),' *Annuaire de l'Institut de Philologie et d'Histoire Orientales et Slaves*, Université Libre de Bruxelles, 10 (1950): 115–126.
Chartier, *Order*	Roger Chartier, *The Order of Books*, translated by Lydia G. Cochrane (Stanford 1992).
CHCL-1	P. E. Easterling and B. M. W. Knox, eds, *Cambridge History of Classical Literature*. I *Greek Literature* (Cambridge 1985).
CHCL-2	E. J. Kenney and W. V. Clausen, eds, *Cambridge History of Classical Literature*. II *Roman Literature* (Cambridge 1982).
Chitiri/Willows 1994a	Helena-Fivi Chitiri and Dale M. Willows, 'Word Recognition in Two Languages and Orthographies: English and Greek,' *Memory and Cognition* 22 (1994): 313–325.
CIG	A. Boeckh, *Corpus Inscriptionum Graecarum* (Berlin 1828–1877).
CIL	*Corpus Inscriptionum Latinarum* (Berlin 1862–).
Civiltà	M. Cristofani, *Civiltà degli etruschi* (Milan 1985).
Clanchy, *Memory*	M. T. Clanchy, *From Memory to Written Record. England 1066–1307*, 2nd edn (Oxford and Cambridge, MA 1993).
Clark, *Libraries*	J. W. Clark, *Libraries in the Medieval and Renaissance Periods* (1894, rpt Chicago 1968).
Clarkson 1992a	Mark A. Clarkson, 'The Information Theater,' *Byte* (November 1992): 145–152.
Clarysse 1993a	Willy Clarysse, 'Egyptian Scribes Writing Greek,' *Chronique d'Égypte* 68 Fasc. 135–136 (1993): 186–201.
Clay 1992a	Diskin Clay, 'Plato's First Words,' *Yale Classical Studies* 29 (1992): 113–129.
Cockle 1984a	W. E. H. Cockle, 'State Archives in Graeco-Roman Egypt from 30 BC to the Reign of Septimius Severus,' *Journal of Egyptian Archaeology* 70 (1984): 106–122.
Cohen-Mushlin 1992a	Aliza Cohen-Mushlin, 'On Learned Scribes,' in Jacqueline Hamesse, ed., *Les problèmes posés par l'édition critique des textes anciens et médiévaux* (Louvain-la-Neuve 1992), pp. 197–206.
Cohon 1991/92a	Robert Cohon, 'Hesiod and the Order and Naming of the Muses in Hellenistic Art,' *Boreas* 14/15 (1991/92): 67–83.

Cole 1996a — Thomas Cole, Review of Steiner, *Tyrant* in *American Journal of Philology* 17 (1996): 145–148.

Cole, *OrigRhet* — Thomas Cole, *The Origins of Rhetoric in Ancient Greece* (Baltimore and London 1991).

Cole/Scribner, *CT* — Michael Cole and Sylvia Scribner, *Culture and Thought. A Psychological Introduction* (New York 1974).

Coleman, *Memories* — Janet Coleman, *Ancient and Medieval Memories* (Cambridge 1992).

Connors 1993a — Robert J. Connors, 'Actio: A Rhetoric of Written Delivery (Iteration Two),' in Reynolds, *RhetMem*, pp. 65–77.

Conway/Gathercole 1990a — Martin A. Conway and Susan E. Gathercole, 'Writing and Long-Term Memory: Evidence for a "Translation" Hypothesis,' *The Quarterly Journal of Experimental Psychology* 42A (1990): 513–527.

Cook 1989a — Neil McLaughlin Cook, 'The Applicability of Verbal Mnemonics for Different Populations: a Review,' *Applied Cognitive Psychology* 3 (1989): 3–22.

Corbier 1991a — M. Corbier, 'L'écriture en quête de lecteurs,' *Journal of Roman Archaeology*, Supplementary Series 3 (1991): 99–118.

Cornoldi/De Beni 1991a — Cesare Cornoldi and Rossana De Beni, 'Memory for Discourse: Loci Mnemonics and the Oral Presentation Effect,' *Applied Cognitive Psychology* 5 (1991): 511–518.

Corsi, *Loom* — Pietro Corsi, ed., *The Enchanted Loom. Chapters in the History of Neuroscience*, History of Neuroscience 4 (New York and Oxford 1991).

Coulson 1976a — William D. E., 'The Reliability of Pliny's Chapters on Greek and Roman Sculpture,' *Classical World* 69 (1976): 361–372.

Coulson et al., *AAADem* — William Coulson, Olga Palagia, T. L. Shear, Jr., H. A. Shapiro, and F. J. Frost, eds, *The Archaeology of Athens and Attica under the Democracy*, Oxbow Monograph 37 (Oxford 1994).

Cowie 1985a — Roddie Cowie, 'Reading Errors and Clues to the Nature of Reading,' *Progress in the Psychology of Language* 1 (1985): 73–107.

Crawford, *RRC* — Michael H. Crawford, *Roman Republican Coinage* (Cambridge 1974).

Cribiore, *WTS* — Raffaella Cribiore, *Writing, Teachers and Students in Graeco-Roman Egypt*, Ph.D. Dissertation, Columbia University (Atlanta 1997).

Croisille, *NatM* — Jean-Michel Croisille, *Les natures mortes campaniennes*, Collection Latomus 76 (Brussels 1965).

Cromer, *Uncommon* — Alan Cromer, *Uncommon Sense. The Heretical Nature of Science* (New York and Oxford 1993).

Crowder/Wagner — Robert G. Crowder and Richard K. Wagner, *The Psychology of Reading. An Introduction*, 2nd edn (Oxford 1992).

CUE 2.2 — Gabriele Cateni, *Urne volterrane. 2. Il Museo Guarnacci. Corpus delle urne etrusche di età ellenistica* 2 (Pisa 1986).

Culham 1989a	P. Culham, 'Archives and Alternatives in Republican Rome,' *Classical Philology* 84 (1989): 100–115.
Culham 1991a	Phyllis Culham, 'Documents and *Domus* in Republican Rome,' *Libraries and Culture* 26 (1991): 119–134.
Curtis 1984/86a	Robert I. Curtis, 'Product Identification and Advertising on Roman Commercial Amphorae,' *Ancient Society* 15–17 (1984–1986): 209–228.
Cytowic, *Tasted*	Richard E. Cytowic, *The Man Who Tasted Shapes. A Bizarre Medical Mystery Offers Revolutionary Insights into Emotions, Reasoning, and Consciousness* (New York 1993).
Dagenais, *Ethics*	John Dagenais, *The Ethics of Reading in Manuscript Culture. Glossing the Libro de buen amor* (Princeton 1994).
Daly	Lloyd W. Daly, *Contributions to a History of Alphabetization in Antiquity and the Middle Ages*, Collection Latomus 90 (Brussels 1967).
Dalzell 1955a	Alexander Dalzell, 'C. Asinius Pollio and the Early History of Public Recitation at Rome,' *Hermathena* 86 (1955): 20–28.
D'Andrade 1987a	Roy D'Andrade, 'A Folk Model of the Mind' in Holland/Quinn, pp. 112–148.
Davies 1971a	J. C. Davies, 'Was Cicero Aware of Natural Beauty?,' *Greece & Rome*, s. 2, vol. 18 (1971): 152–165.
De Franceschini, *Adriana*	Marina de Franceschini, *Villa Adriana. Mosaici – Pavimenti – Edifici* (Rome 1991).
DeFrancis 1996a	John DeFrancis, 'How Efficient is the Chinese Writing System?,' *Visible Language* 30 (1996): 6–44.
De Hamel, *Scribes*	C. De Hamel, *Scribes and Illuminators* (Toronto 1992).
Delaissé *et al.*	L. M. J. Delaissé, H. Liebaers, and F. Masai, *Mittelalterliche Miniaturen von der burgundischen Bibliothek zum Handschriftenskabinett der königlich belgischen Bibliothek* (Cologne 1959).
Delia 1992a	Diana Delia, 'From Romance to Rhetoric: The Alexandrian Library in Classical and Islamic Traditions,' *American Historical Review* 97 (1992): 1449–1467.
Della Corte 1982a	Francesco Della Corte, 'Tecnica espositiva e struttura della *Naturalis Historia*,' in *Plinio*, pp. 19–39.
Demougin, *MémPerdu*	Ségolène Demougin, ed., *La mémoire perdue. A la recherche des archives oubliées, publiques et privées, de la Rome antique* (Paris 1994).
Den Boer, *ArtMem*	W. Den Boer, *The Art of Memory and Its Mnemotechnical Traditions* (Amsterdam, Oxford, and New York 1986).
Denis 1987a	Michel Denis, 'Individual Imagery Differences and Prose Processing,' in McDaniel/Pressley, pp. 204–217.
De Romilly 1988a	Jacqueline De Romilly, 'Plutarch and Thucydides or the Free Use of Quotations,' *Phoenix* 42 (1988): 22–34.
Derrida, *Dissem*	Jacques Derrida, *Dissemination*, translated by Barbara Johnson (Chicago 1981).
Desrochers/Begg 1987a	Alain Desrochers and Ian Begg, 'A Theoretical Account September 21, 1996 of Encoding and Retrieval Processes in the Use of Imagery-Based Mnemonic

	Techniques: The Special Case of the Keyword Method,' in McDaniel/Pressley, pp. 56–77.
Detienne, *Savoirs*	Marcel Detienne, ed., *Les savoirs de l'écriture en Grèce ancienne* (Lille 1988).
Detienne, *Vérité*	Marcel Detienne, *Les maîtres de vérité dans la Grèce archaïque*, 2nd edn (Paris 1973).
Devine/Stephens 1993a	A. M. Devine and Laurence D. Stephens, 'Evidence from Experimental Psychology for the Rhythm and Metre of Greek Verse,' *Transactions of the American Philological Association* 123 (1993): 379–403.
Devine/Stephens, *Prosody*	A. M. Devine and Laurence D. Stephens, *The Prosody of Greek Speech* (New York and Oxford 1994).
Diamond, *Chimp*	Jared Diamond, *The Third Chimpanzee. The Evolution and Future of the Human Animal* (New York 1993).
Dilke, *Maps*	O. A. W. Dilke, *Greek and Roman Maps* (Ithaca 1985).
Dilke, *Math*	O. A. W. Dilke, *Mathematics and Measurement* (London 1988).
Dimarogonas 1995a	Andrew D. Dimarogonas, 'Pliny the Elder on the Making of Papyrus Paper,' *Classical Quarterly* 89 (n.s. 45) (1995): 588–590.
Dix, *Libraries*	Thomas Keith Dix, *Private and Public Libraries at Rome in the First Century B.C.: A Preliminary Study in the History of Roman Libraries*, Ph.D. Dissertation, University of Michigan, 1986.
Donald	Merlin Donald, *Origins of the Modern Mind* (Cambridge, MA and London 1991).
Dorandi 1984a	Tiziano Dorandi, 'Sillyboi,' *Scrittura e Civiltà* 8 (1984): 185–199.
Dorandi 1991a	Tiziano Dorandi, 'Den Autoren über die Schulter geschaut Arbeitsweise und Autographie bei den antiken Schriftstellern,' *Zeitschrift für Papyrologie und Epigraphik* 87 (1991): 11–33.
Dorandi 1993a	Tiziani Dorandi, 'Zwischen Autographie und Diktat: Momente der Textualität in der antiken Welt,' in Kullmann/Althoff, pp. 71–83.
Dorandi 1995a	Tiziano Dorandi, 'La 'Villa dei Papiri,' a Ercolano e la sua biblioteca,' *Classical Philology* 90 (1995): 168–182.
Dorr 1994a	Aimée Dorr, 'What Constitutes Literacy in a Culture with Diverse and Changing Means of Communication?' in Deborah Keller-Cohen, ed., *Literacy: Interdisciplinary Conversations* (Cresskill, NJ 1994), pp. 129–153.
Dudley, *Urbs*	Donald R. Dudley, *Urbs Roma. A Source Book of Classical Texts on the City and Its Monuments* (New York 1967).
EAA	*Enciclopedia dell'arte antica, classica e orientale*, 1–7 (Rome 1958–1966).
Einstein *et al.* 1990a	Gilles O. Einstein, Mark A. McDaniel, Patricia D. Owen, and Nathalie C. Coté, 'Encoding and Recall of Texts: The Importance of Material Appropriate Processing,' *Journal of Memory and Language* 29 (1990): 566–581.
Einstein/McDaniel 1987a	Gilles O. Einstein and Mark A. McDaniel, 'Distinc-

tiveness and the Mnemonic Benefits of Bizarre Imagery,' in McDaniel/Pressley, pp. 78–102.

Eisenberg 1996a — Anne Eisenberg, 'These Key Words for Hire,' *Scientific American* 275 No. 3 (September 1996): 48.

Eisenstein, *PrintRev* — Elizabeth L. Eisenstein, *The Printing Revolution in Early Modern Europe* (Cambridge 1983).

Ellis/Beattie — Andrew Ellis and Geoffrey Beattie, *The Psychology of Language & Communication* (New York and London 1986).

Elsner, *Art* — Jaś Elsner, editor, *Art and Text in Roman Culture* (Cambridge 1996).

Ericsson/Polson 1988a — K. A. Ericsson and P. G. Polson, 'A Cognitive Analysis of Exceptional Memory for Restaurant Orders,' in M. Chi, R. Glaser, and M. Farr, eds, *The Nature of Expertise* (Hillsdale, NJ 1988), pp. 23–70.

Ernest 1987a — Carole H. Ernest, 'Imagery and Memory in the Blind,' in McDaniel/Pressley, pp. 218–238.

Ésperandieu 7 — Ésperandieu, E., *Recueil général des bas-reliefs, statues et bustes de la Gaule romaine* 7 (Paris 1918).

Evans, *Herodotus* — J. A. S. Evans, *Herodotus, Explorer of the Past: Three Essays* (Princeton 1991).

Everson, *Psych* — Stephen Everson, ed., *Psychology, Companions to Ancient Thought* 2 (Cambridge 1991).

Eyre/Baines 1989a — Christopher Eyre and John Baines, 'Interactions between Orality and Literacy in Ancient Egypt,' in Schousboe/Larsen, pp. 91–119.

Ezzell 1991a — Carol Ezzell, 'Watching the Remembering Brain at Work,' *Science News* 140 (23 November 1991): 333.

Fantham, *RLC* — Elaine Fantham, *Roman Literary Culture. From Cicero to Apuleius* (Baltimore and London 1996).

Farah 1988a — Martha J. Farah, 'Is Visual Imagery Really Visual? Overlooked Evidence from Neuropsychology,' *Psychological Review* 95 (1988): 307–317.

Farah, *Visual* — Martha J. Farah, *Visual Agnosia. Disorders of Object Recognition and What they Tell Us about Normal Vision* (Cambridge, MA and London 1990).

Farah *et al.* 1988a — Martha J. Farah, Katherine M. Hammond, David N. Levine, and Ronald Calvanio, 'Visual and Spatial Mental Imagery: Dissociable Systems of Representation,' *Cognitive Psychology* 20 (1988): 439–462.

Fedeli 1988a — Paolo Fedeli, 'Biblioteche private e pubbliche a Roma e nel mondo Romano,' in Cavallo, *Biblio*, pp. 29–64.

Ferraro 1975a — V. Ferraro, 'Il numero delle fonti, dei volumi e dei fatti della *Naturalis Historia* di Plinio,' *Annali della Scuola Normale Superiore di Pisa, Cl. di Lettere e Filosofia* 5 (1975): 519–533.

FgrH — F. Jacoby, *Fragmente der griechischen Historiker* (Berlin 1923–).

Finnegan 1985a — Ruth Finnegan, 'Oral Composition and Oral Literature in the Pacific,' in Gentili/Paioni, pp. 125–154.

Finnegan, *Oral* — Ruth Finnegan, *Oral Poetry. Its Nature, Significance and*

	Social Context (Cambridge 1977, rpt Bloomington and Indianapolis 1992).
Foden 1993a	Giles Foden, 'Fear of the Glyph. Between Hypertext and hors-texte,' *TLS* 4700 (30 April 1993): 5.
Fornara, *NatHist*	Charles William Fornara, *The Nature of History in Ancient Greece and Rome* (Berkeley and Los Angeles 1983).
Fowler 1991a	D. P. Fowler, 'Narrate and Describe: The Problem of Ekphrasis,' *Journal of Roman Studies* 81 (1991): 25–35.
Frakes 1995a	R. M. Frakes, 'Cross-References to the Lost Books of Ammianus Marcellinus,' *Phoenix* 49 (1995): 232–246.
Frankfort, *Before Phil*	H. and H. A. Frankfort, John A. Wilson, and Thorkild Jacobsen, *Before Philosophy. The Intellectual Adventure of Ancient Man* (Baltimore 1963; rpt of Chicago 1946).
Fraser, *Alexandria*	P. M. Fraser, *Ptolemaic Alexandria* (Oxford 1972; rpt 1984, 1986).
Freedman, *Brainmakers*	David H. Freedman, *Brainmakers* (New York 1994).
French/Greenaway	Roger French and Frank Greenaway, eds, *Science in the Early Roman Empire: Pliny the Elder, His Sources and Influence* (Totowa, New Jersey 1986).
Friend 1927a	A. M. Friend, Jr., 'The Portraits of the Evangelists in Greek and Latin Manuscripts,' *Art Studies* 5 (1927): 115–147.
Friend 1929a	A. M. Friend, Jr., 'The Portraits of the Evangelists in Greek and Latin Manuscripts,' *Art Studies* 7 (1929): 3–29.
Freund, *Objects*	Thatcher Freund, *Objects of Desire* (New York 1993).
Frost 1980a	Frank J. Frost, 'Plutarch and Clio,' in Burstein/Okin, pp. 155–170.
Frost 1994a	Ram Frost, 'Prelexical and Postlexical Strategies in Reading: Evidence from a Deep and a Shallow Orthography,' *Journal of Experimental Psychology: Learning, Memory, and Cognition* 20 (1994): 116–129.
Frost/Katz, *OPMM*	Ram Frost and Leonard Katz, eds, *Orthography, Phonology, Morphology, and Meaning, Advances in Psychology* 94 (Amsterdam 1992).
Gabba 1981a	Emilio Gabba, 'True History and False History in Classical Antiquity,' *Journal of Roman Studies* 71 (1981): 50–62.
Gaiser, *PhilMos*	K. Gaiser, *Das Philosophen Mosaik in Neapel, AbhHeidelberg,* 2 (1980).
Galaburda, *Reading*	Albert M. Galaburda, ed., *From Reading to Neurons* (Cambridge 1989).
Gallagher, *Power*	Winifred Gallagher, *The Power of Place. How Our Surroundings Shape Our Thoughts, Emotions, and Actions* (New York 1993).
Gallop 1963a	D. Gallop, 'Plato and the Alphabet,' *Philosophical Review* 72 (1963): 364–376.
Galotti, *CogPsych*	Kathleen M. Galotti, *Cognitive Psychology in and Out of the Laboratory* (Pacific Grove, CA 1994).
Gamble, *Books*	Harry Y. Gamble, *Books and Readers in the Early Church.*

A History of Early Christian Texts (New Haven and London 1995).

Ganz, *TirNoten* — Peter Ganz, ed., *Tironische Noten*, Wolfenbütteler Mittelalter-Studien 1 (Wiesbaden 1990).

Gardner 1993a — Martin Gardner, 'The False Memory Syndrome,' *The Skeptical Inquirer* 17 (1993): 370–375.

Gaur, *Writing* — Albertine Gaur, *A History of Writing* (London 1987).

Gell-Mann, *Quark* — Murray Gell-Mann, *The Quark and the Jaguar. Adventures in the Simple and the Complex* (New York 1994).

Genest 1989a — J.-F. Genest, 'Le mobilier des bibliothèques d'après les inventaires medievaux,' in Weijers, *VocLivre*, pp. 136–154.

Gentili/Cerri 1978a — B. Gentili and G. Cerri, 'Written and Oral Communication in Greek Historiographical Thought,' in Havelock/Hershbell, pp. 137–155.

Gentili/Paioni — Bruno Gentili and Giuseppe Paioni, eds, *Oralità. Cultura, Letteratura, Discorso* (Rome 1985).

Georgoudi 1988a — Stella Georgoudi, 'Manières d'archivage et archives de cités,' in Detienne, *Savoirs*, pp. 221–247.

Gibson-Wood 1987a — Carol Gibson-Wood, 'The *Utrecht Psalter* and the Art of Memory,' *Canadian Art Review* 14 (1989): 9–15.

Gigante, *Philodemus* — Marcello Gigante, *Philodemus in Italy. The Books from Herculaneum*, translated by Dirk Obbink (Ann Arbor 1995).

Gill/Wiseman, *Lies* — Christopher Gill and T. P. Wiseman, eds, *Lies and Fiction in the Ancient World* (Austin 1993).

Giuliano, *MNR* — Antonio Giuliano, ed., *Museo Nazionale Romano. Le Sculture* (Rome 1979–).

Glasgow *et al.*, *Diag* — Janice Glasgow, N. Nari Narayanan, and B. Chandrasekaran, eds, *Diagrammatic Reasoning: Cognitive and Computational Perspective* (Cambridge, MA and London 1995).

Gleitman *et al.* 1989a — Lila Gleitman, Henry Gleitman, Barbara Landau, and Eric Wanner, 'Great Expectations,' in Galaburda, *Reading*, pp. 91–132.

Goldhill 1994a — Simon Goldhill, 'The Naive and Knowing Eye: Ecphrasis and the Culture of Viewing in the Hellenistic World,' in Goldhill/Osborne, pp. 197–223.

Goldhill/Osborne — Simon Goldhill and Robin Osborne, eds, *Art and Text in Ancient Greek Culture* (Cambridge 1994).

Goleman 1994a — Daniel Goleman, 'Miscoding Is Seen as the Root of False Memories,' *New York Times* (31 May 1994): C1, C8.

Goody, *Interface* — Jack Goody, *The Interface between the Written and the Oral* (Cambridge 1987).

Gordon, *LatEpig* — Arthur E. Gordon, *Illustrated Introduction to Latin Epigraphy* (Berkeley and Los Angeles 1983).

Gordon, *LetNames* — Arthur E. Gordon, *The Letter Names of the Latin Alphabet*, University of California Publications, Classical Studies 9 (Berkeley 1973).

Gould, *Bully* — Stephen Jay Gould, *Bully for the Brontosaurus. Reflections in Natural History* (New York and London 1991).

Grafton 1980a   Anthony T. Grafton, 'The Importance of Being Printed,' *Journal of Interdisciplinary History* 11 (1980): 265–286.

Grant, *Annals*   Michael Grant, translator, *Tacitus. The Annals of Imperial Rome* (Baltimore 1956).

Graver 1993a   Margaret Graver, '*Quaelibet Audendi*: Fortunatus and the Acrostic,' *TAPA* 123 (1993): 219–245.

Grayeff 1956a   Felix Grayeff, 'The Problem of the Genesis of Aristotle's Text,' *Phronesis* 1 (1956): 105–122.

Grayeff, *Aristotle*   Felix Grayeff, *Aristotle and His School* (London 1974).

Greene 1994a   Kevin Greene, 'Technology and Innovation in Context: The Roman Background to Mediaeval and Later Developments,' *Journal of Roman Archaeology* 7 (1994): 22–33.

Gregory, *Mind*   Richard L. Gregory, ed., *The Oxford Companion to the Mind* (Oxford 1987).

Gruneberg *et al.* 1978a   M. M. Gruneberg, P. E. Morris, and R. N. Sykes, eds, *Practical Aspects of Memory* (London, New York, and San Francisco 1978).

Gruneberg *et al.* 1988a   M. M. Gruneberg, P. E. Morris, and R. N. Sykes, eds, *Practical Aspects of Memory* (Chichester 1988).

Haas, *WritTech*   Christina Haas, *Writing Technology: Studies in the Materiality of Literature* (Mahwah, NJ 1996).

Hadas   Moses Hadas, *Ancilla to Classical Reading* (New York 1954).

Halverson 1991a   John Halverson, 'Olson on Literacy,' *Language in Society* 20 (1991): 619–640.

Halverson 1992a   John Halverson, 'Goody and the Implosion of the Literacy Thesis,' *Man* n.s. 27 (1992): 301–317.

Halverson 1992b   John Halverson, 'Havelock on Greek Orality and Literacy,' *Journal of the History of Ideas* 53 (1992): 148–163.

Hankins 1991a   James Hankins, 'Forging Links with the Past,' *Journal of the History of Ideas* 52 (1991): 509–518.

Hanson 1991a   Ann Ellis Hanson, 'Ancient Illiteracy,' *Journal of Roman Archaeology*, Supplementary Series 3 (1991): 159–198.

Harrington 1996a   Spencer P. M. Harrington, 'Sanctuary of the Gods,' *Archaeology* 49 No. 1 (March/April 1996): 28–35.

Harris 1989a   Roy Harris, 'How Does Writing Restructure Thought?,' *Language & Communication* 9 (1989): 99–106.

Harris 1991a   William V. Harris, 'Why Did the Codex Supplant the Book-Roll' in John Monfasani and Ronald G. Musto, eds, *Renaissance Society and Culture. Essays in Honor of Eugene F. Rice, Jr.* (New York 1991), pp. 71–85.

Harris 1995a   William V. Harris, '*Instrumentum domesticum* and Roman Literacy,' in *ACEL*, pp. 19–27.

Harris, *Inscribed*   William V. Harris, ed., *The Inscribed Economy. Production and Distribution in the Roman Empire in the Light of Instrumentum domesticum, Journal of Roman Archaeology* Supplement 6 (Ann Arbor 1993).

Harris, *Literacy*   William V. Harris, *Ancient Literacy* (Cambridge, MA 1989).

338

Harris, *OrigWr*	Roy Harris, *The Origin of Writing* (London 1986).
Harrison/Verrall	Jane E. Harrison and Margaret de G. Verrall, *Mythology & Monuments of Ancient Athens* (London 1890).
Hartley 1991a	James Hartley, 'Psychology, Writing and Computers: A Review of Research,' *Visible Language* 15 (1991): 339–375.
Hartley 1992a	James Hartley, 'The Visual Chunking of Text. Commentary on Small on Skoyles on Reading,' *Psycoloquy* 92.3.66.reading.11.hartley (136 lines).
Hartley 1993a	James Hartley, 'Recalling Structured Text: Does What Goes in Determine What Comes Out?,' *British Journal of Educational Technology* 24 (1993): 84–91.
Haslam 1994a	Michael W. Haslam, 'The Homer Lexicon of Apollonius Sophista. I. Composition and Constituents,' *Classical Philology* 89 (1994): 1–45.
Haslam 1994b	Michael W. Haslam, 'The Homer Lexicon of Apollonius Sophista. II. Identity and Transmission,' *Classical Philology* 89 (1994): 107–119.
Havelock, *LitRev*	Eric A. Havelock, *The Literate Revolution in Greece and Its Cultural Consequences* (Princeton 1982).
Havelock, *Muse*	Eric A. Havelock, *The Muse Learns to Write* (New Haven and London 1986).
Havelock, *Preface*	Eric A. Havelock, *Preface to Plato* (Cambridge, MA 1963).
Havelock/Hershbell	Eric A. Havelock and Jackson P. Hershbell, eds, *Communication Arts in the Ancient World* (New York 1978).
Heffernan, *Museum*	James Heffernan, *Museum of Words: The Poetics of Ekphrasis from Homer to Ashberry* (Chicago and London 1993).
Helbig[4]	H. Speier, ed., *W. Helbig – Führer durch die öffentlichen Sammlungen klassischer Altertümer in Rom*, 4th edn (Tübingen 1963–1972).
Hembold/O'Neill	W. C. Hembold and E. N. O'Neill, *Plutarch's Quotations* (Baltimore 1959).
Henderson 1992a	Edmund H. Henderson, 'The Interface of Lexical Competence and Knowledge of Written Words,' in Shane Templeton and Donald R. Bear, eds, *Development of Orthographic Knowledge and the Foundations of Literacy* (Hillsdale, NJ 1992), pp. 1–30.
Herbig, *Götter*	Reinhard Herbig, *Götter und Dämonen der Etrusker*, edited and revised by Erika Simon (Mainz 1965).
Herescu 1956a	N. I. Herescu, 'Le mode de composition des écrivains ("dictare"),' *Revue des études latines* 34 (1956): 132–146.
Hexter/Selden	Ralph Hexter and Daniel Selden, eds, *Innovations of Antiquity* (New York and London 1992).
Hibbert, *Greville*	Christopher Hibbert, ed., *Greville's England. Selections from the Diaries of Charles Greville 1818–1860* (London 1981).
Higbee *et al.* 1991a	Kenneth L. Higbee, Stephen K. Markham, and Steven Crandall, 'Effects of Visual Imagery and Familiarity on Recall of Sayings Learned with an Imagery Mnemonic,' *Journal of Mental Imagery* 15 (1991): 65–76.

Hindman, *Printing* — Sandra L. Hindman, ed., *Printing the Written Word. The Social History of Books, circa 1450–1520* (Ithaca 1991).

Hitt, *Word* — Jack Hitt, ed., *In a Word. A Dictionary of Words That Don't Exist, But Ought To* (New York 1992).

Hofter, *Kaiser* — M. Hofter, ed., *Kaiser Augustus und die verlorene Republik*, Exhibition in the Martin-Gropius-Bau, Berlin 7 June–14 August 1988 (Berlin 1988).

Holford-Strevens — Leofranc Holford-Strevens, *Aulus Gellius* (London 1988).

Holland/Quinn — Dorothy Holland and Naomi Quinn, eds, *Cultural Models in Language and Thought* (Cambridge 1987).

Holtz 1989a — Louis Holtz, 'Les mots latins désignant le livre au temps d'Augustin,' in Blanchard, *Codex*, pp. 105–113.

Hoogendijk 1985a — F. A. J. Hoogendijk, 'Business Letter on an Ostracon,' in P. W. Pestman, ed., *Textes et études de papyrologie grecque, démotique et copte, Papyrologie Lugduno-Batava* 23 (Leiden 1985), pp. 7–8.

Horowitz 1991a — Rosalind Horowitz, 'A Reexamination of Oral versus Silent Reading,' *Text* 11 (1991): 133–166.

Horsfall 1979a — Nicholas Horsfall, 'Stesichorus at Bovillae?,' *Journal of the Historical Society* 99 (1979): 26–48.

Horsfall 1981a — Nicholas Horsfall, 'Some Problems of Titulature in Roman Literary History,' *Bulletin of the Institute of Classical Studies of the University of London* 28 (1981): 103–114.

Horsfall 1983a — Nicholas Horsfall, 'The Origins of the Illustrated Book,' *Aegyptus* 63 (1983): 199–216.

Horsfall 1991a — Nicholas Horsfall, 'Statistics or States of Mind,' *Journal of Roman Archaeology*, Supplementary Series 3 (1991): 59–76.

Horsfall 1993a — Nicholas Horsfall, 'Empty Shelves on the Palatine,' *Greece & Rome* 40 (1993): 58–67.

Horsfall 1995a — Nicholas Horsfall, 'Rome without Spectacles,' *Greece & Rome* 42 (1995): 50–56.

Horsfall, *Nepos* — Nicholas Horsfall, *Cornelius Nepos, A Selection, Including the Lives of Cato and Atticus* (Oxford 1989).

Howell, *Martial* — Peter Howell, *A Commentary on Book I of the Epigrams of Martial* (London 1980).

Howes, *Sensory* — David Howes, ed., *The Varieties of Sensory Experience. A Sourcebook in the Anthropology of the Sense* (Toronto 1991).

Howes/Classen 1991a — David Howes and Constance Classen, 'Conclusion: Sounding Sensory Profiles,' in Howes, *Sensory*, pp. 257–288.

Huby 1989a — Pamela M. Huby, 'Cicero's *Topics* and Its Peripatetic Sources,' *Rutgers University Studies in Classical Humanities* 4 (1989): 61–72.

Huff, *Rise* — Toby E. Huff, *The Rise of Early Modern Science. Islam, China, and the West* (Cambridge 1993).

Hughes, *Words* — Geoffrey Hughes, *Words in Time. A Social History of the English Vocabulary* (Oxford 1988).

Hull, *Touching* — John M, Hull, *Touching the Rock. An Experience of Blindness* (New York 1990).

Hunt/Agnoli 1991a — Earl Hunt and Franca Agnoli, 'The Whorfian Hypothesis: A Cognitive Psychology Perspective,' *Psychological Review* 98 (1991): 377–389.

Hunt/Banaji 1988a — Earl Hunt and Mahzarin R. Banaji, 'The Whorfian Hypothesis Revisited: A Cognitive View of Linguistic and Cultural Effects on Thought,' in Berry *et al.*, pp. 57–83.

Hunter 1962a — Ian M. L. Hunter, 'An Exceptional Talent for Calculative Thinking,' *British Journal of Psychology* 53 (1962): 243–258.

Hunter 1979a — Ian M. L. Hunter, '1. Memory in Everyday Life,' in M. M. Gruneberg and P. E. Morris, *Applied Problems in Memory* (London, New York, and San Francisco 1979): 1–24.

Hunter 1985a — Ian M. L. Hunter, 'Lengthy Verbatim Recall: The Role of Text,' *Progress in the Psychology of Language* 1 (1985): 207–235.

Huot 1992a — Sylvia Huot, 'Visualization and Memory: The Illustration of Troubadour Lyric in a Thirteenth-Century Manuscript,' *Gesta* 31 (1992): 3–14.

IG — *Inscriptiones Graecae* (Berlin 1873–).

Immerwahr 1960a — Henry R. Immerwahr, 'ERGON: History as a Monument in Herodotus and Thucydides,' *American Journal of Philology* 81 (1960): 261–290.

Immerwahr 1964a — Henry R. Immerwahr, 'Book Rolls on Attic Vases,' in Charles Henderson, Jr., ed., *Classical Mediaeval and Renaissance Studies in Honor of Berthold Louis Ullman* (Rome 1964), pp. 17–48.

Immerwahr, *Script* — Henry R. Immerwahr, *Attic Script. A Survey* (Oxford 1990).

Inhoff *et al.* 1992a — Albrecht Werner Inhoff, Deborah Briihl, Gregory Bohemier, and Jian Wang, 'Eye–Hand Span and Coding of Text during Copytyping,' *Journal of Experimental Psychology: Learning, Memory, and Cognition* 18 (1992): 298–306.

Isager — Jacob Isager, *Pliny on Art and Society. The Elder Pliny's Chapters on the History of Art* (Odense 1991).

Jager 1990a — Eric Jager, 'Speech and the Chest in Old English Poetry: Orality or Pectorality?,' *Speculum* 65 (1990): 845–859.

Jager 1996a — Eric Jager, 'The Book of the Heart: Reading and Writing the Medieval Subjects,' *Speculum* 71 (1996): 1–26.

Jandreau/Bever 1992a — S. Jandreau and T. G. Bever, 'Phrase-Spaced Formats Improve Comprehension in Average Readers,' *Journal of Applied Psychology* 77 (1992): 143–146.

Janko 1990a — 'The *Iliad* and Its Editors: Dictation and Redaction,' *Classical Antiquity* 9 (1990): 326–334.

Jannot, *RelChiusi* — J.-R. Jannot, *Les reliefs archaïques de Chiusi. Collection de l'École Française de Rome* 71 (Rome 1984).

Janson, *Prefaces* — Tore Janson, *Latin Prose Prefaces. Studies in Literary Conventions* (Stockholm 1964).

341

JerBibComm	Raymond E. Brown, Joseph A. Fitzmyer, and Roland E. Murphy, eds, *The New Jerome Biblical Commentary*, 2nd edn (Englewood Cliffs 1990).
Johnson 1980a	Richard R. Johnson, 'Parchment in the Hellenistic Age,' in Burstein/Okin, pp. 133–142.
Johnson 1993a	William A. Johnson, 'Pliny the Elder and Standardized Roll Heights in the Manufacture of Papyrus,' *Classical Philology* 88 (1993): 46–50.
Johnson 1993b	Wiliam A. Johnson, 'Is Oratory Written on Narrower Columns? A Papyrological Rule of Thumb Reviewed,' *Proceedings of the Twentieth International Congress of Papyrology* (Copenhagen 1993): 423–427.
Johnson 1993c	William A. Johnson, 'Column Layout in Oxyrhynchus Literary Papyri: Maas's Law, Ruling and Alignment Dots,' *Zeitschrift für Papyrologie und Epigraphik* 96 (1993): 211–215.
Johnson 1994a	William A. Johnson, 'The Function of the Paragraphus in Greek Literary Prose Texts,' *Zeitschrift für Papyrologie und Epigraphik* 100 (1994): 65–68.
Johnson 1994b	William A. Johnson, '*Macrocollum*,' *Classical Philology* 89 (1994): 62–64.
Johnson 1994c	William A. Johnson, 'Oral Performance and the Composition of Herodotus' *Histories*,' *Greek, Roman, and Byzantine Studies* 35 (1994): 229–254.
Johnson Forthcoming a	William A. Johnson, 'The Aesthetics of the Luxury Book Roll,'
Johnson, *Library*	L. L. Johnson, *The Hellenistic and Roman Library: Studies Pertaining to Their Architectural Form*, Ph.D. Dissertation, Brown University, 1984.
Johnson *et al.* 1993a	Marcia K. Johnson, Shahin Hashtroudi, and D. Stephen Lindsay, 'Source Monitoring,' *Psychological Bulletin* 114 (1993): 3–28.
Jolly, *HBF*	Claude Jolly, ed., *Histoire des bibliothèques françaises. Les bibliothèques sous l'Ancien Régime 1530-1789* (Paris 1988).
Jolowicz/Nicholas	H. F. Jolowicz and Barry Nicholas, *Historical Introduction to the Study of Roman Law*, 3rd edn (Cambridge 1972).
Jones 1959a	D. M. Jones, 'Cicero as Translator,' *Bulletin of the Institute of Classical Studies of the University of London* 6 (1959): 22–34.
Jones, *Plutarch*	C. P. Jones, *Plutarch and Rome* (Oxford 1971).
Jousse, *Oral*	Marcel Jousse, *The Oral Style*, translated by Edgard Sienart and Richard Whitaker (New York and London 1990).
Kaeppler 1991a	Adrienne L. Kaeppler, 'Memory and Knowledge in the Production of Dance,' in Küchler/Melion, pp. 109–120.
Kajava 1995a	Mika Kajava, 'Some Remarks on the Erasure of Inscriptions in the Roman World (with Special Reference to the Case of Cn. Piso, cos. 7 BC),' in *ACEL*, pp. 201–210.

Kampen 1979a | Natalie Boymel Kampen, 'Observations on the Ancient Uses of the Spada Reliefs,' *L'Antiquité Classique* 48 (1979): 583–600.

Kampen 1981a | Natalie Boymel Kampen, 'Biographical Narration and Roman Funerary Art,' *American Journal of Archaeology* 85 (1981): 47–58.

Kaster, *Suetonius* | Robert A. Kaster, editor and translator, *C. Suetonius Tranquillus. De Grammaticis et Rhetoribus* (Oxford 1995).

Keaney 1973a | John J. Keaney, 'Alphabetization in Harpocration's *Lexicon*,' *Greek, Roman and Byzantine Studies* 14 (1973): 415–423.

Keesing 1987a | Roger M. Keesing, 'Models, "Folk" and "Cultural." Paradigms Regained?,' in Holland/Quinn, pp. 369–393.

Kennedy, *AristRhet* | George A. Kennedy, translator, *Aristotle On Rhetoric. A Theory of Civic Discourse* (Oxford 1991).

Kennedy, *RhetRom* | George A. Kennedy, *The Art of Rhetoric in the Roman World* (Princeton 1972).

Kenney 1982a | E. J. Kenney, 'Books and Readers in the Roman World,' in *CHCL-2* pp. 3–32.

Kitzinger | Ernst Kitzinger. *Byzantine Art in the Making* (Cambridge, MA 1977).

Kleberg 1973a | Tönnes Kleberg, 'Book Auctions in Ancient Rome?,' *Libri* 23 (1973): 1–5.

Kleiner, *RomSculp* | D. E. E. Kleiner, *Roman Sculpture* (New Haven and London 1992).

Kleve *et al.* 1991a | K. Kleve, A. Angeli, M. Capasso, B. Fosse, R. Jensen, and F. C. Störmer, 'Three Technical Guides to the Papyri of Herculaneum. How to Unroll. How to Remove Sovrapposti. How to Take Pictures,' *Cronache Ercolanesi* 21 (1991): 111–124.

Knauer 1993a | Elfriede R. Knauer, 'Roman Wall Paintings from Boscotrecase: Three Studies in the Relationship between Writing and Painting,' *Metropolitan Museum Journal* 28 (1993): 13–46.

Knox 1968a | B. M. W. Knox, 'Silent Reading in Antiquity,' *Greek, Roman and Byzantine Studies* 9 (1968): 421–435.

Knox 1985a | B. M. W. Knox, 'Books and Readers in the Greek World,' in *CHCL-1*, pp. 1–41.

Koch/Sichtermann | Guntram Koch and Hellmut Sichtermann, *Römische Sarkophage, Handbuch der Archäologie* (Munich 1982).

KP | Konrat Ziegler and Walther Sontheimer, eds, *Der Kleine Pauly. Lexikon der Antike* (Munich 1975–1979).

Koeppel 1983a | Gerhard Koeppel, 'Die historischen Reliefs der römischen Kaiserzeit I: Stadtrömische Denkmäler unbekannter Bauzugehörigkeit aus augusteischer und Julisch-claudischer Zeit,' *Bonner Jahrbücher* 183 (1983): 61–144.

Koeppel 1985a | Gerhard Koeppel, 'Die historischen Reliefs der römischen Kaiserzeit III: Stadtrömische Denkmäler unbekannter Bauzugehörigkeit aus trajanischer Zeit,' *Bonner Jahrbücher* 185 (1985): 143–213.

Koriat/Goldsmith 1996a   Asher Koriat and Morris Goldsmith, 'Memory Metaphors and the Laboratory/Real-Life Controversy: Correspondence versus Storehouse Views of Memory,' *Behavioral and Brain Sciences* 19 (1996): 167–228.

Kosslyn, *Image*   Stephen M. Kosslyn, *Image and Brain. The Resolution of the Imagery Debate* (Cambridge 1994).

Kouymjian 1981   Dickran Kouymjian, 'The Eastern Case: The Classical Tradition in Armenian Art and the *Scaenae Frons*,' in Margaret Mullett and Roger Scott, eds, *Byzantium and the Classical Tradition. University of Birmingham Thirteenth Spring Symposium of Byzantine Studies 1979* (Birmingham 1981), pp. 155–171.

Kraus 1994a   Christina S. Kraus, '"No Second Troy": Topoi and Foundation in Livy, Book V,' *Transactions of the American Philological Association* 124 (1994): 267–289.

Kraus, *Pompeii*   Theodor Kraus and Leonard von Matt, *Pompeii and Herculaneum. The Living Cities of the Dead* (New York 1975).

Kristeller 1990a   Paul Oskar Kristeller, 'The Modern System of the Arts,' *Journal of the History of Ideas* 12 (1951): 496–527 and *Journal of the History of Ideas* 13 (1952): 17–46, reprinted together in Paul Oskar Kristeller, *Renaissance Thought and the Arts: Collected Essays*, expanded edn (Princeton 1990), pp. 163–227.

Kruglanski 1989a   Arie W. Kruglanski, 'The Psychology of Being "Right": The Problem of Accuracy in Social Perception and Cognition,' *Psychological Bulletin* 106 (1989): 395–409.

Küchler/Melion   Susanne Küchler and Walter Melion, eds, *Images of Memory. On Remembering and Representation* (Washington and London 1991).

Kullmann/Althoff   Wolfgang Kullmann and Jochen Althoff, eds, *Vermittlung und Tradierung von Wissen in der griechischen Kultur*, *ScriptOralia* 61 (Tübingen 1993).

Kuttner 1993a   Ann Kuttner, 'Vitruvius and the Second Style,' *Journal of Roman Archaeology* 6 (1993): 341–347.

Lakoff, *Talking*   Robin Tolmach Lakoff, *Talking Power. The Politics of Language* (New York 1990).

Lalou, *Tablettes*   Élisabeth Lalou, ed., *Les tablettes à écrire de l'Antiquité à l'Époque Moderne*, *Bibliologia* 12 (Turnhout 1992).

Lanham, *ElecWord*   Richard A. Lanham, *The Electronic Word. Democracy, Technology, and the Arts* (Chicago 1993).

Larmour 1992a   David H. J. Larmour, 'Making Parallels: *Synkrisis* and Plutarch's Themistocles and Camillus,' *ANRW* pt. 2 vol. 33.6 (1992): 4154–4200.

Larsen 1988a   Steen F. Larsen, 'Remembering without Experiencing: Memory for Reported Events,' in Neisser/Winograd, pp. 326–355.

Latham   Ronald Latham, translator, *Lucretius. On the Nature of the Universe* (Baltimore 1951).

Lattimore 1958a   Richmond Lattimore, 'The Composition of the *History* of Herodotus,' *Classical Philology* 53 (1958): 9–21.

Lattimore, *Iliad*	Richmond Lattimore, translator, *The Iliad of Homer* (Chicago 1951).
Lattimore, *Ody*	Richmond Lattimore, translator, *The Odyssey of Homer* (New York 1967).
Laudan, *SciRel*	Larry Laudan, *Science and Relativism. Some Key Controversies in the Philosophy of Science* (Chicago and London 1990).
Lavie, *Sleep*	Peretz Lavie, *The Enchanted World of Sleep,* translated by Anthony Berris (New Haven and London 1996).
Lawton, *ADR*	Carol L. Lawton, *Attic Document Reliefs. Art and Politics in Ancient Athens* (Oxford 1995).
Laymon, *InterpComm*	Charles M. Laymon, ed., *Interpreter's One-Volume Commentary on the Bible* (Nashville and New York 1971).
Leach, *RhetSpace*	Eleanor Winsor Leach, *The Rhetoric of Space. Literary and Artistic Representations of Landscape in Republican and Augustan Rome* (Princeton 1988).
Lee 1973a	Sir Desmond Lee, 'Science, Philosophy, and Technology in the Greco-Roman World: I,' *Greece and Rome,* s. 2 vol. 20 (1973): 65–78.
Lehmann-Hartleben 1941a	Karl Lehmann-Hartleben, 'The *Imagines* of the Elder Philostratus,' *Art Bulletin* 23 (1941): 16–44.
Levin 1993a	Joel R. Levin, 'Mnemonic Strategies and Classroom Learning: A Twenty-Year Report Card,' *The Elementary School Journal* 94 (1993): 235–244.
Lewin, *Life*	Roger Lewin, *Life at the Edge of Chaos* (New York 1992).
Lewis and Short	Charlton T. Lewis and Charles Short, *A Latin Dictionary* (Oxford 1879).
LCL	Leob Classical Library (London and Cambridge, MA).
LIMC	*Lexicon Iconographicum Mythologiae Classicae* (Zurich and Munich 1981–1997).
Ling 1991a	Roger Ling, 'The Architecture of Pompeii,' *Journal of Roman Archaeology* 4 (1991): 248–256.
Ling, *RomPaint*	Roger Ling, *Roman Painting* (Cambridge 1991).
Lloyd, *EGS*	G. E. R. Lloyd, *Early Greek Science: Thales to Aristotle* (New York 1970).
Lloyd, *GrSciA*	G. E. R. Lloyd, *Greek Science after Aristotle* (New York 1973).
Lloyd, *RevWisdom*	G. E. R. Lloyd, *The Revolutions of Wisdom. Studies in the Claims and Practice of Ancient Greek Science* (Berkeley and Los Angeles 1987).
Locher 1986a	A. Locher, 'The Structure of Pliny the Elder's Natural History,' in French/Greenaway, pp. 20–29.
Loftus 1991a	Loftus, Elizabeth F., ed., 'The Glitter of Everyday Memory . . . and the Gold,' *American Psychologist* 46 (1991): 16–48, 74–79 (numerous commentaries in response to Banaji/Crowder 1989a).
Loftus, *Witness*	Elizabeth Loftus and K. Ketcham, *Witness for the Defense. The Accused, the Eyewitness, and the Expert Who Puts Memory on Trial* (New York 1991).
Long, *HellPhil*	A. A. Long, *Hellenistic Philosophy. Stoics, Epicureans, Sceptics,* 2nd edn (Berkeley and Los Angeles 1986).

Loraux 1988a   Patrice Loraux, 'L'art platonicien d'avoir l'air d'écrire,' in Detienne, *Savoirs*, pp. 420–455.

Lord, *Singer*   Albert B. Lord, *The Singer of Tales* (Cambridge, MA 1960).

Lord 1985a   Albert B. Lord, 'Memory, Meaning, and Myth in Homer and Other Oral Epic Traditions,' in Gentili/Paioni, pp. 37–67.

LSJ   H. G. Liddell, R. Scott, H. S. Jones, and R. McKenzie, *A Greek-English Lexicon*, 9th edn (Oxford 1968).

LTUR   Eva Margareta Steinby, ed., *Lexicon Topographicum Urbis Romae* (Rome 1993–).

Luce 1989a   T. J. Luce, 'Ancient Views on the Causes of Bias in Historical Writing,' *Classical Philology* 84 (1989): 16–31.

Luce 1990a   T. J. Luce, 'Livy, Augustus, and the Forum Augustum,' in Raaflaub/Toher, pp. 123–138.

Luce, *Livy*   T. J. Luce, *Livy. The Composition of His History* (Princeton 1977).

Luck 1981a   Georg Luck, 'Textual Criticism Today,' *American Journal of Philology* 102 (1981): 164–194.

Lullies/Hirmer   Reinhard Lullies and Max Hirmer, *Greek Sculpture* (New York 1960).

Luppe 1977a   W. Luppe, 'Rückseitentitel auf Papyrusrollen,' *Zeitschrift für Papyrologie und Epigraphik* 27 (1977): 89–99.

Luria, *Mnemonist*   A. R. Luria, *The Mind of a Mnemonist. A Little Book about a Vast Memory*, translated by Lynn Solotaroff (Cambridge, MA 1987).

Lycan, *Mind*   William G. Lycan, *Mind and Cognition. A Reader* (Oxford 1990).

McArthur, *EngLang*   Tom McArthur, ed., *The Oxford Companion to the English Language* (Oxford 1992).

McArthur, *Worlds*   Tom McArthur, *Worlds of Reference* (Cambridge 1986).

McCormick 1985a   M. McCormick, 'The Birth of the Codex and the Apostolic Life-Style,' *Scriptorium* 39 (1985): 150–158.

McCormick/Levin 1987a   Christine B. McCormick and Joel R. Levin, 'Mnemonic Prose-Learning Strategies,' in McDaniel/Pressley, pp. 392–406.

McDaniel *et al.* 1995a   Mark A. McDaniel, Edward L. DeLosh, Gilles O. Einstein, Cindi P. May, and Paul Brady, 'The Bizarreness Effect: It's Not Surprising, It's Complex,' *Journal of Experimental Psychology: Learning, Memory, and Cognition* 21 (1995): 422–435.

McDaniel/Pressley   Mark A. McDaniel and Michael Pressley, eds, *Imagery and Related Mnemonic Processes. Theories, Individual Differences, and Applications* (New York 1987).

McIlwaine 1990a   I. C. McIlwaine, 'Herculaenum: A Guide to Printed Sources. Supplement,' *Cronache Ercolanesi* 20 (1990): 87–128.

McKane, *Proverbs*   William McKane, *Proverbs. A New Approach* (Philadelphia 1970).

Mandelbaum, *Aeneid*   Allen Mandelbaum, *The Aeneid of Virgil* (New York 1971).

Marrou, *HistEduc*
H. I. Marrou, *A History of Education in Antiquity*, translated by George Lamb (Madison 1956).

Marsden 1995a
Richard Marsden, 'Job in His Place: The Ezra Miniature in the Codex Amiatinus,' *Scriptorium* 49 (1995): 3–15.

Marshall 1976a
Anthony J. Marshall, 'Library Resources and Creative Writing at Rome,' *Phoenix* 30 (1976): 252–264.

Marvin 1989a
Miranda Marvin, 'Copying in Roman Sculpture: The Replica Series,' in Kathleen Preciado, ed., *Retaining the Original. Multiple Originals, Copies, and Reproductions, Studies in the History of Art* 20 (Washington 1989), pp. 29–45.

Mathews, *Clash*
Thomas F. Mathews, *The Clash of Gods. A Reinterpretation of Early Christian Art* (Princeton 1993).

Mathews/Sanjian
Thomas F. Mathews and Avedis K. Sanjian, *Armenian Gospel Iconography. The Tradition of the Glajor Gospel, Dumbarton Oaks Studies* 29 (Washington, DC 1991).

Matsen *et al.*
Patricia P. Matsen, Philip B. Rollinson, and Marion Sousa. eds, *Readings from Classical Rhetoric* (Edwardsville, IL 1990).

Matthews 1995a
Roger Matthews, 'Writing and Civilization in Early Mesopotamia,' *Cambridge Archaeological Journal* 5 (1995): 309–314.

Mau, *Pompeii*
August Mau, *Pompeii. Its Life and Art*, translated by Francis W. Kelsey (New Rochelle, NY 1982).

Maurois, *Titans*
André Maurois, *The Titans. A Three-Generation Biography of the Dumas*, translated by Gerard Hopkins (New York 1957).

Mejer, *DiogLaert*
Jörgen Mejer, *Diogenes Laertius and His Hellenistic Background, Hermes*, Einzelschriften 40 (Wiesbaden 1978).

Menci 1985a
Giovanna Menci, 'Χάρτης ἔληξε,' *Yale Classical Studies* 28 (1985): 261–266.

Merton, *OTSOG*
Robert K. Merton, *On the Shoulders of Giants. A Shandean Postscript* (San Diego, New York, and London 1965).

Messerschmidt 1931a
F. Messerschmidt, 'Die schreibenden Gottheiten in der etruskischen Religion,' *Archiv für Religionswissenschaft* 29 (1931): 60–69.

Metzger, *HistLit*
Bruce M. Metzger, *Historical and Literary Studies. Pagan, Jewish, and Christian* (Leiden 1968).

Metzger, *TextNT*
Bruce M. Metzger, *The Text of the New Testament. Its Transmission, Corruption, and Restoration*, 3rd edn (New York and Oxford 1992).

Mieder, *AmerProv*
Wolfgang Mieder, ed., *A Dictionary of American Proverbs* (New York and Oxford 1992).

Miles, *Livy*
Gary B. Miles, *Livy. Reconstructing Early Rome* (Ithaca and London 1995).

Millard 1994a
Alan R. Millard, 'Re-creating the Tablets of the Law,' *Bible Review* 10 no. 1 (February 1994): 48–53.

Miller 1956a
George A. Miller, 'The Magic Number Seven, Plus or Minus Two: Some Limits on Our Capacity for

Processing Information,' *Psychological Review* 63 (1956): 81–97.

Miller 1994a — George A. Miller, 'The Magic Number Seven, Plus or Minus Two: Some Limits on Our Capacity for Processing Information,' *Psychological Review* 101 (1994): 343–352.

Miller 1994b — Michael J. Miller, 'Big PCs for Little Rascals,' *PC Magazine* 13 no. 12 (28 June 1994): 80.

Minchin 1992a — Elizabeth Minchin, 'Scripts and Themes: Cognitive Research and the Homeric Epic,' *Classical Antiquity* 11 (1992): 229–241.

Mitscherling 1982a — J. Mitscherling, 'Xenophon and Plato,' *Classical Quarterly* n.s. 32 (1982): 468–469.

Moffitt 1993a — John F. Moffitt, 'Medieval *Mappaemundi* and Ptolemy's *Chorographia*,' *Gesta* 32 (1993): 59–68.

Moles 1993a — J. L. Moles, 'Truth and Untruth in Herodotus and Thucydides,' in Gill/Wisemann, *Lies*, pp. 99–121.

Momigliano 1978a — Arnaldo Momigliano, 'The Historians of the Classical World and Their Audiences: Some Suggestions,' *Annali della Scuola Normale Superiore di Pisa*, series 3, vol. 8, fasc. 1 (1978): 59–75, reprinted in *idem*, *Sesto Contributo* (Rome 1980), pp. 361–376.

Moravcsik 1971a — Julius Moravcsik, 'Learning As Recollection,' in Gregory Vlastos, ed., *Plato. A Collection of Critical Essays I: Metaphysics and Epistemology* (Garden City, NY 1971), pp. 53–69.

Moray 1959a — N. Moray, 'Attention in Dichotic Listening: Affective Cues and the Influence of Instructions,' *Quarterly Journal of Experimental Psychology* 11 (1959): 56–60.

Morgan — Morris Hicky Morgan, translator, *Vitruvius. The Ten Books on Architecture* (New York 1960).

Morrison 1987a — Ken Morrison, 'Stabilizing the Text: The Institutionalization of Knowledge in Historical and Philosophic Forms of Argument,' *Canadian Journal of Sociology* 12 (1987): 242–274.

Moser, *Rationality* — Paul K. Moser, ed., *Rationality in Action. Contemporary Approaches* (Cambridge 1990).

Murray 1981a — Penelope Murray, 'Poetic Inspiration in Early Greece,' *Journal of Hellenic Studies* 101 (1981): 87–100.

Murray 1989a — Penelope Murray, 'Poetic Genius and its Classical Origins,' in Penelope Murray, ed., *Genius: The History of an Idea* (Oxford 1989), pp. 9–31.

Nagy 1992a — Gregory Nagy, 'Mythological Exemplum in Homer,' in Hexter/Selden, pp. 311–331.

Nagy 1992b — Gregory Nagy, 'Homeric Questions,' *Transactions of the American Philological Association* 122 (1992): 17–60.

Nagy, *Best* — Gregory Nagy, *The Best of the Achaeans* (Baltimore 1979).

Nagy, *PoetPerf* — Gregory Nagy, *Poetry as Performance. Homer and Beyond* (Cambridge 1996).

Naissance — *Naissance de l'écriture. Cunéiformes et hiéroglyphes*, Exhibition Galeries nationales du Grand Palais, 7 May to 9 August 1982 (Paris 1982).

Nash, *PDAR* — E. Nash, *Pictorial Dictionary of Ancient Rome*, 2nd edn (New York and Washington 1968).

Neel, *Plato* — Jasper P. Neel, *Plato, Derrida, and Writing* (Carbondale and Edwardsville 1988).

Negroponte, *Being* — Nicholas Negroponte, *Being Digital* (New York 1995).

Neisser 1981a — Ulric Neisser, 'John Dean's Memory: A Case Study,' *Cognition* 9 (1981): 1–22. Reprinted in Neisser, *MemObs*, pp. 139–159.

Neisser 1982a — Ulric Neisser, 'Memory: What Are the Important Questions?,' in Neisser, *MemObs*, pp. 3–19.

Neisser 1988a — Ulric Neisser, 'Time Present and Time Past,' in Gruneberg *et al.* 1988a, pp. 545–560.

Neisser 1988b — Ulric Neisser, 'What Is Ordinary Memory the Memory of?,' in Neisser/Winograd, pp. 356–373.

Neisser *et al.* 1996a — Ulric Neisser, Eugene Winograd, Erik T. Bergman, Charles A. Schreiber, Stephen E. Palmer, and Mary Susan Weldon, 'Remembering the Earthquake: Direct Experience vs. Hearing the News,' *Memory* 4 (1996): 337–357.

Neisser, *MemObs* — Ulric Neisser, *Memory Observed. Remembering in Natural Contexts* (New York 1982).

Neisser/Fivush — Ulric Neisser and Robyn Fivush, eds, *The Remembering Self: Construction and Accuracy in the Self-Narrative* (Cambridge 1994).

Neisser/Winograd — Ulric Neisser and Eugene Winograd, eds, *Remembering Reconsidered. Ecological and Traditional Approaches to the Study of Memory* (Cambridge 1988).

Nelson/Roediger — Douglas L. Nelson and Henry L. Roediger III, eds, 'Special Issue on Illusions of Memory,' *Journal of Memory and Language* 35 no. 1 (April 1996).

Neudecker, *Skulp* — Richard Neudecker, *Die Skulpturen-Ausstattung Römischer Villen in Italien* (Mainz 1988).

Neusner, *MemTorah* — Jacob Neusner, *The Memorized Torah. The Mnemonic System of the Torah* (Chico, CA 1985).

Nicolet, *Space* — Claude Nicolet, *Space, Geography, and Politics in the Early Roman Empire* (Ann Arbor 1991).

Nieddu 1984a — Gian Franco Nieddu, 'La metafora della memoria come scrittura e l'immagine dell'animo come *deltos*,' *Quaderni di Storia* 10 no. 19 (1984): 213–219.

Nisetich, *Pindar* — Frank J. Nisetich, *Pindar's Victory Songs* (Baltimore 1980).

Nock 1972a — Arthur Darby Nock, 'Word-Coinage in Greek,' in Zeph Stewart, ed., *Arthur Darby Nock. Essays on Religion and the Ancient World*, vol. 2 (Cambridge, MA 1972), pp. 642–652; reprint of 'Word-Coinage in the Hermetic Writings,' *Coniectanea Neotestamentica* II (1947): 163–178.

Norman 1960a — A. F. Norman, 'The Book Trade in Fourth-Century Antioch,' *Journal of Hellenic Studies* 80 (1960): 122–126.

Norman, *PsychEv*	Donald A. Norman, *The Psychology of Everyday Things* (New York 1988).
Norman, *Things*	Donald A. Norman, *Things That Make Us Smart. Defending Human Attributes in the Age of the Machine* (Reading, MA 1993).
Norman, *TurnSig*	Donald A. Norman, *Turn Signals Are the Facial Expressions of Automobiles* (Reading, MA 1992).
North 1995a	Robert North, 'Did Ancient Israelites Have a Heart?,' *Bible Review* 11 No. 3 (June 1995): 33.
Notopoulos 1938a	J. A. Notopoulos, 'Mnemosyne in Oral Literature,' *Transactions of the American Philological Association* 69 (1938): 465–493.
OCD ^{2}	N. G. L. Hammond and H. H. Scullard, *The Oxford Classical Dictionary*, 2nd edn, reprinted with corrections (Oxford 1973).
O'Connor, *Letters*	*Letters of Flannery O'Connor. The Habit of Being*, Edited by Sally Fitzgerald (New York 1979).
OED ^{2}	J. A. Simpson and E. S. C. Weiner, *The Oxford English Dictionary*, 2nd edn (Oxford 1989).
Ofshe/Watters	Richard Ofshe and Ethan Watters, *Making Monsters. False Memory, Psychotherapy, and Sexual Hysteria* (New York 1994).
Ogilvie, *Comm*	R. M. Ogilvie, *A Commentary on Livy Books 1–5* (Oxford 1970).
OHCA	John Boardman, ed., *The Oxford History of Classical Art* (Oxford 1993).
OHCW	John Boardman, Jasper Griffin, and Oswyn Murray, eds, *The Oxford History of the Classical World* (Oxford and New York 1988).
OLD	P. G. W. Glare, ed., *Oxford Latin Dictionary* (Oxford 1982).
Olmert, *Books*	M. Olmert, *The Smithsonian Book of Books* (Washington, DC 1992).
Olson 1993a	David R. Olson, 'How Writing Represents Speech,' *Language & Communication* 12 (1992): 1–17.
Olson, *Paper*	David R. Olson, *The World on Paper* (Cambridge 1994).
Olson/Astington 1990a	David R. Olson and Janet W. Astington, 'Talking about Text: How Literacy Contributes to Thought,' *Journal of Pragmatics* 14 (1990): 705–721.
Olson/Torrance	David R. Olson and Nancy Torrance, eds, *Literacy and Orality* (Cambridge 1991).
Ong, *Orality*	Walter J. Ong, *Orality and Literacy. The Technologizing of the Word* (London and New York 1982).
Onians, *Origins*	Richard Broxton Onians, *The Origins of European Thought about the Body, the Mind, the Soul, the World, Time, and Fate* (Cambridge 1951, rpt 1988).
Onions, *ODEE*	C. T. Onions, ed., *The Oxford Dictionary of English Etymology* (Oxford 1966 (rpt 1969 with corrections)).
Osborne 1973a	Michael J. Osborne, 'The Stoichedon Style in Theory and Practice,' *Zeitschrift für Papyrologie und Epigraphik* 20 (1973): 249–270.
Packer 1993a	James Packer, 'The West Library in the Forum of

Trajan: The Architectural Problems and Some Solutions,' in Russell T. Scott and Ann Reynolds Scott, eds, *Eius Virtutis Studiosi: Classical and Postclassical Studies in Memory of Frank Edward Brown (1908–1988), Studies in the History of Art* 43 (Hanover and London 1993), pp. 420–444.

Padel, *Mind* Ruth Padel, *In and out of the Mind. Greek Images of the Tragic Self* (Princeton 1992).

Parássoglou 1979a G. M. Parássoglou, 'ΔΕΞΙΑ ΧΕΙΡ ΚΑΙ ΓΟΝΥ. Some Thoughts on the Postures of the Ancient Greeks and Romans When Writing on Papyrus Rolls,' *Scrittura e Civiltà* 3 (1979): 5–21.

Parássoglou 1985a G. M. Parássoglou, 'A Roll upon His Knees,' *Yale Classical Studies* 28 (1985): 273–275.

Parkes, *Pause* M. B. Parkes, *Pause and Effect. An Introduction to the History of Punctuation in the West* (Berkeley and Los Angeles 1993).

Parkinson/Quirke Richard Parkinson and Stephen Quirke, *Papyrus* (Austin 1995).

PastPersp I. S. Moxon, J. D. Smart, and A. J. Woodman, eds, *Past Perspectives. Studies in Greek and Roman Historical Writing* (Cambridge 1986).

Pease, *CicDiv* Arthur Stanley Pease, ed., *M. Tulli Ciceronis de Divinatione Libri Duo* (Darmstadt 1977).

Pelliccia, *Mind* Hayden Pelliccia, *Mind, Body, and Speech in Homer and Pindar, Hypomnemata* 107 (Göttingen 1995).

Pelling 1979a C. B. R. Pelling, 'Plutarch's Method of Work in the Roman Lives,' *Journal of Hellenic Studies* 99 (1979): 74–96.

Pelling 1980a C. B. R. Pelling, 'Plutarch's Adaptation of His Source-Material,' *Journal of Hellenic Studies* 100 (1980): 127–140.

Pelling 1990a C. B. R. Pelling, 'Truth and Fiction in Plutarch's *Lives*,' in D. A. Russell, ed., *Antonine Literature* (Oxford 1990).

Pennisi 1994a E. Pennisi, 'Mice, Flies Share Memory Molecule,' *Science News* 146 (15 October 1994): 244.

Pernoud/Vigne R. Pernoud and Jean Vigne, *La plume et le parchemin* (Paris 1983).

Petitmengin/Flusin 1984a Pierre Petitmengin and Bernard Flusin, 'Le livre antique et la dictée. Nouvelles recherches,' in E. Lucchesi and H. D. Saffrey, eds, *Mémorial André-Jean Festugière. Antiquité païenne et chrétienne* (Geneva 1984), pp. 247–262.

Petroski, *Evolution* Henry Petroski, *The Evolution of Useful Things* (New York 1992).

PHI Latin Disk Packard Humanities Institute, Palo Alto, CA: CD-ROM #5.3, Latin Texts.

Phillips 1986a John J. Phillips, 'Atticus and the Publication of Cicero's Works,' *Classical World* 79 (1986): 227–237.

Piccaluga 1994a 'La specificità dei *libri lintei* romani,' *Scrittura e Civiltà* 18 (1994): 5–22.

351

Pine-Coffin, *Conf*
R. S. Pine-Coffin, translator, *Saint Augustine Confessions* (London and New York 1961).

Plato, Bollingen
Edith Hamilton and Huntington Cairns, eds, *Plato. The Collected Dialogues*, Bollingen Series 71 (New York 1961).

Platthy, *Sources*
Jenö Platthy, *Sources on the Earliest Greek Libraries with the Testimonia* (Amsterdam 1968).

Podlecki/Duane 1992a
Anthony J. Podlecki and Sandra Duane, 'Work on Plutarch's Greek Lives, 1951–1988,' *ANRW* pt. 2, vol. 33.6 (New York 1992), pp. 4053–4127.

Pollard 1962a
Graham Pollard, 'The Construction of English Twelfth-Century Bindings,' *The Library*, 5th series, 17 no. 1 (March 1962): 1–22.

Pollini 1984a
John Pollini, '*Damnatio Memoriae* in Stone: Two Portraits of Nero Recut to Vespasian in American Museums,' *American Journal of Archaeology* 88 (1984): 547–555.

Pollitt, *AncView*
J. J. Pollitt, *The Ancient View of Greek Art: Criticism, History, and Terminology* (New Haven and London 1974).

Pomeroy, *Xenophon*
Sarah B. Pomeroy, *Xenophon Oeconomicus. A Social and Historical Commentary* (Oxford 1994).

Posner
Ernst Posner, *Archives in the Ancient World* (Cambridge, MA 1972).

Posner/Raichle, *Images*
Michael I. Posner and Marcus E. Raichle, *Images of Mind* (New York 1994).

Powell 1981a
Marvin A. Powell, 'Three Problems in the History of Cuneiform Writing: Origins, Direction of Script, Literacy,' *Visible Language* 15 (1981): 419–440.

Powell, *Homer*
Barry Powell, *Homer and the Origin of the Greek Alphabet* (Cambridge 1991).

Pratt 1995a
Louise Pratt, 'The Seal of Theognis, Writing, and Oral Poetry,' *American Journal of Philology* 116 (1995): 171–184.

Pritchard, *ANET-A*
James B. Pritchard, ed., *The Ancient Near East. An Anthology of Texts and Pictures* (Princeton 1958).

Pritchett, *DionHal*
W. Kendrick Pritchett, translator and annotator, *Dionysius of Halicarnassus: On Thucydides* (Berkeley, Los Angeles, and London 1975).

Pucci, *Hesiod*
Pietro Pucci, *Hesiod and the Language of Poetry* (Baltimore and London 1977).

Pullum
Geoffrey K. Pullum, *The Great Eskimo Vocabulary Hoax and Other Irreverent Essays on the Study of Language* (Chicago and London 1991).

Quinn 1982a
Kenneth Quinn, 'The Poet and His Audience in the Augustan Age,' *ANRW* II 30.1 (Berlin and New York 1982), pp. 75–180.

Raaflaub/Toher
Kurt A. Raaflaub and Mark Toher, eds, *Between Republic and Empire. Interpretations of Augustus and His Principate* (Berkeley, Los Angeles, and Oxford 1990).

Radding/Clark
Charles M. Radding and William W. Clark, *Medieval Architecture, Medieval Learning* (New Haven 1992).

352

Radice, *PlinyY* — Betty Radice, translator, *The Letters of the Younger Pliny* (Baltimore 1963).

Rafti 1988a — Patrizia Rafti, 'L'interpunzione nel libro manoscritto: mezzo secolo di studi,' *Scrittura e Civiltà* 12 (1988): 239–298.

Raloff/Lipkin 1995a — Janet Raloff and Richard Lipkin, 'A Digital Notary,' *Science News* 147 no. 9 (4 March 1995): 138.

Raskin 1994a — Robin Raskin, 'Stop the Real World, I Want to Get Off,' *PC Magazine* 13 no. 10 (31 May 1994): 30.

Rawson, *IntellLife* — Elizabeth Rawson, *Intellectual Life in the Late Roman Republic* (Baltimore 1985).

RE — A. Pauly and G. Wissowa, *Realencyclopädie der classischen Altertumswissenschaft* (Munich 1893 to 1978).

Reber, *DictPsych* — Arthur S. Reber, *The Penguin Dictionary of Psychology* (London 1985).

Reggiani — Anna Maria Reggiani, *Educazione e scuola* (Rome 1990).

Reinach, *RP* — Salomon Reinach, *Répertoire des peintures grecques et romaines* (Paris 1922).

Reinach, *Textes* — Adolphe Reinach, *Textes grecs et latins relatifs à l'histoire de la peinture ancienne* (Paris 1921; rpt Chicago 1981).

Reynolds, *RhetMem* — John Frederick Reynolds, ed., *Rhetorical Memory and Delivery. Classical Concepts for Contemporary Composition and Communication* (Hillsdale, NJ 1993).

Reynolds/Wilson — L. D. Reynolds and N. G. Wilson, *Scribes & Scholars. A Guide to the Transmission of Greek & Latin Literature*, 3rd edn (Oxford 1991).

RHUD — Stuart Berg Flexner, ed., *Random House Unabridged Dictionary*, 2nd edn (New York 1987).

Richardson, *NTDAR* — L. Richardson, Jr., *A New Topographical Dictionary of Ancient Rome* (Baltimore and London 1992).

Richter, *Furniture* — G. M. A. Richter, *The Furniture of the Greeks, Etruscans and Romans*, 2nd edn (London 1966).

Richter, *Perspective* — G. M. A. Richter, *Perspective in Greek & Roman Art* (London and New York 1974).

Richter, *Portraits* — G. M. A. Richter, *The Portraits of the Greeks*, 3 vols (London 1965).

Richter, *TopRom* — Otto Richter, *Topographie der Stadt Rom. Handbuch der klassischen Altertumswissenschaft*, vol. 3, part 3, second half, 2nd edn (Munich 1901).

Ridgway, *HelSculp I* — Brunilde Sismondo Ridgway, *Hellenistic Sculpture I. The Styles of c. 331–200 B.C.* (Madison 1990).

Ridgway, *Princeton* — Brunilde Sismondo Ridgway, ed., *Greek Sculpture in the Art Museum, Princeton University: Greek Originals, Roman Copies and Variants* (Princeton 1994).

Riding 1985a — Stewart Riding, 'Plato's κήρινον ἐκμαγεῖον and Memory Models in Current Psychology,' *Platon* 37 (1985): 101–120.

Robb, *LitPaid* — Kevin Robb, *Literacy and Paideia in Ancient Greece* (New York and Oxford 1994).

Roberts 1992a — Beth Roberts, 'The Evolution of the Young Child's Concept of *Word* as a Unit of Spoken and Written

Language,' *Reading Research Quarterly* 27 (1992): 124–138.

Roberts/Skeat, *Codex* C. H. Roberts and T. C. Skeat, *The Birth of the Codex* (London 1987).

Rochette 1995a Bruno Rochette, 'Du grec au latin et du latin au grec. Les problèmes de la traduction dans l'antiquité gréco-latine,' *Latomus* 54 (1995): 245–261.

Roediger 1980a Henry L. Roediger, III, 'Memory Metaphors in Cognitive Psychology,' *Memory & Cognition* 8 (1980): 231–246.

Rogers, *Cliches* James Rogers, *The Dictionary of Cliches* (New York 1987).

Rollins, *Imagery* Mark Rollins, *Mental Imagery. On the Limits of Cognitive Science* (New Haven 1989).

Rose, *Memory* Steven Rose, *The Making of Memory. From Molecules to Mind* (New York 1992).

Rottländer 1986a R. C. A. Rottländer, 'The Pliny Translation Group of Germany,' in French/Greenaway, pp. 11–19.

Rouse, *Plato* W. H. D. Rouse, translator, *Great Dialogues of Plato* (New York 1956).

Rouse/Rouse 1982a Richard H. Rouse and Mary A. Rouse, '*Statim invenire*: Schools, Preachers, and New Attitudes to the Page,' in Benson/Constable, pp. 201–225.

Rouse/Rouse 1989a Richard H. Rouse and Mary A. Rouse, 'Wax Tablets,' *Language & Communication* 9 (1989): 175–191.

Rouse/Rouse 1989b Richard H. Rouse and Mary A. Rouse, 'The Vocabulary of Wax Tablets,' in Weijers, *VocLivre*, pp. 220–230.

Rouse/Rouse 1991a Richard H. Rouse and Mary A. Rouse, 'The Development of Research Tools in the Thirteenth Century,' in Richard H. Rouse and Mary A. Rouse, eds, *Authentic Witnesses: Approaches to Medieval Texts and Manuscripts* (Notre Dame 1991), pp. 221–255.

Rouveret 1987a Agnès Rouveret, '"Toute la mémoire du monde": La notion de collection dans la *NH* de Pline,' *Helmantica* 38 (1987): 115–133.

Rouveret, *HistImag* Agnès Rouveret, *Histoire et imaginaire de la peinture ancienne (Ve siècle av. J.-C. – Ier siècle ap. J.-C.)*, Bibliothèque des Écoles Françaises d'Athènes et de Rome 274 (Rome 1989).

Rubin, *AutobioMem* David C. Rubin, ed., *Autobiographical Memory* (Cambridge 1986).

Rubin, *MemOral* David C. Rubin, *Memory in Oral Traditions. The Cognitive Psychology of Epic, Ballads, and Counting-out Rhymes* (New York and Oxford 1995).

Rubin, *Remembering* David C. Rubin, ed., *Remembering Our Past: Studies in Autobiographical Memory* (Cambridge 1996).

Rubincam 1989a C. I. R. Rubincam, 'Cross-references in the *Bibliotheke Historike* of Diodoros,' *Phoenix* 43 (1989): 39–61.

Rybczynski, *Home* W. Rybczynski, *Home. A Short History of an Idea* (New York 1986).

Ryle 1960a Gilbert Ryle, 'Letters and Syllables in Plato,' *Philosophical Review* 69 (1960): 431–451.

Sacks, *Mars*	Oliver Sacks, *An Anthropologist on Mars* (New York 1995).
Sadoski/Quast 1990a	Mark Sadoski and Zeba Quast, 'Reader Response and Long-Term Recall for Journalistic Text: The Roles of Imagery, Affect, and Importance,' *Reading Research Quarterly* 25 (1990): 256–272.
Sadurska, *Tables*	Anna Sadurska, *Les tables iliaques* (Warsaw 1964).
Saenger 1982a	Paul Saenger, 'Silent Reading: Its Impact on Late Medieval Script and Society,' *Viator* 13 (1982): 367–414.
Saenger 1990a	Paul Saenger, 'The Separation of Words and the Order of Words: the Genesis of Medieval Reading,' *Scrittura e Civiltà* 14 (1990): 49–74.
Saenger 1991a	Paul Saenger, 'The Separation of Words and the Physiology of Reading,' in Olson/Torrance, pp. 198–214.
Saenger/Heinlen 1991a	Paul Saenger and Michael Heinlen, 'Incunable Description and Its Implication for the Analysis of Fifteenth-Century Reading Habits,' in Hindman, *Printing*, pp. 225–258.
Salles, *Lire*	Catherine Salles, *Lire à Rome* (Paris 1992).
Sampson, *Writing*	Geoffrey Sampson, *Writing Systems. A Linguistic Introduction* (Stanford 1985).
Savage-Rumbaugh/ Lewin, *Kanzi*	Sue Savage-Rumbaugh and Roger Lewin, *Kanzi. The Ape at the Brink of the Human Mind* (New York 1994).
Schacter, *Searching*	Daniel L. Schacter, *Searching for Memory. The Brain, the Mind, and the Past* (New York 1996).
Schank, *Connoisseur*	Roger C. Schank, *The Connoisseur's Guide to the Mind* (New York 1991).
Schank, *Tell*	Roger C. Schank, *Tell Me a Story. A New Look at Real and Artificial Memory* (New York 1990).
Schefold, *SB* 5	Karl Schefold and Franz Jung, *Die Sagen von den Argonauten, von Theben und Troia in der klassischen und hellenistischen Kunst* (Munich 1989).
Schefold, *WP*	Karl Schefold, *Die Wände Pompejis* (Berlin 1957).
Schenkeveld 1992a	Dirk M. Schenkeveld, 'Prose Usages of ἀκούειν "To Read",' *Classical Quarterly* 42 (1992): 129–141.
Schlott, *Schrift*	Adelheid Schlott, *Schrift und Schreiber im Alten Ägypten* (Munich 1989).
Schmitt, *Object*	Marilyn Schmitt (general ed.), Elizabeth Bakewell, William O. Beeman, and Carol McMichael Reese, *Object – Image – Inquiry. The Art Historian at Work* (Santa Monica, CA 1988).
Scholes/Willis 1991a	Robert J. Scholes and Brenda J. Willis, 'Linguists, Literacy, and the Intensionality of Marshall McLuhan's Western Man,' in Olson/Torrance, pp. 215–235.
Schousboe/Larsen	K. Schousboe and M. T. Larsen, *Literacy and Society* (Copenhagen 1989).
Schultze 1986a	Clemence Schultze, 'Dionysius of Halicarnassus and his Audience,' *PastPersp*, pp. 121–141.
Schwarz/Sudman	Norbert Schwarz and Seymor Sudman, eds, *Autobiographical Memory and the Validity of Retrospective Reports* (New York, Berlin, Heidelberg 1994).

355

Scisco 1994a — Peter Scisco, 'Review of *Creative Writer*,' *PC Magazine* 13 no. 11 (14 June 1994): 477–478.

Scott-Kilvert, *Polybius* — *Polybius: The Rise of the Roman Empire*, translated by Ian Scott-Kilvert (Harmondsworth 1979).

Scott-Kilvert, *Plutarch* — *Plutarch. The Rise and Fall of Athens. Nine Greek Lives*, translated by Ian Scott-Kilvert (Harmondsworth 1960).

Scribner/Cole — Sylvia Scribner and Michael Cole, *The Psychology of Literacy* (Cambridge, MA 1981).

Scrivere Etrusco — Giorgio Bombi and Silvia Guagliumi, *Scrivere Etrusco* (Milan 1985).

Serbat 1986a — Guy Serbat, 'Pline l'Ancien. Etat présent des études sur sa vie, son oeuvre et son influence,' *ANRW* II vol. 32 pt. 4 (Berlin 1986).

Settis, *ColTraiana* — S. Settis, ed., *La Colonna Traiana* (Torino 1988).

Shackleton Bailey, *Atticus* — D. R. Shackleton Bailey, translator, *Cicero's Letters to Atticus* (Harmondsworth 1978).

Shackleton Bailey, *Cicero* — D. R. Shackleton Bailey, *Cicero* (New York 1971).

Shackleton Bailey, *Friends* — D. R. Shackleton Bailey, translator, *Cicero's Letters to His Friends* (Harmondsworth 1978).

Shankweiler/ Lundquist 1992a — Donald Shankweiler and Eric Lundquist, 'On the Relations between Learning to Spell and Learning to Read,' in Frost/Katz, *OPMM*, pp. 179–192.

Shelton 1983a — Kathleen J. Shelton, 'The Consular Muse of Flavius Constantius,' *Art Bulletin* 65 (1983): 7–23.

Shelton, *Romans* — Jo-Ann Shelton, *As the Romans Did. A Sourcebook in Roman Social History* (New York and Oxford 1988).

Sherk, *RDGE* — Robert K. Sherk, *Roman Documents from the Greek East. Senatus Consulta and Epistulae to the Age of Augustus* (Baltimore 1969).

Shiffrin/Nosofsky 1994a — Richard M. Shiffrin and Robert M. Nosofsky, 'Seven Plus or Minus Two: A Commentary on Capacity Limitations,' *Psychological Review* 101 (1994): 357–361.

Shimron/Sivan 1994a — Joseph Shimron and Tamar Sivan, 'Reading Proficiency and Orthography: Evidence from Hebrew and English,' *Language Learning* 44 (1994): 5–27.

Shipley, *OriginMind* — Thorne Shipley, *Intersensory Origin of Mind. A Revisit to Emergent Evolution* (London and New York 1995).

Shubert 1993a — Steven Blake Shubert, 'The Oriental Origins of the Alexandrian Library,' *Libri* 43 (1993): 142–172.

Shupak 1985a — N. Shupak, 'Some Idioms Connected with the Concept of "Heart" in Egypt and the Bible,' in *Pharaonic Egypt. The Bible and Christianity*, edited by Sarah Israelit-Groll (Jerusalem 1985), pp. 202–212.

Sider 1990a — Sandra Sider, 'Herculaneum's Library in 79 A.D.: The Villa of the Papyri,' *Libraries and Culture* 25 (1990): 534–542.

SIG — W. Dittenberger, ed., *Sylloge Inscriptionum Graecarum*, 3rd edn (Leipzig 1915 to 1924).

Sirat 1994a — Colette Sirat, 'Handwriting and the Writing Hand,' in Watt, *WritSys*, pp. 375–460.

Skeat 1956a — T. C. Skeat, 'The Use of Dictation in Ancient Book-

	Production,' *Proceedings of the British Academy* 41 (1956): 179–208.
Skeat 1981a	T. C. Skeat, 'Two Notes on Papyrus,' in Edda Bresciani *et al.*, eds, *Scritti in onore di Orsolina Montevecchi* (Bologna 1981), pp. 373–378.
Skeat 1982a	T. C. Skeat, 'The Length of the Standard Papyrus Roll and the Cost-Advantage of the Codex,' *Zeitschrift für Papyrologie und Epigraphik* 45 (1982): 169–175.
Skeat 1990a	T. C. Skeat, 'Roll versus Codex – A New Approach?,' *Zeitschrift für Papyrologie und Epigraphik* 84 (1990): 297–298.
Skeat 1994a	T. C. Skeat, 'The Origin of the Christian Codex,' *Zeitschrift für Papyrologie und Epigraphik* 102 (1994): 263–268.
Skydsgaard, *Varro*	Jens Erik Skydsgaard, *Varro the Scholar. Studies in the First Book of Varro's de Re Rustica* (Copenhagen 1968).
Small 1987a	Jocelyn Penny Small, 'Left, Right, and Center: Direction in Etruscan Art,' *Opuscula Romana* 16 no. 7 (1987): 125–135.
Small 1991a	Jocelyn Penny Small, 'The Tarquins and Servius Tullius at Banquet,' *Mélanges d'Archéologie et d'Histoire de l'École Française de Rome* 103 (1991): 247–264.
Small 1992a	Jocelyn Penny Small, 'Historical Development of Writing and Reading. Commentary on Skoyles on Reading,' *Psycoloquy* 92.3.61 (1992), 211 lines.
Small 1993a	Jocelyn Penny Small, 'Visual Display of Text Affects Visual Display of Recall: Evidence from Antiquity. Commentary on Hartley on Small on Skoyles on Reading,' *Psycoloquy* 93.4.20 (1993), 193 lines.
Small 1994a	Jocelyn Penny Small, 'Eat, Drink, and Be Merry: Etruscan Banquets,' in Richard De Puma and Jocelyn Penny Small, eds, *Murlo and the Etruscans* (Madison 1994), pp. 85–94.
Small 1994b	Jocelyn Penny Small, 'Why We Learn by Heart in English and French,' in Marie-Odile Jentel and Gisèle Deschênes-Wagner, eds, *Tranquillitas. Mélanges en l'honneur de Tran tam Tinh* (Quebec 1994), pp. 557–565.
Small 1995a	Jocelyn Penny Small, 'Artificial Memory and the Writing Habits of the Literate,' *Helios* 22 (1995): 159–166, 175–179.
Small, Forthcoming	Jocelyn Penny Small, 'On Doctors and Fingers: Auctor ad Herennium 3.20.33–34,' *Biblos*.
Smith/Marx	Merritt Roe Smith and Leo Marx, *Does Technology Drive History? The Dilemma of Technological Determinism* (Cambridge, MA 1994).
Snowman 1987a	Jack Snowman, 'Explorations in Mnemonic Training,' in McDaniel/Pressley, pp. 392–406.
Sorabji, *Memory*	Richard Sorabji, translator, *Aristotle. On Memory* (Providence 1972).
Sprenger/Bartoloni	M. Sprenger and G. Bartoloni, *The Etruscans – Their History, Art, and Architecture* (New York 1983).

Stapleford 1994a	Richard Stapleford, 'Intellect and Intuition in Botticelli's *Saint Augustine*,' *Art Bulletin* 76 (1994): 69–80.
Starr 1981a	Raymond J. Starr, 'Cross-References in Roman Prose,' *American Journal of Philology* 102 (1981): 431–437.
Starr 1987a	Raymond J. Starr, 'The Circulation of Literary Texts in the Roman World,' *Classical Quarterly*, n.s. 37 (1987): 213–223.
Starr 1990a	Raymond J. Starr, 'The Used-Book Trade in the Roman World,' *Phoenix* 44 (1990): 148–157.
Starr 1991a	Raymond J. Starr, 'Reading Aloud: *Lectores* and Roman Reading,' *Classical Journal* 86 (1991): 337–343.
Stein 1994a	Harry Stein, 'Our Times,' *TV Guide* 42 no. 47 (Issue 2173) (19–25 November 1994): 53.
Steiner 1955a	Grundy Steiner, 'The Skepticism of the Elder Pliny,' *The Classical Weekly* 48 no. 10, 1189 (21 March 1955): 137–143.
Steiner, *Tyrant*	Deborah Tarn Steiner, *The Tyrant's Writ. Myths and Images of Writing in Ancient Greece* (Princeton 1994).
Sterelny 1986a	Kim Sterelny, 'The Imagery Debate,' *Philosophy of Science* 53 (1986): 560–583; rpt in Lycan, *Mind*, pp. 607–626.
Stewart 1994a	Ian Stewart, 'The New Metrology of Beastly Numbers,' *Scientific American* 270 no. 3 (March 1994): 110–113.
Stewart, *GrSculp*	Andrew Stewart, *Greek Sculpture* (New Haven and London 1990).
Stirewalt, *Epistolography*	M. Luther Stirewalt, Jr., *Studies in Ancient Greek Epistolography* (Atlanta, GA 1993).
Störmer *et al.* 1990a	F. C. Störmer, I. Lorentzen, B. Fosse, M. Capasso, and K. Kleve, 'Ink in Herculaneum,' *Cronache Ercolanesi* 20 (1990): 183.
Stout, *Scribe*	Selatie Edgar Stout, *Scribe and Critic at Work in Pliny's Letters. Notes on the History and the Present Status of the Text* (Bloomington 1954).
Strocka 1981a	Volker Michael Strocka, 'Römische Bibliotheken,' *Gymnasium* 88 (1981): 298–329.
Stückelberger, *Bild*	Alfred Stückelberger, *Bild und Wort. Das illustrierte Fachbuch in der antiken Naturwissenschaft, Medizin und Technik* (Mainz am Rhein 1994).
Stump, *Boethius*	Eleonore Stump, translator, *Boethius's De topicis differentiis* (Ithaca and London 1978).
Sullivan 1994a	Shirley Darcus Sullivan, 'The Relationship of Person and θυμός in the Greek Lyric Poets (excluding Pindar and Bacchylides): Part One,' *Studi Italiani di Filologia Classica* 87 s. 3 no. 12 (1994): 12–37.
Sullivan, *Phren*	Shirley Darcus Sullivan, *Psychological Activity in Homer: A Study of Phren* (Ottawa 1988).
Svenbro 1989a	Jesper Svenbro, 'Phrasikleia – An Archaic Theory of Writing,' in Schousboe/Larsen, pp. 229–246.
Svenbro, *Phrasikleia*	Jesper Svenbro, *Phrasikleia. An Anthropology of Reading in Ancient Greece* (Ithaca and London 1993).
Tait 1988a	William John Tait, 'Rush and Reed: the Pens of

Egyptian and Greek Scribes,' in Basil G. Mandilaras, ed., *Proceedings of the XVIII International Congress of Papyrology. Athens 25–31 May 1986*, vol. 2 (Athens 1988), pp 477–481.

Tarrant 1987a R. J. Tarrant, 'Toward a Typology of Interpolation in Latin Poetry,' *Transactions of the American Philological Association* 117 (1987): 281–298.

Tatum 1995a James Tatum, 'Aunt Elvie's Quilt on the Bed of Odysseus: The Role of Artifacts in Natural Memory,' *Helios* 22 (1995): 167–177.

Teitler, *Notarii* H. C. Teitler, *Notarii and Exceptores. Dutch Monographs on Ancient History and Archaeology* 1 (Amsterdam 1985).

Thalmann, *Form* William G. Thalmann, *Conventions of Form and Thought in Early Greek Epic Poetry* (Baltimore and London 1984).

Theophilidou 1984a E. Theophilidou, 'Die Musenmosaiken der römischen Kaiserzeit,' *Trierer Zeitschrift* 47 (1984): 239–348.

Thomas Rosalind Thomas, *Oral Tradition and Written Record in Classical Athens* (Cambridge 1989).

Thomas 1993a Rosalind Thomas, 'Performance and Written Publication in Herodotus and the Sophistic Generation,' in Kullmann/Althoff, pp. 225–244.

Thomas, *LitOral* Rosalind Thomas, *Literacy and Orality in Ancient Greece* (Cambridge 1992).

Thompson 1994a Dorothy J. Thompson, 'Literacy and Power in Ptolemaic Egypt,' in Bowman/Woolf, pp. 67–83.

Thompson *et al.*, *MemSearch* Charles P. Thompson, Thaddeus M. Cowan, and Jerome Frieman, *Memory Search by a Memorist* (Hillsdale, NJ 1993).

TLG *Thesaurus Linguae Graecae*, University of California, Santa Barbara, CA: Pilot CD-ROM #C.

TLS *Times Literary Supplement* (London).

Tortorella 1992a Stefano Tortorella, 'I rilievi del Louvre con suovetaurile: un documento del culto imperiale,' *Ostraka* 1 (1992): 81–104.

Travlos, *PDAA* John Travlos, *Pictorial Dictionary of Ancient Athens* (New York 1971).

Trianti 1994a Ismene Trianti, 'Παρατηρήσεις σε δύο ομάδες γλυπτών του τέλους του 6ου αιώνα από την Ακρόπολη,' in Coulson *et al.*, *AAADem*, pp. 83–91.

Trianti 1994b Ismene Trianti, 'Sculpture from the Time of Cleisthenes,' *American Journal of Archaeology* 98 (1994): 284 (abstract of paper).

Tufi 1981a Sergio Rinaldi Tufi, 'Frammenti delle statue dei *summi viri* nel foro di Augusto,' *Dialoghi di Archeologia* n.s. 3 (1981): 69–84.

Turner 1978a Eric G. Turner, 'The Terms Recto and Verso. The Anatomy of the Papyrus Roll,' *Actes du XVᵉ Congrès International de Papyrologie, Papyrologica Bruxellensia* 16 pt. 1 (Brussels 1978).

Turner 1983a Eric G. Turner, 'Sniffing Glue,' *Cronache Ercolanesi* 13 (1983): 7–14.

Turner, *GrMss*   Eric G. Turner, *Greek Manuscripts of the Ancient World*, 2nd edn, revised and enlarged by P. J. Parsons (London 1987).

Turner, *GrPap*   Eric G. Turner, *Greek Papyri. An Introduction* (Oxford 1980, rpt of 1968).

Tversky/Kahneman 1974a   Amos Tversky and Daniel Kahneman, 'Judgment under Uncertainty: Heuristics and Biases,' *Science* 185 (1974): 1124–1131, rpt in Moser, *Rationality*, pp. 171–188.

Tversky/Kahneman 1983a   Amos Tversky and Daniel Kahneman, 'Extensional Versus Intuitive Reasoning: The Conjunction Fallacy in Probability Judgment,' *Psychological Review* 90 (1983): 293–315.

Tye, *Imagery*   Michael Tye, *The Imagery Debate* (Cambridge, MA and London 1991).

Van Groningen 1963a   B. A. Van Groningen, 'ΕΚΔΟΣΙΣ,' *Mnemosyne* s. 4, vol. 16 (1963): 1–17.

Van Ophuijsen 1994a   Jan M. van Ophuijsen, 'Where Have the Topics Gone?,' *Rutgers University Studies in Classical Humanities* 6 (1994): 131–173.

Van Sickle 1980a   John van Sickle, 'The Book-Roll and Some Conventions of the Poetic Book,' *Arethusa* 13 no. 1 (1980): 5–42.

Vansina, *OralTrad*   Jan Vansina, *Oral Tradition As History* (Madison 1985).

Vasaly, *Reps*   Ann Vasaly, *Representations: Images of the World in Ciceronian Oratory* (Berkeley and Lost Angeles 1993).

Vegetti 1988a   Mario Vegetti, 'Dans l'ombre de Thoth. Dynamique de l'écriture chez Platon,' in Detienne, *Savoirs*, pp. 387–419.

Vernet, *HBF*   André Vernet, ed., *Histoire des bibliothèques françaises. Les bibliothèques médiévales du VIe siècle à 1530* (Paris 1989).

Vezin 1989a   Jean Vezin, 'Le mobilier des bibliothèques,' in Vernet, *HBF*, pp. 364–371.

Vogl/Thompson 1995a   Rodney J. Vogl and Charles P. Thompson, 'The Specificity and Durability of Rajan's Memory,' in Alice F. Healy and Lyle E. Bourne, Jr., eds, *Learning and Memory of Knowledge and Skills: Durability and Specificity* (Thousand Oaks, CA 1995): 320–342.

Wagner 1978a   Daniel A. Wagner, 'Culture and Mnemonics,' in Gruneberg *et al.* 1978a, pp. 180–188.

Waldrop, *Complexity*   M. Mitchell Waldrop, *Complexity. The Emerging Science at the Edge of Order and Chaos* (New York 1992).

Walker 1993a   Andrew W. Walker, '*Enargeia* and the Spectator in Greek Historiography,' *Transactions of the American Philological Association* 123 (1993): 353–377.

Wallace 1994a   Wanda T. Wallace, 'Memory for Music: Effect of Melody on Recall of Text,' *Journal of Experimental Psychology: Learning, Memory, and Cognition* 20 (1994): 1471–1485.

Wallace/Rubin 1988a   Wanda T. Wallace and David C. Rubin, '"The Wreck of the Old 97'': A Real Event Remembered in Song,' in Neisser/Winograd, pp. 283–310.

Walsh 1958a — P. G. Walsh, 'The Negligent Historian: "Howlers" in Livy,' *Greece & Rome* s. 2 vol. 5 (1958): 83–88.

Walsh/Zlatic 1981a — Thomas M. Walsh and Thomas D. Zlatic, 'Mark Twain and the Art of Memory,' *American Literature* 53 (1981): 214–231.

Wang/Thomas 1995a — Alvin Y. Wang and Margaret H. Thomas, 'Effect of Keywords on Long-Term Retention: Help or Hindrance?,' *Journal of Educational Psychology* 87 (1995): 468–475.

Ward-Perkins/Claridge, *Pompeii* — John Ward-Perkins and Amanda Claridge, *Pompeii A.D. 79*, Exhibition Catalogue, Museum of Fine Arts, Boston, 2 vols (Boston 1978).

Warden 1991a — P. Gregory Warden, 'The Sculptural Program of the Villa of the Papyri,' *Journal of Roman Archaeology* 4 (1991): 257–261.

Warden/Romano 1994a — P. Gregory Warden and David Gilman Romano, 'The Course of Glory: Greek Art in a Roman Context at the Villa of the Papyri at Herculaneum,' *Art History* 17 (1994): 228–254.

Watling, *Seneca* — E. F. Watling, translator, *Seneca: Four Tragedies and Octavia* (Harmondsworth 1966).

Watt, *WritSys* — W. C. Watt, ed., *Writing Systems and Cognition: Perspectives from Psychology, Physiology, Linguistics and Semiotics, Neurology and Cognition* 6 (Dordrecht 1994).

Wegner, *MusenSark* — Max Wegner, *Die Musensarkophage, Die antiken Sarkophagreliefs*, vol. 5 pt. 3 (Berlin 1966).

Weijers, *VocLivre* — O. Weijers, *Vocabulaire du livre et de l'écriture au Moyen Age* (Turnhout 1989).

Weitzmann, *AncBk* — Kurt Weitzmann, *Ancient Book Illumination* (Cambridge, MA 1959).

Weitzmann, *LateAnt* — Kurt Weitzmann, *Late Antique and Early Christian Book Illumination* (New York 1977).

Weitzmann, *Roll* — Kurt Weitzmann, *Illustrations in Roll and Codex. A Study of the Origin and Method of Text Illustration* (Princeton 1947, 2nd printing with addenda 1970).

Weitzmann, *Spirit* — Kurt Weitzmann, ed., *Age of Spirituality. Late Antique and Early Christian Art, Third to Seventh Century* (New York and Princeton 1979).

Weitzmann, *Studies* — Kurt Weitzmann, *Studies in Classical and Byzantine Manuscript Illumination*, edited by Herbert L. Kessler (Chicago 1971).

White, *Birth* — John White, *The Birth and Rebirth of Pictorial Space*, 3rd edn (Cambridge, MA 1987).

Wightman, *Trier* — E. M. Wightman, *Roman Trier and the Treveri* (New York and Washington 1971).

Wilamowitz-Moellendorff, *AnalEur* — Ulrich von Wilamowitz-Moellendorff, *Analecta Euripidea* (Berlin 1875, rpt Hildesheim 1963).

Williams 1992a — G. D. Williams, 'Representations of the Book-Roll in Latin Poetry: Ovid, *Tr.* 1,1,3–14 and Related Texts,' *Mnemosyne* 45 (1992): 178–189.

Williams 1972a — Ronald J. Williams, 'Scribal Training in Ancient Egypt,' *Journal of the American Oriental Society* 92 (1972): 214–221.

Williamson 1987a — Callie Williamson, 'Monuments of Bronze: Roman Legal Documents on Bronze Tablets,' *Classical Antiquity* 6 (1987): 160–183.

Williamson 1995a — Callie Williamson, 'The Display of Law and Archival Practice in Rome,' in *ACEL*, pp. 239–251.

Williamson, *Euseb* — G. A. Williamson, translator, *Eusebius. The History of the Church from Christ to Constantine* (Harmondsworth 1965).

Williamson, *Sappho* — Margaret Williamson, *Sappho's Immortal Daughters* (Cambridge, MA and London 1995).

Willinsky, *Empire* — John Willinsky, *Empire of Words. The Reign of the OED* (Princeton 1954).

Willows/Houghton 1 — Dale M. Willows and Harvey A. Houghton, eds, *The Psychology of Illustration: 1 Basic Research* (New York 1987).

Willows/Houghton 2 — Dale M. Willows and Harvey A. Houghton, eds, *The Psychology of Illustration: 2 Instructional Issues* (New York 1987).

Winograd/Neisser — Eugene Winograd and Ulric Neisser, eds, *Affect and Accuracy in Recall: Studies of 'Flashbulb Memories'* (Cambridge 1992).

Wiseman 1993a — T. P. Wiseman, 'Living Historians: Seven Types of Mendacity,' in Gill/Wiseman, *Lies*, pp. 122–146.

Wiseman, *Clio* — T. P. Wiseman, *Clio's Cosmetics. Three Studies in Greco-Roman Literature* (Leicester 1979).

Wollen/Margres 1987a — Keith A. Wollen and Matthew G. Margres, 'Bizarreness and the Imagery Multiprocess Model,' in McDaniel/Pressley, pp. 103–127.

Woodbury 1976a — Leonard Woodbury, 'Aristophanes' *Frogs* and Athenian Literacy: *Ran.* 52–53, 1114,' *Transactions of the American Philological Association* 106 (1976): 349–357.

Woodhead — A. G. Woodhead, *The Study of Greek Inscriptions* (Cambridge 1967).

Woodman, *RhetHist* — A. J. Woodman, *Rhetoric in Classical Historiography* (London and Sydney 1988).

Woodruff, *Plato* — Paul Woodruff, *Plato Two Comic Dialogues: Ion. Hippias Major* (Indianapolis 1983).

Wormald, *EngDraw* — F. Wormald, *English Drawings of the Tenth and Eleventh Centuries* (London 1952).

Wrede 1981a — Henning Wrede, 'Scribae,' *Boreas* 4 (1981): 106–116.

Wyatt/Edmonson 1984a — William F. Wyatt, Jr. and Colin N. Edmonson, 'The Ceiling of the Hephaisteion,' *American Journal of Archaeology* 88 (1984): 135–167.

Yates, *Memory* — Frances A. Yates, *The Art of Memory* (Chicago 1966).

Zanker, *Power* — Paul Zanker, *The Power of Images in the Age of Augustus*, translated by Alan Shapiro (Ann Arbor 1988).

Zeitlin 1994a — Froma Zeitlin, 'The Artful Eye: Vision, Ecphrasis and Spectacle in Euripidean Theatre,' in Goldhill/Osborne, pp. 138–196.

Zetzel 1973a   J. E. G. Zetzel, '*Emendavi ad Tironem*: Some Notes on Scholarship in the Second Century AD,' *Harvard Studies in Classical Philology* 77 (1973): 225–243.

Zetzel 1975a   J. E. G. Zetzel, 'On the History of Latin Scholia,' *Harvard Studies in Classical Philology* 79 (1975): 335–354.

Zoller *et al.* 1989a   Carrie L. Zoller, Jeff S. Workman, and Neal E. A. Kroll, 'The Bizarre Mnemonic: The Effect of Retention Interval and Mode of Presentation,' *Bulletin of the Psychonomic Society* 27 (1989): 215–218.

INDEX OF TRANSLATED PASSAGES

Note: non-bold numbers refer to source texts; bold numbers refer to pages.

GENERAL INDEX

Abeita 156, 169
Abelson, R. 197, 200
acrostics 66–7, 124–5
Adams, Hazard 35
Adams, Marilyn 6, 24
Aeneid, The (Vergil) 74; Achilles's shield
  compared to Aeneas's 225–7;
  descendants of Aeneas 233; Evander
  and Aeneas among the monuments
  in Rome 234; rough drafts 211–12
Aeschylus: Dionysius the Elder uses
  tablets 154; memory tablets of the
  lungs/mind 131–2
Agar, Michael 192
Aitken, Alexander Craig 125–6, 128
Albertus Magnus 115
Alcibiades: drops musical instruction
  73; on editions of Homer 30–1
Alexander the Great: on Darius's
  scrinium 50; reads silently 22
Alexandria library 44–6; Homeric texts
  222; Muses 78, 162; 'official' texts
  221; Seneca on 42; storage 48
Allen, T. W. 30
alphabet: Etruscans adopt Phoenician
  alphabet 185–6; mnemotechnics
  87–8, 123–4; storage and retrieval
  61–7
alphabetization 61–5
Ambrose, St 173
Antigonus of Carystus 14
Antisthenes 129
Antonius, Marcus 209
Apellicon of Teos 43
Apollo Sosianus 77
Apollonius Sophista 63, 187
Aquinas, St Thomas 173
argument 92–4

Aristarchus of Samothrace 13
Aristides 149–50
Aristophanes of Byzantium 129
Aristotle: on accents 13; beauty from
  size and order 230–1; Cicero's
  'translation' of *Topics* 217–19;
  difference between history and
  poetry 192; lecture audiences 37;
  logic 243; memory of poetry 75;
  mnemotechnics 100, 111, 118, 126,
  238; organization of texts 187–8;
  personal library 43; published versus
  delivered speeches 206–7; sensory
  experience 97, 230; slips of the
  tongue xviii–xix; thoughts in lungs
  132; *topoi* and memory 87–94; use of
  letters in diagrams 66
arts: craft versus fine arts 73
Athena 73, 77
Athenaeus: alphabetization 62, 124;
  library catalogues 46; on Plato and
  memory 86; titles 33, 34
Atropos, a Fate 77
Attic Nights (Aulus Gellius): table of
  contents 19
Atticus, Titus Pomponius 212, 220
Auctor ad Herennium, The 81, 82;
  colonnades for remembering 99,
  101, 233; memory as treasury 178;
  mental imagery 112, 113–15; size,
  perception and memory 230; system
  of *loci* 98–101; way vision works 107
audiences 36, 39–40
Augustine, St 123; acrostics 124–5;
  reading at a table 167
Augustus: composes in the bath 183;
  handwriting 29; reads speeches

367

193–4, 194, 198–9; on lectures 37; memory 127, 220–1; method of composition 186; on ostracism of Aristides 149–50; peripatetic philosophers 164; praises library of Lucullus 31; on Themistocles 128

Poetics (Aristotle) 88; difference between history and poetry 192; size and beauty 230

poetry 12, 14

Politics (Aristotle) 92

Pollio, Gaius Asinius 77, 162

Polybios: mistranslated by Livy 220; parade of ancestors 233; plausible liars 200; questioning eyewitnesses 190–1; on Roman retrieval of documents 55–6; speeches 207

Polyhymnia, Muse of dance, pantomime and geometry 72, 73

Pomponius Musa, Quintus 77

Powell, Marvin 143–4

Pre-Socratic philosophers 221

Pressley, Michael 127

printing 15–16

Probus, Marcus Valerius: proofing copies 30; *On the Secret Meaning of the Letters* 67

Proclus of Naucratis 44

Protagoras 90

psyche 132

Ptolemaeus, Claudius 22

Ptolemy I Euregetes 44

public readings/performances 35–40; ability to perform 38–40; lecture attendees 37; mnemotechnics 84; venues 38

Pulena, Laris 166

punctuation 13, 14, 18; aural aspect 20–2; *paragraphos* 13–14, 15

Punic War (Naevius) 13

Pythians (Pindar) 171

Quast, Zeba 195

Quinn, Kenneth 38

Quintilian (Marcus Fabus Quintilianus): on the alphabet 64–5; archaic forms in old books 32; commonplaces 90–1; defines digression 215; importance of memory 82, 103, 179; lecture notes 37–8; *loci* 97; on memory performance 127, 128; mnemotechnics 88; neologisms

69–70; note-taking techniques 169; practical advice on memorizing 74–5, 115, 117–22; on research assistants 175; revisions and drafts 210, 213; on saying everything xx; on Simonides's mnemotechnics 83, 84–5; system of *loci* 109–11; thinking out composition 21, 181–3; on using wax tablets 143, 146; Vergil quotations 222; writing out speeches 207, 208–9

quotations and citations 219–23

Raskin, Robin 110

reading: aural aspect 20–5; continuous writing 19; Greek words for 187; learning 23–4; modern methods 23–5; organization of a book 15; silently 22–3, 167; speed and information density 19–20, 25

reading stands 155–8

Reagan, Ronald 196

Reber, Arthur 119–20

religion 55

Republic, The (Plato): first lines worked over 211; parable of the cave 97

research 160; assistants 174–5; excerpting 168; note-taking 169–74; scholars 161; *see also* libraries

retrieval and storage xvi–xvii; alphabetization 61–7, 84; documents and records 54–6; filing cabinets 141; indexes 67–71; sequential orders 84; slaves as storage 130

Reynolds, L. D. 13

rhetoric 37–8, 74, 91–2, 95, 118, 182, 241; memory 82–3; speeches 206–9; tools 241

Roberts, C. H. 12

rolls 148–9, 151–4, 158; Homer 12; libraries 164–5, 167–9

Rome: art 108; engraved laws 55–7; libraries 47, 160–2; places as *loci* for remembering 231–5; portrayal of ancestors 232–4; records of Senate discussions 59–60; sense of place 95–6

Rose, Stephen 199

Rouse, Richard H. and Mary A. 45, 67–8

Rossano Gospels 168

Rouveret, Agnès 236

Sabinus, Calvisius 130
Sacks, Oliver 106–7
Sadoski, Mark 195
Saenger, Paul 15, 23, 50, 147, 167
Sallust (Gaius Sallustius Crispus) 233
Sapir, Edward 142
Sappho 221
Saussure, Ferdinand de 38
Scaevola, Gaius Mucius 151
Schank, Roger 197, 199–200
Schenkeveld, Dirk M. 22
Scholar, The (Pliny the Elder) 189
Scholes, Robert 5–6
science and mathematics 72–4
Scipio, Lucius 128
Scopas 82–3
scribes: dictation 170–4; final drafts 26–7; status 151, 152, 153–4; take the blame 31
Scribner, Sylvia 4, 98
scrinia 49–50
scriptio continua 12–13, 14, 17–18, 19, 23; children's inclination 242; reading aloud 21–2
Semitic languages 19
Seneca the Elder 132; attribution of sayings 196; deathlessness of writing 10; powerful memory 127–8, 128, 189; on Vergil's readings 38–9
Seneca the Younger: dictation 173; flower arrangment of excerpts 180–1; on libraries 47, 161; on possessing books 42; reading aloud 21; on relationship between writing and memory 9; research assistants 175; on Sabinus's memory slaves 130; on shorthand 61; storage at libraries 48; treasure-house of memory 179
sensory experience 97, 101
sentence 254 n. 64
Serbo-Croatian singers 5, 7–8, 202–3
Shannon, Claude 20
Shaw, George Bernard 65, 171
Shepard, Roger 105
Shereshevskii ('S.') 101–5
Shimron, Joseph 20, 25
shorthand 60–1
Sibylline Books 66–7
Simonides of Keos: Cicero's view 96; compared to Shereshevskii 103; inventor of mnemotechnics 4, 82–3;

mnemotechnics 87–8, 90; pay for poetry 36
Sirat, Colette 143, 153
Sivan, Tamar 20, 25
Skeat, T. C. 12, 155, 171
Slak, S. 126
slaves and freedmen: research assistants 174–5; *see also* scribes
sleep 122
Socrates: and Ischomachus 227; mnemotechnics 86; reads rolls with boys 164–5; *see also* Plato
Sorabji, Richard 93
speeches and spoken words: Cicero's literary requirements for dialogue 205–6; conversations and dialogues 202–6; revisions 209–10; written versus delivered speech 204–9
Stephens, Laurence D. 76
Strabo 31, 43
Stump, Eleanor 218
stylus *see* pens
Suetonius (Gaius Suetonius Tranquillus): on Augustus 29, 69; book storage 49; Caligula's published laws 57; on Claudius's new letters 65; falsification of documents 58–9; on Naevius 13; numerology 67; on proofing copies 30; shorthand 60–1; on Vergil's readings 39
Svenbro, Jesper 22–3
syllogism 88, 243
synaesthesia 103–4

Table Alphabetical (Cowdrey) 68
tachygraphy *see* shorthand
Tacitus, Publius Cornelius 187; poets' audiences 40; swapped drafts with Pliny 210–11
technē 73–4, 81
Temple of Mars Ultor 232–3
Terence: success of *The Eunuch* 35
Terpsichore, Muse of the lyre 72
texts: abridgements 177–8; annotations and marginalia 70–1, 121–2, 169; as artifacts 3; capitals and lower case 13, 18; commentary 13–14; 'continuous' writing 12, 14, 17–18, 23, 120–1, 187; individually produced 16; origins 7; partial or fragmented survival 221; process of writing affected by medium 141–5;